The Wechsler Intelligence Scales and *Gf-Gc* Theory

The Wechsler Intelligence Scales and *Gf-Gc* Theory

A Contemporary Approach to Interpretation

Dawn P. Flanagan
St. John's University, New York

Kevin S. McGrew
St. Cloud State University

Samuel O. Ortiz
San Diego State University

Foreword by Alan S. Kaufman

Allyn and Bacon
Boston ■ London ■ Toronto ■ Sydney ■ Tokyo ■ Singapore

Series editor: Becky Pascal
Series editorial assistant: Susan Hutchinson
Marketing manager: Caroline Croley

Library of Congress Cataloging-in-Publication Data

Flanagan, Dawn P.
    The Wechsler intelligence scales and Gf-Gc theory : a contemporary
approach to interpretation / Dawn P. Flanagan, Kevin S. McGrew, and
Samuel O. Ortiz.
        p.   cm.
    Includes bibliographical references and index.
    ISBN 0-205-29271-2
    1. Wechsler Adult Intelligence Scale.   2. Intelligence tests.
3. Intellect.   I. McGrew, Kevin S.   II. Ortiz, Samuel O.
III. Title.
BF432.5.W4F53   1999
153.9'32--dc21
                                        99-35058
                                        CIP

Printed in the United States of America

10   9   8   7   6   5   4   3   2   03   02   01   00

In Memory of David Wechsler
(1896–1981)

Every step of progress the world has made has been
from scaffold to scaffold, and from stake to stake
—Wendell Phillips, 1851

This book is dedicated to those scholars whose work
has provided us with a scaffold on which to build

David Wechsler
For developing a rich clinical instrument that has provided
important insights into the theoretical construct of intelligence
and the cognitive capabilities of individuals

Raymond B. Cattell and John L. Horn
For developing the Gf-Gc theory of intelligence, a theory that
demonstrates that an individual's intelligence is not a single
ability, but rather a mosaic of many distinct cognitive abilities

John B. Carroll
For articulating a comprehensive, empirically supported
cognitive ability taxonomic foundation that can be used to bridge
intelligence test theory and practice

Richard W. Woodcock
For modeling how to bridge the Gf-Gc theory/measurement gap
with Gf-Gc designed test batteries and for first recognizing that
"crossing" different batteries may be necessary to measure a
great breadth of a person's Gf-Gc cognitive abilities

Samuel Messick
For reminding psychologists that all psychological measures are
not created equal and that all psychological tests must be based
on strong theory-based construct validity evidence

Alan S. Kaufman
For providing the "intelligent testing" interpretive framework—
a framework that captures the delicate balance between the art
and science of intelligence test interpretation

CONTENTS

PART THREE: *Gf-Gc* Cross-Battery Assessment and Interpretation Using the Wechsler Scales

FOREWORD

ALAN S. KAUFMAN
Clinical Professor of Psychology
Yale University School of Medicine

The history of intelligence testing has often been chronicled—from Galton to Binet to Wechsler—and that type of historical perspective can be useful for understanding contemporary test practices and controversies. Sometimes, however, it is even more prudent to stand back and ponder the history of the *interpretation* of intelligence tests. That history is less often discussed, but has its own place in making sense out of the vitriolic bile that seems to follow IQ tests like a shadow. This book by Flanagan, McGrew, and Ortiz has stirred my own memory bank regarding the history of IQ test interpretation—in part because of their summary of Kamphaus, Petoskey, and Morgan's (1997) division of the history of IQ test interpretation into four *waves,* and in part because the comprehensive theory-based approach to Wechsler interpretation that forms the crux of the Flanagan, McGrew, Ortiz text reflects the crest of the fourth wave, "applying theory to intelligence test interpretation."

My own work, primarily *Intelligent Testing with the WISC-R* (Kaufman, 1979), was credited with forming an aspect of the third wave (psychometric profile analysis), in conjunction with the pioneering factor-analytic studies published by the recently deceased Jacob Cohen (i.e., Cohen, 1959), and paving the way for the fourth wave of theoretical applications. Yet, I know that other people were far more influential than I was in forming the bridge between the third and fourth waves, and that a serendipitous set of circumstances tilled the soil for the interpretive method that would be attributed to me. Let me explain.

First, there was the burgeoning learning disabilities movement that began to gain steam during the decade of the 1960s. At the end of the decade of the 1950s, the old Stanford-Binet was still the king of assessment, with the Wechsler scales merely the pretenders to the throne. But spokespersons for the learning disabilities movement such as Sam Kirk, more likely to reside in Departments of Special Education than Educational Psychology, made it clear that multiscore IQ tests were essential for proper diagnosis and remediation and that the one-score Binet was as outmoded as the Model T Ford. Waiting in the wings was the 1949 WISC, until then a bridesmaid, ready to take over the field. In a way, the Wechsler takeover of the Binet was similar to Binet's ultimate triumph over Galton's psychophysical measure of intelligence. Binet had been developing tasks in his laboratory and gathering data on children's abilities since the mid-1880s—Galton's time as reigning King. When the French government knocked on Binet's door in the early 1900s to weed out the slow thinkers from the crème-de-la-crème in Paris's school system, Binet delivered his 1905 test in record time; he had it ready and waiting, and just needed to dust off a few parts. Similarly, when the Binet scale was found wanting by the learning disabilities leaders in the United States more than a half-century later, the three-IQ and multiple-scaled-score WISC, waiting a decade for its opportunity, stepped to the forefront of the testing scene.

Arm in arm with Cohen's factor loadings (fine-tuned with "g" loadings and estimates of subtest specificity), and given renewed life by new interpretive heroes like Alex Bannatyne, the WISC began its reign.

During the early 1970s, two fortuitous occurrences happened to me. In 1970, I began working with master clinician and genius David Wechsler, the same year I earned my Ph.D. under master psychometrician and genius Robert L. Thorndike, at Columbia University. In my clinical courses on IQ interpretation, I was taught the clinical profile analysis that the second wave featured, as promoted by Rapaport and others, that somehow was only able to interpret low scores on Information in terms of the Oedipal conflict, and the inability to reverse digits in terms of hostility and a weak super-ego. In my psychometric theory courses, Thorndike's bent dominated, and the Cohen statistics assumed primacy. The latter influence was the strongest in my own development, constantly reinforced by my superiors at The Psychological Corporation—most of whom, I found out, were also trained by Robert L. Thorndike (although one went back to his father, E. L. Thorndike). Despite Dr. Wechsler's frequent attempts to get his dull-witted student (me) to see things through an astute clinician's eye (his), I always fell back on the psychometric approach. When I wrote an article on the factor analysis of the WISC-R (Kaufman, 1975), one that continued the work of Cohen and was to be frequently cited, I was a practicing and devout coward; I didn't even have the courage to change the name of Cohen's Freedom from Distractibility factor, even though my instincts told me that it measured some cognitive ability or other, and I could barely spell the damn thing.

All the while that Wechsler was trying to hammer some sense into my head, so was my wife and colleague, Nadeen, who was also in a doctoral program at Columbia, but one that didn't rely on psychologists to interpret IQ tests and whose clinical and diagnostic coursework barely overlapped with the coursework in Psychology programs. Nadeen was in the Learning Disabilities and Neuroscience division of the Department of Special Education, and she learned IQ tests not by begging her neighbor to volunteer their children for practice testing, but by testing individuals of all ages in the Learning Disabilities clinic under the watchful eye of some superb clinicians. She was being taught to focus on intraindividual differences, to apply theory to the test-score profile, and to integrate behavioral observations with the profile of scores. Her mentors, Dr. Margaret Jo Shepherd and the late Dr. Jeannette Fleischner, were using different words than my mentor, Dr. Wechsler, but their messages had a similar ring: Focus on the client, not the profile of test scores; understand this profile in terms of theory and clinical observations of behavior, background information, and reasons for referral; and use the IQ test to understand the person's strengths and weaknesses so that the test results can be used productively. However, I listened with half a brain, convinced that the real answers could be found by sticking to psychometric formulas.

Then I left my ivory tower and took a position in the School Psychology program at the University of Georgia, taught the IQ course, and had to grade case reports. Help! I conferred with Nadeen. I called Dr. Wechsler. This time I listened with both hemispheres, integrated what they taught me with my own strait-laced psychometric background, and developed the method that ultimately was seen as transitioning from wave three to wave four in the Kamphaus and colleagues (1997) scheme of interpretive history.

And now Flanagan, McGrew, and Ortiz have taken my pleas for an integrated research-based and theoretical approach to IQ test interpretation to a new level. In my writings, I asked for research results to be applied to profile interpretation. This book, *The Wechsler Intelligence Scales and* Gf-Gc *Theory: A Contemporary Approach to Interpretation,* is based on an impressive compilation and integration of research investigations. Every chapter has research at its foundation. I asked for theory to be applied to profile interpretation. Flanagan, McGrew, and Ortiz have achieved more than anyone else in operationalizing my plea into action. They have accomplished their ambitious goal of applying Carroll's (1993a) research-based, comprehensive theory to the complex task of interpreting Wechsler's intelligence and memory tests, and have done it in a way that translates to a veritable guide for examiners to follow. One of the basic tenets of my approach to IQ test interpretation is to supplement Wechsler's scales with pertinent tasks to round out the assessment and to follow-up hunches and hypotheses. This psychoeducational approach to assessment (courtesy of patient, hands-on teaching by Nadeen, and vicarious mentorship from Dr. Shepherd and Dr. Fleischner) has been implemented to near perfection by Flanagan and colleagues via their numerous valuable tables that systematically categorize tasks from the diversity of other IQ tests that are available to clinicians. The authors of this text have also systematically applied research concerning the inclusion of basic concepts in the directions to children, the need to understand item difficulty gradients, and other subtle aspects of Wechsler's tasks, in their development of helpful interpretive sheets for each component subtest.

The 1990s have witnessed two major sophisticated, high-quality psychometric approaches to intelligence test interpretation: The research conducted by Glutting, McDermott, and their colleagues on profile interpretation and the research by Flanagan, McGrew, and their colleagues on the cross-battery technique. Both sets of research programs have been based, either directly or indirectly, on the now controversial approach to profile interpretation espoused by me, Randy Kamphaus, Jack Naglieri, Alex Bannatyne, and others, and tracing its roots both to Wechsler's clinical use of test scores and Kirk's psycholinguistic use of test scores. Both groups of researchers have contributed significantly to the test-interpretation scene by advancing the application of psychometrics to profile analysis.

Yet Glutting and McDermott have used the results of their research as an obstacle for clinicians, as purveyors of gloom-and-doom for anyone foolish enough to engage in profile interpretation. In contrast, Flanagan and McGrew have applied their research findings to elevate profile interpretation to a higher level, to add theory to psychometrics and thereby to improve the quality of the psychometric assessment of intelligence.

In a footnote to a reference to a Glutting and McDermott study, Anastasi and Urbina (1997) state: "One problem with several of the negative reviews of Kaufman's approach is that they seem to assume that clinicians will use it to make decisions based solely on the magnitude of scores and score differences. While it is true that the mechanical application of profile analysis techniques can be very misleading, this assumption is quite contrary to what Kaufman recommends, as well as to the principles of sound assessment practice" (p. 513).

One thing is obvious to me. Flanagan, McGrew, and Ortiz have internalized sound assessment principles. And they might even understand my method of profile interpretation better than I do.

A. S. K.

PREFACE

This book has one overarching goal—to modernize the interpretation of the Wechsler Intelligence Scales by applying *Gf-Gc* theory and the cross-battery approach to intellectual assessment and interpretation. This book represents a focused extension of the *Intelligence Test Desk Reference (ITDR): Gf-Gc Cross-Battery Assessment* (McGrew & Flanagan, 1998), in which the cross-battery approach was first introduced. The *Gf-Gc cross-battery approach* is a time-efficient method of intellectual assessment that allows practitioners to measure validly a wider range (or a more in-depth but selective range) of cognitive abilities than that represented by any one intelligence battery in a manner consistent with contemporary psychometric theory and research. Whereas the ITDR briefly described how to use the cross-battery approach to supplement the major intelligence batteries (including the Wechsler scales), this book provides an *in-depth treatment* of how to use cross-battery principles and techniques to augment the Wechsler Intelligence Scales (WPPSI-R, WISC-III, WAIS-III) in a psychometrically defensible manner and interpret the results of Wechsler-based cross-battery assessments within the context of current theory and research.

In the process of writing this book and applying the *Gf-Gc* cross-battery approach to the Wechsler Intelligence Scales, we have gained a greater appreciation of the foundational sources of information on which our assessment approach is based. In particular, this book builds on the seminal work of David Wechsler, Raymond Cattell, John Horn, John Carroll, Richard Woodcock, Samuel Messick, and Alan Kaufman. Through their extensive research, ideas, and writings, these scholars have contributed significantly to our development of the Wechsler-based *Gf-Gc* cross-battery approach in several important ways.

First, few psychologists would argue the fact that David Wechsler's Intelligence Scales currently dominate the practice of intelligence testing. Although we have been critical of certain aspects of the Wechsler Scales in our writings, there is little doubt in the pages that follow that our work has been influenced directly and indirectly by the writings of David Wechsler.

According to one who knew him well, Wechsler succeeded largely because he was able to anticipate the needs of practitioners and had the courage to challenge the prevailing Stanford-Binet monopoly (Kaufman, 1990a). Similarly, it is our hope that the Wechsler *Gf-Gc* cross-battery approach presented in this book will meet the emerging needs of assessment professionals who have recognized the gap between intelligence theory and practice. However, because our ideas and procedures necessitate a change in thinking and practice with regard to the Wechsler Intelligence Scales, our recommended use and interpretation of these batteries may be met with resistance by some, this time due to the prevailing Wechsler monopoly, which carries with it a limited test-kit focus. Our approach suggests a shift in focus from a circumscribed set of measures (as represented by a single intelligence battery) to a theory-driven method of organizing assessments and making interpretations. Thus, our Wechsler-based *Gf-Gc* cross-battery approach is not intended to denigrate the Wechsler Scales, but rather, to modernize these measures thereby extending Wechsler's legacy.

Second, the seminal theoretical work of Raymond Cattell, John Horn, and John Carroll played a prominent role in the development of our assessment approach. Cattell, Horn, and Carroll's contributions have, in our judgement, provided a convincing argument that a hierarchical multiple-ability theory, such as those represented by the Horn-Cattell *Gf-Gc* and Carroll *Three-Stratum* models, best describes the structure of human intelligence. Furthermore, the network of validity evidence (e.g., substantive, structural, and external) that supports the *Gf-Gc* structure of intelligence argues strongly for the use of this framework as a guide to the selection and interpretation of all intelligence batteries.

Third, readers familiar with the *ITDR* will recognize the "three pillars of cross-battery assessment" presented in Chapter 6 of this book. Briefly, the *Gf-Gc* cross-battery approach is predicated on three major sources of information: (1) the *Gf-Gc* theory of intelligence, (2) cross-battery factor-analysis-based classifications of the individual tests in all major intelligence batteries at the *broad* (stratum II) level of the *Gf-Gc* model, and (3) expert consensus-based classifications of individual tests at the *narrow* (stratum I) level of the *Gf-Gc* model. All three pillars provide evidence from which valid inferences can be drawn from cross-battery organized test scores. The second and third pillars focus on increasing validity through the reduction of *construct irrelevant variance* and *construct underrepresentation*, respectively—two ubiquitous sources of invalidity in traditional assessment and interpretation approaches. The three cross-battery pillars (the latter two in particular) are best conceptualized as being part of a larger overarching theory-based construct validity framework that rests solidly on the work of Samuel Messick. The writings of Messick have allowed us to more accurately place the Wechsler-based *Gf-Gc* cross-battery approach within a "big picture" construct validity structure.

Fourth, the application of the cross-battery approach to the Wechsler Intelligence Scales is consistent with the influential writings of Alan Kaufman. Kaufman's prominent "intelligent" approach to Wechsler intelligence test interpretation is at the core of our teaching, writing, research, and practice. To be sure, Kaufman's approach to intelligence test interpretation—an approach that recognizes that "clinical assessment is part art, part science" (Kaufman, 1994, p. 27)—permeates much of the Wechsler-based *Gf-Gc* cross-battery approach presented in this text.

In summary, the process of extending the *Gf-Gc* cross-battery approach to the interpretation of the Wechsler Intelligence Scales has made us more cognizant of the shoulders on which we stand—Wechsler, Cattell, Horn, Carroll, Woodcock, Messick, and Kaufman. We hope our humble efforts to integrate their contributions and extend them to the use and interpretation of the Wechsler Intelligence Scales do justice to their work.

Organization

This book is organized in three sections. Part I (Linking Contemporary Intelligence Theory and Practice: An Overview) consists of three chapters. In Chapter 1, the Wechsler Intelligence Scales are placed in historical and contemporary perspective. This chapter is arranged around Kamphaus's conceptualization of intelligence test interpretation as representing four waves, beginning in the late 1900s through present day. The Wechsler Scales have been an integral part of each wave of test interpretation. This book is an attempt to ground the Wechsler Scales firmly in the fourth, *theory-based wave* of intelligence test interpretation. Chapter 2 provides an overview of the current state-of-the-art of intellectual assessment, and describes the progress that has been made in both psychometric theory development and intelligence test development. An integrated Cattell-Horn-Carroll *Gf-Gc* model is presented and defined in this chapter. Support for the *Gf-Gc* framework as the most well validated and researched theoretical model of multiple cognitive abilities within the psychometric tradition is presented in this chapter. Also, the Wechsler Scales are described according to the extent to which they operationalize prominent abilities specified in the *Gf-Gc* structure of intelligence. In Chapter 3, the extant literature on the validity of the Wechsler Intelligence Scales is evaluated according to substantive, structural, and external validation criteria. This chapter shows how *Gf-Gc* theory can be linked to the applied measurement of cognitive abilities using the Wechsler Scales. Specifically, we impose a strong substantive framework to the interpretation of the Wechsler Intelligence Scales via McGrew and Flanagan's (1998) *Gf-Gc* cross-battery approach. The end result is the derivation of more valid inferences from Wechsler test scores. Together, Chapters 1 through 3 of this book provide the foundational knowledge on which our approach to using and interpreting the Wechsler Intelligence Scales was based.

Part II of this text (Descriptions and Evaluations of the Wechsler Intelligence and Wechsler-Linked Memory Scales) provides a comprehensive review of the psychometric, theoretical, and qualitative characteristics of the individual subtests of the WPPSI-R, WISC-III, WAIS-III, WMS-III, and CMS. Chapter 4 describes these test characteristics in detail and relates each characteristic to the test interpretation process. In addition, the psychometric (e.g., reliability, *g* loading, floors/ceilings), theoretical (e.g., *Gf-Gc* broad and narrow ability classifications), and qualitative (e.g., individual/situational factors that influence performance, degree of cultural loading, degree of linguistic demand) characteristics for each individual test of the Wechsler Scales are presented on summary pages (one page per test) in an easy-to-read, visual-graphic format at the end of Chapter 4. Chapter 5 provides a brief description of the importance of *supplemental* cognitive ability tests in the assessment and interpretation process. All cognitive ability tests included in this chapter are described according to the *Gf-Gc* theoretical model and are used in subsequent chapters to supplement the Wechsler Intelligence Scales. Finally, like Chapter 4, Chapter 5 provides test characteristic summary pages for the Wechsler-linked memory batteries (i.e., WMS-III and CMS).

Part III describes the product of grounding cognitive ability assessment and interpretation with the Wechsler Scales in strong theory and research—the *Wechsler-based* Gf-Gc *cross-battery approach*. The foundation, rationale, and application of this approach are presented in Chapter 6. In this chapter, we argue strongly for a theory- and research-based approach and highlight the utility of this approach in uncovering intracognitive strengths and weaknesses particularly as it applies to the identification and diagnosis of learning disabilities. Chapter 7 provides a comprehensive approach to interpreting *Gf-Gc* cross-battery data using a case example. Finally, Chapter 8 extends the Wechsler-based *Gf-Gc* cross-battery approach to multicultural and multilingual populations. Numerous tables, figures, flowcharts, and *Gf-Gc* cross-battery worksheets are provided throughout this book to assist the reader in the process of infusing this material in their current practice. In addition, the appendices provide valuable information, such as a *Gf-Gc* cross-battery interpretive report, a "user-friendly" guide to understanding *Gf-Gc* abilities, a percentile and standard score conversion table, and information about ability-achievement discrepancy analyses, that is also intended to assist Wechsler users in the application of the psychometrically and theoretically defensible cross-battery approach.

Intended Audience

This book is intended for practitioners, researchers, and scholars who seek to infuse current theory and research in their use and interpretation of the Wechsler Intelligence Scales. Practitioners, university trainers, students, researchers and other professionals in school, clinical, counseling, and educational psychology as well as neuropsychology, who use the Wechsler Intelligence and Memory Scales in applied settings would find this book valuable. This book would be appropriate for a graduate course in beginning or advanced intelligence testing, measurement, and psychoeducational assessment. This book is also particularly valuable for those who seek an organized, systematic, and theory-based method for evaluating cognitive functioning in children, adolescents, and adults, including those from culturally and linguistically diverse backgrounds.

Acknowledgments

We are grateful to a number of individuals who facilitated the preparation of this book. Our deepest appreciation is extended to Jennifer Mascolo who spent endless hours preparing tables, organizing materials, conducting library research, editing, and performing countless other tasks related to the preparation of this book. Jennifer Mascolo's dedication, commitment, insightfulness, energy, and attention to detail greatly enhanced the quality of this work. We also wish to thank Matthew Broudy, Bhupin Butaney, Theresa Huettl, Jennifer Jablonski, Dennis Russell, and Joe Wehrman for their assistance in locating articles, entering data, and participating in an extensive review of the literature on the validity of the Wechsler Intelligence and Memory Scales. We are particularly grateful for the diligence of Jennifer Jablonski who carefully edited earlier drafts of this manuscript.

Our appreciation also goes to the following reviewers for their valuable thoughts and comments on an initial draft of this manuscript: Vincent C. Alfonso, Fordham University; Michael E. Gerner, President, Consulting Psychologists, Flagstaff, AZ; Steven K. Kaplan, Lesley College; Cynthia A. Riccio, Texas A&M University; Alexander I. Troster, The University of Kansas Medical Center; Christopher Tolsdorf, University of Connecticut; Glenna B. Rubin, St. John's University.

Finally, the contributions of Sean Wakely, Susan Hutchinson, and the rest of the staff at Allyn and Bacon are gratefully acknowledged. Their expertise and pleasant and cooperative working style made this book an enjoyable and productive endeavor.

D. P. F.
K. S. M.
S. O. O.

CHAPTER

1

The Wechsler Scales in Perspective

Historical and Contemporary Views

No theory is good unless it permits, not rest, but the greatest work. No theory is good except on condition that one use it to go on beyond.

—André Gide (1913)

Few things in life achieve preeminent stature without some merit. Substance is, after all, the fundamental criteria against which we assess greatness in nearly every case. Within the field of applied psychological assessment, the substantive elements underlying the Wechsler Intelligence Scales have served to propel these instruments to positions of dominance and popularity unrivaled in the history of intellectual assessment. The concepts, methods, and procedures embodied in the design of the Wechsler Scales have been so influential, that they have guided the majority of development and research in the field over the last half century. Virtually every reviewer of these scales, including those who voice significant concerns about the test, acknowledge the monumental impact and position of central importance that the scales have occupied in scientific endeavors aimed at understanding the nature of human intelligence and cognitive abilities. For example, despite the critical content and tone of their review, McDermott, Fantuzzo, and Glutting (1990) assert their "deep respect for most of the Wechsler heritage" by stating that "were we to say everything we might about the Wechsler Scales and their contributions to research and practice, by far our comments would be quite positive" (p. 291).

Kamphaus (1993) has also observed that praise flows from the pages of the majority of those who have written about the Wechsler Scales. The titles of many articles in the professional literature continue to illustrate the heights to which the Wechsler Scales have been elevated; for example, "King WISC the third assumes the throne" (Kaufman, 1994b). Although such praise of the Wechsler Scales has always exceeded their criticisms, they have not been without their detractors. In fact, critics of the Wechsler Scales offer compelling arguments that outline one or more significant deficiencies in these instruments (e.g., Braden, 1995; Little, 1992; McGrew, 1994; Shaw, Swerdlik, & Laurent, 1993; Sternberg,

1993; Witt & Gresham, 1985). Nonetheless, it remains clear that when viewed from a historical perspective, the importance, influence, and contribution of David Wechsler's instruments to the science of intellectual assessment can neither be disputed nor diminished.

The purpose of this chapter is neither to pay another tribute to the Wechsler Scales nor present a thesis regarding its failings. Rather, the purpose of this chapter is to provide factual and historical information regarding the Wechsler Scales and to trace developments that have occurred in attempts to interpret and derive meaning from the Wechsler scores.

The Wechsler Scales: History and Approaches to Interpretation

Kamphaus, Petoskey, and Morgan (1997) offered an extended treatment of the historical precedents and contemporary developments regarding interpretive approaches with the Wechsler Scales. These authors describe the history of intelligence test interpretation in terms of four waves: (1) quantification of a general level; (2) clinical profile analysis; (3) psychometric profile analysis; and (4) application of theory to intelligence test interpretation. Kamphaus and colleagues' four-wave framework will be used to organize the current treatment of the development of the Wechsler Scales and, more importantly, the evolution of approaches to interpreting the Wechsler Scales.

The First Wave: Quantification of General Level

To a large extent, the widespread acceptance of the early intelligence tests (the Stanford-Binet, in particular) was grounded in the conclusion that intelligence tests offered an objective method for creating distinct groups of people differentiated on the basis of their general intelligence. According to Kamphaus and colleagues (1997), this represented the first wave of intelligence test interpretation and was driven by practical considerations related to classification of individuals into separate groups.

During this period, the focus in interpretation for most all individually administered intelligence tests was on the omnibus IQ. The dominant influence of Spearman's g theory of intelligence and the age-based Stanford-Binet Scale, combined with the fact that factor-analytic and psychometric methods were not available for the identification of multiple cognitive abilities, contributed to an almost exclusive focus on using a global IQ to classify individuals. In turn, a number of classification systems were proposed for organizing individuals according to their global IQ.

Some of these early classification systems used labels that corresponded to medical and legal terminology (e.g., *idiot, imbecile,* and *moron*). Although the Wechsler Scales did not contribute to the early classification efforts during most of this interpretive wave, Wechsler eventually made a significant contribution. He proposed a classification scheme that relied less on evaluative terminology (albeit, it still contained the terms *defective* and *borderline*) and more on meaningful deviations from the mean that reflected the "prevalence of certain intelligence levels in the country at that time" (Kamphaus et al., 1997, p. 35). With some refinements, interpretation of intelligence tests in the present day continue to be based on this type of classification system, as distinctions are still made between individuals who are mentally retarded, learning disabled, and gifted, for example.

It appears that Wechsler accepted the prevailing ideas regarding *g* and the definition of intelligence as a global entity along the lines already postulated by Terman, Binet, Spearman, and others (Reynolds & Kaufman, 1990) when he offered his own definition of intelligence as being "the aggregate or global capacity of the individual to act purposefully, to think rationally and to deal effectively with his environment." Wechsler specified that this definition "avoids singling out any ability, however esteemed (e.g., abstract reasoning), as crucial or overwhelmingly important" (Wechsler, 1939, p. 3) and implies that any one intelligence subtest is readily interchangeable with another.

The Second Wave: Clinical Profile Analysis

Kamphaus and colleagues (1997) identified the second wave in interpretation as *clinical profile analysis* and suggested that the publication of the Wechsler-Bellevue (W-B; Wechsler, 1939) was pivotal in spawning the profile approach to interpretation, an approach that sought to understand individuals beyond identification of their global intellectual ability. The relationship between the development of the Wechsler Scales and the second wave of interpretation, as well as subsequent historical and conceptual developments of the Wechsler Scales and approaches to interpretation, is summarized in Figure 1.1.

The Wechsler-Bellevue Intelligence Scale, Form I, published in 1939 (a slightly updated version, Form II, was published in 1946), represented an approach to intellectual assessment in adults that was differentiated clearly from other instruments available at that time (e.g., the Binet scales). The W-B was comprised of 11 separate subtests, including Information, Comprehension, Arithmetic, Digit Span, Similarities, Vocabulary, Picture Completion, Picture Arrangement, Block Design, Digit Symbol, and Coding. Perhaps the most notable feature introduced with the W-B that contributed to an emphasis in interpretation on more than a global IQ was the grouping of subtests into the now familiar Verbal and Performance dichotomy, an organizational structure that was based on the notion that intelligence could be expressed and measured through both verbal and nonverbal modes of communication. In attempting to clarify his use of and the distinction between the verbal and nonverbal methods for assessing intelligence, Wechsler asserted that this dichotomy:

> [D]oes not imply that these are the only abilities involved in the tests. Nor does it presume that there are different kinds of intelligence, e.g., verbal, manipulative, etc. It merely implies that these are different ways in which intelligence may manifest itself. (Wechsler, 1958, p. 64)

Another important feature pioneered in the W-B revolved around the construction and organization of subtests. At the time, the Binet Scale was ordered and administered sequentially according to developmental age, irrespective of the task. In contrast, Wechsler utilized only 11 subtests, each scored by points rather than age, and each with a sufficient range of item difficulties to encompass the entire age range of the scale.

In his writings, Wechsler often shifted between conceptualizing intelligence as a singular entity (the first wave) and conceptualizing it as a collection of primary mental abili-

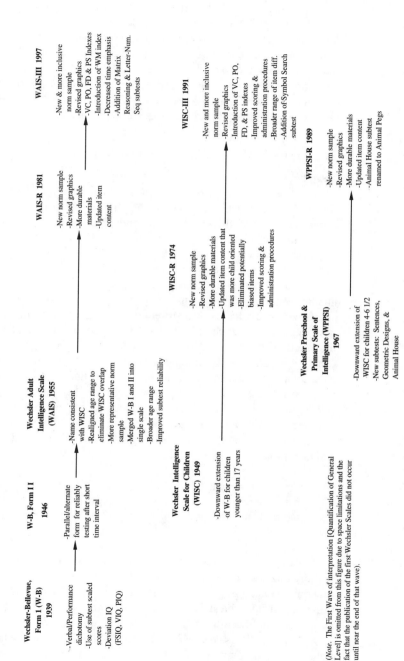

FIGURE 1.1 Timeline of Wechsler Intelligence Scale Revisions and Corresponding Interpretive Approaches

ties, a notion more consistent with the emphasis on profile interpretation during the second wave. At times he appeared to encourage the practice of individual interpretation of subtests, and suggested that each one represented a relatively distinct and different measure of intellectual ability (McDermott, Fantuzzo, & Glutting, 1990). To many, this position seems to represent a theoretical contradiction to his prior meticulous attempts not to equate general intelligence with the sum of separate intellectual abilities. This shift in viewpoint may have been responsible, in part, for the development of methods for interpreting the constructs underlying individual subtests that established the trend toward profile analysis.

Unquestionably, the structure, organization, and innovations found in the original W-B were impressive, practical, and in many respects, superior to any other instruments available in 1939. More importantly, the structure and organization of the W-B scale stimulated the pioneering efforts of Rapaport, Gill, and Schafer (1945–46) to invent approaches to test interpretation that focused on understanding the meaning behind the shape of a person's profile of subtest scores. According to Kamphaus and colleagues (1997), a new method of test interpretation developed under the assumption that "patterns of high and low subtest scores could presumably reveal diagnostic and psychotherapeutic considerations" (p. 36). Thus, during the second wave of intelligence test interpretation, the W-B (Wechsler, 1939) provided the major impetus for developing a variety of procedures for deriving diagnostic and prescriptive meaning from not only the shape of Wechsler subtest profiles, but also Verbal and Performance discrepancies and, in some cases, individual item responses.

In addition to the enormous scope of Rapaport and colleagues' (1945–46) diagnostic suggestions, their approach to understanding profile shape triggered a furious rush of investigations that sought to establish the psychological functions underlying the infinite variety of profile patterns and the nature of their relationships to each other. Perhaps as a consequence of the enormous clinical appeal of the approach espoused by Rapaport and colleagues, Wechsler (1944) helped relegate general level assessment to the back burner while increasing the heat on the analysis of profile shape.

The search for meaning in discrepancies and profiles was carried over to interpretation of the Wechsler Intelligence Scale for Children (WISC; Wechsler, 1949), a downward extension of the W-B. The WISC was comprised of the same 11 subtests used in the W-B, but was modified to assess intellectual functioning in children within the age range of 6 to 16 years. The subtests were grouped into the verbal and performance categories as before, with Information, Comprehension, Arithmetic, Digit Span, Similarities, and Vocabulary making up the verbal subtests, and Picture Completion, Picture Arrangement, Block Design, Object Assembly, and Coding comprising the performance subtests. The WISC also provided scaled scores for each subtest and yielded the ubiquitous Wechsler composite scores: Full Scale IQ (FSIQ), Verbal IQ (VIQ), and Performance IQ (PIQ).

Although the search for diagnostic meaning in differences between Wechsler scores represented a more sophisticated approach to intelligence test interpretation, it also created additional methodological problems. With enough practice, just about any astute clinician could provide a rational interpretation of an obtained profile to fit the known functional or dysfunctional patterns of any individual. Notwithstanding, simple analysis of profile shape or scatter did not create diagnostic or treatment utility automatically. Although the next wave in intelligence test interpretation sought to address such methodological flaws with the clinical profile analysis method, this dominant interpretive approach remains in practice today (Kamphaus et al., 1997).

The Third Wave: Psychometric Profile Analysis

As presented in Figure 1.1, the original W-B scales were revised and updated into a single instrument in 1955. The name was aligned with the existing juvenile version (i.e., WISC) and became known as the Wechsler Adult Intelligence Scale (WAIS; Wechsler, 1955). Major changes and revisions included incorporating Forms I and II of the W-B into a single scale with a broader range of item difficulties, realigning the target age range to include ages 16 years and older (which eliminated overlap with the WISC, creating a larger and more representative norm sample) and refining the subtests to improve reliability.

Within this general time period, technological developments in the form of computers and readily accessible statistical software packages to assist in intelligence test interpretation, provided the impetus for what Kamphaus and colleagues (1997) called the third wave of interpretation—*psychometric profile analysis*. The work of Cohen (1959), which was based extensively on the then new WAIS (Wechsler, 1955), sharply criticized the clinical profile analysis tradition that defined the second wave. For example, Cohen's factor-analytic procedures revealed a viable three-factor solution which rivaled the dichotomous Verbal-Performance model and remained the de facto standard for the Wechsler Scales for decades. Also, by examining and removing the variance shared between subtests, Cohen demonstrated that the majority of Wechsler subtests had very poor specificity (i.e., reliable, specific variance). Thus, the frequent clinical practice of interpreting subtests as reliable measures of a *presumed* construct was not supported. Kamphaus and colleagues (1997) summarize Cohen's significant contributions that largely defined the third wave of test interpretation as threefold: (1) empirical support for the Full Scale IQ based on analysis of shared variance between subtests; (2) development of the three-factor solution for interpretation of the Wechsler Scales; and (3) revelation of limited subtest specificity questioning individual subtest interpretation.

The most vigorous and elegant application of psychometric profile analysis to intelligence test interpretation occurred with the revision of the venerable WISC (Wechsler Intelligence Scale for Children—Revised; Wechsler, 1974). Briefly, as summarized in Figure 1.1, the WISC-R utilized a larger, more representative norm sample than its predecessor, included more contemporary-looking graphics and updated items, eliminated content that was differentially familiar to specific groups, and included improved scoring and administration procedures. Armed with the WISC-R, Kaufman (1979) articulated the essence of the psychometric profile approach to intelligence test interpretation in his seminal book, *Intelligent Testing with the WISC-R* (now superceded by *Intelligent Testing with the WISC-III;* Kaufman, 1994).

Kaufman emphasized flexibility in interpretation and provided a logical and systematic approach that utilized principles grounded in measurement theory. Reflective of the underlying philosophy of the psychometric profile analysis wave, Kaufman's approach required the examiner to have a greater level of psychometric expertise than might ordinarily be possessed by the average clinician. Anastasi (1988) lauded and recognized that "the basic approach described by Kaufman undoubtedly represents a major contribution to the clinical use of intelligence tests. Nevertheless, it should be recognized that its implementation requires a sophisticated clinician who is well informed in several fields of psychology" (p. 484). In some respects, publication of Kaufman's work can be viewed as an indictment against the poorly reasoned and unsubstantiated interpretation of the Wechsler Scales that had sprung up in the second wave (clinical profile analysis). Kaufman's focal message was the notion that interpretation of Wechsler intelligence test performance must be conducted with a higher than usual degree of psychometric precision and must be based on credible and dependable evidence, rather than merely the clinical lore which surrounded earlier interpretive methods. The psychometric profile analysis approach was also applied readily to Wechsler's downward extension of the WISC (i.e., the Wechsler Preschool and Primary Scale of Intelligence; WPPSI; Wechsler, 1967).

Despite the enormous body of literature that has mounted over the years regarding profile analysis of the Wechsler Scales, this form of interpretation, even when upgraded with the rigor of psychometrics, must be regarded as a perilous endeavor, because it is largely without empirical support, and it is not grounded in a well-validated theory of intelligence. With over 75 different profile types discussed in a variety of areas, including neuropsychology, personality, learning disabilities, and juvenile delinquency (McDermott, Fantuzzo, & Glutting, 1990), there is considerable temptation to believe that such analysis is reliable. It must be remembered, however, that many studies (e.g., Hale, 1979; Hale & Landino, 1981; Hale & Saxe, 1983) have demonstrated consistently that "profile and scatter analysis is not defensible" (Glutting, McDermott, Watkins, Kush, & Konold, 1997; Kavale & Forness, 1984, p. 136). In a meta-analysis of 119 studies of the WISC-R subtest data, Mueller, Dennis, and Short (1986) concluded that using profile analysis with the WISC-R in an attempt to differentiate various diagnostic groups is clearly not supported. Recent evaluations regarding the merits of profile analysis have produced similar results (e.g., Glutting, McDermott, & Konold, 1997; Glutting et al., 1997b; Kamphaus, 1993; McDermott, Fantuzzo, Glutting, Watkins, & Baggaley, 1992; Watkins & Kush, 1994). The nature of the controversy surrounding clinical profile analysis, with or without the application of psychometric theory, was brought to the forefront by McDermott and colleagues (1990) in their substantive discussion of the subject. After extensively reviewing the subtest analysis literature and investigating the diagnostic utility of Wechsler subtest scatter based on their own sound analyses of nationally representative datasets, McDermott and colleagues concluded, "until preponderant and convincing evidence shows otherwise, we are compelled to advise that psychologists 'just say no' to subtest analysis" (p. 299).

The Fourth Wave: Application of Theory

The third wave's less-than-impressive results at improving intelligence test interpretation set the stage for the fourth and current wave, described by Kamphaus and colleagues (1997) as *application of theory*. The need to integrate theory and research in the intelligence test interpretation process was articulated best by Kaufman (1979). Specifically, Kaufman commented that problems with intelligence test interpretation can be attributed largely to the lack of a specific theoretical base to guide the practice. He suggested that it was possible to enhance interpretation significantly by reorganizing subtests into clusters specified by a particular theory. In essence, the end of the third wave of intelligence test interpretation and beginning of the fourth wave was marked by Kaufman's pleas for practitioners to ground their interpretations in theory, as well as his efforts to demonstrate the importance of linking intellectual measurement tools to empirically supported and well-established conceptualizations of human cognitive abilities.

In contrast to the Wechsler Scales' central role in the development of new approaches to test interpretation (e.g., clinical and psychometric profile analysis), recent revisions of the Wechsler trilogy (i.e., WPPSI-R, WISC-III, WAIS-R/WAIS-III) have (unfortunately) failed to ride the next wave of test interpretation (i.e., the fourth "theoretical" wave). As seen in Figure 1.1, since the early 1980s the WPPSI and WISC-R have undergone one revision each (WPPSI-R; WISC-III) and the WAIS has undergone two revisions (WAIS-R; WAIS-III). However, neither instrument changed substantially from its predecessor. Changes to the basic structure, item content, and organization of the WPPSI-R and WISC-III were relatively minimal, with the most obvious changes being cosmetic. However, the WISC-III introduced four new composite score indexes, Verbal Comprehension (VC), Perceptual Organization (PO), Freedom from Distractibility (FD), and Processing Speed (PS), to supplement the subtest scaled scores and the FSIQ, VIQ, and PIQ. This version of the WISC also contains one new subtest, Symbol Search.

In terms of structure, organization, and content, the WAIS-R did not represent a significant departure from the WAIS. As summarized in Figure 1.1, the more salient changes reflected in the WAIS-R included a new norm sample, revised item graphics, more durable materials, and updated item content. The WAIS-III, however, reflected more substantive revisions, including more careful attention to the factor structure and statistical linkage to other measures of cognitive functioning and achievement. Of course, the WAIS-III also included the more typical changes, such as the use of updated color graphics with improved item content, and the adoption of the composite indexes first introduced with the WISC-III. The WAIS-III, like the WISC-III, yields a VC, PO, and PS index; however, the FD index was renamed the *Working Memory (WM) Index* in the WAIS-III. This change most likely reflected the considerable controversy over whether FD was a viable construct, as well as the increasing recognition of the importance of working memory in understanding (predicting) specific academic skills. Adding a working memory construct to the underlying factor structure of the WAIS-III led to the development of a working memory test (i.e., Letter-Number Sequencing) and a slight reorganization of subtests, based on the results of factor analyses (Wechsler, 1997). The organization of subtests according to the respective underlying factor structures of the WPPSI-R, WISC-III, and WAIS-III is presented in Table 1.1.

Although the latest versions of the WISC-III and WAIS-III provide more factor-based composite scores for interpretation than their predecessors (i.e., VC, PO, FD, PS, and WM), the fact remains that nearly all current options for interpreting Wechsler test performance are not grounded in any contemporary theoretical model of intelligence. This failure to ground the latest revisions of the Wechsler Scales in a contemporary theoretical model is at variance with Kaufman's (1979) admonition for intelligence tests and intelligence test interpretation to become more theory-based.

The fact that the Wechsler Intelligence Scales lack theoretical substance cannot, in his absence, be attributed to David Wechsler. Admittedly, David Wechsler was not often considered a theoretician in his own right and the name "*Wechsler*" is rarely followed by the word *theory* in the professional literature. Discussions of his work invariably refer to

TABLE 1.1 Factor Indexes and Organization of Subtests in the Current Wechsler Intelligence Scales

TEST	FACTOR	SUBTEST
WPPSI-R	Verbal Comprehension (VC)	Information Similarities Vocabulary Comprehension Arithmetic Sentences
	Perceptual Organization (PO)	Picture Completion Block Design Mazes Animal Pegs Geometric Designs
WISC-III	Verbal Comprehension (VC)	Information Similarities Vocabulary Comprehension
	Perceptual Organization (PO)	Picture Completion Picture Arrangement Block Design Object Assembly
	Freedom from Distractibility (FD)	Arithmetic Digit Span
	Processing Speed (PS)	Coding Symbol Search
WAIS-III	Verbal Comprehension (VC)	Information Similarities Vocabulary Comprehension
	Perceptual Organization (PO)	Picture Completion Block Design Matrix Reasoning
	Working Memory (WM)	Arithmetic Digit Span Letter–Number Sequencing
	Processing Speed (PS)	Digit Symbol-Coding Symbol Search

Wechsler's *views*, or Wechsler's *definition*, and not Wechsler's *theory*. However, if he were alive today, the possibility exists that the Wechsler Scales would have kept abreast with the theoretical focus of contemporary intelligence test development and, may have even led these efforts.

Although Wechsler's name is still listed as the author of all revisions since his death in 1981, this most likely reflects contractual obligations. The publisher of the Wechsler Scales, as well as the members of the work groups organized by the publisher, are more accurately responsible for the slow, incremental changes in the Wechsler Scales. Historical continuity and tradition apparently has played a stronger role than theoretical considerations in the revisions of the Wechsler Scales.

In addition to a greater focus on the development and revision of intelligence tests based on a theoretical framework during the fourth wave, Kamphaus (1993, 1998) extended the portion of Kaufman's intelligent testing approach that espouses a method for integrating theory and hypothesis validation in the test interpretation process. Briefly, Kamphaus warned against the practice of using results from intelligence tests in isolation, without the benefit of other supporting data. In addition, he emphasized the need to base interpretations on research evidence and theory. Central to this approach is the *a priori* specification of hypotheses relevant to the referral questions. The development of such hypotheses changes the nature of the assessment and interpretive process from exploratory to confirmatory. Typical clinically based profile analyses generally require the clinician to gather a wide variety of evidence and, subsequently, engage in attempts to make sense of it *a posteriori*. Conversely, Kamphaus suggested that a hypothesis should arise from already existing evidence and then be tested specifically (see case study presentation in Chapter 7). A crude analogy of this distinction may be expressed as the difference between a leisurely fishing trip and a hunting expedition—catching anything that bites versus setting out for specific game.

The primary purpose of this book is to provide a method for guiding interpretation of the Wechsler Scales from an underlying modern theoretical foundation. The theory-based interpretive approach outlined in the subsequent chapters represents an attempt to move the Wechsler Scales into the currents of the fourth wave of intelligence test interpretation (i.e., application of theory). Figure 1.2 illustrates the various theoretical, empirical, and interpretive components that are combined and integrated to create the basic principles of the proposed assessment and interpretive approach.

The approach described herein is an outgrowth of the publication of the *Intelligence Test Desk Reference (ITDR): Gf-Gc Cross-Battery Assessment* (McGrew & Flanagan, 1998), which introduced a comprehensive application of theory-driven assessment and interpretation known as the *cross-battery approach*. One of the core components of the cross-battery approach rests on the adoption and application of an empirically supported, modern theory of intelligence. The two upper boxes on the left side of Figure 1.2 illustrate the development of an integrated Carroll (1989; 1993a) and Horn-Cattell (Horn, 1985; 1988; 1989; 1991) *Gf-Gc* theoretical model that is supported with considerable empirical research that establishes construct validity. The arrows leading from these boxes indicate their integration as the foundation for the *Gf-Gc* based classification of intelligence batteries and supplemental tests according to the broad (Stratum II) and narrow (Stratum I) abilities they measure. In other words, theory specifies the structure and empiricism supports

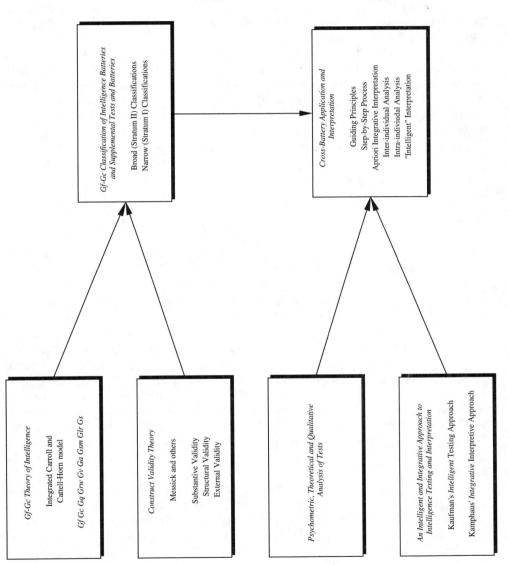

FIGURE 1.2 Major Developmental and Structural Components of *Gf-Gc* Cross-Battery Application and Interpretation

it. The two lower boxes on the left side of Figure 1.2 illustrate the integration of knowledge related to the psychometric, theoretical, and qualitative properties of tests with a rational and sound approach to assessment and interpretation (e.g., Kaufman's intelligent testing approach). The arrows leading from these boxes indicate their integration into a comprehensive, systematic, hypothesis-driven approach to cross-battery based assessment and interpretation, which also rests on the knowledge base of the broad and narrow *Gf-Gc* classifications described in the previous text.

Each of these major developmental and structural components are presented and discussed in detail in the chapters that follow, including the manner in which they may be applied in the assessment of culturally and linguistically diverse populations (see Chapter 8). As such, the remaining chapters of this book offer a formal Wechsler-based *Gf-Gc* cross-battery approach that merges intelligent testing with intelligent interpretation. When fully integrated, we believe that the resulting cross-battery approach represents a pioneering effort in line with the fourth wave of intelligence test interpretation.

Conclusion

The contributions to the science of intellectual assessment made by David Wechsler through his intelligence scales are many and substantial, if not landmark. Although he is not recognized as an important theoretician in the strictest sense, this neither detracts from his accomplishments nor diminishes his innovations in applied psychometrics. Wechsler was a well-known clinician and, as such, he intentionally placed significant importance in developing tasks that had practical, clinical value, and not merely theoretical value. Thus, the driving force behind the development of the Wechsler Scales was no doubt based equally, if not more, on practical considerations rather than theoretical ones. Zachary (1990) stated, "when David Wechsler published the original Wechsler-Bellevue Scales in 1939, he said relatively little about the theoretical underpinnings of his new instrument; rather, he followed a pragmatic approach. He selected a set of tasks that were easy to administer and score" (p. 276). Detterman (1985) also attributed much of the popularity of the Wechsler family of tests to their "ease of administration fostered by an organization of subtests that are brief... and have long clinical histories" (p. 1715). For better or worse, Wechsler's primary motivation for constructing his tests was to create an efficient, easy-to-use tool for clinical purposes; operationalizing them on a specific theory of intelligence was not of paramount importance.

It can be argued reasonably that the popularity and longevity of the Wechsler Scales is more strongly attributed to atheoretical features. Wechsler introduced numerous innovations into the arena of applied intelligence testing that had an immediate appeal to assessment professionals and aided in creating the Wechsler Scales as a viable challenger and alternative to the Binet scales (Reynolds & Kaufman, 1990). Some of the more notable features introduced with the various Wechsler Intelligence Scales included: (1) separate norms for children and adults (with the introduction of the WISC; Wechsler, 1949); (2) the provision for the calculation of subtest standard scores, which made the test open to profile interpretation; (3) multiple-channel assessment that allowed for a fairer method of determining performance through verbal and nonverbal means; and (4) calculation of a new type of standard score, the Deviation IQ, which greatly reduced the theoretical and statistical inadequacies of the Ratio IQ (Zimmerman & Woo-Sam, 1985). In addition, there is some evidence that Wechsler's instruments might have reached their preeminent status precisely because of his reputation as a clinician (Zimmerman & Woo-Sam, 1985). Irrespective of the true reasons for the immediate acceptance and lasting popularity of the Wechsler Scales, their influence on the research and practice of psychology is unparalleled.

In spite of these accomplishments and accolades, under the critical eye of subsequent advancements in the field, the failure of the Wechsler Scales to keep abreast of contemporary intelligence research cannot be ignored. As will be described in Chapters 2 and 3, the extant literature reveals that the Wechsler Scales lack a modern theoretical base, prefer historical continuity over scientific innovation, and are dominated by practical rather than theoretical considerations—all of which raise doubts about the validity of inferences drawn from some of the Wechsler subtest and composite scores. It is clear that meaningful use and interpretation of the Wechsler Scales require the adoption of an alternative (fourth wave) approach in which contemporary theory, research, measurement principles, and hypothesis validation are integrated. Such alternative approaches to measuring intelligence with the Wechsler Scales are necessary in order to reliably and validly assess a broader and more in-depth range of abilities than that which can be accomplished through traditional methods.

Previous attempts have been made to adapt the Wechsler Scales in ways that improve diagnostic precision and interpretive accuracy. However, the research into clinical and psychometric profile analyses is not convincing, and the reliability and validity of such practices are questionable. We believe that clinical judgment and experience are insufficient stanchions on which defensible interpretations can be built. In contrast, the application of theory to intelligence test use and interpretation is beginning to form a solid empirical base. The *Gf-Gc* cross-battery approach offered in this book has considerable promise as an efficient, theoretically and statistically defensible method for assessing and interpreting the broad array of cognitive abilities specified in contemporary psychometric theory. The subsequent chapters of this book demonstrate how the principles and procedures of this approach can be applied to the Wechsler Scales in order to advance the science of measuring multiple cognitive abilities when using these instruments as the core battery in assessment, including the assessment of individuals from diverse cultural and linguistic backgrounds.

CHAPTER

2

Theories and Measures of Intelligence

A Continuum of Progress within the Psychometric Tradition

> *Classification is arguably one of the most central and generic of all our conceptual exercises...without classification, there could be no advanced conceptualization, reasoning, language, data analysis, or for that matter, social science research.*
>
> —K. D. Bailey (1994)

Although the approaches varied across the four waves of intelligence test interpretation described in Chapter 1, they all shared a common goal—the classification of individuals according to their cognitive abilities. The process of analyzing and classifying human cognitive abilities "has intrigued scientists for centuries" (Kamphaus et al., 1997, p. 33) and is a manifestation of the longstanding quest, since the beginning of our existence, to understand the world by creating order. Intelligence tests (such as the Wechsler Scales) have served as the taxonomic or classification tools of researchers and practitioners who have sought to understand and create order within the domain of human cognitive abilities.

Intelligence Tests as Taxonomic Tools

Systematic attempts to classify various parts of the world date back to the Greeks, notably Aristotle, who developed an elaborate taxonomic system for classifying the animal kingdom (Dunn & Everitt, 1982; Lorr, 1983). Today classification is an "activity that is essential to all scientific work" (Dunn & Everitt, 1982, p. 9). Indeed, a specialized science of classification of empirical entities known as *taxonomy* (Bailey, 1994; Prentky, 1994) is ubiquitous in all fields of study, because it guides our search for information or truth.

For centuries, we have both observed and sought to classify and understand differences between people. For example, Plato believed in assigning individuals to tasks for which they were best suited, and Aristotle studied gender and racial differences in mental characteristics (Minton & Schneider, 1980). These early observations and attempts to classify individuals illustrate one of the few irrefutable laws in psychology—the law of individual differences.

Individual differences are evident in the considerable variability that exists across all human traits such as weight, height, temperament, intellect, social skills, and facial characteristics. Thurstone (1935) captured the essence of individual difference in cognitive abilities when he stated:

> A large class of human activity is that which differentiates accomplishments. Just as it is convenient to postulate physical forces in describing the movements of physical objects, so it is natural to postulate abilities and their absence as primary causes of the successful completion of a task by some individual and of the failure of other individuals in the same task. (p. 45)

More recently, Neisser and colleagues (1996) conveyed a similar theme when they stated that "individuals differ from one another in their ability to understand complex ideas, to adapt effectively to the environment, to learn from experience, to engage in various forms of reasoning, to overcome obstacles by taking thought" (p. 77). Thus, for many years scholars have offered the trait or construct of *intelligence* to explain and clarify the complex set of phenomena that account for individual differences in various cognitive capabilities.

Attempts to define the construct of intelligence and to explain and classify individual differences in intellectual functioning have spanned decades and have been characterized by significant variability. The differences between theories of intelligence is exemplified by the various multiple intelligences models that have been offered or revised recently to explain the structure of intelligence (some of which serve as the theoretical foundation of current fourth wave attempts to improve test interpretation). These include Carroll's Three-Stratum Theory of Cognitive Abilities, Gardner's Theory of Multiple Intelligences, the Cattell-Horn Fluid-Crystallized *(Gf-Gc)* theory, Feurestein's theory of Structural Cognitive Modifiability (SCM), the Luria-Das Model of Information Processing, and Sternberg's Triarchic Theory of Intelligence (see Flanagan, Genshaft, & Harrison, 1997, for a comprehensive description of these theories). Each of these theories represents an attempt to comprehend a class of phenomena and, ultimately, fulfill the chief goal of science—to minimize the mental effort needed to understand complex phenomena through classification (Thurstone, 1935, p. 45). To achieve this goal, each theory of intelligence provides a taxonomic framework for classifying and analyzing the nature of the cognitive characteristics that account for the variability in observed intellectual performance among and between individuals.

The remainder of this chapter presents a summary of the state-of-the-art theories of intelligence and provides the context within which the Wechsler Intelligence Scales are evaluated according to contemporary *Gf-Gc* theory, the theory that we believe provides the best framework for moving the interpretation of the Wechsler Scales into credible theory-based (fourth wave) interpretation.

Three General Paradigms for Conceptualizing and Measuring Intelligence

"There is an unlimited number of ways in which nature can be comprehended" (Thurstone, 1935, p. 47). At a general level, the variability in the theories and measures of intelligence can be explained by differences in underlying research traditions in psychological measurement. Taylor (1994) suggests that the psychometric, information processing, and cognitive modifiability theories are the most prominent approaches used to conceptualize the measurement of intelligence.[1]

The *psychometric* or structural approach "attempts to measure performance along dimensions which are purported to constitute the fundamental structure of the psychological domain" (Taylor, 1994, p. 185). In the psychometric approach, psychological tests that yield scores on quantitative scales are used. Correlational and factor analytic methods are employed typically to analyze these scores and identify ability dimensions that form the structure of individual differences in cognitive ability (Gustafsson & Undheim, 1996). The Wechsler Scales and the various approaches to the interpretation of intelligence tests that characterized all four waves of test interpretation (described in Chapter 1) are all products of the psychometric approach to measuring intelligence.

Information-processing theories are more recent in origin (largely since the 1960s) and, in general, have taken a cognitive-rational view of human intellectual functioning using the computer analogy of humans as information processors. In general, information processing theories are "limited capacity theories of cognitive competence" (Taylor, 1994, p. 185) that are concerned with how information is processed efficiently during problem solving and everyday tasks. Information processing approaches view individuals who can process information efficiently through one or more "bottlenecks" as being competent or intelligent. For example, working memory is considered to be a bottleneck because it is a limited-capacity system that can only hold and process a finite amount of information at any one time. As a result, if information is not processed efficiently through working memory, the entire system does not perform at an optimal level. Individuals who have developed skills and strategies for efficient processing of information through working memory can perform at higher levels and are thus considered to be more intelligent (Taylor, 1994).

Information processing research typically uses fine-grained computer-administered chronometric measures of human performance and functioning (e.g., inspection time, average evoked potentials, nerve conduction velocity, reaction time). Currently, practical adaptations of chronometric measures to applied intelligence testing have yet to surface. However, the recent addition of a test of working memory (viz., Letter-Number Sequencing) to the WAIS-III (Wechsler, 1997) and the third edition of the Woodcock-Johnson (WJ-III; Woodcock et al., in press), as well as tests of attention, planning, and rapid automatic naming to the WJ-III and Cognitive Assessment System (CAS: Das & Naglieri, 1997) suggests that information processing concepts are beginning to influence the design and interpretation of intelligence batteries.

Cognitive modifiability theories are based primarily on Vygotsky's (1978) view that cognitive development is a social phenomenon. In particular, they have focused on the "capacity of humans to adapt to circumstantial demands—in other words, to learn to function effectively in their environment" (Taylor, 1994, p. 187). Underlying this conception of cognitive development is the belief that intelligence is dynamic, modifiable, and changeable. Dynamic assessment, which evolved from cognitive modifiability theories, "refers to approaches to the development of decision-specific information that most characteristically involve interaction between the examiner and the examinee, focus on learner metacognitive processes and responsiveness to intervention, and follow a pretest-intervene-posttest administration format (Lidz, 1987; 1991)" (Lidz, 1997, p. 281).

Three general approaches to dynamic assessment have been proposed (Laughon, 1990). In general, dynamic assessment approaches are characterized by an attempt to measure processes through the integration of teaching into the assessment process. With the exception of the Kaufman Adolescent and Adult Intelligence Test (KAIT) and the Woodcock-Johnson series of intelligence batteries (Woodcock & Johnson, 1977; 1989; Woodcock et al., in press), none of the major individually administered intelligence tests include actual learning tasks, let alone tasks and procedures that are consistent with the dynamic assessment model. Kaufman's (1979) criticism of the WISC-R's failure to include actual learning tasks, especially of higher-order cognitive abilities, continues to apply to all revisions of the Wechsler trilogy. The reader is referred to Budoff (1968; 1974; 1987), Feuerstein (1970; 1972; 1979), and Campione and Brown (1987) for a description of the varying dynamic assessment procedures. The interested reader is also referred to Feuerstein, Feuerstein, and Gross's (1997) cogent description of perhaps the most well-known of the dynamic assessment procedures, the Learning Potential Assessment Device.

In summary, the psychometric approach to understanding the structure of intelligence is the oldest and most established of the three approaches, dating back to Galton's attempt, in the late 1800s, to measure intelligence with psychophysical measures (Sternberg & Kaufman, 1998). It is also the approach that is the most research based and that has produced the most economically efficient and practical instruments for measuring intelligence (e.g., Wechsler Scales) (Neisser et al., 1996; Taylor, 1994). Psychometric theories and measures continue to be the dominant force even during the current theory-based wave of interest in test interpretation. On the other hand, to date, the newer information processing and cognitive modifiability theories have produced little in the way of practical measurement tools. The reader is referred to Carroll (1993a), Gustafsson and Undheim (1996), Ittenbach, Esters, and Wainer (1997), Kamphaus (1993), Sattler (1988), and Thorndike and Lohman (1990) for historical information on the development of psychometric theories of intelligence.

Psychometric Theories and Measures of Intelligence: Where Do the Wechsler Intelligence Scales Fit?

The evolution of research on intelligence measures and psychometric theories chronicles the many attempts and progressions toward specifying a "complete" taxonomy of human cognitive abilities. In lieu of a detailed discussion of this research literature, an adaptation and extension of Woodcock's (1994) "continuum of progress in theories of multiple intelligences" is presented. This continuum, shown in the top of Figure 2.1, summarizes the *that was then-this is now* progression of psychometric theories of intelligence. In addition to this continuum, the bottom of Figure 2.1 depicts a parallel continuum of prominent approaches to the applied measurement of intelligence. Through an examination of Figure 2.1, the relation between the respective theoretical benchmarks and intelligence measures is readily apparent. It is important to note that the continua presented in Figure 2.1 do not portray linear *timelines;* rather, they portray the *progress* in understanding and measuring the structure of human intelligence. Note also that the specific theories listed under the theory continuum are illustrative examples and are not intended to represent a complete list of theories.

That Was *Then:* Early or "Incomplete" Taxonomic Theories and Models of Intelligence

Spearman's *g*-Factor Theory

Sir Francis Galton is considered by many to be the father of differential psychology. However, the birth of the psychometric research tradition, by and large, is considered to have begun with Spearman's (1904; 1927) presentation of the general or *g*-factor theory of intelligence and his development and application of factor analytic methods to general mental ability measures (Jensen, 1998). In fact, Spearman's 1904 paper, "General Intelligence Objectively Determined and Measured," is "perhaps the single most important paper in the history of differential psychology and psychometrics" (Jensen, 1998, p. 21). The fundamental premise of Spearman's theory is that a single *g* or general intelligence ability accounts for the performance of individuals on most all types of cognitive tasks. As discussed in Chapter 1, Spearman's general factor theory was largely responsible for the focus on the quantification of a general level of intellectual functioning during the first wave of intelligence test interpretation.

Although Spearman's *g* theory is typically described as a single-factor theory (as displayed in Figure 2.1), this characterization is not completely accurate. In addition to the large *g* factor, Spearman's theory also includes smaller specific *(s)* factors. Spearman eventually became interested in specific cognitive ability factors and, together with Karl Holziner, developed the *bi-factor* model. According to Carroll (1993a), if Spearman had lived beyond 1945, he most likely would have converged on a multiple abilities model similar to the ones proposed by other researchers (e.g., Thurstone's primary mental abilities, which is discussed later in this chapter). As shown in Figure 2.1, the most notable applied measure of intelligence that reflects the *g* model was the omnibus Stanford-Binet Intelligence Scale (Terman, 1916; Terman & Merrill, 1937; Terman & Merrill, 1960; Terman & Merrill, 1972), which provided a single composite intelligence score. The *g*-based Binet was the intelligence test that achieved preeminent status during the first wave of intelligence test interpretation.

Dichotomous Theories and Models

The demise of Spearman's bi-factor model had begun as early as 1909, primarily as a result of the evidence presented by Sir Cyril Burt in favor of *group factors*. According to Jensen (1998), by 1911, Burt's data had convinced most psychologists that it was more reasonable

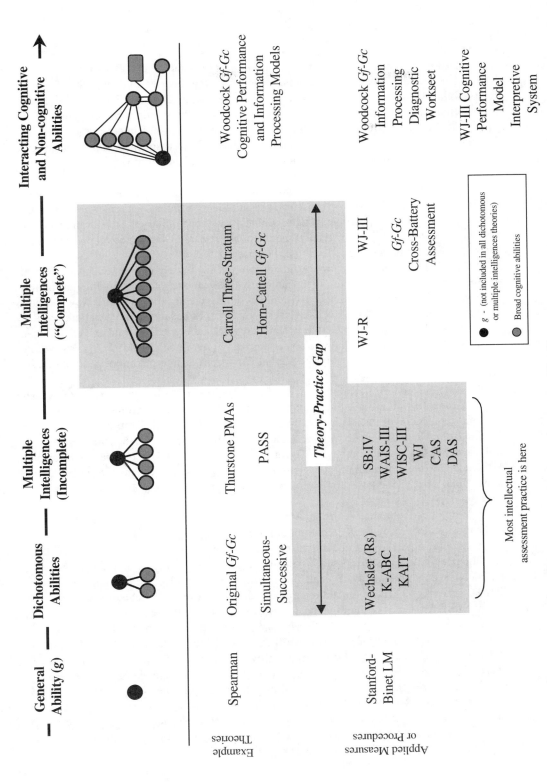

FIGURE 2.1 Progress in Psychometric Theories and Applied Measures of Intelligence

19

to accept the existence of group factors, in addition to *g* and *s*. The evidence for factors beyond *g* resulted in a variety of attempts to develop both theories and measures of group-factor abilities. The recognition that a complete understanding of intelligence required the measurement and interpretation of abilities beyond *g* set the stage for the eventual development and interpretation of new intelligence tests, or the post-hoc interpretation of existing intelligence tests (viz., the Binet) in a more differentiated manner (e.g., the clinical and psychometric profile analyses that characterized the second and third wave of test interpretation, respectively).

One of the more prominent dichotomous models of intelligence was Cattell's (1941; 1957) original *fluid (Gf)* and *crystallized (Gc)* intelligence theory. Cattell, who earned his doctoral degree under Spearman, suggested that *g* was not a unitary trait, but rather a composite of two different types of general factors or abilities representing novel problem solving *(Gf)* and consolidated knowledge *(Gc)* (Jensen, 1998).

The dichotomous *Gf-Gc* theory did not result in any widely used practical assessment instrument at the time. However, many attempts were made to interpret intelligence batteries according to the dichotomous *Gf-Gc* model during the second and third waves of test interpretation. In the case of Wechsler's tests, differences between the Verbal and Performance scales have been suggested to be "indicative of differences in fluid and crystallized ability rather than in verbal and nonverbal thinking" (Kaufman, 1994, p. 167). As will be seen in subsequent chapters, only the Verbal/*Gc* Wechsler interpretation is supported by contemporary research.

Although the KAIT (Kaufman & Kaufman, 1993) is a relatively new intelligence battery, its organization around the dichotomous *Gf-Gc* model has warranted its placement near the "older" end of the theory continuum in Figure 2.1. As will be presented later in this section, John Horn's program of research had a significant impact on the evolution of Cattell's model into a multidimensional group-factor theory. This theory has significantly influenced the development of theory-based intelligence tests, as well as the current fourth wave theory-based methods for interpreting intelligence test performance (McGrew & Flanagan, 1998).

Without a doubt, the Wechsler *verbal/nonverbal* (performance) model of intelligence is the most widely recognized dichotomous model of cognitive abilities. It is also the model that has produced the most frequently used intelligence batteries to date (viz., the Wechsler Intelligence Scales). As discussed in Chapter 1, David Wechsler designed his first scale based on a combination of clinical, practical, and empirical considerations (Kaufman, 1990a; Zachary, 1990) and did not regard the Verbal-Performance dichotomy as representing two different types of intelligence. Rather, his intent was to organize the tests to reflect the two different ways (i.e., two different "languages") through which intelligence can be expressed (Kamphaus, 1993; Reynolds & Kamphaus, 1990; Zachary, 1990). Although verbal abilities represent a valid cognitive ability construct (i.e., crystallized intelligence), there is no such thing as *nonverbal ability*—only abilities that are expressed nonverbally. While the above information is presented in greater detail in the "theory" section of this book, it should serve to remind assessment professionals that the various versions of Wechsler's Scales *were not (and are not) based on an empirically supported theory of intelligence*. The relation between the Wechsler model and contemporary empirically based models of intelligence is discussed later in this chapter.

Finally, since the early to mid 1980s there has been interest in developing tests that have their roots in a neuropsychological model of cognitive processing advanced by Soviet neuropsychologist, A. R. Luria (Sternberg, 1997). Luria's work (1966; 1970; 1973; 1980), plus related experimental and cognitive psychological research (Anokhin, 1969; Broadbent, 1958; Das, Kirby & Jarman, 1979; Hunt & Lansman, 1986), has suggested a model of cognitive processing based on two to four mental operations (Kamphaus, 1990; 1993; Kamphaus & Reynolds, 1984; Kaufman, 1984; Kaufman & Kaufman, 1983; Naglieri, 1997; Naglieri & Das, 1990).

As reflected in Figure 2.1, the two-factor *simultaneous/successive* processing model of intelligence spawned the development of the Kaufman Assessment Battery for Children (K-ABC; Kaufman & Kaufman, 1983). *Simultaneous processing,* primarily associated with the right cerebral hemisphere, is involved in the integration or synthesis of stimuli into groups when the individual components of the stimuli are interrelated (Kaufman, 1994; Naglieri, 1997). In contrast, *successive processing,* typically associated with left-hemisphere functioning, is involved when the individual stimuli are processed in a serial order and there is no point in time at which the stimuli are interrelated.

The K-ABC was the first norm-referenced cognitive battery that was designed primarily to operationalize the simultaneous and successive processing dichotomy. When evaluated in the context of current psychometric research and theory, the K-ABC has been found to assess only a very limited range of known mental abilities, namely visual processing and short-term memory (Carroll, 1993a; McGrew & Flanagan, 1998; Woodcock, 1990). According to Carroll (1993a), visual processing and short-term memory factors have been included in the cognitive factor analytic research literature well before the publication of the K-ABC; therefore, "there is little if anything that is new in the K-ABC test" (p. 703).

Attempts have also been made to interpret the Wechsler Scales from the simultaneous/successive processing framework (Kaufman, 1994). From this perspective the Wechsler perceptual organization tests (viz., Picture Completion, Block Design, and Object Assembly) are interpreted as measures of simultaneous processing, while the Picture Arrangement, Digit Span (forward) and Coding tests are interpreted as indicators of successive processing. The reader is referred to Kaufman (1994) for details regarding the application of this dichotomous model to the Wechsler Scales.

"Incomplete" Multiple Intelligences Theories and Models

The earliest attempt to identify multiple intelligences—a development that contributed to the proliferation of attempts to understand a person's profile of abilities via clinical and psychometric analysis—was undoubtedly Thurstone's factor-analysis-based efforts to identify *primary mental abilities* (*PMA;* Thurstone, 1938; Thurstone & Thurstone, 1941). The PMA theory suggested that, rather than being a function of *g,* performance on psychometric tests of cognitive ability was due to a number of primary mental abilities or faculties such as Space, Perceptual Speed, Number, Verbal Meaning, Word Fluency, Memory, and Inductive Reasoning (Kamphaus, 1993). Thurstone's PMA model is significant, as most modern test construction tends to be based on it (Taylor, 1994). Although some of the primary mental abilities are reflected in certain Wechsler tests (e.g., Verbal Meaning and the Vocabulary test; Number and the Arithmetic test), these are post-hoc interpretations; the original Wechsler Scales and subsequent revisions were not explicitly constructed to operationalize all or part of the PMA model. Other examples of factor analytically based models are seen in the works of Burt (1949), French, Eckstrom, and Price (1963), and Vernon (1961). Given the benefit of hindsight, the generation of multiple intelligences theories described thus far is now seen as being relatively "incomplete."

As depicted in Figure 2.1, the simultaneous/successive processing model has recently evolved into a four-construct *Planning, Attention, Simultaneous,* and *Successive* model (*PASS;* Das & Naglieri, 1997; Naglieri & Das, 1997) based on the work of A. R. Luria (1966). *Planning,* which has been an important construct in the neuropsychological arena, is one of a number of activity-related executive functions used to identify and organize steps required to achieve a goal or carry out an intention. It is characterized by forward thinking, the generation of alternatives, the weighing and making of choices, and the development of a framework or structure that provides direction in the completion of a plan (Lezak, 1995). According to Naglieri (1997), *attention* involves those processes that allow individuals to focus and respond to a particular stimulus while concurrently ignoring competing stimuli.

The *Cognitive Assessment System* (*CAS;* Das & Naglieri, 1997) is a psychometric intelligence battery specifically designed to operationalize the PASS model. Thus, it is an example of a recent attempt to move test interpretation into the fourth wave. Based on independent research and reviews (Carroll, 1993a; 1995a; Kranzler, Flanagan, & Keith, 1999; Kranzler & Keith, in press; Kranzler & Weng, 1995), the CAS is classified as an incomplete measure of cognitive abilities and its underlying theory. In addition to the above sources, the reader is referred to McGrew and Flanagan (1998), Das, Naglieri, and Kirby (1994), Naglieri (1997), and Chapter 5 of this book for additional information regarding the differing interpretations of the constructs measured by the CAS.

There have been recent attempts to interpret the Wechsler Scales from the perspective of the PASS model. Naglieri (1997) suggested the following: (1) the Wechsler Performance scale is primarily (but not exclusively) a measure of simultaneous processing; (2) Digit Span (forward only) measures successive processing; and (3) the Verbal scale represents verbal/achievement abilities that involve a variety of PASS processes. Although Naglieri believes that planning and attention are not adequately assessed by the Wechsler Scales, Kaufman (1994) suggested that the Wechsler Scales Processing Speed Index measures planning ability and that the Arithmetic, Digit Span, and Digit-Symbol/Coding subtests, which fall under the Freedom from Distractibility factor, measure attention. The reader is referred to Das and colleagues (1994), Kaufman (1994), and Naglieri (1997) for detailed discussions of hypothesized PASS interpretations of the Wechsler Scales. As will be demonstrated in Chapter 3, the extant cognitive abilities factor analytic research does not support either Naglieri's (1997) or Kaufman's (1994) interpretations of the Wechsler-PASS relationship. Rather, this research suggests that the Wechsler subtests are best understood as measures of a narrow range of *Gf-Gc* abilities.

As presented in Figure 2.1, the majority of currently used intelligence batteries are classified as incomplete measures of multiple cognitive abilities (viz., CAS, Differential Abilities Scales [DAS; Elliott, 1990a], Stanford-Binet Intelligence Scale: Fourth Edition

[SB:IV; Thorndike, Hagen, & Sattler, 1986], and the original Woodcock-Johnson Psycho-Educational Battery [WJ; Woodcock & Johnson, 1977]). Of these three batteries, the DAS appears to assess the broadest array of cognitive abilities (McGrew, 1997).

As presented in Figure 2.1, the most recent Wechsler Intelligence Scales (i.e., Wechsler Intelligence Scale for Children—Third Edition [WISC-III; Wechsler, 1991] and WAIS-III) represent progress in the evolution of these batteries. However, the WISC-III and WAIS-III are still classified as "incomplete" since they measure only a subset of the known broad cognitive abilities (viz., three to five *Gf-Gc* abilities). However, as will be discussed in later chapters, when combined with other measures (e.g., the Children's Memory Scale [CMS; Cohen, 1997]; Wechsler Memory Scale—Third Edition [WMS-III; Wechsler, 1997]; WJ-III), the Wechsler system of instruments can aid in narrowing the intelligence theory-practice gap.

This Is *Now:* Contemporary or "Complete" Taxonomic Theories and Models of Intelligence

As portrayed in Figure 2.1, psychometric intelligence theories have converged recently on a more "complete" (in a relative sense, no theory is ever complete) *Gf-Gc* multiple intelligences taxonomy, reflecting a review of the extant factor analytic research conducted over the past 50 to 60 years. This taxonomy serves as the organizational framework for both the Carroll and Cattell-Horn models (Carroll, 1983; 1989; 1993a; 1997; Gustafsson, 1984; 1988; Horn, 1988; 1991; 1994; Horn & Noll, 1997; Lohman, 1989; Snow, 1986), the two most prominent psychometric theories of intelligence proposed to date (McGrew & Flanagan, 1998; Sternberg & Kaufman, 1998).

As depicted in Figure 2.1, only the Woodcock-Johnson Psycho-Educational Battery—Revised (WJ-R; Woodcock & Johnson, 1989) and the Woodcock-Johnson Psycho-Educational Battery—Third Edition (WJ-III; Woodcock et al., in press) come close to measuring the broad abilities specified in the more "complete" psychometrically based *Gf-Gc* multiple intelligences theories. This is not surprising given that the *Gf-Gc* framework drove the design of both the WJ-R and WJ-III. Recent joint or cross-battery factor analyses of the major intelligence batteries with the WJ-R (e.g., Flanagan & McGrew, 1998; McGhee, 1993; McGrew, 1997; Woodcock, 1990) indicated that the majority of these batteries do not adequately assess the complete range of *broad Gf-Gc* abilities included in either Horn's (1991; 1994) or Carroll's (1993a; 1997) model of the structure of intelligence. The one possible exception is the WJ-III which was designed to measure the greatest practically feasible range of *Gf-Gc* abilities. But even the WJ-III may benefit from supplementation via *Gf-Gc* cross-battery procedures (McGrew & Flanagan, 1998), particularly when attempting to assess more thoroughly a person's specific or narrow cognitive abilities.

Finally, while research continues to focus on identifying major abilities in the multiple intelligences taxonomy (Carroll, 1993a), a number of researchers are attempting to push the far end of the intelligence theory continuum by proposing models that describe and explain cognitive performance as a composition of both cognitive and noncognitive variables within an information processing framework (see Figure 2.1). For example, Woodcock (1993; 1997; 1998) has presented a *Gf-Gc Cognitive Performance Model (CPM)* and an *Information Processing Model (IPM)*. These recent theoretical developments, which are described later in this chapter, will continue to stimulate efforts in theory-based interpretation (i.e., the fourth wave) and may eventually contribute to a (yet to be identified) fifth wave of interpretation.

What Is *Gf-Gc* Theory?

Gf-Gc theory is the most comprehensive and empirically supported psychometric theory of intelligence. Therefore, we believe that the *Gf-Gc* theory should serve as a foundation for the development and interpretation of intelligence batteries. In order to implement a *Gf-Gc*-based approach to assessing and interpreting cognitive functioning with the Wechsler Intelligence Scales, it is necessary to understand the major components of the theory.

The Evolution of *Gf-Gc* Theory

Cattell (1941; 1957) first postulated *Gf-Gc* theory as consisting of two major types of cognitive abilities (i.e., *Gf* and *Gc*). Fluid Intelligence *(Gf)* was thought to include inductive and deductive reasoning, abilities thought to be influenced by both biological and neurological factors and incidental learning through interaction with the environment (Taylor, 1994). In contrast, Crystallized Intelligence *(Gc)* was believed to consist primarily of abilities (especially knowledge) that reflected the influences of acculturation (viz., verbal-conceptual knowledge; Gustafsson, 1994; Taylor, 1994). Thus, the original *Gf-Gc* theory was a dichotomous conceptualization of human cognitive ability. Unfortunately (or fortunately, depending on one's belief in maintaining the historical integrity of a theory), the *Gf-Gc* label has been retained as the acronym for this theory, despite the fact that the theory has not been conceived of as a dichotomy since the 1960s (Gustafasson &Undheim, 1986; Horn & Noll, 1997; Woodcock, 1993). As a result, *Gf-Gc* theory is misunderstood often as being a two-factor model of the structure of intelligence.

As early as the mid-1960s, Horn (1965) expanded the *Gf-Gc* model to include four additional cognitive abilities, including visual perception or processing *(Gv)*, short-term memory (Short-Term Acquisition and Retrieval—SAR or *Gsm*), long-term storage and retrieval (Tertiary Storage and Retrieval—TSR or *Glr*), and speed of processing *(Gs)*. By 1968, Horn had refined the definition of *Gv, Gs,* and *Glr,* and added auditory processing ability *(Ga)*. More recently, factors representing a person's quantitative ability or knowledge *(Gq)* and facility with reading and writing *(Grw)* (Horn, 1985; 1988; 1991; Woodcock, 1994) were added to the model, resulting in a ten-factor ability structure.

The Hierarchical Structure of *Gf-Gc* Theory

In his review of the extant factor-analytic research literature, Carroll (1993a) differentiated factors or abilities by three strata that varied according to the "relative variety and diversity of variables" (Carroll, 1997, p. 124) included at each level. The various *"G"* abilities are the most prominent and recognized abilities in the model. They include *Gf, Gc,* and so on. These abilities are classified as broad or stratum II abilities in Carroll's model. The *broad abilities* represent "basic constitutional and longstanding characteristics of individuals that can govern or influence a great variety of behaviors in a given domain" and they vary in their emphasis on process, content, and manner of response (Carroll, 1993a, p. 634). What is often not immediately clear when discussing *Gf-Gc* theory is that the broad abilities subsume a large number of narrow or stratum I abilities (currently approximately 70 have been identified; Carroll, 1993a; 1997). *Narrow abilities* "represent greater specializations of abilities, often in quite specific ways that reflect the effects of experience and learning, or the adoption of particular strategies of performance" (Carroll, 1993a, p. 634). The hierarchical structure of *Gf-Gc* theory is demonstrated for the domain of visual processing *(Gv)* in Figure 2.2.

In the *Gf-Gc* taxonomy, *Gv* is classified as a broad stratum II cognitive ability. The 11 narrow or stratum I visual abilities that comprise *Gv* clearly demonstrate the "broadness" or breadth of this factor (see Figure 2.2). Figure 2.2 conveys that 11 different narrow or specialized visual processing abilities have been identified. The broad and narrow *Gv* abilities presented in Figure 2.2, as well as the other *Gf-Gc* broad and narrow abilities, are defined later in this chapter. The significant moderate to high intercorrelations displayed by these narrow abilities suggests the presence of a broader factor or construct that accounts for this shared visual processing variance. The broad *Gv* factor is hypothesized to represent this higher-order explanatory construct and is believed to exert a significant common effect (reflected by the direction of the arrows in Figure 2.2) on the narrow abilities. When extended to the nine other broad cognitive domains, all of which also subsume a number of narrow abilities, it is clear that the contemporary hierarchical *Gf-Gc* theory is extremely comprehensive.

Even without the benefit of the information presented in subsequent chapters of this book, after reflecting on Figure 2.2, the experienced Wechsler user should be able to identify relations between narrow *Gv* abilities and certain Wechsler nonverbal tests (e.g., the narrow ability of Spatial Relations and the Block Design tests). The experienced Wechsler

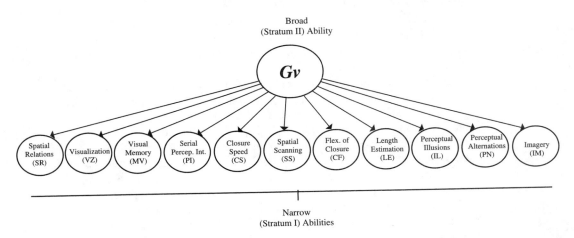

FIGURE 2.2 A Visual Processing *(Gv)* Example Demonstrating the Hierarchical Structure of *Gf-Gc* Theory

user may also observe that the Wechsler Performance scale only measures a subset of the entire *Gv* domain, and that some tests do not seem to fit the empirical taxonomy (e.g., Picture Arrangement). Such observations should set the stage for assessment professionals to recognize the breadth of coverage of certain *Gf-Gc* abilities (or lack thereof) by their favorite intelligence batteries. This will be discussed in detail in subsequent chapters.

The broadest or most general level of ability in the *Gf-Gc* model is represented by stratum III, located at the apex of the Carroll (1993a) hierarchy. This single cognitive ability which subsumes both broad (stratum II) and narrow (stratum I) abilities, is interpreted by Carroll as representing a general factor (i.e., *g*) that is involved in complex higher-order cognitive processes (Gustafsson & Undheim, 1996).

Finally, it is important to recognize that the abilities within each level of the hierarchical *Gf-Gc* model typically display non-zero positive intercorrelations (Carroll, 1993a; Gustafsson & Undheim, 1996). For example, similar to the *Gv* discussion above, the different stratum I (narrow) abilities that define the various *Gf-Gc* domains are correlated positively to varying degrees. These intercorrelations give rise to and allow for the estimation of the stratum II (broad) ability factors. Likewise, the positive non-zero correlations among the stratum II (broad) *Gf-Gc* abilities allows for the estimation of the stratum III (general) *g* factor. The positive factor intercorrelations within each level of the *Gf-Gc* hierarchy indicates that the different *Gf-Gc* abilities do not reflect independent (uncorrelated or orthogonal) traits.

The Carroll and Cattell-Horn *Gf-Gc* Models

The simplified (i.e., narrow abilities omitted) Cattell-Horn and Carroll *Gf-Gc* models are presented together in Figure 2.3. A review of Figure 2.3 reveals a number of notable similarities and differences between the two models. In general, these models are similar in that they both include some form of fluid *(Gf)*, crystallized *(Gc)*, short-term memory and/or learning *(Gsm or Gy)*, visual *(Gv)*, auditory *(Ga or Gu)*, retrieval *(Glr or Gr)*, processing speed *(Gs)*, and decision and/or reaction time speed *(CDS or Gt)* abilities. Although there are some differences in broad ability definitions and in the narrow abilities subsumed by the respective broad *Gf-Gc* abilities, the major differences between the two models are primarily four-fold (McGrew, 1997).

First, the Carroll and Cattell-Horn models differ in their inclusion of *g* at stratum III. According to Carroll (1993a; 1997), the general intelligence factor at the apex of his three-stratum theory is analogous to Spearman's *g*. The off-center placement of *g* (to the left side of Figure 2.3) in the Carroll model is intended to reflect the strength of the relations between *g* and the respective broad *Gf-Gc* abilities. As represented in the Carroll model portion of Figure 2.3 (i.e., the top half of the figure), *Gf* has been reported to have the strongest association with *g,* followed next by *Gc,* and continuing on through the remaining abilities to the two broad abilities that are weakest in association with *g* (i.e., *Gs* and *Gt*).[2]

Carroll (1997) believes that the evidence for *g* is overwhelming. Horn disagrees with Carroll (see Horn, 1991; Horn & Noll, 1997), and instead posits what Jensen (1998) calls a *truncated hierarchical model,* a model that does not contain a single *g* factor at the apex. Debates about the nature and existence of *g* have waxed and waned for decades and have been some of the liveliest debates in differential psychology (Gustafsson & Undheim, 1996; Jensen, 1997). Much of the debate has been theoretical in nature with definitions of *g* ranging from an index of neural cognitive efficiency, general reasoning ability or mental energy to a mere statistical irregularity (Neisser et al., 1996). After being more or less banned from the scientific scene (Gustafsson & Undheim, 1996), the prominent position of *g* in contemporary models of intelligence (e.g., Carroll's Three-Stratum model and Jensen's [1998] seminal *g* factor treatise) has helped it to once again take center stage in intelligence research and dialogue. Interested readers are directed to the writings of Carroll (1993a; 1997), Horn (1991), Horn and Noll (1997), and Jensen (1997; 1998) for further discussion of the *g*-related issues and research.

Second, in the Cattell-Horn model, quantitative knowledge and quantitative reasoning abilities together represent a distinct broad ability, as depicted by the *Gq* rectangle in the bottom half of Figure 2.3. Carroll (1993a), on the other hand, considers quantitative ability to be "an inexact, unanalyzed popular concept that has no scientific meaning unless it is referred to the structure of abilities that compose it. It cannot be expected to constitute a higher-level ability" (p. 627). Therefore, Carroll classifies quantitative reasoning as a nar-

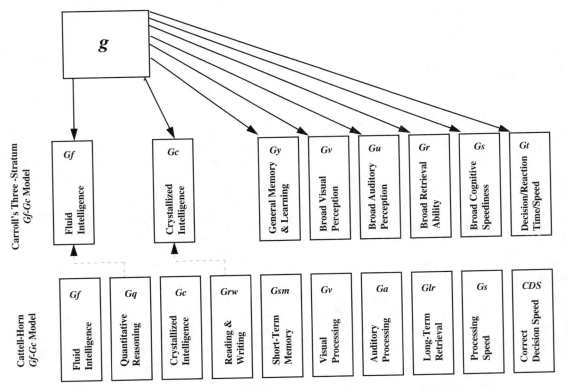

FIGURE 2.3 The Broad and General Strata of the Cattell-Horn and Carroll *Gf-Gc* Models

row ability subsumed by *Gf,* as indicated by the arrow leading from the *Gq* rectangle in the Cattell-Horn model to the *Gf* rectangle in the Carroll model in Figure 2.3. Furthermore, Carroll included mathematics achievement and mathematics knowledge factors in a separate chapter in his book which described a variety of knowledge and achievement abilities (e.g., technical and mechanical knowledge; knowledge of behavioral content) that are not included in his theoretical model.

Third, recent versions of the Cattell-Horn model have included a broad English-language reading and writing ability *(Grw)* that is depicted in the bottom half of Figure 2.3 (McGrew, 1997; Woodcock, 1993). Carroll, however, considers reading and writing to be narrow abilities subsumed by *Gc,* as reflected by the arrow leading from the *Grw* rectangle in the Cattell-Horn model to the *Gc* rectangle in the Carroll model in Figure 2.3.

Finally, the Carroll and Cattell-Horn models differ in their treatment of certain narrow memory abilities. Carroll combines both short-term memory and the narrow abilities of associative, meaningful, and free recall memory (defined later in this chapter) with learning abilities under his General Memory and Learning factor *(Gy).* Horn (1991) makes a distinction between immediate apprehension (e.g., short-term memory span) and storage and retrieval abilities, while Carroll combines them into a single broad ability *(Gy).* However, Horn (1988) indicated that it is often difficult to distinguish short-term memory and storage from retrieval abilities. For example, in some of his writings Horn (1991) referred to associative memory as a narrow ability subsumed by short-term memory. However, Horn (1988) listed the Delayed Recall tests of the WJ-R (Woodcock & Johnson, 1989), which are measures of associative memory (McGrew, 1997), under the long-term storage and retrieval ability *(Glr).*

Seeking a Standard Nomenclature: An Integrated Cattell-Horn-Carroll *Gf-Gc* Model

Notwithstanding the important differences between the Cattell-Horn and Carroll models, in order to realize the practical benefits of the calls for more theory-based interpretation (Kaufman, 1979; Kamphaus et al., 1997), it would be useful if a single *Gf-Gc* taxonomy is used to classify the individual tests in intelligence batteries. A first effort to create a single *Gf-Gc* taxonomy for use in the evaluation and interpretation of intelligence batteries was the integrated Cattell-Horn-Carroll model (McGrew, 1997). McGrew and Flanagan (1998) subsequently presented a slightly revised integrated model, which has been further revised in the current work via two changes (i.e., the splitting of Phonetic Coding into separate analysis and synthesis abilities under *Ga* and the inclusion of working memory under *Gsm;* see Figure 2.4).

The exclusion of *g* in Figure 2.4 does not mean that the integrated model used in this text does not subscribe to a separate general human ability or that *g* does not exist. Rather, it was omitted by McGrew (1997) and McGrew and Flanagan (1998) as it was judged to have little practical relevance to *Gf-Gc* cross-battery assessment and interpretation. That is, their cross-battery approach was designed to improve psychological and psychoeducational assessment practice by describing the unique *Gf-Gc* pattern of abilities of individuals. This pattern of abilities can then be related to important occupational and achievement outcomes as well as other human traits (McGrew & Flanagan, 1998).

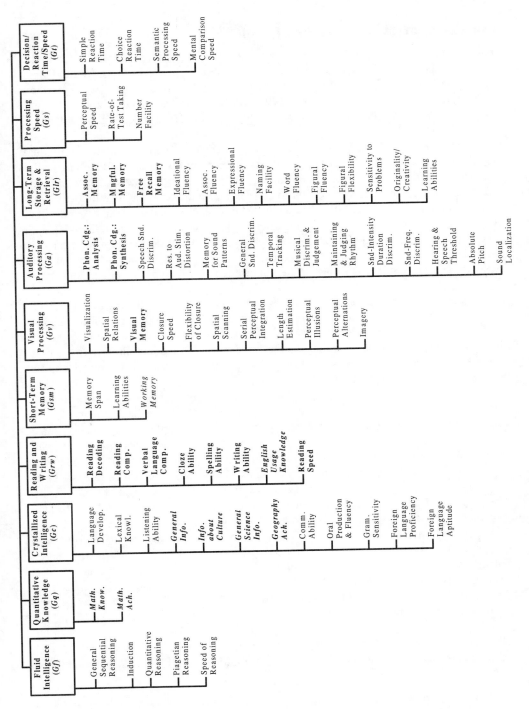

FIGURE 2.4   An Integrated Cattell-Horn-Carroll *Gf-Gc* Model of the Structure of Cognitive Abilities

Note: Italic font indicates abilities that were not included in Carroll's three-stratum model but were included by Carroll in the domains of knowledge and achievement. **Bold font** indicates abilities that are placed under different *Gf-Gc* broad abilities than in Carroll's model. These changes are based on the Cattell-Horn model and/or recent research (see McGrew, 1997, and McGrew & Flanagan, 1998). See Table 2.1 for definitions of narrow abilities.

Broad and Narrow *Gf-Gc* Ability Definitions

In this section the definitions of the broad and narrow abilities included in the *Gf-Gc* model are presented. These definitions are consistent with those presented in McGrew and Flanagan (1998). They were derived from an integration of the writings of Carroll (1993a), Gustafsson and Undheim (1996), Horn (1991), McGrew (1997), McGrew and colleagues (1991), and Woodcock (1994). The narrow ability definitions are presented in Table 2.1.

Fluid Intelligence (Gf). *Fluid Intelligence* refers to mental operations that an individual may use when faced with a relatively novel task that cannot be performed automatically. These mental operations may include forming and recognizing concepts, drawing inferences, comprehending implications, problem solving, and extrapolating. Inductive and deductive reasoning are generally considered to be the hallmark narrow-ability indicators of *Gf*. What may come as a surprise to experienced Wechsler users is the finding that, with the exception of the WAIS-III Matrix Reasoning test, the Wechsler Intelligence Scales do not measure much in the way of *Gf* abilities, one of the primary indicators of intelligent behavior. Definitions of the narrow abilities subsumed by *Gf* are presented in Table 2.1.

Crystallized Intelligence (Gc). *Crystallized Intelligence* refers to the breadth and depth of a person's acquired knowledge of a culture and the effective application of this knowledge. This store of primarily verbal or language-based knowledge represents those abilities that have been developed largely through the "investment" of other abilities during educational and general life experiences (Horn & Noll, 1997). Almost half of the tests in the Wechsler Scales measure various aspects of *Gc*.

Schematically, *Gc* might be represented by the interconnected nodes of a fishing net. Each node of the net represents an acquired piece of information, and the filaments between nodes (with many possible filaments leading to and from multiple nodes) represent links between different bits of stored information. A person high in *Gc* abilities would have a rich "fishing net" of information with many meaningfully organized and interconnected nodes. *Gc* is one of the abilities mentioned most often by lay persons when asked to describe an intelligent person (Horn, 1988). The image of a sage captures the essence of *Gc*.

Gc includes both declarative (static) and procedural (dynamic) knowledge. Declarative knowledge is held in long-term memory *(Glr)* and is activated when related information is in working memory *(Gsm)*. Declarative knowledge includes factual information, comprehension, concepts, rules, and relationships, especially when the information is verbal in nature. *Declarative knowledge* refers to knowledge "that something is the case, whereas procedural knowledge is knowledge of how to do something" (Gagne, 1985, p. 48). *Procedural knowledge* refers to the process of reasoning with previously learned procedures in order to transform knowledge. For example, a child's knowledge of his or her street address would reflect declarative knowledge, while a child's ability to find his or her way home from school would require procedural knowledge (Gagne, 1985). The breadth of *Gc* is apparent from the number of narrow abilities (i.e., 12) that it subsumes (see Table 2.1).

Quantitative Knowledge (Gq). *Quantitative Knowledge* represents an individual's store of acquired quantitative declarative and procedural knowledge. The *Gq* store of acquired knowledge represents the ability to use quantitative information and manipulate numeric symbols. The Wechsler Arithmetic test is an indicator of an aspect of *Gq*.

It is important to understand the difference between *Gq* and the Quantitative Reasoning (RQ) ability that is subsumed by *Gf*. *Gq* represents an individual's store of acquired mathematical knowledge, while RQ represents the ability to reason inductively and deductively when solving quantitative problems. *Gq* would be evident when a task requires mathematical skills and general mathematical knowledge (e.g., knowing what the square root symbol means). RQ would be required in order to solve for a missing number in a number series task (e.g., 2 4 6 8 ___). Two narrow abilities are listed and defined under *Gq* in Table 2.1.

Reading/Writing Ability (Grw). *Reading/Writing Ability* is an acquired store of knowledge that includes basic reading and writing skills required for the comprehension of written language and the expression of thought via writing. It includes both basic (e.g., reading decoding, spelling) and complex abilities (e.g., reading comprehension and the ability to write a story). Currently, this ability domain has been neither well defined nor extensively researched within the *Gf-Gc* framework. Also, in typical practice, *Grw* (and *Gq*) are considered to be *achievement* domains and are therefore measured by achievement tests and not intelligence tests. In Carroll's (1993a) three-stratum model, eight narrow reading and writing abilities are subsumed by *Gc* in addition to other abilities. In the *Gf-Gc* models presented by McGrew (1997), McGrew and Flanagan (1998), and the current authors (see Figure 2.4), these eight narrow abilities define the broad *Grw* ability. These *Grw* narrow abilities are defined in Table 2.1.

Short-Term Memory (Gsm). *Short-Term Memory* is the ability to apprehend and hold information in immediate awareness and then use it within a few seconds. *Gsm* is a limited capacity system, as most individuals can only retain seven "chunks" of information (plus or minus two chunks) in this memory system at one time. The ability to remember a telephone number long enough to dial it, or the ability to retain a sequence of spoken directions long enough to complete a task specified in the directions, are examples of *Gsm*. Given the limited amount of information that can be held in short-term memory, information is typically retained for only a few seconds before it is lost. As most individuals have experienced, it is difficult to remember an unfamiliar telephone number for more than a few seconds unless one consciously employs a cognitive learning strategy (e.g., continually repeating or rehearsing the numbers). Once a new task requires an individual to use their *Gsm* abilities to store new information the previous information held in short-term memory is either lost or must be stored in the acquired stores of knowledge (i.e., *Gc, Gq, Grw*) through the use of *Glr*.

More recently, the related construct of working memory has received considerable attention in the cognitive psychology literature, resulting in the inclusion of practical tests of working memory in recent revisions of two intelligence batteries (viz., WAIS-III; WJ-III). Working memory is considered to be the "mechanism responsible for the temporary storage and processing of information" (Richardson, 1996, p. 23). However, the integration of working memory into the *Gf-Gc* framework is hindered by the lack of a universally accepted definition of the construct (Logie, 1996). Working memory has been referred to

(text continued on page 42)

TABLE 2.1 Narrow *Gf-Gc* Stratum I Ability Definitions and Task Examples

Gf-Gc Broad Stratum II Ability

Narrow stratum I name (code)	Definition	Task Example
Fluid Intelligence (Gf)		
General Sequential Reasoning (RG)	Ability to start with stated rules, premises, or conditions, and to engage in one or more steps to reach a solution to a novel problem.	An examinee is presented with an incomplete logic puzzle and must deduce the missing components following careful analysis of the presented stimuli.
Induction (I)	Ability to discover the underlying characteristic (e.g., rule, concept, process, trend, class membership) that governs a problem or a set of materials.	An examinee is presented with a certain pattern of related stimuli and must select one of several stimuli that would complete or continue the pattern.
Quantitative Reasoning (RQ)	Ability to inductively and deductively reason with concepts involving mathematical relations and properties.	An examinee is presented with an incomplete series of related numbers and must select the number(s) that best complete the series.
Piagetian Reasoning (RP)	Seriation, conservation, classification and other cognitive abilities as defined by Piaget's developmental theory.	An examinee must demonstrate knowledge of conservation of mass or volume when presented with transformations of either the actual state of the object or items extraneous to the object, such as a container holding the object (e.g., When 5 ounces of water is transformed to ice is there a change in the amount of water?).
Speed of Reasoning (RE)	(Not clearly defined by existing research.)	An examinee must say the days of the week while counting by 3's as quickly as possible (e.g., Monday, 3, Tuesday, 6, Wednesday, 9, etc.).
Quantitative Knowledge (Gq)		
Mathematical Knowledge (KM)	Range of general knowledge about mathematics.	An examinee is asked to demonstrate knowledge of basic mathematical facts and operations.
Mathematical Achievement (A3)	Measured mathematics achievement.	An examinee is required to perform simple mathematical calculations using pencil and paper.

Crystallized Intelligence (Gc)

Language Development (LD)	General development, or the understanding of words, sentences, and paragraphs (*not* requiring reading), in spoken native language skills.	An examinee is presented with two words and must describe the common relation or similarity between them.
Lexical Knowledge (VL)	Extent of vocabulary that can be understood in terms of correct word meanings.	An examinee must provide oral definitions for words of increasing difficulty.
Listening Ability (LS)	Ability to listen and comprehend oral communications.	An examinee is presented with an incomplete verbal passage and must provide a word that completes the passage.
General (verbal) Information (K0)	Range of general knowledge.	An examinee must provide specific responses to questions of general factual information (e.g., In what direction does the sun rise?).
Information about Culture (K2)	Range of cultural knowledge (e.g., music, art).	An examinee is presented with pictorial depictions of major artistic works (e.g., the Mona Lisa) and must correctly identify the name of the work or the artist.
General Science Information (K1)	Range of scientific knowledge (e.g., biology, physics, engineering, mechanics, electronics).	An examinee must correctly respond to questions demonstrating general knowledge of basic scientific ideas or facts (e.g., What is the largest planet in our solar system? What is the ozone layer?).
Geography Achievement (A5)	Range of geographic knowledge.	An examinee must identify capitals of countries around the world.
Communication Ability (CM)	Ability to speak in "real life" situations (e.g., lecture, group participation) in an adult-like manner.	An examinee is required to view a picture of a small town with stores and streets and must describe the scene and give directions from one store in the picture to another.
Oral Production and Fluency (OP)	More specific or narrow oral communication skills than reflected by Communication Ability (CM).	An examinee is presented with a starting stimulus word and must use the word properly in a sentence.
Grammatical Sensitivity (MY)	Knowledge or awareness of the grammatical features of the native language.	An examinee must correctly label the parts of speech contained in a sentence or correct those parts of speech that are utilized incorrectly (e.g., disparate tenses in a sentence).

(continued)

TABLE 2.1 Continued

Gf-Gc Broad Stratum II Ability

Narrow stratum I name (code)	Definition	Task Example
Foreign Language Proficiency (KL)	Similar to Language Development (LD) but for a foreign language.	An examinee is presented with two words in a foreign language and must describe the common relation or similarity between them.
Foreign Language Aptitude (LA)	Rate and ease of learning a new language.	An examinee is presented with several translated words that are paired with pictorial stimuli and must pair the words with the pictures following a single presentation.
	Reading/Writing (Grw)	
Reading Decoding (RD)	Ability to recognize and decode words or pseudowords in reading.	An examinee is required to accurately pronounce a list of nonsense words.
Reading Comprehension (RC)	Ability to comprehend connected discourse during reading.	An examinee is required to read a short passage and respond to questions about the passage.
Verbal (printed) Language Comprehension (V)	General development, or the understanding of words, sentences, and paragraphs in native language, as measured by *reading* vocabulary and *reading* comprehension tests.	An examinee must read a list of four vocabulary words and choose two of the four words that belong together in some meaningful way.
Cloze Ability (CZ)	Ability to supply words deleted from prose passages that must be read.	An examinee is required to read a short passage and supply a missing word that best corresponds to the theme or content of the passage.
Spelling Ability (SG)	Ability to spell.	An examinee must spell a series of increasingly difficult orally presented words.
Writing Ability (WA)	Ability to write with clarity of thought, organization, and good sentence structure.	An examinee is given a starting stimulus and must write a well-organized story that adheres to the structural rules of writing (e.g., examinee starts a new paragraph when he or she presents a new idea).

Term	Definition	Task
English Usage Knowledge (EU)	Knowledge of writing in the English language with respect to capitalization, punctuation, usage, and spelling.	An examinee must correct sentences with respect to capitalization, punctuation, spelling, and usage errors.
Reading Speed (RS)	Time required to silently read a passage or series of sentences as quickly as possible.	An examinee is asked to silently read a passage for one minute. Reading speed reflects words per minute read.

Short-Term Memory (Gsm)

Term	Definition	Task
Memory Span (MS)	Ability to attend to and immediately recall temporally ordered elements in the correct order after a single presentation.	An examinee is presented with a series of numbers or words and must repeat them orally in the same sequence as presented.
Working Memory (MW)	Ability to temporarily store and perform a set of cognitive operations on information that requires divided attention and the management of the limited capacity of short-term memory.	An examinee is presented a series of numbers and words in a mixed-up order and is then required to reorder and say the complete list of numbers first in order followed by the words in order.
Learning Abilities (L1)	A number of factors that are specific to particular kinds of learning situations and memory [Also listed under *Glr*]. (Not clearly defined by existing research.)	An examinee must learn paired-associate material to a criterion during a study phase that is followed by an intervening task and finally a "relearning" testing phase.

Visual Processing (Gv)

Term	Definition	Task
Spatial Relations (SR)	Ability to rapidly perceive and manipulate relatively simple visual patterns or to maintain orientation with respect to objects in space.	An examinee is required to view a stimulus pattern or design and reproduce the design using blocks or cubes.
Visual Memory (MV)	Ability to form and store a mental representation or image of a visual stimulus and then recognize or recall it later.	An examinee is required to reproduce or recognize a previously presented visual stimulus that has been removed.
Visualization (Vz)	Ability to mentally manipulate objects or visual patterns and to "see" how they would appear under altered conditions.	The examinee is presented with a visual image and must draw how the image would look upside down.
Closure Speed (CS)	Ability to quickly combine disconnected, vague, or partially obscured visual stimuli or patterns into a meaningful whole, *without knowing in advance* what the pattern is.	An examinee is required to identify an object from a line drawing that has portions of the lines missing.

(continued)

TABLE 2.1 Continued

Gf-Gc Broad Stratum II Ability

Narrow stratum I-name (code)	Definition	Task Example
Flexibility of Closure (CF)	Ability to find, apprehend, and identify a visual figure or pattern embedded in a complex visual array, *when knowing in advance* what the pattern is.	An examinee must identify ten animals that are embedded in a complex visual scene.
Spatial Scanning (SS)	Ability to accurately and quickly survey a spatial field or pattern and identify a path through the visual field or pattern.	An examinee is required to complete a series of increasingly difficult mazes within a specified time period.
Serial Perceptual Integration (PI)	Ability to apprehend and identify a pictorial or visual pattern when parts of the pattern are presented rapidly in serial or successive order.	An examinee is required to correctly identify or name a stimulus when portions of the stimuli are presented serially (e.g., portions of a line drawing of a cat are passed through a small "window").
Length Estimation (LE)	Ability to accurately estimate or compare visual lengths and distances without using measurement instruments.	An examinee is presented with a series of paired double-arrow lines of differing orientations and determine whether they are the same length or different.
Perceptual Illusions (IL)	Ability to resist being affected by perceptual illusions involving geometric figures.	An examinee is presented with pictures of geometric shapes that have superimposed patterns and must correctly identify the dominant geometric shape present in the picture.
Perceptual Alternations (PN)	Consistency in the rate of alternating between different visual perceptions.	An examinee is asked to view a series of flashing bars with one constant bar in the middle and must indicate whether or not the bars are going behind the middle bar or are flashing simultaneously at its side.
Imagery (IM)	Ability to vividly mentally manipulate abstract spatial forms. (Not clearly defined by existing research.)	An examinee is given a starting stimulus (e.g., a square) and must follow a series of verbal transformations to determine the resultant stimuli (e.g., a triangle)

Auditory Processing (Ga)

Phonetic Coding: Analysis (PC:A)	Ability to segment larger units of speech sounds into smaller units of speech sounds.	An examinee is presented with the pronunciation of a word and must identify the beginning and ending sounds.
Phonetic Coding: Synthesis (PC:S)	Ability to blend smaller units of speech together into larger units of speech.	An examinee is presented with the isolated sounds for a word and must blend the sounds together and identify the word.
Speech Sound Discrimination (US)	Ability to detect differences in speech sounds under conditions of little distraction or distortion.	An examinee is presented with a series of tape-recorded phonetically nonmeaningful sounds and must identify whether the sounds are the same or different.
Resistance to Auditory Stimulus Distortion (UR)	Ability to understand speech and language that has been distorted or masked in one or more ways.	An examinee must identify monosyllabic and multisyllabic words while listening to an increasing level of noise presented through earphones.
Memory for Sound Patterns (UM)	Ability to retain on a short-term basis auditory events such as tones, tonal patterns, and voices.	An examinee is presented with a series of tone patterns and later must identify whether subsequently presented patterns were among those originally heard.
General Sound Discrimination (U3)	Ability to discriminate tones, tone patterns, or musical materials with regard to pitch, intensity, duration, and rhythm.	An examinee is presented with two short musical patterns and must identify whether the patterns are similar or different and, if different, how they differ (e.g., by duration, intensity)
Temporal Tracking (UK)	Ability to track auditory temporal events so as to be able to count, rearrange, or anticipate them.	An examinee is presented with a steady pattern of musical beats and must identify the note that is to come next after the music has stopped.
Musical Discrimination and Judgment (U1, U9)	Ability to discriminate and judge tonal patterns in music with respect to melodic, harmonic, and expressive aspects (e.g., phrasing, tempo, and intensity variations).	An examinee is presented with tape-recorded samples of musical pieces from different musical genres presented in either major or minor keys and must describe the differences in the music in terms of its harmonic complexity and mood.

(continued)

TABLE 2.1 Continued

Narrow stratum I name (code)	Definition	Task Example
	Gf-Gc **Broad Stratum II Ability**	
Maintaining and Judging Rhythm (U8)	Ability to recognize and maintain a musical or equal time beat.	An examinee is presented with a tape-recorded metronome keeping 4/4 time (i.e., one measure) that is comprised of quarter notes and must demonstrate knowledge of equal time beat by tapping out eighth notes.
Sound-Intensity/Duration Discrimination (U6)	Ability to discriminate sound intensities and to be sensitive to the temporal/rhythmic aspects of tonal patterns.	An examinee must listen to a series of tape-recorded sounds and indicate by raising their hand when one sound becomes more intense than the previously presented sound.
Sound-Frequency Discrimination (U5)	Ability to discriminate frequency attributes (pitch and timbre) of tones.	An examinee is presented with random tape-recorded notes played on the high, middle, and low ends of a piano keyboard and must describe the relationship of the second note played to the first note played (e.g., higher, lower).
Hearing and Speech Threshold Factors (UA, UT, UU)	Ability to hear pitch and varying sounds over a range of audible frequencies.	An examinee is presented with a series of 15 tape-recorded sounds and must indicate by writing a check mark in a response booklet whenever they hear a sound.
Absolute Pitch (UP)	Ability to perfectly name or identify the pitch of tones.	An examinee is presented with a tape-recorded note of a piano key (e.g., C or F sharp) and is required to name the note.
Sound Localization (UL)	Ability to localize heard sounds in space.	An examinee is presented with earphones and must indicate whether a presented sound was heard in the left, right, or both sides of the headset.
	Long-Term Storage and Retrieval (Glr)	
Associative Memory (MA)	Ability to recall one part of a previously learned but unrelated pair of items when the other part is presented (i.e., paired-associative learning).	An examinee is presented with a set of visual stimuli paired with nonsense words and must correctly identify the nonsense word that had been presented with a certain visual stimulus.

	Ability	Task
Meaningful Memory (MM)	Ability to recall a set of items where there is a meaningful relation between items or the items comprise a meaningful story or connected discourse.	An examinee is presented with a short story and must retell the story as accurately as possible immediately following a single presentation.
Free Recall Memory (M6)	Ability to recall as many unrelated items as possible, in any order, after a large collection of items is presented.	An examinee is presented with a series of objects and, after they are removed, must recall the objects in any order.
Ideational Fluency (FI)	Ability to rapidly produce a series of ideas, words, or phrases related to a specific condition or object. Quantity not quality is emphasized.	An examinee must rapidly name as many square objects as he can within a specified time limit.
Associational Fluency (FA)	Ability to rapidly produce words or phrases associated in meaning (semantically associated) with a given word or concept.	An examinee must name as many examples of objects that fit into a specified category (e.g., name as many fruits as you can think of) within a specified time limit.
Expressional Fluency (FE)	Ability to rapidly think of and organize words or phrases into meaningful complex ideas under high general or more specific cueing conditions.	An examinee must rapidly name a category that bests represents a series of presented words (e.g., Pattern, material, thread . . . things to make clothing.)
Naming Facility (NA)	Ability to rapidly produce names for concepts when presented with a pictorial or verbal cue.	An examinee must rapidly provide the general name of a category when shown specific pictorial stimuli (e.g., a picture of an apple, shirt, and bus, would require the reply: fruit, clothing, transportation)
Word Fluency (FW)	Ability to rapidly produce words that have specific phonemic, structural, or orthographic characteristics (independent of word meanings).	An examinee must name as many words as he can think of that start with the "sh" sound within a specified time limit.
Figural Fluency (FF)	Ability to rapidly draw or sketch several examples or elaborations when given a starting visual or descriptive stimulus.	An examinee must draw as many things as he can when presented with a nonmeaningful starting visual stimulus.
Figural Flexibility (FX)	Ability to quickly change set in order to generate new and different solutions to figural problems.	An examinee is presented with five geometric shapes and must manipulate those shapes to create objects described by the examiner (e.g., build a house, build a car).

(continued)

TABLE 2.1 Continued

Gf-Gc **Broad Stratum II Ability**

Narrow stratum I name (code)	Definition	Task Example
Sensitivity to Problems (SP)	Ability to identify and state practical problems in a given situation or rapidly think of and state various solutions to, or consequences of, such problems.	An examinee is required to answer questions such as "What is the thing to do if you lock your keys in the car?"
Originality/Creativity (FO)	Ability to rapidly produce original, clever, or uncommon verbal or ideational responses to specified tasks.	An examinee is given a starting stimulus word such as "car" and must construct as many words as he can using those three letters in the word (e.g., carrot, care, carton, racecar, macaroon)
Learning Abilities (L1)	A number of factors that are specific to particular kinds of learning situations and memory [Also listed under *Gsm*]. (Not clearly defined by existing research).	An examinee must learn paired-associate material to a criterion during a study phase that is followed by an intervening task and finally a "relearning" testing phase.
Processing Speed (Gs)		
Perceptual Speed (P)	Ability to rapidly search for and compare known visual symbols or patterns presented side by side or separated in a visual field.	An examinee must rapidly view rows of stimuli and cross out those stimuli that are similar within the presented row within a specified time limit.
Rate of Test Taking (R9)	Ability to rapidly perform tests which are relatively easy or that require very simple decisions.	An examinee is required to pair numbers with symbols according to a presented key as rapidly as possible.
Number Facility (N)	Ability to rapidly and accurately manipulate and deal with numbers, from elementary skills of counting and recognizing numbers to advanced skills of adding, subtracting, multiplying, and dividing numbers.	An examinee is required to complete a series of arithmetic problems using paper and pencil in a specified time limit.

Decision/Reaction Time or Speed (Gt)

Simple Reaction Time (R1)	Reaction time to the presentation of a single visual or auditory stimulus.	An examinee is required to quickly depress a computer key when presented with a specific geometric figure (e.g., a square) that appears intermittently in a series of other figures on the computer screen.
Choice Reaction Time (R2)	Reaction time to one of two or more alternative stimuli, depending on which alternative is signaled.	An examinee is required to rapidly depress one of two computer keys depending on the type of stimulus presented (e.g., press green key when square is presented and red key when a circle is presented).
Semantic Processing Speed (R4)	Reaction time when the decision requires some encoding and mental manipulation of stimulus content.	An examinee is required to rapidly depress a key when the stimulus viewed is opposite to a stimulus description provided (e.g., the examinee would depress a key when he/she viewed a star beneath a cross after initially viewing the star above the cross).
Mental Comparison Speed (R7)	Reaction time where the stimuli must be compared for a particular attribute.	An examinee is required to rapidly depress a key when presented with two identical geometric shapes and refrain from pressing when the shapes differ.

Note: Most all definitions were derived from Carroll (1993a). Two-letter factor codes (e.g., RG) are from Carroll (1993a). Information in this table was adapted from McGrew (1997) with permission from Guilford Press.

41

as the "mind's scratchpad" (Jensen, 1998, p. 220) and most models of working memory postulate a number of subsystems or temporary *buffers*. The phonological or articulatory loop processes auditory-linguistic information while the visuospatial sketch/scratchpad (Baddeley, 1986; 1992; Logie, 1996) is the temporary buffer for visually processed information. Most working memory models posit a central executive or processor mechanism that coordinates and manages the activities and subsystems in working memory.

Carroll (1993a) is skeptical of the working memory construct as reflected in his conclusion that "although some evidence supports such a speculation, one must be cautious in accepting it because as yet there has not been sufficient work on measuring working memory, and the validity and generality of the concept have not yet been well established in the individual differences research" (p. 647). Respecting the judgement of one of the primary architects of the *Gf-Gc* model (i.e., Carroll), we have chosen not to elevate working memory to the status of a broad stratum II ability. Instead, we feel that at this time, current knowledge argues for the classification of working memory as a narrow ability under *Gsm*. This makes logical sense given that working memory shares a number of cognitive processes with Memory Span (MS) yet also includes additional processes that differentiate the two abilities. Given that Carroll includes Learning Abilities under his *Gsm* factor (which he calls *Gy*), it is clear that the *Gsm* portion of the *Gf-Gc* framework requires additional research to elucidate the relations between the various narrow memory abilities that currently comprise *Gsm*.

To allow working memory "membership" in the *Gf-Gc* taxonomy, we suggest herein that the *Gf-Gc* taxonomic code system (e.g., MS = Memory Span; see Table 2.1) be expanded to include *MW* for working memory. Given that Carroll questions the validity of the working memory construct, we propose this MW code primarily for practical use and ease of communication. Additional research is necessary before a consensus can be reached about the inclusion (or exclusion) of working memory in the *Gf-Gc* model of intelligence. Practitioners need to recognize the somewhat tenuous nature of the *Gsm* domain when using the cross-battery assessment approach outlined in subsequent chapters.

Visual Processing (Gv).   *Visual Processing (Gv)* is the ability to generate, perceive, analyze, synthesize, store, retrieve, manipulate, transform, and think with visual patterns and stimuli (Lohman, 1994). These abilities are measured frequently by tasks that require the perception and manipulation of visual shapes and forms, usually of a figural or geometric nature (e.g., the Wechsler Block Design and Object Assembly tests). An individual who can effectively mentally reverse and rotate objects, interpret how objects change as they move through space, perceive and manipulate spatial configurations, and maintain spatial orientation would be regarded as having a strength in *Gv* abilities. The various narrow abilities subsumed by *Gv* are listed and defined in Table 2.1.

Auditory Processing (Ga).   In the broadest sense, auditory abilities "are cognitive abilities that depend on sound as input and on the functioning of our hearing apparatus" (Stankov, 1994, p. 157) and reflect "the degree to which the individual can cognitively control the perception of auditory stimulus inputs" (Gustafsson & Undheim, 1996, p. 192). *Auditory Processing* is the ability to perceive, analyze, and synthesize patterns among auditory stimuli, and discriminate subtle nuances in patterns of sound (e.g., complex musical structure) and speech when presented under distorted conditions. While *Ga* abilities do not require the comprehension of language (*Gc*), they may be very important in the development of language skills. *Ga* subsumes most of those abilities referred to as phonological awareness/processing. However, as can be seen from the list of narrow abilities subsumed by *Ga* (Table 2.1), this domain is very broad.

A change from McGrew and Flanagan's (1998) discussion of *Ga* is the splitting of Carroll's Phonetic Coding (PC) narrow ability into separate analysis (PC:A) and synthesis (PC:S) abilities. Support for two different PC abilities comes primarily from four sources. First, in a sample of kindergarten students, Yopp (1988) reported evidence in favor of two phonemic awareness factors: simple phonemic awareness (required one operation to be performed on sounds) and compound phonemic awareness (required holding sounds in memory while performing another operation on them). Second, in what appears to be the most comprehensive *Ga* factor-analytic study to date, Stankov and Horn (1980) presented evidence for seven different auditory abilities, two of which had tests of sound blending (synthesis) and incomplete words (analysis) as factor markers. Third, the WJ-R Sound Blending and Incomplete Words tests (which are almost identical in format to the tests used by Stankov and Horn) correlated only moderately (0.37 or 13.7% shared or common variance) across the kindergarten to adult WJ-R norm sample, a correlation that suggests that these tests are measuring different aspects of PC. Finally, using confirmatory factor-analytic methods, Wagner, Torgesen, Laughton, Simmons, and Rashotte (1993) presented a model of phonological processing that included separate auditory analysis and synthesis factors.

Although the features of these different auditory factors across respective studies are not entirely consistent, there are a number of similarities. For example, Yopp's (1988) simple phonemic factor appears to be analogous to Wagner and colleagues' (1993) synthesis factor and the factor Stankov and Horn (1980) identified with the aid of sound blending tasks. Also, Yopp's (1988) compound phonemic factor bears similarities to Wagner and colleagues' (1993) analysis factor and the Stankov and Horn (1980) factor, identified in part by an incomplete words task. At this time, we conclude that Wagner and colleagues' (1993) analysis/synthesis distinction is probably the most useful. According to Wagner and colleagues (1993), analysis and synthesis can be defined as "the ability to segment larger units of speech into smaller units" and "the ability to blend smaller units of speech to form larger units" (p. 87), respectively. As a result, in the current model (Figure 2.4) we proposed that PC be split into separate PC:A and PC:S narrow abilities.

Long-Term Storage and Retrieval (Glr). *Long-Term Storage and Retrieval* is the ability to store information in and fluently retrieve new or previously acquired information (e.g., concepts, ideas, items, names) from long-term memory. *Glr* abilities have been prominent in creativity research where they have been referred to as idea production, ideational fluency, or associative fluency. It is important to not confuse *Glr* with *Gc, Gq,* and *Grw*, a person's stores of acquired knowledge. *Gc, Gq,* and *Grw* represent *what* is stored in long-term memory, while *Glr* is the *efficiency* by which this information is initially stored in and later retrieved from long-term memory. Using the *Gc* fishing net analogy discussed earlier in this chapter (where the nodes and links of the net represent the knowledge that is stored in long-term memory), *Glr* is the process by which individuals efficiently add new nodes and links to their "fishing net" of stored knowledge and then later retrieve information from their net of knowledge.

Different processes are involved in *Glr* and *Gsm*. Although the word *long-term* frequently carries with it the connotation of days, weeks, months, and years in the clinical literature, long-term storage processes can begin within a few minutes or hours of performing a task. Therefore, the time lapse between the initial task performance and the recall of information related to that task is not of critical importance in defining *Glr*. More important is the occurrence of an intervening task that engages short-term memory during the interim before the attempted recall of the stored information (e.g., *Gc;* Woodcock, 1994). In the present *Gf-Gc* model, 13 narrow memory and fluency abilities are included under *Glr* (see Table 2.1).

Processing Speed (Gs).   *Processing Speed* or mental quickness is often mentioned when talking about intelligent behavior (Nettelbeck, 1994). Processing speed is the ability to fluently and automatically perform cognitive tasks, especially when under pressure to maintain focused attention and concentration. *Attentive speediness* encapsulates the essence of *Gs*. *Gs* is measured typically by fixed-interval timed tasks that require little in the way of complex thinking or mental processing (e.g., the Wechsler Animal Pegs, Symbol Search, and Digit Symbol/Coding tests).

Recent interest in information processing models of cognitive functioning has resulted in a renewed focus on *Gs* (Kail, 1991; Lohman, 1989). A central construct in information processing models is that of limited processing resources (e.g., the limited capacities of short-term or working memory). That is, "many cognitive activities require a person's deliberate efforts and that people are limited in the amount of effort they can allocate. In the face of limited processing resources, the speed of processing is critical because it determines in part how rapidly limited resources can be reallocated to other cognitive tasks" (Kail, 1991, p. 152). Woodcock (1994) likens *Gs* to a valve in a water pipe. The rate at which water flows in the pipe (i.e., *Gs*) increases when the valve is wide open and it decreases when the valve is partially closed. Three different narrow speed of processing abilities are subsumed by *Gs* in the present *Gf-Gc* model (see Table 2.1).

Decision/Reaction Time or Speed (Gt).   In addition to *Gs,* both Carroll and Horn include a second broad speed ability in their respective *Gf-Gc* models. Processing Speed (Decision/ Reaction Time or Speed; *Gt*), the ability proposed by Carroll, subsumes narrow abilities that reflect an individual's quickness in reacting (reaction time) and making decisions (decision speed). Correct Decision Speed (CDS), what Horn proposed as the second speed ability (*Gs* being the first) is typically measured by recording the time an individual requires to provide an answer to problems on a variety of tests (e.g., letter series, classifications, vocabulary; Horn, 1988; 1991). Because CDS appears to be a much narrower ability than *Gt,* it is subsumed by *Gt* in the *Gf-Gc* model used in this book.

Gt should not be confused with *Gs*. *Gt* abilities reflect the immediacy with which an individual can react (typically measured in seconds or parts of seconds) to stimuli or a task, while *Gs* abilities reflect the ability to work quickly over a longer period of time (typically measured in intervals of 2 to 3 minutes). Being asked to read a passage (on a self-paced scrolling video screen) as quickly as possible and, in the process, touch the word *the* with a stylus pen each time it appears on the screen, is an example of *Gs*. The individual's *Gs* score would reflect the number of correct responses (taking into account errors of omission and commission). In contrast, *Gt* may be measured by requiring a person to read the same text at their normal rate of reading and press the space bar as quickly as possible whenever a light is flashed on the screen. In this latter paradigm, the individual's score is based on the average response latency or the time interval between the onset of the stimulus and the individual's response.

Recent *Gf-Gc* Theory Developments

Research and development regarding the *Gf-Gc* theory is not static. Two general lines of research that are germane to the current work are providing insights into potential future refinements and extensions of the *Gf-Gc* theory.

Refining the Structural Taxonomy

Recent research (Roberts & Stankov, 1998; Roberts, Stankov, Pallier, & Dolph, 1997) has suggested possible modifications to the *Gf-Gc* model of cognitive abilities. Roberts and associates (1997) presented evidence that suggests that tactile-kinesthetic (TK) abilities may represent either a narrow stratum I ability influenced by both *Gv* and *Gf*, or a broad stratum II ability closely related to *Gv* and *Gf*. According to Roberts and associates, the TK factor consists of a complex set of abilities that are related to *Gf* and may involve tactile, visual, and working memory processes.

TK measures are not included in any of the major intelligence batteries. However, instruments such as the Wechsler Scales are often supplemented with a variety of TK tests (e.g., examinees must identify numbers written on their fingertips; examinees must place geometrically shaped blocks into a form board while blindfolded). This is a common practice in neuropsychological assessment. For example, the recently published NEPSY (Korkman, Kirk, & Kemp, 1997) includes a test that requires an examinee to identify the finger or fingers the examiner touches (Finger Discrimination). Further research in the TK domain is important given the salient role these abilities have played in neuropsychological assessment and aging research (i.e., cognitive decline due to *decrements* in sensory processes).

The other major *Gf-Gc* domain that has been the subject of active exploration recently is cognitive speed (*Gs* and *Gt*). Roberts and Stankov (1998), for example, have presented evidence for a four-level hierarchical structure of cognitive speed in which they identify speed factors at the narrow (stratum I) and broad (stratum II) levels, and suggest the presence of intermediate levels between and below these strata. Roberts and Stankov identified a single *broad* speed ability (*Gt*—Cognitive Speed) and five *narrow* speed abilities (viz., Clerical/Perceptual Speed, Induction Speed, Visual/Auditory [Perceptual] Test-Taking Speed, General Decision Speed, and Movement Time). In addition, these researchers posited a Psychometric Speed ability "in limbo" between the narrow and broad stratum speed abilities. Finally, below the five narrow (stratum I) abilities exists the possibility of three more specific decision speed and movement time abilities, respectively. Currently, the Wechsler Intelligence Scales and other intelligence batteries only include tests that tap the Clerical/Perceptual *(Gs)* portion of the Roberts and Stankov model (e.g., WISC-III Coding).

The addition of a TK ability and a more complex and specific cognitive speed hierarchy to the *Gf-Gc* model has primarily theoretical implications at this time. Additional research is needed to determine the replicability of these findings in additional samples of varying ages and, more importantly, to determine their practical implications for psychological assessment.

Gf-Gc and Information Processing Theory: Pushing the Edge of the Theory Envelope

As mentioned earlier in this chapter (see Figure 2.1 and related discussion), a number of researchers have proposed theoretical models that describe and explain cognitive performance as a composition of both cognitive and noncognitive variables within an information processing framework. Most prominent within the context of *Gf-Gc* theory are Woodcock's (1993; 1997; 1998) *Gf-Gc Cognitive Performance Model (CPM)* and *Information Processing Model (IPM)*. According to Woodcock (1998, p. 143) these models are not intended to extend *Gf-Gc* theory, but rather, to "nudge current theory further into clinical and research practice." The basis of the CPM model is that a person's cognitive performance is a complex interaction of many different components that can be differentiated by function. The most recent revision of the CPM is presented schematically in Figure 2.5.

Briefly, *Acquired Knowledge,* represented by the *Gc, Gq,* and *Grw* abilities, includes knowledge stores of factual (declarative) and automatized cognitive processes and procedures (procedural knowledge) within a domain. For example, being able to identify Σ as the statistical summation symbol is a type of *Gq* declarative knowledge. Knowing how *to do* the summation process is a form of *Gq* procedural knowledge. With the exception of the Digit Span test, the entire Wechsler Verbal scale is comprised of acquired knowledge indicators (viz., *Gc* and *Gq*).

Thinking Abilities (viz., *Gv, Ga, Glr, Gf*) are involved in the cognitive processing of information that is placed in short-term memory *(Gsm)* but cannot be processed automatically. These abilities are often what many professionals think of when talking about intelligence, because they are involved in new learning or performing tasks that an individual cannot complete or solve automatically. All of the Wechsler performance tests (except Symbol Search, Animal Pegs, and Digit-Symbol/Coding) are measures of *Gv* thinking abilities.

Cognitive Efficiency includes abilities that influence the speed *(Gs)* or automaticity of cognitive functioning through the efficient allocation of mental resources within the limited capacity short-term and working memory systems *(Gsm)*. Using the *Gq* example described above, two individuals who have the same overall level and pattern of thinking abilities and stores of acquired *Gq* knowledge may vary in the speed and accuracy by which they can mentally sum a series of five numbers, due to differences in overall speed of cognitive processing, automaticity of mathematical facts, and ability to hold information in working memory via the use of cognitive strategies. The various Wechsler processing speed tests (i.e., Symbol Search, Animal Pegs, Digit Symbol/Coding) are considered measures of one aspect of cognitive efficiency (i.e., *Gs*) while the short-term and working memory tests (i.e., Digit Span, Sentences, Letter-Number Sequencing) are classified as *Gsm.*

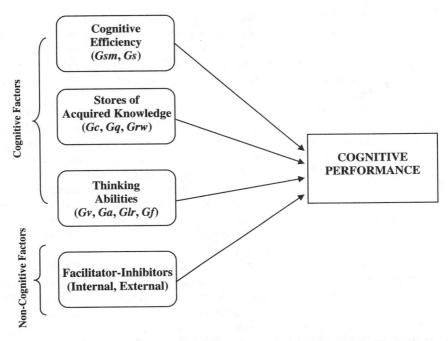

FIGURE 2.5   A Schematic Representation of Woodcock's Cognitive Performance Model

Facilitators-Inhibitors are internal (e.g., health, attention and concentration, cognitive style, emotional state) and external (e.g., distracting stimuli) variables that can "modify cognitive performance for better or for worse, often overriding the effects of strengths and weaknesses in the previously described cognitive abilities" (Woodcock, 1998, p. 146). For example, two individuals with similar overall levels and patterns of thinking abilities and cognitive efficiency may differ in their ability to sum the previously discussed five numbers, due to differences in concentration, intrinsic motivation, or state of health at the time of performance. The collective participation of these four functional cognitive and noncognitive components aids in explaining intraindividual and interindividual variation in the performance of complex cognitive activities.

Woodcock (1993; 1998) extended the CPM into a more complex *Gf-Gc Information Processing Model (IPM)* that integrates *Gf-Gc* abilities and other aspects of cognition within an information processing framework. Woodcock's grounding of the CPM and IPM in the Cattell-Horn *Gf-Gc* theory is consistent with Taylor's (1994) conclusion that a "positive feature of the Cattell model is that it is amenable to dynamic, learning, or developmental interpretations" (p. 185). The IPM is admittedly complex and cannot be described in sufficient detail in this book. The interested reader is referred to Woodcock (1997; 1998) for a discussion of the model and a description of a practical *Gf-Gc Diagnostic Worksheet* that could be applied to the Wechsler Scales when they are supplemented via the Wechsler-based *Gf-Gc* cross-battery approach described in Part III of this book.

Another notable effort along these lines is Snow's (1989) attempt to use new forms of psychometric theory to measure information processing constructs such as declarative knowledge acquisition, proceduralization, and automatization (Anderson, 1985). Snow's work was not specifically designed to extend *Gf-Gc* theory, but it shares the same general goal of integrating cognitive and noncognitive constructs to better understand cognitive performance.

Briefly, Snow suggested that cognitive constructs need to be combined with affective and conative (i.e., noncognitive) constructs to fully measure an individual's aptitudes for learning (Snow, Corno, & Jackson, 1996). According to Snow (1989), learners approach tasks with previously developed *conceptual structures* and *procedural skills* (i.e., initial states) that subsume *Gf-Gc*-type cognitive constructs (e.g., *Gc, Gv, Gsm*). In addition, conative personal characteristics in the broad domains of *learning strategies, self-regulatory functions,* and *motivational orientation* are viewed as interacting with the cognitive constructs during cognitive performance. The important common feature of Woodcock and Snow's attempts to explain cognitive performance is that both dynamic models include cognitive and noncognitive constructs.

Although the Wechsler Intelligence Scales (and for that matter all major intelligence batteries) do not directly measure noncognitive constructs, David Wechsler was at the forefront in highlighting the important link between cognitive and noncognitive factors when trying to explain real-world intelligent behavior. Throughout his career, Wechsler was interested in how a variety of *nonintellectual factors* (e.g., persistence, curiosity, and motivation) influenced the expression of intelligent behavior (Zachary, 1990). In 1943 Wechsler stated:

> When our scales measure the nonintellective as well as intellectual factors in intelligence, they will more nearly measure what in actual life corresponds to intelligent behavior. (Wechsler, 1944, p. 103)

Even Spearman, who is almost exclusively associated with intelligence and cognition, recognized the importance of nonintellectual factors. In his seminal book "The Abilities of Man," Spearman (1927) stated that: "the process of cognition cannot possibly be treated apart from those of conation and affection, seeing that all these are but inseparable aspects in the instincts and behavior of a single individual, who himself, as the very name implies, is essentially indivisible" (p. 2). The work of Woodcock and Snow suggests that current theory and research are catching up with the pioneering ideas of David Wechsler and Charles Spearman.

Gardner, Sternberg, and Guilford's Theories: Relevance to Contemporary Psychometric Theories

In addition to the increased interest in the psychometric *Gf-Gc* theory of intelligence, there has been considerable attention (particularly in the popular press) in Gardner's theory of *Multiple Intelligences* (Chen & Gardner, 1997; Gardner, 1983; 1993; 1994) and Sternberg's *Triarchic* theory of intelligence (Sternberg, 1994; 1997). Guilford's *Structure-of-*

Intellect model, although now more of historical interest, also continues to receive prominent treatment in most books or book chapters on intelligence. Given the movement toward theory-based intelligence test interpretation, the utility of these three theories for practical test development and interpretation warrant comment. These three theories are briefly described here with a particular emphasis on their relationship to contemporary *Gf-Gc* theory.

Gardner's Theory of Multiple Intelligences

The description of *Gf-Gc* theory as a multiple intelligences theory often causes confusion when individuals try to reconcile this model with Gardner's multiple intelligences (MI) theory (Chen & Gardner, 1997; Gardner, 1983; 1993; 1994). Although Gardner's MI theory has yet to serve as the foundation for an individually administered norm-referenced battery of tests, the concepts have received considerable attention in the popular press.

Gardner (1983) originally proposed seven intelligences which included (together with a brief example): (1) linguistic—used in reading or writing of poetry; (2) logical-mathematical—used by scientists or mathematicians to solve problems; (3) spatial—used by architects to visualize and draw building plans; (4) musical—used by musicians to compose songs; (5) bodily-kinesthetic—used by athletes or dancers when performing or competing; (6) interpersonal—used by therapists to understand and interact with clients; and (7) intrapersonal—used by individuals to gain insight about themselves. Recently, Gardner (1998) has added an eighth intelligence dealing with the ability to discern patterns in nature (i.e., the *naturalist*) (Meyer, 1997). He also suggested the possibility of two additional types of intelligence (viz., *spiritual* and *existential*), although the evidence he presented for the latter two is preliminary in nature. The terms Gardner uses to label his eight intelligences are dramatically different from the terminology of *Gf-Gc* theory. What are the differences and similarities between the *Gf-Gc* and Gardner multiple intelligences theories?

Sternberg (1997) suggested that Gardner's theory (and his own triarchic theory of intelligence) differs from traditional psychometric theories in that it specifies a "system of interacting abilities rather than just specifying a set of abilities" (p. 1134). McGrew (1993; 1995) suggested that the fundamental differences between the two theories is that *Gf-Gc* theory is concerned with *describing the basic domains or building blocks of intelligent behavior* in the cognitive domain, while Gardner's theory focuses on *how these different domains or building blocks are combined,* along with other personal competencies (e.g., motor and social skills), in patterns representing different forms of aptitude or expertise (i.e., adult end-states valued by a culture) (Chen & Gardner, 1997).

Using Greenspan's model of personal competence (Greenspan & Driscoll, 1997), a model that includes the broad domains of physical and emotional competence and conceptual, practical, and social intelligence as an overarching framework, McGrew (1994) suggested that Gardner's seven intelligences represent unique combinations or patterns of human cognitive abilities that, together with other personal competencies, help to explain, understand, or predict aptitude, expertise, or talent. For example, Gardner's logical-mathematical intelligence reflects a sensitivity to and capacity for processing logical and/or numerical patterns and the ability to manage long sequences or chains of reasoning. Scientists and mathematicians would most likely be high on logical-mathematical intelligence. An individual who has high logical-mathematical intelligence may have high fluid intelligence, quantitative knowledge and reasoning, and visual-spatial abilities, abilities that are central in contemporary *Gf-Gc* theory. It is the specific combination of *Gf-Gc* strengths that a person exhibits that defines him or her as being high in logical-mathematical intelligence. Furthermore, individuals who are high in Gardner's bodily-kinesthetic intelligence, for example, may have specific *Gf-Gc* strengths (e.g., visual-spatial), *plus* strengths in other personal competence domains such as physical competence that help to explain their overall level of bodily-kinesthetic performance.

Thus, according to McGrew (1994), Gardner's theory is not an attempt to isolate the basic domains or elements of intelligence (a function performed by *Gf-Gc* theory), rather, it describes different patterns of expertise or aptitude based on specific combinations of *Gf-Gc* abilities *and other personal competencies*. In this regard, Gardner's different intelligences are conceptually similar to Snow's (1989; 1991; 1992) *aptitude complexes* which define aptitudes in the broadest sense (i.e., including both cognitive and conative structures).

Although Gardner's MI theory has considerable appeal, there has been no empirical evaluation of the validity of the theory as a whole (Sternberg & Kaufman, 1998), and the available empirical evaluations have been found wanting. In a review of Gardner's (1983) *Frames of Mind,* the book that first outlined his MI theory, Lubinski and Benbow (1995) concluded that there is "little empirical support for or against the unique features of Gardner's ideas. Before MI theory can be taken seriously by the scientific community and policy makers, Gardner's (1983) bold theoretical skeleton is in need of empirical flesh" (p. 937). According to Carroll (1993a), Gardner "discounts multifactorial theories of intelligence . . . because, he claims, they fail to account for the full diversity of abilities that can be observed. Generally, Gardner has neglected the evidence on the basis of which the present three-stratum theory has been constructed" (p. 641). Furthermore, in a review and comparison of structural *Gf-Gc* theory, Gardner's multiple intelligences theory, and Sternberg's Triarchic theory (Sternberg, 1985), Messick (1992) characterized Gardner's (as well as Sternberg's) theory as appealing selectively to factor-analytic research while ignoring or downplaying research that challenged his model.

It seems clear that the descriptions of Gardner's seven multiple intelligences "do not derive from any consistent set of empirical data and can be tied to data only in piecemeal fashion, thereby being constantly threatened by the perverse human tendency to highlight results that are consonant with the theory's logic over findings that are dissonant" (Messick, 1992; p. 368). Bouchard (1984), Gustafsson and Undheim (1996), Scarr (1985), and Snow (1985) also questioned the empirical support for Gardner's theory. Despite the lack of a strong program of validity research, Gardner's theory has produced many school-based educational interventions. According to Sternberg and Kaufman (1998), evidence to support these interventions is also limited.

Sternberg's Triarchic Theory

The Triarchic theory of intelligence (Sternberg, 1994; 1997) is an attempt to describe the processes that underlie intelligent thought by understanding the way in which intelligence relates to the internal and external world and experiences of individuals (Messick, 1992). Sternberg suggested that three major elements or *components* influence intelligent thought.

First, three sets of processing components or mental processes (i.e., knowledge acquisition, performance, metacomponents) allow individuals to solve problems (Sternberg, 1994; 1997). *Knowledge acquisition components* allow individuals to learn new information, while *performance* and *metacomponents* are involved in working with problems to produce solutions and executing and monitoring the problem-solving processes, respectively (Eggen & Kauchak, 1997). Second, *experiential components* are involved in relating new experiences and knowledge to old experiences and knowledge and recognizing and creating new patterns of information. Third, *contextual components* are concerned with adaptation—that is, explaining how a person's intelligence allows him or her to select new environments or adapt or modify existing environments (Eggen & Kauchak, 1997; Travers, Elliott, & Kratochwill, 1993).

According to Messick (1992), Sternberg's focus on culturally relevant conceptions of intelligence in relation to individual experiences results in a "focus on five critical aspects of intelligence—problem solving, verbal ability, social and practical competence, coping with novelty, and the automatization of performance" (p. 376). A consideration of these concepts suggests that the Triarchic theory includes parts of the *Gf-Gc* model, namely *Gf, Gc, Glr,* and *Gs,* respectively (Messick, 1992).

More recently, Sternberg (1996) proposed a theory of *successful intelligence* which "involves an individual's discerning his or her pattern of strengths and weaknesses, and the figuring out ways to capitalize upon the strengths and at the same time to compensate for weaknesses" (Sternberg & Kaufman, 1998, p. 494). Much like Gardner's theory of multiple intelligences, Sternberg's successful intelligence is comprised of abilities drawn from a broader array of personal competencies than those typically associated with traditional notions of intelligence. These include analytical, creative, and practical abilities. As is the case with much of Sternberg's theoretical concepts, analytical abilities are broadly defined (e.g., identifying a problem, defining the nature of the problem, devising a strategy to solve the problem, and monitoring the solution process). Analytical abilities more than likely include some that are *Gf-Gc* abilities and others that are yet to be determined. In contrast, creative and practical abilities are best thought of as including abilities from *other* competence domains (e.g., practical intelligence in Greenspan's model of personal competence).

To date, little validity evidence exists in support of Sternberg's theory of successful intelligence, due, in part, to its recency. However, Sternberg's Triarchic theory, like Gardner's MI theory, has not fared well when evaluated against established standards of validity. Messick (1992) indicated that "several aspects of Sternberg's theory are simply nonfactual...the theory is construct dense....In the process, he [Sternberg] forgoes relations of strict deductibility and tends to rely on metaphorical descriptions...but they are not conducive to the derivation of empirical consequences instrumental to theory testing" (p. 379). Messick's less than positive treatment of Sternberg's Triarchic theory is echoed in Cronbach's (1986) response to some of Sternberg's claims:

> We don't have much theory, and I don't favor using the word loosely for almost any abstraction or point of view.... I would reserve the word *theory* for substantial, articulated, somewhat validated constructions. Rather than an emperor with no clothes, we have theory being used as an imperial cloak that has no emperor inside. (p. 23)

Guilford's Structure-of-Intellect Model

Anyone who has read any psychology book that covers the topic of intelligence has probably seen the "Rubik's cube" of intelligence theories. As a result of an ambitious and largely factor analytically based program of research, J. P. Guilford and associates proposed a three-dimensional *Structure-of-Intellect (SOI)* model (which has been presented typically as a three-dimensional cube) where all cognitive abilities were classified in terms of *operations* (cognitive, memory, divergent and convergent production, evaluation), *contents* (visual, auditory, symbolic, semantic, behavioral), and *products* (units, classes, relations, systems, transformations, implications). Based on the SOI model, understanding intelligence would require the classification and measurement of well over 100 discrete abilities. The SOI model probably represents the most detailed and comprehensive attempt to develop a precise and systematic taxonomy of cognitive abilities.

Although SOI interpretations of the Wechsler Intelligence Scales have been offered (Meeker, 1969; 1975), they no longer are used with much frequency due to both practical constraints (i.e., too time consuming and eclectic; Kaufman, 1994), and more importantly, a lack of supporting empirical evidence (Carroll, 1993a; Cronbach & Snow, 1977; Gustafsson & Undheim, 1996; Messick, 1992; Vernon, 1961). Carroll (1993a) rendered a particularly harsh judgement when he concluded that the SOI model "is fundamentally defective" (p. 59) and should be "marked down as a somewhat eccentric aberration in the history of intelligence models; that so much attention has been paid to it is disturbing, to the extent that textbooks and other treatments of it have given the impression that the model is valid and widely accepted, when clearly it is not" (p. 60).

Gardner, Sternberg, and Guilford: Concluding Comments

Currently, Gardner's MI, Sternberg's Triarchic, and Guilford's SOI models of intelligence are not likely to have significant impact on intelligence test interpretation. The SOI model had its day in the court of intelligence research and theory and was judged to be lacking in the validity evidence necessary for sound intelligence test interpretation. Although Gardner's and Sternberg's theories are receiving much attention in the popular press, they have been found to be data-poor. They both attend selectively to or ignore features of the extensive *Gf-Gc* research literature. Hence, if Sternberg (and Gardner) "had treated factorial theories and research on human abilities in more depth, their empirical and scholarly efforts might have systematically built upon (or undercut) these structural formulations and advanced the science of intellect in cumulative rather than idiosyncratic fashion" (Messick, 1992, p. 382). Although the MI and Triarchic theories may appear to be judged too harshly here and by others we cite, this does not diminish the possibility that these theories may eventually help broaden our understanding and measurement of intelligence. The MI and Triarchic theories are *different* from traditional psychometric theories of intelligence and, therefore, may require the development of different measurement approaches if they are to have a signficant influence on the practice of measuring intelligence.

Moving the Wechslers from Then to Now: Narrowing the Theory-Practice Gap

As depicted in Figure 2.1, there currently exists a significant theory-practice gap in the field of intellectual assessment. This is particularly true in the case of the WPPSI-R, K-ABC, and KAIT batteries which measure only two to three broad *Gf-Gc* abilities adequately (McGrew & Flanagan, 1998). The K-ABC primarily measures *Gv* and *Gsm,* and to a much lesser extent, *Gf,* while the KAIT primarily measures *Gf, Gc,* and *Glr,* and to a much lesser extent *Gv* and *Gsm.* And while the CAS, DAS, SB:IV, and WJ (1997) batteries do not provide sufficient coverage to narrow the theory-practice gap, their comprehensive measurement of four to five *Gf-Gc* abilities is nonetheless an improvement over the above mentioned batteries (McGrew & Flanagan, 1998).

Although the most recent versions of two Wechsler Scales (i.e., WAIS-III and WISC-III) measure a greater breadth of *Gf-Gc* abilities than their predecessors, a significant theory-practice gap remains. The WPPSI-R provides for adequate coverage of *Gc* and *Gv,* and partial measurement of *Gs, Gq,* and *Gsm.* The WISC-III and WAIS-III represent improvements over the WPPSI-R as both provide for good coverage of *Gs* in addition to *Gc* and *Gv.* Like the WPPSI-R, the WISC-III allows for only partial measurement of *Gq* and *Gsm.* However, the WAIS-III includes a single *Gf* test (viz., Matrix Reasoning) and expanded coverage of *Gsm.* These recent developments, although much welcomed and necessary, reflect slow incremental progress. As such, even when the WISC-III and WAIS-III are combined with the two memory batteries to which they are statistically linked (i.e., Children's Memory Scale and Wechsler Memory Scale—Third Edition, respectively), the end result does not represent an effective narrowing of the theory-practice gap. This is not unexpected given that the third generation of the Wechsler Scales have not been influenced overtly by contemporary *Gf-Gc* theory and research.

In defense of the Wechsler Scales, the serious attention that has focused on developing tests that are firmly grounded in empirically supported theories of intelligence is a relatively recent trend in the history of intelligence test development (Kamphaus, 1998; Sternberg & Kaufman, 1998). In terms of a single battery, currently the WJ-III comes closest to narrowing the gap between practice and contemporary *Gf-Gc* theory. As stated earlier, however, most major intelligence batteries need to be supplemented with other measures in order to narrow the *Gf-Gc* theory-practice gap.

Conclusion

There is little doubt that the Wechsler Intelligence Scale verbal/nonverbal (performance) model has exerted, and continues to exert, a significant influence on the measurement, classification, and interpretation of intellectual behavior. Because of the historical dominance of the Wechsler Scales in psychological assessment, it is understandable that many assessment professionals have internalized the belief that a verbal/nonverbal taxonomy is one of the best models for understanding intelligence test performance. However, the Wechsler verbal/nonverbal model is not based on an empirically derived theory of intelligence. Therefore, it should come as no surprise that comprehensive reviews of the extant cognitive abilities factor analysis research reveal a convergence on a hierarchical *Gf-Gc* model of intelligence and not a dichotomous verbal/nonverbal model. From the perspective of *Gf-Gc* theory, the Wechsler-based verbal/nonverbal model measures only a small portion of the 10 empirically supported broad *Gf-Gc* abilities. Carroll (1993a; 1993b) concluded that the Wechsler Verbal scale is an approximate measure of crystallized intelligence *(Gc)* and the Performance scale is an approximate measure of both broad visual perception *(Gv)* and, somewhat less validly, fluid intelligence *(Gf)*. Recent cross-battery factor analysis studies of the Wechsler Scales and other intelligence batteries (see Chapter 3) support Carroll's (1993b) *Gf-Gc* analysis of the Wechsler Scales. However, the Wechsler Performance scale is now being viewed as a measure of predominantly *Gv,* and not *Gf,* abilities (Elliott, 1994; Kaufman & Kaufman, 1993; McGrew & Flanagan, 1996; 1998; Woodcock, 1990). Carroll (1993a) provided a succinct judgement regarding the Wechsler Scales when he concluded that "presently available knowledge and technology would permit the development of tests and scales that would be much more adequate for their purpose than the Wechsler Scales" (p. 702).

We believe that the less than positive results from the second and third waves of intelligence test interpretation of the Wechsler Scales (i.e., clinical and psychometric profile analysis) were largely due to the use of either clinical, empirical, or theoretical taxonomies that were based on little or no sound empirical evidence. We believe that *Gf-Gc* theory is currently the *best* and most advanced taxonomy from which to understand human cognitive abilities and from which to improve the practice of theory-based intelligence test interpretation. *Gf-Gc* theory has provided a useful framework from which to analyze and interpret intelligence tests (e.g., the *Intelligence Test Desk Reference (ITDR): Gf-Gc Cross-Battery Assessment* [McGrew & Flanagan, 1998] is organized around the *Gf-Gc* taxonomy; Prentky, 1994). Furthermore, the *Gf-Gc* framework has provided a standard set of names or terms for the components of the entity (i.e., a standard nomenclature), an important feature of good taxonomies. Such an established nomenclature increases the effective communication among researchers and practitioners so that a "knowledge base can be accumulated" (Reynolds & Lakin, 1987).

Based on our review, the Wechsler verbal/nonverbal model (as well as a number of other theoretical models of intelligence) cannot be considered a *good* taxonomic system from which to organize thinking regarding intelligence tests. *The Wechsler verbal/nonverbal model does not represent a theoretically or empirically supported model of the structure of intelligence.* Unfortunately, a by-product of the Wechsler Scales' success is that many assessment professionals have grounded their practices in a largely atheoretical taxonomy of human cognitive abilities, a practice that was found to be seriously wanting in the second and third waves of intelligence test interpretation and a practice that constrains interpretation from benefiting from the now recognized need for theory-based interpretation. The staying power of this venerable (and out-of-date) taxonomy is at variance with viable taxonomies that are flexible and evolving. The premature hardening of the taxonomic categories can result in a deformation of the scientific process by "hermetically sealing of the boundaries of knowledge" (Prentky, 1994, p. 507).

We recognize that other theories of intelligence, including many of those reviewed briefly in this chapter, have either made important contributions to the intelligence knowledge base or posses new and/or unique features that will make new contributions and perhaps illuminate the limitations of the *Gf-Gc* theory. Contemporary *Gf-Gc* theory was presented as the most researched, empirically supported, and comprehensive descriptive hierarchical psychometric framework from which to organize thinking about intelligence test interpretation. According to Gustafsson and Undheim (1996), "the empirical evidence in favor of a hierarchical arrangement of abilities is overwhelming" (p. 204). An integrated Cattell-Horn-Carroll *Gf-Gc* model was presented here as the taxonomic framework around which the practice of intelligence testing and interpretation should be organized. The remainder of this book is devoted to describing how the interpretation of the Wechsler Intelligence Scales can be moved into the current emphasis on more theory-based intelligence test interpretation. In particular, we seek to modernize the Wechsler Scales by wrapping them in the *Gf-Gc* theory and taxonomy of human intelligence.

ENDNOTES

1. Piaget's theory of cognitive development is not included in this discussion since his work focuses primarily on universal cognitive changes and not on individual differences in cognitive development (Niesser et al., 1996).
2. It is important to not confuse low correlations with *g* as meaning those abilities that are furthest to the right in Carroll's model are not important. For example, Kamphaus (1997) has stated that the Wechsler Coding test is not important since it represents an ability *(Gs)* which is to the far right in Carroll's model. Abilities (and thus tests) may be low in *g* but may correlate significantly with other criteria. For example, a review of the literature has shown the *Gs* abilities are important for reading, math, and writing during the elementary school years (see Chapter 3). Claims that certain abilities are not important because of lower internal validity (i.e., not a strong measure of *g*) fail to recognize that internal and external validity are different forms of validity and that both are important for different reasons.

3

Contemporary *Gf-Gc* Theory and Wechsler Test Interpretation

Validity is an integrated evaluative judgment of the degree to which empirical evidence and theoretical rationales support the adequacy *and* appropriateness *of* inferences *and* actions *based on test scores or other modes of assessment.*

—Messick (1989, p. 13)

In Chapter 2 it was concluded that most individually administered intelligence batteries, including the Wechsler Scales, fall short in the valid measurement of the full range of known *Gf-Gc* abilities. This conclusion is grounded in the notion that the ability to draw valid inferences about theoretical constructs from observable measures (e.g., tests) is a function of the extent to which the underlying program of validity research attends to both the *theoretical* and *empirical* domains of the focal constructs (Bensen, 1998; Bensen & Hagtver, 1996). The purpose of this chapter is to describe the characteristics of strong programs of test validation research, explain why parts of the Wechsler Intelligence Scales (as organized and typically interpreted) are judged *not* to be based on a strong validation research program, and finally, to demonstrate how the application of the *Gf-Gc* theory can strengthen the validity of the inferences drawn from Wechsler test scores.

Strong Theory: A Necessary Prerequisite for Strong Construct Validity

Similar to the calls for theory-based intelligence test interpretation in Chapter 1, leading scholars in the area of test validity (Cronbach, 1971; Cronbach & Meehl, 1955; Loevinger, 1957; Messick, 1989; Nunnally, 1978) stress the prominent role theory should play in the construction, validation, and interpretation of psychological tests (Bensen, 1998). Therefore, it is essential that the underlying theory of any psychological test be based on a solid foundation of evidence. In Chapter 2, *Gf-Gc* theory was described as the most comprehensive and empirically supported psychometric theory of intelligence and the theory around which intelligence tests should be developed and interpreted. Given the salient role theory plays in test validation, it is first necessary to provide evidence which supports the use of *Gf-Gc* theory in the interpretation of the Wechsler Intelligence Scales.

Supporting Evidence for *Gf-Gc* Theory

Extensive and robust factor-analytic evidence supports the validity of the *Gf-Gc* theory of intelligence. Unfortunately, since the factor-analytic literature on cognitive abilities is typically the only evidence cited in support of *Gf-Gc* theory, there is a common misconception that *Gf-Gc* theory is only a factor-analytic-based theory. However, support for the hierarchical *Gf-Gc* theory has been documented through five major forms of validity evidence (Gustafsson & Undheim, 1996; Horn, 1994; Horn & Noll, 1997). Each is discussed briefly in the text following.

Structural Evidence

Structural evidence, or evidence based on the individual differences, factor-analytic research tradition, has been the most prominent evidential base for the *Gf-Gc* constructs (Taylor, 1994). This source of evidence is based on the principle of concomitant variation. That is, if measures covary repeatedly across studies that differ in sample characteristics, time, and place, then this covariation suggests the plausibility of a common underlying function (Horn & Noll, 1997). The extant factor-analytic research over the past 50 to 60 years has converged consistently on models of intelligence similar to the *Gf-Gc* models presented in Figure 2.4 (in Chapter 2). Furthermore, the *Gf-Gc* structure presented in Figure 2.4 has been found to be invariant across different gender, ethnic, and racial groups (Carroll, 1993a). Carroll (1993a) concluded that "with reference to the major types of cognitive ability, there is little evidence that factorial structure differs in any systematic way across male and female groups, different cultures, racial groups, and the like" (p. 687).

Given the wide age range covered by the family of Wechsler Intelligence Scales, it is important to know if the *Gf-Gc* model presented in Figure 2.4 is invariant across ages. Historically, both logical and theoretical considerations have suggested that cognitive abilities become more differentiated with age (the age-differentiation hypothesis) (Carroll, 1993a). Carroll's massive review of the cognitive ability factor-analytic research addressed the age-differentiation issue given that it included studies with subjects from as young as 6 to 11 months to 70 years. Carroll (1993a) stated that "my general conclusion on age-differentiation of cognitive ability factors is that it is a phenomenon whose existence is hard to demonstrate ... the question of the age differentiation is probably of little scientific interest except possibly at very young ages ... the same factors are found throughout the life span" (p. 681). The apparent invariance of the *Gf-Gc* factors across the life span, male and female groups, and different cultures and racial groups supports the application of the *Gf-Gc* cross-battery approach to intelligence test interpretation for most of the population.

Developmental Evidence

The validity of the *Gf-Gc* constructs is supported also by differential developmental changes in the growth and decline of cognitive abilities across the life span (Carroll, 1993a; Dixon, Kramer, & Baltes, 1985). This type of evidence typically takes the form of comparing *Gf-Gc* growth curves. *Developmental evidence* has shown that different *Gf-Gc* abilities follow divergent developmental trajectories with increasing age (Horn, 1982; 1985; Horn & Cattell, 1967; Schaie, 1979; 1983; 1994). For example, from young adulthood to old age, increases in *Gc* and *Glr* (maintained abilities) and decreases in *Gf, Gs,* and *Gsm* (vulnerable abilities) have been reported (see Horn & Noll, 1997 for a summary). The finding of maintained and vulnerable abilities and differential ability growth curves across the lifespan suggests that different mechanisms or determinants (e.g., education, genes, injuries, lifestyle factors) operate differentially in the development and decline of *Gf-Gc* abilities, evidence that supports the validity of the different *Gf-Gc* constructs (Carroll, 1983; Horn & Noll, 1997).

Neurocognitive Evidence

Neurocognitive evidence exists in the form of empirical relations between measures of *Gf-Gc* abilities and physiological and neurological functioning (Horn & Noll, 1997). For example, the norepinephrine system of the brain has been associated with neurological arousal that is characteristic of *Gf* abilities (Horn, 1982; 1985; Iverson, 1979). The localization of specific cognitive abilities in certain regions of the brain (e.g., verbal or *Gc*-type abilities are often reported to be localized mainly in the left hemisphere) is another example of neurocognitive evidence (see Kaufman, 1990 and Lezak, 1995 for summaries). Differential declines in different *Gf-Gc* abilities that are associated with age-related central nervous system deterioration (e.g., the development of senile plaques apparent in Alzheimer's patients) suggest that different *Gf-Gc* abilities are supported by different underlying brain structures and functions—a finding that further supports the construct validity of the different abilities.

Heritability Evidence

Another form of support for the different *Gf-Gc* abilities is *heritability evidence,* evidence concerned with the "proportion of phenotypic (observed) differences among individuals in a population that can be attributed to genetic differences among them" (Plomin & Petrill, 1997, p. 57). Although at times controversial and theoretically and methodologically complex (see McArdle & Prescott, 1997), behavioral-genetic research has suggested that different sets of genes may determine different structures and functions of the brain (Plomin & Petrill, 1997). Although no definitive conclusions have been reached, different heritability estimates have been reported for different cognitive abilities in some studies (Carroll, 1993; McGue & Bouchard, 1989; Plomin, DeFries, & McClearn, 1990; Scarr & Carter-Saltzman, 1982; Vandenberg & Volger, 1985). For example, Vanderberg and Volger (1985) cite parent-offspring research that suggests that spatial (*Gv*-Spatial Relations) and verbal *(Gc)* abilities have higher heritabilities than visual memory (*Gv*-Visual Memory) and perceptual speed (*Gs*-Perceptual Speed). In studies of twins, McGue and Bouchard (1989) reported that genetic influences were largest for spatial (*Gv*-Spatial Relations) abilities and smallest for visual memory (*Gv*-Visual Memory) abilities. Some behavioral genetic research has suggested that different *Gf-Gc* abilities may be influenced by separate genetic and environmental factors. When combined with research that has reported the differentiation of cognitive abilities at early ages (Carroll, 1993), Horn and Noll (1997) concluded that "the outlines for different intelligences can be seen in early childhood" (p. 81).

Outcome-Criterion Evidence

Finally, differential achievement or *outcome-criterion evidence* supports the existence of separate *Gf-Gc* abilities. Supporting outcome-criterion evidence is found in research studies that have investigated the relations between *Gf-Gc* abilities and academic achievement, occupational success, and other human traits. This outcome-criterion evidence is important, as *Gf-Gc*-based intellectual assessments will be of little practical value if they fail to produce valid interpretations of intellectual functioning that contribute to improved diagnostic and classification decisions, predictions about performance, and interventions. A first step on the road to using *Gf-Gc* theory to improve the practice of intellectual assessment is to understand the relations between *Gf-Gc* abilities and other variables.

McGrew and Flanagan (1998) presented a summary of more than a decade of research that has examined the relations between different *Gf-Gc* constructs and measures and other non-*Gf-Gc* constructs and measures. An abstracted summary of their review is presented in Table 3.1. In general, the information presented in Table 3.1 indicates that different *Gf-Gc* constructs (and valid measures of the constructs) are significantly and differentially related to different academic, occupational, interest, and personality variables.[1] This form of evidence provides additional support for the validity of the different *Gf-Gc* constructs.

Supporting Evidence: Concluding Comments and Cautions

The validity evidence present for the *Gf-Gc* theory approximates the desired standard of validity evidence—a nomological network of different types of validity evidence (viz., structural, developmental, neurocognitive, heritability, and achievement or outcome criteria). This conclusion is similar to that reached by Messick (1992), who, after comparing the validity evidence for the *Gf-Gc* theory and two other theories of multiple cognitive abilities (i.e., Gardner's and Sternberg's theories), concluded that the *Gf-Gc* theories of intelligence "fare somewhat better . . . because they reflect many decades of programmatic research" (p. 382). Messick went as far as to state that *Gf-Gc* "multifactor theory and measurement provide a partial standard of validity for both Gardner and Sternberg" (1992, p. 366). It seems clear that *Gf-Gc*-organized Wechsler-based cross-battery assessments (described in Chapters 7 and 8) have the potential to contribute meaningfully to research studies and reviews on the relations between cognitive abilities and many different outcome criteria, because they are organized within this well-articulated and researched theoretical framework.

TABLE 3.1 Select *Gf-Gc* External Validity Evidence Summarized by McGrew and Flanagan (1998)

	Reading Achievement	Math Achievement	Occupational Performance	Interest Traits	Personality Traits
Gf	Inductive (I) and general sequential reasoning (RG) abilities play a moderate role in reading comprehension.	Inductive (I) and general sequential (RG) reasoning abilities are consistently very important at all ages.	Mathematician Scientist	Realistic Investigative Enterprising (–)	Openness to Experiences
Gc	Language development (LD), lexical knowledge (VL), and listening ability (LS) are important at all ages. These abilities become increasingly important with age.	Language development (LD), lexical knowledge (VL), and listening abilities (LS) are important at all ages. These abilities become increasingly more important with age.	Accountant Leader (military)/Soldier Lawyer Poet Scholar Scientist	Realistic Investigative Artistic Conventional (–)	Typical Intelligence Engagement Test Anxiety
Gsm	Memory span (MS) is important especially when evaluated within the context of working memory.	Memory span (MS) is important especially when evaluated within the context of working memory.		Realistic Enterprising (–)	Openness to Experiences Test Anxiety (–)
Gv		May be important primarily for higher level or advanced mathematics (e.g., geometry, calculus).	Carpenter Engineer Leader (military)/Soldier Machinist Photographer Teacher Architect/Draftsperson Artist/Sculptor Electrician Navigator/Pilot Air traffic controller Designer Mathematician Scientist		Typical Intelligence Engagement
Ga	Phonetic coding (PC) or "phonological awareness" is very important during the elementary school years.		Musician Musical composer Sonar Operator		
Glr	Naming facility (NA) or "rapid automatic naming" is very important during the elementary school years. Associative memory (MA) may be somewhat important at select ages (e.g., age 6 years).				
Gs	Perceptual speed (P) abilities are important during all school years, particularly the elementary school years.	Perceptual speed (P) abilities are important during all school years, particularly the elementary school years.	Accountant Leader (military)/Soldier Clerk/Typist Proofreader	Conventional	Conventional Test Anxiety (–)

Note: (–) Indicates a negative correlation between the *Gf-Gc* ability and the interest and/or personality trait.

Although there is considerable support for the *Gf-Gc* theory of intelligence, it should not be considered *the* definitive theory. *Gf-Gc* theory is not without limitations. Horn and Noll (1997) summarized four major limitations of *Gf-Gc* theory. Carroll (1995b; 1997) also provided appropriate words of caution about the limits of *Gf-Gc* theory.

First, *Gf-Gc* theory is more a descriptive, empirical generalization of research findings than a deductive explanation of these findings. A research tradition has evolved in which the *Gf-Gc* variables included in successive studies are based on the variables included in prior studies, a situation that does not include the requisite *a priori* theoretical basis for validating a theory. Horn and Noll (1997) acknowledge this limitation, but point out that all scientific theory is the result of a research history and culture, and it "evolves out of a repetitive spiral of building on what is known (induction), which leads to deductions that generate empirical studies and more induction, which leads to further deductions, which spawn further induction, and so on" (p. 83).

Second, the structure implied in the *Gf-Gc* theory is a limitation. Although the statistical method of factor analysis can produce neat hierarchically organized factors, these empirically based frameworks most likely do not represent accurately the organization of actual human cognitive abilities. That is, *Gf-Gc* theory is largely a product of linear equations (viz., factor analysis). Natural phenomena most likely are nonlinear in nature. As Horn and Noll (1997) stated, "The equations that describe the outer structure and convolutions of brains must be parabolas, cycloids, cissoids, spirals, folliums, exponentials, hyperboles, and the like. It is likely that the equations that best describe the inner workings of brains—human capabilities—are of the same forms, not those that describe city blocks and buildings" (p. 84).

Third, *Gf-Gc* theory provides little information on how the *Gf-Gc* abilities develop or how the cognitive processes work together. The theory is largely product oriented and provides little guidance on the dynamic interplay of variables (i.e., the processes) that occur in human cognitive processing (Gustafsson & Undheim, 1996). However, as described in Chapter 2, recently Woodcock (1993, 1997) has articulated a *Cognitive Performance Model* and a *Gf-Gc Information Processing Model* of intellectual performance that specify relations between and among *Gf-Gc* abilities, information processing constructs, and noncognitive variables. Currently these models are largely speculative and need further study.

Fourth, Carroll (1997), one of the primary architects of the *Gf-Gc* taxonomy, humbly pointed out that additional work needs to be completed in the factor-analytic study of human cognitive abilities. "The map of abilities provided by the three-stratum theory undoubtedly has errors of commission and omission, with gaps to be filled in by further research" (Carroll, 1997, p. 128). Carroll (1995) stated that certain aspects of the hierarchical structure may need to be refined and/or revised, including the identification of additional narrow abilities, the clarification of already identified narrow abilities, and the clarification of the number and structure of broad abilities. Although Carroll's wise words should temper the tendency to believe that we have now discovered the "holy taxonomic grail" of human cognitive abilities, the *Gf-Gc* taxonomy is currently the most comprehensive and empirically supported psychometric framework from which to understand the structure of human intelligence.

Linking *Gf-Gc* Theory and Applied Measurement: The Importance of a Strong Program of Construct Validation Research

The benefits accrued from the identification of a valid theory of intelligence (i.e., *Gf-Gc* theory) are wasted if the development of operational measures of the relevant cognitive constructs is not based on a strong program of construct validation research (Benson, 1998; Cronbach, 1989). But just what is a "strong" program of construct validation research and how does it relate to the development and interpretation of the Wechsler Intelligence Scales?

Many leading researchers and scholars in the area of psychological measurement have, at one time or another, described similar validation stages or components that are necessary for strong test validity (see, for example, Cronbach, 1971; Cronbach & Meehl, 1955; Loevinger, 1957; Messick, 1989; Nunnally, 1978). In general, a common theme among these voices is that the test validation process is similar to that used to develop and evaluate scientific theories and involves the evaluation of both theory and measures in a concurrent iterative process. Benson's (1998) synthesis of the various validity concepts and components is particularly useful for understanding the interplay between theory and measurement. According to Benson (1998), the steps that allow for valid inferences to be drawn from test scores are those illustrated in Figures 3.1 and 3.2.

The Substantive Stage of Construct Validation: A Conceptual Explanation

The information presented in Figures 3.1 and 3.2 conveys the message that a strong theory is a necessary foundation from which to develop and interpret valid measures of intelligence. A strong theory of intelligence is needed in order to specify, define, and circumscribe both the theoretical and empirical domains of the focal constructs. This point will be illustrated within the domain of visual intelligence or processing *(Gv)*.

As illustrated in Figure 3.1, the first step toward developing valid measures of the *Gv* construct is the identification of a strong theory. We have already presented ample evidence to support the conclusion that *Gf-Gc* theory is a strong theory. Therefore, the *Gf-Gc* framework and the *Gv* domain (which is part of this framework) constitute the *theoretical domain* (see Figure 3.1) from which to develop measures during the substantive stage (see Figure 3.2) in this example.

The next step in the substantive stage of construct validation is to develop and evaluate possible measures of the theoretical constructs (i.e., the *empirical domain*) (see Figure 3.1). During this step a variety of methods and concepts should be employed to "flesh out" the potential measures in the empirical domain (see Figure 3.2). For example, definitions of the theoretical constructs must be specified in order to circumscribe the constructs to be measured. Typically, this is followed by the development of test formats, the generation of

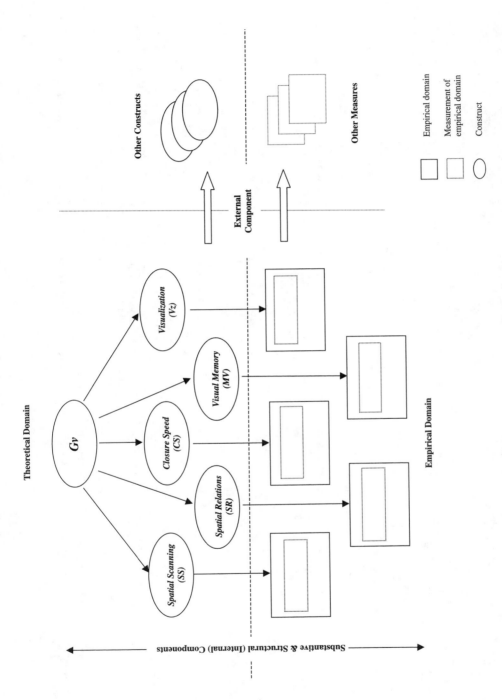

FIGURE 3.1 Relationship between Three Stages/Components of Strong Construct Validation Research Programs: A *Gv* Example

Note: The *Gv* narrow abilities of Flexibility of Closure (CF), Serial Perceptual Integration (PI), Length Estimation (LE), Perceptual Illusions (IL), Perceptual Alternations (PN), and Imagery (IM) are excluded from this figure.

	Substantive Stage/Component	Structural Stage/Component	External Stage/Component
Purpose	• Define the *theoretical* and *empirical* domains of intelligence	• Examine the *internal* relations among the measures used to operationalize the theoretical construct domain (i.e., intelligence)	• Examine the *external* relations among the focal construct (i.e., intelligence) and other constructs and/or subject characteristics
Question Asked	• How should intelligence be defined and operationally measured?	• Do the observed measures "behave" in a manner consistent with the theoretical domain definition of intelligence?	• Do the focal constructs and observed measures "fit" within a network of expected construct relations (i.e., the nomological network)?
Methods & Concepts	• Theory development & validation • Generate definitions • Item and scale development • Content validation • Evaluate construct underrepresentation and construct irrelevancy	• Internal domain studies • Item/subscale intercorrelations • Exploratory/confirmatory factor analysis • Item response theory (IRT) • Multitrait-Multimethod matrix • Generalizability theory	• Group differentiation • Structural equation modeling • Correlation of observed measures with other measures • Multitrait-Multimethod matrix
Characteristics of *strong* validation programs	• A strong psychological theory plays a prominent role • Theory provides a well-specified and bounded domain of constructs • The empirical domain includes measures of all potential constructs (i.e., adequate construct representation) • The empirical domain includes measures that only contain reliable variance related to the theoretical constructs (i.e., construct relevance)	• Moderate item internal consistency • Measures covary in a manner consistent with the intended theoretical structure • Factors reflect trait rather than method variance • Items/measures are representative of the empirical domain • Items fit the theoretical structure • The theoretical/empirical model is deemed plausible (especially when compared against other competing models) based on substantive and statistical criteria	• Focal constructs vary in theorized ways with other constructs • Measures of the constructs differentiate existing groups that are known to differ on the constructs • Measures of focal constructs correlate with other validated measures of the same constructs • Theory-based hypotheses are supported, particularly when compared to rival hypotheses

FIGURE 3.2 A Continuum of Stages for Strong Construct Validation Research Programs

Note: Information in this table is based on Benson, J. (1988). Developing a strong program of construct validation: A test anxiety example. *Educational Measurement: Issues and Practice.*

test items, the gathering of item calibration data, and the use of various item analysis procedures (e.g., Rasch scaling) to evaluate the adequacy of the items and scales. Essential to the process are activities directed at insuring adequate *content validity* of the measures that will be used to represent the theoretical construct (Benson, 1998; Messick, 1989).

Briefly, *content* or *construct representation* is concerned with the extent to which the items/tests within an empirical domain adequately reflect the major aspects of the theoretical domain of constructs (Bensen, 1998). In Figure 3.1, adequate *Gv* construct representation would be insured through the development of tests for the abilities of Spatial Scanning, Spatial Relations, Closure Speed, Visual Memory, and Visualization. The development and use of a single test indicator (e.g., a test of Visual Memory) or two similar indicators (e.g., two different tests that measure Visual Memory) to represent the *Gv* construct would not result in accurate and valid inferences regarding the complete *Gv* construct. In general, the most valid measures of intellectual ability constructs (i.e., *Gf-Gc* abilities) would be those that include the largest number of different tests (within practical constraints), each measuring a unique aspect of every one of the broad theoretical constructs.

Substantive Validity of the Wechsler Scales

With the benefit of hindsight, it is now clear that the Wechsler Intelligence Scales are not grounded in a strong theory of intelligence and thus, have a weak substantive foundation. In addition to the material summarized in previous chapters, evidence that supports this conclusion is the paucity of substantive Wechsler Scale validity research studies. A comprehensive literature review of validity studies conducted with the Wechsler Intelligence and Memory Scales since 1989 was completed by the present authors. A summary of this review is provided in Appendix A (Network of Validity Evidence of the Wechsler Scales). The studies included in this appendix were classified by the present authors as fitting into one of these categories: substantive, structural, and external. The information presented in Figure 3.2 guided our classifications.[2]

Because the *Gf-Gc* taxonomy "provides what is essentially a 'map' of all known cognitive abilities . . . [it] can be used in interpreting scores on the many tests used in individual assessment" (Carroll, 1993a, p. 127). In other words, the *Gf-Gc* taxonomy can serve as a blueprint from which to evaluate the content validity of intelligence tests. The first systematic attempt to map the major intelligence batteries to the *Gf-Gc* structural framework was presented by Woodcock (1990). Woodcock's (1990) classifications, which were only at the broad (stratum II) level, were extended to the narrow (stratum I) level by McGrew (1997). McGrew and Flanagan (1998) subsequently refined McGrew's classifications and extended the classifications to over 200 cognitive ability measures. The Wechsler *Gf-Gc* test classifications presented by McGrew and Flanagan are used here to evaluate the content or substantive validity of the Wechsler Intelligence Scales.

The Wechsler *Gf-Gc* classifications required that each test be classified at both the broad (stratum II) and narrow (stratum I) ability levels. The broad abilities measured by tests coincide with the *broad Gf-Gc* abilities in the Integrated Cattell-Horn-Carroll model described in Chapter 2. Figure 3.3 presents an example of a *Gf-Gc* broad- and narrow-ability test mapping for five Wechsler tests.

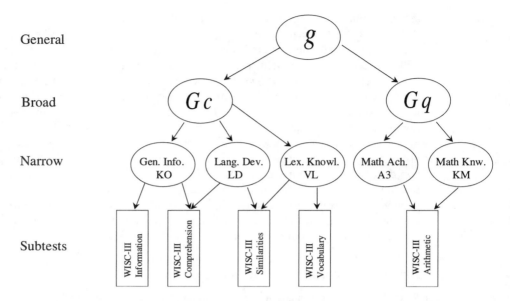

FIGURE 3.3   The Relations between Five WISC-III Tests and the Three Strata (Narrow, Broad, and General) of the *Gf-Gc* Model of Intelligence

Note: There are additional narrow abilities in the domains of *Gc* and *Gq* that are not included in this figure.

Figure 3.3 shows that the broad ability of *Gc* subsumes the specialized narrow abilities of General Information, Language Development, Lexical Knowledge, and others not included in the figure. The rectangles in Figure 3.3 represent five tests from the WISC-III. In this figure, the Information, Comprehension, Similarities, and Vocabulary tests are all classified as indicators of the broad *Gc* ability. The Arithmetic test is classified as an indicator of the broad *Gq* ability. The complete *Gf-Gc* content validity evaluation of the Wechsler Scales is presented in Figure 3.4. The broad *Gf-Gc* test classifications presented in Figure 3.4 were derived from a series of confirmatory cross-battery intelligence test factor analysis studies (described below). The narrow-ability classifications of the Wechsler subtests, as well as the expert consensus procedures on which they are based, are described in McGrew (1997) and McGrew and Flanagan (1998) and are summarized in Chapter 4.

A review of Figure 3.4 reveals that the Wechsler Intelligence Scales have weak content validity when evaluated according to the *Gf-Gc* theoretical model. This is not a surprising conclusion given that the Wechsler scales have, by and large, maintained their ancestral link with David Wechsler's largely atheoretical notions of intelligence. Of the *Gf-Gc* domains that are represented across the Wechsler Intelligence batteries (viz., *Gf, Gc, Gsm, Gv, Ga, Glr, Gs*), *Gc* and *Gv* are the only abilities that have strong content or construct representation (defined by the measurement of three or more narrow abilities under a broad ability). In addition to *Gc* and *Gv,* the WISC-III adequately represents the construct of *Gs* (i.e., it measures at least two distinct narrow abilities that define this broad ability) while the WAIS-III adequately represents *Gs* and *Gsm.*

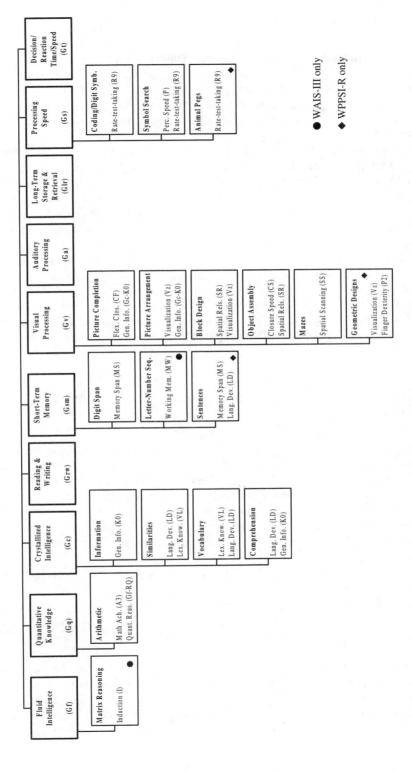

FIGURE 3.4 Wechsler *Gf-Gc* Empirical-Theoretical Domain Mapping Based on Strong Substantive and Structural Validity Evidence: The Foundation of the Wechsler *Gf-Gc* Cross-Battery Approach

The Wechsler Intelligence Scales do not contain any measures of *Ga* and *Glr*. In the *Gf* domain, the WAIS-III has weak construct representation (i.e., it only measures one narrow ability within this domain), while the WPPSI-R and WISC-III do not contain any strong measures of *Gf*. Similarly, *Gsm* is underrepresented on the WPPSI-R and WISC-III (i.e., each scale provides only one measure of this construct) and *Gs* is underrepresented on the WPPSI-R.

This content validity analysis suggests that, from the perspective of *Gf-Gc* theory, the Wechsler Intelligence Scales have a weak substantive foundation. This is primarily due to the fact that during the development and subsequent revisions of the Wechsler Intelligence Scales, no explicit attempt was made to specify and circumscribe the theoretical domain (and subdomains) of intelligence. As a result, the Wechsler Intelligence Scales have not benefited from a test development process where measures were operationalized according to a theory-based "blueprint" similar to that portrayed in Figure 3.1. The continuum represented in Figure 3.2 suggests that the lack of a strong substantive component is the Achilles heel of the Wechsler Intelligence Scales. The largely atheoretical foundation of the Wechsler Scales places a number of constraints on the validity of inferences that can be drawn from all of the Wechsler tests and composite scores. As will be demonstrated in the remainder of this chapter, the lack of a sound theory constrains the degree to which interpretation of the Wechsler Scales can benefit from current efforts to make test interpretation more theory based.

The Structural Stage of Construct Validation: A Conceptual Explanation

As highlighted in Figure 3.2, the *structural stage* of test validation has an internal focus on the collection of tests designed to measure the theoretical domain (e.g., *Gv*). A variety of internal domain studies and methods are used to evaluate whether the tests measure the construct(s) they are purported to measure. That is, does empirical evidence support a strong link between the empirical and theoretical domains of the focal constructs? Although a theory of intelligence may have considerable popular appeal or supporting evidence, the lack of psychometrically sound measures of the focal constructs of a theory will limit its practical utility.

As is the case with all major intelligence batteries, Appendix A reveals that the primary structural validity tool of the Wechsler Scales has been *factor analysis,* a statistical procedure that groups together measures (tests) that intercorrelate positively with one another. The use of factor-analytic methods in the investigation of the structural validity of intelligence batteries can be organized along two dimensions. The first dimension is the *method* of factor analysis that is employed (i.e., exploratory or confirmatory, both of which subsume a variety of different procedures). *Exploratory* factor analysis allows the data to "speak for themselves," since it identifies the factor structure of an intelligence battery with no *a priori* model in mind. In contrast, *confirmatory* factor analysis typically examines the extent to which an *a priori* hypothesized factor structure or model fits the data, as well as how the fit of the model compares to alternative models, and how the model might be modified to fit the data better. Confirmatory factor methods are becoming particularly prominent in theory-based test development and research activities (Keith, 1997).

The second dimension of factor-analytic methods involves the breadth of cognitive ability indicators (or tests) that are analyzed. *Within-battery* factor analysis is confined to the tests from a single intelligence battery (e.g., the 13 WISC-III tests). *Cross-battery* (or joint) factor analysis, includes tests from more than one intelligence battery (e.g., WISC-III and WJ-III).

In the *Gv* example presented in Figure 3.1, if tests of Spatial Scanning, Spatial Relations, Closure Speed, Visual Memory, and Visualization are factor analyzed together with indicators of other *Gf-Gc* constructs, structural or internal construct validity evidence would emerge in the grouping (i.e., loading) of these five specific tests on a *Gv* factor while other non-*Gv* tests would load on separate and uniquely different factors. In the case of intelligence tests like the Wechsler Scales, positive structural evidence would be inferred if the tests selected or developed from the empirical domain are determined to be valid measures of the corresponding constructs in the theoretical domain (see Figure 3.1).

Structural Validity of the Wechsler Scales

David Wechsler appeared to have strong convictions regarding the tasks in his scales and their ability to measure a range of cognitive functions sufficient to assess general intelligence validly (Wechsler, 1958; Zachary, 1990). As such, he may have felt little need to include much information regarding validity in the technical manuals of his tests. The little evidence that was presented in support of the early Wechsler Scales' validity reflected, for the most part, a content-description orientation (e.g., some data concerning the correlation between the Wechsler Scales and other global measures of intelligence such as the Stanford-Binet, the latter of which hovered around 0.80). Although there were references to the underlying factor structure of the Wechsler Scales, the early manuals never addressed the issue empirically. Rather, it was left to the auspices of independent researchers to provide such data, which they did in abundance.

Unlike the earlier versions, the current Wechsler Scales come with manuals that are replete with validity data. For example, nearly half of the entire WAIS-III manual (not including appendices) is devoted to the topic of validity. Like their predecessors, the validity data reported in the current Wechsler manuals continue to be supported by extensive independent investigations (see Appendix A). It is clear that validity has emerged as the preeminent concern for the publishers of the Wechsler Scales. Below we present a summary of the factor-analytic construct validity evidence that has been reported for the Wechsler Scales.

Within-Battery Structural Research.   The preponderance of structural validity studies included in Appendix A support the internal validity of the Wechsler Scales. Within-battery factor-analytic studies of the early Wechsler Scales invariably revealed a two-factor solution involving a verbal and nonverbal (or perceptual-organizational) factor (Gutkin & Reynolds, 1981; Kaufman, 1975; Leckliter, Matarazzo, & Silverstein, 1986; Silverstein, 1982). A number of the WAIS-R factor analysis studies listed in Appendix A (e.g., Gutkin, Reynolds & Galvin, 1984; Parker, 1983; Silverstein, 1982) were included in a recent literature review in which the reviewers concluded that the WAIS-R was characterized best by three factors—namely, Verbal Comprehension (VC), Perceptual Organization (PO), and Working Memory/Freedom From Distractibility (WMFFD) (Leckliter, Matarazzo, & Silverstein, 1986). A similar but more recent example listed in Appendix A is Keith and Witta's (1997) multisample hierarchical confirmatory factor analysis of the WISC-III standardization data. These researchers found support for similar VC and PO factors as well as a similar FFD-like factor they called Quantitative Reasoning. Consistent with the WISC-III factor-based index interpretation system, Keith and Witta found support for a separate Processing Speed (PS) factor.

The large number of within-battery factor-analytic studies reported in Appendix A supports the current consensus that a three- or four-factor structure characterizes the various permutations of the 11 common core Wechsler subtests. These factors include Verbal Comprehension (VC), Perceptual Organization (PO), Processing Speed (PS), and Working Memory (WM) (or Freedom From Distractibility, depending on the Scale). In lieu of a detailed and lengthy discussion of all the within-battery factor analysis studies of the various versions of the Wechsler Scales, Figure 3.5 is used to summarize and illustrate how the extant factor analysis research findings have changed the face of the Wechsler interpretive framework over time.

Figure 3.5 shows that the Verbal and Performance two-factor structure was believed to best represent the structural characteristics of the Wechsler Scales until the late 1970s. Alan Kaufman's research and writings on the WISC-R (Kaufman, 1979) were particularly instrumental in the acceptance of the familiar three-factor (VC, PO, FFD) structure. As demonstrated in Figure 3.5, this more differentiated WISC-R factor structure occurred through the splitting off of the Arithmetic and Digit Span subtests from the Verbal Scale, and their marriage with the Coding subtest (which split off from the Performance Scale) to form the new FFD triad.

Movement toward an even more differentiated factor structure occurred with the publication of the WISC-III (Wechsler, 1991). The addition of the Symbol Search test resulted in the splitting of the FFD factor into separate FFD and PS factors in factor analysis studies. Likewise, the addition of two new tests (i.e., Letter-Number Sequencing and Matrix Reasoning) to the Wechsler subtest family with the publication of the WAIS-III resulted in a "fine-tuning" of the four-factor structure of the Wechsler Scales. In addition to the WISC-III-like VC and PS factors, the latest Wechsler battery has expanded the composition of the PO factor with the addition of the Matrix Reasoning test. In addition, the new Letter-Number Sequencing test has resulted in a reconceputalization of the FFD factor into a three-test Working Memory (WM) factor.

The movement away from the original Verbal and Performance Scales in the direction of the four factor indexes (VC, PO, PS, WM), a change that is supported by a substantial body of systematic within-battery factor analysis research within the past 10 to 15 years (see Appendix A), reflects incremental improvement in the internal or structural validity of the factor-based interpretation schemes of the Wechslers as manifest in the most recent Wechsler Scale (i.e., WAIS-III). This improvement in the structural validity of the WAIS-III, in particular, suggests a harbinger of changes in the next revisions of the WPPSI-R and WISC-III.

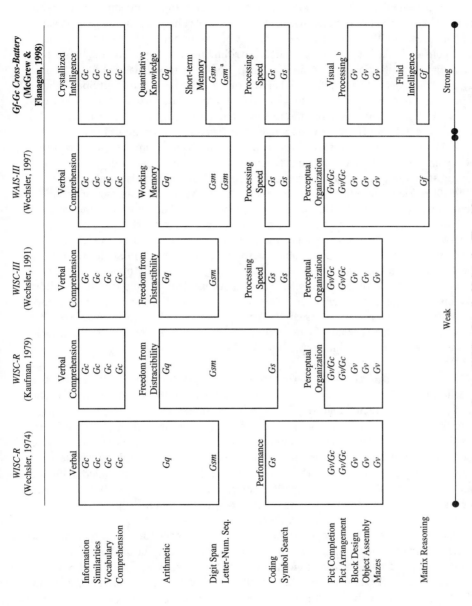

FIGURE 3.5 A Comparison of Wechsler Intelligence Scale Interpretation Schemes Based on Within-Battery and Cross-Battery Structural Validity Research

[a]Working memory (MW) has been integrated into the *Gsm* factor domain in the current work (see Chapter 2).

[b]Picture Completion and Picture Arrangement are not included as they are *mixed* measures of two constructs (*Gv* and *Gc*).

Although the within-battery factor analysis research of the most recent Wechsler Scales generally support the internal validity of the batteries, the ever changing interpretation of two of the original FFD tests (viz., Digit Span and Arithmetic) should give pause for concern (McGrew, 1999). As reflected in Figure 3.5, within-battery factor analyses of the various Wechsler Scales have shown that the Arithmetic and Digit Span subtests have changed their factor allegiance from their original Verbal factor to that of FFD, and more recently, WM. The ever changing factorial nature of the Arithmetic and Digit Span subtests raises concerns about the validity of the factor-based interpretations that have been offered for these subtests. Not unexpectedly, the factorial ambiguity of these two tests resulted in independent researchers offering a wide range of interpretations for the FFD factor (Kamphaus, 1993). For example, this factor has been suggested to measure short-term memory, math achievement, attention and concentration, sequential processing, and executive problem-solving strategies, as well as a variety of personality and emotional constructs (Kaufman, 1994; Wielkiewicz, 1990). How can this be? Even Alan Kaufman, whose name has become synonymous with the FFD label, has expressed frustration with the interpretative quagmire as reflected in his statement, "I cringe whenever I read 'Kaufman's Freedom from Distractibility factor.' It's not mine, and I don't want it" (Kaufman, 1994, p. 212).

The authors believe that the variable interpretations for the Arithmetic, Digit Span, and Coding/Digit Symbol tests reflect, in large part, the fallout from the weak substantive or theoretical foundation of the Wechsler Scales. It seems clear that the structural validity of the Wechsler Scales can be improved on significantly through the application of theory-based cross-battery factor analysis research. The application of *Gf-Gc* organized cross-battery factor analysis to the Wechsler Scales represents, in a sense, a post-hoc structural validity repair to the substantive foundation of the Wechsler Scales.

Cross-Battery Structural Research Defined.   Cross-battery (or joint) factor analysis, as stated earlier, includes tests from *more than one* intelligence battery in the analysis. Theory-based cross-battery factor analysis intelligence test studies are consistent with the focus of the fourth wave of intelligence test interpretation since these investigations organize the analyses from the perspective of a particular theory of intelligence. That is, the measures from the various intelligence batteries are freed from the confines of their own battery and are allowed to, or are specified to, load on the various cognitive factors included in the theoretical domain. Thus, the tests from the different individual batteries are allowed to *cross* battery boundaries in order to mingle with other tests and subsequently load on the theoretical factors specified by the theory of intelligence.

Consistent with the call for more theory-based intelligence test interpretation, the authors believe that the *Gf-Gc* theory of intelligence, if imposed on the analysis of the complete collection of Wechsler subtests together with measures from other intelligence batteries, will facilitate understanding of the structural characteristics and validity of the Wechsler Intelligence Scales. Fortunately, there have been a series of recent *Gf-Gc*-designed cross-battery factor analysis studies with a number of major intelligence batteries. These confirmatory cross-battery studies, which collectively will be referred to as the *CB studies* hereafter, included Woodcock's (1990) analyses of the WJ-R, Wechsler's, SB:IV (Thorndike, Hagen, & Sattler, 1986), and K-ABC (Kaufman & Kaufman, 1983); McGhee's (1993) analyses of the WJ-R, Differential Ability Scales (DAS; Elliott, 1990a), and Detroit Tests of Learning Aptitude-3 (DTLA-3; Hammill & Bryant, 1991); Flanagan and McGrew's (1998) WJ-R and Kaufman Adult Intelligence Test (KAIT: Kaufman & Kaufman, 1993) analyses, and joint WJ-R and DAS analyses (Laurie Ford, personal communication, August, 1998). McGrew and Flanagan (1998) recently synthesized the resulting *Gf-Gc* classifications for all the tests from all the major intelligence batteries based on Flanagan and McGrew's (1997) and McGrew's (1997) summaries of the extant *Gf-Gc* CB research.

The CB studies differ substantially from the within-battery structural validity studies described previously in a number of important ways. First, the Horn-Cattell *Gf-Gc* model of intelligence was the theoretical model used to organize each confirmatory factor analysis study. Second, all the data sets included tests from the WJ-R, a battery that has empirically validated indicators of eight broad *Gf-Gc* abilities (McGrew, 1994; McGrew et al., 1991; Reschly, 1990; Woodcock, 1990; Ysseldyke, 1990). As a result, each of the major intelligence batteries was analyzed together with a common set of empirically supported *Gf-Gc* test indicators from the WJ-R. That is, the *Gf-Gc* analyses of all the major intelligence batteries used the WJ-R *Gf-Gc*-designed battery as a common reference point. Thus, most of the broad *Gf-Gc* ability test classifications assigned by the authors of this textbook were based on empirical research studies. These *Gf-Gc* classifications provide evidence for the construct validity of the tests within individual intelligence batteries. A summary of these broad *Gf-Gc* classifications for nine major intelligence batteries is presented in Table 3.2. Table 3.2 represents an update of the broad ability classifications presented in McGrew and Flanagan (1998).

As summarized in Table 3.2, most intelligence batteries measure a rather limited range of *Gf-Gc* abilities. When using a criterion of at least two qualitatively different indicators (a cross-battery assessment guiding principle) for adequate construct representation (see Chapter 6 for a discussion), it is clear that most major intelligence batteries measure only *three* or *four* *Gf-Gc* abilities well. These data demonstrate that it is necessary to *cross* batteries (i.e., supplement an intelligence test with tests from another battery or other batteries) in order to obtain a comprehensive evaluation of cognitive function (e.g., when determining appropriate early intervention services; Wilson, 1992). The information presented in Table 3.2 is discussed further in Chapter 4.

Cross-Battery Structural Research Applied to the Wechsler Scales.   The importance of the CB study approach to understanding the structural validity of all intelligence batteries, and the Wechsler Scales in particular, is demonstrated when a comparison is made between the CB study results and a typical within-battery exploratory factor analysis. For example, as summarized in Figure 3.5, three factors (VC, PO, FFD) typically were reported for the WISC-R (Kaufman, 1979). The previously mentioned three-factor structure has evolved more recently into a VC, PO, PS, and FFD/WM structure. The latter four-factor structure, which is based on within-battery structural validity research, contrasts with the *Gf-Gc* cross-battery-based interpretation of the Wechsler Scales also presented in Figure 3.5. A comparison of the within-battery and *Gf-Gc* cross-battery Wechsler interpretations reveals a number of important insights.

When considered within the context of *Gf-Gc* theory, the VC and PO factors are interpreted as measuring mainly *Gc* and *Gv* abilities, respectively (Carroll, 1993b; McGrew

TABLE 3.2 *Gf-Gc* Broad (Stratum II) Empirical Classifications of Intelligence Batteries (Based on Cross-Battery Studies Since 1990)

Gf-Gc Factor	WJ-R/III	Wechslers	SB:IV	DAS*	K-ABC*	KAIT
Long-Term Retrieval (*Glr*)	**Memory for Names** **Visual–Auditory Learning** **Delayed Recall-MN** **Delayed Recall-VAL** Retrieval Fluency (*Gs*) Rapid Picture Naming (*Gs*)	...	...	†	...	**Rebus Learning** **Delayed Recall Rebus Learning** Delayed Recall Auditory Comprehension
Short-Term Memory (*Gsm*)	**Memory for Words** **Numbers Reversed** Auditory Working Memory Memory for Sentences (*Gc*)	**Digit Span** Letter-Number Sequence	**Memory for Digits** Memory for Objects Memory for Sentences (*Gc*) Bead Memory (*Gv*)	**Recall of Designs**	**Number Recall** **Word Order** Hand Move (*Gq*)	**Memory for Block Design**
Processing Speed (*Gs*)	**Visual Matching** Cross Out (*Gv*) Decision Speed (*Gv*) Pair Cancellation	**Coding/Digit Symbol** **Symbol Search**	...	†	...	...
Auditory Processing (*Ga*)	**Incomplete Words** **Sound Blending** **Auditory Attention** **Sound Patterns**	...	...	...	...	...
Visual Processing (*Gv*)	**Spatial Relations** **Picture Recognition** Visual Closure	**Block Design** **Object Assembly** Mazes Picture Comprehension (*Gc*) Picture Arrangment (*Gc*)	**Pattern Analysis** Copying Paper Folding (*Gq*)	Pattern Construction	**Triangles** Gestalt Closure Spatial Memory Math Analogies (*Gf*) Photo Series (*Gf*)	...
Crystallized Intelligence (*Gc*)	**Picture Vocabulary** **Oral Vocabulary** **Verbal Comprehension** **General Information** **Oral Comprehension**	**Information** **Similarities** **Vocabulary** **Comprehension**	**Vocabulary** **Verbal Relations** Comprehension Absurdities	**Word Definitions** **Similarities**	**Faces and Places** **Riddles** Expressive Vocabulary	**Famous Faces** Definitions (*Grw*) Double Meanings (*Grw*) Auditory Comprehension (*Gsm*)
Fluid Reasoning (*Gf*)	**Analysis-Synthesis** **Concept Formation** Planning (*Gv*) Verbal Analogies (*Gc*)	**Matrix Reasoning**	**Matrices**	**Matrices** Seq-Quant Reasoning (*Gq*)	...	**Logical Steps** **Mystery Codes**
Quantitative Ability (*Gq*)	**Calculation** **Applied Problems** Math Concepts (*Gf*) Math Fluency (*Gs*)	**Arithmetic**	**Quantitative** **Number Series** **Equation Building**	†	**Arithmetic**	...

Note: Strong measures of *Gf-Gc* factors are reported in bold type; measures not in bold type are moderate or mixed indicators of *Gf-Gc* abilities. Primary measures of *Gf-Gc* factors for the WJ-R are based on the empirical analyses of Woodcock (1990) and McGrew and Flanagan (1998); *Gf-Gc* factor classifications of the SB:IV, Wechslers, and K-ABC are reported in Woodcock (1990); classifications for the DAS and KAIT are reported in McGhee (1993) and Flanagan and McGrew (1998), respectively. For additional information on *Gf-Gc* factor classifications of major intelligence test batteries see McGrew and Flanagan (1998). *Gf-Gc* codes reported in parentheses next to subtest names identify the factor(s) on which the subtest has a secondary factor loading. These subtests are mixed measures of abilities. Information in this table was adapted from Flanagan and McGrew (1997) with permission from Guilford Press.

*Only a subset of DAS and K-ABC tests were joint factor analyzed by McGhee (1993) and Woodcock (1990), respectively. Therefore, only the tests that were included in these analyses are reported in this table. The *Gf-Gc* factor classifications of *all* DAS and K-ABC tests following a logical task analysis and expert consensus are reported in McGrew and Flanagan (1998).

†Tests measuring these abilities (i.e., *Glr*, *Gs*, *Gq*) are included on the DAS battery but have yet to be included in *Gf-Gc* organized confirmatory cross-battery factor analyses.

& Flanagan, 1996; 1998). It is also important to note that the FFD factor was not consistent with or similar to any broad ability within the *Gf-Gc* taxonomy. Is the taxonomy wrong, or was the FFD factor suspect?

Based on logical content analysis, it seems clear that the three WISC-R FFD tests (Arithmetic, Digit Span, Coding) are likely "loner" indicators of *Gq, Gsm,* and *Gs,* respectively. This hypothesis has been supported in *Gf-Gc* CB studies of the WISC-R and WJ-R (Woodcock, 1990) and the WISC-III and WJ-III (Phelps, Bowen, Chaco, Howard, Leahy, & Lucenti, 1999). For example, when the WISC-R tests were analyzed together with empirically validated indicators of a broad range of *Gf-Gc* abilities from the WJ-R (Woodcock, 1990; 1998), the results revealed that the traditional FFD tests loaded on three separate factors. The WISC-R FFD tests abandoned one another to "hang out" (i.e., correlate) with indicators of other *Gf-Gc* abilities with which they had more in common. Specifically, Arithmetic, Digit Span, and Coding loaded strongly on the *Gq, Gsm,* and *Gs* factors, respectively. Thus, in within-battery factor analysis studies, the so-called FFD factor appears to have been an invalid factor that consisted of tests that had no counterparts that measured similar cognitive ability constructs with which they could correlate to form valid factors (McGrew, 1999).

This conclusion is supported further by comparing the within-battery WISC-R and within-battery WISC-III analyses. With the addition of one new test (Symbol Search) in the third edition of the WISC, Coding abandoned its tried-and-true counterparts (Arithmetic and Digit Span) and formed a separate and, indeed, more appropriate *Gs* factor, as both Coding and Symbol Search involve perceptual speed and rate of test taking. Because the WISC-R FFD factor consists of tests that are indicators of *different Gf-Gc* abilities, it did not represent a valid theoretical cognitive construct. Given that two indicators (and preferably three or more) are needed to define a factor in factor analysis (Zwick & Velicer, 1986), it is not surprising that the Wechsler's loner tests loaded together on the so-called FFD factor. There simply were not enough indicators present in the within-battery WISC-R and WISC-III factor analyses (i.e., one or two more tests each of *Gq, Gsm,* and *Gs*) to identify clearly the separate abilities measured by the FFD tests. Furthermore, as is reflected in Figure 3.5, contemporary *Gf-Gc* research suggests that even the most recent recommended WAIS-III interpretation of the Arithmetic and Digit Span subtests as measures of working memory is suspect. *Gf-Gc* organized CB research suggests that Arithmetic and Digit Span subtests are primarily measures of *Gq* and *Gsm,* respectively. The ever changing nature of the original FFD factor, and the chameleon nature of Arithmetic and Digit Span in particular, demonstrate how valid test interpretation can be compromised when tests are developed and/or interpreted on the basis of a weak substantive foundation (McGrew, 1999).

The importance of the *Gf-Gc* CB study approach is also apparent when one examines the Wechsler PO tests. The PO tests have a long history of being interpreted as measures of *Gf* abilities (e.g., Kaufman, 1979; 1994). However, as summarized in Figure 3.5, cross-battery analyses with the WISC-R (Woodcock, 1990) and WISC-III (Phelps et al., 1999) show that the PO tests do not load on the *Gf* factor (defined by the WJ Analysis-Synthesis and Concept Formation tests). These results, as well as other exploratory cross-battery analyses of the Wechsler's with the DAS (Elliot, 1994; Stone, 1992) and KAIT (Kaufman & Kaufman, 1993), call into question the traditional *Gf* interpretation of the Wechsler PO tests (McGrew & Flanagan, 1996).

The recent addition of a test of *Gf* (i.e., Matrix Reasoning) to the WAIS-III, and hopefully a similar addition to the next versions of the WPPSI-R and WISC-III, is a step in the direction of better representation of the theoretical domain of intelligence. However, the inclusion of the Matrix Reasoning test in the PO index is a step backward in the empirical-theory match of the Wechsler index scores. As will be discussed in Chapter 4, matrix reasoning tests are strong measures of *Gf*, not *Gv*. In fact, matrix analogy or reasoning tests are considered to be one of (if not) the best indicators of *Gf* (Carroll, 1993a). The inclusion of the Matrix Reasoning test in the WAIS-III PO index results in the PO index now being comprised of measures of *Gv, Gf,* and to a lesser extent, *Gc*. We believe that this further muddying of the construct validity waters of the PO index is due to the lack of a strong theoretical or substantive foundation to the Wechsler program of validity research.

The Structural Validity of the Wechsler Scales: Concluding Comments

Systematic and strong programs of theory-based construct validity research are becoming increasingly important during the fourth wave of theory-based intelligence test interpretation. The *construct validity* of a test "is the extent to which the test may be said to measure a theoretical construct or trait" (Anastasi & Urbina, 1997, p.126). In the case of intelligence tests, the constructs of interest are the different cognitive abilities included in the theoretical domain of intelligence. The appropriate evaluation of the construct validity of tests requires the embedding of the constructs of interest in a conceptual framework (APA, 1985; Messick, 1995) and the examination of tests via research studies that include substantive, structural (internal), and external components. We believe that *Gf-Gc* theory is currently the best supported framework of cognitive abilities on which a strong program of test construct validation can be based (Bensen, 1998).

The primary conclusion reached from the preceding discussion is that *the Wechsler Intelligence Scales' continued allegiance to a largely practical and atheoretical model of intelligence limits the validity of the inferences that can be drawn from some of the Wechsler subtest and composite scores*. Figure 3.5 illustrated how the lack of a strong theory (which is the cornerstone of the substantive stage of validation) can result in the completion of structural or internal validity studies with a collection of tests that have significant content validity limitations, which in turn can significantly confound attempts to draw valid inferences from some of the test and index scores (e.g., Wechsler FFD tests). Although most of the internal structural validity studies reported for the Wechsler Scales have provided evidence for a within-battery factor structure of these instruments (see Appendix A), this evidence does not portray accurately their underlying theoretical constructs, as was evidenced through an evaluation of the individual Wechsler tests within a strong construct validation framework.

The Wechsler *Gf-Gc* cross-battery interpretations proposed by McGrew and Flanagan (1998) (summarized in the far right portion of Figure 3.5), interpretations which are based on structural analysis studies of a collection of measures (from many intelligence batteries) that collectively have strong substantive or content validity, provides a strong theory-based and construct-validated approach to interpreting the Wechsler Intelligence Scales. This is the beginning of the *Gf-Gc* empirical-theoretical domain match that is the foundation for the Wechsler Scale cross-battery interpretive approach described in subsequent chapters.

The External Stage of Construct Validation: A Conceptual Explanation

Although positive structural evidence is a necessary condition for establishing construct validity for tests, it does not meet the sufficient condition (Nunnally, 1978). The necessary and sufficient conditions for construct validity are both met when structurally valid measures demonstrate expected convergent and divergent relations with measures of constructs external to the focal measures (Benson, 1998; Benson & Hagtvet, 1996). This "looking outside" of the focal theoretical and empirical domains represents the *external* stage or component of a strong program of construct validity research.

As depicted in Figure 3.1, the external component of test and construct validation examines the nature and strength of significant relations between the focal theoretical constructs and a network of "other" constructs and measures "outside" of or external to the theoretical and empirical domains of primary interest. In the *Gv* example depicted in Figure 3.1, evidence for the construct validity of individual *Gv* tests (e.g., in the case of the Wechsler Scales, tests like Block Design and Object Assembly) or composite scores (e.g., Wechsler PO index) might take the form of moderate to high correlations between the focal *Gv* tests and composites and other *Gv* tests (e.g., SB:IV Pattern Analyses; WJ-R Spatial Relations) or composites (e.g., WJ-R Visual Processing Cluster) concurrent with low or nonsignificant relations with valid measures of distinctly different constructs (e.g., the WJ-R Auditory Processing Cluster consisting of the Sound Blending and Incomplete Words tests). Additional evidence might take the form of the finding that the *Gv* tests add important incremental information to the prediction of success in certain occupations that require strong visual-spatial skills (e.g., mathematics, sculpture, architecture). In other words, valid tests of cognitive constructs should (1) correlate significantly with "other" (external) tests of the same constructs; (2) either not correlate or correlate at low levels with tests of distinctly different constructs; and (3) make theoretically consistent predictions of a number of outcome variables (see Figure 3.2).

In light of the preceding discussion, ideally, all intelligence test authors and publishers should strive to achieve the comprehensive validity evidence. That is, they should provide substantive, structural, and external validity evidence that supports the recommended inferences that can be made from their individual intelligence test and composite scores. A review of Appendix A indicates that a significant body of research literature supports the external validity of the Wechsler Scales. This conclusion is similar to Zimmerman and Woo-Sam's (1997) recent synthesis of the criterion-related validity of the WISC-III. Zimmerman and Woo-Sam reported an average correlation (across 55 samples) of 0.75 between the WISC-III Full Scale score and 11 different ability measures. They also reported correlations ranging from 0.50 to 0.65 between the WISC-III Full Scale score and various achievement tests. A review of all the external validity evidence listed in Appendix A produces conclusions similar to those of Zimmerman and Woo-Sam.

The positive external validity studies reported for the Wechsler Scales would, on initial inspection, raise doubts about the validity of the claim that a strong substantive or theoretical foundation is required in order for an intelligence test to possess strong construct validity. In other words, how can the Wechsler Scales demonstrate significant external validity evidence in the absence of a strong substantive foundation? The answer lies in the fact that although positive external validity evidence has been reported, some of which provides strong evidence for some of the Wechsler tests and indexes, a portion of this evidence is not what it appears to be. Problems with the external validity evidence provided in support of the Wechsler Scales are discussed briefly below.

External Validity of Confounded Measures

Space limitations do not allow a detailed discussion and evaluation of the Wechsler external validity research presented in Appendix A. Many of the research studies reported in Appendix A provide external validity evidence for many of the Wechsler tests and scores. For example, consistent with the *Gf-Gc* outcome-criterion validity evidence summarized in Table 3.1, many of the studies listed in Appendix A report significant relations between the Wechsler VC index and other measures of verbal or *Gc* abilities. Furthermore, a number of these studies report that the Wechsler verbal subtests are significantly related to school achievement. Overall, considerable evidence supports the validity of inferences drawn from the tests comprising the Wechsler VC index. This is most likely due to the strong Wechsler VC-*Gc* empirical-theoretical domain match.

The same, however, cannot be said for the Wechsler FFD index—the primary example of poor construct validity research in this chapter. At first glance, the extant external validity research would appear to support the validity of the FFD index. Numerous studies have reported significant relations between the Wechsler FFD index and many external variables ranging from reading and math achievement to personality and emotional disturbance (Wielkiewicz, 1990). Even more impressive is Kaufman's (1994a) list of 15 different diagnostic categories of children who score low on the FFD tests. The list includes children with reading and learning disabilities, children with leukemia who received cranial irradiation therapy, children with epilepsy, and "believe it or not—normal children, especially girls, living in the Western part of the United States" (Kaufman, 1994a, p. 213), to name a few.

Although a diverse and impressive number of studies, Kaufman's (1994a) comment that the "FD subtests are like a land mine that explodes on a diversity of abnormal populations but leaves most normal samples unscathed" (p. 213) should serve as a reminder that the mere presence of significant relations between intelligence test scores and external variables is not always indicative of strong validity. In fact, patterns of significant correlations that do not "behave" in a manner consistent with theory may cast doubt on the construct validity of the test scores.

The indiscriminate nature of the FFD external evidence is difficult to explain. Just what is the nature of the construct underlying the FFD score that is related to both reading and math achievement, developmental language disorders, attention deficit disorder, schizophrenia, and Duchenne muscular dystrophy (Kaufman, 1994a)? According to Wielkiewicz (1990), "the studies available so far do not define any single construct that could connect this wide range of findings" (p. 93). When evaluated within a validity framework similar to the *Gv* example presented in Figure 3.1, the authors believe that the promiscuous statistical tendencies of the FFD index are due to a breakdown in the substantive and structural stages of construct validation. That is, the FFD factor is not a valid indicator of a valid theoretical construct within a valid theoretical model of intelligence (Carroll, 1993a). As stated earlier, the original FFD tests are best considered to be indicators of three separate *Gf-Gc* abilities (i.e., Arithmetic *[Gq]*; Digit Span *[Gsm]*; Coding *[Gs]*). The lack of a substantive theoretical foundation for the Wechsler tests has resulted in the post-hoc emergence of the FFD and its relations to a variety of disorders, the interpretations of which are similarly not grounded in any substantive theoretical domain. Therefore, it is not surprising that the external validity evidence for the FFD index is limited and confusing. In many ways a score on the FFD index is like a thermometer. Its wide range of significant external validity correlations suggests that it may help identify when something is amiss or atypical, but it contributes little in the way of explanation or prescription and, in fact, may result in the selection of the wrong interpretative hypotheses or subsequent recommendations (McGrew, 1999).

The meaning of the Wechsler PO index score, both from internal and external validity perspectives, also suffers from a poor theoretical-empirical domain match. For example, the current WISC-III PO index score, although predominately a measure of *Gv* abilities, also includes two tests (i.e., Picture Completion and Picture Arrangement) that the extant factor analytic research has consistently found to be measures of both *Gv* and *Gc*. Furthermore, although the addition of a measure of *Gf* (i.e., Matrix Reasoning) is a much welcomed improvement in the WAIS-III, the positive impact of this addition is minimized by its inclusion in the PO index. The result is a WAIS-III PO index that is a mixed measure of *Gv, Gc,* and *Gf* abilities. Although such a factorially complex measure may have important purposes in certain situations, factorial complexity makes it difficult to understand and interpret significant relations between the PO index and external validity criteria. Thus, significant correlations between the Wechsler PO index and other external criteria, notwithstanding the interpretation, is indeterminate.

Strong Construction Validation Models
Do Make a Difference

Recently, Flanagan (1999) presented results from a series of causal models where the relations between the WISC-R factors and reading achievement factors were examined in a sample of 166 normal elementary school-aged subjects. Figure 3.6 summarizes the major findings from two causal models that were consistent with the atheoretical Wechsler model, a model that has been described in this chapter as being based on a "weak" program of construct validity research. The simple *g* model revealed a strong and significant relation between the WISC-R *g* score (i.e., Full Scale) and Reading (which included three different aspects of reading). The 0.64 structural path between the WISC-R *g* factor and Reading, a relation that indicates that the Wechsler *g* factor accounted for approximately 41 percent of the Reading factor variance, is strong external validity evidence for the WISC-R.

Even more impressive are the results of the WISC-R *g*+specific abilities causal model in the bottom half of Figure 3.6, a model that included, in addition to the *g*/Reading

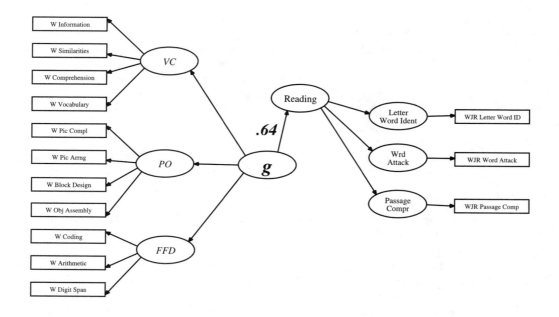

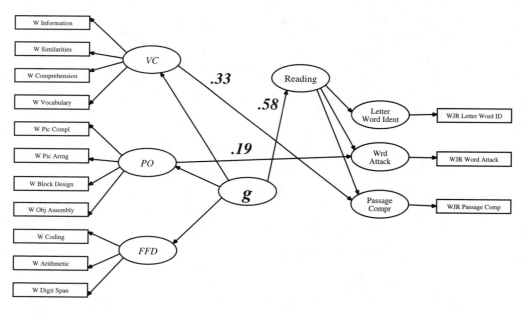

FIGURE 3.6   Example of External Validity Evidence for Atheoretical Within-Battery-Based Wechsler Factor Models: Summary of Flanagan's (1999) *g* and *g*+Specific Abilities and Reading Achievement Causal Models

Note: Factor loadings are omitted for readability purposes.

causal path, significant paths between specific cognitive abilities (i.e., VC, PO, and FFD) and specific reading abilities (i.e., Letter Word Identification, Word Attack, and Passage Comprehension)[3]. In addition to a significant *g*/Reading path (0.58), significant structural paths were identified between VC and Passage Comprehension (0.33) and PO and Word Attack (0.19). These results indicate that even though the WISC-R factor scores may be based on a weak atheoretical construct validity model, positive external validity evidence still exists for the WISC-R Full Scale and VC and PO scores. On initial inspection, these findings might argue against the central tenet of this chapter, namely, the need for measures of intelligence to be grounded in a strong program of construct validation. However, support for this central tenet is found in the significant improvement in external validity reported by Flanagan (1999) when the *Gf-Gc* cross-battery framework was superimposed on the WISC-R. These results are summarized in Figure 3.7.

Briefly, the Wechsler Scales can be "modernized" by taking the *Gf-Gc* interpretation of the Wechsler scales (as summarized in Figures 3.4 and 3.5) and "fleshing out" a more valid interpretation of the scales via the cross-battery approach (McGrew & Flanagan, 1998). As summarized in Figure 3.7, Flanagan (1999) used this approach and specified a causal model where the four-factor WISC-R model in Figure 3.6 was replaced with a *Gf-Gc* WISC-R cross-battery cognitive model (accomplished by supplementing the strong WISC-R *Gf-Gc* test indicators with strong WJ-R *Gf-Gc* test indicators). A number of important differences in the findings reported in Figure 3.6 and Figure 3.7 should be noted.

In the simple *g*/Reading model, the structural coefficient increased from 0.64 (Figure 3.6) to 0.81 (Figure 3.7), reflecting an increase in prediction/explanation of 24 percent of the total Reading variance (65% to 41%). A similar pattern is reported in the *g*+specific abilities models where a stronger *g*/Reading path was present for the WISC-R *Gf-Gc* cross-battery model (0.71) when compared to the simple WISC-R model (0.58). Also, the number and nature of the significant specific cognitive abilities to specific reading abilities paths changed. More importantly, the significant specific paths in the WISC-R *Gf-Gc* cross-battery model are more consistent with the extant *Gf-Gc* reading research literature (see Table 3.1).

In both figures the significant *Gc*/Passage Comprehension (0.42) and WISC-R VC/Passage Comprehension (0.33) paths are consistent with the *Gc*/reading research reported in Table 3.1. In contrast, the significant WISC-R PO/Word Attack path (0.19) in Figure 3.6 is difficult to interpret in light of the extant research literature which provides little, if any, support for a significant relation between word attack skills and a factor (PO) that is primarily *Gv* in nature (see Table 3.1). The lack of a significant relation between the valid *Gv* factor and reading achievement in Figure 3.7 is more consistent with the research literature. A possible explanation, and one that would further support the tenet that the atheoretical basis of the Wechsler Scales has constrained and confounded the external validity evidence for the scales, is that the significant PO/Word Attack path (0.19) in Figure 3.6 may be due to the *Gc* variance present in the Wechsler Picture Completion and Picture Arrangement subtests.

Even more interesting is the identification of the significant *Gs*/Passage Comprehension (0.14) and *Ga*/Word Attack (0.26) paths in Figure 3.7 and their absence in Figure 3.6 (WISC-R data). The significant *Ga*/Word Attack path is consistent with research that has demonstrated a strong relation between phonological awareness and beginning reading (see

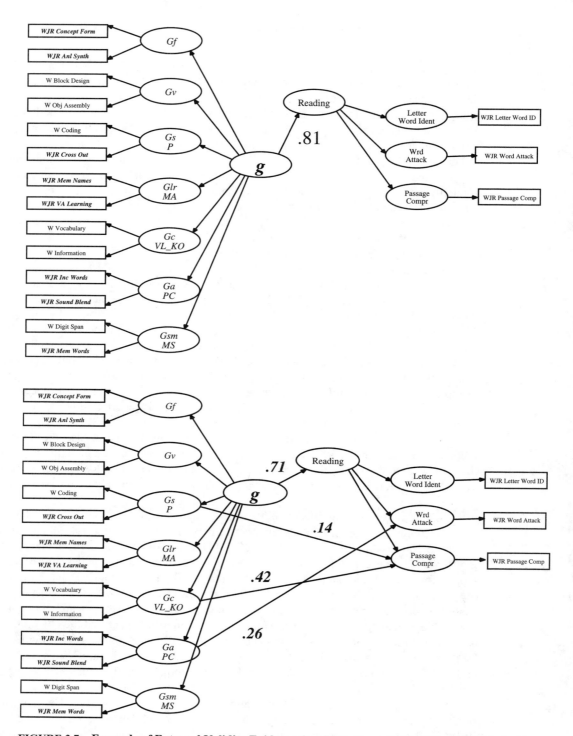

FIGURE 3.7   Example of External Validity Evidence for *Gf-Gc* Cross-Battery-Based Wechsler Factor Models: Summary of Flanagan's (1999) *g* and *g*+Specific Abilities and Reading Achievement Causal Models

Note: Factor loadings are omitted for readability purposes.

Table 3.1). This path did not surface in the traditional WISC-R model (Figure 3.6) simply because the Wechsler Scales do not include measures of this construct (see Figures 3.4 and 3.5, and Table 3.2), a situation that is largely due, in our judgement, to the limited attention paid to the substantive stage of construct validation in the development and revision of the Wechsler Scales.

Finally, the absence of a significant *Gs*/Passage Comprehension path in Figure 3.6 and the presence of a significant *Gs*/Passage Comprehension path (0.14) in Figure 3.7, is most likely due to the previously discussed problems with the WISC-R FFD factor. Contemporary research has shown that the WISC-R Coding test is a strong indicator of one aspect of *Gs* (see Table 3.2). However, as seen in Figure 3.6, it's potential contribution to prediction/explanation of reading is degraded in the WISC-R via its combination of two other tests (i.e., Arithmetic and Digit Span) that measure other cognitive abilities (i.e., *Gq* and *Gsm*). Fortunately this situation has been rectified in the WISC-III and WAIS-III through the addition of another measure of *Gs* (i.e., Symbol Search), a revision that has made possible the emergence of a separate and valid *Gs* factor index in these two batteries.

External Validity and the Wechsler Scales: Concluding Comments

In summary, it should be clear from the difficulties associated with the interpretation of the confounded Wechsler FFD factor-based index and the research results reported by Flanagan (1999) that a number of conclusions regarding the external validity of certain aspects of the Wechsler Scales may be inaccurate. Although significant correlations have been reported between the Wechsler FFD and PO indexes and important outcome criteria (e.g., school achievement), the inferences that can be drawn from these correlations are suspect due to the confounded (factorially complex) nature of these index scores. Furthermore, the failure to include indicators of cognitive abilities (e.g., *Ga* and *Glr*) that substantive analysis has identified as important abilities to include in an intelligence test that is used to predict and understand school achievement, reveals a significant limitation of the atheoretical Wechsler Scales. Finally, the significant improvement in the prediction/explanation of total reading (24 percent increase in reading variance explained) which occurred when the WISC-R substantive and structural shortcomings were "ameliorated" via a *Gf-Gc* cross-battery approach, suggests that a more substantive theory-based approach to constructing and interpreting test batteries can result in stronger external validity.

The remainder of this book outlines a theoretically and empirically based Wechsler *Gf-Gc* cross-battery approach that provides the Wechsler Scales with a much needed substantive foundation, which, in our judgement, will improve the internal and external validity of intellectual assessments that are based on the Wechsler Scales. Ultimately, this approach will provide a viable means of propelling the Wechsler Scales into the theory-based fourth wave of intelligence test interpretation.

Conclusion

"Those who are enamoured of the practice without science are like a pilot who goes into a ship without a rudder or compass and never has any certainty where he is going. Practice should always be based on a sound knowledge of theory" (Leonardo da Vinci). Similarly, we believe that the applied science of intelligence testing must be based on solid empirical and theoretical knowledge. This stated belief, which is a cornerstone of this entire book, should not be misconstrued as an indictment of the original Wechsler Intelligence Scales. Historical hindsight is 20/20. It must be kept in mind that David Wechsler's original test was intentionally grounded in practical and clinical considerations rather than theoretical deliberations. Also, only portions of the *Gf-Gc* terrain were emerging at the time when David Wechsler was developing his first scales. The original Verbal and Performance factors made sense at the time and were quite valuable and useful.

In order to improve the validity of inferences drawn from the various Wechsler scores, it is important to understand that "that was then and this is now." The recent application of *Gf-Gc*-organized cross-battery factor analyses to the major intelligence batteries (McGrew & Flanagan, 1998) has produced a closer correspondence between the empirical and theoretical domains of intelligence. The left and right sides of Figure 3.5 represent the *then* and *now* of Wechsler Scale test interpretation, respectively. An even more refined *now* *Gf-Gc* interpretation of the Wechsler Scales was presented in Figure 3.4.

The imposition of the *Gf-Gc* framework and the breaking down of the secular within-battery confines of the Wechsler Intelligence Scales (i.e., adopting a cross-battery perspective) reflects a necessary post-hoc attempt to shore up the weak substantive foundation of the Wechsler interpretative system. Research presented in this chapter demonstrated how the lack of a strong substantive foundation has undermined certain aspects of the internal and external validity of the Wechsler Scales. Furthermore, research showed that the imposition of a valid substantive foundation (i.e., contemporary *Gf-Gc* theory) can significantly improve this state of affairs. The empirical-theoretical construct mapping presented in Figure 3.4 is intended to "right" the Wechsler construct validity ship. It is our belief that the imposition of a strong substantive framework to the interpretation of the Wechsler Intelligence Scales via McGrew and Flanagan's (1998) *Gf-Gc* cross-battery approach will result in a greater alignment of the Wechsler *Gf-Gc* empirical-theoretical domains. The end result should be the derivation of more valid inferences from Wechsler test scores.

E N D N O T E S

1. For a detailed explanation of this table, see McGrew and Flanagan (1998).

2. At least two of the three authors classified every study according to the criteria summarized in Figure 3.2. In addition to the authors' classifications, two upper-level doctoral students in a clinical psychology program classified every study included in Appendix A. This process resulted in four ratings for each study. In the few instances in which disagreement was found among the raters, the consensus reached by the authors constituted the final classification. The positive (+) and negative (–)

signs throughout Appendix A indicate whether the individual investigations provided or failed to provide validity evidence for the Wechsler Scales, respectively. A review of this Appendix demonstrates a lack of substantive validity support for the Wechsler Scales.

3. The rationale and methods used by Flanagan (1999) mirror those that are described in detail in McGrew, Flanagan, Keith, and Vanderwood (1997). The reader is directed to this latter source for specific details of this type of methodology.

CHAPTER

4

Psychometric, Theoretical, and Qualitative Characteristics of the Wechsler Intelligence Scales

Almost any kind of information about a test can contribute to an understanding of score meaning, but the contribution becomes stronger if the degree of fit of the information with the theoretical rationale underlying score interpretation is explicitly evaluated.

—Messick (1998, p. 246)

Theory, theory, theory. It should be obvious from Chapters 1 through 3 that the approach to interpretation presented in this book is an attempt to chart a course that will allow assessment professionals to ride Kamphaus, Petoskey, and Morgan's (1997) fourth wave to theory-based (and valid) interpretation of the Wechsler Intelligence Scales. Although a theory-based framework is a necessary condition for increased validity of test score inferences, it is not a sufficient condition. Somehow, the abstractions inherent in a theory must be linked to the practical realities of intellectual assessment and interpretation.

To illustrate, consider the following analysis. A captain of a large ship would have a difficult time navigating large waves in the open sea armed only with the knowledge of abstract concepts such as tidal currents, weather systems, how radar works, and so on. The captain needs practical instruments (e.g., sonar) with acceptable technical properties (i.e., reliable). Equally important is a working knowledge of the technical properties of the instruments. The prerequisites for effective navigation are analogous to those for effective test interpretation. In order to translate the benefits of theory-based intelligence test interpretation to practice, assessment professionals must have an intimate knowledge of the various nuances of each of the individual tests. This chapter provides the necessary information about the various instruments (i.e., tests) that practitioners can use (or not use if found to be wanting) when aligning their practice of test interpretation with the theory-based emphasis of the fourth wave of intelligence test interpretation. A failure to use this information during interpretation could result in the same fate awaiting a captain who "sailed by the seat of his or her pants"—veering off course and riding the wrong waves to the wrong place.

This chapter provides a description of the critical psychometric, theoretical, and qualitative characteristics of the Wechsler Intelligence Scales (WPPSI-R, WISC-III, WAIS-III). By including this information, we are acknowledging the benefits derived from the third wave of intelligence test interpretation, benefits that should not be denigrated due to the less-than-positive results of the psychometric analysis wave which we and others (e.g., Kaufman, 1979; 1994) believe was largely due to the absence of strong (valid) theories and measures of intelligence.

The primary purpose of this chapter is to provide important test characteristic information for the individual tests of the Wechsler Scales. Following a brief description of pertinent psychometric, theoretical, and qualitative test characteristics, each Wechsler Scale will be presented, test-by-test, in a visual-graphic, "consumer's report" format. Each test of each battery is evaluated according to *common criteria* adapted from McGrew and Flanagan (1998). Specifically, the information pertaining to each individual Wechsler test is presented using a *standard nomenclature* and is displayed in a *uniform format* in summary pages (located at the end of this chapter). The psychometric and qualitative information presented in this chapter is critical to understanding individual Wechsler test performance. Furthermore, the meaning of Wechsler test scores is enhanced when interpretations are grounded in a contemporary theory of the structure of intelligence. This may be achieved by evaluating the theoretical test characteristic information presented here and using it in a systematic and organized manner consistent with current research (as described in Part III of this book).

Understanding What the Wechsler Scales Measure: A Conceptual Framework

Skillful interpretation of intelligence tests requires practitioners to "know thy instrument" (McGrew, 1994, p. 4). This requires knowledge of the important variables that may aid in understanding an individual's performance on a given test. Figure 4.1 presents a conceptual framework for understanding the most significant variables that may contribute to a person's individual test score. This model, which was first presented in a narrative form by McGrew (1999) and fully illustrated by McGrew and Flanagan (1998), serves as the overarching interpretive framework on which the Wechsler Scales (and other cognitive instruments presented in this text, namely in Chapter 5) are described and interpreted. It is important to note that Figure 4.1 is a *conceptual* representation of psychometric concepts. It is not intended to be a perfect depiction of the relations between psychometric concepts and the procedures used to calculate them. Also, the conceptual model presented in Figure 4.1 represents an evolution of the empirical domain portion of Figure 3.1, which illustrated the relations between the empirical and theoretical domains in construct validity research. Figure 4.1 extends this model by illustrating how the quantitative and qualitative characteristics of the empirical domain indicators of intelligence constructs can be understood and evaluated.

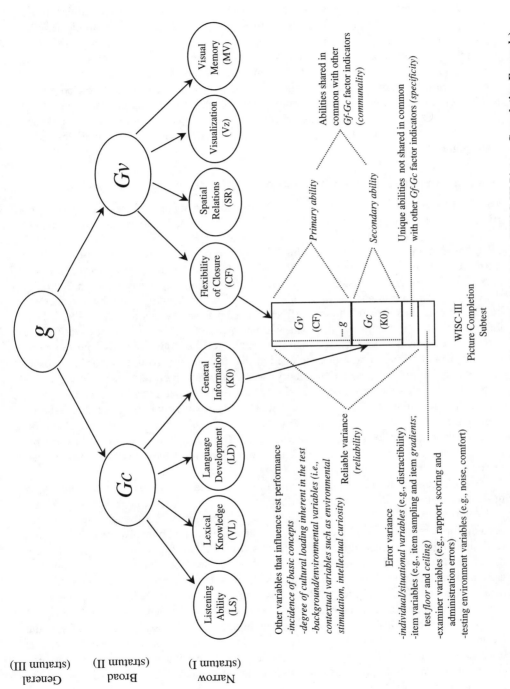

FIGURE 4.1   A Conceptual Model of the Variables   Considered in Test Interpretation (WISC-III Picture Completion Example)

Note: There are additional narrow abilities in the domains of *Gc* and *Gv* that are not included in this figure; the rectangle represents the total score variance of the WISC-III Picture Completion test; the italicized terms represent the test characteristic information that is presented for the Wechsler Scales in Table 4.2 and in the Wechsler Scale summary pages.

To illustrate how this conceptual framework is used to interpret intelligence test scores, a single test (i.e., WISC-III Picture Completion) is presented as an example. Briefly, the WISC-III Picture Completion test requires the examinee to identify essential missing parts in a series of pictures of common objects and scenes. The top portion of Figure 4.1 demonstrates that cognitive abilities located at different strata in the *Gf-Gc* model account for different proportions of the total reliable test score variance of the Picture Completion test (which is represented by the rectangle in Figure 4.1). Understanding what an individual test measures requires an appreciation of which variables account for the total reliable and unreliable variance of a test score (i.e., the total area represented by the rectangle) and to what degree.

General, Broad, and Narrow Cognitive Abilities

The most general influence on the Picture Completion test score performance is *g* (stratum III or general intelligence) which is mediated indirectly through two broad (stratum II) *Gf-Gc* abilities (i.e., *Gv* and *Gc*) (see Figure 4.1). The broad abilities of *Gv* and *Gc*, in turn, effect performance on the Picture Completion test through their respective influences on the narrow (stratum I) abilities of Flexibility of Closure (CF) and General Information (K0) (see Table 2.1 for definitions of these narrow abilities). Thus, appropriate interpretation of the Picture Completion test requires an appreciation of the degree to which the respective general, broad, and narrow abilities influence performance on this test. In a sense, these three interpretive levels (general, broad, and narrow) reflect the evolution of intelligence test interpretation. The first wave's focus on general level of functioning is represented by the recognition of *g*. The abilities included at the broad and narrow levels (although not always couched in terms of *Gf-Gc* theory) were, in many interpretive schemes, the raw material that fueled the second and third wave attempts, respectively, to move interpretation in the direction of a more differentiated ability taxonomy. Thus, the theory-based approach to intelligence test interpretation described in this book does not reflect a complete break from past waves of test interpretation. Rather, it reflects an effort to mine the jewels of past efforts and include them among the jewels recently mined from present theory and research.

The degree to which *g* influences performance on a test is represented typically by the test's loading on a factorially derived *g* factor. Moving down the cognitive ability hierarchy portrayed in Figure 4.1, the degree to which the different broad and narrow abilities account for portions of an individual test's variance is estimated typically by examining the test's loadings on the respective ability factors (the ovals in Figure 4.1) in appropriately designed factor-analytic studies. In the case of the Picture Completion test, the *g* and *Gf-Gc* common factor loadings provide empirical estimates of the extent to which this test measures *g* and *Gf-Gc* abilities. Collectively, the amount of the Picture Completion test score reliable variance that can be attributed to cognitive abilities within the *Gf-Gc* model (as represented by ovals with arrows that point directly, or indirectly in the case of *g*, to the Picture Completion rectangle) is referred to as *communality* or *common variance*. That is, the reliable portion of the Picture Completion test score variance represents the variance shared in common with all other indicators (or tests) that constitute the *Gf-Gc* factors (in factor analysis).

As illustrated in Figure 4.1, the *g*, *Gv* (CF), and *Gc* (K0) abilities account for the largest proportion of the Picture Completion reliable test score variance. Thus, these cognitive abilities should receive priority consideration when interpreting an individual's score on the Picture Completion test. The portion of the Picture Completion reliable test score variance that may be attributable to the influence of *g* is represented by the dashed line within the rectangle. Tests such as Picture Completion that are moderately related to *g* have proportionally more of their reliable variance accounted for by the general factor than tests that are minimally related to *g*.

The division of the reliable common variance of the Picture Completion test into two portions signifies that Picture Completion is a *factorially complex* measure of more than one broad ability (viz., *Gv* and *Gc*). This means that the interpretation of an individual's score on the Picture Completion test should focus on both *Gv* and *Gc* abilities. Furthermore, in this example the influence of *Gv* on Picture Completion is depicted as being greater than *Gc* (i.e., *Gv* represents the larger area of the rectangle). Thus, *Gv* is the *primary* cognitive ability measured by the Picture Completion test. *Gc* is the *secondary* cognitive ability that should be considered when interpreting performance on this test. Furthermore, the narrow stratum I classifications suggest that the most likely *Gv* interpretation is that of Flexibility of Closure (CF), whereas General Information (K0) likely accounts for the *Gc* influence on the Picture Completion test. The primary abilities and, in the case of factorially complex measures, primary and secondary abilities, of all the individual Wechsler tests are listed in the visual-graphic test characteristic summary pages located at the end of this chapter.

Other Sources of Test Score Variance: Uniqueness and Error

As can be seen in Figure 4.1, the *Gf-Gc* general, broad, and narrow cognitive abilities account for the largest portion of the Picture Completion test score variance. However, two additional portions of test score variance need to be considered in the interpretation process—uniqueness and error. As presented in Chapter 1 (Figure 1.1), a pivotal event that helped spawn the psychometric approach to intelligence test interpretation was Cohen's (1959) Wechsler factor analysis studies, studies that brought to professionals' attention the importance of incorporating knowledge of subtest uniqueness (or specificity) and measurement error in the interpretive process.

Subtest *uniqueness* is the reliable proportion of the Picture Completion test score variance that is attributed to abilities not represented in the *Gf-Gc* cognitive model. This test characteristic is also referred to as *specificity*. As can be seen in Figure 4.1, the amount of the Picture Completion reliable test score variance that is specific or unique to this test is proportionally much less than that attributable to *Gf-Gc* abilities (i.e., common variance or communality). Together the common *Gv* and *Gc* variance and specific variance represent the total reliable variance (i.e., *reliability*) of the Picture Completion test. In Figure 4.1 the combined *Gv*, *Gc*, and unique ability areas within the rectangle represent what is measured reliably by the Picture Completion test.

The abilities that account for reliable score variance should be the primary focus of interpretation of tests in intelligence batteries. Furthermore, the degree to which different abilities should be emphasized in the interpretation of a test is directly proportional to the amount of reliable score variance they explain. In the case of the Picture Completion test example, this means that *Gv* abilities should be the primary focus of interpretation, followed by *Gc* abilities and, to a much lesser extent, unique abilities.

The portion of Picture Completion test score variance that is not reliable (i.e., *error variance*) is that which is not accounted for by the common and unique abilities. In Figure 4.1 the Picture Completion error variance is represented by the area at the bottom of the rectangle. An inspection of the figure shows that the amount of the Picture Completion test score variance that is due to error (or unreliability) is relatively small when compared to the reliable variance. A test that has poor reliability has a proportionally larger amount of error variance and, therefore, less reliable variance to interpret. As summarized in Figure 4.1, a variety of variables can contribute to unreliability or error in a test, including examiner variables (e.g., failure to establish rapport, scoring and administration errors) and variables related to the testing environment (e.g., noise, comfort level). Other variables that can contribute to error in a test include *individual/situational* variables (e.g., distractibility) and *item* variables (e.g., poor *item gradients, floors* or *ceilings*).

Contextual Variables

Finally, understanding an individual's test performance requires an appreciation of the contextual variables that influenced the development of the person's abilities measured by the test. For example, performance on the *Gc* (K0) component of the Picture Completion test would most likely be related to contextual variables that contribute to the development of an individual's fund of general information. These variables may include the extent of environmental stimulation, direct and indirect educational instruction, and level of acculturation, as well as the individual's intellectual curiosity, to name a few. In Figure 4.1, these variables are called *background/environmental variables*.

Retaining a Focus on the Individual in Interpretation

According to Kaufman (1994a), "[w]hen you use the WISC-III and related tests, you're dealing with *individuals*" (p. 36). The authors agree. However, the preceding interpretive conceptual explanation of intelligence test performance is based on *group-centered* statistical procedures that may not translate perfectly to a single individual. Statements about the proportion of a test's score variance that is accounted for by different *Gf-Gc* abilities "only has meaning as a statement that refers to a distribution of scores" (Gustafsson & Undheim, 1996, p. 217) and value for the interpretation of ability factors. Because *Gf-Gc* test interpretations presented in this book are group-centered, the proportional relations between different *Gf-Gc* abilities, unique abilities, and error variance differ from that found across persons. Therefore, practitioners need to consider the *Gf-Gc* ability classifications presented herein as empirically grounded interpretative *starting points* which should be modified (if necessary) based on the individual nuances of a particular case. As cogently stated by Kaufman (1994a), clinical assessment involves both art and science.

Improving Test Interpretation:
The Cross-Battery Perspective

As portrayed in Figure 4.1, factor analysis research indicates that the WISC-III Picture Completion test measures both *Gv* and *Gc* abilities. However, would this interpretation differ if the factor analyses that included the Picture Completion test did not contain other tests of *Gv* or *Gc* abilities? The answer is *yes*.

In Chapter 3 the statistical procedure of factor analysis was described briefly. To summarize, factor analysis represents a collection of data reduction statistical procedures that group together measures (tests) that intercorrelate. Furthermore, it was argued in Chapter 3 that in order to establish a link between what intelligence batteries measure and the *Gf-Gc* taxonomy of cognitive abilities, the ideal research design is a *Gf-Gc* organized confirmatory cross-battery factor analysis study. Confirmatory procedures allow the *Gf-Gc* theoretical model to drive the analyses, and the cross-battery design ensures that a sufficient breadth of indicators is present to represent adequately the major *Gf-Gc* abilities. Furthermore, a comparison of within- and cross-battery factor analyses of the Wechsler Scales presented in Chapter 3 demonstrated that for some of the Wechsler subtests and scales, the largely atheoretically driven within-battery structural validity research has resulted in some misinterpretations of certain Wechsler subtests (e.g., FFD subtests).

With this brief background information, the answer to the question posed above should be clear. If the factor analyses that included the WISC-III Picture Completion test did not contain strong indicators of *Gc*, for example, then the interpretation of an individual's performance on this test would be quite different from that suggested by Figure 4.1. That is, if a factor analysis contained only indicators of *Gv* and *Gsm*, for example, then Picture Completion would have its strongest loading on the *Gv* factor and most likely an insignificant loading on *Gsm*. Under this circumstance, the influence of *Gc* on Picture Completion test performance would not be apparent, resulting in potentially misleading or erroneous interpretation. Although it appears that a sufficient breadth of tests are included on the Wechslers to interpret the Picture Completion test adequately, this is not the case for all tests (e.g., Arithmetic, Digit Span). Moreover, many important *Gf-Gc* abilities are not measured or not measured adequately by the Wechsler Scales (e.g., *Ga, Gf, Glr*). We believe that the understanding of what individual tests in intelligence batteries measure is understood best through theoretically driven (viz., *Gf-Gc* theory) cross-battery factor-analytic studies that include a sufficient number and breadth of *Gf-Gc* indicators that allow for adequate representation of the major *Gf-Gc* factors.

Identifying *g* and Specificity Test Characteristics

The problem with within-battery factor analyses also affects the estimation of other psychometric test characteristics. For example, a test's loading on the general intelligence *(g)* factor will depend on the specific mixture of tests used in the analysis (Gustafsson & Undheim, 1996; Jensen, 1998; Jensen & Weng, 1994; McGrew, Untiedt, & Flanagan, 1996; Woodcock, 1990). If a single vocabulary test is combined with nine visual processing tests, the vocabulary test will most likely display a relatively low g loading, because the general factor will be defined primarily by the visual processing measures. In contrast, if the vocabulary test is included in a battery of tests that is an even mixture of verbal and visual processing measures, the loading of the vocabulary test on the general factor will probably be higher. It is important to understand that test g loadings, as typically reported, only reflect each test's relation to the general factor *within a specific intelligence battery*. Although in many situations a test's g loading will not change dramatically when computed in the context of a different collection of diverse cognitive tests (Jensen, 1998; Jensen & Weng, 1994), this will not always be the case.

Just as g loading estimates may change as a function of the diversity and complexity of tasks included in a single test battery, so may the estimates of test specificity. Using the example described above, a single vocabulary test embedded within a battery with nine other visual processing tests would most likely demonstrate high specificity because of its low common or shared variance with the visual processing tests. If the same vocabulary test is then examined in the context of a ten-test battery that has an even mixture of verbal and visual processing tests, then the vocabulary test specificity value would most likely drop appreciably due to the abilities shared in common with four other verbal tests within the battery (which results in an increase in common variance and a proportional decrease in specific variance). Although the example of a test battery with a nine-to-one visual processing/verbal test mixture is extreme, it illustrates that traditionally computed test g and specificity estimates are interpretable primarily within the confines of a single intelligence battery.

A Within- and Cross-Battery WISC-III Example

When tests from different batteries are combined in the cross-battery approach, the battery-bound g and specificity estimates for some tests may be altered significantly. To illustrate this point, the authors calculated within- and cross-battery g and communality (which is the major variance component used to calculate specificity) estimates for the WISC-III. These estimates were derived from a sample of 150 subjects who were administered the WISC-III and WJ-III cognitive tests as part of the Phelps validity study reported for the WJ-III technical manual (McGrew & Woodcock, in press). Within-battery g estimates were calculated with the WISC-III data based on the first unrotated principal component and within-battery specificity estimates were based on squared multiple correlations. Consistent with the belief that Gf-Gc theory provides the most empirically supported psychometric theory from which to interpret intelligence tests, cross-battery g and specificity estimates were calculated in the same way using the combined set of WISC-III and WJ-III tests. The cross-battery factor analysis allowed for an examination of the g and specificity characteristics of the WISC-III tests vis-à-vis the comprehensive Gf-Gc model underlying the WJ-III. The WISC-III results are summarized in Table 4.1.

A review of Table 4.1 shows that the within- and cross-battery WISC-III g loadings are similar for many of the individual tests. For example, the within- and cross-battery test g loadings are generally similar (i.e., do not differ by more than 0.05) for the Similarities (0.76 vs. 0.71), Vocabulary (0.78 vs. 0.74), Digit Span (0.48 vs. 0.49), Block Design (0.60 vs. 0.61), Object Assembly (0.50 vs. 0.45), and Symbol Search (0.57 vs. 0.54) tests. These

TABLE 4.1   Example of Within- and Cross-Battery *g* Loading and Communality Estimates for the WISC-III Tests

Subtest	*g* Loadings		Communality	
	Within-Battery	Cross-Battery	Within-Battery	Cross-Battery
Information	0.77	0.68	0.57	0.44
Similarities	0.76	0.71	0.55	0.49
Arithmetic	0.70	0.64	0.42	0.39
Vocabulary	0.78	0.74	0.59	0.53
Comprehension	0.59	0.51	0.29	0.24
Digit Span	0.48	0.49	0.17	0.22
Picture Completion	0.50	0.40	0.19	0.15
Picture Arrangement	0.37	0.31	0.10	0.08
Block Design	0.60	0.61	0.28	0.34
Object Assembly	0.50	0.45	0.18	0.18
Coding	0.46	0.37	0.16	0.12
Symbol Search	0.57	0.54	0.25	0.27

Note: Estimates are based on 150 subjects who had been administered the WISC-III and 28 tests from WJ-III Tests of Cognitive Abilities in the Phelps validity study reported in the WJ-III manual (McGrew & Woodcock, in press). The *g* loading estimates are based on the first unrotated principal component. Communality estimates are squared multiple correlations.

six WISC-III tests appear to have similar *g* characteristics when examined from the perspective of either the WISC-III or *Gf-Gc* frameworks. However, the cross-battery *g* loadings are noticeably lower than the within-battery *g* loadings (i.e., lower by 0.06 or more) for Information (0.77 vs. 0.68), Arithmetic (0.70 vs. 0.64), Comprehension (0.59 vs. 0.51), Picture Completion (0.50 vs. 0.40), Picture Arrangement (0.37 vs. 0.31), and Coding (0.46 vs. 0.37). These results suggest that the latter WISC-III tests are relatively weaker *g* indicators than is suggested by within-battery WISC-III *g* analysis.

In the case of the WISC-III communality estimates, four tests displayed noticeable differences (i.e., greater than 0.05) between their respective cross- and within-battery values. Three verbal tests (viz., Information, Similarities, and Vocabulary) displayed lower communality in the cross-battery analysis. The lower communality estimates indicate that these three verbal tests have *higher* specificities when examined within the *Gf-Gc* framework. This is most likely due to the fact that approximately half of the WISC-III is comprised of verbal *(Gc)* tests, and thus, these three tests have many other similar *Gc* tests with which they share common variance in the WISC-III. However, when analyzed together with a collection of tests that assess a broader array of *Gf-Gc* abilities, the proportional amount of shared variance attributable to *Gc* abilities is less. Thus, the Information, Similarities, and Vocabulary tests have less in common with the other tests, and as a result, have more uniqueness (i.e., higher specificities in appropriately designed *Gf-Gc* cross-battery factor analyses). In contrast, Block Design increased in communality from the within- to cross-battery analyses, a situation that results in a lower specificity estimate for this test when evaluated within the context of contemporary *Gf-Gc* theory.

This example demonstrates the potential chameleon nature of test *g* and specificity estimates that are calculated within the confines of individual intelligence batteries when compared to those calculated within the comprehensive *Gf-Gc* model (via cross-battery analyses). Thus, when practitioners combine the Wechsler tests with tests from other batteries according to the *Gf-Gc* cross-battery approach, it is important to understand the impact that this may have on the psychometric characteristics of *g* and specificity. Although the Wechsler summary pages provide both within- and cross-battery *g* and specificity estimates for the tests of the Wechsler Intelligence Scales, we believe that the most appropriate values for interpretation are those estimated from the cross-battery perspective. Selective attention to certain within-battery psychometric test characteristics—characteristics that for most intelligence batteries are based typically on incomplete theoretical models of the structure of cognitive abilities—may result in erroneous and inappropriate test interpretation. We believe that the previously described problems with atheoretical within-battery-derived psychometric test characteristic information contributed, in part, to the less-than-positive outcomes achieved during the third wave of intelligence test interpretation.

A Description of Important Psychometric Characteristics

"Psychometrics developed as a substantively nontheoretical technology for reliably measuring individual differences and validating the practical use of the measurements for making decisions and predictions about individuals" (Jensen, 1998, p. 108). Psychometrics is the specialty within psychology that uses agreed-upon measurement procedures to operationalize the concepts of reliability and validity. Given that the individual tests of the Wechsler Scales provide the foundation for interpretation either at the individual test or composite score level, it is essential that practitioners understand the psychometric characteristics of each test. According to Reynolds and Kaufman (1990), "[t]he clinical evaluation of test performance must be directed by careful analyses of the statistical properties of the test scores, the internal psychometric characteristics of the test, and the data regarding its relationship to external factors" (p. 131). Otherwise, interpretation of tests may become an idiosyncratic enterprise dependent on the individual skills and whims of different practitioners (McGrew, 1994).

The psychometric characteristics presented in this chapter for the Wechsler Scales are reliability, *g* loadings, specificity, test floors and ceilings, item gradients, and construct validity (i.e., *Gf-Gc* broad and narrow ability classifications) (see Figure 4.1 and the related discussion for information on the relations between these different psychometric characteristics). Sources that were used to establish the evaluative psychometric criteria are defined and discussed at length in McGrew and Flanagan (1998). These criteria were established using the following publications: the *Standards for Educational and Psychological Testing* (APA, 1985*)*; *A Consumer's Guide to Tests in Print* (Hammill, Brown, & Bryant, 1992); and a review of recent literature that focused on the evaluation of the major intelligence batteries (e.g., Alfonso & Flanagan, 1999; Bracken, 1986; 1987; Flanagan & Alfonso, 1995; Flanagan, Alfonso, Kaminer, & Rader, 1995; Harrison, Flanagan, & Genshaft, 1997; McGrew, 1997). Based on these sources and the subsequent set of criteria presented in McGrew and Flanagan (1998), the technical adequacy of the Wechsler Scales were evaluated. The results of this evaluation are located on the summary pages at the end of this chapter.

Only the *individual tests* of the Wechsler Scales are included and evaluated in this chapter. Wechsler battery composites (or indexes) are not included and evaluated because they are generally not consistent with the *Gf-Gc* broad abilities specified in contemporary *Gf-Gc* theory and research (i.e., some contain confounded or mixed measures). Since the primary purpose of this book is to aid practitioners in selecting the most technically adequate and theoretically pure tests for inclusion in *Gf-Gc* cross-battery assessment, individual test information is considered most critical. Based on the information provided in this chapter (as well as Chapter 5), *relatively pure Gf-Gc broad ability clusters* can be constructed (using the Wechsler Scales as the core batteries) that more adequately represent the cognitive abilities specified in contemporary theory than the clusters (or composites) of most intelligence batteries.

The next section of this chapter briefly defines each psychometric, theoretical, and qualitative test characteristic that is used in this text to describe the individual tests in the Wechsler batteries. Specifically, the importance of each test characteristic is highlighted, and the procedures for reporting and evaluating the technical and descriptive data are presented. The definitions of the psychometric, theoretical, and qualitative test characteristics and corresponding evaluative criteria as well as the interpretive relevance of these test features are presented in Table 4.2.

Reliability

Reliability "refers to the consistency of scores obtained by the same persons when they are reexamined with the same test on different occasions, or with different sets of equivalent items, or under other variable examining conditions" (Anastasi & Urbina, 1997, p. 84). The reliability of a scale affects interpretation of the test results because it guides decisions regarding the range of scores (i.e., standard error of measurement) likely to occur as the result of irrelevant chance factors. Test reliability, in its broadest sense, indicates the extent to which individual differences are attributed to true differences in the characteristics under investigation or to chance errors (Anastasi & Urbina, 1997). The degree of confidence that can be placed in the precision of a test score is related directly to the estimated reliability of the test score. Unreliable test scores can contribute to misdiagnosis and inappropriate placement and treatment. This problem can be reduced by selecting tests that have good reliability and thus relatively little error associated with their scores or by combining individual test scores into composite scores. For in-depth treatment of reliability concepts, the reader is referred to Anastasi and Urbina (1997), APA (1985), Crocker and Algina (1986), Lord and Novick (1968), Salvia and Ysseldyke (1991), and Sattler (1992).

(text continued on page 106)

TABLE 4.2 Definitions of Psychometric, Theoretical, and Qualitative Test Characteristics, Evaluative Criteria, and Interpretive Relevance

Category Characteristic Evaluative Criteria	Definition	Interpretive Relevance
Psychometric		
Reliability	The precision of a test score (i.e., free from errors of measurement).	Important for making accurate educational and/or diagnostic decisions.
High	Coefficients of 0.90 or above.	Test scores are sufficiently reliable and can be used to make diagnostic decisions.
Medium	Coefficients from 0.80 to 0.89 inclusive.	Test scores are moderately reliable and can be used to make *screening* decisions or can be combined with other tests to form a composite with *high* reliability.
Low	Coefficients below 0.80.	Test scores are not sufficiently reliable and cannot be used to make important screening or diagnostic decisions. Need to be combined with other tests to form a composite with *medium* or *high* reliability.
Within-Battery g Loading	Each test's loading on the first unrotated factor or component in principal factor or component analysis with all other tests from a specific intelligence battery.	Important indicator of the degree to which a test of an individual battery measures general intelligence. Aids in determining the extent to which a test score can be expected to vary from other scores within a profile.
Cross-Battery g Loading	A test's loading on the first unrotated factor or component in principal joint factor or component analysis with all other tests from a specific intelligence battery together with the WJ-R.*	Important indicator of the degree to which a test measures general intelligence when it is included in *Gf-Gc*-organized cross-battery analyses. Aids in determining the extent to which a test score can be expected to vary from other scores in an appropriately designed *Gf-Gc* cross-battery profile.
High	General factor or *g* loading of 0.70 or higher.	Tests with high *g* loadings are not expected to vary greatly from the mean of the profile and are considered good indicators of general intelligence.

Medium	A loading of 0.51 to 0.69.	Tests with medium g loadings may vary from the mean of the profile as tests with this classification are considered fair indicators of general intelligence.
Low	A loading of 0.50 or lower.	Tests with low g loadings can be expected to vary from the mean of the profile as tests with this classification are considered poor indicators of general intelligence.
Within-Battery Specificity	The portion of a test's variance that is reliable and unique to the test. Within-battery specificity is calculated by subtracting the communality estimate of the test (the squared multiple correlation between each test and all other tests within the battery) from the total reliable variance (a value obtained by subtracting a test's reliability coefficient from unity).	Important for determining the degree to which a test measures an ability that is distinct and specific to an individual test that is part of a particular intelligence battery.
Cross-battery Specificity	The portion of a test's variance that is reliable and unique to the test. Cross-battery specificity is calculated by subtracting the communality estimate of the test (the squared multiple correlation between each test and all other tests within the battery together with the WJ-R*) from the total reliable variance (a value obtained by subtracting a test's reliability coefficient from unity).	Important for determining the degree to which a test measures an ability that is distinct and specific to an individual test that is part of an appropriately designed Gf-Gc cross-battery assessment comprised of two or more batteries.
High	A test's unique reliable variance is equal to or above 25% of the total test variance and it exceeds error variance (1-reliability).	A test with high specificity may be interpreted as measuring an ability distinct or specific to that test (or battery of tests).
Medium	When a test meets only one of the criteria for high.	A test with medium specificity should be interpreted cautiously as measuring an ability distinct or specific to that test (or battery of tests).
Low	When a test does not meet either of the criteria for high.	A test with low specificity should not be interpreted as representing a unique ability but may prove useful in interpretation when it is considered as part of a composite or cluster of other similar tests.

(continued)

TABLE 4.2 Continued

Category Characteristic Evaluative Criteria	Definition	Interpretive Relevance
Test Floor	The test contains a sufficient number of easy items to reliably distinguish between individuals functioning in the average, low average, and borderline ranges of ability.	
Adequate	A raw score of 1 is associated with a standard score that is more than 2 standard deviations below the normative mean of the test.	A test with an adequate floor can distinguish reliably between individuals functioning in the average, low average, and borderline ranges of ability. Moreover, tests with adequate floors can discriminate reliably between various degrees of mental retardation (i.e., mild, moderate).
Inadequate	A raw score of 1 is associated with a standard score that is *not* more than 2 standard deviations below the normative mean of the test.	A test with an inadequate floor, or an insufficient number of easy items, may not distinguish reliably between individuals functioning in the average, low average, and borderline ranges of ability. Moreover, tests with inadequate floors cannot discriminate reliably between various degrees of mental retardation (i.e., mild, moderate).
Test Ceiling	The test contains a sufficient number of difficult items to reliably distinguish between individuals functioning in the average, high average, and superior ranges of ability.	
Adequate	The maximum raw score for the test is associated with a standard score that is more than 2 standard deviations above the normative mean of the test.	A test with an adequate ceiling can distinguish reliably between individuals functioning in the average, high average, and superior ranges of intellectual ability. Moreover, tests with adequate ceilings can discriminate reliably between various levels of giftedness.

Inadequate	A test with an inadequate ceiling, or an insufficient number of difficult items, will not distinguish reliably between individuals who function in the average, high average, and superior ranges of intellectual ability. A test with an inadequate ceiling cannot discriminate reliably between various levels of giftedness.
	The maximum raw score is associated with a standard score that is *not* more than 2 standard deviations above the normative mean of the test.
Item Gradients[†]	A test with good item gradient characteristics has items that are approximately equally spaced in difficulty along the entire test scale, and the spacing between items is small enough to allow reliable discrimination between individuals on the latent trait measured by the test. An item gradient *violation* occurs when a one unit increase in raw score points results in a change of more than one-third standard deviation in standard score values. Item gradient violations are identified for each test by calculating the standard score change for every possible raw score change in the test.
Good	Items are approximately equally spaced in difficulty along the entire test scale and spacing between items is small enough to allow for reliable discrimination between individuals on the latent trait measured by the test.
	≤ 5% violations.
Fair	Items are not equally spaced in difficulty at certain points along the entire test scale, resulting in fair discrimination between individuals on the latent trait measured by the test.
	>5% to ≤ 15% violations.
Poor	Items are inconsistently spaced in difficulty at various points along the entire test scale, resulting in generally unreliable discrimination between individuals on the latent trait measured by the test.
	>15% violations.
Theoretical Gf-Gc *Broad (stratum II) Ability Classification*	A description of the broad abilities that underlie intelligence tests based on an examination of appropriately designed *Gf-Gc* confirmatory cross-battery factor analysis research studies.
	Useful for guiding interpretation and discussing performance at the broad level of ability (viz., in terms of the basic, long-standing ability underlying a specific cluster of tests).

(continued)

TABLE 4.2 Continued

Category Characteristic Evaluative Criteria	Definition	Interpretive Relevance
Empirical: Strong	A test having a substantial factor loading (≥ 0.50) on a primary factor and a secondary factor loading (if present) that is equal to or less than $\frac{1}{2}$ of its loading on the primary factor.	The test may be interpreted as a relatively *pure* indicator of the factor (i.e., latent trait) on which it loads.
Empirical: Moderate	A test having a primary factor loading of < 0.50 and a secondary factor loading (if present) that is less than $\frac{1}{2}$ of the primary loading, or any primary factor loading and secondary loading between $\frac{1}{2}$ and $\frac{7}{10}$ of the primary loading.	The test may be interpreted as a moderate indicator of the factor (i.e., latent trait) on which it loads.
Empirical: Mixed	A test having a factor loading on a secondary factor that is greater than $\frac{7}{10}$ of its loading on the primary factor.	The test may be interpreted as measuring aspects of two distinct factors on which it loads. When tests measure two or more abilities they are psychologically ambiguous and difficult to interpret.
Gf-Gc Narrow (stratum I) Ability Classification[≠]	A description of the narrow abilities that underlie intelligence tests based on expert content validity consensus.	Important in determining the degree of confidence one can place in discussing performance in terms of the specific ability or abilities measured by the test.
Probable	Classifications in which there was a clear correspondence between the content and task demands of a test and a particular *Gf-Gc* narrow-ability definition.	Test scores may be interpreted confidently as a measure of a particular narrow ability.
Possible	Classifications in which there was a moderate degree of correspondence between the content and task demands of a test and a particular *Gf-Gc* narrow ability definition.	Test scores should be interpreted cautiously as a measure of a narrow ability. Other sources of data should be gathered to support the interpretation.

Qualitative

Incidence of Basic Concepts in Test Directions	The degree to which the directions in intelligence batteries place conceptual demands on the examinee. Excessive conceptual demands (defined as conceptual knowledge required to understand test directions above age level) may pose a threat to the construct validity of the test. This is particularly important when evaluating preschool aged children.	Important when interpreting scores obtained on tests in which performance is dependent, in part, on the degree of basic conceptual knowledge that is required to comprehend test directions (e.g., WPPSI-R Object Assembly). When a large number of difficult basic concepts is included in test directions, the construct validity of the test may be jeopardized for individuals with a limited conceptual knowledge base.
Typical Age of Concept Attainment	A p value of 0.75 or greater, indicating that the basic concept is understood by at least 75% of preschoolers (aged 3–5 years).	
Degree of Cultural Loading	The degree to which U.S. cultural knowledge or experience is required to perform the task. It is assumed that an examinee's level of acculturation to mainstream U.S. culture will affect his or her performance to a greater extent on tests that are dependent on accumulated knowledge and acquired experiences (that result from exposure to U.S. culture) than on tests that measure basic learning processes.	Important in determining the extent to which knowledge of cultural information and conventions can impact test performance.
High	Test performance is highly influenced by exposure to mainstream U.S. culture.	Scores obtained from culturally diverse examinees should not be interpreted as a valid estimate of ability as they are likely to be spuriously low.
Medium	Test performance is moderately influenced by exposure to mainstream U.S. culture.	Scores obtained from culturally diverse examinees should be interpreted with caution as they may be spuriously low.
Low	Test performance is minimally influenced by exposure to mainstream U.S. culture.	Scores obtained from culturally diverse examinees may be considered to be minimally affected by cultural influences.
Degree of Linguistic Demand	The extent to which a test requires verbal and nonverbal communication to be properly administered, as well as, the degree of language proficiency required by the examinee in order to understand the test instructions and provide an appropriate response.	Important in determining the extent to which the language demands necessary to perform a test may compromise optimal performance.

(continued)

TABLE 4.2 Continued

Category Characteristic Evaluative Criteria	Definition	Interpretive Relevance
High	Test administration requires a high level of expressive/receptive language. Optimal test performance requires a high level of language proficiency on the part of the examinee.	Test scores obtained from linguistically diverse examinees or those with limited English proficiency may not be valid indicators of ability.
Medium	Test administration requires a moderate level of expressive/receptive language. Optimal test performance requires a moderate level of language proficiency on the part of the examinee.	Test scores obtained from linguistically diverse examinees or those with limited English proficiency should be interpreted with caution as scores may be spuriously low.
Low	Test administration has minimal expressive/receptive language requirements. Test performance is less dependent on the examinee's level of language proficiency.	Test scores obtained from linguistically diverse examinees or those with limited English proficiency are minimally influenced by language demands. Therefore, scores may be interpreted as estimates of their respective underlying cognitive ability when supported by other sources of data.
Background/Environmental Influences		
Hearing Difficulties	A past history of significant problems in the perception of auditory stimuli that may affect the extent to which an examinee can accurately discriminate auditory stimuli.	Important when interpreting scores obtained on tests that require the examinee to process or discriminate effectively auditory stimuli prior to providing a response (e.g., WPPSI-R Sentences).
Vision Difficulties	A past history of significant problems in the perception of visual stimuli that may affect the extent to which an examinee can accurately discriminate visual stimuli.	Important when interpreting scores obtained on tests that require the examinee to perceive or discriminate effectively visual information prior to providing a response (e.g., WAIS-III Matrix Reasoning).
Reading Difficulties	A past history of significant problems with reading.	Important when interpreting scores obtained on tests in which the examinee's ability to read information can impact directly on his or her ability to respond and/or the quality of response (e.g., later items on WISC-III Arithmetic test).

102

Math Difficulties	A past history of significant problems with mathematics.	Important when interpreting scores obtained on tests requiring the examinee to perform or comprehend mathematical operations or rules (e.g., Wechsler Arithmetic tests).
Language Stimulation	The extent to which an examinee's verbal communication skills have been influenced by frequent interaction with the environment.	Important when interpreting scores obtained on tests involving a moderate to high degree of verbal stimuli (e.g., Wechsler Vocabulary tests).
Cultural Opportunities and Experiences	The extent to which an examinee has been exposed to a wide array of opportunities and experiences that impart knowledge of mainstream U.S. culture.	Important when interpreting scores obtained on tests that contain items that (directly or indirectly) assume knowledge of specific or general cultural conventions or facts on the part of the examinee (e.g., Wechsler Comprehension tests).
Educational Opportunities and Experiences	The extent to which an examinee has been exposed to a wide array of formal and informal educational experiences.	Important when interpreting scores obtained on tests measuring general (verbal) information acquired through both direct and indirect instruction (e.g., Wechsler Information tests).
Alertness to the Environment	The extent to which an examinee is attentive to his or her surroundings.	Important when interpreting scores obtained on tests measuring knowledge that is acquired informally by individuals who are alert to their surroundings (e.g., Comprehension).
Intellectual Curiosity	The extent to which an examinee displays a tendency to seek out and explore knowledge and new learning.	Important when interpreting scores obtained on tests involving information that is often acquired through informal instruction and learning experiences (e.g., WAIS-III Matrix Analogies).
Individual/Situational Influences *Attention Span/Distractibility*	An examinee's ability to focus on two or more competing stimuli simultaneously (divided attention) or a specific stimuli under distracting conditions (selective attention).	Important when interpreting scores obtained on tests in which attentiveness can either facilitate or inhibit an examinee's performance to a significant degree or in which competing or distracting stimuli can significantly affect performance (e.g., WISC-III Digit Span, Coding, Symbol Search, WAIS-III Letter-Number Sequencing).

(continued)

TABLE 4.2 Continued

Category Characteristic Evaluative Criteria	Definition	Interpretive Relevance
Concentration	An examinee's ability to focus on stimuli for a sustained period of time (sustained attention).	Important when interpreting scores obtained on tests in which optimal performance requires a sustained, concentrated effort on the part of the examinee (e.g., WISC-III Coding; WAIS-III Digit-Symbol Coding).
Ability to Perform Under Time Pressure	The extent to which an examinee is capable of maintaining an optimal level of performance during a specified period of time (vigilance).	Important when interpreting scores obtained on speeded tests from the Wechsler Performance Scales (e.g., Symbol Search).
Visual-Motor Coordination	An examinee's ability to coordinate the movement of his or her eyes, hands, and fingers when holding or manipulating objects.	Important when interpreting scores obtained from most Wechsler Performance Scale tests (e.g., Mazes).
Color Blindness	A congenital visual defect which results in an examinee's inability to identify and distinguish certain colors from other colors.	Important when interpreting scores obtained from tests that require the accurate perception of chromatic stimuli (e.g., WAIS-III Matrix Reasoning).
Reflectivity vs. Impulsivity	An examinee's consistent tendency to respond either deliberately (reflective) or quickly (impulsive) when confronted with problem-solving situations.	Important when interpreting scores obtained from tests in which performance can be facilitated or inhibited by the examinee's carefulness in responding (e.g., timed tests involving problem solving such as Picture Arrangement).
Field Dependence vs. Independence	The examinee's tendency to be significantly affected (dependent) or not affected (independent) by irrelevant factors or stimuli in a perceptual field.	Important when interpreting scores obtained on tests that are moderately to highly susceptible to performance errors when irrelevant stimuli become the focus of the examinee's attention (e.g., Picture Completion).
Verbal Rehearsal	The strategy of verbally repeating (covertly or overtly) information in short-term memory to facilitate the immediate use of the information.	Important when interpreting scores obtained on tests in which the examinee's use of verbal rehearsal strategies can facilitate performance (e.g., WISC-III Digit Span; WAIS-III Letter-Number Sequencing).

Term	Description	Interpretation Note
Verbal Elaboration	The strategy of verbally relating new information to already existing information to facilitate the transfer of the information to the store of acquired knowledge (i.e., long-term memory).	Important when interpreting scores obtained on tests in which novel stimuli can be encoded verbally to facilitate performance (e.g., Coding; associative memory tasks).
Visual Elaboration	The strategy of visually relating new information to already existing information to facilitate the transfer of the information to the store of acquired knowledge (i.e., long-term memory).	Important when interpreting scores obtained on tests in which visual representations of test stimuli can be used to facilitate performance (e.g., WAIS-III Letter-Number Sequencing; associative memory tasks).
Organization	The strategy of grouping together several different "chunks" or clusters of information to aid in the retrieval of information.	Important when interpreting scores obtained on tests that require the examinee to perceive, and later retrieve, moderate amounts of information (e.g., WAIS-III Letter-Number Sequencing).
Planning	The process of developing efficient methods or solutions (i.e., plans or "forward thinking") to a problem prior to starting the problem.	Important when interpreting scores obtained on tests in which optimal performance may be facilitated through careful contemplation of the task prior to responding (e.g., Mazes).
Monitoring/Regulating	The process of assessing how well a selected strategy or plan is working, and then deciding whether to continue, modify, or discontinue the strategy or plan.	Important when interpreting scores obtained from tests in which the examinee has an opportunity to modify or retain their current mode of responding to facilitate performance (e.g., Mazes).

*Tests 1–14 from the WJ-R were used in the analysis. These tests provide 2 relatively pure measures for each of seven *Gf-Gc* abilities.

†This test characteristic is often referred to as item density.

≠*Gf-Gc* narrow (stratum I) definitions can be found in Carroll (1993a), McGrew (1997), McGrew and Flanagan (1998), and Chapter 2 of this text.

The reliabilities reported for the individual Wechsler tests were drawn from their respective technical manuals (Wechsler, 1989; 1991; 1997). With the exception of the speeded tests, all reported reliabilities were estimates of how consistently examinees performed across items or subsets of items in a single test administration (i.e., internal consistency). For speeded tests, reported reliabilities were estimates of how consistently examinees performed on the same set of items at different times (i.e., test-retest or stability reliability). The internal consistency or test-retest reliabilities of the individual Wechsler tests, as reported at different age levels in their respective manuals, are included in the Wechsler summary pages at the end of this chapter. The criteria used to evaluate the reliability of the individual Wechsler tests as well as the interpretive relevance of this test characteristic are described in Table 4.2.

g Loadings

Intelligence tests have been interpreted often as reflecting a general mental ability referred to as *g* (Anastasi & Urbina, 1997; Bracken & Fagan, 1990; Carroll, 1993a; French & Hale, 1990; Horn, 1988; Jensen, 1984; 1998; Kaufman, 1979; 1994; Keith, 1997; Sattler, 1992; Sattler & Ryan, 1999; Thorndike & Lohman, 1990). As presented in Chapter 2, the *g* concept was associated originally with Spearman (1904; 1927) and is considered to represent an underlying general intellectual ability (viz., the apprehension of experience and the eduction of relations) that is the basis for most intelligent behavior.

As with the controversy surrounding the nature and meaning of *g* (see Chapter 2), disagreements exist about how best to calculate and report psychometric *g* estimates. All methods are based on some variant of principal component, principal factor, hierarchical factor, or confirmatory factor analysis (Jensen, 1998; Jensen & Weng, 1994). Although a hierarchical analysis is generally preferred (see Jensen, 1998, p. 86), as long as the number of tests factored is relatively large, the tests have good reliability, a broad range of abilities is represented by the tests, and the sample is heterogeneous (preferably a large random sample of the general population), the psychometric *g*s produced by the different methods are typically very similar (Jensen, 1998; Jensen & Weng, 1994). Given that the focus of this book is on the Wechsler Scales, which are standardized on large, nationally representative samples and which include a relatively large number of reliable tests that measure a range of different abilities, differences in *g* loadings that may occur as a function of factor-analytic method are most likely trivial. For the interested reader, Jensen's (1998) recent treatise on *g* *(The g Factor)* is suggested, as it represents the most comprehensive and contemporary integration of the *g*-related theoretical and research literature.

Within- and Cross-Battery Procedures for Estimating g.   Traditionally, most reported within-battery psychometric *g* estimates for individual intelligence tests are based on each test's loading on the first unrotated factor or component in principal factor or component analysis. Published within-battery *g* estimates included in the Wechsler Scale summary sheets were derived from these customary procedures via analysis of the correlation matrices included in the respective technical manuals (Wechsler, 1989; 1991; 1997).

Ideally, *Gf-Gc* cross-battery *g* estimates should be based on the analyses of large, nationally representative samples of subjects at different age levels who have been administered multiple intelligence batteries. Unfortunately, such an undertaking is impractical.

The strategy adopted by McGrew and Flanagan (1998) for calculating cross-battery *g* estimates (and specificity estimates) was to use available data sets where subjects had been administered a common set of empirically validated *Gf-Gc* indicators (viz., WJ-R) together with another major intelligence battery. The cross-battery *g* estimates calculated here used a similar strategy.

The critical feature of the datasets used by McGrew and Flanagan (1998) was the common use of the WJ-R, a battery that includes empirically validated indicators of eight broad *Gf-Gc* abilities (McGrew, Werder, & Woodcock, 1991; Reschly, 1990; Woodcock, 1990; Ysseldyke, 1990). As a result, each of the major intelligence batteries (e.g., WPPSI-R) was analyzed together with the same set of empirically supported *Gf-Gc* test indicators (viz., the WJ-R). In a sense, the WJ-R *Gf-Gc* tests served as *reference* or *marker* variables from which the tests in other intelligence batteries were analyzed. For each of the cross-battery analyses conducted by McGrew and Flanagan, test *g* loadings and communality estimates (needed for calculation of specificities, described below) were calculated separately for each battery (e.g., WPPSI-R alone) as well as together with the same set of strong reference indicators (tests) of seven *Gf-Gc* abilities (clusters) from the WJ-R battery (e.g., WJ-R and WPPSI-R combined). McGrew and Flanagan compared these results in a manner consistent with the data presented in Table 4.1. In addition, they calculated the proportional change between the within-battery and cross-battery estimates for each test. They used these values as scaling factors and applied them to all the standardization sample-based *g* and specificity values available for each test (i.e., reported within-battery values) in the major intelligence batteries. This resulted in "adjusted" norm-based cross-battery test *g* and specificity values. The Wechsler cross-battery *g* and specificity values calculated here were derived from the same technique using a combination of Wechsler and WJ (WJ-R and WJ-III) datasets. In simple terms, the Wechsler *g* and specificity cross-battery estimates are *anchored* or *referenced* to the best available battery (viz., WJ-R, WJ-III) that measures the greatest breadth of abilities represented in the *Gf-Gc* model of intelligence. The results of these analyses are reported in the summary pages at the end of this chapter.

It is important to note that the cross-battery *g* estimates likely contain an unknown degree of error and, therefore, should be used with caution. The potential impact of this error is minimized by the reporting of within- and cross-battery statistical estimates in categories (i.e., high, medium, low). Although the exact cross-battery *g* or specificity estimates for a particular test (if computed through an ideal set of cross-battery studies) would likely differ from the adjusted values reported here, in many cases the amount of the precise difference may not result in a test changing in its qualitative categorization (e.g., from high to medium). Also, we believe that the risks associated with using the cross-battery estimates are less than the risks associated with test interpretations based on within-battery estimates because, for some tests, these latter estimates are clearly inaccurate when considered within the extant literature on the structure of intelligence. Cross-battery psychometric test characteristics are more consistent with the emphasis on theory in current efforts to increase the validity of intelligence test interpretation.

Specificity

Test *specificity* refers to the portion of a test's variance that is reliable and unique to the test "that is, not shared or held in common with other tests of the same scale" (Reynolds &

Kaufman, 1990, p. 151). Across different factor-analytic studies, specificity estimates are the least consistent characteristic of tests because, as described in the preceding text, "the amount of specific variance in a test is a function of the number and variety of the other tests in the factor analysis" (Jensen, 1998, p. 84; see also, McGrew, Untiedt, & Flanagan, 1996). Thus, if the number of tests in a factor analysis remained constant while varying the variety of tests, then an increase in test variety would result in an increase in specificity and vice versa. As variety decreases (i.e., tests are very similar in content and demand) the variance that would otherwise be specific contributes to common factor variance (Jensen, 1998). Alternatively, if the variety of tests in a factor analysis was held constant and the number of tests was varied, then as the number of tests increased, specificity would decrease. This is because it is likely that the additional tests would be similar to many of the tests already included in the analysis, resulting in increased common variance and a concomitant decrease in residual variance (which includes specificity) (Jensen, 1998). When the Wechsler Coding test constituted the only measure of Gs on earlier editions of the Wechsler Scales (e.g., the WISC-R), its specificity was proportionately higher as compared to its specificity when included in a battery that contained another similar measure of Gs (e.g., WISC-III). As stated earlier, because of the arbitrariness of specificity estimates, interpretations should not be made solely on the basis of a test's uniqueness.

Within- and Cross-Battery Procedures for Calculating Specificity Estimates.   A number of different methods have been suggested for the calculation of test specificity (Jensen, 1998; Kaufman, 1990a; Keith, 1990). In the most frequently cited method (Kaufman, 1979; 1990a; Silverstein, 1976), an estimate of each test's common or shared variance with all other tests within a specific intelligence battery is obtained by calculating the squared multiple correlation between each test and all other tests within the battery. This value is called the test's communality estimate. Each test's communality estimate is then subtracted from the total reliable variance for each test (a value that is obtained by subtracting each test's reliability coefficient from unity). The difference between the total reliable variance and the communality estimate represents the amount of reliable test score variance that is unique to (not shared in common with) each test within the intelligence battery (i.e., specificity). The sources of the test specificity estimates reported for the individual Wechsler tests are the same as those reported above for estimating g. The procedures used to develop cross-battery specificity estimates were described previously in the discussion of the cross-battery g estimates.

As may be seen in Table 4.2, we followed the recommendation of McGrew (1994) and used the terms *high, medium,* and *low* in place of the terms *ample, adequate, inadequate,* and *good, fair,* and *poor* for specificity and g loadings, respectively. Although these latter terms have been used for decades to describe test specificity and g loading characteristics, they connote a "good-bad" continuum and, therefore, can be misleading. For example, because it is recommended that tests classified as *inadequate* with regard to specificity not be interpreted as representing a unique ability, it is assumed often that these measures are not as valuable as those that are classified as *ample* in specificity. This, however, is not the case. First, tests with *inadequate* specificity (as well as tests that are *poor* indicators of g) may be very valuable to the interpretive process when they are part of a composite or cluster with other similar tests. Second, since a test's level of specificity and g loading are related to the breadth or diversity of tests included in the battery, these test characteristics are relative and somewhat arbitrary. In order to circumvent misleading interpretations or judgements about tests characterized as having inadequate specificity or poor *g* loadings, standard terminology was replaced with the terms *high, medium,* and *low* for specificity and *g* loading test characteristics (see Wechsler summary pages at the end of this chapter). Table 4.2 includes the criteria used to evaluate within- and cross-battery specificity estimates, as well as a description of the interpretive relevance of this test characteristic.

Test Floors and Ceilings

Intelligence batteries with adequate floors and ceilings will yield scores that effectively discriminate among various degrees of functioning at the extremes of the cognitive ability continuum. A test with an *inadequate floor,* or an insufficient number of easy items, may not distinguish adequately between individuals functioning in the average, low average, and borderline ranges of ability. Moreover, tests with inadequate floors cannot reliably discriminate between degrees of mental retardation (i.e., mild, moderate). Likewise, a test with an *inadequate ceiling,* or an insufficient number of difficult items, may not distinguish adequately between individuals who function in the average, high average, and superior ranges of intellectual ability. A test with an inadequate ceiling cannot reliably discriminate between various levels of giftedness. Thus, an intelligence battery that does not have adequate floors or ceilings may not provide information with sufficient precision for diagnostic, classification, or placement decisions, especially with individuals who are suspected of developmental delay or intellectual giftedness, respectively.

Information about individual Wechsler test floors and ceilings was derived from the published norm tables of each Wechsler battery. A simple raw score to standard score conversion at each norm table age grouping was used to examine the adequacy of individual test floors and ceilings across the age range of all individual Wechsler tests in a manner similar to that of Bracken (1987) and Flanagan and Alfonso (1995) and reported in McGrew and Flanagan (1998). Table 4.2 contains the criteria used to evaluate the adequacy of the Wechsler test floors and ceilings as well as additional information regarding the interpretive relevance of these test characteristics.

Item Gradients

Item gradient information describes the extent to which a test effectively differentiates among various ability levels across the entire range of ability in contrast to the floors and ceilings that focus on the ends of the ability scale (Bracken, 1987). This characteristic is related to the density of items across a test's latent trait scale (Woodcock, 1978). Item density or gradient information is concerned with how big the average ability "steps" are between adjacent test items. In other words, a test with good item gradient characteristics has items that are approximately equally spaced in difficulty along the entire test scale. Furthermore, spacing between items is small enough to allow for precise (reliable) discrimination between individuals on the latent trait measured by the test. Thus, a test with good item gradient or density characteristics allows for precise measurement.

A test with good item gradient characteristics is akin to a ruler with equally spaced "tic" or interval marks. The "ruler" (i.e., test) allows for reliable measurement and ranking of individuals who are positioned anywhere on the ruler. A test with poor item gradients or density information is less precise. It is akin to a ruler with unequal or inconsistently spaced interval or tic marks—a ruler that would not measure and rank all individuals precisely. Consider a portion of a special 10-foot ruler that has tic marks at 2, 5, and 7 feet. The farther one's actual height falls from these respective tic marks, the less precision one has in estimating actual height. Item gradient information is concerned with the extent to which changes of single raw score points on a test result in excessively large changes in ability scores.

Item gradient information has received relatively little attention in the test development and evaluation literature. Woodcock (1978) was one of the first to highlight the importance of item density information in the development of psychoeducational tests, while Bracken (1987) was one of the first researchers to present procedures and evaluative criteria for understanding item gradient characteristics in the assessment literature. Several years later, Flanagan and Alfonso (1995) reported item gradient information, using a slight modification of Bracken's procedure, for the most current intelligence batteries with norms for preschoolers. Flanagan and Alfonso (1995) adopted Bracken's (1987) definition of an *item gradient violation* as a one unit increase in raw score points that resulted in a change of more than $1/3$ standard deviation in standard score values.

Likewise, McGrew and Flanagan (1998) used this definition to identify item gradient violations for each individual test in eight major intelligence batteries (including the Wechsler Scales) by calculating the standard score change for every possible raw score change for each age-based norm table for each test. The data from the published norm tables for the respective intelligence batteries were used in their calculations. Following the procedures outlined by Flanagan and Alfonso (1995) for dealing with the different norm table age groupings (e.g., 1-month intervals on the WJ-R, 3-month intervals on the DAS, 5-month intervals on the WPPSI-R), an item gradient violation was counted once for each 1-month interval for which it occurred (see Flanagan & Alfonso, 1995, for details).

Building on Bracken's (1987) evaluative criteria, McGrew and Flanagan (1998) tallied the number of item gradient violations and compared that number to the total number of possible item gradient violations for the test. For example, if a test had 2 item gradient violations out of a possible 50 (i.e., 50 possible raw score changes across the entire scale), the test was characterized as having 4 percent (2 of 50) item gradient violations. McGrew and Flanagan then calculated the total percent of item gradient violations for each test of the major intelligence batteries at every age level. Through an examination of the distribution of the percentage of item gradient violations, a system of item gradient evaluation was established (see Table 4.2). This system was used to evaluate the item gradients of the Wechsler Scales. The resultant information can be found in the summary pages at the end of this chapter. Table 4.2 provides information about how the quality of a test's item gradients impacts interpretation. (For a more detailed discussion see McGrew & Flanagan, 1998.)

Construct Validity:
Gf-Gc Broad and Narrow Test Classifications

Chapter 3 was devoted primarily to a discussion of test *construct validity* which "is the extent to which the test may be said to measure a theoretical construct or trait" (Anastasi & Urbina, 1997, p.126). Furthermore, the results of *Gf-Gc* organized confirmatory factor analysis studies were summarized (see Table 3.2). This summary provided the starting point for subsequent detailed narrow-ability mapping of the Wechsler subtests as presented in Figure 3.4. In this section we describe in greater detail the rationale for the broad and narrow *Gf-Gc* ability classifications for the Wechsler Scales as well as the individual tests in all the major intelligence batteries.

The broad-ability test classifications reported in Table 3.2 coincide with the broad *Gf-Gc* abilities in the integrated Cattell-Horn-Carroll model (see Chapter 3). An example of the *Gf-Gc* broad- and narrow-ability test mapping also was demonstrated for five Wechsler tests in Chapter 3 (see Figure 3.3). The CB studies summarized in the previous chapter allowed for the broad *Gf-Gc* test classifications to be categorized further. That is, a broad-ability test classification could be either logical or empirical.

Logical classifications are based on a task analysis of the content and demands of tests that were not included in CB analyses, within the context of the *Gf-Gc* taxonomy (see McGrew & Flanagan, 1998). *Empirical* classifications, such as those presented in Table 3.2, are derived from a review of the results of CB studies. Typically in these studies, tests were found to have significant or salient factor loadings on *one Gf-Gc* factor (these tests are printed in bold-faced type in Table 3.2). This was considered the tests' primary *Gf-Gc* ability interpretation. However, some tests were factorially complex or mixed, displaying salient loadings on *two or more Gf-Gc* factors (e.g., the tests with a *Gf-Gc* code reported in parentheses after them in Table 3.2). In this situation, the *Gf-Gc* factor on which the test displayed its highest factor loading was considered the primary ability measured, and the other less salient factor loading(s) for the test was interpreted as a secondary ability (see Figure 4.1 and the related discussion for an illustration of this point). Tests appearing in regular type in Table 3.2 that do not have a secondary factor loading were moderate indicators of the latent trait corresponding to the *Gf-Gc* factors on which they loaded.

The CB studies summarized in Table 3.2 were designed to provide information about the abilities measured by intelligence tests at the *broad (stratum II) level* of the *Gf-Gc* structural model. Empirically based narrow-ability classification factor analysis studies would be a major undertaking and have yet to be completed. In their absence, McGrew (1997) extended the broad *Gf-Gc* test classifications of Woodcock (1990) by applying a logically based expert consensus process to the narrow *Gf-Gc* ability classification of the tests in the major intelligence batteries. This involved asking a number of intelligence test experts (including most of the intelligence test authors) to match the content and task demands of each test within a battery to the narrow *Gf-Gc* ability definitions reported in Table 2.1 (see Chapter 2). In essence, this is a form of *Gf-Gc content validity* (APA, 1985) for the tests of the major intelligence batteries.

McGrew and Flanagan (1998) reviewed every narrow-ability test classification originally reported by McGrew (1997) in light of a greater understanding of the narrow-ability definitions. This was achieved through a review of *Gf-Gc*-organized CB studies (published between 1990 and 1999), a re-reading of Carroll's (1993a) text, and communication with intelligence scholars and test authors. As a result, a handful of the narrow-ability classifications originally provided by McGrew (1997) were modified by McGrew and Flanagan (1998). The narrow-ability classifications of all the individual Wechsler tests included on the summary pages at the end of this chapter are essentially the same as those presented in McGrew and Flanagan (1998). Slight modifications were necessary based on logical analyses and recent *Gf-Gc*-organized factor analyses. Expert consensus notwithstanding, the *Gf-Gc* narrow-ability classifications presented here (like McGrew's [1997] original classifications) may undergo modification as a result of future research and scholarly dialogue.

In the absence of empirical data on which to evaluate and categorize the logically based narrow-ability test classifications, McGrew and Flanagan (1998) adopted McGrew's (1997) system. This classification system also was used here to categorize the narrow abilities presumed to underlie all individual Wechsler tests (see summary pages). In this system, a *probable* designation indicates that there was a clear correspondence between the content and task demands of a test and a particular *Gf-Gc* narrow-ability definition in the expert consensus process. These were also the narrow-ability test classifications for which there was the most expert consensus. A *possible* categorization reflects narrow test classifications in which there was less agreement during the expert consensus process, or the correspondence between a test's content and task demands and the narrow-ability definition was present, but less obvious.

Other Variables That Influence Test Performance

Based on a review of the literature on variables that influence test performance, the following characteristics were considered most salient: (1) incidence of basic concepts in intelligence test directions (applicable for instruments with norms for preschoolers); (2) degree of U.S. mainstream cultural loading on test performance; (3) degree of linguistic demand required to perform a task; and (4) background/environmental and individual/situational variables that influence test performance. It is particularly critical to consider these variables in test interpretation because such influences may contaminate test scores in a manner irrelevant to the interpreted construct—a condition (called *construct-irrelevant variance*) that poses a threat to construct validity (Messick, 1995).

The two types of construct-irrelevant variance are construct-irrelevant difficulty and construct-irrelevant easiness. When *construct-irrelevant difficulty* is operating, "aspects of the task that are extraneous to the focal construct make the test irrelevantly difficult for some individuals or groups" (Messick, 1998, p. 244). For example, the excessive intrusion of math knowledge requirements in a test of inductive reasoning may lead to invalidly low (inductive reasoning) scores for individuals who do not excel in mathematics. Likewise, excessive intrusion of reading comprehension requirements in a test of general knowledge may lead to spuriously low scores for individuals who are poor readers or for whom English is a second language. In both examples, undue math and reading requirements, respectively, constitute construct-irrelevant difficulty (see Messick, 1998).

When *construct-irrelevant easiness* is operating, "extraneous clues in item or task formats permit some individuals to respond correctly or appropriately in ways irrelevant to the construct being assessed" (Messick, 1998, p. 248). For example, when an individual is exposed to or trained in specific test content, a test containing similar content will be *irrelevantly easy* for the individual previously exposed to such items. When a task is irrelevantly easy for a particular individual, the resultant test score is an invalidly high estimate of the construct under investigation. In some instances, background/environmental and individual/situational variables, for example, may be responsible for invalidly high or low scores because they affect assessment in a manner irrelevant to the construct being interpreted. In other instances, these variables may help to explain high or low test scores that are considered valid estimates of the measured trait. Careful attention to these variables within the context of a comprehensive case study will allow the practitioner to evaluate properly whether a test score is likely a valid estimate (or, alternatively an under- or over-estimate) of the ability under investigation. The aforementioned variables are described briefly in the text that follows. The Wechsler Scale summary pages at the end of this chapter include a list of variables that were considered likely to influence performance on a given test.

Basic Concepts in Test Directions

Practitioners who use intelligence batteries to assess the cognitive functioning of preschool children (aged 3 to 5 years) should be cognizant of the basic concepts that are used during standard test administration procedures, as well as the likelihood that a young child's understanding (or conversely, misunderstanding) of these concepts may influence test performance. Many researchers have stressed the need to evaluate the difficulty of intelligence test directions by examining the incidence of basic concepts that are used during standard administration procedures, because the linguistic knowledge of preschoolers is limited (Bracken, 1986; Flanagan et al., 1995; Flanagan, Mascolo, & Genshaft, 1998; Glutting & Kaplan, 1990; Kaufman, 1978; 1990b).

Based on the results of prior investigations, it is evident that practitioners ought not to assume that preschoolers comprehend fully the standard directions of most major intelligence batteries. For instance, intelligence test directions that include "difficult" basic concepts (e.g., without, over, after), long sentences, or the passive voice may not be understood by preschool children (Alfonso & Flanagan, 1999; Boehm, 1991; Bracken, 1986; Flanagan et al., 1995; Kaufman, 1978; 1990b). A child who does not understand test directions because of complex conceptual knowledge demands may not perform optimally and, as a result, his or her obtained scores may underestimate his or her ability. Moreover, intelligence batteries with directions that require conceptual or linguistic knowledge that is above age level may pose a threat to the construct validity of the instrument (Bracken, 1986). The extent to which intelligence batteries require excessive conceptual knowledge demands is important to consider when evaluating the performance of preschoolers and children from economically or socially disadvantaged or culturally diverse backgrounds (see Alfonso & Flanagan, 1999; Bracken, 1986; Flanagan et al., 1995; Kaufman, 1978).

The incidence of basic concepts in intelligence test directions was evaluated for the WPPSI-R only, because no other Wechsler Scale contains norms for preschool children. To evaluate the extent to which basic concepts have an impact on the difficulty of WPPSI-R test directions, three characteristics of basic concepts were considered: (1) the presence (i.e., number) of basic concepts in individual test directions; (2) the percentage of the preschool population who understand each basic concept; and (3) the frequency with which basic concepts occur in individual test directions (cited in Flanagan et al., 1995). These characteristics were examined using the Bracken Basic Concept Scale (BBCS; Bracken, 1984). The standardized test directions included in the WPPSI-R administration and scoring manual (Wechsler, 1989) provided the necessary information. The specific procedure for identifying basic concepts in the directions of the WPPSI-R (and other preschool intelligence tests) can be found in McGrew and Flanagan (1998).

The authors' review of basic concepts in the WPPSI-R test directions included only directions that are used to guide, direct, or give feedback to the child. A restricted analysis of this kind was preferable because it eliminates the basic concepts that are inextricably bound to the ability to perform a cognitive task and includes only those directions that are essentially unrelated to the abilities or skills necessary for successful performance (Flanagan et al., 1995). Thus, if the basic concepts that are revealed by this type of analysis are not understood by a preschool child, it is likely that the child's obtained score will underestimate his or her true ability.

Based on this criterion, certain tests were not included in the present analysis. For example, the directions of the WPPSI-R Similarities test were not included because the child must understand the concept *alike* in order to perform the cognitive task (Flanagan et al., 1995). In addition, tests that directly assessed a child's knowledge of basic concepts, were deleted from the analysis. Inter-rater reliability coefficients were calculated and revealed greater than 90 percent agreement among raters with respect to the presence and frequency of basic concepts in intelligence test directions (see McGrew & Flanagan, 1998). See Table 4.2 for the criteria used to evaluate the incidence of basic concepts in test directions and for information regarding the interpretive relevance of this test characteristic. The incidence of basic concepts in the WPPSI-R test directions can be found on the summary pages for this scale at the end of this chapter.

Degree of Cultural Loading in Cognitive Ability Tests

Most major theorists include *culture* (either implicitly or explicitly) as a critical component in their conceptualizations of intelligence to explain how differing experiences facilitate or inhibit intellectual behavior (e.g., Carroll, 1993a; Feuerstein, Feuerstein, & Schun, 1995; Gardner, 1983; Horn, 1991; Sternberg, 1985; 1997). As such, performance on all intelligence batteries reflects, in part, the extent to which the examinee is familiar with the conventions of the mainstream culture in which the battery was constructed and normed.

Newland's (1971) process-dominant/product-dominant continuum is often used to evaluate the extent to which culture may influence test performance. The application of this to the Wechsler Scales assumes that an examinee's level of acculturation, or learning of mainstream U.S. culture will impact his or her performance to a greater extent on tests that are dependent on accumulated knowledge and acquired experiences (product-dominant) than on tests that purport to measure fundamental learning processes (process-dominant) (Newland, 1971). For example, it is assumed that an individual who is not acculturated (i.e., not familiar with the mainstream societal conventions of the United States) generally will perform relatively lower on product-dominant tests (i.e., tests that are highly influenced by U.S. culture such as Information and Comprehension) as compared to process-dominant tests, which are typically less influenced by exposure to mainstream U.S. culture, such as tasks that involve analysis and synthesis of visual stimuli. It is further assumed that individuals who do not have the knowledge and experiences that accumulate gradually through the largely informal and indirect process of acculturation (in contrast to formal and direct processes like schooling) are apt to earn product-dominant test or cluster scores that are spuriously low. Because all intelligence batteries include process-dominant and product-dominant tests or some combination of the two, none is *culture-free* (Humphreys, 1992). The Wechsler Scales (indeed, all intelligence batteries) appear to measure cognitive abilities that "result from the interaction between the person's neurophysiology and the environment" (Elliott, 1990b, p. 2). Therefore, the degree to which individual intelligence tests are *culturally loaded* most likely varies.

Knowledge of the degree to which U.S. cultural knowledge and experience are required to perform a task may aid in the selection of the most appropriate cognitive tests for use with individuals whose cultural backgrounds differ from mainstream U.S. culture and in making more appropriate interpretations regarding cultural demands on test performance (see Alfonso & Flanagan, 1999; Armour-Thomas, 1992; Barona & Barona, 1991; Esters et al., 1997; Helms, 1997; Lopez, 1997; Rogoff & Chavajay, 1995; Valdés & Figueroa, 1994; Vernon, Jackson, & Messick, 1988 for discussions of the importance of considering cultural influences on test performance).

Like Newland's process-dominant/product-dominant continuum, *Gf-Gc* abilities can be thought of as lying on a continuum, with abilities that depend little on direct instruction and formal learning (e.g., *Gf*) at one end, and abilities that depend extensively on breadth and depth of knowledge of a culture, including the ability to communicate (especially verbally) and reason through the application of previously learned procedures (e.g., *Gc*), at the other. The remaining *Gf-Gc* abilities lie somewhere between *Gf* and *Gc* on the continuum with their location depending on the degree to which they differ as a function of relative emphasis on process, content, and manner of response (Carroll, 1993a).[1] Thus, classifications of all cognitive tests according to a well-researched and validated theory is a necessary step prior to considering how culture impacts test performance (Flanagan & Alfonso, 1994; Hessler, 1993).

Flanagan and Alfonso (1994), Alfonso and Flanagan (1999), and most recently, the present authors, used the *Gf-Gc* theoretical framework as a basis for understanding the abilities and processes that underlie the individual Wechsler tests (as well as the tests of other major intelligence batteries). Specifically, these authors examined the tests of the major intelligence batteries according to underlying process, nature of the content to be processed, and type of response to determine the degree (i.e., high, medium, low) to which test performance is likely to be influenced by U.S. culture. The degree of cultural loading classifications presented in the Wechsler Scale summary pages represent an extension of the authors' earlier work. That is, the present authors reviewed the degree of cultural loading classifications for the Wechsler Scales presented in McGrew and Flanagan (1998) and, where appropriate, modified them vis-à-vis current research and feedback from experts in multicultural/multilingual assessment. These classifications represent the degree to which U.S. cultural knowledge or experience is required to perform the task (see Chapter 8 for a more in-depth discussion).

The classifications of all individual Wechsler tests as either high, medium, or low with respect to the degree to which cultural loading impacts test performance are admittedly subjective. They are based predominantly on our judgments and therefore should be used only as a guide for selecting tests that may more appropriately meet the needs of culturally diverse populations. The cultural loading of a particular test or item represents only one form of potential bias in assessment. A consideration of how the cultural loading of cognitive ability tests is likely to influence test performance cannot eliminate entirely the bias in test performance of individuals with different cultural backgrounds. The classifications presented at the end of this chapter (and in McGrew & Flanagan, 1998) may provide the necessary framework for conducting research on the relationship between U.S. cultural demands and test performance.

Degree of Linguistic Demand in Cognitive Ability Tests

It is also important to understand the degree to which language demands can impact test performance. To evaluate this impact, two factors were considered. First, tests were evaluated according to the extent to which proper administration required the use of verbal and nonverbal communication on the part of the assessor. Some tests have lengthy, verbose instructions (e.g., Wechsler Block Design test, WJ-R Analysis-Synthesis test) and, as such, requires significant verbal communication, whereas others may be administered using only gestures or minimal oral language (e.g., Comprehensive Test of Nonverbal Intelligence [CTONI; Hammill, Pearson, & Wiederholt, 1996], Leiter-Revised [Leiter-R; Roid & Miller, 1997], Universal Nonverbal Intelligence Test [UNIT; McCallum & Bracken, 1998]).

In addition, tests were evaluated on the basis of the level of language proficiency required by the examinee in order to comprehend the assessor's instructions and provide an appropriate response. Responses on some tests require considerable expressive language skills (e.g., Wechsler Vocabulary and Comprehension tests), while others can be accomplished without a word (e.g., Wechsler Symbol Search and Mazes tests). Final classifications were based on the joint consideration of both factors using a three-dimensional categorization system that reflects the continuous nature of these variables (i.e., low, medium, high). The degree of linguistic demand inherent in the individual Wechsler tests is reported on the summary pages at the end of this chapter. Also, these categories are presented alongside the cultural loading categories in Table 8.2 (in Chapter 8 page 306) and are arranged in order of increasing language demands. This information is used in Chapter 8 to guide the construction of Wechsler-based cross-battery assessments, which are more appropriate for estimating the cognitive capabilities of linguistically diverse individuals (e.g., second language learners) than traditional approaches. The reader is referred to Chapter 8 for an in-depth discussion and treatment of linguistic barriers to reliable test performance.

Background/Environmental and Individual/Situational Variables

Two additional broad categories of variables that are important when interpreting performance on intelligence tests include background/environmental and individual/situational variables. These variables place the interpretation of an individual's test performance within an appropriate and meaningful context. Background/environmental variables typically have a distal (far or remote) influence on an examinee's test performance whereas individual/situational variables usually have a proximal (near or immediate) influence.

Background/environmental variables (e.g., language stimulation, educational opportunities, and experiences) refer to distal influences—that is, prior developmental or environmental factors that may have contributed to the development of the skill being evaluated or that may negatively influence performance on other tasks that require this skill. For example, when interpreting a very low score on a verbal comprehension test requiring auditory processing *(Ga)*, the meaning of this score would likely be different for a child with a long history of hearing difficulties due to chronic inner ear infections when compared to a similar level of performance for a child with no history of hearing difficulties. For the child with the history of hearing difficulties, a possible hypothesis may be that the presence of hearing difficulties hindered the development of the child's *Ga* abilities which, in turn, made the verbal comprehension task *irrelevantly difficult.*

Individual/Situational variables include characteristics of the examinee that might exert a situational influence on test performance (either in a positive or negative direction) during the testing session. For example, when the text of a reading comprehension passage is highly familiar to a particular individual, his or her resultant score will likely be invalidly high because the task was *irrelevantly easy* due to prior exposure (Messick, 1998). Conversely, if an examinee is highly distractible and inattentive during a task of perceptual speed, then his or her performance may be influenced negatively. As a result, the individual's score on this test may not accurately portray his or her level on the trait being measured (i.e., *Gs*). In the context of the interpretive framework presented in Figure 4.1, the size of the test indicator rectangle that represents error variance may be relatively larger for this individual (resulting in a reduction of the reliable variance of the person's score).

Knowledge of the environmental, background, individual, and situational variables that may influence performance on an individual test is necessary for appropriate test interpretation. Close attention to individual and situational factors, in particular, allows a practitioner to make informed judgments about the extent to which the proportion of reliable variance for a test (which is the primary focus of interpretation) is a valid indicator of the abilities that are measured by the test. In addition, a consideration of contextual variables assists in determining whether the measured construct was affected by construct-irrelevant difficulty or easiness. Failure to consider the possibility that certain environmental, situation specific, or individual characteristics may influence test performance would be akin to blindly evaluating the running performance of a world-class sprinter based on her reported 100-meter dash time without knowledge of the unique variables that were operating during the performance (e.g., Was it raining and/or windy? Was the sprinter performing with a slightly pulled hamstring muscle?).

A list of background/environmental and individual/situational variables along with the definitions of each variable may be found in Table 4.2. These variables were presented originally in McGrew and Flanagan (1998). They were generated from a synthesis of similar variables that have been presented in the intelligence test interpretation literature. Specifically, McGrew and Flanagan reviewed the published interpretive material for the DAS (Elliott, 1990), K-ABC (Kaufman & Kaufman, 1983), KAIT (Kaufman & Kaufman, 1993), Wechsler Scales (Kaufman, 1979; 1990a; 1994a), and the WJ-R (McGrew, 1994), as well as a major reference book on intelligence test interpretation (i.e., Sattler, 1988; 1992). Based on this review, they compiled a table of the cross-referenced terms and statements.

For example, the phrases "school learning," "effect of schooling and education," and "quality of schooling" were judged to be referring to the same variable. As a result, they referred to this variable as "educational opportunities/experiences" (see Table 4.2). McGrew and Flanagan's (1998) list of environmental/background and individual/situational variables included those terms that were repeated most frequently across the above mentioned sources. For more details on the general guidelines and procedures of this consensus process, see McGrew and Flanagan (1998).

Using the terms and definitions presented in Table 4.2, each individual test in each Wechsler battery was judged according to whether one or more of these variables may potentially influence test performance. With few exceptions, the contextual variables listed on the WPPSI-R, WISC-III, and WAIS-III summary pages at the end of this chapter are identical to those reported by McGrew and Flanagan (1998). It is important to note that the process of classifying each test according to background/environmental and individual/situational variables was not based on specific objective criteria. Rather, the test classifications presented here are the authors' consensus-based judgement as to whether performance on a test may or may not be influenced by a particular variable. The process involved a simple dichotomous (yes or no) classification.

The Wechsler Intelligence Test
Characteristic Summary Pages

Proper interpretation of intelligence tests is a complex activity that often has significant implications (e.g., diagnostic, treatment, placement) for the individual being evaluated. It is incumbent on those who use intelligence batteries to consider all available information about each test in the assessment and interpretation process. In order to facilitate this process, general information about each Wechsler Scale is reported in Table 4.3 in the following broad categories:

- *General information.* Author(s); publisher; date of publication; age range of tests; and typical administration time.
- *Composite measure information.* Number and type of broad and lower-order composite scores.
- *Score information.* Type of peer comparison scores; range of standard scores; mean floor of tests.
- *Norming information.* Number of tests normed at each age; conorming features; person and community variables in the norming plan; size of the norming sample; age blocks used in norm tables.

Knowledge of this general information as well as mastery and use of the wide range of psychometric, theoretical, and qualitative test characteristic information described in this chapter for the individual tests of all Wechsler batteries is a daunting (but necessary) task for practitioners. To facilitate the infusion of this critical test characteristic information into the day-to-day assessment practices of practitioners, this section of the chapter presents a summary page for each individual test of each individually administered Wechsler battery.

TABLE 4.3 Select Content, Scoring, and Norming Features of the Wechsler Scales

	WPPSI-R	WISC-III	WAIS-III
General Information			
Author	David Wechsler	David Wechsler	David Wechsler
Publisher	The Psychological Corporation	The Psychological Corporation	The Psychological Corporation
Publication Date	1949–1989	1949–1991	1939–1997
Age Range	2:11 to 7:3 years	6:0 to 16:11 years	16 to 89 years
Administration Time	50 to 70 minutes Optional tests: 10 to 15 minutes	50 to 70 minutes Optional tests: 10 to 15 minutes	60 to 90 minutes Optional tests: 10 to 15 minutes
Composite Measure Information			
Broad	Full Scale IQ (FSIQ)	Full Scale IQ (FSIQ)	Full Scale IQ (FSIQ)
Lower-Order Composites	Verbal Scale Performance Scale	Verbal Scale Performance Scale Verbal Comprehension Index Perceptual Organization Index Processing Speed Index Freedom from Distractibility Index	Verbal Scale Performance Scale Verbal Comprehension Index Perceptual Organization Index Processing Speed Index Working Memory Index
Score Information			
Peer Comparison Scores	Percentile Rank IQ/Index	Percentile Rank IQ/Index	Percentile Rank IQ/Index
Range of Standard Scores for Total Test Composite	41 to 160	40 to 160	45 to 155
Mean Floor of Tests at Age 3:0	−1.6	N/A	N/A
Norming Information			
Number of Tests Normed at Each Age	12 across age range	13 across age range	14 across age range

(continued)

Conormed with Other Measures	No (Equated scores for WIAT; *n* = 84) Reading Mathematics Language Writing	No (Equated scores for WIAT; *n* = 1,100) Reading Mathematics Language Writing No (Equated scores for CMS)	No (Equated scores with WIAT for ages 16–89; *n* = 142) Reading Mathematics Language Writing Yes. WMS-III (*n* = 437)
Person Variables in Norming Plan	Gender Race/Ethnicity (confounding race and Hispanic origin) Family SES (occupation and education)	Gender Race/Ethnicity (confounding race and Hispanic origin) Family SES (occupation and education)	Gender Race/Ethnicity (confounding race and Hispanic origin) Family SES (occupation and education)
Community Variables in Norming Plan	Location Size	Location Size	Location Size
Size of Norming Sample for the Broad Measure of General Intelligence	*N* = 1,700 Average number per year: 183	*N* = 2,200 Average number per year: 200	*N* = 2,450 Average number per age group: 200
Age Blocks in Norm Table	3-month blocks	4-month blocks	2-year blocks (Age 16 to 19) 5-year blocks (Age 20 to 34; 65 to 89) 10-year blocks (Age 35 to 64)

A summary page for the WPPSI-R Object Assembly test is presented in Figure 4.2 and will be used to explain the information that is available for all Wechsler tests.

As may be seen in Figure 4.2, the name of the battery and individual test as well as the age range for which norms are provided are located at the top of the summary page. A brief description of the test follows. A section called, Basic Psychometric Characteristics appears next in Figure 4.2. Here, information about each test's reliability, within- and cross-battery g loadings, specificity, and item gradients is presented by age in a visual-graphic format. The evaluation of each of these test characteristics, according to the psychometric criteria presented in Table 4.2, is accomplished by simply locating the appropriate age level and inspecting the tone of the shading in the small square associated with that age. The meaning of the shaded box is understood by referring to the key for each test characteristic located on the top right half of the summary pages. For example, at age five, the WPPSI-R Object Assembly test is classified as having *low* reliability, *medium* within-battery g loadings, *low* cross-battery g loadings, *low* within-battery specificity, *high* cross-battery specificity, and *good* item gradients.[2] In addition to these psychometric characteristics, the adequacy of test floors and ceilings is reported on the summary pages. For example, Figure 4.2 shows that the Object Assembly test has *adequate* test floors and ceilings across most of the age range. The manner in which this psychometric information is useful in the interpretive process is made apparent in Part III of this book.

Inspection of the middle of the summary page for the Object Assembly test in Figure 4.2 provides information about how to interpret this test from the *Gf-Gc* theoretical framework. This section shows that the *primary* focus of interpretation for this test should be Visual Processing *(Gv)*. Specifically, the narrow abilities of Closure Speed (CS) and Spatial Relations (SR) appear to be necessary to perform this test. The classifications included in this section, for the broad *Gf-Gc* abilities, namely *Empirical: strong, Empirical: moderate, Empirical: mixed* were explained earlier in this chapter and are described in Table 4.2. Likewise, the *probable* and *possible* classifications for the narrow *Gf-Gc* abilities listed in this section of the summary pages were described earlier.

The Other Variables section of the summary pages provides information about variables that may influence an examinee's test performance either positively or negatively. For example, Figure 4.2 shows that factors such as reflectivity/impulsivity, field dependence/independence, and planning ability, as well as the ability to perform under time pressure may impact performance on the Object Assembly test. Also, data in this section shows that when interpreting Object Assembly test performance, practitioners need to consider whether the examinee was generally alert and attentive during test administration.

The cube on the bottom right portion of the summary page in Figure 4.2 provides information about the degree of cultural loading and linguistic demand inherent in the Object Assembly test. As shown in this figure, performance on the Object Assembly test is moderately influenced by exposure to U.S. mainstream culture as indicated by the *medium* classification in the degree of cultural loading grid. Additionally, the Object Assembly test is judged to be characterized as having a *low* degree of linguistic demand, particularly because of the length of its directions. When interpreting Object Assembly test scores, this information suggests that practitioners should consider the degree to which exposure to U.S. culture and the extent to which receptive language demands may impact performance,

Battery: WPPSI-R   **Test: Object Assembly**   **Age Range: 3 to 7 years**

Description of test: The examinee is required to assemble a set of puzzles of common objects into meaningful wholes. This is a timed test.

	BASIC PSYCHOMETRIC CHARACTERISTICS	Low / Medium / High	Poor / Fair / Good	(Item gradients only)

	3 4 5 6 7 8 9 10 11 12 13 14 15 16 17 18 19	20 25 30 35 40 45 50 55 60 65 70 75 80 / 24 29 34 39 44 49 54 59 64 69 74 79 84 85+
Reliability		
g loading / **g loading** [a]		
Specificity / **Specificity** [a]		
Item gradients		

Inadequate at ages:	**Test floor**	**Test ceiling**
		Ages 6:5 to 7:3

Gf-Gc CLASSIFICATIONS (Broad:stratum II / *Narrow:stratum I*)

Visual Processing (*Gv*): The ability to generate, perceive, analyze, synthesize, manipulate, transform, and think with visual patterns and stimuli (Empirical: strong).
- *Closure Speed* (CS): Ability to quickly combine disconnected, vague, or partially obscured visual stimuli or patterns into a meaningful whole, without knowing in advance what the pattern is (probable).
- *Spatial Relations* (SR): Ability to rapidly perceive and manipulate visual patterns or to maintain orientation with respect to objects in space (possible).

OTHER VARIABLES THAT MAY INFLUENCE TEST PERFORMANCE

Background and Environmental
- Alertness to the environment

Individual and Situational
- Reflectivity/impulsivity
- Field dependence/independence
- Planning
- Ability to perform under time pressure

Degree of Linguistic Demand

	L	M	H
Degree of Cultural Loading — L			
M	■		
H			

Typical Age (in years) of Concept Attainment

Basic Concepts in Test Directions (Frequency of occurrence)	3	4	5	> 5	Data not available
	in (5) / big (2)	together (6) / through (2) / fast (5)	like (1) / pieces (12) / all (2)	some (1)	

[a] Cross-battery estimates. See Table 4-2 for the definition of the terms and keys used on this page.

FIGURE 4.2   Wechsler Summary Page (WPPSI-R Object Assembly Example)

especially for individuals who are not fully acculturated or for whom English is not the native language.

Finally, the bottom portion of the summary page in Figure 4.2 includes information about the incidence of basic concepts in the Object Assembly test. For example, Figure 4.2 shows that the basic concepts of "together," "through," and "fast" were found in the Object Assembly test directions. These basic concepts are listed in the column for 4-year-olds on the summary page. This indicates that these basic concepts are understood by at least 75 percent of 4-year-olds. Therefore, children younger than age 4 may have difficulty understanding the directions of the Object Assembly test.

The summary pages that follow are presented for the WAIS-III first, followed by the WISC-III and WPPSI-R. The Wechsler individual tests are presented alphabetically rather than the recommended order of test administration reported in the respective Wechsler administration and scoring manuals. The alphabetical order makes it easier to locate information about a specific test. (For additional critical reviews of the Wechsler Scales, the reader is referred to the bibliography in Appendix B.)

Conclusion

We believe that the breadth of information presented in this chapter collectively exemplifies Keith's (1994) admonition, "Intelligence *is* important, intelligence *is* complex" (p. 209, emphasis in the original). This chapter was designed to facilitate a greater understanding of this important and complex construct through the grounding of psychometric, theoretical, and qualitative test characteristic information in cognitive psychology and through the presentation of this information in an easy-to-read format. The primary goal of this chapter is to make it easier for assessment professionals to strengthen and use the *science* half of the *art and science* of intelligence test interpretation.

In light of the numerous test features that must be considered in order to use and interpret the Wechsler Scales, it was not possible to include all variables that might play a role in this process. For example, variables such as the ease of use and scoring, the trade-off between psychometric sophistication and user-friendliness, the use of item response theory procedures in test development, and so on, were not included (see Harrison, Flanagan, & Genshaft, 1997, for information on the technical, administration, content, and interpretive features of the major intelligence batteries as well as Appendix B for other test reviews). This chapter includes only those psychometric, theoretical, and qualitative test characteristics that were judged to be most important in the use and interpretation of the Wechsler Scales. Furthermore, it is important to note that many of the test characteristic concepts included in this book first reached prominence during the psychometric analysis wave of test interpretation (i.e., Kamphaus and colleagues' third wave, 1997), a wave that has received considerable criticism. In the current work these test characteristics are conceptualized and/or are based on analysis embedded in a contemporary model of intelligence that has strong validity. This later approach is representative of current theory-based efforts to improve the validity of intelligence tests and the interpretations based on the scores they provide—a fourth wave approach (Kamphaus, 1997).

It is hoped that the test characteristic information presented here will promote more psychometrically and theoretically sound interpretations of the Wechsler Scales within the context of relevant noncognitive factors (e.g., educational opportunities, cultural experiences, etc.). Part III of this book will demonstrate how the test characteristic information presented in this chapter can facilitate the construction of Wechsler-based *Gf-Gc* cross-battery assessments that are psychometrically sound, theory-based, and consistent with current research on the structure of intelligence.

Summary Pages for the
Wechsler Intelligence Scales

Battery: WAIS-III   **Test: Arithmetic**   **Age Range: 16 to 89 years**

Description of test: The examinee is required to mentally solve a series of orally presented arithmetic problems and respond orally.

BASIC PSYCHOMETRIC CHARACTERISTICS	Low ☐ Medium ▨ High ■	Poor ☐ Fair ▨ Good ■	(Item gradients only)

	3 4 5 6 7 8 9 10 11 12 13 14 15	16 17 18 19	20 25 30 35 40 45 50 55 60 65 70 75 80 / 24 29 34 39 44 49 54 59 64 69 74 79 84 85+
Reliability			
g loading **g loading** [a]			
Specificity **Specificity** [a]			
Item gradients			

	Test floor	Test ceiling
Inadequate at ages:		

Gf-Gc CLASSIFICATIONS (Broad:stratum II / *Narrow:stratum I*)

Quantitative Knowledge (Gq): An individual's store of acquired quantitative declarative and procedural knowledge (Empirical: strong).
- *Mathematical Achievement* (A3): Measured mathematics achievement (probable).

Fluid Intelligence (Gf): The ability to solve relatively novel tasks that cannot be performed automatically by forming and recognizing concepts, identifying relations, perceiving relationships among patterns, drawing inferences, comprehending implications, problem solving, extrapolating, and reorganizing or transforming information (Logical).
- *Quantitative Reasoning* (RQ): Ability to inductively and deductively reason with concepts involving mathematical relations and properties (possible).

OTHER VARIABLES THAT MAY INFLUENCE TEST PERFORMANCE

Background and Environmental
- Math difficulties
- Educational opportunities/experiences
- Hearing difficulties

Individual and Situational
- Attention span/distractibility
- Concentration
- Distractibility
- Visual elaboration

Degree of Linguistic Demand

		L	M	H
Degree of	L			
Cultural	M		■	
Loading	H			

[a] Cross-battery estimates. See Table 4-2 for the definition of the terms and keys used on this page.

Battery: WAIS-III   **Test: Block Design**   **Age Range: 16 to 89 years**

Description of test: The examinee is required to replicate a set of modeled or printed two-dimensional geometric patterns using two-color cubes. This is a timed test.

BASIC PSYCHOMETRIC CHARACTERISTICS	Low Medium High		Poor Fair Good	(Item gradients only)

	3	4	5	6	7	8	9	10	11	12	13	14	15	16	17	18	19	20 24	25 29	30 34	35 39	40 44	45 49	50 54	55 59	60 64	65 69	70 74	75 79	80 84	85+
Reliability																															
g loading **g loading** [a]																															
Specificity **Specificity** [a]																															
Item gradients																															

	Test floor	Test ceiling
Inadequate at ages:		

Gf-Gc CLASSIFICATIONS (**Broad:stratum II** / *Narrow:stratum I*)

Visual Processing (*Gv*): The ability to generate, perceive, analyze, synthesize, manipulate, transform, and think with visual patterns and stimuli (Empirical: strong).
- *Spatial Relations* (SR): Ability to rapidly perceive and manipulate visual patterns or to maintain orientation with respect to objects in space (probable).
- *Visualization* (Vz): Ability to mentally manipulate objects or visual patterns and to "see" how they would appear under altered conditions (possible).

OTHER VARIABLES THAT MAY INFLUENCE TEST PERFORMANCE

Background and Environmental	**Individual and Situational**
	• Reflectivity/impulsivity • Field dependence/independence • Flexibility/inflexibility • Planning • Ability to perform under time pressure

Degree of Linguistic Demand

		L	M	H
Degree of Cultural Loading	L			
	M			
	H			

[a] Cross-battery estimates. See Table 4-2 for the definition of the terms and keys used on this page.

Battery: WAIS-III   **Test: Comprehension**   **Age Range: 16 to 89 years**

Description of test: The examinee is required to respond orally to orally presented questions that focus on everyday problems or understanding of social rules and concepts.

BASIC PSYCHOMETRIC CHARACTERISTICS	Low — Poor
	Medium — Fair
	High — Good
	(Item gradients only)

Reliability

g loading
g loading [a]

Specificity
Specificity [a]

Item gradients

Inadequate at ages:	Test floor	Test ceiling

Gf-Gc **CLASSIFICATIONS** (**Broad:stratum II** / *Narrow:stratum I*)

Crystallized Intelligence (Gc): The breadth and depth of a person's acquired knowledge of a culture and the effective application of this knowledge (Empirical: strong).
- *Language Development* (LD): General development, or the understanding of words, sentences, and paragraphs (not requiring reading) in spoken native language skills (probable).
- *General Information* (K0): Range of general knowledge (probable).

OTHER VARIABLES THAT MAY INFLUENCE TEST PERFORMANCE

Background and Environmental   **Individual and Situational**

- Language stimulation
- Environmental stimulation
- Educational opportunities/experiences
- Alertness to the environment

Degree of Linguistic Demand

	L	M	H
Degree of Cultural Loading L			
M			
H			■

[a] Cross-battery estimates. See Table 4-2 for the definition of the terms and keys used on this page.

Battery: WAIS-III	Test: Digit Span	Age Range: 16 to 89 years

Description of test: The examinee is required to repeat verbatim or in a reversed order a series of orally presented number sequences.

BASIC PSYCHOMETRIC CHARACTERISTICS	Low Medium High	Poor Fair Good	(Item gradients only)

20 25 30 35 40 45 50 55 60 65 70 75 80
3 4 5 6 7 8 9 10 11 12 13 14 15 16 17 18 19 24 29 34 39 44 49 54 59 64 69 74 79 84 85+

Reliability

g loading
g loading [a]

Specificity
Specificity [a]

Item gradients

	Test floor	Test ceiling
Inadequate at ages:		

Gf-Gc CLASSIFICATIONS (**Broad:stratum II** / *Narrow:stratum I*)

Short-Term Memory (*Gsm*): The ability to apprehend and hold information in immediate awareness and then use it within a few seconds (Empirical: strong).
  • *Memory Span* (MS): Ability to attend to and immediately recall temporally ordered elements in the correct order after a single presentation (probable).

OTHER VARIABLES THAT MAY INFLUENCE TEST PERFORMANCE

Background and Environmental	**Individual and Situational**
• Hearing difficulties	• Attention span/distractibility
	• Concentration
	• Distractibility
	• Verbal rehearsal
	• Visual elaboration
	• Organization

Degree of Linguistic Demand

		L	M	H
Degree of Cultural Loading	L		■	
	M			
	H			

[a] Cross-battery estimates. See Table 4-2 for the definition of the terms and keys used on this page.

Battery: WAIS-III   **Test: Digit Symbol-Coding**   **Age Range: 16 to 89 years**

Description of test: The examinee is required to draw symbols that are paired with a series of numbers according to a key. The examinee is required to perform this task as quickly as possible. This is a timed test.

BASIC PSYCHOMETRIC CHARACTERISTICS	Low ☐ Poor	(Item
	Medium Fair	gradients only)
	High Good	

	3 4 5 6 7 8 9 10 11 12 13 14 15 16 17 18 19	20 25 30 35 40 45 50 55 60 65 70 75 80 24 29 34 39 44 49 54 59 64 69 74 79 84 85+
Reliability		
g loading **g loading** [a]		
Specificity **Specificity** [a]		
Item gradients		

Inadequate at ages:	**Test floor**	**Test ceiling**

Gf-Gc* CLASSIFICATIONS (Broad:stratum II /** *Narrow:stratum I)**

Processing Speed (*Gs*): The ability to fluently perform cognitive tasks automatically, especially when under pressure to maintain focused attention and concentration (Empirical: strong).
- *Rate-of-Test-Taking* (R9): Ability to rapidly perform tests that are relatively easy or that require very simple decisions (probable).

OTHER VARIABLES THAT MAY INFLUENCE TEST PERFORMANCE

Background and Environmental	**Individual and Situational**	Degree of Linguistic Demand
• Vision difficulties	• Attention span/distractibility • Concentration • Distractibility • Visual acuity • Reflectivity/impulsivity • Verbal elaboration • Visual elaboration • Planning • Ability to perform under time pressure	Degree of Cultural Loading

Degree of Linguistic Demand table:

	L	M	H
L		■	
M			
H			

[a] Cross-battery estimates. See Table 4-2 for the definition of the terms and keys used on this page.

Battery: WAIS-III   **Test: Information**   **Age Range: 16 to 89 years**

Description of test: The examinee is required to respond to a series of orally presented questions that tap one's knowledge about common events, objects, places, and people.

BASIC PSYCHOMETRIC CHARACTERISTICS

Low / Medium / High — Poor / Fair / Good — (Item gradients only)

Reliability

g loading / g loading [a]

Specificity / Specificity [a]

Item gradients

Test floor   Test ceiling

Inadequate at ages:

***Gf-Gc* CLASSIFICATIONS (Broad:stratum II / *Narrow:stratum I*)**

Crystallized Intelligence (*Gc*): The breadth and depth of a person's acquired knowledge of a culture and the effective application of this knowledge (Empirical: strong).
- *General Information* (K0): Range of general knowledge (probable).

OTHER VARIABLES THAT MAY INFLUENCE TEST PERFORMANCE

Background and Environmental   **Individual and Situational**

- Environmental stimulation
- Educational opportunities/experiences
- Alertness to the environment
- Intellectual curiosity

Degree of Linguistic Demand

	L	M	H
Degree of Cultural Loading — L			
M			
H			■

[a] Cross-battery estimates. See Table 4-2 for the definition of the terms and keys used on this page.

Battery: WAIS-III   **Test: Letter-Number Sequencing**   **Age Range: 16 to 89 years**

Description of test: The examinee is presented orally a series of letters and numbers in a mixed-up order and is required to say the complete list with the numbers first in ascending order and then the letters in alphabetical order.

BASIC PSYCHOMETRIC CHARACTERISTICS	Low Medium High	Poor Fair Good	(Item gradients only)

	20 25 30 35 40 45 50 55 60 65 70 75 80
	3 4 5 6 7 8 9 10 11 12 13 14 15 16 17 18 19 24 29 34 39 44 49 54 59 64 69 74 79 84 85+

Reliability

g loading
g loading [a]

Specificity
Specificity [a]

Item gradients

	Test floor	Test ceiling
Inadequate at ages:		

Gf-Gc CLASSIFICATIONS (**Broad:stratum II** / *Narrow:stratum I*)

Short-Term Memory (*Gsm*): The ability to apprehend and hold information in immediate awareness and then use it within a few seconds (Logical).
- *Working Memory* (MW): Ability to temporarily store and perform a set of cognitive operations on information that that requires divided attention and the management of the limited capacity of short-term memory.

OTHER VARIABLES THAT MAY INFLUENCE TEST PERFORMANCE

Background and Environmental

- Hearing difficulties

Individual and Situational

- Attention span/distractibility
- Concentration
- Distractibility
- Verbal rehearsal
- Visual elaboration

Degree of Linguistic Demand

	L	M	H
Degree of Cultural Loading — L			■
M			
H			

---

[a] Cross-battery estimates. See Table 4-2 for the definition of the terms and keys used on this page.

Battery: WAIS-III   **Test: Matrix Reasoning**   **Age Range: 16 to 89 years**

Description of test: The examinee is presented a series of geometric shapes in an incomplete grid and must identify the correct answer that completes the grid from five different options.

BASIC PSYCHOMETRIC CHARACTERISTICS	Low / Medium / High	Poor / Fair / Good	(Item gradients only)

	3	4	5	6	7	8	9	10	11	12	13	14	15	16	17	18	19	20–24	25–29	30–34	35–39	40–44	45–49	50–54	55–59	60–64	65–69	70–74	75–79	80–84	85+

Reliability

g loading
g loading [a]

Specificity
Specificity [a]

Item gradients

	Test floor	Test ceiling
Inadequate at ages:		

Gf-Gc CLASSIFICATIONS (**Broad:stratum II** / *Narrow:stratum I*)

Fluid Intelligence (*Gf*): The ability to solve relatively novel tasks that cannot be performed automatically by forming and recognizing concepts, identifying relations, perceiving relationships among patterns, drawing inferences, comprehending implications, problem solving, extrapolating, and reorganizing or transforming information (Logical).
- *Induction* (I): Ability to discover the underlying characteristic (e.g., rule, concept, process, trend, class membership) that governs a problem or a set of materials (probable).

OTHER VARIABLES THAT MAY INFLUENCE TEST PERFORMANCE

Background and Environmental	**Individual and Situational**	Degree of Linguistic Demand
• Vision difficulties	• Reflectivity/impulsivity • Field dependence/independence • Flexibility/inflexibility • Planning • Color blindness	Degree of Cultural Loading

Degree of Linguistic Demand

	L	M	H
L	■		
M			
H			

[a] Cross-battery estimates. See Table 4-2 for the definition of the terms and keys used on this page.

Battery: WAIS-III   **Test: Object Assembly**   **Age Range: 16 to 89 years**

Description of test: The examinee is required to assemble a set of puzzles of common objects into meaningful wholes. This is a timed test.

BASIC PSYCHOMETRIC CHARACTERISTICS   Low / Medium / High   Poor / Fair / Good   (Item gradients only)

| | 3 | 4 | 5 | 6 | 7 | 8 | 9 | 10 | 11 | 12 | 13 | 14 | 15 | 16 | 17 | 18 | 19 | 20-24 | 25-29 | 30-34 | 35-39 | 40-44 | 45-49 | 50-54 | 55-59 | 60-64 | 65-69 | 70-74 | 75-79 | 80-84 | 85+ |

Reliability

g loading
g loading [a]

Specificity
Specificity [a]

Item gradients

	Test floor	**Test ceiling**
Inadequate at ages:		

Gf-Gc CLASSIFICATIONS (**Broad:stratum II** / *Narrow:stratum I*)

Visual Processing (*Gv*): The ability to generate, perceive, analyze, synthesize, manipulate, transform, and think with visual patterns and stimuli (Empirical: strong).
- *Closure Speed* (CS): Ability to quickly combine disconnected, vague, or partially obscured visual stimuli or patterns into a meaningful whole, without knowing in advance what the pattern is (probable).
- *Spatial Relations* (SR): Ability to rapidly perceive and manipulate visual patterns or to maintain orientation with respect to objects in space (possible).

OTHER VARIABLES THAT MAY INFLUENCE TEST PERFORMANCE

Background and Environmental
- Alertness to the environment

Individual and Situational
- Reflectivity/impulsivity
- Field dependence/independence
- Planning
- Ability to perform under time pressure

Degree of Linguistic Demand: L M H
Degree of Cultural Loading: L M H

[a] Cross-battery estimates. See Table 4-2 for the definition of the terms and keys used on this page.

Battery: WAIS-III   **Test: Picture Arrangement**   **Age Range: 16 to 89 years**

Description of test: The examinee is required to arrange a set of pictures, presented in a mixed-up order, into a logical story sequence. This is a timed test.

BASIC PSYCHOMETRIC CHARACTERISTICS

Low		Poor	
Medium		Fair	(Item
High		Good	gradients only)

	3 4 5 6 7 8 9 10 11 12 13 14 15 16 17 18 19	20 25 30 35 40 45 50 55 60 65 70 75 80 / 24 29 34 39 44 49 54 59 64 69 74 79 84 85+

Reliability

g loading
g loading [a]

Specificity
Specificity [a]

Item gradients

	Test floor	Test ceiling
Inadequate at ages:	Ages 65 to 89	

Gf-Gc CLASSIFICATIONS (Broad:stratum II / *Narrow:stratum I*)

Visual Processing (*Gv*): The ability to generate, perceive, analyze, synthesize, manipulate, transform, and think with visual patterns and stimuli (Empirical: mixed).
- *Visualization* (Vz): Ability to mentally manipulate objects or visual patterns and to "see" how they would appear under altered conditions (possible).

Crystallized Intelligence (*Gc*): The breadth and depth of a person's acquired knowledge of a culture and the effective application of this knowledge (Empirical: mixed).
- *General Information* (K0): Range of general knowledge (possible).

OTHER VARIABLES THAT MAY INFLUENCE TEST PERFORMANCE

Background and Environmental
- Alertness to the environment
- Educational opportunities/experiences
- Vision difficulties

Individual and Situational
- Reflectivity/impulsivity
- Flexibility/inflexibility
- Planning
- Ability to perform under time pressure

Degree of Linguistic Demand

		L	M	H
Degree of Cultural Loading	L			
	M		■	
	H			

[a] Cross-battery estimates. See Table 4-2 for the definition of the terms and keys used on this page.

Battery: WAIS-III   **Test: Picture Completion**   **Age Range: 16 to 89 years**

Description of test: The examinee is required to identify an important part that is missing from a set of pictures of common objects and scenes.

		BASIC PSYCHOMETRIC CHARACTERISTICS	Low / Medium / High	Poor / Fair / Good	(Item gradients only)

	3 4 5 6 7 8 9 10 11 12 13 14 15 16 17 18 19	20 25 30 35 40 45 50 55 60 65 70 75 80 / 24 29 34 39 44 49 54 59 64 69 74 79 84 85+
Reliability		
g loading / **g loading** [a]		
Specificity / **Specificity** [a]		
Item gradients		

	Test floor	Test ceiling
Inadequate at ages:		

Gf-Gc CLASSIFICATIONS (Broad:stratum II / *Narrow:stratum I*)

Visual Processing (*Gv*): The ability to generate, perceive, analyze, synthesize, manipulate, transform, and think with visual patterns and stimuli (Empirical: mixed).
- *Flexibility of Closure* (CF): Ability to identify a visual figure or pattern embedded in a complex visual array, when knowing in advance what the pattern is (possible).

Crystallized Intelligence (*Gc*): The breadth and depth of a person's acquired knowledge of a culture and the effective application of this knowledge (Empirical: mixed).
- *General Information* (K0): Range of general knowledge (possible).

OTHER VARIABLES THAT MAY INFLUENCE TEST PERFORMANCE

Background and Environmental	**Individual and Situational**
• Vision difficulties	• Visual acuity
• Alertness to the environment	• Field dependence/independence

Degree of Linguistic Demand

		L	M	H
Degree of Cultural Loading	L			
	M			
	H	■		

[a] Cross-battery estimates. See Table 4-2 for the definition of the terms and keys used on this page.

Battery: WAIS-III   **Test: Similarities**   **Age Range: 16 to 89 years**

Description of test: The examinee is presented pairs of words orally and is required to explain the similarity of the common objects or concepts they represent.

BASIC PSYCHOMETRIC CHARACTERISTICS	Low Medium High	Poor Fair Good	(Item gradients only)

	3	4	5	6	7	8	9	10	11	12	13	14	15	16	17	18	19	20 24	25 29	30 34	35 39	40 44	45 49	50 54	55 59	60 64	65 69	70 74	75 79	80 84	85+
Reliability																															
g loading **g loading** [a]																															
Specificity **Specificity** [a]																															
Item gradients																															

	Test floor	Test ceiling
Inadequate at ages:		

Gf-Gc CLASSIFICATIONS (Broad:stratum II / *Narrow:stratum I*)

Crystallized Intelligence (*Gc*): The breadth and depth of a person's acquired knowledge of a culture and the effective application of this knowledge (Empirical: strong).
- *Language Development* (LD): General development, or the understanding of words, sentences, and paragraphs (not requiring reading) in spoken native language skills (probable).
- *Lexical Knowledge* (VL): Extent of vocabulary that can be understood in terms of correct word meanings (possible).

OTHER VARIABLES THAT MAY INFLUENCE TEST PERFORMANCE

Background and Environmental   **Individual and Situational**

- Language stimulation
- Environmental stimulation
- Educational opportunities/experiences

Degree of Linguistic Demand

		L	M	H
Degree of	L			
Cultural	M			
Loading	H			■

---

[a] Cross-battery estimates. See Table 4-2 for the definition of the terms and keys used on this page.

Battery: WAIS-III   **Test: Symbol Search**   **Age Range: 16 to 89 years**

Description of test: The examinee is required to scan a series of paired groups of symbols, each pair consisting of a target group and a search group, and indicate whether or not a target symbol appears in the search group. The examinee is required to perform this task as quickly as possible. This is a timed test.

BASIC PSYCHOMETRIC CHARACTERISTICS

	Low		Poor	
	Medium		Fair	(Item
	High		Good	gradients only)

	3	4	5	6	7	8	9	10	11	12	13	14	15	16	17	18	19	20 24	25 29	30 34	35 39	40 44	45 49	50 54	55 59	60 64	65 69	70 74	75 79	80 84	85+

Reliability

g loading
g loading [a]

Specificity
Specificity [a]

Item gradients

	Test floor	Test ceiling
Inadequate at ages:		

Gf-Gc CLASSIFICATIONS (Broad:stratum II / *Narrow:stratum I*)

Processing Speed (*Gs*): The ability to fluently perform cognitive tasks automatically, especially when under pressure to maintain focused attention and concentration (Logical).
- *Perceptual Speed* (P): Ability to rapidly search for and compare visual symbols presented side or separated in a visual field (probable).
- *Rate-of-Test-Taking* (R9): Ability to rapidly perform tests that are relatively easy or that require very simple decisions (probable).

OTHER VARIABLES THAT MAY INFLUENCE TEST PERFORMANCE

Background and Environmental	**Individual and Situational**
• Vision difficulties	• Attention span/distractibility
	• Concentration
	• Distractibility
	• Visual acuity
	• Reflectivity/impulsivity
	• Verbal elaboration
	• Visual elaboration
	• Planning
	• Ability to perform under time pressure

Degree of Linguistic Demand

		L	M	H
Degree of	L		■	
Cultural	M			
Loading	H			

[a] Cross-battery estimates. See Table 4-2 for the definition of the terms and keys used on this page.

Battery: WAIS-III   **Test: Vocabulary**   **Age Range: 16 to 89 years**

Description of test: The examinee is required to orally define a series of orally presented words.

| | BASIC PSYCHOMETRIC CHARACTERISTICS | Low Medium High | Poor Fair Good | (Item gradients only) |

| | 3 4 5 6 7 8 9 10 11 12 13 14 15 16 17 18 19 | 20 25 30 35 40 45 50 55 60 65 70 75 80 / 24 29 34 39 44 49 54 59 64 69 74 79 84 85+ |

Reliability

g loading
g loading [a]

Specificity
Specificity [a]

Item gradients

	Test floor	Test ceiling
Inadequate at ages:		

Gf-Gc CLASSIFICATIONS (**Broad:stratum II** / *Narrow:stratum I*)

Crystallized Intelligence (*Gc*): The breadth and depth of a person's acquired knowledge of a culture and the effective application of this knowledge (Empirical: strong).
- *Language Development* (LD): General development, or the understanding of words, sentences, and paragraphs (not requiring reading) in spoken native language skills (probable).
- *Lexical Knowledge* (VL): Extent of vocabulary that can be understood in terms of correct word meanings (probable).

OTHER VARIABLES THAT MAY INFLUENCE TEST PERFORMANCE

Background and Environmental   **Individual and Situational**

- Language stimulation
- Environmental stimulation
- Educational opportunities/experiences
- Alertness to the environment
- Intellectual curiosity

Degree of Linguistic Demand

		L	M	H
Degree of Cultural Loading	L			
	M			
	H			■

[a] Cross-battery estimates. See Table 4-2 for the definition of the terms and keys used on this page.

Battery: WISC-III   **Test: Arithmetic**   **Age Range: 6 to 16 years**

Description of test: The examinee is required to mentally solve a series of orally presented arithmetic problems and respond orally.

BASIC PSYCHOMETRIC CHARACTERISTICS	Low / Medium / High	Poor / Fair / Good	(Item gradients only)

	20 25 30 35 40 45 50 55 60 65 70 75 80
	3 4 5 6 7 8 9 10 11 12 13 14 15 16 17 18 19 24 29 34 39 44 49 54 59 64 69 74 79 84 85+

Reliability

g loading
g loading [a]

Specificity
Specificity [a]

Item gradients

	Test floor	**Test ceiling**
Inadequate at ages:		

Gf-Gc CLASSIFICATIONS (Broad:stratum II / *Narrow:stratum I*)

Quantitative Knowledge (*Gq*): An individual's store of acquired quantitative declarative and procedural knowledge (Empirical: strong).
- *Mathematical Achievement* (A3): Measured mathematics achievement (probable).

Fluid Intelligence (*Gf*): The ability to solve relatively novel tasks that cannot be performed automatically by forming and recognizing concepts, identifying relations, perceiving relationships among patterns, drawing inferences, comprehending implications, problem solving, extrapolating, and reorganizing or transforming information (Logical).
- *Quantitative Reasoning* (RQ): Ability to inductively and deductively reason with concepts involving mathematical relations and properties (possible).

OTHER VARIABLES THAT MAY INFLUENCE TEST PERFORMANCE

Background and Environmental
- Math difficulties
- Educational opportunities/experiences
- Hearing difficulties

Individual and Situational
- Attention span/distractibility
- Concentration
- Distractibility
- Visual elaboration

Degree of Linguistic Demand

	L	M	H
Degree of Cultural Loading	L		
	M	■	
	H		

[a] Cross-battery estimates. See Table 4-2 for the definition of the terms and keys used on this page.

Battery: WISC-III   **Test: Block Design**   **Age Range: 6 to 16 years**

Description of test: The examinee is required to replicate a set of modeled or printed two-dimensional geometric patterns using two-color cubes. This is a timed test.

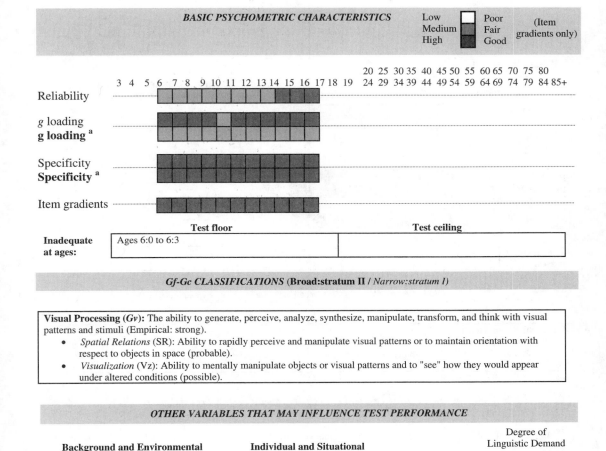

Gf-Gc CLASSIFICATIONS (**Broad:stratum II** / *Narrow:stratum I*)

Visual Processing (*Gv*): The ability to generate, perceive, analyze, synthesize, manipulate, transform, and think with visual patterns and stimuli (Empirical: strong).
- *Spatial Relations* (SR): Ability to rapidly perceive and manipulate visual patterns or to maintain orientation with respect to objects in space (probable).
- *Visualization* (Vz): Ability to mentally manipulate objects or visual patterns and to "see" how they would appear under altered conditions (possible).

OTHER VARIABLES THAT MAY INFLUENCE TEST PERFORMANCE

Background and Environmental	**Individual and Situational**
	• Reflectivity/impulsivity
	• Field dependence/independence
	• Flexibility/inflexibility
	• Planning
	• Ability to perform under time pressure

Degree of Linguistic Demand

	L	M	H
Degree of Cultural Loading — L		■	
M			
H			

[a] Cross-battery estimates. See Table 4-2 for the definition of the terms and keys used on this page.

Battery: WISC-III   **Test: Coding**   **Age Range: 6 to 16 years**

Description of test: The examinee is required to draw symbols that are paired with a series of simple shapes (Coding A) or numbers (Coding B) according to a key. The examinee is required to perform the task as quickly as possible. The test is timed.

BASIC PSYCHOMETRIC CHARACTERISTICS

Low / Medium / High — Poor / Fair / Good — (Item gradients only)

| | 3 4 5 6 7 8 9 10 11 12 13 14 15 16 17 18 19 | 20 25 30 35 40 45 50 55 60 65 70 75 80 / 24 29 34 39 44 49 54 59 64 69 74 79 84 85+ |

Reliability

g loading / **g loading** [a]

Specificity / **Specificity** [a]

Item gradients

| Inadequate at ages: | **Test floor** | **Test ceiling** |

Gf-Gc CLASSIFICATIONS (**Broad:stratum II** / *Narrow:stratum I*)

Processing Speed (*Gs*): The ability to fluently perform cognitive tasks automatically, especially when under pressure to maintain focused attention and concentration (Empirical: strong).
- *Rate-of-Test-Taking* (R9): Ability to rapidly perform tests that are relatively easy or that require very simple decisions (probable).

OTHER VARIABLES THAT MAY INFLUENCE TEST PERFORMANCE

Background and Environmental
- Vision difficulties

Individual and Situational
- Attention span/distractibility
- Concentration
- Distractibility
- Visual acuity
- Reflectivity/impulsivity
- Verbal elaboration
- Visual elaboration
- Planning
- Ability to perform under time pressure

Degree of Linguistic Demand

	L	M	H

Degree of Cultural Loading
L
M
H

[a] Cross-battery estimates. See Table 4-2 for the definition of the terms and keys used on this page.

Battery: WISC-III   **Test: Comprehension**   **Age Range: 6 to 16 years**

Description of test: The examinee is required to respond orally to orally presented questions that focus on everyday problems or understanding of social rules and concepts.

BASIC PSYCHOMETRIC CHARACTERISTICS	Low Medium High	Poor Fair Good	(Item gradients only)

	3 4 5 6 7 8 9 10 11 12 13 14 15 16 17 18 19	20 25 30 35 40 45 50 55 60 65 70 75 80 24 29 34 39 44 49 54 59 64 69 74 79 84 85+
Reliability		
g loading **g loading** [a]		
Specificity **Specificity** [a]		
Item gradients		

	Test floor	**Test ceiling**
Inadequate at ages:		

Gf-Gc CLASSIFICATIONS (**Broad:stratum II** / *Narrow:stratum I*)

Crystallized Intelligence (*Gc*): The breadth and depth of a person's acquired knowledge of a culture and the effective application of this knowledge (Empirical: strong).
- *Language Development* (LD): General development, or the understanding of words, sentences, and paragraphs (not requiring reading) in spoken native language skills (probable).
- *General Information* (K0): Range of general knowledge (probable).

OTHER VARIABLES THAT MAY INFLUENCE TEST PERFORMANCE

Background and Environmental   **Individual and Situational**

- Language stimulation
- Environmental stimulation
- Educational opportunities/experiences
- Alertness to the environment

Degree of Linguistic Demand

		L	M	H
Degree of	L			
Cultural	M			
Loading	H			

[a] Cross-battery estimates. See Table 4-2 for the definition of the terms and keys used on this page.

Battery: WISC-III   **Test: Digit Span**   **Age Range: 6 to 16 years**

Description of test: The examinee is required to repeat verbatim or in a reversed order a series of orally presented number sequences.

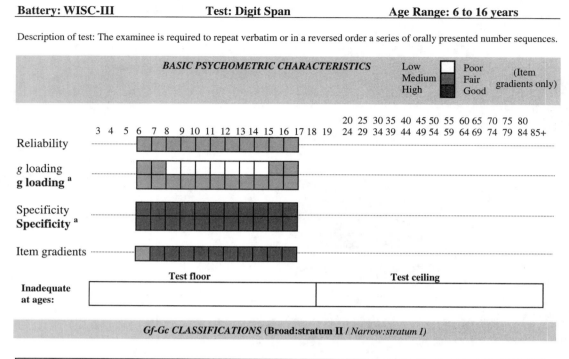

Gf-Gc CLASSIFICATIONS (**Broad:stratum II** / *Narrow:stratum I*)

Short-Term Memory (*Gsm*): The ability to apprehend and hold information in immediate awareness and then use it within a few seconds (Empirical: strong).
- *Memory Span* (MS): Ability to attend to and immediately recall temporally ordered elements in the correct order after a single presentation (probable).

OTHER VARIABLES THAT MAY INFLUENCE TEST PERFORMANCE

Background and Environmental
- Hearing difficulties

Individual and Situational
- Attention span/distractibility
- Concentration
- Distractibility
- Verbal rehearsal
- Visual elaboration
- Organization

Degree of Linguistic Demand

	L	M	H
Degree of Cultural L		■	
Loading M			
H			

[a] Cross-battery estimates. See Table 4-2 for the definition of the terms and keys used on this page.

Battery: WISC-III   **Test: Information**   **Age Range: 6 to 16 years**

Description of test: The examinee is required to respond to a series of orally presented questions that tap knowledge about common events, objects, places, and people.

BASIC PSYCHOMETRIC CHARACTERISTICS

	Low		Poor	
	Medium		Fair	(Item
	High		Good	gradients only)

| | 20 25 30 35 40 45 50 55 60 65 70 75 80 |
| 3 4 5 6 7 8 9 10 11 12 13 14 15 16 17 18 19 | 24 29 34 39 44 49 54 59 64 69 74 79 84 85+ |

Reliability

g loading
g loading [a]

Specificity
Specificity [a]

Item gradients

	Test floor	**Test ceiling**
Inadequate at ages:	Ages 6:0 to 6:3	

Gf-Gc CLASSIFICATIONS (Broad:stratum II / Narrow:stratum I)

Crystallized Intelligence (Gc): The breadth and depth of a person's acquired knowledge of a culture and the effective application of this knowledge (Empirical: strong).
- *General Information* (K0): Range of general knowledge (probable).

OTHER VARIABLES THAT MAY INFLUENCE TEST PERFORMANCE

Background and Environmental   **Individual and Situational**

- Environmental stimulation
- Educational opportunities/experiences
- Alertness to the environment
- Intellectual curiosity

Degree of Linguistic Demand

		L	M	H
Degree of	L			
Cultural	M			
Loading	H			■

---

[a] Cross-battery estimates. See Table 4-2 for the definition of the terms and keys used on this page.

Battery: WISC-III　　　　　　**Test: Mazes**　　　　　　**Age Range: 6 to 16 years**

Description of test: The examinee is required to solve, with a pencil, a series of increasingly difficult mazes.

BASIC PSYCHOMETRIC CHARACTERISTICS	Low ☐ Poor	(Item
	Medium ▨ Fair	gradients only)
	High ■ Good	

	3 4 5 6 7 8 9 10 11 12 13 14 15 16 17 18 19	20 25 30 35 40 45 50 55 60 65 70 75 80 / 24 29 34 39 44 49 54 59 64 69 74 79 84 85
Reliability		
g loading / **g loading** [a]		
Specificity / **Specificity** [a]		
Item gradients		

	Test floor	Test ceiling
Inadequate at ages:		

Gf-Gc CLASSIFICATIONS (**Broad:stratum II** / *Narrow:stratum I*)

Visual Processing (*Gv*): The ability to generate, perceive, analyze, synthesize, manipulate, transform, and think with visual patterns and stimuli (Empirical: strong).
- *Spatial Scanning* (SS): Ability to accurately and quickly survey a spatial field or pattern and identify a path through the visual field or pattern (probable).

OTHER VARIABLES THAT MAY INFLUENCE TEST PERFORMANCE

Background and Environmental

- Vision difficulties

Individual and Situational

- Visual-motor coordination
- Reflectivity/impulsivity
- Field dependence/independence
- Planning
- Ability to perform under time pressure

Degree of Linguistic Demand

Degree of Cultural Loading		L	M	H
	L			
	M	■		
	H			

[a] Cross-battery estimates. See Table 4-2 for the definition of the terms and keys used on this page.

Battery: WISC-III   **Test: Object Assembly**   **Age Range: 6 to 16 years**

Description of test: The examinee is required to assemble a set of puzzles of common objects into meaningful wholes. This is a timed test.

BASIC PSYCHOMETRIC CHARACTERISTICS	Low Medium High	Poor Fair Good	(Item gradients only)

	3 4 5 6 7 8 9 10 11 12 13 14 15 16 17 18 19	20 25 30 35 40 45 50 55 60 65 70 75 80 24 29 34 39 44 49 54 59 64 69 74 79 84 85+
Reliability		
g loading **g loading** [a]		
Specificity **Specificity** [a]		
Item gradients		

	Test floor	Test ceiling
Inadequate at ages:		

Gf-Gc CLASSIFICATIONS (**Broad:stratum II** / *Narrow:stratum I*)

Visual Processing (*Gv*): The ability to generate, perceive, analyze, synthesize, manipulate, transform, and think with visual patterns and stimuli (Empirical: strong).
- *Closure Speed* (CS): Ability to quickly combine disconnected, vague, or partially obscured visual stimuli or patterns into a meaningful whole, without knowing in advance what the pattern is (probable).
- *Spatial Relations* (SR): Ability to rapidly perceive and manipulate visual patterns or to maintain orientation with respect to objects in space (possible).

OTHER VARIABLES THAT MAY INFLUENCE TEST PERFORMANCE

Background and Environmental	**Individual and Situational**	Degree of Linguistic Demand

			L	M	H

- Alertness to the environment

- Reflectivity/impulsivity
- Field dependence/independence
- Planning
- Ability to perform under time pressure

Degree of Cultural Loading

	L	M	H
L			
M	■		
H			

[a] Cross-battery estimates. See Table 4-2 for the definition of the terms and keys used on this page.

<u>**Battery: WISC-III**</u>   <u>**Test: Picture Arrangement**</u>   <u>**Age Range: 6 to 16 years**</u>

Description of test: The examinee is required to arrange a set of pictures, presented in a mixed-up order, into a logical story
          sequence. This is a timed test.

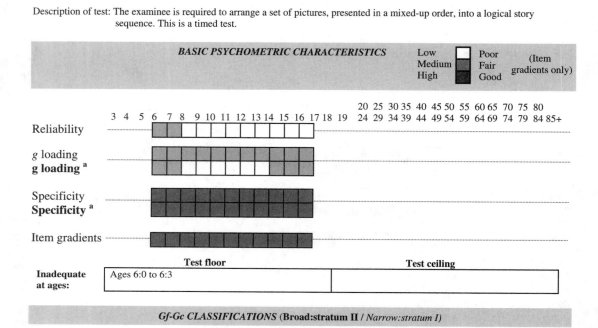

^a Cross-battery estimates. See Table 4-2 for the definition of the terms and keys used on this page.

Battery: WISC-III · · · · · · · · **Test: Picture Completion** · · · · · · · · **Age Range: 6 to 16 years**

Description of test: The examinee is required to identify an important part that is missing from a set of pictures of common objects and scenes.

BASIC PSYCHOMETRIC CHARACTERISTICS

Low / Medium / High □ Poor / Fair / Good (Item gradients only)

	3 4 5 6 7 8 9 10 11 12 13 14 15 16 17 18 19	20 25 30 35 40 45 50 55 60 65 70 75 80 / 24 29 34 39 44 49 54 59 64 69 74 79 84 85+
Reliability		
g loading / g loading a		
Specificity / Specificity a		
Item gradients		

Test floor · · · Test ceiling

Inadequate at ages:		

***Gf-Gc* CLASSIFICATIONS** (**Broad:stratum II** / *Narrow:stratum I*)

Visual Processing (*Gv*): The ability to generate, perceive, analyze, synthesize, manipulate, transform, and think with visual patterns and stimuli (Empirical: mixed).
- *Flexibility of Closure* (CF): Ability to identify a visual figure or pattern embedded in a complex visual array, when knowing in advance what the pattern is (possible).

Crystallized Intelligence (*Gc*): The breadth and depth of a person's acquired knowledge of a culture and the effective application of this knowledge (Empirical: mixed).
- *General Information* (K0): Range of general knowledge (possible).

OTHER VARIABLES THAT MAY INFLUENCE TEST PERFORMANCE

Background and Environmental
- Vision difficulties
- Alertness to the environment

Individual and Situational
- Visual acuity
- Field dependence/independence

Degree of Linguistic Demand

		L	M	H
Degree of Cultural Loading	L			
	M			
	H	■		

a Cross-battery estimates. See Table 4-2 for the definition of the terms and keys used on this page.

Battery: WISC-III   **Test: Similarities**   **Age Range: 6 to 16 years**

Description of test: The examinee is presented pairs of words orally and is required to explain the similarity of the common objects or concepts they represent.

	BASIC PSYCHOMETRIC CHARACTERISTICS	Low		Poor	
		Medium		Fair	(Item
		High		Good	gradients only)

		20 25 30 35 40 45 50 55 60 65 70 75 80
	3 4 5 6 7 8 9 10 11 12 13 14 15 16 17 18 19	24 29 34 39 44 49 54 59 64 69 74 79 84 85+

Reliability

g loading
g loading [a]

Specificity
Specificity [a]

Item gradients

	Test floor	**Test ceiling**
Inadequate at ages:	Ages 6:0 to 6:3	

Gf-Gc CLASSIFICATIONS (**Broad:stratum II** / *Narrow:stratum I*)

Crystallized Intelligence (*Gc*): The breadth and depth of a person's acquired knowledge of a culture and the effective application of this knowledge (Empirical: strong).
- *Language Development* (LD): General development, or the understanding of words, sentences, and paragraphs (not requiring reading) in spoken native language skills (probable).
- *Lexical Knowledge* (VL): Extent of vocabulary that can be understood in terms of correct word meanings (possible).

OTHER VARIABLES THAT MAY INFLUENCE TEST PERFORMANCE

Background and Environmental   **Individual and Situational**

- Language stimulation
- Environmental stimulation
- Educational opportunities/experiences

Degree of
Linguistic Demand

		L	M	H
Degree of	L			
Cultural	M			
Loading	H			

[a] Cross-battery estimates. See Table 4-2 for the definition of the terms and keys used on this page.

Battery: WISC-III	Test: Symbol Search	Age Range: 6 to 16 years

Description of test: The examinee is required to scan a series of paired groups of symbols, each pair consisting of a target group and a search group, and indicate whether or not a target symbol appears in the search group. The examinee is required to perform this task as quickly as possible. This is a timed test.

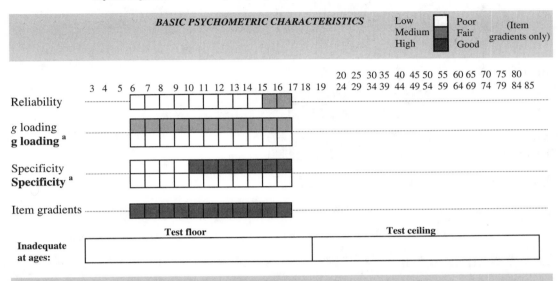

BASIC PSYCHOMETRIC CHARACTERISTICS

Low — Poor
Medium — Fair
High — Good
(Item gradients only)

Reliability

g loading
g loading [a]

Specificity
Specificity [a]

Item gradients

Test floor   Test ceiling

Inadequate at ages:

Gf-Gc CLASSIFICATIONS (**Broad:stratum II** / *Narrow:stratum I*)

Processing Speed (*Gs*): The ability to fluently perform cognitive tasks automatically, especially when under pressure to maintain focused attention and concentration (Logical).
- *Perceptual Speed* (P): Ability to rapidly search for and compare visual symbols presented side or separated in a visual field (probable).
- *Rate-of-Test-Taking* (R9): Ability to rapidly perform tests that are relatively easy or that require very simple decisions (probable).

OTHER VARIABLES THAT MAY INFLUENCE TEST PERFORMANCE

Background and Environmental
- Vision difficulties

Individual and Situational
- Attention span/distractibility
- Concentration
- Distractibility
- Visual acuity
- Reflectivity/impulsivity
- Verbal elaboration
- Visual elaboration
- Planning
- Ability to perform under time pressure

Degree of Linguistic Demand

	L	M	H
Degree of Cultural Loading — L		■	
M			
H			

[a] Cross-battery estimates. See Table 4-2 for the definition of the terms and keys used on this page.

Battery: WISC-III   **Test: Vocabulary**   **Age Range: 6 to 16 years**

Description of test: The examinee is required to define orally a series of orally presented words.

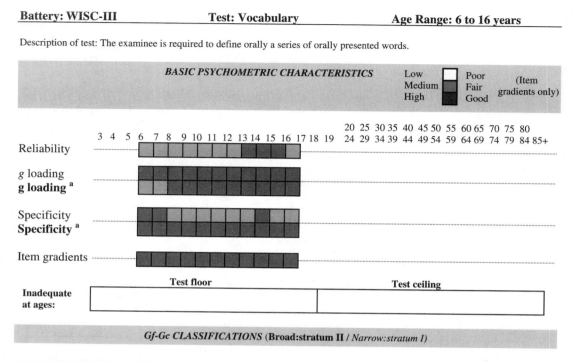

	Low		Poor	
	Medium		Fair	(Item
	High		Good	gradients only)

BASIC PSYCHOMETRIC CHARACTERISTICS

	3 4 5 6 7 8 9 10 11 12 13 14 15 16 17 18 19	20 25 30 35 40 45 50 55 60 65 70 75 80 / 24 29 34 39 44 49 54 59 64 69 74 79 84 85+
Reliability		
g loading / **g loading** [a]		
Specificity / **Specificity** [a]		
Item gradients		

	Test floor	Test ceiling
Inadequate at ages:		

Gf-Gc **CLASSIFICATIONS (Broad:stratum II** / *Narrow:stratum I*)

Crystallized Intelligence (Gc): The breadth and depth of a person's acquired knowledge of a culture and the effective application of this knowledge (Empirical: strong).
- *Language Development* (LD): General development, or the understanding of words, sentences, and paragraphs (not requiring reading) in spoken native language skills (probable).
- *Lexical Knowledge* (VL): Extent of vocabulary that can be understood in terms of correct word meanings (probable).

OTHER VARIABLES THAT MAY INFLUENCE TEST PERFORMANCE

Background and Environmental   **Individual and Situational**

- Language stimulation
- Environmental stimulation
- Educational opportunities/experiences
- Alertness to the environment
- Intellectual curiosity

Degree of Linguistic Demand

		L	M	H
Degree of	L			
Cultural	M			
Loading	H			■

[a] Cross-battery estimates. See Table 4-2 for the definition of the terms and keys used on this page.

Battery: WPPSI-R	Test: Animal Pegs	Age Range: 3 to 7 years

Description of test: The examinee is required to place colored pegs in holes on a board according to a key at the top of the board. This is a timed test.

BASIC PSYCHOMETRIC CHARACTERISTICS	Low	☐ Poor	(Item
	Medium	☐ Fair	gradients only)
	High	■ Good	

	3 4 5 6 7 8 9 10 11 12 13 14 15 16 17 18 19	20 25 30 35 40 45 50 55 60 65 70 75 80 / 24 29 34 39 44 49 54 59 64 69 74 79 84 85+
Reliability		
g loading / g loading [a]		
Specificity / Specificity [a]		
Item gradients		

Inadequate at ages:	Test floor	Test ceiling
	Ages 2:11 to 4:2	

Gf-Gc CLASSIFICATIONS (Broad:stratum II / Narrow:stratum I)

Processing Speed (Gs): The ability to fluently perform cognitive tasks automatically, especially when under pressure to maintain focused attention and concentration (Logical).
- *Rate-of-Test-Taking* (R9): Ability to rapidly perform tests that are relatively easy or that require very simple decisions (probable).

OTHER VARIABLES THAT MAY INFLUENCE TEST PERFORMANCE

Background and Environmental
- Vision difficulties

Individual and Situational
- Attention span/distractibility
- Concentration
- Distractibility
- Visual acuity
- Reflectivity/impulsivity
- Verbal elaboration
- Visual elaboration
- Planning
- Ability to perform under time pressure

Degree of Linguistic Demand

		L	M	H
Degree of Cultural Loading	L			
	M		■	
	H			

Typical Age (in years) of Concept Attainment

	3	4	5	> 5	Data not available
Basic Concepts in Test Directions (Frequency of occurrence)	up (1) in (2)	white (3) under (2) top (1) fast (1)	piece (1) different (1) next (1)	right (2) after (1)	black (1) blue (3) yellow (1) row (2) with (7)

[a] Cross-battery estimates. See Table 4-2 for the definition of the terms and keys used on this page.

Battery: WPPSI-R   **Test: Arithmetic**   **Age Range: 3 to 7 years**

Description of test: The examinee is required to mentally solve and respond orally to a series of orally presented arithmetic problems.

BASIC PSYCHOMETRIC CHARACTERISTICS		
Low	Poor (white)	
Medium	Fair (gray)	(Item gradients only)
High	Good (black)	

	3 4 5 6 7 8 9 10 11 12 13 14 15 16 17 18 19	20 25 30 35 40 45 50 55 60 65 70 75 80 / 24 29 34 39 44 49 54 59 64 69 74 79 84 85+
Reliability		
g loading / **g loading** [a]		
Specificity / **Specificity** [a]		
Item gradients		

	Test floor	**Test ceiling**
Inadequate at ages:	Ages 2:11 to 3:8	Ages 6:8 to 7:3

Gf-Gc CLASSIFICATIONS (Broad:stratum II / Narrow:stratum I)

Quantitative Knowledge (Gq): An individual's store of acquired quantitative declarative and procedural knowledge (Empirical: strong).
- *Mathematical Achievement* (A3): Measured mathematics achievement (probable).

Fluid Intelligence (Gf): The ability to solve relatively novel tasks that cannot be performed automatically by forming and recognizing concepts, identifying relations, perceiving relationships among patterns, drawing inferences, comprehending implications, problem solving, extrapolating, and reorganizing or transforming information (Logical).
- *Quantitative Reasoning* (RQ): Ability to inductively and deductively reason with concepts involving mathematical relations and properties (possible).

OTHER VARIABLES THAT MAY INFLUENCE TEST PERFORMANCE

Background and Environmental
- Math difficulties
- Educational opportunities/experiences
- Hearing difficulties

Individual and Situational
- Attention span/distractibility
- Concentration
- Distractibility
- Visual elaboration

Degree of Linguistic Demand

	L	M	H
Degree of Cultural Loading — L			
M		■	
H			

Typical Age (in years) of Concept Attainment

	3	4	5	> 5	Data not available
Basic Concepts in Test Directions (Frequency of occurrence)	on (4) in (2)				some (7)

[a] Cross-battery estimates. See Table 4-2 for the definition of the terms and keys used on this page.

Battery: WPPSI-R	Test: Block Design	Age Range: 3 to 7 years

Description of test: The examinee is required to replicate a set of modeled or printed two-dimensional geometric patterns using two-color cubes. This is a timed test.

BASIC PSYCHOMETRIC CHARACTERISTICS

	Low	Poor	
	Medium	Fair	(Item
	High	Good	gradients only)

Age columns: 3 4 5 6 7 8 9 10 11 12 13 14 15 16 17 18 19 | 20-24 25-29 30-34 35-39 40-44 45-49 50-54 55-59 60-64 65-69 70-74 75-79 80-84 85+

Reliability

g loading
g loading [a]

Specificity
Specificity [a]

Item gradients

	Test floor	Test ceiling
Inadequate at ages:	Ages 2:11 to 4:5	

Gf-Gc CLASSIFICATIONS (Broad:stratum II / *Narrow:stratum I*)

Visual Processing (*Gv*): The ability to generate, perceive, analyze, synthesize, manipulate, transform, and think with visual patterns and stimuli (Empirical: strong).
- *Spatial Relations* (SR): Ability to rapidly perceive and manipulate visual patterns or to maintain orientation with respect to objects in space (probable).
- *Visualization* (Vz): Ability to mentally manipulate objects or visual patterns and to "see" how they would appear under altered conditions (possible).

OTHER VARIABLES THAT MAY INFLUENCE TEST PERFORMANCE

Background and Environmental

Individual and Situational
- Reflectivity/impulsivity
- Field dependence/independence
- Flexibility/inflexibility
- Planning
- Ability to perform under time pressure

Degree of Linguistic Demand

	L	M	H
Degree of	L	■	
Cultural	M		
Loading	H		

Typical Age (in years) of Concept Attainment

Basic Concepts in Test Directions (Frequency of occurrence)	3	4	5	> 5	Data not available
	red (1) up (1) on (1)	one (1) white (3) together (1) through (1)	side (1) like (>15) sample (2)	some (1) another (1)	next to (1)

[a] Cross-battery estimates. See Table 4-2 for the definition of the terms and keys used on this page.

Battery: WPPSI-R   **Test: Comprehension**   **Age Range: 3 to 7 years**

Description of test: The examinee is required to respond orally to orally presented questions that focus on everyday problems or understanding of social rules and concepts.

BASIC PSYCHOMETRIHARACTERISTICS	Low Medium High	Poor Fair Good	(Item gradients only)

	3 4 5 6 7 8 9 10 11 12 13 14 15 16 17 18 19	20 25 30 35 40 45 50 55 60 65 70 75 80 24 29 34 39 44 49 54 59 64 69 74 79 84 85
Reliability		
g loading **g loading** [a]		
Specificity **Specificity** [a]		
Item gradients		

	Test floor	**Test ceiling**
Inadequate at ages:	Ages 2:11 to 4:8	

Crystallized Intelligence (*Gc*): The breadth and depth of a person's acquired knowledge of a culture and the effective application of this knowledge (Empirical: strong).
- *Language Development* (LD): General development, or the understanding of words, sentences, and paragraphs (not requiring reading) in spoken native language skills (probable).
- *General Information* (K0): Range of general knowledge (probable).

OTHER VARIABLES THAT MAY INFLUENCE TEST PERFORMANCE

Background and Environmental   **Individual and Situational**   Degree of Linguistic Demand

- Language stimulation
- Environmental stimulation
- Educational opportunities/experiences
- Alertness to the environment

Degree of Cultural Loading		L M H
	L	
	M	
	H	■

Typical Age (in years) of Concept Attainment

	3	**4**	**5**	**> 5**	**Data not available**
Basic Concepts in Test Directions (Frequency of occurrence)	in (1)	one (1)		another (1)	sick (1) before (1) hot (2) cold (1)

[a] Cross-battery estimates. See Table 4-2 for the definition of the terms and keys used on this page.

Battery: WPPSI-R	Test: Geometric Design	Age Range: 3 to 7 years

Description of test: The examinee is required to examine a simple set of designs, and, with the stimulus in view, point to a design that is exactly like it from an array of four designs. The examinee is then required to draw geometric designs from a printed model.

BASIC PSYCHOMETRIC CHARACTERISTICS	Low Poor (Item Medium Fair gradients only) High Good

	3 4 5 6 7 8 9 10 11 12 13 14 15 16 17 18 19	20 25 30 35 40 45 50 55 60 65 70 75 80 24 29 34 39 44 49 54 59 64 69 74 79 84 85+
Reliability		
g loading **g loading** [a]		
Specificity **Specificity** [a]		
Item gradients		

	Test floor	Test ceiling
Inadequate at ages:	Ages 2:11 to 3:11	Ages 6:5 to 7:3

Gf-Gc CLASSIFICATIONS (Broad:stratum II / *Narrow:stratum I*)

Visual Processing (*Gv*): The ability to generate, perceive, analyze, synthesize, manipulate, transform, and think with visual patterns and stimuli (Logical).
- *Visualization* (Vz): Ability to mentally manipulate objects or visual patterns and to "see" how they would appear under altered conditions (probable).

Psychomotor: (Logical).
- *Finger Dexterity* (P2): Ability to make skillful, coordinated movements of the fingers (probable).

OTHER VARIABLES THAT MAY INFLUENCE TEST PERFORMANCE

Background and Environmental	**Individual and Situational**	Degree of Linguistic Demand
• Vision difficulties • Environmental stimulation	• Visual-motor coordination	L M H Degree of L Cultural M Loading H

	Typical Age (in years) of Concept Attainment				
	3	**4**	**5**	**> 5**	**Data not available**
Basic Concepts in Test Directions (Frequency of occurrence)	up (1) finished (1)	two (2) both (1)	like/alike (>15)		

[a] Cross-battery estimates. See Table 4-2 for the definition of the terms and keys used on this page.

Battery: WPPSI-R   **Test: Information**   **Age Range: 3 to 7 years**

Description of test: The examinee is required to respond to a series of orally presented questions that measure one's knowledge about common events, objects, places, and people.

BASIC PSYCHOMETRIC CHARACTERISTICS	Low Medium High	☐ ▨ ■	Poor Fair Good	(Item gradients only)

	3 4 5 6 7 8 9 10 11 12 13 14 15 16 17 18 19	20 25 30 35 40 45 50 55 60 65 70 75 80 / 24 29 34 39 44 49 54 59 64 69 74 79 84 85+
Reliability	▨▨☐☐☐	
g loading / g loading [a]	▨▨▨▨▨	
Specificity / Specificity [a]	▨▨▨☐☐	
Item gradients	■■■■■	

	Test floor	**Test ceiling**
Inadequate at ages:	Ages 2:11 to 3:11	

Gf-Gc CLASSIFICATIONS (Broad:stratum II / Narrow:stratum I)

Crystallized Intelligence (Gc): The breadth and depth of a person's acquired knowledge of a culture and the effective application of this knowledge (Empirical: strong).
- *General Information* (K0): Range of general knowledge (probable).

OTHER VARIABLES THAT MAY INFLUENCE TEST PERFORMANCE

Background and Environmental   **Individual and Situational**   Degree of Linguistic Demand

- Environmental stimulation
- Educational opportunities/experiences
- Alertness to the environment
- Intellectual curiosity

		L	M	H
Degree of Cultural Loading	L			
	M			
	H			■

Typical Age (in years) of Concept Attainment

	3	4	5	> 5	Data not available
Basic Concepts in Test Directions (Frequency of occurrence)	on (5) in (2)	two (3) together (1)	pieces (1)	another (1) before (1)	four (1) night (1) after (1) wood (1)

[a] Cross-battery estimates. See Table 4-2 for the definition of the terms and keys used on this page.

Battery: WPPSI-R   **Test: Mazes**   **Age Range: 3 to 7 years**

Description of test: The examinee is required to solve, with a pencil, a series of increasingly difficult mazes.

BASIC PSYCHOMETRIC CHARACTERISTICS		Low Medium High	Poor Fair Good	(Item gradients only)

	3 4 5 6 7 8 9 10 11 12 13 14 15 16 17 18 19	20 25 30 35 40 45 50 55 60 65 70 75 80 / 24 29 34 39 44 49 54 59 64 69 74 79 84 85
Reliability		
g loading / g loading ᵃ		
Specificity / Specificity ᵃ		
Item gradients		

	Test floor	Test ceiling
Inadequate at ages:	Ages 2:11 to 3:8	

Gf-Gc CLASSIFICATIONS (Broad:stratum II / Narrow:stratum I)

Visual Processing (Gv): The ability to generate, perceive, analyze, synthesize, manipulate, transform, and think with visual patterns and stimuli (Empirical: moderate).
- *Spatial Scanning* (SS): Ability to accurately and quickly survey a spatial field or pattern and identify a path through the visual field or pattern (probable).

OTHER VARIABLES THAT MAY INFLUENCE TEST PERFORMANCE

Background and Environmental
- Vision difficulties

Individual and Situational
- Visual-motor coordination
- Reflectivity/impulsivity
- Field dependence/independence
- Planning
- Ability to perform under time pressure

Degree of Linguistic Demand

	L	M	H
Degree of Cultural Loading — L			
M	■		
H			

Typical Age (in years) of Concept Attainment

	3	4	5	> 5	Data not available
Basic Concepts in Test Directions (Frequency of occurrence)	on (6) in (2) up (1) out of (1) boy (2) little (2) finished (1)	inside (4) into (7) middle (1)	like (2) wrong (1) all (5)	without (4) another (1) over [direction] (3)	over [time] (2)

ᵃ Cross-battery estimates. See Table 4-2 for the definition of the terms and keys used on this page.

Battery: WPPSI-R   **Test: Object Assembly**   **Age Range: 3 to 7 years**

Description of test: The examinee is required to assemble a set of puzzles of common objects into meaningful wholes. This is a timed test.

BASIC PSYCHOMETRIC CHARACTERISTICS	Low	☐ Poor	
	Medium	▨ Fair	(Item
	High	▨ Good	gradients only)

	3 4 5 6 7 8	9 10 11 12 13 14 15 16 17 18 19	20 25 30 35 40 45 50 55 60 65 70 75 80 / 24 29 34 39 44 49 54 59 64 69 74 79 84 85+
Reliability	☐☐☐☐☐		
g loading / **g loading** [a]	▨▨▨☐		
Specificity / **Specificity** [a]	▨☐☐☐ / ▨▨▨▨		
Item gradients	▨▨▨▨		

Inadequate at ages:	**Test floor**	**Test ceiling**
		Ages 6:5 to 7:3

Gf-Gc CLASSIFICATIONS (Broad:stratum II / *Narrow:stratum I*)

Visual Processing (Gv): The ability to generate, perceive, analyze, synthesize, manipulate, transform, and think with visual patterns and stimuli (Empirical: strong).
- *Closure Speed* (CS): Ability to quickly combine disconnected, vague, or partially obscured visual stimuli or patterns into a meaningful whole, without knowing in advance what the pattern is (probable).
- *Spatial Relations* (SR): Ability to rapidly perceive and manipulate visual patterns or to maintain orientation with respect to objects in space (possible).

OTHER VARIABLES THAT MAY INFLUENCE TEST PERFORMANCE

Background and Environmental
- Alertness to the environment

Individual and Situational
- Reflectivity/impulsivity
- Field dependence/independence
- Planning
- Ability to perform under time pressure

Degree of Linguistic Demand

		L	M	H
Degree of Cultural Loading	L			
	M	■		
	H			

Typical Age (in years) of Concept Attainment

Basic Concepts in Test Directions (Frequency of occurrence)	3	4	5	> 5	Data not available
	in (5) big (2)	together (6) through (2) fast (5)	like (1) pieces (12) all (2)	some (1)	

[a] Cross-battery estimates. See Table 4-2 for the definition of the terms and keys used on this page.

Battery: WPPSI-R   **Test: Picture Completion**   **Age Range: 3 to 7 years**

Description of test: The examinee is required to identify an important part that is missing from a set of pictures of common objects and scenes. This is a timed test.

BASIC PSYCHOMETRIC CHARACTERISTICS		Low	☐	Poor	(Item
		Medium	◨	Fair	gradients only)
		High	■	Good	

| | 3 | 4 | 5 | 6 | 7 | 8 | 9 | 10 | 11 | 12 | 13 | 14 | 15 | 16 | 17 | 18 | 19 | 20 24 | 25 29 | 30 34 | 35 39 | 40 44 | 45 49 | 50 54 | 55 59 | 60 64 | 65 69 | 70 74 | 75 79 | 80 84 | 85+ |

Reliability
g loading
g loading [a]
Specificity
Specificity [a]
Item gradients

	Test floor	**Test ceiling**
Inadequate at ages:	Ages 2:11 to 3:11	

Gf-Gc CLASSIFICATIONS (Broad:stratum II / *Narrow:stratum I*)

Visual Processing (*Gv*): The ability to generate, perceive, analyze, synthesize, manipulate, transform, and think with visual patterns and stimuli (Empirical: mixed).
- *Flexibility of Closure* (CF): Ability to identify a visual figure or pattern embedded in a complex visual array, when knowing in advance what the pattern is (possible).

Crystallized Intelligence (*Gc*): The breadth and depth of a person's acquired knowledge of a culture and the effective application of this knowledge (Empirical: mixed).
- *General Information* (K0): Range of general knowledge (possible).

OTHER VARIABLES THAT MAY INFLUENCE TEST PERFORMANCE

Background and Environmental
- Vision difficulties
- Alertness to the environment

Individual and Situational
- Visual acuity
- Field dependence/independence

Degree of Linguistic Demand

Degree of Cultural Loading	L	M	H
L			
M			
H	■		

Typical Age (in years) of Concept Attainment

	3	4	5	> 5	Data not available
Basic Concepts in Test Directions (Frequency of occurrence)	in (>15)		missing (>15)		

[a] Cross-battery estimates. See Table 4-2 for the definition of the terms and keys used on this page.

Battery: WPPSI-R   **Test: Sentences**   **Age Range: 3 to 7 years**

Description of test: The examinee is required to repeat verbatim sentences that are presented orally.

BASIC PSYCHOMETRIC CHARACTERISTICS	Low ☐	Poor ☐	(Item
	Medium ▨	Fair ▨	gradients only)
	High ■	Good ■	

	3	4	5	6	7	8	9 10 11 12 13 14 15 16 17 18 19	20 25 30 35 40 45 50 55 60 65 70 75 80 / 24 29 34 39 44 49 54 59 64 69 74 79 84 85
Reliability	▨	▨	☐	☐	☐	☐		
g loading / **g loading** [a]	■	■	▨	▨	▨			
	☐	☐	☐	☐	☐			
Specificity / **Specificity** [a]	■	■	■	■	■			
	☐	☐	☐	☐	☐			
Item gradients	▨	■	■	▨	■			

	Test floor	**Test ceiling**
Inadequate at ages:	Ages 2:11 to 3:8	

Gf-Gc CLASSIFICATIONS (Broad:stratum II / *Narrow:stratum I*)

Short-Term Memory (*Gsm*): The ability to apprehend and hold information in immediate awareness and then use it within a few seconds (Logical).
- *Memory Span* (MS): Ability to attend to and immediately recall temporally ordered elements in the correct order after a single presentation (probable).

Crystallized Intelligence (*Gc*): The breadth and depth of a person's acquired knowledge of a culture and the effective application of this knowledge (Logical).
- *Language Development* (LD): General development, or the understanding of words, sentences, and paragraphs (not requiring reading) in spoken native language skills (probable).

OTHER VARIABLES THAT MAY INFLUENCE TEST PERFORMANCE

Background and Environmental
- Hearing difficulties
- Language stimulation

Individual and Situational
- Attention span/distractibility
- Concentration
- Distractibility
- Verbal rehearsal
- Visual elaboration

Degree of
Linguistic Demand

	L	M	H
L			
M			■
H			

Degree of
Cultural
Loading

		Typical Age (in years) of Concept Attainment			
	3	**4**	**5**	**> 5**	**Data not available**
Basic Concepts in Test Directions (Frequency of occurrence)			same (1)	after (1)	

[a] Cross-battery estimates. See Table 4-2 for the definition of the terms and keys used on this page.

Battery: WPPSI-R	Test: Similarities	Age Range: 3 to 7 years

Description of test: The examinee is presented pairs of words orally and is required to explain the similarity of the common objects or concepts they represent.

BASIC PSYCHOMETRIC CHARACTERISTICS

Low / Medium / High — Poor / Fair / Good   (Item gradients only)

	3 4 5 6 7 8 9 10 11 12 13 14 15 16 17 18 19	20 25 30 35 40 45 50 55 60 65 70 75 80 / 24 29 34 39 44 49 54 59 64 69 74 79 84 85+
Reliability		
g loading / **g loading** [a]		
Specificity / **Specificity** [a]		
Item gradients		

	Test floor	Test ceiling
Inadequate at ages:	Ages 2:11 to 4:2	

Gf-Gc CLASSIFICATIONS (Broad:stratum II / Narrow:stratum I)

Crystallized Intelligence (Gc): The breadth and depth of a person's acquired knowledge of a culture and the effective application of this knowledge (Empirical: strong).
- *Language Development* (LD): General development, or the understanding of words, sentences, and paragraphs (not requiring reading) in spoken native language skills (probable).
- *Lexical Knowledge* (VL): Extent of vocabulary that can be understood in terms of correct word meanings (possible).

OTHER VARIABLES THAT MAY INFLUENCE TEST PERFORMANCE

Background and Environmental   **Individual and Situational**

- Language stimulation
- Environmental stimulation
- Educational opportunities/experiences

Degree of Linguistic Demand

	L	M	H
Degree of Cultural Loading L			
M			
H			■

Typical Age (in years) of Concept Attainment

	3	4	5	> 5	Data not available
Basic Concepts in Test Directions (Frequency of occurrence)	in (2) up (1)	together (1) both (1)	like/alike (4) all (4)	another (5)	nickel (1) penny (1)

[a] Cross-battery estimates. See Table 4-2 for the definition of the terms and keys used on this page.

Battery: WPPSI-R   **Test: Vocabulary**   **Age Range: 3 to 7 years**

Description of test: The examinee is required to orally define a series of orally presented words.

BASIC PSYCHOMETRIC CHARACTERISTICS	Low ▢ Poor
	Medium ▨ Fair (Item gradients only)
	High ▣ Good

	3	4	5	6	7	8	9	10	11	12	13	14	15	16	17	18	19	20–24	25–29	30–34	35–39	40–44	45–49	50–54	55–59	60–64	65–69	70–74	75–79	80–85

Reliability

g loading
g loading [a]

Specificity
Specificity [a]

Item gradients

	Test floor	**Test ceiling**
Inadequate at ages:	Ages 2:11 to 3:2	

Gf-Gc CLASSIFICATIONS **(Broad:stratum II** / *Narrow:stratum I*)

Crystallized Intelligence (*Gc*): The breadth and depth of a person's acquired knowledge of a culture and the effective application of this knowledge (Empirical: strong).
- *Language Development* (LD): General development, or the understanding of words, sentences, and paragraphs (not requiring reading) in spoken native language skills (probable).
- *Lexical Knowledge* (VL): Extent of vocabulary that can be understood in terms of correct word meanings (probable).

OTHER VARIABLES THAT MAY INFLUENCE TEST PERFORMANCE

Background and Environmental   **Individual and Situational**   Degree of Linguistic Demand

- Language stimulation
- Environmental stimulation
- Educational opportunities/experiences
- Alertness to the environment
- Intellectual curiosity

	L	M	H
Degree of Cultural Loading — L			
M			
H			■

Typical Age (in years) of Concept Attainment

	3	4	5	> 5	Data not available
Basic Concepts in Test Directions (Frequency of occurrence)				some (2)	

---

[a] Cross-battery estimates. See Table 4-2 for the definition of the terms and keys used on this page.

ENDNOTES

1. This continuum refers to *Gf, Gc, Gsm, Ga, Gv,* and *Gs* abilities. *Gq* and *Grw* were not included because they reflect achievement-like content and are typically measured with achievement tests. If they were to be included on such a continuum, then they would lie at the far end of the continuum (leaving *Gc* somewhere in the middle) because the development of both *Gq* and *Grw* is highly dependent on direct instruction and formal learning.

2. It is important to note that the classification and shading of the respective reliabilities, *g* loadings, and specificities for each test in the summary pages are based on sample statistics that were "fine-tuned" to better approximate the population parameters by reducing the effect of sampling error through the use of data smoothing procedures that are commonly used in the development of test norms (see McGrew, 1994; McGrew & Wrightson, 1997).

CHAPTER

5 The Wechsler Memory Scales and Other Supplements to the Wechsler Intelligence Scales

A WISC-III detective strives to use ingenuity, clinical sense, a thorough grounding in psychological theory and research, and a willingness to administer supplementary cognitive tests to reveal the dynamics of a child's scaled-score profile.

—Kaufman (1994a, p. 271)

The Importance of Supplementary Cognitive Tests

Practitioners often administer supplemental or special purpose tests to provide additional information about cognitive capabilities beyond that provided by the Wechsler Intelligence Scales. The term *supplemental test* will be used in this chapter to refer to instruments that can be used in a systematic, psychometrically, and theoretically defensible way to augment the Wechsler Intelligence Scales via cross-battery assessment procedures (to be described in Chapter 6). Additional or supplemental information is sought by Wechsler users for a variety of reasons, including the following: (1) testing hypotheses about cognitive strengths or weaknesses initially identified by a Wechsler Scale; (2) gaining information about abilities that a Wechsler Scale either does not measure or does not measure adequately (e.g., fluid reasoning, long-term storage and retrieval, auditory processing, short-term memory); (3) seeking a "fairer" measure of cognitive potential in individuals from diverse cultural or linguistic backgrounds; (4) determining the cognitive capabilities of individuals with speech/communication disorders or hearing impairments; (5) determining the cognitive capabilities of individuals with motor impairments; (6) assessing cognitive processes in individuals with neurological impairments or traumatic brain injury; and (7) assessing selective, sustained, and divided attention in individuals suspected of attention deficit disorder (ADD).

Because many Wechsler tests have extensive receptive and expressive language requirements, individuals with limited hearing abilities, individuals with receptive and expressive language disabilities, or learners of English as a second language (i.e., dual-language learners) may be at a disadvantage when assessed by conventional tests that rely heavily on verbal communication between the examiner and examinee. Also, because these instruments, like other individually administered intelligence tests and batteries, were defined and developed from a unique cultural perspective (viz., U.S. mainstream culture), individuals with diverse cultural backgrounds or with sociolinguistic patterns that differ substantially from those of the test's developer(s) may again be at a disadvantage when assessed with the Wechsler Scales. Furthermore, many supplemental tests provide norm-referenced information about abilities and processes (e.g., memory, attention) that is not available through the conventional Wechsler Intelligence Scales. Thus, many supplemental tests have the potential to (1) offer practitioners an alternative means to assessing people whose performance is likely to be underestimated by the Wechsler Scales, and (2) yield information about abilities and/or processes not adequately or directly measured by these traditional batteries.

It is important to understand, however, that supplemental tests possess many of the same types of problems as the Wechsler Intelligence Scales. The major problem is not so much with linguistic differences or cultural bias, but rather with the fundamental norms on which the Wechslers and other major intelligence batteries are based. While such factors as gender, socioeconomic status, geographic location, and ethnicity are well controlled in major intelligence batteries, acculturation and language proficiency are *not*. In the majority of cases where there is a cultural difference, there is often a concomitant language difference. Because all children entering the public school system in the United States are taught to speak and use English, the United States population contains many students who vary widely in their English language proficiency. Thus, tests with appropriate norms for such children are currently lacking.

Limitations in test norms notwithstanding, a good Wechsler "detective" can supplement the WPPSI-R, WISC-III, and/or WAIS-III in a systematic and referral-relevant way through the application of cross-battery principles and procedures (see Chapter 6) to gain important, meaningful and practical information beyond that available through the administration of a single battery. A willingness to augment the Wechsler Intelligence Scales following cross-battery procedures will undoubtedly "reveal the dynamics of a child's scaled-score profile" and lead to valid interpretations that have practical value (Kaufman, 1994a, p. 271). However, knowing the requisite circumstances for supplementing the Wechsler batteries requires critical thinking and clinical sense; knowing how to interpret the results of a cross-battery evaluation requires a firm understanding of psychometric theory and related research (see Flanagan, Mascolo, & Genshaft, in press; Kaufman, 1994a).

Purpose

The purpose of this chapter is to describe commonly used intelligence batteries, the Wechsler-Linked Memory Scales, and other select supplemental cognitive tests in terms of the *Gf-Gc* abilities they measure, so that they can be used in Wechsler-based cross-battery and selective cross-battery assessments. In Chapter 4, the tests of the Wechsler Intelligence Scales were classified according to the broad (stratum II) and narrow (stratum I) *Gf-Gc* abilities they measure. Most of the classifications at the broad level were empirical (i.e., based on the results of a series of *Gf-Gc*-organized cross-battery factor analyses). All of the classifications at the narrow-ability level were logical (i.e., based on expert consensus). The *Gf-Gc* classifications were reported to (1) aid practitioners in making Wechsler test interpretations that are grounded in contemporary theory and research; and (2) to provide the necessary foundation for organizing Wechsler-based cross-battery assessments. The use of *Gf-Gc* theory to classify all Wechsler tests and select supplementary measures allows practitioners to choose the most appropriate tests for the assessment of abilities that are not measured or not measured adequately by a given Wechsler Scale. *Gf-Gc* classifications of a variety of supplemental cognitive ability measures are described and presented in the following section.

Description of Major Intelligence Batteries and Supplemental Cognitive Tests within the *Gf-Gc* Framework

Table 5.1 includes 20 supplemental tests or batteries consisting of 152 individual cognitive measures. These supplemental measures include the major intelligence batteries (i.e., DAS, K-ABC, KAIT, SB:IV, WJ-R/III), as well as other cognitive ability batteries (CAS, DTLA-3/4, Leiter-R, UNIT, WASI), neuropsychological batteries (e.g., NEPSY), Memory Scales (i.e., WMS-III and CMS) and measures of auditory processing abilities. The definition and age range are included for every test listed in Table 5.1 along with the classifications of the broad (stratum II) and narrow (stratum I) *Gf-Gc* abilities that are believed to be measured by these tests.

The *Gf-Gc* classifications presented in Table 5.1 were made in the following way: All broad *Gf-Gc* classifications for intelligence batteries (i.e., DAS, DTLA-3, K-ABC, KAIT, SB:IV, WJ-R) and recently published batteries of cognitive abilities and processes (e.g., UNIT) were based on *Gf-Gc*-organized cross-battery factor analyses in a manner consistent with McGrew and Flanagan (1998; as reported in Chapter 4). The narrow ability classifications for these tests were based on the expert consensus process discussed in Chapter 4 and originally presented in McGrew (1997). Thus, the broad and narrow *Gf-Gc* ability classifications of the DAS, DTLA-3, K-ABC, KAIT, SB:IV and WJ-R are identical to those reported in McGrew and Flanagan (1998). For newer tests (e.g., CAS, WJ-III) the broad-ability classifications presented in Table 5.1 are the result of recent *Gf-Gc*-organized confirmatory factor analyses conducted by independent researchers (e.g., Kranzler, Keith, & Flanagan, 1999; McGrew & Woodcock, in press). The narrow-ability classifications for the CAS were reported in McGrew and Flanagan (1998), whereas the narrow-ability classifications for the WJ-III were reported in McGrew and associates (in press) using the information and procedures described in McGrew (1997) and McGrew and Flanagan (1998) as a guide.

In instances where a test or battery was not included in *Gf-Gc*-organized cross-battery analyses (e.g., CMS, DTLA-4, Leiter-R, NEPSY, WMS-III), the following procedure

(text continued on page 181)

TABLE 5.1 Description of Cognitive Ability Tests within the *Gf-Gc* Framework

Battery	Age Range	Test[1]	BROAD (STRATUM II) ABILITY (code) Narrow (Stratum I) Ability (code) Test Description
			FLUID INTELLIGENCE (*Gf*) **Tests of Induction (I)**
DAS	6-17	**MATRICES**	The examinee is required to complete a matrix of abstract designs by choosing the correct design from among four or six designs.
DAS	2-5	Picture Similarities	The examinee is required to match a target picture to one of four stimulus pictures.
KAIT	11-85+	**MYSTERY CODES**	The examinee is required to study the identifying codes associated with a set of pictorial stimuli and then figure out the code of a novel pictorial stimulus.
SB:IV	7-24	**MATRICES**	When presented with figural matrices, in which one portion of the matrix is missing, the examinee is required to identify the missing elements from multiple-choice alternatives.
WJ-R/III	2-85+	**CONCEPT FORMATION**	The examinee is required to identify the rules for concepts when shown illustrations of instances of the concept and non-instances of the concepts. This is a controlled-learning task that involves categorical reasoning based on principles of formal logic. The examinee is given feedback regarding the correctness of each response.
CAS	5-17	Nonverbal Matrices	The examinee is required to select one of six options to complete a nonverbal progressive matrix.
DTLA-3/4	6-17	**SYMBOLIC RELATIONS**	The examinee is presented with a series of geometric or line drawings in which one design is absent. The examinee is then presented with six possible designs and is required to choose the missing design.
Leiter-R	2-6	Classification	The examinee is required to categorize objects or geometric designs.
Leiter-R	5-18+	Design Analogies	The examinee is presented with 2x2 and 4x2 matrices and is required to complete these matrices using geometric shapes.
Leiter-R	2-18+	Repeated Patterns	The examinee is presented with patterns of pictorial or figural objects. These patterns are presented again and the examinee is required to supply the "missing" portion of the pattern by moving response cards into alignment with the easel.
Leiter-R	2-18+	Sequential Order	The examinee is presented with a progressive series of pictorial or figural objects and is required to select appropriate items that fit the progression.
UNIT	5-17	**ANALOGIC REASONING**	The examinee completes the matrix analogies task using common objects (e.g., hand/glove, foot/____?) and novel geometric figures.
WASI	6-89	Matrix Reasoning	The examinee is presented with a series of matrices, in which one part of the matrix is missing, and is required to identify the missing part from a series of presented alternatives.

(continued)

169

TABLE 5.1   Continued

Battery	Age Range	Test[1]	BROAD (STRATUM II) ABILITY (code) / Narrow (Stratum I) Ability (code) / Test Description
			FLUID INTELLIGENCE (Gf) — **Tests of General Sequential Reasoning (RG)**
KAIT	11-85+	LOGICAL STEPS	The examinee is required to attend to logical premises presented both visually and aurally, and then respond to a question by making use of the logical premise.
WJ-R/III	4-85+	ANALYSIS-SYNTHESIS	The examinee is required to analyze the presented components of an incomplete logic puzzle and to identify the missing components. This is a controlled-learning task in which the examinee is given instructions on how to perform an increasingly complex procedure. The examinee is given feedback regarding the correctness of his or her response.
Leiter-R	2-10	Picture Context	The examinee is required to recognize an object that has been removed from a larger display using visual context clues.
Leiter-R	6-18+	Visual Coding	The examinee is required to code symbols associated with pictorial objects, geometric objects, and numbers.
UNIT	5-17	CUBE DESIGN	The examinee completes a three-dimensional block design task using between 1 and 9 green and white blocks.
			FLUID INTELLIGENCE (Gf) — **Tests of Quantitative Reasoning (RQ)**
DAS	6-17	SEQ & QUANT REASONING	The examinee is required to complete a series/sequence of abstract designs by identifying the missing designs or provide the missing number to match a pattern of numbers. This test may also involve induction (I).
SB:IV	12-24	EQUATION BUILDING	The examinee is required to take numerals and mathematical signs and resequence them in order to produce a correct solution (i.e., equation).
SB:IV	7-24	Number Series	After reviewing a series of four or more numbers, the examinee is required to generate the next two numbers in the series in a matter consistent with the principle underlying the number series.
			CRYSTALLIZED INTELLIGENCE (Gc) — **Tests of Language Development (LD)**
DAS	6-17	SIMILARITIES	The examinee is required to say how three words are similar to one another.
DAS	2-5	Verbal Comprehension	The examinee is required to manipulate objects or identify objects in pictures in response to oral instructions given by the examiner. This test may also involve listening ability (LS).
SB:IV	12-24	VERBAL RELATIONS	When given four words, the examinee is required to state how three words out of the four-word set are similar.
SB:IV	2-24	Comprehension	For items 1-6, the examinee is required to identify body parts on a card with a picture of a child. For items 7-42, the examinee is required to respond to questions about everyday problem situations ranging from survival behavior to civic duties. This test may also involve general information (K0).
SB:IV	2-14	Absurdities	The examinee is required to point to or describe the absurdity in a presented situation that is contrary to common sense.

Battery	Age Range	Test[1]	BROAD (STRATUM II) ABILITY (code) Narrow (Stratum I) Ability (code) Test Description
			CRYSTALLIZED INTELLIGENCE (*Gc*) **Tests of Language Development (LD) (cont'd)**
DTLA-3/4	6-17	Word Opposites	After the examiner presents a word, the examinee is required to present a word that is opposite in meaning.
DTLA-3/4	6-17	Story Construction	The examinee is required to make up stories about a series of pictures.
WASI	6-89	Similarities	The examinee is required to determine how two objects or concepts are alike. This test may also involve lexical knowledge (VL).
WASI	6-89	Vocabulary	The examinee is required to define a series of orally presented words. This test may also involve lexical knowledge (VL).
			CRYSTALLIZED INTELLIGENCE (*Gc*) **Tests of Lexical Knowledge (VL)**
DAS	6-17	**WORD DEFINITIONS**	The examinee is required to define words. This test may also involve language development (LD).
DAS	2-5	Naming Vocabulary	The examinee is required to name objects or pictures of objects. This test may also involve language development (LD).
SB:IV	2-24	**VOCABULARY**	The examinee either is required to point to pictures named by the examiner or (later) orally define words. This test may also involve language development (LD).
WJ-III	2-85+	**VERBAL COMPREHENSION**	In part A (Synonyms), the examinee is required to state a word similar in meaning to the word presented. In part B (Antonyms), the examinee must state a word that is opposite in meaning to the word presented. In part C (Picture Vocabulary) the examinee is required to name familiar and unfamiliar pictured objects. In part D (Verbal Analogies) the examinee is required to provide a word that completes a verbal analogy. This test may also involve language development (LD) and general information (K0).
WJ-R	2-85+	**ORAL VOCABULARY**	In part A (Synonyms), the examinee is required to state a word similar in meaning to the word presented. In part B (Antonyms), the examinee must state a word that is opposite in meaning to the word presented. This test may also involve language development (LD).
WJ-R	2-85+	**PICTURE VOCABULARY**	The examinee is required to name familiar and unfamiliar picture objects. This test may also involve general information (K0).
NEPSY	3-4	Body Part Naming	The examinee is required to name specific body parts presented on a stimulus card. This test may also involve general information (K0).
			CRYSTALLIZED INTELLIGENCE (*Gc*) **Tests of Listening Ability (LS)**
WJ-R/III	4-85+	**LISTENING COMP**[2]	The examinee is required to listen to a short tape-recorded passage and supply the single word missing at the end of the passage. This test may also involve language development (LD).
NEPSY	3-12	Comp of Instructions	The examinee is required to listen to and respond quickly to a series of increasingly complex verbal instructions (e.g., point to the little, bright star). Later, the examinee must point to items that are not as readily identifiable (point to a shape that is not blue and is in between two triangles and under a circle). This test may also involve language development (LD).

(continued)

TABLE 5.1 Continued

Battery	Age Range	Test[1]	BROAD (STRATUM II) ABILITY (code) Narrow (Stratum I Ability (code) Test Description
			CRYSTALLIZED INTELLIGENCE (Gc) **Tests of General Information (K0)**
DTLA-3/4	6-17	Basic Information	The examinee is required to verbally answer a series of common knowledge questions.
WJ-III	2-85+	**GENERAL INFORMATION**	The examinee is required to answer orally presented questions regarding the common or typical characteristics of certain objects.
			CRYSTALLIZED INTELLIGENCE (Gc) **Tests of Information About Culture (K2)**
KAIT	11-85+	**FAMOUS FACES**	The examinee is required to name people of current or historical fame, based on their photographs and a verbal cue about them.
			VISUAL PROCESSING (Gv) **Tests of Spatial Relations (SR)**
DAS	3-17	Pattern Construction	The examinee is required to use flat squares or blocks to construct a series of designs.
K-ABC	4-12	**TRIANGLES**	The examinee is required to reproduce a printed two-dimensional design using two-color triangles.
SB:IV	2-24	**PATTERN ANALYSIS**	For the first six items, the examinee is required to place puzzle pieces into a form board. In subsequent items the examinee reproduces patterns with blocks. This is a timed test.
Leiter-R	11-18+	Figure Rotation	The examinee is required to mentally rotate a two- or three-dimensional object or geometric figure. This test may also involve visualization (Vz).
UNIT	5-17	Cube Design	The examinee completes a three-dimensional block design task using between one and nine green and white blocks. This test may also involve visualization (Vz).
WASI	6-89	Block Design	The examinee is required to reproduce a series of designs using blocks. This test may also involve visualization (Vz).
			VISUAL PROCESSING (Gv) **Tests of Visualization (Vz)**
DAS	2-3	Block Building	The examinee is required to copy two- or three-dimensional designs with wooden blocks.
DAS	4-5	Matching Letter-like Forms	The examinee is required to find an identical match of a target letter-like shape.
WJ-R/III	4-85+	**SPATIAL RELATIONS**	The examinee is required to match shapes visually. The examinee must select, from a series of shapes, the component parts needed to make a given whole shape. This test may also involve spatial relations (SR).
Leiter-R	2-10	Matching	The examinee is presented with a series of visual stimuli and is required to select response cards to match these stimuli.
Leiter-R	2-18+	Form Completion	The examinee is required to recognize a "whole object" from a randomly displayed array of its parts. This test may also involve spatial relations (SR).
Leiter-R	11-18+	Paper Folding	The examinee is required to mentally "fold" an unfolded object displayed in two dimensions and match it to a target.
NEPSY	3-12	Block Construction	The examinee is required to construct a series of three dimensional designs using monochromatic blocks.

Battery	Age Range	Test[1]	BROAD (STRATUM II) ABILITY (code) Narrow (Stratum I) Ability (code) Test Description
			VISUAL PROCESSING (Gv) **Tests of Visual Memory (MV)**
DAS	6-17	**RECALL OF DESIGNS**	The examinee is required to reproduce abstract line drawings from memory.
DAS	3-7	Recognition of Pictures	The examinee is required to view pictures of objects and identify those objects in a second picture that has a larger array of objects.
K-ABC	2-4	Face Recognition	The examinee is required to select from a group photograph the one or two faces that were shown briefly in a proceeding photograph.
KAIT	11-85+	**MEM. FOR BLOCK DESIGNS**	The examinee is required to study a printed abstract design that is exposed briefly and then copy the design from memory using six yellow and black wooden blocks and a tray.
SB:IV	2-24	**Bead Memory**	For the first 10 items, the examinee is required to recall which one of two beads was exposed. For items 11 through 42, the examinee is required to place beads on the stick in the same sequence as shown in a picture.
SB:IV	7-24	**Memory for Objects**	The examinee is required to identify objects in the correct order from a larger array of presented objects.
WJ-R/III	4-85+	**Picture Recognition**	The examinee is required to recognize a subset of previously presented pictures within a field of distracting pictures.
DTLA-3/4	6-17	Design Sequences	The examinee is presented with a series of pictured designs for 5 seconds and is required to replicate the designs with a group of cubes.
DTLA-3/4	6-17	Design Reproduction	The examinee is presented with a geometric figure for a specified time and is required to draw the figure from memory.
Leiter-R	4-10	Immediate Recognition	A stimulus array of pictured objects is shown for 5 seconds. After its removal the examinee is required to discriminate between objects that are present and objects that are absent.
Leiter-R	2-18+	Forward Memory	After the examiner points to a series of pictures in a given sequence, the examinee is required to repeat the pointing sequence.
UNIT	5-17	**OBJECT MEMORY**	The examinee is shown a visual array of common objects (e.g., shoes, telephone, tree) for 5 seconds, after which the examinee identifies the pictured objects from a larger array of pictured objects.
UNIT	5-17	**SPATIAL MEMORY**	The examinee is required to remember and recreate the placement of black and/or green chips on a 3x3 or 4x4 cell grid.
UNIT	5-17	**SYMBOLIC MEMORY**	The examinee is required to recall and recreate sequences of visually presented universal symbols (e.g., green boy, black woman).
WMS-III	16-89	Visual Reproduction I	The examinee is required to briefly view a design and draw it from memory.
CMS	5-16	Dot Locations	The examinee is required to place chips on an empty grid to replicate a previously presented dot pattern.
CMS	5-16	Dot Locations 2	The examinee is required to replicate the previously presented dot patterns shown in the immediate condition, after a 25-35 minute delay.
CMS	5-16	Picture Locations	The examinee is presented with pictures located on a grid and, when the stimulus card is removed from view, must place response chips on a blank grid to denote the locations of the previously presented pictures.

(continued)

TABLE 5.1 Continued

Battery	Age Range	Test[1]	BROAD (STRATUM II) ABILITY (code) Narrow (Stratum I) Ability (code) Test Description
			VISUAL PROCESSING (*Gv*) (cont'd) **Tests of Visual Memory (MV)**
NEPSY	3-12	Imitating Hand Positions	The examinee is required to imitate a series of hand positions as demonstrated by the examiner using both the preferred and nonpreferred hands within a specified time limit (e.g., 20 seconds).
			VISUAL PROCESSING (*Gv*) **Tests of Closure Speed (CS)**
K-ABC	2-12	**Gestalt Closure**	The examinee is required to name an object or scene pictured in a partially completed "ink blot" drawing.
WJ-R	2-85+	**Visual Closure**	The examinee is required to identify a drawing or picture of a simple object that is represented by disconnected lines. The test requires the subject to visually combine the disconnect lines into a meaningful whole.
DTLA-3	6-17	Picture Fragments	The examinee is presented with a series of pictures in which different elements are missing from otherwise common objects and is required to verbally identify the names of these objects in the pictures.
			VISUAL PROCESSING (*Gv*) **Tests of Spatial Scanning (SS)**
WJ-III	4-85+	**PLANNING**	The examinee is required to plan and initialize a tracing route that covers as many segments of a dotted line drawing as possible without lifting the pencil or tracing over the same segment twice. The test requires "forward thinking" in that the examinee is required to plan a sequence of steps prior to initializing the plan.
UNIT	5-17	**Mazes**	The examinee completes a maze task by tracing a path through each maze from the center starting point to an exit.
NEPSY	5-12	Route Finding	The examinee is presented with a drawing of a target house in a small schematic map and is required to find a route to that house. Later, the examinee must find the target house again when it is presented within a larger map containing other houses and streets.
			VISUAL PROCESSING (*Gv*) **Tests of Flexibility of Closure (CF)**
CAS	5-17	Figure Memory	The examinee is required to identify a geometric figure that is within a more complex design. This test may also involve visual memory (MV).
Leiter-R	2-18+	Figure Ground	The examinee is required to identify imbedded figures or designs within a complex stimulus.
			VISUAL PROCESSING (*Gv*) **Tests of Serial Perceptual Integration (PI)**
K-ABC	2-4	Magic Window	The examinee is required to identify a picture that is exposed by moving it past a narrow slit or "window" (making the picture only partially visible throughout the presentation).
			SHORT-TERM MEMORY(*Gsm*) **Tests of Memory Span (MS)**
DAS	3-17	Recall of Digits	The examinee is required to repeat a series of orally presented digits.
K-ABC	2-12	**NUMBER RECALL**	The examinee is required to repeat verbatim orally presented number sequences.
K-ABC	4-12	**WORD ORDER**	The examinee is required to touch a series of pictures in the same sequence as named by the examiner.

Battery	Age Range	Test[1]	BROAD (STRATUM II) ABILITY (code) Narrow (Stratum I) Ability (code) Test Description
			SHORT-TERM MEMORY (Gsm) **Tests of Memory Span (MS) (cont'd)**
SB:IV	7-24	**MEMORY FOR DIGITS**	The examinee is required to repeat digits exactly as they were stated by the examiner and, from some items, in reverse order. This test may also involve working memory (MW).
WJ-R/III	4-85+	**MEMORY FOR WORDS**	The examinee is required to repeat lists of unrelated words in the correct sequence after they are presented auditorily by use of a tape player, or, in special cases, by an examiner.
CAS	5-17	Word Series	The examinee is required to repeat a series of words in the same order as presented by the examiner.
WMS-III	16-89	Digit Span	The examinee is required to repeat a series of digits both forward and backward. This test may also involve working memory (MW).
CMS	5-16	Numbers	The examinee is required to repeat a series of orally presented number sequences either verbatim or in reverse order. This test may also involve working memory (MW).
CMS	5-16	Sequences	The examinee is required to perform a series of simple tasks such as saying the names of the months forward and backward as quickly as possible. This test may also involve working memory (MW).
DTLA-3/4	6-17	Word Sequences	The examinee is required to repeat a series of unrelated words that were previously read by the examiner.
NEPSY	3-12	Sentence Repetition	The examinee must repeat a series of increasingly complex and lengthy sentences.
NEPSY	5-12	Rep of Nonsense Words	The examinee is required to repeat a series of tape recorded nonsense words.
			SHORT-TERM MEMORY (Gsm) **Tests of Working Memory**
WJ-III	4-85+	AUD WORKING MEM	The examinee is required to retain two types of orally presented information (numbers and words) and then repeat them in a specified order. The task requires the examinee to perform two different mental operations simultaneously (i.e., retain and manipulate stimuli).
WMS-III	16-89	Mental Control	The examinee is required to perform a series of simple tasks, that gradually increase in complexity, as quickly as possible (e.g., saying the months of the years forward and backward).
WJ-R/III	4-85+	**NUM REVERSED**	The examinee is required to repeat a series of number sequences presented auditorily by use of a tape player.
WMS-III	16-89	Letter-Number Sequencing	The examinee is required to listen to orally presented letter-number sequences and repeat the sequence back by arranging the numbers in ascending order, followed by the letters in alphabetical order.
NEPSY	5-12	Knock and Tap	The examinee is required to watch the examiner produce different motor movements and must respond in a specified manner (e.g., if the examiner knocks, the examinee must tap).
			LONG-TERM RETRIEVAL (Glr) **Tests of Associative Memory (MA)**
KAIT	11-85+	**REBUS LEARNING**	The examinee is required to learn the word or concept associated with a particular rebus (drawing) and then "read" phrases sentences and phrases composed of these rebuses.
KAIT	11-85+	**REBUS DEL. RECALL**	The examinee is required to "read" phrases and sentences composed of rebuses they learned about 45 minutes earlier during the rebus learning test.

(continued)

TABLE 5.1 Continued

Battery	Age Range	Test[1]	BROAD (STRATUM II) ABILITY (code) / Narrow (Stratum I) Ability (code) / Test Description
			LONG-TERM RETRIEVAL (*Glr*) (cont'd) / **Tests of Associative Memory (MA)**
WJ-R	2-85+	**MEMORY FOR NAMES**	The examinee is required to learn associations between unfamiliar auditory and visual stimuli (an auditory-visual association test).
WJ-R/III	2-85+	**VISUAL AUDITORY LEARNING**	The examinee is required to associate novel visual symbols (rebuses) with familiar words in oral language and to translate a series of symbols into verbal sentences (a visual-auditory association task). This test is a controlled-learning test in which the examinee's errors are corrected. This task simulates a learning-to-read test. This test may also involve meaningful memory (MM).
WJ-R	4-85+	**DEL REC: MEM FOR NAMES**	The examinee is required to recall (after 1 to 8 days) the space creatures presented in the Memory for Names test. The examinee is not told that subsequent testing will occur.
WJ-R/III	4-85+	**Del Rec: Visual-Auditory Learning**	The examinee is required to recall (after 1 to 8 days) the symbols (rebuses) presented in the Visual-Auditory Learning test. The examinee is not told that subsequent testing will occur. This test is a controlled-learning test in which the examinee's errors are corrected. This is a recall and "relearning" test in the WJ-III.
Leiter-R	4-10	Delayed Recognition	After a 20-minute delay the examinee is required to recognize the objects associated in the Associated Pairs test.
Leiter-R	2-18+	Associated Pairs	Pairs of pictured objects are displayed for 5 to 10 seconds. After their removal the examinee is required to make meaningful and nonmeaningful associations. This test may also involve meaningful memory (MM).
Leiter-R	6-18+	Delayed Pairs	After a 20-minute delay the examinee is required to recognize the objects associated in the Associated Pairs test. This test may also involve meaningful memory (MM).
WMS-III	16-89	Verbal Paired Associates I	The examinee is required to listen to eight novel word pairs, and, upon the presentation of the first word of each pair, the examinee must provide the second word of the pair.
WMS-III	16-89	Verbal Paired Associates II	The examinee is presented with the first word of each pair learned in Verbal Paired Associates I and must provide the corresponding word that completes the pair. Later, the examinee is read a list containing 24 word pairs and must identify each pair as a previously learned or newly presented pair.
CMS	5-16	Word Pairs	The examinee is read a list of word pairs and, following the presentation of the first word pair, the examinee must provide the second word of the pair. After 3 trials, the examinee is required to provide both words of the pairs from memory.
CMS	5-16	Word Pairs 2	Following a 25-35 minute delay, the examinee is asked to recall previously learned word pairs. Later, the examinee is presented with word pairs and must identify the pairs as previously learned or newly presented pairs.
NEPSY	5-12	Memory for Names	The examinee is presented with a series of pictures depicting children and is given the name of each child. Following this presentation, the examinee is presented with the stimulus cards in random order and must provide the correct name. There is a delayed portion of this test. This test may also involve meaningful memory (MM).

Battery	Age Range	Test[1]	BROAD (STRATUM II) ABILITY (code) Narrow (Stratum I Ability) (code) Test Description
			LONG-TERM RETRIEVAL (*Glr*) **Tests of Free Recall Memory (M6)**
DAS	4-17	Recall of Objects	The examinee is required to view a picture card with 20 objects and recall the names of these objects after the card is removed.
WMS-III	16-89	Word Lists I	The examinee is required to recall as many words from a list of 12 orally presented, unrelated words. Later, a new word list is presented and the examinee must recall as many words from the first list as he or she can.
WMS-III	16-89	Word Lists II	The examinee is required to recall the original word list given in Word Lists I. Later, the examinee is read 24 words and must identify the word as belonging or not belonging to the original list. This test may also involve associative memory (MA).
CMS	5-16	Word Lists	The examinee is required to recall as many words as possible in any order, from an orally presented list. Later, the examinee is presented with those words omitted in the first recall and asked to recall those words as well as the original words recalled from the first list.
CMS	5-16	Word Lists 2	After a 20-35 minute delay, the examinee is required to recall as many words he or she can from Word List I. Later, the examinee is presented with a list of words and must identify the words as newly presented or previously presented words. This test may also involve associative memory (MA).
NEPSY	7-12	List Learning	The examinee is required to listen to a list of orally presented words and repeat as many words as he/she can remember, in any order. Later, the examinee is presented with a new list of words and must recall those words, in addition to the original list or words, in any order.
			LONG-TERM RETRIEVAL (*Glr*) **Tests of Meaningful Memory (MM)**
WMS-III	16-89	Logical Memory II	The examinee is asked to retell two previously presented stories from Logical Memory I and respond to close-ended (e.g., yes/no) questions about both sets of stories.
CMS	5-16	Stories 2	The examinee is asked to retell two previously presented stories from Stories in the absence of any stimulus cues. Later, the examinee is required to answer questions presented by the examiner for each story.
			LONG-TERM RETRIEVAL (*Glr*) **Tests of Ideational Fluency (FI)**
WJ-III	4-85+	RETRIEVAL FLUENCY	The examinee is required to fluently retrieve the names of objects. The subject is asked to state as many items as they can of three different types, "things to eat or drink", "names of people", and "animals"
			LONG-TERM RETRIEVAL (*Glr*) **Tests of Naming Facility (NA)**
WJ-III	4-85+	RAPID PIC NAM	Measures the ability to rapidly identify and orally name pictures of common objects. This test may also involve Rate-of-test-taking (R9)
CAS	5-17	Expressive Attention	The examinee must rapidly name characteristics (e.g., size, color) when presented with a series of stimulus items.
NEPSY	5-12	Speeded Naming	The examinee is required to rapidly name the color, size, and shape of a series of stimulus items.
			LONG-TERM RETRIEVAL (*Glr*) **Tests of Figural Fluency (FF)**
NEPSY	5-12	Design Fluency	The examinee is required to make as many unique designs as possible by connecting a series of dots.

(continued)

TABLE 5.1 Continued

Battery	Age Range	Test[1]	BROAD (STRATUM II) ABILITY (code) Narrow (Stratum I) Ability (code) Test Description
			AUDITORY PROCESSING (_Ga_) **Tests of Phonetic Coding- Analysis (PC-A)**
WJ-R/III	2-85+	INCOMPLETE WORDS	After hearing a recorded word that has one or more phonemes missing, the examinee is required to identify the correct word.
NEPSY	3-12	Phonological Process.	The examinee is required to identify words from word segments. Later, the examinee is required to construct a new word by either omitting a syllable or phoneme or by substituting a phoneme in one word for another. This test may also involve phonetic coding – synthesis (PC:S).
W-ADT	4-8		The examinee is required to recognize the fine differences between phonemes used in English speech by indicating, verbally or gesturally, whether the words in each pair are the same or different.
GFW-TAD	3-70+		The examinee is required to discriminate speech sounds against two different backgrounds - quiet and noise. This test may also involve resistance to auditory distortion (UR).
G-FTA	2-16+		The examinee is required to produce spontaneous and imitative sounds and correctly produce a previously misarticulated sound following a demonstration by the examiner.
TOPA	5-8		The examinee is required to isolate individual phonemes in spoken words.
TPAT	5-9	Segmentation	The examinee is required to divide sentences into words by clapping out the number of words in the sentences and divide words into syllables by clapping out the number of syllables in the word. Later, the examinee must segment words by phoneme or sound.
TPAT	5-9	Isolation	The examinee must identify the initial, medial, and final phonemes in a series of presented words.
TPAT	5-9	Deletion	The examinee is required to say a word then repeat it leaving out a root word, syllable, or phoneme.
TPAT	5-9	Rhyming	The examinee is required to identify whether or not two presented words rhyme. Later, the examinee must produce a word that rhymes with a given stimulus word.
			AUDITORY PROCESSING (_Ga_) **Tests of Phonetic Coding- Synthesis (PC-S)**
WJ-R/III	4-85+	SOUND BLENDING	The examinee is required to integrate and then say whole words after hearing part (syllables and/or phonemes) of the words presented via an audio tape player.
TPAT	5-9	Substitution	The examinee must construct words by using blocks that represent sounds. Later, the examinee is required to transform a given word into a new word by changing one sound. This test may also involve phonetic coding - analysis (PC-A).
TPAT	5-9	Blending	The examinee is required to blend together given sound units (e.g., syllables, phonemes) to construct words.
			AUDITORY PROCESSING (_Ga_) **Tests of Speech/General Sound Discrimination (US/U3)**
WJ-III	4-85+	AUD. ATTENTION	The examinee is required to discriminate similar sounding words in the presence of increasing noise. This test requires selective attention and may also involve resistance to auditory stimulus distortion (UR).
WJ-R	4-85+	Sound Patterns	The examinee is required to indicate whether pairs of complex sound patterns presented via an audio tape player are the same or different. The patterns may differ in pitch, rhythm, or content.

Battery	Age Range	Test[1]	BROAD (STRATUM II) ABILITY (code) Narrow (Stratum I) Ability (code) Test Description
			PROCESSING SPEED (Gs) **Tests of Perceptual Speed (P)**
WJ-R/III	4-85+	**VISUAL MATCHING**	The examinee is required to locate and circle the two identical numbers in a row of six numbers. The task proceeds in difficulty from single-digit numbers to triple-digit numbers and has a 3-minute time trial. For younger examinees, the task requires the examinee to identify two identical pictures of assorted shapes and colors by pointing. This test may also involve rate-of-test-taking (R9).
WJ-R	4-85+	**CROSS OUT**	The examinee is required to scan and compare visual information quickly. The examinee must mark the five drawings in a row of 20 drawings that are identical to the first drawings in the row. The examinee is given a 3-minute time limit to complete as many rows of items as possible. This test may also involve rate-of-test-taking (R9).
CAS	5-17	Matching Numbers	The examinee is required to develop a plan to find two identical numbers on several rows. This test may also involve rate-of-test-taking (R9).
CAS	5-17	Receptive Attention	The examinee is required to identify pairs of pictures or letters while resisting distractions. This test may also involve semantic processing speed (R4).
Leiter-R	2-18+	Attention Sustained	The examinee is required to identify specific stimuli among an array of different stimuli. This test may also involve rate-of-test-taking (R9).
			PROCESSING SPEED (Gs) **Tests of Rate -of-test-taking (R9)**
CAS	5-17	Planned Codes	The examinee is required to use a strategy to match symbols to letters as quickly as possible.
WJ-III	4-85+	**PAIR CANCELLATION**	The examinee is required to draw circles around two images when they occur under certain conditions only. This is a speeded, vigilance type test.
			PROCESSING SPEED (Gs) **Tests of Mental Comparison Speed (R7)**
DAS	6-17	Speed of Information Processing	The examinee is required to mark on each row the largest number or the circle with the most boxes as quickly as possible. This test may also involve rate-of-test-taking (R9).
CAS	5-17	Number Detection	The examinee is required to find specific numbers to match a sample while resisting response to distracting numbers. This test may also involve rate-of-test-taking (R9).
WJ-III	4-85+	**DECISION SPEED**	The examinee is required to rapidly scan a row of pictures and decide which of the two drawings are conceptually related. The decisions become slightly more abstract as the test progresses. This test may also involve semantic processing speed (R4) or correct decision speed (CDS)

[1] Tests printed in bold/uppercase letters are strong measures as defined empirically; tests printed in bold/lowercase letters are moderate measures as defined empirically; tests printed in regular type/lowercase letters were classified logically (see McGrew and Flanagan, 1998). In the case where tests have two narrow ability classifications, the second classification is reported in parentheses following the test description. Tests of the major batteries that were classified either empirically or logically as mixed measures are not included in this table.

Note: The WPPSI-R, WISC-III, and WAIS-III are not included in this table because they measure in Chapter 4 of this text. CAS= Cognitive Assessment System; CMS= Children's Memory Scale; DAS= Differential Ability Scales; DTLA-3= Detroit Tests of Learning Aptitude—3;DTLA-4= Detroit Tests of Learning Aptitude—4; G-FTA= Goldman-Fristoe Test of Articulation; G-FTAD= Goldman-Fristoe-Woodcock Test of Auditory Discrimination; K-ABC= Kaufman Assessment Battery for Children; KAIT= Kaufman Adolescent and Adult Intelligence Test; Leiter-R= Leiter International Performance Scale-Revised; NEPSY = Neurological Psychological; SB:IV= Stanford-Binet Intelligence Scale—Fourth Edition; TOPA= Test of Phonological Awareness; TPAT= The Phonological Awareness Test; UNIT= Universal Nonverbal Intelligence Test; WASI= Wechsler Abbreviated Scale of Intelligence; W-ADT=Wepman's Auditory Discrimination Test —Second Edition; WMS-III= Wechsler Memory Scale—Third Edition; WJ-R= Woodcock-Johnson Psychoeducational Battery—Revised; WJ-III= Woodcock- Johnson Psychoeducational Battery—Third Edition.

Because the NEPSY is a neuropsychological battery, some of its measures do not "fit" well within the *Gf-Gc* structural framework. Only those NEPSY tests that had a clear match to an ability specified in contemporary *Gf-Gc* theory are included in this table.

led to *Gf-Gc* ability classifications. Each test was compared to the 150-plus tests reported in this book and in McGrew and Flanagan (1998)—tests that were included in *Gf-Gc*-guided factor analyses (i.e., empirically classified tests)—to determine similarity in content and task demands. When a test was found to be similar (or identical) in content and task demand to an empirically classified test, the broad- and narrow-ability classifications of the empirically classified test were adopted for the supplemental test and reported in Table 5.1. If a supplemental test appeared to measure an ability not directly measured by any empirically classified test, it was classified by the authors. The classifications were made based on an understanding of Carroll's (1993a) text, the results of *Gf-Gc*-organized factor analytic studies, and communication with intelligence scholars and test authors. Because of the subjective nature of the latter classification process, the narrow (and perhaps some broad) *Gf-Gc* ability classifications presented in Table 5.1 may require modification following future research and scholarly dialogue.

It is important to note that the list of tests presented in Table 5.1 is not exhaustive. There are literally hundreds of cognitive ability tests available (see McGrew & Flanagan, 1998 for a more extensive listing). Those selected for inclusion in Table 5.1 are the major intelligence batteries, other frequently used cognitive ability tests, and new tests that appear likely to gain widespread use. As such, it is probable that users of the Wechsler Intelligence Scales may also have access to one or more batteries or tests listed in Table 5.1. Collectively, these tests measure a wide range of *Gf-Gc* abilities, many of which are not measured or not measured well by the Wechsler batteries—namely, Fluid Intelligence *(Gf)*, Long-Term Storage and Retrieval *(Glr)*, Short-Term Memory/Working Memory *(Gsm)*, and Auditory Processing *(Ga)*. Because these broad abilities are related differentially to various achievement and/or occupational outcomes across the lifespan, they can be used systematically to supplement the Wechsler Intelligence Scales in a variety of ways, depending on the purpose of the assessment. It is also noteworthy that while the Wechsler Intelligence Scales provide good coverage of *Gc* and *Gv* abilities, coverage of additional broad *Gf-Gc* abilities across various supplemental batteries exceeds that of these conventional tests. For example, Table 5.1 shows that the Leiter-R includes six measures of *Gf*, representing two *different* narrow abilities within that domain (i.e., Induction and General Sequential Reasoning).

While the WPPSI-R and WISC-III do not include any strong measures of *Gf*, the WAIS-III contains one (i.e., Matrix Reasoning). According to one of the principles underlying the cross-battery approach, two or more *qualitatively different* narrow abilities must be measured within a broad *Gf-Gc* area before making generalizations about ability in that domain. None of the Wechsler Intelligence Scales meets this criterion for the broad ability of *Gf*. However, in addition to the Leiter-R, *Gf* is represented amply among many of the supplemental batteries listed in Table 5.1.

For example, Table 5.1 shows that the DAS, KAIT, SB:IV and WJ-R/III measure *Gf* adequately, as they include at least two qualitatively different narrow-ability indicators of this broad ability. Moreover, supplemental batteries such as the Leiter-R and UNIT are capable of assessing *Gf* (as well as other important *Gf-Gc* abilities) without the use (or interference) of expressive and receptive language requirements. That is, these batteries can be administered entirely in pantomime (i.e., nonverbally). However, this should not be construed to mean that bias related to language is entirely eliminated through this method.

Rather, it is important to recognize that although such tests do reduce the linguistic demands on the examinee, effective nonverbal communication must still be established and maintained between the examiner and examinee. Such nonverbal communication and the degree to which it is successful (which is often predicated on culturally specific behavior) thus remains a crucial factor affecting performance. Nevertheless, because the Leiter-R and UNIT were normed using a nonverbal communication format, test scores can often be compared to an appropriate norm group (see McCallum & Bracken, 1997, for a discussion). In addition, many of the batteries listed in Table 5.1 include tests of the progressive matrices type, which by their nature typically have significantly reduced language requirements (viz., minimal receptive language requirements and no expressive language requirements). These *Gf* tests appear to be useful for assessing inductive reasoning in a variety of populations (e.g., dual-language learners).

Because of the importance of *Gf* in predicting school learning as well as other important outcome criteria, it should be considered one of the more important abilities to include in a battery designed to assess cognitive functioning. Part III of this text will demonstrate how to supplement the Wechsler Intelligence Scales with measures of *Gf* in both comprehensive and selective cross-battery assessments.

Yet another important ability within the *Gf-Gc* taxonomy is *Ga*. Because the phonological awareness/processing abilities subsumed by *Ga* are important in the development of reading decoding skills in the early elementary school years, it is critical to assess *Ga* in children who are referred due to poor progress in reading achievement. Table 5.1 includes several measures of *Ga,* including Phonetic Coding tests, that can be used to supplement the Wechsler Intelligence Scales, especially in reading-related referrals.

It is also noteworthy that certain broad *Gf-Gc* areas are covered in supplemental batteries with greater depth than they are in the Wechsler Intelligence Scales. For example, Table 5.1 shows that both the WJ-III and the WMS-III contain several qualitatively different narrow-ability measures of *Glr:* The WJ-III contains tests of Associative Memory (MA), Ideational Fluency (FI) and Naming Facility (NA), and the WMS-III contains tests of MA, Meaningful Memory (MM), and Free Recall Memory (M6). On the other hand, none of the Wechsler Intelligence Scales measures the broad ability of *Glr* (McGrew & Flanagan, 1998). Therefore, when an individual is suspected of having significant long-term memory and retrieval difficulties, it is necessary to supplement the Wechsler Scales (as well as most major intelligence batteries) to assess functioning in this area adequately.

In Part III of this text, the information from Table 5.1 is translated into worksheets that can be used to design Wechsler-based cross-battery assessments to measure a wide range (or select but in-depth range) of abilities, including those abilities found in current research to be most closely associated with common academic referral concerns.

Wechsler-Linked Memory Scales

The Wechsler Memory Scale—Third Edition (WMS-III; Wechsler, 1997) and the Children's Memory Scale (CMS; Cohen, 1997) are individually administered tests of learning and memory functioning for individuals ages 16 to 89 years and 5 to 16 years, respectively. Descriptions of the general features of these batteries are provided in Tables 5.2 and 5.3. As with the Wechsler scales, it is important to recognize and consider all available information about the individual tests that comprise the memory scales in the assessment and interpretation process. In order to facilitate this process, general information about each Wechsler-Linked Memory battery is reported here and more specific psychometric, theoretical, and qualitative characteristics of the individual memory tests are described in the next section. Tables 5.2 and 5.3 include the following categories of information for the WMS-III and CMS, respectively:

- General information. Author(s); publisher, date of publication; age range of tests; and typical administration time.

- Composite measure information. Number and type of broad and lower-order composite scores.

- Score information. Type of peer comparison scores; range of standard scores.

- Norming information. Number of tests normed at each age; conorming features; norms for ability-memory discrepancies; person and community variables in the norming plan; size of the norming sample; age blocks used in norm tables.

The information in these tables shows that both batteries consist of several core tests and several optional tests. These tests are combined in various ways to yield eight Primary Indexes in each battery, allowing for a comprehensive appraisal of various aspects of an individual's memory abilities. Individual tests are based on a mean of 10 and a standard deviation of 3, while indexes are based on a mean of 100 and a standard deviation of 15.

The Primary Indexes of the WMS-III provide information about aspects of memory functioning that are temporal (i.e., immediate and delayed abilities) and sensory specific (i.e., visual and auditory abilities). Many indexes also provide information about an individual's recall and recognition abilities. Thus, the WMS-III was organized according to three *dimensions* in order to facilitate the interpretation of memory test performance: Immediate versus Delayed *(Temporal)*; Auditory versus Visual *(Modality)*; and Recall versus Recognition *(Test Format)*. The indexes of the CMS are constructed and organized similarly with regard to dimension. For either battery, evaluating performance across these indexes can help practitioners understand the test taker's ability to (1) learn and retain new information; (2) learn and retain information presented visually versus auditorily; (3) learn information quickly; (4) retrieve information following a delay; and (5) retrieve information following a cue (The Psychological Corporation, 1997). The more specific information about the individual tests of the WMS-III and CMS provided in the summary pages at the end of this chapter is similar to that provided in Chapter 4 to describe important individual Wechsler Intelligence test characteristics. The WMS- III and CMS summary pages are described in the following section.

The Memory Scale Test Characteristic Summary Pages

To facilitate the infusion of critical test characteristic information (viz., the general information provided in Tables 5.2 and 5.3; psychometric, theoretical, and qualitative test characteristic information for individual tests of both Wechsler-Linked Memory batteries) into

TABLE 5.2   Select Content, Scoring, and Norming Features of the WMS-III

	WMS-III
General Information	
Author	David Wechsler
Publisher	The Psychological Corporation
Publication Date	1945–1997
Age Range	16:0 to 89:0 years
Administration Time	30 to 35 minutes
Composite Measure Information	
Primary Indexes	Auditory Immediate
	Auditory Delayed
	Auditory Recognition Delayed
	Visual Immediate
	Visual Delayed
	General Memory
	Immediate Memory
	Working Memory
Supplementary Composites	Single-Trial Learning
	Learning Slope
	Retention
	Retrieval
Score Information	
Peer Comparison Scores	Percentile Rank Index
Range of Standard Scores for Total Test Composite	45 to 155
Norming Information	
Number of Tests Normed at Each Age	11 across age range
Conormed with Tests of Intelligence	Yes. WAIS-III
Norms for Ability-Memory Discrepancies	Actual Discrepancy Norms
Person Variables in Norming Plan	Gender
	Race/Ethnicity (confounding race and Hispanic origin)
	Education level (parent education used for 16 to 19 year olds)
Community Variables in Norming Plan	Location
	Size
Size of Norming Sample for the Broad Measure of General Intelligence	$N=1,250$
	Average number per age group: 100
Age Blocks in Norm Table	2-year blocks (Age 16 to 19)
	5-year blocks (Age 20 to 34; 65 to 89)
	10-year blocks (Age 35 to 64)

Note: WMS-III = Wechsler Memory Scale—Third Edition (Wechsler, 1997).

TABLE 5.3   Select Content, Scoring, and Norming Features of the CMS

	CMS
General Information	
Author	Morris Cohen
Publisher	The Psychological Corporation
Publication Date	1997
Age Range	5:0 to 16:0 years
Administration Time	20 to 25 minutes
Composite Measure Information	
Primary Indexes	Verbal Immediate
	Verbal Delayed
	Visual Immediate
	Visual Delayed
	Delayed Recognition
	General Memory
	Learning
	Attention/Cognition
Supplementary Composites	Percent Retention
	Thematic Gist Unit Analysis
	Numbers Forward/ Numbers Backward
Score Information	
Peer Comparison Scores	Percentile Rank
	Index
Range of Standard Scores for Total Test Composite	50 to 150
Norming Information	
Number of Tests Normed at Each Age	9 across age range
Conormed with Tests of Intelligence	No. Linked to WPPSI-R ($n = 27$) and WISC-III ($n = 273$)
Norms for Ability-Memory Discrepancies	Pseudo-discrepancy Norms
Person Variables in Norming Plan	Gender
	Race/Ethnicity
	Parental Education level
Community Variables in Norming Plan	Location
	Size
Size of Norming Sample for the Broad Measure of General Intelligence	$N=1,000$
	Average number per age group: 100
Age Blocks in Norm Table	1-year blocks (Age 5 to 12)
	2-year blocks (Age 13 to 16)

Note: CMS = Children's Memory Scale (Cohen, 1997).

the day-to-day assessment practices of practitioners, this section of the chapter presents a summary page for each individual test of each individually administered memory battery. The summary pages contain tests which are presented in alphabetical order beginning with the tests comprising the WMS-III, followed by the tests comprising the CMS. The first test listed for the WMS-III (i.e., Digit Span) will be used to explain the information that is available for all individual tests of the Wechsler-Linked Memory Scales.

As may be seen in the summary pages at the end of this chapter, the individual test name and definition are provided first, followed by a section called, Basic Psychometric Characteristics. In this latter section, information about each test's reliability and item gradients is presented by age in a visual-graphic format. The evaluation of each of these test characteristics, according to the psychometric criteria presented in Chapter 4 (see Table 4.2), is accomplished by simply locating the appropriate age level and inspecting the tone of the shading in the small square associated with that age. The meaning of the shaded boxes is explained in the key located at the top right half of the summary page. For example, at age 16, the WMS-III Digit Span test is classified as having *medium* reliability and *good* item gradients.[1] It is noteworthy that while the item gradients of the individual memory tests are generally good, a significant number of these tests from both batteries are not sufficiently reliable (i.e., they received a rating of *low,* as indicated by the unshaded boxes) to make individual judgements about test performance.

Due to the poor reliability of many individual Wechsler-Linked Memory tests, it is recommended that only indexes and composites (and not individual tests) be interpreted.[2] Notwithstanding the low reliabilities associated with many individual WMS-III and CMS tests, interpretation at the *individual test level* (e.g., subtest analysis) is ill-advised for the following reasons: (1) it relies on subtest uniqueness (which is typically the smallest portion of the test's reliable variance); (2) it is not grounded in a well-validated theory and/or current research; and (3) the ipsatized scores yielded by subtest analysis lack construct validity support (see Flanagan, Andrews, & Genshaft, 1997 for a discussion).

Although many tests of the Wechsler-Linked Memory Scales have medium to low reliability at various ages, they fare somewhat better with regard to their floors and ceilings. An evaluation of test floors and ceilings can be found along with evaluations of test reliability and item gradient characteristics on the summary pages. Here, the ages at which a given test has an *inadequate* floor and/or ceiling are listed in the floor and ceiling boxes, respectively. The summary page for the Digit Span test shows that this test has *adequate* floors and ceilings across its age range as indicated by the absence of information in the test floor and test ceiling boxes.

Below the Basic Psychometric Characteristics section of the summary page is information about each test's underlying *Gf-Gc* construct(s). The Digit Span summary page shows that the *primary* focus of interpretation for this test is Short-Term Memory *(Gsm).* More specifically, the narrow abilities of Memory Span (MS) and Working Memory (MW) (for digit span backwards) appear to be necessary to perform this test.

The Other Variables section of the summary pages provides information about factors that may positively or negatively influence an examinee's test performance. For example, the summary page for the Digit Span test shows that factors such as attention span, concentration, distractibility, verbal rehearsal, visual elaboration, and organization may impact performance on this measure (see *individual/situational variables*). Data in this section also shows that when interpreting Digit Span test performance, practitioners should be aware of whether or not the examinee has a history of hearing difficulties (see *background/ environmental variables*). An understanding of individual/situational and background/ environmental variables is critical to the interpretive process because it provides a basis from which to evaluate the integrity of test scores.

Finally, the cube on the bottom right portion of the summary pages provides information about the degree of cultural loading and linguistic demand of an individual test. Performance on the Digit Span test, for example, is considered to be minimally influenced by exposure to U.S. mainstream culture as indicated by the *low* classification in the degree of cultural loading grid. The Digit Span test is also characterized as having a *moderate* degree of linguistic demand (i.e., some receptive language skills are requisite for optimal test performance). When evaluating individuals who are not fully acculturated to the U.S. mainstream, knowledge of the degree of linguistic demand and cultural loading of the Wechsler-Linked Memory tests can be valuable in the interpretive process (this issue is discussed at length in Chapter 8).[3]

The Wechsler-Linked Memory Scales in Perspective

Despite their psychometric limitations, both the WMS-III and CMS provide a comprehensive set of measures that can be used to evaluate individuals with difficulties in learning and remembering. Because the WMS-III was conormed with the WAIS-III and the CMS was linked with the WISC-III and WPPSI-R, these batteries are valuable when used together to evaluate developmental changes in learning and memory (The Psychological Corporation, 1997). Specifically, it has been suggested that evaluating the discrepancy between the Wechsler IQs and the Wechsler-Linked Memory Scale Indexes is analogous to conducting an ability-achievement discrepancy analysis (see The Psychological Corporation, 1997, for details). In such an analysis, the IQ represents an individual's memory potential (i.e., premorbid memory functioning) and the extent and direction of the deviation between IQ and memory provides information about the nature and severity of memory impairment or specific memory deficits. It is important to note that, unlike many ability-achievement discrepancy procedures, the ability-memory discrepancy analysis method recommended for the WMS-III and CMS is technically valid. That is, the discrepancy method (1) is based on conormed (or linked) measures; (2) takes into account regression toward the mean; and (3) provides base rate data for determining the meaningfulness of the ability-memory discrepancy. In short, there appears to be little doubt that a combination of Wechsler Individual Intelligence tests and Wechsler-Linked Memory tests may have clinical utility in the evaluation of a variety of suspected disorders (e.g., learning disability, neurological disorders, Alzheimer's disease).

Even when the nature of a disorder or suspected learning problem is not readily apparent, it still may not be necessary to administer an entire Memory Scale. For example, if a comprehensive evaluation of cognitive functioning is needed to obtain a baseline set of measures prior to delivering intervention services, then a practitioner would most likely start by assessing a broad range of abilities rather than conducting an in-depth assessment in any given domain, such as memory. That is, the practitioner would probably attempt to "touch all of the major cognitive areas" (e.g., through cross-battery procedures), emphasizing those most suspect vis-à-vis history, observation, and on-going test results (Wilson, 1992, p. 382). In these situations, selected tests from the Wechsler-Linked Memory Scales can be used to supplement the Wechsler Intelligence Scales so that a *sampling* of memory functioning can be achieved in addition to the measurement (or sampling) of several other broad-ability domains.

In order to include the Memory Scales in Wechsler-based cross-battery assessments, it was necessary to classify all Wechsler-Linked Memory tests according to the *Gf-Gc* taxonomy. These classifications were discussed earlier and can be found in Table 5.1. Chapter 6 offers a set of principles and steps that guide the practitioner through a systematic method of augmenting the Wechsler Intelligence Scales with select Wechsler-Linked Memory tests when a sampling (rather than comprehensive evaluation) of memory functioning is warranted.

Conclusion

It is clear from the information presented to this point that none of the currently available major intelligence batteries measure the breadth and depth of cognitive abilities that define the structure of intelligence according to contemporary *Gf-Gc* theory and research. When considering the Wechsler Intelligence Scales in particular, *Gf, Ga, Gsm,* and *Glr* are not measured or not measured adequately, and therefore, these batteries require supplementing in instances where one or more of the aforementioned abilities are deemed necessary to evaluate. This chapter demonstrated that, *depending on the purpose of assessment,* each Wechsler Intelligence Scale may need to be supplemented with other tests to better assess these abilities (i.e., *Gf, Ga, Gsm, Glr*) or to obtain a more valid and complete evaluation of intellectual functioning. The supplemental batteries and tests presented in Table 5.1 serve as valuable additions to the Wechsler Intelligence Scales. The Wechsler-Linked Memory Scales were highlighted as particularly valuable supplements to the Wechsler Intelligence Scales because they were either conormed with or linked to these batteries and offer in-depth evaluation of short-term memory, long-term storage and retrieval and working memory. Other supplemental tests have unique features (e.g., reduced language demands or culture loading) that make them useful in the assessment of culturally and linguistically diverse populations.

The next section of this book demonstrates how supplemental tests can be used in Wechsler-based *Gf-Gc* cross-battery assessment. It is through this process that Wechsler users can improve their detective skills (Kaufman, 1994a). Specifically, they will learn how to measure a wider (and often more in-depth) range of broad cognitive abilities, uncover more meaningful profiles of test scores than that which is revealed through the use of any single intelligence battery, and make informed interpretations of these scaled-score profiles within the context of contemporary theory and research.

Wechsler Memory Scale and Children's Memory Scale Summary Pages

WMS-III Digit Span: The examinee is required to repeat a series of orally presented digits verbatim. Later, the examinee must repeat a different series of digits in reverse sequence.

Basic Psychometric Characteristics

	20 25 30 35 40 45 50 55 60 65 70 75 80		
	16 17 18 19 24 29 34 39 44 49 54 59 64 69 74 79 84 85+		
Reliability		Low	Poor (Item
Item gradients		Medium	Fair gradients only)
		High	Good

Inadequate at ages:	Test floor	Test ceiling

Gf-Gc Classifications

Broad stratum II (Narrow stratum I)
Gsm (MS), (MW)

Other Variables

Background & Environmental	**Individual and Situational**	Degree of Linguistic Demand
• Hearing Difficulties	• Attention span	L M H
	• Concentration	
	• Distractibility	Degree of L
	• Verbal rehearsal	Cultural M
	• Visual elaboration	Loading H
	• Organization	

(Degree of Cultural Loading × Degree of Linguistic Demand: L row, M column filled)

WMS-III Faces I: The examinee is presented with a set of 24 photographs that they are told to remember and must identify those faces from a set of 48 photographs.

Basic Psychometric Characteristics

	20 25 30 35 40 45 50 55 60 65 70 75 80		
	16 17 18 19 24 29 34 39 44 49 54 59 64 69 74 79 84 85+		
Reliability		Low	Poor (Item
Item gradients		Medium	Fair gradients only)
		High	Good

Inadequate at ages:	Test floor	Test ceiling

Gf-Gc Classifications

Broad stratum II (Narrow stratum I)
Gv (MV); *Glr* (MM)

Other Variables

Background & Environmental	**Individual and Situational**	Degree of Linguistic Demand
	• Concentration	L M H
	• Reflectivity/impulsivity	
	• Verbal elaboration	Degree of L
		Cultural M
		Loading H

(Degree of Cultural Loading × Degree of Linguistic Demand: H row, L column filled)

WMS-III Faces II: The examinee is required to identify those faces they were asked to remember in Faces I from a set of 48 photographs

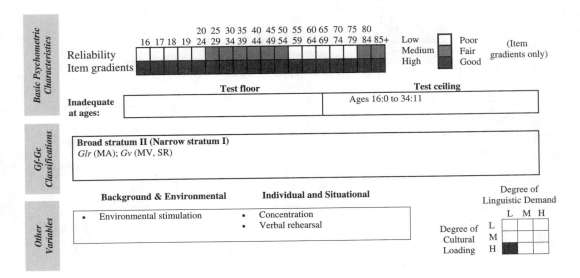

WMS-III Family Pictures I: The examinee is required to view and remember four scenes containing individuals (i.e., family members) engaged in specific activities. Following the presentation of all four scenes, the examinee is asked to recall information such as identifying characters in a particular scene, their respective locations in the scene, and the activities they were engaging in.

WMS-III Family Pictures II: The examinee is required to provide all of the information requested in Family Pictures I in the absence of any pictures.

Basic Psychometric Characteristics

20 25 30 35 40 45 50 55 60 65 70 75 80
16 17 18 19 24 29 34 39 44 49 54 59 64 69 74 79 84 85+

Reliability
Item gradients

Low / Medium / High   Poor / Fair / Good   (Item gradients only)

	Test floor	Test ceiling
Inadequate at ages:	Ages 85:0 to 89:11	Ages 16:0 to 34:11

Gf-Gc Classifications

Broad stratum II (Narrow stratum I)
Glr (MA); *Gv* (MV, SR)

Other Variables

Background & Environmental
- Environmental stimulation

Individual and Situational
- Concentration
- Verbal rehearsal

Degree of Linguistic Demand
L M H
Degree of Cultural Loading: L, M, H

WMS-III Letter-Number Sequencing: The examinee is required to listen to orally presented letter-number sequences and repeat the sequence back by arranging the numbers in ascending order, followed by the letters in alphabetical order. The length of the sequences is gradually increased over trials.

Basic Psychometric Characteristics

20 25 30 35 40 45 50 55 60 65 70 75 80
16 17 18 19 24 29 34 39 44 49 54 59 64 69 74 79 84 85+

Reliability
Item gradients

Low / Medium / High   Poor / Fair / Good   (Item gradients only)

	Test floor	Test ceiling
Inadequate at ages:		

Gf-Gc Classifications

Broad stratum II (Narrow stratum I)
Gsm (MW)

Other Variables

Background & Environmental

Individual and Situational
- Attention span
- Concentration
- Distractibility
- Verbal rehearsal
- Visual elaboration

Degree of Linguistic Demand
L M H
Degree of Cultural Loading: L, M, H

WMS-III Logical Memory I: The examinee is required to listen to two orally presented short stories and immediately retell the stories from memory following each presentation

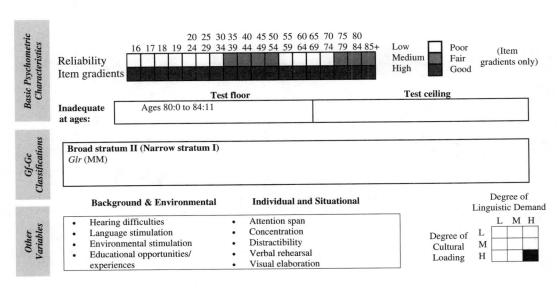

WMS-III Mental Control: The examinee is required to perform a series of simple tasks such as saying the alphabet, the days of the week, and the months of the year as rapidly as possible. The complexity of the task gradually increases to having the examinee perform multi-skill tasks such as saying the days of the week while counting by sixes.

Basic Psychometric Characteristics

	16 17 18	19	20 24	25 29	30 34	35 39	40 44	45 49	50 54	55 59	60 64	65 69	70 74	75 79	80 84	85+

Reliability
Item gradients

Low / Medium / High · Poor / Fair / Good (Item gradients only)

Test floor · **Test ceiling**

Inadequate at ages:

Gf-Gc Classifications

Broad stratum II (Narrow stratum I)
Gsm (MW)

Other Variables

Background & Environmental · **Individual and Situational**
- Attention span
- Concentration
- Distractibility
- Reflectivity/impulsivity

Degree of Linguistic Demand — Degree of Cultural Loading: H-M shaded

---

WMS-III Spatial Span: The examinee is required to point to a series of blocks on a three-dimensional board in the same sequence as presented by the examiner. In the backward condition, the examinee must perform the examiner's pointing sequence in reverse order.

Basic Psychometric Characteristics

Reliability
Item gradients

Low / Medium / High · Poor / Fair / Good (Item gradients only)

Test floor · **Test ceiling**

Inadequate at ages:

Gf-Gc Classifications

Broad stratum II (Narrow stratum I)
Gsm (MS); *Gv* (MV)

Other Variables

Background & Environmental · **Individual and Situational**
- Attention span
- Concentration
- Distractibility
- Verbal rehearsal
- Visual elaboration

Degree of Linguistic Demand — Degree of Cultural Loading: L-M shaded

WMS-III Verbal Paired Associates I: The examinee is required to listen to the oral presentation of eight novel word pairs, and, upon the presentation of the first word of each pair, the examinee must provide the second word of the pair

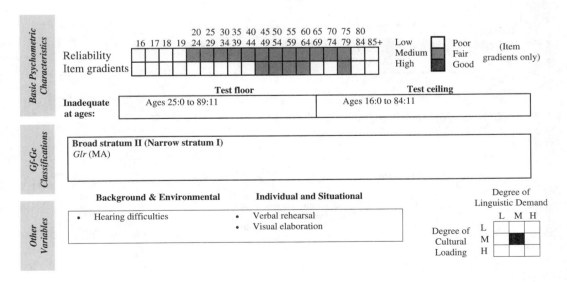

WMS-III Visual Reproduction I: The examinee is required to briefly view a design and draw it from memory.

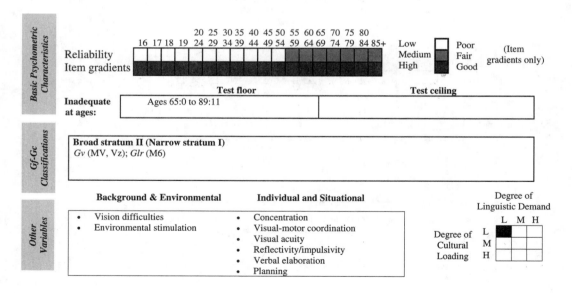

WMS-III Visual Reproduction II: A total of four conditions are presented to the examinee that require the examinee to draw designs from Visual Reproduction I in any order they can remember, identify the original designs they were shown from a series of 48 designs, reproduce designs while looking at them, and select one design from a group of six that matches a target design located at the top of a stimulus page.

WMS-III Word Lists I: The examinee is required to recall as many words as he or she can from a list of 12 orally presented, unrelated words. The process is repeated over a period of four learning trials. Later, the examinee is presented with a new word list and is required to recall as many words from the first list as he or she can.

Basic Psychometric Characteristics

				20 25 30 35 40 45 50 55 60 65 70 75 80
			16 17 18 19	24 29 34 39 44 49 54 59 64 69 74 79 84 85+

Reliability
Item gradients

Low · Medium · High

Poor · Fair · Good   (Item gradients only)

Test floor	Test ceiling

Inadequate at ages:

Gf-Gc Classifications

Broad stratum II (Narrow stratum I)
Glr (M6)

Other Variables

Background & Environmental	Individual and Situational
• Hearing difficulties	• Attention span
	• Concentration
	• Distractibility
	• Verbal rehearsal
	• Visual elaboration

Degree of Linguistic Demand

	L	M	H
Degree of Cultural Loading — L			
M			■
H			

WMS-III Word Lists II: The examinee is required to recall the original word list given in Word Lists I. Later, the examinee is read 24 words and is required to identify the word as belonging or not belonging to the original list.

Basic Psychometric Characteristics

				20 25 30 35 40 45 50 55 60 65 70 75 80
			16 17 18 19	24 29 34 39 44 49 54 59 64 69 74 79 84 85+

Reliability
Item gradients

Low · Medium · High

Poor · Fair · Good   (Item gradients only)

Test floor	Test ceiling
Ages 18:0 to 89:11	Ages 16:0 to 64:11

Inadequate at ages:

Gf-Gc Classifications

Broad stratum II (Narrow stratum I)
Glr (M6), (MA)

Other Variables

Background & Environmental	Individual and Situational
• Hearing difficulties	• Attention span
	• Concentration
	• Distractibility
	• Verbal rehearsal
	• Visual elaboration

Degree of Linguistic Demand

	L	M	H
Degree of Cultural Loading — L			
M			■
H			

CMS Dot Locations: The examinee is presented with a stimulus card containing a series of blue dots on a grid. After the card is removed from view, the examinee must place response chips on an empty grid to replicate the previously viewed dot locations. Later, the examinee is presented with additional stimulus cards with red dots that he or she must replicate. Finally, the examinee must replicate the first designs shown in trials 1-3 in the absence of any stimulus cards.

Basic Psychometric Characteristics

Reliability
Item gradients

| 5 | 6 | 7 | 8 | 9 | 10 | 11 | 12 | 13 | 14 | 15 | 16 |

Low — Poor   (Item
Medium — Fair   gradients only)
High — Good

	Test floor	Test ceiling
Inadequate at ages:		Ages 5:0 to 16:11

Gf-Gc Classifications

Broad stratum II (Narrow stratum I)
Gv (MV)

Other Variables

Background & Environmental   **Individual and Situational**

- Concentration
- Verbal rehearsal

Degree of Linguistic Demand

Degree of Cultural Loading

	L	M	H
L		■	
M			
H			

CMS Dot Locations 2: After 25-35 minutes, the examinee is required to replicate the original designs presented in Dot Locations

Basic Psychometric Characteristics

Reliability
Item gradients

| 5 | 6 | 7 | 8 | 9 | 10 | 11 | 12 | 13 | 14 | 15 | 16 |

Low — Poor   (Item
Medium — Fair   gradients only)
High — Good

	Test floor	Test ceiling
Inadequate at ages:	Ages 5:0 to 6:11	Ages 5:0 to 16:11

Gf-Gc Classifications

Broad stratum II (Narrow stratum I)
Gv (MV); *Glr* (MA)

Other Variables

Background & Environmental   **Individual and Situational**

- Concentration
- Verbal rehearsal

Degree of Linguistic Demand

Degree of Cultural Loading

	L	M	H
L		■	
M			
H			

CMS Faces: The examinee is presented with a series of 12 or 16 faces depending on their age. Following a presentation of all of the faces, the examinee must identify those faces they were asked to remember.

Basic Psychometric Characteristics

Reliability
Item gradients

| 5 | 6 | 7 | 8 | 9 | 10 | 11 | 12 | 13 | 14 | 15 | 16 |

Low □ Poor
Medium ▨ Fair (Item gradients only)
High ■ Good

Test floor   **Test ceiling**

Inadequate
at ages:

Gf-Gc Classifications

Broad stratum II (Narrow stratum I)
Gv (MV); *Glr* (MM)

Other Variables

Background & Environmental   **Individual and Situational**

- Concentration
- Reflectivity/impulsivity
- Verbal elaboration

Degree of
Linguistic Demand

	L	M	H
Degree of L			
Cultural M	■		
Loading H			

CMS Faces 2: The examinee must identify faces as either those they were asked to remember in Faces or as those they were not asked to remember.

Basic Psychometric Characteristics

Reliability
Item gradients

| 5 | 6 | 7 | 8 | 9 | 10 | 11 | 12 | 13 | 14 | 15 | 16 |

Low □ Poor
Medium ▨ Fair (Item gradients only)
High ■ Good

Test floor   **Test ceiling**

Inadequate
at ages:

Gf-Gc Classifications

Broad stratum II (Narrow stratum I)
Gv (MV); *Glr* (MM)

Other Variables

Background & Environmental   **Individual and Situational**

- Concentration
- Reflectivity/impulsivity
- Verbal elaboration

Degree of
Linguistic Demand

	L	M	H
Degree of L			
Cultural M	■		
Loading H			

CMS Family Pictures: The examinee is required to view and remember four scenes containing individuals (i.e., family members) engaged in specific activities. Following the presentation of all four scenes, the examinee is asked to recall information such as identifying characters in a particular scene, their respective locations in the scene, and the activities they were engaging in.

Basic Psychometric Characteristics

	5 6 7 8 9 10 11 12 13 14 15 16		Low		Poor	(Item
Reliability			Medium		Fair	gradients only)
Item gradients			High		Good	

	Test floor	**Test ceiling**
Inadequate at ages:		Ages 11:0 to 16:11

Gf-Gc Classifications

Broad stratum II (Narrow stratum I)
Glr (MA); *Gv* (MV), (SR)

Other Variables

Background & Environmental
- Environmental stimulation

Individual and Situational
- Concentration
- Verbal rehearsal

Degree of Linguistic Demand

		L M H
Degree of	L	
Cultural	M	■
Loading	H	

CMS Family Pictures 2: The examinee is presented with a family portrait stimulus card and is required to provide all of the information requested in Family Pictures I in the absence of any stimulus pictures.

Basic Psychometric Characteristics

	5 6 7 8 9 10 11 12 13 14 15 16		Low		Poor	(Item
Reliability			Medium		Fair	gradients only)
Item gradients			High		Good	

	Test floor	**Test ceiling**
Inadequate at ages:		Ages 11:0 to 16:11

Gf-Gc Classifications

Broad stratum II (Narrow stratum I)
Glr (MA); *Gv* (MV), (SR)

Other Variables

Background & Environmental
- Environmental stimulation

Individual and Situational
- Concentration
- Verbal rehearsal

Degree of Linguistic Demand

		L M H
Degree of	L	
Cultural	M	■
Loading	H	

CMS Numbers: The examinee is presented with a series of number sequences and is required to repeat the sequence verbatim. Later, the examinee is required to repeat number sequences in the reverse order as presented by the examiner.

Basic Psychometric Characteristics

Reliability
Item gradients

5 6 7 8 9 10 11 12 13 14 15 16

Low
Medium
High

Poor
Fair
Good

(Item gradients only)

	Test floor	**Test ceiling**
Inadequate at ages:		

Gf-Gc Classifications

Broad stratum II (Narrow stratum I)
Gsm (MS)

Other Variables

Background & Environmental
- Hearing Difficulties

Individual and Situational
- Attention span
- Concentration
- Distractibility
- Verbal rehearsal
- Visual elaboration
- Organization

Degree of Linguistic Demand

Degree of Cultural Loading

	L	M	H
L		■	
M			
H			

CMS Picture Locations: The examinee is presented with pictures located on a grid and, when the stimulus card is removed from view, must place "response chips" on a blank grid to denote the locations of the previously presented pictures.

Basic Psychometric Characteristics

Reliability
Item gradients

5 6 7 8 9 10 11 12 13 14 15 16

Low
Medium
High

Poor
Fair
Good

(Item gradients only)

	Test floor	**Test ceiling**
Inadequate at ages:		Ages 8:0 to 8:11

Gf-Gc Classifications

Broad stratum II (Narrow stratum I)
Gsm (MS); *Gv* (MV)

Other Variables

Background & Environmental

Individual and Situational
- Attention span
- Concentration
- Distractibility
- Verbal rehearsal
- Visual elaboration

Degree of Linguistic Demand

Degree of Cultural Loading

	L	M	H
L			
M		■	
H			

CMS Sequences: The examinee is required to perform a series of simple tasks such as saying the names of the month forward and backward as quickly as possible. This is a timed test.

Basic Psychometric Characteristics

Reliability
Item gradients

5 6 7 8 9 10 11 12 13 14 15 16

Low   Poor
Medium   Fair   (Item
High   Good   gradients only)

Test floor	Test ceiling
Inadequate at ages:	Ages 5:0 to 5:11	

Gf-Gc Classifications

Broad stratum II (Narrow stratum I)
Gsm (MW)

Other Variables

Background & Environmental

Individual and Situational

- Attention span
- Concentration
- Distractibility
- Reflectivity/impulsivity

Degree of
Linguistic Demand

	L	M	H
Degree of Cultural Loading L			
M			■
H			

CMS Stories: The examinee is required to listen to two orally presented stories. Following each individual presentation, the examinee is required to retell the story.

Basic Psychometric Characteristics

Reliability
Item gradients

5 6 7 8 9 10 11 12 13 14 15 16

Low   Poor
Medium   Fair   (Item
High   Good   gradients only)

Test floor	Test ceiling
Inadequate at ages:	Ages 5:0 to 5:11	

Gf-Gc Classifications

Broad stratum II (Narrow stratum I)
Glr (MM); *Gc* (LS)

Other Variables

Background & Environmental

- Hearing difficulties
- Language stimulation
- Environmental stimulation
- Educational opportunities/ experiences

Individual and Situational

- Attention span
- Concentration
- Distractibility
- Verbal rehearsal
- Visual elaboration

Degree of
Linguistic Demand

	L	M	H
Degree of Cultural Loading L			
M			
H			■

CMS Stories 2: The examinee is required to retell both stories that were presented in Stories I in the absence of any stimulus cues. Later, the examinee is required to answer questions presented by the examiner for each story.

CMS Word Lists: In trial 1, following the oral presentation of a word list, the examinee is required to recall as many words as possible in any order. In trials 2-4, the examinee is presented with those words omitted in their first recall and asked to recall those words as well as the original words recalled from trial 1. Finally, a new list is presented to the examinee and he or she must recall, in any order, as many words as possible from the first list.

CMS Word Lists 2: After a 20-35 minute delay, the examinee is required to recall as many words he or she can from Word List I. Later, the examinee is presented with a list of words and must identify the words as newly presented or previously presented words.

Basic Psychometric Characteristics

Reliability
Item gradients

5 6 7 8 9 10 11 12 13 14 15 16

Low — Poor
Medium — Fair   (Item gradients only)
High — Good

	Test floor	Test ceiling
Inadequate at ages:	Ages 5:0 to 7:11	Ages 8:0 to 8:11; 12:0 to 16:11

Gf-Gc Classifications

Broad stratum II (Narrow stratum I)
Glr (M6), (MA)

Other Variables

Background & Environmental	Individual and Situational
• Hearing difficulties	• Attention span • Concentration • Distractibility • Verbal rehearsal • Visual elaboration

Degree of Linguistic Demand

	L	M	H
Degree of Cultural Loading — L			
M			■
H			

CMS Word Pairs: The examinee is read a list of word pairs and, following the presentation of the first word pair, the examinee must provide the second word of the pair. After 3 trials, the examinee is required to provide both words of the pairs from memory.

Basic Psychometric Characteristics

Reliability
Item gradients

5 6 7 8 9 10 11 12 13 14 15 16

Low — Poor
Medium — Fair   (Item gradients only)
High — Good

	Test floor	Test ceiling
Inadequate at ages:		

Gf-Gc Classifications

Broad stratum II (Narrow stratum I)
Glr (MA)

Other Variables

Background & Environmental	Individual and Situational
• Hearing difficulties	• Verbal rehearsal • Visual elaboration

Degree of Linguistic Demand

	L	M	H
Degree of Cultural Loading — L			
M		■	
H			

CMS Word Pairs 2: Following a 25-35 minute delay, the examinee is asked to recall previously learned word pairs. Later, the examinee is presented with word pairs and must identify the pairs as previously learned or newly presented pairs.

Basic Psychometric Characteristics

Reliability
Item gradients

| 5 | 6 | 7 | 8 | 9 | 10 | 11 | 12 | 13 | 14 | 15 | 16 |

Low   Poor   (Item
Medium   Fair   gradients only)
High   Good

	Test floor	**Test ceiling**
Inadequate at ages:	Ages 5:0 to 7:11	

Gf-Gc Classifications

Broad stratum II (Narrow stratum I)
Glr (MA)

Other Variables

Background & Environmental	**Individual and Situational**
• Hearing difficulties	• Verbal rehearsal
	• Visual elaboration

Degree of
Linguistic Demand

	L	M	H
Degree of Cultural Loading — L			
M		■	
H			

ENDNOTES

1. It is important to note that the classification and shading of the respective reliabilites for each test in the summary pages are based on sample statistics that were fine-tuned to better approximate the population parameters. In other words, the effect of sampling error was reduced through the use of data smoothing procedures that are commonly used in the development of test norms (see McGrew, 1994; McGrew & Wrightson, 1997).

2. When indexes are associated with a reliability rating of *low,* they should not be interpreted or they should only be interpreted if performance is consistent across various sources of data.

3. We acknowledge The Psychological Corporation's (1997) warning to avoid using the WMS-III and CMS with linguistically diverse populations. We have taken the proper safeguards in our approach to using the *degree of linguistic demand* classifications with these batteries and recommend their use in a manner consistent with The Psychological Corporation's suggestions.

6

The *Gf-Gc* Cross-Battery Approach

Foundation, Rationale, and Application to the Wechsler Intelligence Scales

> *An individual who is unduly concerned with the Full Scale IQ is saying implicitly that a child's intellectual abilities can be summarized by a single score. . . Each new [Wechsler] profile should represent a challenge to prove emphatically that the child's abilities defy encapsulation in a single numerical value or even in a range of values.*
>
> —Kaufman (1994a, p. 271)

Since the late 1930s, the Wechsler Intelligence Scales have made significant contributions to research and practice in psychology and to special education. Although they remain the most widely used individually administered intelligence batteries, Part I of this text demonstrated that they do not adequately measure many of the broad cognitive abilities that contemporary psychometric theory and research deems important in understanding learning and problem solving. Thus, currently a gap exists between the known structure of cognitive abilities and the traditional practice of measuring these abilities (viz., through the use of the Wechsler Intelligence Scales). In order to narrow this theory-practice gap, the Wechsler Scales need to be modernized so that a broader range of cognitive abilities can be both measured and interpreted validly.

As discussed in Chapter 2, Horn and Cattell's *Gf-Gc* theory (Horn, 1985; 1988; 1991; 1994; Horn & Noll, 1997) and Carroll's (1993a; 1997b) hierarchical three-stratum theory of human cognitive abilities are the most widely accepted and well validated of the psychometric theories of multiple intelligences to date. The structure of intelligence that has emerged from this body of research (i.e., the integrated Cattell-Horn-Carroll *Gf-Gc* model presented in Chapter 2) is significantly different from the conceptualization of intelligence that underlies the Wechsler Scales. Given the extensive body of supporting evidence for the Horn and Carroll *Gf-Gc* models (summarized in Chapter 3), it is clear that the contemporary *Gf-Gc* taxonomy provides the most appropriate basis for understanding and interpreting the cognitive constructs that underlie intelligence tests (Carroll, 1997b; 1998; Flanagan, Genshaft, & Harrison, 1997; Flanagan & McGrew, 1995; 1997; Genshaft & Gerner, 1998; McGrew, 1997; McGrew & Flanagan, 1998; Woodcock, 1990; Ysseldyke, 1990).

The purpose of this chapter is to demonstrate how the *Gf-Gc* theoretical framework can be used as a foundation for understanding the breadth and depth of abilities that are measured (and conversely, not measured) by the Wechsler Intelligence Scales. This chapter is organized according to three broad categories of information. These categories include the *foundation* and *rationale* for and *application* of the *Gf-Gc* cross-battery approach. The organization of topics within these categories is displayed in Figure 6.1. This figure shows that the foundation of the cross-battery approach consists of three *pillars* (i.e., theory, stratum II test classifications, stratum I test classifications). These three pillars provide the *Gf-*

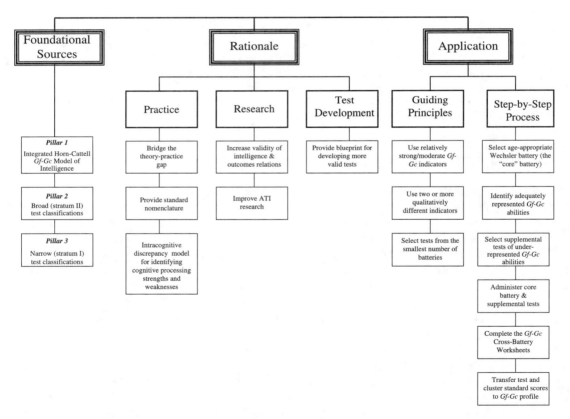

FIGURE 6.1   Foundation, Rationale, and Application of the *Gf-Gc* Cross-Battery Approach: An Organizational Structure

Gc taxonomic system requisite to effective selection of assessment tools and scientifically based interpretation of cognitive performance. Next, the rationale for the *Gf-Gc* cross-battery approach will be presented. This section demonstrates the significant benefits that will likely result when a transition from being test-kit focused to theory focused is made in practice, research, and test development. Finally, the application of the *Gf-Gc* cross-battery approach to the Wechsler Scales will be described. In this section, a set of guiding principles is offered for augmenting each Wechsler Scale with psychometrically sound and theoretically pure tests (e.g., those presented in Chapter 5). In addition to general guiding principles, a step-by-step approach to Wechsler-based cross-battery assessment is offered as a means of improving the reliability and validity of intellectual assessment, thereby narrowing the intelligence testing theory-practice gap. In this step-by-step presentation, the reader is "walked through" an actual case study using the WISC-III as the core battery in assessment. The WISC-III-based cross-battery data presented here are interpreted in Chapter 7 and described in a focused psychological report in Appendix F.

Unless an effort is made to devise new ways of measuring cognitive abilities, "we shall remain limited by obsolescent testing methods that do not reflect modern theories of cognition" (Hunt, 1990, p. 238). The "crossing" of batteries described here is not a new method of intellectual assessment per se, as it is commonplace in neuropsychological assessment (e.g., Lezak, 1976; 1995; Wilson, 1992). However, a method for crossing intelligence batteries was not formally operationalized until just recently (see McGrew & Flanagan, 1998). The cross-battery approach defined here provides a systematic means for practitioners to make valid, *up-to-date* interpretations of the Wechsler Intelligence Scales, in particular, and to augment them in a way that is consistent with the empirically supported *Gf-Gc* theoretical model. Through an understanding of the breadth and depth of broad (stratum II) *Gf-Gc* cognitive abilities and their relationship to outcome criteria, it will become clear that the measurement of these abilities, via Wechsler-based cross-battery assessment, supercedes global IQ in the evaluation of learning and problem-solving capabilities. The intracognitive data gleaned from Wechsler-based cross-battery assessments can be translated into educational recommendations (e.g., in a manner consistent with Mather, 1991). Moving beyond the boundaries of a single Wechsler test kit via the adoption of psychometrically and theoretically defensible cross-battery principles represents an improvement in the measurement of cognitive abilities (Carroll, 1998).

The Foundation of the *Gf-Gc* Cross-Battery Approach

The *Gf-Gc* taxonomy of human cognitive abilities "appears to prescribe that individuals should be assessed with regard to the *total range* of abilities the theory specifies" (Carroll, 1997b, p. 129). Because "any such prescription would of course create enormous problems," Carroll indicated that "[r]esearch is needed to spell out how the assessor can select what abilities need to be tested in particular cases" (p. 129). The *Gf-Gc* cross-battery approach (McGrew & Flanagan, 1998) was developed to spell out how practitioners can conduct assessments that approximate the total range of broad cognitive abilities more adequately than any single intelligence battery. According to Carroll (1998), McGrew and

Flanagan's *Gf-Gc* cross-battery approach "can be used to develop the most appropriate information about an individual in a given testing situation" (p. xi). This approach will be applied directly to the Wechsler Intelligence Scales in this chapter.

The *Wechsler-based Gf-Gc cross-battery approach* is a time-efficient method of cognitive assessment that is grounded in contemporary psychometric theory and research on the structure of intelligence. More specifically, it allows practitioners to validly measure a wider range (or a more in-depth but selective range) of abilities than that represented by a single Wechsler Scale. The cross-battery approach is based on three foundational sources or pillars of information: the integrated Cattell-Horn-Carroll *Gf-Gc* model of cognitive abilities; the *Gf-Gc* broad (stratum II) classifications of cognitive ability tests; and the *Gf-Gc* narrow (stratum I) classifications of cognitive ability test (Flanagan & McGrew, 1997; McGrew & Flanagan, 1998). Together, the three pillars provide the knowledge base necessary to organize theory-based, comprehensive, reliable and valid measures of cognitive abilities.

Cross-Battery Pillar 1: The Integrated Cattell-Horn-Carroll *Gf-Gc* Model

According to Kamphaus (1993), "[k]nowledge of theory is important above and beyond research findings as theory allows the clinician to do a better job of conceptualizing a child's score" (p. 44). Assessment and interpretation of cognitive functioning, therefore, should be grounded firmly in contemporary theory. The first pillar of the cross-battery approach is the *integrated Cattell-Horn-Carroll Gf-Gc model* of cognitive abilities (presented in Chapter 2). Because this model was described at length earlier in this text, it will not be explained again here. The *Gf-Gc* model is the one around which Wechsler-based cross-battery assessments are designed, because it has a more comprehensive network of validity evidence than other multidimensional conceptualizations of intelligence (Horn, 1994; Horn & Noll, 1997; Messick, 1992) (see also Chapter 3).

Cross-Battery Pillar 2: *Gf-Gc* Broad (Stratum II) Classifications

The second pillar of the cross-battery approach is the *Gf-Gc broad (stratum II) classifications* of cognitive ability tests. These classifications were reported originally by McGrew (1997) and subsequently were refined by McGrew and Flanagan (1998) based on their interpretation of a series of *Gf-Gc*-organized joint factor-analytic studies. Broad *Gf-Gc* ability classifications were necessary because they ensure that the *Gf-Gc* constructs which underlie cross-battery assessments are minimally affected by construct irrelevant variance (Messick, 1989; 1995), thus increasing the validity of score inference.

Construct irrelevant variance is present when an "assessment is too broad, containing excess reliable variance associated with other distinct constructs...that affects responses in a manner irrelevant to the interpreted constructs" (Messick, 1995, p. 742). For example, Figure 6.2 shows that the WISC-III Performance IQ (PIQ) has construct irrelevant variance because, in addition to its four indicators of *Gv* (i.e., Block Design, Object Assembly, Picture Completion, Picture Arrangement), it has one indicator of *Gs* (i.e., Cod-

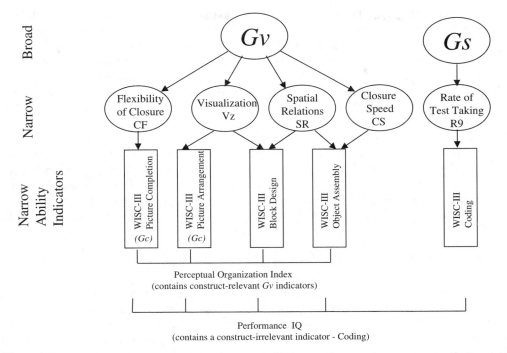

FIGURE 6.2   Examples of WISC-III Construct Relevant and Construct Irrelevant *Gv* Composites and Subtests

ing). Therefore, the PIQ is a *mixed* measure of two distinct, broad *Gf-Gc* abilities (*Gv* and *Gs*); it contains reliable variance (associated with *Gs*) that is irrelevant to the interpreted construct of *Gv*. This represents a grouping together of subtests on the basis of face validity (e.g., grouping tests together that *appear* to measure perceptual organization or nonverbal ability), an inappropriate aggregation of subtests which can actually decrease reliability and validity (Epstein, 1983). Before aggregating subtests for interpretive purposes, "it is desirable to establish through psychometric procedures, such as item-whole test correlations or factor analysis, that the different items contribute to the measurement of a common concept" (Epstein, 1983, p. 371).

Like the WISC-III PIQ, the WISC-III Picture Completion (PC) and Picture Arrangement (PA) tests, contain construct irrelevant variance. While both tests primarily measure *Gv*, they also share common variance with *Gc* tests (this is depicted in Figure 6.2 by the *Gc* code located in the PC and PA test rectangles). Specifically, in factor-analytic studies, the PC and PA tests consistently have displayed salient secondary loadings on a *Gc* factor. As such, these tests are factorially complex—a situation that complicates interpretation of these tests in isolation (e.g., is poor performance due to visual processing problems or low crystallized intelligence, or both?) and as part of a composite (e.g., did weaknesses in crystallized abilities attenuate the PIQ?).

Interpretation is far less complicated when composites are derived from relatively pure measures of the underlying construct. As shown in Figure 6.2, the Perceptual Organization Index is a purer measure of *Gv* than the PIQ. However, when considering the individual WISC-III visual processing tests, the purest *Gv* aggregate consist of the Block Design (BD) and Object Assembly (OA) tests. The BD and OA tests have strong loadings on a *Gv* factor and insignificant loadings on all other factors in *Gf-Gc*-designed joint factor analyses. Therefore, the BD and OA aggregate contains mainly construct *relevant* (i.e., *Gv*) variance.

Composite scores provide valid estimates of broad *Gf-Gc* abilities when they contain at least two reliable measures of two distinctly different narrow (stratum I) abilities subsumed by that broad ability[1]. Composite scores that contain excess reliable variance (i.e., measures of narrow abilities subsumed by two or more broad abilities) will confound interpretation. "[A]ny test that measures more than one common factor to a substantial degree yields scores that are psychologically ambiguous and very difficult to interpret" (Guilford, 1954, p. 356; cited in Briggs & Cheek, 1986). Therefore, cross-battery assessments are designed using only empirically strong or moderate (but not mixed) measures of *Gf-Gc* abilities (Woodcock, 1990) based on McGrew and Flanagan's (1998) classification system.[2]

We have added to and modified the classifications presented in McGrew and Flanagan (1998) using the information from recent *Gf-Gc*-organized joint factor-analytic studies. These *Gf-Gc* classifications and modifications are reported in Chapters 4 and 5. To date, over 250 *Gf-Gc* broad-ability classifications have been made based primarily on the results of joint factor-analytic studies (see Chapter 4 for details). These empirically based classifications of cognitive ability tests assist practitioners in identifying measures that assess various aspects of the broad cognitive abilities (such as *Gf* or *Gc*).

If constructs are broad and multifaceted, like those represented at stratum II in the *Gf-Gc* model, then each component (i.e., *Gf-Gc* broad ability) "should be specified and measured as *cleanly* as possible" (Briggs & Cheek, 1986, p. 130, emphasis added). Because the cross-battery approach combines only empirically strong (or moderate) measures of *Gf-Gc* abilities into construct relevant composites, this method provides a more valid means of measuring the narrow and broad *Gf-Gc* constructs than that offered by most single intelligence batteries.

Cross-Battery Pillar 3:
Gf-Gc Narrow (Stratum I) Classifications

The third pillar of the cross-battery approach is the *Gf-Gc narrow (stratum I) classifications* of cognitive ability tests. These classifications were originally reported in McGrew (1997) then later reported in McGrew and Flanagan (1998) following minor modifications. Classifications of individual test content and format at the narrow (stratum I) ability level were necessary to further improve on the validity of intellectual assessment and interpretation (see Messick, 1989). Specifically, these narrow-ability classifications were necessary to ensure that the *Gf-Gc* constructs that underlie cross-battery assessments are well represented. According to Messick (1995), *construct underrepresentation* is present when an "assessment is too narrow and fails to include important dimensions or facets of the construct" (p. 742). Two examples of construct underrepresentation inherent in traditional intellectual assessment follow.

First, construct underrepresentation is present when an individual test (i.e., subtest) is interpreted as measuring a broad (stratum II) *Gf-Gc* ability. For example, it is inappropriate to interpret the WAIS-III Vocabulary test as a measure of *Gc*, because *Gc* is a broad ability that subsumes several narrow abilities, including Language Development (LD), Lexical Knowledge (VL), Listening Ability (LS), General Information (K0), and Information about Culture (K2), to name a few (see Table 2.2 in Chapter 2). Although the WAIS-III Vocabulary test measures mainly VL, an important component of *Gc,* it represents only one narrow aspect of this broad ability. In order for a construct to be well represented, *two or more qualitatively different indicators* (i.e., measures of two or more narrow abilities subsumed by the broad ability) are needed (see Comrey, 1988; Messick, 1989; 1995).

According to Messick (1989), failure to represent constructs with more than one measure (or subtest) leads to *nomological noise*. That is, "[b]ecause no single test is a pure exemplar of the construct but contains variance due to other constructs and method contaminants, there is no solid basis for concluding that an observed score relationship stems from that part of the test variance reflective of the construct. By using two or more tests to represent the construct . . . one can disentangle shared variance from unshared variance and discern which aspects of construct meaning, if any, derive from the shared and unshared parts" (Messick, 1989, p. 48).

The Verbal Comprehension Index (VCI) of the WAIS-III, which includes Vocabulary (VL), Similarities (LD), Comprehension (LD), and Information (K0), provides a good estimate of the broad *Gc* ability because each test measures a qualitatively different aspect of *Gc*. Likewise, the VCI of the WISC-III, which includes Information (K0), Comprehension (LD), Similarities (LD), and Vocabulary (VL), is also a good estimate of *Gc*. Despite the fact that the *Gc* construct is well represented on the Wechsler Intelligence Scales, there are few composites among the major intelligence batteries that are both pure (i.e., contain only construct relevant tests) and well represented (i.e., contain qualitatively different measures of the broad ability represented by the composite). In fact, with the exception of the WJ-R/III, most major intelligence batteries yield composites characterized by construct irrelevant variance and have two or more constructs which are underrepresented (McGrew & Flanagan, 1998).

On the WISC-III, for example, the important constructs of *Gsm* and *Gq* are underrepresented. Given that the WISC-III Digit Span subtest measures one narrow ability subsumed by *Gsm* (i.e., Memory Span-MS) and the Arithmetic subtest measures one narrow ability subsumed by *Gq* (i.e., Math Achievement-A3), an interpretation of these tests as measures of the broad *Gsm* and *Gq* (stratum II) abilities, respectively, is inappropriate because there are not enough qualitatively different indicators of these broad abilities to represent them adequately. Therefore, before one can interpret or generalize about an individual's functioning in the broad domains of *Gsm* and *Gq,* the WISC-III must be supplemented with at least one additional, qualitatively different, narrow indicator of *Gsm* and *Gq*. Table 6.1 shows the *Gf-Gc* constructs that are well represented, underrepresented, and not measured by the Wechsler Intelligence Scales. The cross-battery principles, procedures, and steps that follow demonstrate how to augment any Wechsler Scale so that all *Gf-Gc* constructs (or, alternatively, only those constructs considered most important vis-à-vis referral issues) are well represented in assessment.

TABLE 6.1   *Gf-Gc* **Construct Representation on the Wechsler Intelligence Scales**

Wechsler Intelligence Scales

Construct	*Gf*			*Gc*			*Gv*			*Gsm*			*Ga*			*Glr*			*Gs*			*Gq*		
	WPPSI-R	WISC-III	WAIS-III	WPPSI-R	WISC-III	WAIS-III	WPPSI-R	WISC-III	WAIS-III	WPPSI-R	WISC-III	WAIS-III	WPPSI-R	WISC-III	WAIS-III	WPPSI-R	WISC-III	WAIS-III	WPPSI-R	WISC-III	WAIS-III	WPPSI-R	WISC-III	WAIS-III
Well represented				✓	✓	✓	✓	✓	✓											✓	✓			
Underrepresented			✓							✓	✓	✓							✓			✓	✓	✓
Not represented	✓	✓											✓	✓	✓	✓	✓	✓						

When constructs are underrepresented in factor analyses of cognitive ability tests, embedded factors result, which may misinform interpretation. Within-battery factor analyses of the Wechsler Intelligence Scales, for example, (described in Chapter 4) have been misleading (see McGrew & Flanagan, 1998) because they did not contain enough reasonably pure (or clean) measures for each of the factors present to allow the factor structure of the instrument to be identified clearly and interpreted appropriately (see also Woodcock, 1990; Woodcock & McGrew, in press). When a broad ability is represented by only one narrow-ability indicator, it may not emerge as a separate factor (i.e., it remains embedded) because there is an insufficient number of indicators to represent the broad ability. Thus, single narrow-ability indicators of different broad abilities or constructs may form a factor of their own.

For example, on the WISC-III, Digit Span (a narrow-ability indicator of *Gsm*) and Arithmetic (a narrow-ability indicator of *Gq*) formed the Freedom From Distractibility (FFD) factor (Wechsler, 1991). According to Carroll (1993a), the FFD factor is "an artifact of the factor analysis of a severely limited battery of tests, and is not to be considered as a basic primary factor in mental organization" (p. 258). The FFD factor demonstrates that factorial complexity masks the true factor structure of an instrument and confounds or misinforms interpretation (McGrew, 1999). However, this problem in assessment can be minimized in the cross-battery approach, because test classifications are used to organize relatively pure *Gf-Gc* clusters.

A second example of construct underrepresentation is when the aggregate of two or more measures of the same narrow (stratum I) ability is interpreted as measuring a broad (stratum II) *Gf-Gc* ability. For example, the Memory for Names and Visual-Auditory Learning tests of the WJ-R are interpreted as measuring the broad ability of *Glr* even though they are primarily measures of Associative Memory (MA), a narrow ability subsumed by *Glr*.

Similarly, with regard to factor analysis, the results of within-battery analyses may be misleading if they do not contain qualitatively different indicators for each of the factors present (e.g., Comrey, 1988; Woodcock, 1990). Subtests that measure the same narrow abilities should, of course, load on the same factor. However, that factor may be misinterpreted as representing a broad (stratum II) rather than narrow (stratum I) ability construct. For example, a factor composed of two or more subtests that measure Induction (I), a narrow ability subsumed by *Gf,* is most appropriately labeled *I,* not *Gf.* The factor is simply not broad enough to warrant a broad (stratum II) label. Only if the factor contained at least one additional indicator of *Gf* that was different from I, such as General Sequential Reasoning (RG), would a label of *Gf* be appropriate.

"A scale [or broad *Gf-Gc* ability cluster] will yield far more information—and, hence, be a more valid measure of a construct—if it contains more differentiated items [or tests]" (Clarke & Watson, 1995). The cross-battery approach suggests circumventing the misinterpretations that may result from underrepresented constructs by using two or more qualitatively different indicators to represent each broad *Gf-Gc* ability. Likewise, when discrepancies are found within broad ability domains, at least two indicators must be used to represent each narrow ability prior to making inferences or interpretations.

To supplement the broad (stratum II) ability classifications we used a systematic consensus process involving multiple experts (see Chapter 4 for details) to classify cognitive ability tests according to the narrow (stratum I) abilities they measure. The 250-plus tests mentioned above were also classified at the narrow ability level (McGrew & Flanagan, 1998). These classifications aid in the selection of qualitatively different test indicators for each of the broad abilities represented in *Gf-Gc* cross-battery assessments. Thus, construct validity is maximized rather than compromised.

In sum, the latter two cross-battery pillars guard against two ubiquitous sources of invalidity in assessment—construct irrelevant variance and construct underrepresentation. Taken together, the three pillars underlying the cross-battery approach provide the necessary foundation from which to build measures of cognitive abilities which are more theoretically driven, comprehensive, and valid.

Rationale for the *Gf-Gc* Cross-Battery Approach

For the purpose of this text, the *Gf-Gc* cross-battery approach is applied directly to the Wechsler Intelligence Scales, in order to improve on the validity of assessment and interpretation of these instruments (WAIS-III, WISC-III, or WPPSI-R) when either is used as the core battery in assessment. However, because this approach is theory-focused (rather than test-kit-focused), its principles and procedures can be used with any intelligence battery (Flanagan & McGrew, 1997; McGrew & Flanagan, 1998). In the intellectual assessment literature, the notion of "crossing" intelligence batteries to measure all the broad abilities included in contemporary *Gf-Gc* theory was first advanced by Woodcock (1990). However, others also have highlighted the importance of supplementing intelligence batteries to gain a more complete understanding of cognitive functioning (e.g., Kaufman, 1994). The limited utility of the data yielded by single intelligence batteries coupled with the conclusions drawn from *Gf-Gc*-organized cross-battery factor analyses, sparked the development of the cross-battery approach to assessment (Flanagan & McGrew, 1997; McGrew, 1997). The more specific and fundamental reasons for developing the cross-battery method are discussed below as they pertain to practice, research, and test development.

Practice

The cross-battery approach was developed to provide "a much needed and updated bridge between current intellectual theory and research and practice" (Flanagan & McGrew, 1997, p. 322). The results of a series of cross-battery factor analyses demonstrated that, with the possible exception of the WJ-III, none of our current intelligence batteries contain measures that sufficiently approximate the full range of *broad Gf-Gc* abilities that define the structure of intelligence in contemporary theory. According to McGrew and Flanagan (1998), of the eight major intelligence batteries currently in use, six fail to measure three or more broad *Gf-Gc* abilities (viz., *Ga, Glr, Gf, Gs*) that are important in understanding and predicting school achievement. In fact, they found that *Gf,* often considered to be the *essence* of intelligence, was either not measured or not measured adequately by half of the intelligence batteries in their review (i.e., WISC-III, WPPSI-R, WAIS-III, and K-ABC).

With the exception of the WAIS-III Matrix Reasoning test, the Wechsler Scales do not contain any strong indicators (or measures) of *Gf.* This is noteworthy, because the Wechsler Performance tests are often misinterpreted as measures of fluid reasoning (see McGrew & Flanagan, 1996; 1998, for a discussion and Kaufman, 1996, for a counter argument). Also noteworthy is the omission of measures of auditory processing *(Ga)* on all intelligence batteries except the WJ-R/III. Because many reading difficulties are strongly related to problems with phonological processes (one of the most common reasons for referral among elementary school children; Cacace & McFarland, 1998; Felton & Pepper, 1995; McBride-Chang, 1995; Morris et al., 1998; Stahl & Murray, 1994; Torgesen et al., 1994; Wagner et al., 1994), it is essential to assess these processing skills in all children who are experiencing reading problems. Recent research with two major intelligence batteries (i.e., WISC-R and WJ-R) demonstrated that significantly more variance in reading achievement is explained through appropriately designed cross-battery assessments as compared to single-battery assessments, highlighting the fact that most batteries by themselves are limited (i.e., *incomplete*; see Flanagan, 1999). Thus, the procedure of augmenting intelligence batteries through cross-battery assessment brings theory and practice closer together.

As summarized in Chapter 2, a standard *Gf-Gc* nomenclature was introduced to the field that links the major cognitive batteries to the *Gf-Gc* taxonomy. Most scientific disciplines have a common set of terms and definitions (i.e., a standard nomenclature) that facilitates communication among professionals and guards against misinterpretations. For example, in chemistry this standard nomenclature is reflected in the *Table of Periodic Elements.* McGrew and Flanagan (1998) developed the cross-battery approach in an attempt to operationalize a Table of Human Cognitive Elements based largely on their review of Carroll's (1993a) work, thereby advancing a standard nomenclature which might improve communication among practitioners, researchers, test developers, and scholars in the field of intelligence testing (McGrew, 1997).

To illustrate, one aspect of intelligence testing that can cloud the interpretation of cognitive performance is the inconsistency in terminology used to describe similar abilities measured by tests and composites across batteries. Considerable variability exists across batteries, for example, in the labels used by test authors to describe a standard block design test. The SB:IV Pattern Analysis test is purported to measure Abstract-Visual Reasoning (which is subsumed by fluid ability according to the theoretical model underlying the instrument) whereas WISC-III/WAIS-III Block Design, K-ABC Triangles, and DAS Pattern Construction are purported to measure Perceptual Organization, Simultaneous Processing, and Spatial Ability, respectively. Notwithstanding this variability in terms, a standard block design task is often interpreted as a measure of inductive and deductive reasoning (i.e., *Gf*) in the intelligence test literature (e.g., Kaufman, 1994). Considering that the demands of the Pattern Analysis, Block Design, Triangles, and Pattern Construction tests are essentially identical, which label is correct?

With the possible exception of the description offered by the authors of the SB:IV, all labels appear to depict, at least in part, the ability measured by a standard block design task (viz., visual-spatial). However, within the context of contemporary *Gf-Gc* theory and research, *none* of them would be considered accurate. In fact, since these labels are not consistent with the language of current theory and research, they may be misleading. For instance, interpreting any of these block design tests as *strong* or even *moderate measures* of fluid intelligence would be inaccurate. According to the *Gf-Gc* framework, Carroll's (1993a) classification of block-design tests, and the results of recent cross-battery factor analyses, the standard block-design-type tests measure two narrow abilities subsumed by the broad ability of Visual Processing *(Gv)*: Visualization (Vz) and Spatial Relations (SR). These labels are therefore most appropriate for describing block-design-type tests and interpreting the abilities that underlie performance on these tests.

Regardless of a practitioner's or researcher's preferred intelligence battery, the conceptualization and implementation of cross-battery assessments within a common *Gf-Gc* theoretical framework will appropriately reflect similarities across instruments as well as the *Gf-Gc* abilities that underlie all cognitive tests (McGrew & Flanagan, 1998). As a result, communication between and among practitioners, researchers, test developers, and scholars will be enhanced, and misinterpretations of cognitive test performance that result from armchair speculation will be minimized (McGrew, 1997).

Finally, we believe that the cross-battery approach offers practitioners a psychometrically defensible approach to conducting intracognitive discrepancy analyses.

> A major value of detecting severe discrepancies within and between areas of cognition is the focus on cognitive processing components of learning disabilities . . . the limited capacity of standardized instruments to assess isolated cognitive processes creates a major weakness in intracognitive discrepancy models. Although analysis of WAIS-R subtests typically report measures of distinct cognitive abilities, such abilities may not emerge by individual subtests but rather in combination with other subtests . . . Hence, intracognitive profiles, critical to learning disabilities diagnoses, cannot be determined by computing discrepancies between single test and subtest scores. (Brackett & McPherson, 1996, p. 79)

The cross-battery approach addresses this significant limitation of most major intelligence batteries. Specifically, by focusing interpretations on cognitive ability clusters (i.e., combination of subtests) that contain qualitatively different indicators of each of seven *Gf-Gc* broad cognitive abilities and processes, the identification of intracognitive processing strengths and weaknesses via cross-battery procedures is both psychometrically defensible and theoretically sound. In sum, the cross-battery approach addresses the longstanding need within the learning disabilities assessment and research literature for intracognitive discrepancy methods that "provide a greater range of information about the ways individuals learn—the ways individuals receive, store, integrate, and express information" (Brackett & McPherson, 1996, p. 80).

Research

The cross-battery approach was developed to promote a greater understanding of the relationship between cognitive abilities and important outcome criteria. Because cross-battery assessments are based on the empirically supported *Gf-Gc* theory of intelligence, and constructed in a psychometrically defensible manner, they represent a valid means of measuring cognitive constructs. It is noteworthy that when second-order constructs are composed of (moderately) correlated but qualitatively distinct measures, they will tend to have higher correlations with complex criteria (e.g., academic achievement) as compared to lower-order constructs, because they are broader in what they measure (Comrey, 1988). Predictive statements about different achievements (i.e., criterion-related inferences) that are made from cross-battery clusters are based on a more solid foundation than individual subtests (and perhaps many global scores from single intelligence batteries), because the predictor constructs are represented by relatively pure and qualitatively distinct measures of broad *Gf-Gc* abilities. Thus, improving the validity of *Gf-Gc*-ability measures may further elucidate the empirically established relations between specific *Gf-Gc* abilities and different achievement and vocational/occupational outcomes (see McGrew, Flanagan, et al., 1997; and Vanderwood, McGrew, Flanagan, & Keith, 1999 for a discussion).

The cross-battery approach may also lead to improved and more methodologically sound ATI research, because it encourages the use of better measures of *Gf-Gc* constructs than those that have been used typically in such research (Flanagan, Andrews, & Genshaft, 1997; Flanagan & McGrew, 1997). That is, it will allow for the investigation of whether instrumentation that more adequately operationalizes current intelligence theory (i.e., *Gf-Gc* cross-battery assessment) provides information that has direct relevance to treatment (Ysseldyke, 1990).

Test Development

The three pillars of the cross-battery approach represent a guide or "blueprint" for researchers who wish to develop tests with strong content and construct validity (see Kamphaus, Petoskey, & Morgan, 1997; Woodcock, McGrew, & Mather, in press). As already stated, most current intelligence batteries do not measure the full range of *Gf-Gc* abilities, and many fail to measure some important abilities adequately. The cross-battery approach highlights the breadth and depth of coverage of broad cognitive constructs that ought to be included in new or revised intelligence batteries to measure intelligence more completely, advance the field, and narrow the gap between practice and advances in cognitive psychology.

In summary, the cross-battery approach was developed to (1) provide practitioners with a means of conducting more valid and comprehensive intellectual assessments; (2) provide researchers with an arsenal of theory-driven and empirically supported classifications of intelligence tests that can be used to design and improve research studies on human cognitive abilities; and (3) provide test developers with a classification system that can be used to conceptualize new tests or modify existing ones. Because the Wechsler Intelligence Scales assess only a limited range of abilities, this chapter will demonstrate how to apply the cross-battery approach to these scales so that a broader range of *Gf-Gc* abilities can be measured. We believe that the cross-battery approach will advance and inform the use and interpretation of the Wechsler Scales by grounding them in solid psychometric principles, as well as current theory and research.

The Need for a Cross-Battery Assessment Approach

The need for cross-battery assessment techniques is not only apparent in school and clinical psychology (e.g., Kaufman, 1994; Woodcock, 1990), it is also apparent in neuropsychology (e.g., Lezak, 1976; 1995; Wilson, 1992). Neuropsychological assessment has been characterized for years by the crossing of various standardized tests in an attempt to measure a broader range of brain functions than that offered by any single instrument (Lezak, 1976; 1995). Unlike the *Gf-Gc* cross-battery approach however, the omnipresent cross-battery techniques within the field of neuropsychological assessment are not grounded in a systematic approach that is psychometrically and theoretically defensible. Thus, as Wilson (1992) cogently pointed out, the field of neuropsychological assessment is in need of an eclectic approach that would guide practitioners through the selection of measures that would result in more specific and delineated patterns of function and dysfunction—an approach that provides more clinically useful information than one that is "wedded to the utilization of subscale scores and IQs" (p. 382). Indeed, all fields involved in the assessment of cognitive functioning have a need for an approach that would allow practitioners to "touch all of the major cognitive areas, with emphasis on those most suspect on the basis of history, observation, and on-going test findings" (Wilson, 1992, p. 382).

Table 6.2 provides pertinent information regarding how the *Gf-Gc* cross-battery approach meets the most salient needs identified within the psychological assessment literature. Although the theories and conceptual models that underlie neuropsychological assessment may differ from those underlying other types of assessment (e.g., psychoeducational), the *Gf-Gc* cross-battery principles and procedures can be adopted within any assessment field.

Application of the *Gf-Gc* Cross-Battery Approach to the Wechsler Intelligence Scales

Guiding Principles

To accurately implement the Wechsler-based *Gf-Gc* cross-battery assessment approach, the three following guiding principles should be followed.

1. When constructing broad (stratum II) ability composites or clusters one should, include only *relatively pure Gf-Gc indicators* (i.e., those tests that had either *strong* or *mod-*

TABLE 6.2   Parallel Needs in Cognitive Assessment-Related Fields Addressed by *Gf-Gc* Cross-Battery Assessment

Need within the Field of Neuropsychological Assessment (Wilson, 1992)	Need Addressed in Assessment-Related Fields in Psychology by Cross-Battery Assessment Philosophy, Principles and Procedures
Neuropsychology has lagged in the development of conceptual models of the assessment of individuals. There is a need for the development of contemporary models.	School and clinical psychology have lagged in the development of conceptual models of the assessment of individuals. The cross-battery approach was designed to meet this need.
It is likely that there is a need for events external to a field of endeavor to give impetus to new developments and real advances in that field.	Carroll's and Horn's *Gf-Gc* theoretical models and continuing systematic programs of research in cognitive psychology provided the impetus for the cross-battery approach and led to the development of better assessment instruments and procedures.
There is a need for truly unidimensional assessment instruments for children and adults. Without them, valid interpretation of test scores are problematic at best.	Most scale and composite intelligence measures are mixed, containing excess reliable variance associated with a construct irrelevant to the one interpreted. The *Gf-Gc* cross-battery clusters yield estimates of relatively pure abilities represented in the *Gf-Gc* theoretical model, allowing for valid interpretation of multiple unidimensional abilities.
There is a need to utilize a conceptual framework to direct any approach to neuropsychological assessment. This would aid in both the selection of instruments and methods, and in the interpretation of test findings.	The cross-battery approach to assessment is premised on the *Gf-Gc* theoretical framework. Since this approach links all the major intelligence batteries (and a variety of supplemental tests) to the *Gf-Gc* conceptual model of the structure of intelligence, both selection of tests and interpretation of test findings is made easy.
It is necessary that the conceptual framework or model underlying neuropsychological assessment incorporates various aspects of neuropsychological function that can be described in terms of constructs which are recognized in the neuropsychological literature.	The cross-battery approach incorporates various aspects of cognitive function that are described in terms of constructs which are recognized in the extant psychoeducational assessment, intelligence and cognitive psychology literature.
There is a need to adopt a conceptual framework that allows for the measurement of the full range of behavioral functions subserved by the brain. Unfortunately, in neuropsychological assessment there is no inclusive set of measures which is standardized on a single normative population.	*Gf-Gc* cross-battery assessment allows for the measurement of a wide range of broad cognitive abilities specified in contemporary *Gf-Gc* theory. Although a cross-battery norm group does not exist at this time, the characteristics of the normal probability curve are used to interpret cross-battery assessment data effectively.

TABLE 6.2 Continued

Because there are no truly unidimensional measures in psychological assessment, there is a need to select subtests from standardized instruments which appear to reflect the neurocognitive function of interest. In neuropsychological assessment, the aim, therefore, is to select those measures that, on the basis of careful task analysis, appear mainly to tap a given construct.

It is clear that an eclectic approach is needed in the selection of measures, preferably subtests rather that the omnibus tests of cognitive abilities, in order to gain more specificity in the delineation of patterns of function and dysfunction.

There is a need to solve the potential problems that can arise from crossing normative groups as well as sets of measures that vary in reliability.

In neuropsychological assessment, we have found more useful clinical information is potentially available from a more eclectic approach than one that is wedded to the utilization of subscale scores and IQs.

The cross-battery approach is defined by a *Gf-Gc* classification system. Subtests from the major intelligence batteries (and various supplemental instruments) were classified empirically as measures of broad *Gf-Gc* constructs through theoretically-driven joint factor analyses. Subtests were also classified logically as measures of narrow *Gf-Gc* constructs via task analyses conducted by a panel of experts. Through a consideration of both sets of classifications, practitioners can be reasonably confident that a given test taps a given construct.

The cross-battery approach ensures that two or more relatively pure, but qualitatively different, indicators of each *broad* cognitive ability are represented in a complete assessment. Two or more qualitatively similar indicators are necessary to make inferences about *narrow Gf-Gc* abilities. This process is eclectic in its selection of measures, but attempts to represent all broad abilities by using a subset of measures from only two batteries. Additional iterations of assessment that may be necessary to delineate patterns of cognitive strengths and weaknesses may require the introduction of subtests from other batteries.

In cross-battery assessment, one can typically achieve baseline data in cognitive functioning across seven or eight *Gf-Gc* broad abilities through the use of only two well standardized batteries, which minimizes the effects of error due to norming differences. Also, since interpretation of both broad and narrow *Gf-Gc* abilities is made at the cluster (rather than subtest) level, issues related to low reliability are less problematic in this approach. Finally, because confidence intervals have been constructed for all broad and narrow cluster scores, the effects of measurement error are reduced further.

Recent research has demonstrated the potential benefits and increase in clinically relevant information that results through *Gf-Gc* cross-battery (versus single battery) assessment (e.g., Flanagan, 1999; McGrew, Flanagan, Keith, & Vanderwood, 1997).

erate [but not mixed] loadings on their respective *Gf-Gc* factors in cross-battery factor analyses). This factor loading information is available in Chapters 4 and 5, and is included on the Wechsler-based *Gf-Gc* cross-battery worksheets (Figures 6.4 to 6.10, pages 236 to 246) presented in the next section of this chapter (as well as in Appendix C).

There is one exception to this principle: A test that was classified *logically* at the broad (stratum II) level may be used in cross-battery assessments if there is a clear, established relation between it and the format of a test that was classified *empirically*. For example, although the WMS-III Digit Span test has not yet been included in adequately designed *Gf-Gc* cross-battery factor analyses, it is likely to be a good indicator of a narrow ability (i.e., Memory Span-MS) subsumed by the broad ability of *Gsm*. This is because it is very similar in testing format (e.g., administration procedure, task demand, nature of stimuli) to the Wechsler Intelligence Scales' Digit Span tests which had consistent strong loadings on a broad *Gsm* factor in adequately designed cross-battery factor analyses (e.g., Woodcock, 1990). Thus, the WMS-III and the Wechsler Intelligence Scale Digit Span tests measure a narrow ability (viz., MS) subsumed by *Gsm*. A good rule of thumb is to select empirically classified tests over logically classified tests whenever possible. This will ensure that only *construct-relevant* tests are included in cross-battery assessment. (These tests are clearly delineated on the cross-battery worksheets located in Appendix C.)

2. To ensure appropriate construct representation when constructing broad (stratum II) ability composites, *two or more qualitatively different* narrow (stratum I) ability indicators should be included to represent each domain. Without sufficient empirically and/or logically classified tests available to represent constructs adequately, inferences about an individual's broad (stratum II) ability cannot be made. For example, when a composite is derived from two measures of Vocabulary (VL), it is inappropriate to generalize about an individual's *broad Gc* ability, because the *Gc* construct is underrepresented. In this case the composite is best interpreted as a measure of Lexical Knowledge (a narrow stratum I ability) rather than *Gc* (a broad stratum II ability). Alternatively, inferences can be made about an individual's broad *Gc* ability based on a composite that is derived from one measure of Lexical Knowledge and one measure of General Information (i.e., two qualitatively different indicators of *Gc*). Of course, the more broadly an ability is represented (i.e., through the derivation of composites based on *multiple* qualitatively different narrow-ability indicators), the more confidence one has in drawing inferences about that broad ability based on the composite score. A minimum of two qualitatively different indicators per *Gf-Gc* composite is recommended in the cross-battery approach for practical reasons (viz., time efficient assessment).

3. When conducting cross-battery assessments, it is important to select tests from the *smallest number* of batteries to minimize the effect of spurious differences between test scores that may be attributable to differences in the characteristics of independent norm samples (McGrew, 1994). For example, the "Flynn effect" (Flynn, 1984) indicates that, there is, on average, a difference of three standard score points between the intelligence test scores of tests that are standardized 10 years apart. Using the WJ-R to augment the WISC-III or the WJ-III to augment the WAIS-III following the steps outlined below will ensure a valid and comprehensive assessment of most *Gf-Gc* broad abilities. Because the WISC-III and WJ-R, for example, were normed within 2 years of one another and both were found to have exemplary standardization sample characteristics (Kamphaus, 1993; Salvia & Ysseldyke, 1991), this combination of batteries would be appropriate for cross-battery assessments.

There are times, however, when crossing more than two batteries is necessary to gain significant information to test hypotheses about cognitive strengths or weaknesses, to answer specific referral questions, and so forth. For example, because *Glr* is not measured directly by any of the Wechsler Intelligence Scales, it may be necessary to cross one of the Wechsler Scales with more than one intelligence battery or supplemental test of *Glr* (see Chapter 5) in order to conduct an in-depth assessment of an individual's functioning in this area. This crossing of multiple (i.e., more than two) intelligence batteries is often necessary when conducting *selective cross-battery assessments* (discussed in Chapter 7). However, when cross-battery assessments are implemented systematically and adhere to the recommendations for development, use, and interpretation, the potential error introduced due to crossing norm groups is likely negligible and has far *fewer* implications than the error associated with the improper use and interpretation of cognitive ability performance associated with the traditional assessment approach (e.g., subtest analysis).

A Bridge from Theory to Practice

The aforementioned cross-battery pillars and guiding principles provide the foundation from which to conduct a comprehensive assessment of the broad *Gf-Gc* abilities that define the structure of intelligence in current psychometric research. The essence of the cross-battery approach can be understood by reviewing Figure 6.3. This figure graphically summarizes how the three pillars of the cross-battery approach are translated into practice. The first pillar (the empirically supported *Gf-Gc* theory of the structure of intelligence) is represented by the rectangles in the top portion of the figure labeled *Broad (stratum II) Gf-Gc Abilities*. This portion of the figure shows the 10 broad *Gf-Gc* abilities that are included in the integrated Cattell-Horn-Carroll *Gf-Gc* model (i.e., *Gf, Gc, Gq, Grw, etc.*). One of the broad abilities (i.e., *Gv*) is enlarged in Figure 6.3 to demonstrate how the second and third cross-battery pillars are translated into practice.

The center of Figure 6.3, labeled *Test Indicators,* lists the Wechsler tests as well as the tests from Chapter 5 according to their *Gv* classification. The empirically classified *Gv* tests represent the second pillar of the cross-battery approach and should be used instead of the logically classified tests whenever possible. The empirically classified tests are those that practitioners must consider in order to (1) ensure that the measures selected to assess *Gv* are *construct relevant* and (2) adhere to the first guiding principle of the cross-battery approach (i.e., include only relatively pure measures of ability in cross-battery assessment).

Finally, the bottom of Figure 6.3, labeled *Narrow (stratum I) Gf-Gc Abilities,* shows that the broad *Gv* ability subsumes many narrow abilities including Spatial Relations (SR), Visualization (Vz), Visual Memory (MV), Serial Perceptual Integration (PI), Closure Speed (CS), Spatial Scanning (SS), and Flexibility of Closure (CF). Figure 6.3 lists only the narrow abilities for which there are strong or moderate measures among the batteries and tests included in this book. The test indicators were classified according to the type of narrow ability they measure through a consensus among cognitive ability test experts (described in Chapter 4). This classification process represents the third pillar of the cross-

CROSS-BATTERY PILLAR # 1: INTEGRATED HORN-CATTELL/CARROLL *Gf-Gc* MODEL

Broad (str. II) *Gf-Gc* Abilities:

Gf *Gc* *Gq* *Grw* *Gsm* **Gv** *Ga* *Glr* *Gs* *Gt*

CROSS-BATTERY PILLAR # 2: BROAD (STRATUM II) CLASSIFICATION OF TESTS

Test Indicators:

- **WECH. BLK. DES.**
- DAS Patt. Const.
- **K-ABC TRIANGLES**
- **SB:IV PATT. ANALYSIS**
- Leiter-R Figure Rotation
- UNIT Cube Design

- **WPSSI-R** Geometric Des.
- DAS Block Building
- DAS Matching
- Let-Like Forms
- **WJ-R/III SPAT RELATIONS**
- Leiter-R Matching
- Leiter-R Form Completion
- Leiter-R Paper Folding
- NEPSY Block Construction

- WMS-III Vis Repro I
- CMS Dot Locations
- CMS Dot Locations 2
- CMS Picture Locations
- **DAS REC OF DESIGNS**
- DAS Recognition of Pictures
- K-ABC Face Recognition
- **KAIT MEM. BLK. DES.**
- **SB:IV Bead Memory**

- **SB:IV Memory for Objects**
- **WJ-R/III Picture Recognition**
- DTLA-3/4 Design Sequences
- DTLA-3/4 Design Reproduction
- Leiter-R Imm. Recognition
- Leiter-R Forward Memory
- **UNIT OBJECT MEMORY**
- **UNIT SPATIAL MEMORY**
- **UNIT SYMB. MEMORY**
- NEPSY Imitat. Hand Positions

- **WECHSLER OBJ. ASSEM.**
- **K-ABC Gestalt Closure**
- WJ-R/III Visual Closure
- DTLA-3/4 Picture Fragments

- **WISC-III Mazes**
- **WPPSI-R Mazes**
- **UNIT Mazes**
- NEPSY Route Finding

- **CAS Figure Memory**
- Leiter-R Fig. Ground

- K-ABC Magic Window

CROSS-BATTERY PILLAR # 3: NARROW (STRATUM I) CLASSIFICATION OF TESTS

Narrow (str. I) *Gf-Gc* Abilities:

Spatial Rels. SR	Visualization Vz	Visual Memory MV	Closure Speed CS	Spatial Scan. SS	Flex. of Clos. CF	Serial Perc. Int. PI

FIGURE 6.3 Translation of the Three *Gf-Gc* Cross-Battery Pillars into Practice

224

battery approach. Attending to the narrow-ability classifications of tests will ensure appropriate *construct representation,* as well as adherence to the second guiding principle of the cross-battery approach (i.e., to include two or more qualitatively different narrow-ability indicators when constructing *Gf-Gc* broad-ability clusters).

Similar schematic figures could be drawn to show the relations between all the broad and narrow abilities included in the *Gf-Gc* model, as well as between the classifications of the individual tests of the Wechsler Intelligence Scales and a multitude of other cognitive ability tests. However, rather than depict these relations and classifications in figures, this information has been translated into worksheets that can be used by practitioners to guide *Gf-Gc* cross-battery assessments. These worksheets together with a step-by-step approach to cross-battery assessment provide a bridge between *Gf-Gc* theory and practice.

Gf-Gc Cross-Battery Worksheets

Prior to enumerating the steps of the cross-battery approach, it is necessary to describe the *Gf-Gc* Wechsler-based *cross-battery worksheets* that were designed to facilitate more reliable and valid measurement of the broad and narrow abilities within the *Gf-Gc* theoretical model. These worksheets, originally presented in McGrew and Flanagan (1998), have been adapted and modified for use with the Wechsler Intelligence Scales. Seven cross-battery worksheets were constructed in all, one for each of the broad *Gf-Gc* abilities that are considered most critical in comprehensive evaluations of intellectual functioning. These worksheets can be found in Appendix C. Each worksheet contains the tests of the Wechsler Intelligence Scales and supplemental intelligence tests (from Chapter 5) that (1) had either strong or moderate loadings on their respective broad *Gf-Gc* factor (these tests are printed in bold uppercase and bold upper and lowercase letters, respectively, and represent empirically-based classifications); and (2) were classified logically as measures of the respective broad *Gf-Gc* abilities via an expert consensus process (these tests are printed in regular upper and lowercase letters).

Additionally, each worksheet groups the subtests according to the narrow ability that they measure via the expert consensus process. For example, the *Gf* worksheet (see Figure 6.4) groups subtests according to those that measure either Induction (I), General Sequential Reasoning (RG), or Quantitative Reasoning (RQ)—three narrow abilities subsumed by *Gf*. It should be noted that the individual tests included in these worksheets were classified as "probable" or "possible" measures of narrow abilities (see Chapter 4 for details). Only probable classifications are reflected in the worksheets. When a test was classified as a probable measure of two different narrow abilities (subsumed by the same broad ability), it was grouped with other probable measures of one narrow ability and the other narrow ability was reported in parentheses next to the subtest. For example, a review of the *Gc* worksheet (see Figure 6.5 on page 238) shows that the Wechsler Comprehension subtest is a probable measure of Language Development (LD), since it is grouped with other measures of LD on the worksheet. However, because the Comprehension subtest was classified also as a probable measure of General Information (K0), the code *K0* is printed in parentheses next to this subtest. The definitions of the broad and narrow abilities appear on the right side of each worksheet in Appendix C. Although brief, these definitions provide a quick reference and may facilitate test selection, test interpretation, and report writing.

Finally, the tests of the Wechsler Intelligence Scales and Wechsler-Linked Memory Scales (i.e., WMS-III and CMS) appear first on the worksheets, and are encapsulated in a bold border. Worksheets were not constructed for *Gq* and *Grw*, two broad abilities specified in the integrated Cattell-Horn-Carroll *Gf-Gc* model, because these abilities are measured best by comprehensive achievement (not intelligence) batteries (e.g., WIAT, WJ-R/III, ACH). Also, a worksheet for the broad ability of *Gt* was not constructed because this ability (as it is defined currently in Chapter 2) is not measured by any of the major intelligence batteries. Rather, *Gt* is measured best by reaction time (RT) paradigms, many of which are computer administered (Vernon, 1990). Thus, in order to assess the 10 broad *Gf-Gc* abilities in the *Gf-Gc* model, tests other than the Wechsler Intelligence Scales and the supplemental tests and batteries listed in Chapter 5 would need to be administered. However, when the Wechsler-based cross-battery approach is used together with a comprehensive achievement battery, adequate coverage of 9 of the 10 broad cognitive abilities specified in contemporary *Gf-Gc* theory and research can be achieved (leaving only *Gt* unassessed).

It is important to understand that the worksheets are *not* intended to be used in a "cookbook" fashion. They are intended to be used as guides in the selection of tests and as aids to ensure comprehensive assessment across a wide variety of *Gf-Gc* abilities. As will be demonstrated in the remainder of this text, clinical experience and clinical judgment play a necessary role in test selection and interpretation. The worksheets merely provide the clinician with the tools necessary to make certain that test selection and interpretation are grounded firmly in current theory and research on the structure of cognitive abilities. The next section demonstrates how the *Gf-Gc* cross-battery worksheets are used to *guide* more comprehensive and valid intellectual assessments.

A WISC-III-Based Cross-Battery Case Example

A psychoeducational evaluation that employed cross-battery assessment was conducted recently by one of our colleagues and will be used here to demonstrate the various steps of the cross-battery approach. Following is a brief summary of the individual who was evaluated using cross-battery procedures.

Identifying Information

Name of Child: Christine
Chronological Age: 7 years, 9 months
Grade: Second
Home Language: English
Language of Instruction: English

Reason for Referral

Christine was referred by her second grade teacher for a psychoeducational evaluation due to reported difficulty in reading, particularly with word recognition, decoding and sight-word vocabulary skills. Christine's teacher also reported that Christine had difficulty performing academic tasks that required spelling and written expression. This description of Christine's academic difficulties was corroborated by her reading teacher, who noted that Christine had made little progress, relative to her same-age peers. Likewise, Christine's parents agreed that despite additional external tutoring, Christine's progress in reading was slow.

Background Information

Christine resides with her biological mother and father, who each have a high school education. English is the language of Christine's household. Christine's mother reported an uneventful pregnancy. Christine achieved developmental milestones within normal limits. Christine was reported to be in good health and her medical history is otherwise unremarkable.

A review of Christine's academic history revealed difficulty in certain tasks such as learning the letters and sounds of the alphabet and learning to read and spell. In reading, Christine appeared to make progress through the use of visual context clues. Christine's mother reported that Christine has always had difficulty remembering information (e.g., nursery rhymes), despite numerous repetitions. This observation is consistent with teacher reports of Christine's difficulty with retaining and transferring information (e.g., writing words she hears). Despite these academic areas of concern, Christine's teacher reported that she achieves at a level commensurate with her peers in mathematics. However, she also stated that when mathematical problems are complicated by verbal directions, Christine's performance is hampered. Overall, Christine was described by her teachers as a very conscientious child who has good relations with her classmates. Based on a review of Christine's educational records, the nature of and limited progress associated with previous instructional interventions, observations by classroom teachers, and prereferral information given by her parents, Christine's evaluator concluded that further examination of cognitive abilities through standardized testing was warranted.

Tests Administered

Wechsler Intelligence Scale for Children—Third Edition (WISC-III) (selected subtests)

Woodcock-Johnson Psycho-Educational Battery—Revised, Tests of Cognitive Ability and Tests of Achievement (selected subtests)

Children's Memory Scale (CMS) (selected subtests)

NEPSY(Speeded Naming subtest)

Behavioral Observations

Christine approached the evaluation session in a cooperative manner and rapport was established easily. She worked diligently throughout the evaluation and persisted on items she found to be difficult. She also appeared attentive throughout the evaluation and maintained concentration on all tasks. Despite her cooperative and focused manner, Christine exhibited difficulties on tasks that required visual tracking and she often skipped a line when required to read. Furthermore, Christine experienced trouble on a task that required her to reproduce increasingly complex designs using three-dimensional blocks. Specifically, on removal of the lines on the block design stimulus cards, which demarcate the blocks that comprise the design, she failed to produce a correct response.

The manner in which Christine's cognitive abilities were assessed is described below. The steps that follow enumerate the procedures necessary to conduct a comprehensive assessment of a broad range of cognitive abilities. Given that Christine demonstrated little progress despite instructional interventions, Examiner A chose to gather baseline data across all the major cognitive areas with emphasis on those suspect on the basis of history, referral information, and observation. In the event that an assessment of a broad range of cognitive abilities is not necessary, a more selective assessment can be conducted (see Chapter 7).

A Step-by-Step Wechsler-based Approach to *Gf-Gc* Cross-Battery Assessment

Step 1: Begin with the Wechsler Intelligence Scale Appropriate for the Age and Developmental Level of the Examinee.   Based on Christine's chronological age (7 years, 9 months), Examiner A began with the WISC-III as the *core* battery around which a *Gf-Gc* cross-battery assessment will be designed.

Once a core battery is selected, it is necessary to consider whether a Full Scale score is needed. This is because many state and professional classification systems (e.g., DSM:IV; AAMR mental retardation guidelines; Jacobson & Mulick, 1996) regularly use a Full Scale IQ in formulas designed to aid decision making in the diagnosis of learning disabilities and developmental delays. However, many of these formulas (e.g., those used in the discrepancy model for identifying significant ability-achievement differences to assist in diagnosing learning disability) are not only technically invalid, but are invalid for the very purpose for which they are used (e.g., to aid in the diagnosis of LD) (see Appendix H). The Wechsler-based *Gf-Gc* cross-battery approach does not emphasize a Full Scale IQ or recommend that one be calculated using cross-battery clusters.[3] Rather, one of the most effective uses of the cross-battery approach is to generate a broad range of reliable and valid *Gf-Gc* clusters for the purpose of identifying cognitive processing deficits—an important and necessary condition in the diagnosis of learning disabilities. Therefore, rather than continue to use limited batteries to obtain full scale scores for the purpose of plugging them into formulas that lack technical and consequential validity (see Aaron, 1997), the cross-battery approach offers technically valid procedures for identifying cognitive processing strengths and weakness that are grounded in research and a well-validated theory. Issues related to another, often necessary condition, that must be met to diagnose a learning disability (i.e., significant ability-achievement and aptitude-achievement discrepancy) are addressed in Appendix H.

If a complete intelligence battery must be administered to obtain a Full Scale score (or in the case of the WISC-III, a General Ability Index or GAI; Prifitera, Weiss, & Saklofske, 1998), then cross-battery assessment may increase testing time (since individual tests that do not meet the cross-battery guiding principles will need to be administered), depending on the core battery preference of the practitioner. If it is not necessary to use a complete battery to obtain a full scale score because it is either not relevant to the referral question or not required by formal criteria and regulations, then cross-battery testing time will probably remain equivalent to single-battery testing time. Since Examiner A was not constrained by formal guidelines and was most interested in understanding Christine's *intracognitive* strengths and weaknesses, she did not find it necessary to obtain a WISC-III Full Scale IQ.

Given the prominent status that a global IQ assumes in most psychoeducational assessments, regardless of referral, it is necessary to place the importance of a global intelligence score or IQ in perspective prior to proceeding to Step 2. Theoretical debates about *g* aside (see Jensen, 1998), proponents of *g* maintain that due to its undeniable importance in predicting a wide variety of academic and occupational outcomes, intelligence tests should provide a single full scale or composite score that conceptually represents general intelligence. However, the philosophy underlying the cross-battery approach to intellectual assessment focuses on broad (stratum II) *Gf-Gc* abilities rather than a global (stratum III) ability (or *g*) for the following reasons.

First, although a general intelligence factor undeniably accounts for the lion's share of the variance in academic and occupational success, its relevance for intervention is limited. For example, recent research that investigated the relations between *g* and seven *Gf-Gc* specific abilities and general and specific reading achievement (Keith, in press; McGrew, Flanagan et al., 1997; Vanderwood, McGrew, Flanagan, & Keith, 1999) found that *Ga* abilities were strongly related to reading above and beyond the explanation provided by *g*. That is, although the effect of *g* was larger than that for *Ga*, recent research (e.g., Felton & Pepper, 1995; McGuiness et al., 1995; Wagner et al., 1994) has shown that intervention directed at specific *Ga* abilities can improve reading performance. Conversely, attempts to modify general intellectual ability have not resulted in long-standing changes (Gustafsson & Undheim, 1996), with the available research suggesting that specific abilities may be most amenable to modification (Carroll, 1993a). Thus, it is our belief that the probability of developing successful interventions lies not at the apex of the hierarchy of cognitive abilities (i.e., stratum III—*g*), but at lower levels (viz., stratum I and II *Gf-Gc* abilities) (see also Kaufman, 1994).

Second, the cross-battery approach was designed expressly to improve the usefulness of intelligence test interpretation through the delineation of an individual's broad *Gf-Gc* intracognitive strengths and weaknesses. This focus on understanding an individual's functioning across various broad and narrow cognitive abilities has been the preeminent topic of many psychological assessment spokespersons (e.g., Kaufman, 1994; Lezak, 1995).

According to Kaufman (1990a), "the individual tested makes an unspoken plea to the examiner not to summarize his or her intelligence in a single, cold, number; the goal . . . should be to respond to that plea by identifying hypothesized strengths and weaknesses that extend well beyond the limited information provided by FS-IQ, and that will conceivably lead to practical recommendations that help answer the referral questions" (p. 422). Kaufman's comments were echoed by Lezak (1995) who, when discussing the Wechsler Full Scale IQ score in her neuropsychological assessment text, stated that average scores on a WIS battery provide just about as much information as do averaged scores on a school report. There is no question about the performance of students with a four-point average: they can only have had an A in each subject. Nor is there any question about individual grades obtained by students with a zero grade point average. Excluding the extremes, however, it is impossible to predict specific disabilities and areas of cognitive competency or dysfunction from the averaged ability test scores. For these reasons, test data reported in IQ scores have not been presented in this book. (p. 691)

Although we recognize the substantial and undeniable empirical evidence that demonstrates that general ability (or *g*) is "among the most dominant and enduring factors, both causal and corollary, associated with scholastic and occupational success; environmental adaptation; physical propensity and morbidity; scientific, cultural and political acumen" (McDermott, Fantuzzo, & Glutting, 1990, p. 291), we believe that the *Gf-Gc* cross battery approach uncovers the individual skills, abilities, and processes that are more diagnostic of learning and problem solving than a global IQ.

Furthermore, when a broad range of *Gf-Gc* abilities are represented in assessment, it is probable that the cognitive abilities most closely associated with a specific academic deficit will be concomitantly low for an individual who is learning disabled, thus attenuating a Full Scale score. In such cases, although underlying cognitive ability deficits were identified (e.g., through intracognitive analysis) and their relationship to a particular achievement area was established (providing evidence relevant to a learning disability diagnosis) it is unlikely that a significant ability-achievement discrepancy will be found (see Appendix H for a discussion). For example, performance in the *Gf-Gc* domains of *Ga, Glr, Gsm,* and/or *Gs* may be low for a child who is having significant difficulty acquiring reading skills. As a result, the cognitive ability aggregate or Full Scale score (which includes *Ga, Glr, Gsm,* and *Gs* test scores) for this child may be similar in level to her reading achievement performance because it includes performance on cognitive tasks likely to be deficient in individuals with reading difficulties (see Cacace & McFarland, 1998; McGrew, 1993; Morris et al., 1998). Moreover, attempts to demonstrate the validity of identifying poor readers based on discrepancies between global IQ and reading scores have failed (see Aaron, 1997; Morris et al., 1998). This is likely due to the fact that the ability-achievement discrepancy approach is largely atheoretical and does not reflect current research and knowledge on the cognitive bases of reading disability (Morris et al., 1998). In short, since the premise underlying a learning disability is that it is the result of a specific cognitive processing deficit(s), a significant *intracognitive discrepancy* ought to be the primary indicator of learning disability, whereas ability-achievement and intra-achievement discrepancies ought to be secondary (Brackett & McPherson, 1996; Mather, 1993). The *Gf-Gc* cross-battery approach is among the best methods available for examining intracognitive discrepancies. (See Appendix H for a more detailed discussion of the validity and utility of the Ability-Achievement discrepancy model as well as guidelines for interpreting ability-achievement discrepancy results.)

Therefore, we believe that the *Gf-Gc* cross-battery approach represents a "best practices" approach to intellectual assessment, particularly for the purpose of identifying underlying cognitive processing strengths and weaknesses, and concur with Lezak's (1995) position:

[It] has been suggested that examiners retain IQ scores in their reports to conform to the current requirements of . . . various other administrative agencies . . . this is not merely a case of the tail wagging the dog but an example of how outdated practices may be perpetuated even when their invalidity and potential harmfulness has been demonstrated. Clinicians have a responsibility not only to maintain the highest—and most current—practice standards, but to communicate these to the consumer agencies. If every clinician who understands the problems inherent in labeling people with IQ scores ceased using them, then agencies would soon cease asking for them. (p. 691)

A Wechsler-based *Gf-Gc* cross-battery approach allows practitioners to gather information about strong and weak areas of intellectual performance across a wide range of relatively pure cognitive abilities—information that can assist in diagnosis (e.g., identification of underlying cognitive processing deficits) and that may be translated into meaningful educational interventions. The traditional assessment methods of obtaining global IQs do not fare well in this effort.

Step 2: Identify the* Gf-Gc *Abilities That Are Represented Adequately on the Core Battery. This may be achieved by reviewing Table 6.1 or the *Gf-Gc* cross-battery worksheets in Appendix C. Examiner A reviewed Table 6.1 and found that *Gc, Gv,* and *Gs* are represented adequately on the WISC-III. If it is necessary to administer the full core intelligence battery (to obtain a Full Scale score), then all the test indicators of the abilities that are adequately represented on the battery will probably need to be administered (e.g., four WISC-III tests that comprise the VCI, the analogue for *Gc,* rather than two). However, if a Full Scale score is not needed (as in Examiner A's situation), then begin by examining the worksheets (Appendix C) and identifying which two tests will be administered within the *Gf-Gc* domains that are represented adequately on the battery, since in some cases more than two qualitatively different indicators may represent a broad ability.

Examiner A reviewed the *Gc* worksheet and found that four WISC-III subtests (i.e., Comprehension, Similarities, Vocabulary, Information) are strong measures of *Gc* (i.e., they are printed in bold uppercase letters). Based on the guiding principle that a minimum of two qualitatively different indicators are needed to represent a broad ability, Examiner A selected the Vocabulary (a measure of lexical knowledge [VL]) and language development [LD]) and Information (a measure of General Information [K0]) tests for inclusion in her battery. Although Examiner A could just as well have combined Information (K0) and Similarities (LD) to represent *Gc,* the Vocabulary test was selected given the significant relation that has been documented between the narrow ability of Lexical Knowledge (which is measured by Vocabulary tests) and reading achievement (Aaron, 1995; Cacace & McFarland, 1998; Morris et al., 1998). This decision illustrates the need for examiners to select tests within the context of specific referral concerns rather than to follow a blind "cookbook" approach to assesssment.

Similarly, Examiner A selected Block Design (Spatial Relations [SR]) and Object Assembly (Closure Speed [CS]) from the *Gv* worksheet, and Symbol Search (Perceptual Speed [P]) and Coding (Rate-of-Test-Taking [R9]) from the *Gs* worksheet to represent other broad target abilities. Up to this point, Examiner A's battery consists of six WISC-III tests that provide adequate representation of three *Gf-Gc* abilities (i.e., *Gc, Gv,* and *Gs*).

Step 3: Identify the* Gf-Gc *Abilities That Are Both Not Represented and Underrepresented on the Core Battery and Determine the Tests That Will Be Used to Approximate or Ensure Adequate Representation of These Abilities. Identification of *Gf-Gc* abilities that are either not represented or underrepresented on a given Wechsler Intelligence Scale can be achieved by reviewing either Table 6.1 or the *Gf-Gc* cross-battery worksheets in Appendix C. Examiner A located the WISC-III in Table 6.1 and found that the abilities of *Gf, Ga,* and *Glr* are not represented in (i.e., not measured by) this battery.

Keeping in mind that a small number of batteries should be used (preferably two) whenever possible (following the third guiding principle of the cross-battery approach), Examiner A reviewed the *Gf, Ga,* and *Glr* cross-battery worksheets and found that the WISC-III could be supplemented best with the WJ-R battery. For example, the WJ-R includes two strong, qualitatively different indicators of *Gf* (i.e., Concept Formation—a measure of Induction [I], and Analysis-Synthesis—a measure of General Sequential Reasoning [RG]), two strong qualitatively different indicators of *Ga* (i.e., Incomplete Words—a measure of Phonetic Coding: Analysis [PC:A] and Sound Blending—a measure of Phonetic Coding: Synthesis [PC:S]), and two strong indicators of *Glr* (i.e., Memory for Names and Visual-Auditory Learning). However, both *Glr* tests measure Associative Memory (MA), yielding a narrow MA cluster rather than a broad *Glr* cluster. In some instances, it may be sufficient to augment the WISC-III with only associative memory tasks from the WJ-R to sample a narrow aspect of *Glr* (e.g., when gathering baseline data or when screening performance in this domain). However, since memory ability was described *a priori* as an area of concern for Christine, Examiner A chose to cross more than two batteries in order to achieve a broader evaluation of *Glr*. Specifically, Examiner A chose to administer the logically classified test of Free Recall Memory (M6; i.e., Word Lists) from the CMS.

The reasons for selecting M6 from the CMS to broaden the assessment of *Glr* were threefold. First, a logically classified test was selected over an empirically classified test because no empirically classified tests of narrow abilities subsumed by *Glr* (with the exception of MA tests) were available at the time of this evaluation. Second, a test from the CMS was chosen over one from another battery because of its link to the WISC-III (i.e., these two batteries share a common sample). Third, although Stories 2 (another CMS test which measures meaningful memory [MM], a narrow ability involved in Visual-Auditory Learning) is listed on the *Glr* worksheet, it was not selected because Stories (a mixed measure of *Gsm* [Memory Span] and *Gc* [Listening Ability]), a prerequisite for Stories 2, was not administered. Therefore, of the two *Glr* CMS tests, Word Lists represents a *Glr* narrow ability (M6) distinct from Visual-Auditory Learning (MA). Together, Visual-Auditory Learning and Word Lists yield a broad *Glr* cluster.

Up to this point, Examiner A has 12 tests in her battery. In Step 2, six WISC-III tests were identified to represent qualitatively different aspects of *Gc, Gv,* and *Gs*; four WJ-R tests were identified in the present step to represent aspects of *Gf* and *Ga;* and one WJ-R and one CMS test were identified to represent *Glr*.

In addition to the abilities that are not represented on the WISC-III, Table 6.1 reveals the abilities that are underrepresented on this battery (viz., *Gq* and *Gsm*). Since *Gq* is measured best by a comprehensive academic achievement battery (e.g., WIAT) and since mathematics achievement was not a specific referral concern for Christine, it was not considered further in the design of Christine's *Gf-Gc* cross-battery assessment. *Gsm* is underrepresented on the WISC-III; only one narrow ability indicator (i.e., Digit Span) of this broad ability is included. As discussed in Chapter 2, until recently, *Gsm* subsumed only two narrow abilities, namely Memory Span (MS) and Learning Abilities. Because Learning Abilities are not well defined in the cognitive abilities literature (Carroll, 1993a), and because there is little indication (or evidence) that any intelligence tests even measure these abilities. *Gsm* is defined mainly by tests of MS. However, Working Memory (MW) has recently been included as part of the *Gsm* construct, allowing for broader measurement of memory ability (see Chapter 2). Thus, Examiner A chose to broaden and strengthen the measurement of *Gsm* in her evaluation of Christine by including a test of working memory from the CMS (i.e., Sequences).

The fact that some broad (stratum II) *Gf-Gc* abilities (e.g., *Ga, Gsm*) can be represented by *only two or three* qualitatively different narrow abilities (as opposed to *multiple* narrow abilities) highlights the limitations of intelligence instrumentation with respect to diversity of abilities measured and adherence to contemporary theory. Ideally, the "universe" of cognitive ability tests should allow for the selective measurement of multiple narrow (stratum I) abilities that comprise the broad (stratum II) abilities in contemporary *Gf-Gc* theory.

Step 4: Administer the Core Battery Identified in Step 1 and Supplemental Tests Identified in Steps 2 and 3.   Table 6.3 depicts the tests that were selected by Examiner A to be administered in Christine's WISC-III-based cross-battery assessment. As can be seen in this table, two tests (rather than one) will be administered for each of seven *Gf-Gc* abilities to increase the reliability and validity of the obtained cluster scores. It is also evident that all *Gf-Gc* abilities are represented by two qualitatively different indicators, allowing for a broad-ability interpretation across *Gf-Gc* domains. In most instances, the selected test indicators were classified as strong measures of their respective *Gf-Gc* underlying abilities.

Of the seven cognitive clusters that will result from this cross-battery assessment, two include logically classified measures. As stated earlier, less confidence is associated with clusters that are derived using logically classified, as opposed to empirically classified, tests. However, no other option was available for the construction of broad ability clusters in the area of *Glr* and *Gsm* at the time this evaluation was conducted.

Finally, Table 6.3 shows that a seven-test WISC-III battery needed to be supplemented with tests from two other batteries (i.e., the WJ-R and the WISC-III linked CMS) in order to (1) adhere closely to the guiding principles of the cross-battery approach, (2) measure a comprehensive range of broad abilities, and (3) represent well those abilities considered important based on referral concerns (e.g., memory, auditory processing). This cross-battery assessment was designed to provide information about three *Gf-Gc* abilities not currently assessed by the WISC-III (i.e., *Gf, Ga,* and *Glr*) and to yield a more reliable and valid measure of *Gsm,* an ability currently underrepresented on the WISC-III. Also noteworthy is that the increase in test administration time associated with this WISC-III/ WJ-R/CMS cross-battery assessment was negligible. That is, a 14-test battery was administered (i.e., 7 WISC-III plus 5 WJ-R and 2 CMS tests) instead of the more typical 13-test battery (i.e., the WISC-III).

It is important to note that Table 6.3 depicts only one of numerous Wechsler-based cross-battery combinations that may result as a function of the supplemental tests selected

TABLE 6.3   A WISC-III-Based *Gf-Gc* Cross-Battery Case Example

Gf	*Gc*	*Gv*	*Gsm*	*Glr*	*Ga*	*Gs*
ANALYSIS-SYNTHESIS (RG)	*INFORMATION (K0)*	BLOCK DESIGN (SR)	DIGIT SPAN (MS)	VISUAL-AUDITORY LEARNING (MA)	INCOMPLETE WORDS (PC:A)	*CODING (R9)*
CONCEPT FORMATION (I)	*VOCABULARY (VL)*	OBJECT ASSEMBLY (CS)	CMS Sequences (MW)	CMS Word Lists (M6)	SOUND BLENDING (PC:S)	*SYMBOL SEARCH (P)*

Note: The test names in italics are from the WISC-III (the core battery). Tests not in italics are from the WJ-R or CMS (the supplemental batteries). The CMS tests are labeled as such. Tests printed in uppercase/bold letters are strong measures as defined empirically. Tests printed in uppercase and lowercase/no bold letters are logically classified measures that were defined through an expert consensus process.

to augment the core battery and/or the nature of the referral concerns. A WISC-III/WJ-R combination or the WISC-III/WJ-R/CMS combination presented here likely represent the most practical unions of tests in light of the frequency with which the WISC-III is used, the diversity of *Gf-Gc* measures included on the WJ-R/III, and the link between the WISC-III and CMS. Although it is beyond the scope of this book to present every possible combination of supplements to the Wechsler Intelligence Scales, the reader can be certain that other combinations of tests that are derived following the above mentioned cross-battery guiding principles and steps will yield equally valid and useful broad *Gf-Gc* clusters. Also, the various decisions made by Examiner A illustrate that Wechsler-based *Gf-Gc* cross-battery assessment should not be considered a rigid "cookbook" approach to intellectual assessment. Rather, the design of each cross-battery assessment should reflect an attempt to construct the most technically sound assessment within the confines of practical constraints (e.g., time and tests available to the examiner) and the specific referral concerns for an individual.

Step 5: Complete the Gf-Gc Cross-Battery Worksheets.   Examiner A recorded all individual test standard scores on the worksheets in the column marked *SS* and followed the directions printed on the worksheet for recording narrow- and broad-ability standard score averages. Several issues are noteworthy with respect to recording standard scores. First, if a test score is on a standard score scale that does not have a mean of 100 and a standard deviation of 15 (such as the Wechsler individual tests), then the score must be converted to one that is consistent with this metric. A *Percentile Rank and Standard Score Conversion Table* is included in Appendix D for this purpose. Second, while most intelligence batteries have *age-based* norms only, the WJ-R/III has both age- and grade-based norms. Therefore, when the WJ-R/III is used, it is important to derive the standard scores from the age-based norms to allow for comparisons with other batteries.

Third, the WJ-R/III yields *extended standard scores* (i.e., < 40 and > 160; McGrew et al., 1991; Woodcock & McGrew, in press). Although this is a unique and positive feature of the WJ-R/III, it can be problematic when combining or comparing the WJ-R/III standard scores with standard scores from the Wechsler Scales or other tests used in cross-battery assessments. The standard scores for the Wechsler Intelligence Scales and most other intelligence batteries and supplemental tests represent *normalized standard scores* that are based on an area transformation of the raw score distribution. Very low or high normalized standard scores are typically calculated via extrapolation. As a result, low and high extrapolated scores are not based on "real" subjects (Woodcock, 1989). This problem is addressed typically by specifying a cut off score at both the top and bottom of the standard score scale. For example, the WISC-III norm tables include standard scores that range from 40 to 160 (Wechsler, 1991). In contrast, the WJ-R/III standard scores are not extrapolated. They are based on the *linear transformation* of *W (Rasch) scores* that utilize two unique standard deviations to produce the observed 10th and 90th percentiles in the distribution. As a result, the WJ-R/III standard scores can range from 1 to 200 (Woodcock, 1989; Woodcock & McGrew, in press).

Thus, combining extreme WJ-R/III standard scores (i.e., < 40 and > 160) with standard scores from other tests (e.g., WISC-III) that are constrained within a certain range (e.g., 40 to 160 inclusive) could potentially result in misleading cluster averages. Therefore, it is necessary to employ a method for reporting WJ-R/III standard scores that emulate those computed via more traditional methods. Following the logic of Woodcock (1989), whenever a WJ-R/III standard score (or a score from any test) is below 40, a value of 40 should be recorded on the appropriate *Gf-Gc* worksheet. Likewise, whenever a WJ-R/III standard score (or a score from any test) exceeds 160, a score of 160 should be recorded.

Keeping these standard score issues in mind, Examiner A began by recording the standard scores for the WJ-R Concept Formation (SS = 107) and Analysis-Synthesis (SS = 111) tests on the *Gf* cross-battery worksheet (see Figure 6.4). Since the WJ-R test scores are based on a mean of 100 and standard deviation of 15, these scores were recorded directly in the far right column. Next, Examiner A followed the three-step set of directions within each narrow ability section represented on the worksheet. That is, she first summed the standard score columns within the narrow ability domains of Induction (I) and General Sequential Reasoning (RG) and divided this value by the number of tests administered in the respective narrow ability areas (i.e., one test for each area) to obtain the respective *narrow-ability averages*. Since only one test was administered within each of two narrow abilities subsumed by *Gf*, the narrow-ability averages for I and RG are 107 and 111, respectively. In Figure 6.4, shaded lines lead from the rows in which the narrow-ability averages are recorded to a box. Examiner A recorded the *sum* of the narrow-ability averages (i.e., 107 for Concept Formation + 111 for Analysis-Synthesis = 218) and the *number* of narrow-ability averages reported on the worksheet (i.e., 2) in this box. Second, Examiner A recorded the score of 109 (i.e., 218/2 = 109) in the box at the far right side of the worksheet. (Note that averages that result in fractions of one half or more are rounded up to the nearest whole number.) The third and final step that must be carried out on this *Gf* cross-battery worksheet (Figure 6.4) is to indicate whether this cluster score of 109 should be interpreted as a broad or narrow estimate of ability.

A cluster score (or average) would be considered a *broad* estimate of ability if it were derived by summing the standard scores of at least two test indicators of qualitatively different narrow abilities subsumed by the broad ability. As can be seen in Figure 6.4, the clus-

FLUID INTELLIGENCE (*Gf*) CROSS-BATTERY WORKSHEET

Battery or Test	Age	*Gf* Narrow Abilities Tests	SS*	SS (100±15)
		Induction (I)		
WAIS-III	16-89	**MATRIX REASONING**		
DAS	6-17	**MATRICES**		
DAS	2-5	Picture Similarities		
KAIT	11-85+	**MYSTERY CODES**		
SB:IV	7-24	**MATRICES**		
WJ-R/III	2-85+	**CONCEPT FORMATION**		107
CAS	5-17	Nonverbal Matrices		
DTLA-3/4	6-17	**SYMBOLIC RELATIONS**		
Leiter-R	2-6	Classification		
Leiter-R	5-18+	Design Analogies		
Leiter-R	2-18+	Repeated Patterns		
Leiter-R	2-18+	Sequential Order		
UNIT	5-17	**ANALOGIC REASONING**		
Other				
		1. Sum of column		107
		2. Divide by number of tests		1
		3. **Induction** average		107

General Sequential Reasoning (RG)

Battery or Test	Age	*Gf* Narrow Abilities Tests	SS*	SS (100±15)
KAIT	11-85+	**LOGICAL STEPS**		
WJ-R/III	4-85+	**ANALYSIS-SYNTHESIS**		111
Leiter-R	2-10	Picture Context		
Leiter-R	6-18+	Visual Coding		
UNIT	5-17	**CUBE DESIGN**		
Other				
		1. Sum of column		111
		2. Divide by number of tests		1
		3. **General Sequential Reasoning** average		111

Quantitative Reasoning (RQ)

Battery or Test	Age	*Gf* Narrow Abilities Tests	SS*	SS (100±15)
DAS	6-17	**SEQ & QUANT REASONING (I)**		
SB:IV	12-24	**EQUATION BUILDING**		
SB:IV	7-24	Number series		
Other				
		1. Sum of column		
		2. Divide by number of tests		
		3. **Quantitative Reasoning** average		

Name: Christine
Age: 7 years, 9 months
Grade: Second
Examiner: Examiner A
Date of Evaluation: 1/15/98, 1/22/98

**Cluster Average **

✓ Broad (*Gf*)
__ Narrow (___)

218/2   **109**

The Wechsler tests and Wechsler-linked memory tests are enclosed in a bold-faced border. Tests printed in bold/uppercase letters are strong measures as defined empirically; tests printed in regular face/lowercase letters were classified logically. In the case of tests with two "probable" narrow ability classifications, the second classification is reported in parentheses. Only "probable" test classifications are included on the worksheet (tests classified as "possible" measures are not included). Tests that were classified either empirically or logically as mixed measures are not included on the worksheet. This classification system was described in Chapter 4 of this text.

* If a test score is on a standard score scale other than 100 ± 15, record the score in the column marked by an asterisk. Then refer to the *Standard Score Conversion Table* (Appendix D) to convert the score to the scale of 100 ± 15. Record the new score in the next column.

** If the cluster includes two or more qualitatively different *Gf* indicators, place a checkmark (✓) next to the word "Broad" and record "*Gf*" in the parentheses. If the cluster includes indicators from only one narrow ability subsumed by *Gf*, then place a checkmark (✓) next to the word "Narrow" and record the respective narrow ability code in the parentheses (i.e., I, RG, or RQ).

FIGURE 6.4 *Gf* Cross-Battery Worksheet

ter average was computed by summing the standard scores of two test indicators of different narrow abilities subsumed by *Gf* (i.e., Concept Formation [a measure of I] and Analysis-Synthesis [a measure of RG]). Therefore, Examiner A placed a checkmark next to the word *Broad* on the *Gf* worksheet (see Figure 6.4) and recorded the broad (stratum II) code *Gf* in the parentheses adjacent to the word *Broad*. Conversely, if the cluster average was derived by summing the standard scores of two or more test indicators of only one narrow ability subsumed by the broad ability (e.g., two or more measures of RG), then this average would be interpreted most appropriately as representing a narrow (stratum I) ability (i.e., RG), rather than a broad (stratum II) ability (i.e., *Gf*). In this instance the examiner would place a checkmark next to the word *Narrow* and record the narrow (stratum I) code *RG* or *RG-Gf* in the parentheses adjacent to the word *Narrow*. Examiner A completed worksheets for the remaining six *Gf-Gc* abilities that were assessed in this cross-battery evaluation (see Figure 6.5 through Figure 6.10).

Step 6: Transfer* Gf-Gc *Narrow-Ability Test Indicator Standard Scores and Cluster Averages from the* Gf-Gc *Cross-Battery Worksheets to the* Gf-Gc *Profile. A profile for plotting *Gf-Gc* narrow-ability test indicator standard scores and cluster averages from the cross-battery worksheets can be found in Appendix E. The *Gf-Gc* profile includes a place for plotting the broad (or narrow) cluster averages from each of seven *Gf-Gc* worksheets and for plotting the standard scores (based on a mean of 100 and standard deviation of 15) for up to four narrow-ability test indicators from each worksheet. The cluster averages are plotted on the *thick bars* in the profile and the standard scores for the narrow-ability test indicators are plotted on the *thin bars*. The profile contains a total of seven *sets of bars* (i.e., one thick and four thin in each set)—for plotting the scores reported on the seven *Gf-Gc* worksheets. A set of standard scores runs across the outside top of each thick bar on the profile.

The first step is to transfer all the cluster averages and individual test standard scores from the seven *Gf-Gc* worksheets to the appropriate places on the profile. Examiner A first recorded all the cluster averages (by placing a vertical hashmark on the thick bars corresponding to the standard score averages), making sure to indicate whether the average represented a broad or narrow ability (a critical component for test interpretation). As on the worksheets, this was achieved by placing a checkmark next to the word *Broad* or *Narrow* and recording the *Gf-Gc* ability code in the parentheses adjacent to the appropriate descriptor (in the case of Christine, all ability averages are *broad*). Next, the standard scores of the two tests that composed each cluster average were recorded directly below their respective *Gf-Gc* cluster averages. The *Gf-Gc* codes corresponding to the narrow-ability classifications of these tests also were recorded in the parentheses adjacent to the subtest names. Thus, Examiner A recorded a total of 21 scores (i.e., 7 cluster averages and 14 narrow-ability test indicator standard scores) and their corresponding *Gf-Gc* ability codes on Christine's profile.

The next step is to shade in the *confidence band* for each *Gf-Gc* score that was recorded on the profile, as shown in Figure 6.11. Confidence bands for cluster averages and narrow ability test indicator standard scores correspond to ± 1 standard error of measurement (SEM). Confidence bands represent the region in which an individual's true test score most likely will fall. The confidence bands in Figure 6.11 extend from 1 SEM below Chris-

CRYSTALLIZED INTELLIGENCE (*Gc*) CROSS-BATTERY WORKSHEET

Battery or Test	Age	*Gc* Narrow Abilities Tests	SS*	SS (100±15)
		Language Development (LD)		
WECH	3-74	**COMPREHENSION (K0)**		
WECH	3-74	**SIMILARITIES (VL)**		
DAS	6-17	**SIMILARITIES**		
DAS	2-5	Verbal Comprehension (LS)		
SB:IV	12-24	**VERBAL RELATIONS**		
SB:IV	2-24	**Comprehension (K0)**		
SB:IV	2-14	**Absurdities**		
DTLA-3/4	6-17	Word Opposites		
DTLA-3/4	6-17	Story Construction		
Other				
		1. Sum of column		
		2. Divide by number of tests		
		3. **Language Development** average		

Battery or Test	Age	*Gc* Narrow Abilities Tests	SS*	SS (100±15)
		Lexical Knowledge (VL)		
WECH	3-74	**VOCABULARY (LD)**	11	105
DAS	6-17	**WORD DEFINITIONS (LD)**		
DAS	2-5	Naming Vocabulary (LD)		
SB:IV	2-24	**VOCABULARY (LD)**		
WJ-R	2-85+	**ORAL VOCABULARY (LD)**		
WJ-R	2-85+	**PICTURE VOCABULARY (K0)**		
WJ-III	2-85+	**VERBAL COMP (LD)**		
NEPSY	3-4	Body Part Naming		
Other				
		1. Sum of column		105
		2. Divide by number of tests		1
		3. **Lexical Knowledge** average		105

Battery or Test	Age	*Gc* Narrow Abilities Tests	SS*	SS (100±15)
		Listening Ability (LS)		
WJ-R	4-85+	**LISTENING COMP (LD)**		
WJ-III	4-85+	**ORAL COMP (LD)** (in ach. battery)		
NEPSY	3-12	Comprehension of Instructions		
Other				
		1. Sum of column		
		2. Divide by number of tests		
		3. **Listening Ability** average		

Battery or Test	Age	*Gc* Narrow Abilities Tests	SS*	SS (100±15)
		General Information (K0)		
WECH	3-74	**INFORMATION**	9	95
DTLA-3/4	6-17	Basic Information		
WJ-III	2-85+	**GENERAL INFORMATION**		
Other				
		1. Sum of column		95
		2. Divide by number of tests		1
		3. **General Information** average		95

Name: Christine
Age: 7 years, 9 months
Grade: Second
Examiner: Examiner A
Date of Evaluation: 1/15/98, 1/22/98

FIGURE 6.5   *Gc* Cross-Battery Worksheet

Information About Culture (K2)					Sum/No. of Narrow Ability Averages	Cluster Average **
KAIT	11-85+	**FAMOUS FACES**				✓ Broad (_Gc_)
Other						__ Narrow (___)
		1. Sum of column				
		2. Divide by number of tests				
		3. **Information About Culture** average			200/2	100

The Wechsler tests and Wechsler-linked memory tests are enclosed in a bold-faced border. Tests printed in bold/uppercase letters are strong measures as defined empirically; tests printed in regular face/lowercase letters were classified logically. In the case of tests with two "probable" narrow ability classifications, the second classification is reported in parentheses. Only "probable" test classifications are included on the worksheet (tests classified as "possible" measures are not included). Tests that were classified either empirically or logically as mixed measures are not included on the worksheet. This classification system was described in Chapter 4 of this text.

* If a test score is on a standard score scale other than 100 $\pm$ 15, record the score in the column marked by an asterisk. Then refer to the *Standard Score Conversion Table* (Appendix D) to convert the score to the scale of 100 $\pm$ 15. Record the new score in the next column.

** If the cluster includes two or more qualitatively different *Gc* indicators, place a checkmark (✓) next to the word "Broad" and record "*Gc*" in the parentheses. If the cluster includes indicators from only one narrow ability subsumed by *Gc*, then place a checkmark (✓) next to the word "Narrow" and record the respective narrow ability code in the parentheses (i.e., LD, VL, LS, K0, or K2).

FIGURE 6.5   Continued

tine's obtained scores to 1 SEM above Christine's obtained scores. The SEM estimates for all cross-battery cluster averages and individual test standard scores were set at $\pm$ 5 and $\pm$ 7 (representing the average [median] *Gf-Gc* cluster and subtest SEM across all age ranges in the WJ-R norm sample, respectively).[4] The confidence bands that were constructed for the *Gf-Gc* ability scores (based on $\pm$ 1 SEM) are also called *68 percent confidence bands* because they represent the standard score range in which an individual's true score falls two out of three times. Doubling the confidence bands or making them twice as wide (i.e., $\pm$ 2 SEM) would increase one's degree of confidence from 68 percent to 95 percent, representing the standard score range in which an individual's true score falls 19 out of 20 times. The purpose of reporting confidence bands is to demonstrate the degree of precision (or imprecision) that is present in the *Gf-Gc* scores. Examining a test score on a profile as a confidence band (as opposed to a single or exact score) is usually preferred (Woodcock & Mather, 1989; 1990).

Examiner A shaded in the confidence bands for all the *Gf-Gc* standard scores reported on the profile. For example, the confidence band for Christine's broad *Gf* cluster score (i.e., 109 $\pm$ 5) ranged from 104 (i.e., 109–5) to 114 (i.e., 109 + 5). Examiner A made vertical hashmarks through the standard scores of 104 and 114 on the *Gf* bar on the profile and shaded in the area between them. The completed *Gf-Gc* profile (see Figure 6.11) graphically displays Christine's levels of ability. It provides a meaningful basis for making the necessary *Gf-Gc* ability comparisons to evaluate cognitive functioning (e.g., inter- and intra-individual strengths and weaknesses). Procedures for interpreting scores that are plotted on the *Gf-Gc* profile are presented in Chapter 7.

VISUAL PROCESSING (*Gv*) CROSS-BATTERY WORKSHEET

Battery or Test	Age	*Gv* Narrow Abilities Tests	SS*	SS (100±15)
		Spatial Relations (SR)		
WECH	3-74	**BLOCK DESIGN (Vz)**	8	90
DAS	3-17	Pattern Construction		
K-ABC	4-12	**TRIANGLES**		
SB:IV	2-24	**PATTERN ANALYSIS**		
Leiter-R	11-18+	Figure Rotation (Vz)		
UNIT	5-17	Cube Design (Vz)		
Other				
		1. Sum of column		90
		2. Divide by number of tests		1
		3. **Spatial Relations** average		90
		Visualization (Vz)		
WPPSI-R	3-7	Geometric Designs (P2)		
DAS	2-3	Block Building		
DAS	4-5	Matching Letter-like Forms		
WJ-R/III	4-85+	**SPATIAL RELATIONS (SR)**		
Leiter-R	2-10	Matching		
Leiter-R	2-18+	Form Completion (SR)		
Leiter-R	11-18+	Paper Folding		
NEPSY	3-12	Block Construction		
Other				
		1. Sum of column		
		2. Divide by number of tests		
		3. **Visualization** average		
		Visual Memory (MV)		
WMS-III	16-89	Visual Reproduction I		
CMS	5-16	Dot Locations		
CMS	5-16	Dot Locations 2		
CMS	5-16	Picture Locations		
DAS	6-17	**RECALL OF DESIGNS**		
DAS	3-7	Recognition of Pictures		
K-ABC	2-4	Face Recognition		
KAIT	11-85+	**MEM. FOR BLOCK DESIGNS**		
SB:IV	2-24	**Bead Memory**		
SB:IV	7-24	**Memory for Objects**		
WJ-R/III	4-85+	**Picture Recognition**		
DTLA-3/4	6-17	Design Sequences		
DTLA-3/4	6-17	Design Reproduction		
Leiter-R	4-10	Immediate Recognition		
Leiter-R	2-18+	Forward Memory		
UNIT	5-17	**OBJECT MEMORY**		
UNIT	5-17	**SPATIAL MEMORY**		
UNIT	5-17	**SYMBOLIC MEMORY**		
NEPSY	3-12	Imitating Hand Positions		
Other				
		1. Sum of column		
		2. Divide by number of tests		
		3. **Visual Memory** average		

Name: Christine
Age: 7 years, 9 months
Grade: Second
Examiner: Examiner A
Date of Evaluation: 1/15/98, 1/22/98

FIGURE 6.6   *Gv* Cross-Battery Worksheet

VISUAL PROCESSING (*Gv*) CROSS-BATTERY WORKSHEET

Battery or Test	Age	*Gv* Narrow Abilities Tests	SS*	SS (100±15)
Closure Speed (CS)				
WECH	3-74	**OBJECT ASSEMBLY (SR)**	13	115
K-ABC	2-12	**Gestalt Closure**		
WJ-R	2-85+	**Visual Closure**		
DTLA-3	6-17	Picture Fragments		
Other				
		1. Sum of column		115
		2. Divide by number of tests		1
		3. **Closure Speed** average		115
Spatial Scanning (SS)				
WISC-III	6-16	**Mazes**		
WPPSI-R	3-7	**Mazes**		
UNIT	5-17	**Mazes**		
NEPSY	5-12	Route Finding		
Other				
		1. Sum of column		
		2. Divide by number of tests		
		3. **Spatial Scanning** average		
Flexibility of Closure (CF)				
CAS	5-17	Figure Memory (MV)		
Leiter-R	2-18+	Figure Ground		
Other				
		1. Sum of column		
		2. Divide by number of tests		
		3. **Flexibility of Closure** average		
Serial Perceptual Integration (PI)				
K-ABC	2-4	Magic Window		
Other				
		1. Sum of column		
		2. Divide by number of tests		
		3. **Serial Perceptual Integration** average		

Sum/No. of Narrow Ability Averages: **205/2**

**Cluster Average ** **
✓ Broad (*Gv*)
__ Narrow (___)
103

The Wechsler tests and Wechsler-linked memory tests are enclosed in a bold-faced border. Tests printed in bold/uppercase letters are strong measures as defined empirically; tests printed in regular face/lowercase letters were classified logically. In the case of tests with two "probable" narrow ability classifications, the second classification is reported in parentheses. Only "probable" test classifications are included on the worksheet (tests classified as "possible" measures are not included). Tests that were classified either empirically or logically as mixed measures are not included on the worksheet. This classification system was described in Chapter 4 of this text.

* If a test score is on a standard score scale other than 100 ± 15, record the score in the column marked by an asterisk. Then refer to the *Standard Score Conversion Table* (Appendix D) to convert the score to the scale of 100 ± 15. Record the new score in the next column.

** If the cluster includes two or more qualitatively different *Gv* indicators, place a checkmark (✓) next to the word "Broad" and record "*Gv*" in the parentheses. If the cluster includes indicators from only one narrow ability subsumed by *Gv*, then place a checkmark (✓) next to the word "Narrow" and record the respective narrow ability code in the parentheses (i.e., SR, Vz, MV, CS, SS, CF, or PI).

FIGURE 6.6   Continued

SHORT-TERM MEMORY (*Gsm*) CROSS-BATTERY WORKSHEET

Battery or Test	Age	*Gsm* Narrow Abilities Tests	SS*	SS (100±15)
		Memory Span (MS)		
WAIS-III	6-89	**DIGIT SPAN (MW)**		
WISC-III	6-16	**DIGIT SPAN (MW)**	8	90
CMS	5-16	Numbers (MW)		
CMS	5-16	Stories*** (*Gc*-LS)		
WMS-III	16-89	Logical Memory I*** (*Gc*-LS)		
WMS-III	16-89	Digit Span (MW)		
DAS	3-17	Recall of Digits		
K-ABC	2-12	**NUMBER RECALL**		
K-ABC	4-12	**WORD ORDER**		
SB:IV	7-24	**MEMORY FOR DIGITS (MW)**		
WJ-R/III	4-85+	**MEMORY FOR WORDS**		
CAS	5-17	Word Series		
DTLA-3	6-17	Word Sequences		
NEPSY	5-12	Repetition of Nonsense Words		
NEPSY	3-12	Sentence Repetition		
Other				
		1. Sum of column		90
		2. Divide by number of tests		1
		3. **Memory Span** average		90
		Working Memory (MW)		
WAIS-III	16-89	**LETTER-NUMBER SEQ.**		
WMS-III	16-89	Letter-Number Sequencing		
WMS-III	16-89	Mental Control		
CMS	5-16	Sequences	7	85
WJ-R/III	4-85+	**NUMBERS REVERSED**		
WJ-III	4-85+	**AUDITORY WORKING MEM**		
NEPSY	5-12	Knock and Tap		
Other				
		1. Sum of column		85
		2. Divide by number of tests		1
		3. **Working Memory** average		85

Name: Christine
Age: 7 years, 9 months
Grade: Second
Examiner: Examiner A
Date of Evaluation: 1/15/98, 1/22/98

Cluster Average *

✓ Broad (*Gsm*)
__ Narrow (___)

175/2   88

The Wechsler tests and Wechsler-linked memory tests are enclosed in a bold-faced border. Tests printed in bold/uppercase letters are strong measures as defined empirically; tests printed in regular face/lowercase letters were classified logically. In the case of tests with two "probable" narrow ability classifications, the second classification is reported in parentheses. Only "probable" test classifications are included on the worksheet (tests classified as "possible" measures are not included). Tests that were classified either empirically or logically as mixed measures are not included on the worksheet. This classification system was described in Chapter 4 of this text.

* If a test score is on a standard score scale other than 100 ± 15, record the score in the column marked by an asterisk. Then refer to the *Standard Score Conversion Table* (Appendix D) to convert the score to the scale of 100 ± 15. Record the new score in the next column.

** If the cluster includes two or more qualitatively different *Gsm* indicators, place a checkmark (✓) next to the word "Broad" and record "*Gsm*" in the parentheses. If the cluster includes indicators from only one narrow ability subsumed by *Gsm*, then place a checkmark (✓) next to the word "Narrow" and record the respective narrow ability code in the parentheses (i.e., MS, or MW).

*** Although these tests are mixed measures of two *Gf-Gc* abilities (i.e., they also involve Listening Ability in addition to Memory Span), they are included on this worksheet because they are necessary to administer prior to administering Stories 2 and Logical Memory II, respectively (measures of *Glr*- MM).

FIGURE 6.7   *Gsm* Cross-Battery Worksheet

LONG-TERM RETRIEVAL (*Glr*) CROSS-BATTERY WORKSHEET

Battery or Test	Age	*Glr* Narrow Abilities Tests	SS*	SS (100±15)
		Associative Memory (MA)		
WMS-III	16-89	Verbal Paired Associates I		
WMS-III	16-89	Verbal Paired Associates II		
CMS	5-16	Word Pairs		
CMS	5-16	Word Pairs 2		
KAIT	11-85+	**REBUS LEARNING**		
KAIT	11-85+	**REBUS DELAYED RECALL**		
WJ-R	2-85+	**MEMORY FOR NAMES**		
WJ-R/III	2-85+	**VISUAL-AUD LEARNING (MM)**		93
WJ-R	4-85+	**DEL REC: MEM FOR NAMES**		
WJ-R/III	4-85+	**Del Rec: Vis-Aud Learning (MM)**		
Leiter-R	4-10	Delayed Recognition		
Leiter-R	2-18+	Associated Pairs (MM)		
Leiter-R	6-18+	Delayed Pairs (MM)		
NEPSY	5-12	Memory for Names (MM)		
Other				
		1. Sum of column		93
		2. Divide by number of tests		1
		3. **Associative Memory** average		93
		Ideational Fluency (FI)		
WJ-III	4-85+	**RETRIEVAL FLUENCY**		
Other				
		1. Sum of column		
		2. Divide by number of tests		
		3. **Ideational Fluency** average		
		Figural Fluency (FF)		
NEPSY	5-12	Design Fluency		
Other				
		1. Sum of column		
		2. Divide by number of tests		
		3. **Figural Fluency** average		
		Naming Facility (NA)		
WJ-III	4-85+	**RAPID PICTURE NAMING**		
CAS	5-17	Expressive Attention		
NEPSY	5-12	Speeded Naming		
Other				
		1. Sum of column		
		2. Divide by number of tests		
		3. **Naming Facility** average		

Name: Christine
Age: 7 years, 9 months
Grade: Second
Examiner: Examiner A
Date of Evaluation: 1/15/98, 1/22/98

FIGURE 6.8 *Glr* **Cross-Battery Worksheet**

(continued)

LONG-TERM RETRIEVAL (*Glr*) CROSS-BATTERY WORKSHEET

Battery or Test	Age	*Glr* Narrow Abilities Tests	SS*	SS (100±15)	
		Free Recall Memory (M6)			(cont'd prior page)
WMS-III	16-89	Word Lists I			
WMS-III	16-89	Word Lists II (MA)			
CMS	5-16	Word Lists	4	70	
CMS	5-16	Word Lists 2 (MA)			
DAS	4-17	Recall of Objects			
NEPSY	7-12	List Learning			
Other					
		1. Sum of column		70	
		2. Divide by number of tests		1	
		3. **Free Recall Memory** average		70	

Battery or Test	Age	**Meaningful Memory (MM)**			Sum/No. of Narrow Ability Averages	**Cluster Average** **
WMS-III	16-74	Logical Memory II				✓ Broad (*Glr*)
CMS	5-16	Stories 2				__ Narrow (__)
Other						
		1. Sum of column				
		2. Divide by number of tests				
		3. **Meaningful Memory** average			163/2	82

The Wechsler tests and Wechsler-linked memory tests are enclosed in a bold-faced border. Tests printed in bold/uppercase letters are strong measures as defined empirically; tests printed in regular face/lowercase letters were classified logically. In the case of tests with two "probable" narrow ability classifications, the second classification is reported in parentheses. Only "probable" test classifications are included on the worksheet (tests classified as "possible" measures are not included). Tests that were classified either empirically or logically as mixed measures are not included on the worksheet. This classification system was described in Chapter 4 of this text.

* If a test score is on a standard score scale other than 100 ± 15, record the score in the column marked by an asterisk. Then refer to the *Standard Score Conversion Table* (Appendix D) to convert the score to the scale of 100 ± 15. Record the new score in the next column.

** If the cluster includes two or more qualitatively different *Glr* indicators, place a checkmark (✓) next to the word "Broad" and record "*Glr*" in the parentheses. If the cluster includes indicators from only one narrow ability subsumed by *Glr*, then place a checkmark (✓) next to the word "Narrow" and record the respective narrow ability code in the parentheses (i.e., MA, M6, or MM).

FIGURE 6.8   Continued

AUDITORY PROCESSING (*Ga*) CROSS-BATTERY WORKSHEET

Battery or Test	Age	*Ga* Narrow Abilities Tests	SS*	SS (100±15)
		Name: Christine **Age:** 7 years, 9 months **Grade:** Second **Examiner:** Examiner A **Date of Evaluation:** 1/15/98, 1/22/98		

Phonetic Coding: Analysis (PC:A)

Battery or Test	Age	*Ga* Narrow Abilities Tests	SS*	SS (100±15)
W-ADT	4-8	Wepman Aud. Discrim. Test		
GFW-TAD	3-70+	GFW Test of Aud. Discrim.		
G-FTA	2-16+	G-F Test of Articulation		
WJ-R/III	2-85+	**INCOMPLETE WORDS**		83
TOPA	5-8	Test of Phonological Awareness		
TPAT	5-9	Segmentation		
TPAT	5-9	Isolation		
TPAT	5-9	Deletion		
TPAT	5-9	Rhyming		
NEPSY	3-12	Phonological Processing (PC:S)		
Other				
		1. Sum of column		83
		2. Divide by number of tests		1
		3. **Phonetic Coding: Analysis** average		83

Phonetic Coding: Synthesis (PC:S)

Battery or Test	Age	*Ga* Narrow Abilities Tests	SS*	SS (100±15)
WJ-R/III	4-85+	**SOUND BLENDING**		88
TPAT	5-9	Substitution		
TPAT	5-9	Blending		
Other				
		1. Sum of column		88
		2. Divide by number of tests		1
		3. **Phonetic Coding: Synthesis** average		88

Speech/General Sound Discrimination (US/U3)

Battery or Test	Age	*Ga* Narrow Abilities Tests	SS*	SS (100±15)	Sum/No. of Narrow Ability Averages	Cluster Average **
WJ-III	4-85+	**AUDITORY ATTENTION (UR)**				__ Broad (*Ga*)
WJ-R	4-85+	**SOUND PATTERNS**				__ Narrow (__)
Other						
		1. Sum of column				
		2. Divide by number of tests				
		3. **Speech/General Sound Disc.** average			171/2	86

The Wechsler tests and Wechsler-linked memory tests are enclosed in a bold-faced border. Tests printed in bold/uppercase letters are strong measures as defined empirically; tests printed in regular face/lowercase letters were classified logically. In the case of tests with two "probable" narrow ability classifications, the second classification is reported in parentheses. Only "probable" test classifications are included on the worksheet (tests classified as "possible" measures are not included). Tests that were classified either empirically or logically as mixed measures are not included on the worksheet. This classification system was described in Chapter 4 of this text.

* If a test score is on a standard score scale other than 100 ± 15, record the score in the column marked by an asterisk. Then refer to the *Standard Score Conversion Table* (Appendix D) to convert the score to the scale of 100 ± 15. Record the new score in the next column.

** If the cluster includes two or more qualitatively different *Ga* indicators, place a checkmark ( ) next to the word "Broad" and record "*Ga*" in the parentheses. If the cluster includes indicators from only one narrow ability subsumed by *Ga*, then place a checkmark ( ) next to the word "Narrow" and record the respective narrow ability code in the parentheses (e.g., PC:A, PC:S).

FIGURE 6.9   *Ga* Cross-Battery Worksheet

PROCESSING SPEED (*Gs*) CROSS-BATTERY WORKSHEET

Battery or Test	Age	*Gs* Narrow Abilities Tests	SS*	SS (100±15)
Perceptual Speed (P)				
WAIS-III	16-74	**SYMBOL SEARCH (R9)**		
WISC-III	6-16	**SYMBOL SEARCH (R9)**	11	105
WJ-R/III	4-85+	**VISUAL MATCHING (R9)**		
WJ-R	4-85+	**CROSS OUT**		
CAS	5-17	Matching Numbers (R9)		
CAS	5-17	Receptive Attention (R4)		
Leiter-R	2-18+	Attention Sustained (R9)		
Other				
		1. Sum of column		105
		2. Divide by number of tests		1
		3. **Perceptual Speed** Average		105
Rate -of-test-taking (R9)				
WAIS-R	16-74	**DIGIT SYMBOL**		
WISC-III	6-16	**CODING**	7	85
WPPSI-R	3-7	Animal Pegs		
CAS	5-17	Planned Codes		
WJ-III	4-85+	**PAIRED CANCELLATION**		
Other				
		1. Sum of column		85
		2. Divide by number of tests		1
		3. **Rate-of-test-taking** average		85
Mental Comparison Speed (R7)				
DAS	6-17	Speed of Information Processing		
CAS	5-17	Number Detection (R9)		
WJ-III	4-84+	**DECISION SPEED**		
Other				
		1. Sum of column		
		2. Divide by number of tests		
		3. **Mental Comparison Speed** average		

Name: Christine
Age: 7 years, 9 months
Grade: Second
Examiner: Examiner A
Date of Evaluation: 1/15/98, 1/22/98

Sum/No. of Narrow Ability Averages: 190/2

Cluster Average **
✓ Broad (*Gs*)
__ Narrow (__)

95

The Wechsler tests and Wechsler-linked memory tests are enclosed in a bold-faced border. Tests printed in bold/uppercase letters are strong measures as defined empirically; tests printed in regular face/lowercase letters were classified logically. In the case of tests with two "probable" narrow ability classifications, the second classification is reported in parentheses. Only "probable" test classifications are included on the worksheet (tests classified as "possible" measures are not included). Tests that were classified either empirically or logically as mixed measures are not included on the worksheet. This classification system was described in Chapter 4 of this text.

* If a test score is on a standard score scale other than 100 ± 15, record the score in the column marked by an asterisk. Then refer to the *Standard Score Conversion Table* (Appendix D) to convert the score to the scale of 100 ± 15. Record the new score in the next column.

** If the cluster includes two or more qualitatively different *Gs* indicators, place a checkmark (✓) next to the word "Broad" and record "*Gs*" in the parentheses. If the cluster includes indicators from only one narrow ability subsumed by *Gs*, then place a checkmark (✓) next to the word "Narrow" and record the respective narrow ability code in the parentheses (i.e., P, R9, or R7).

FIGURE 6.10   *Gs* Cross-Battery Worksheet

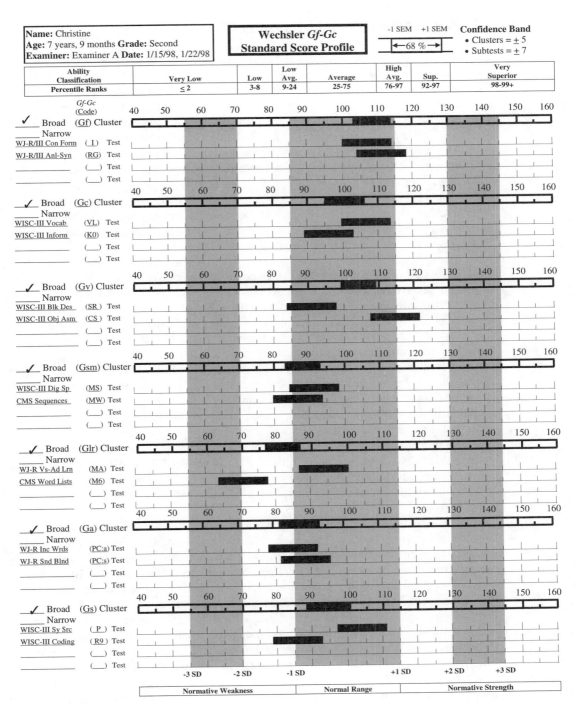

FIGURE 6.11   *Gf-Gc* Cross-Battery Profile

A WAIS-III-Based Cross-Battery Example

The cross-battery guiding principles and procedures described in the WISC-III case example presented above also apply when the WAIS-III is used as the core battery in assessment. An examination of Table 6.1 shows that the constructs of *Gc, Gv, Gsm,* and *Gs* are well represented in the WAIS-III battery, whereas *Gf* is underrepresented and *Glr* and *Ga* are not measured. In order to ensure adequate coverage of *Gf, Glr,* and *Ga,* the WAIS-III would need to be crossed (or supplemented) with another intelligence battery.

The WAIS-III and WJ-R/III appear to represent the most appropriate and practical union of tests for the comprehensive assessment of cognitive functioning in adults for the following reasons: (1) the WAIS-III is the most widely used intelligence battery for this population; (2) the WJ-R/III measures a broader range of *Gf-Gc* cognitive abilities than the other intelligence batteries currently available; and (3) the WAIS-III and WJ-III were normed within a few years of one another. Table 6.4 provides information about the range of *Gf-Gc* abilities measured by the WAIS-III and WJ-R/III batteries.

The tests that appear in shaded boxes in Table 6.4 are recommended in WAIS-III-based cross-battery assessment because they comprise two qualitatively different measures for each of seven broad *Gf-Gc* abilities. As was the case with the WISC-III, supplementing the WAIS-III with appropriate measures from the WJ-R/III leads to a more comprehensive assessment of cognitive abilities and processes with a negligible increase in testing time (i.e., a 14-test WAIS-III/WJ battery versus the more typical 11-test WAIS-III standard battery). It is noteworthy that when the entire WAIS-III battery is administered (i.e., 11 standard battery tests plus 3 optional tests), single-battery testing time is essentially equivalent to cross-battery testing time, since both batteries involve the administration of 14 tests.

In addition to crossing the WAIS-III with the WJ-R/III, the WAIS-III can be administered with the WMS-III to allow for a more comprehensive measurement of memory skills. Table 6.4 includes the tests of the WMS-III battery that were considered to measure relatively pure abilities within the domains of *Gsm* and *Glr,* the short-term and long-term systems that define memory. Together, the WAIS-III/WJ-R/III/WMS-III assess seven narrow *Gf-Gc* memory abilities, including memory span, working memory, associative memory, ideational fluency, naming facility, free recall memory, and meaningful memory (see Table 6.4).

Although it is beyond the scope of this chapter to discuss the concept of memory and its role in the learning process (The Psychological Corporation, 1997; Squire, 1987; 1992), it is clear that this combination of batteries offers a comprehensive means of examining memory functions. As mentioned in Chapter 5, when the conormed WAIS-III/WMS-III batteries are administered, it is possible to examine immediate and delayed memory across modalities (visual and auditory) as well as assess recall versus recognition functions. A comparison of the WMS-III indexes to WAIS-III IQs may aid in understanding the nature and severity of memory impairment or specific memory deficits. Alternatively, tests measuring the narrow *Gsm* and *Glr* abilities presented in Table 6.4 may be more sensitive to the patterns of deficit in memory functions associated with neurological and psychological conditions (see Lezak, 1995). It is noteworthy that, with the exception of Visual Memory tests (in the *Gv* domain), the memory tests included in Table 6.4 are largely verbal in nature

TABLE 6.4 Possible Supplements to the WAIS-III in *Gf-Gc* Cross-Battery Assessment

Gf-Gc Broad (stratum II) ability / Narrow (stratum I) ability	WAIS-III	WJ-R/III	WMS-III
Gf			
(I) Induction	MATRIX REASONING	CONCEPT FORMATION	
(RG) General Sequential Reasoning		ANALYSIS-SYNTHESIS	
(RQ) Quantitative Reasoning			
Gc[1]			
(LD) Language Development	COMPREHENSION (K0) SIMILARITIES (VL)		
(VL) Lexical Knowledge	VOCABULARY (LD)	ORAL VOCABULARY (LD) PICTURE VOCABULARY (VL) VERBAL COMPREHENSION	
(LS) Listening Ability		LISTENING COMP (LD) ORAL COMP (LD)[2]	
(K0) General Information	INFORMATION	GENERAL INFORMATION	
(K2) Information About Culture			
Gv			
(SR) Spatial Relations	BLOCK DESIGN (Vz)	SPATIAL RELATIONS (SR)	
(Vz) Visualization			
(MV) Visual Memory		Picture Recognition	Visual Reproduction I
(CS) Closure Speed	OBJECT ASSEMBLY (SR)	Visual Closure	

(continued)

TABLE 6.4 Continued

Gf-Gc Broad (stratum II) ability / Narrow (stratum I) ability	WAIS-III	WJ-R/III	WMS-III
(SS) Spatial Scanning			
(CF) Flexibility of Closure			
(PI) Serial Perceptual Integration			
Gsm			
(MS) Memory Span	**DIGIT SPAN (MW)**	**MEMORY FOR WORDS**	Logical Memory I[3] (*Gc-LS*) **DIGIT SPAN (MW)**
(MW) Working Memory	**LETTER-NUMBER SEQUENCING**	**NUMBERS REVERSED AUDITORY WORKING MEMORY**	Letter-Number Sequencing Mental Control
Glr[1]			
(MA) Associative Memory		**MEMORY FOR NAMES VIS-AUD LEARNING (MM) DEL REC: MEMORY FOR NAMES** Del Rec: Visual-Auditory Learning (MM)	Verbal Paired Associates I Verbal Paired Associates II
(FI) Ideational Fluency		**RETRIEVAL FLUENCY**	
(NA) Naming Facility		**RAPID PICTURE NAMING**	
(M6) Free Recall Memory			Word Lists I Word Lists II (MA)
(MM) Meaningful Memory			Logical Memory II

TABLE 6.4 Continued

Gf-Gc Broad (stratum II) ability / Narrow (stratum I) ability	WAIS-III	WJ-R/III	WMS-III
Ga			
(PC:A) Phonetic Coding: Analysis		**INCOMPLETE WORDS**	
(PC:S) Phonetic Coding: Synthesis		**SOUND BLENDING**	
(US/U3) Speech/General Sound Discrimination		AUDITORY ATTENTION SOUND PATTERNS	
Gs			
(P) Perceptual Speed	**SYMBOL SEARCH (R9)**	**VISUAL MATCHING (R9)** CROSS OUT	
(R9) Rate-of-test-taking	**DIGIT SYMBOL-CODING**		
(R7) Mental Comparison Speed		DECISION SPEED	

Note: Tests printed in bold/uppercase letters are strong measures as defined empirically; tests printed in bold/lowercase letters are moderate measures as defined empirically; tests printed in regular type lowercase letters were classified logically. In the case of tests with two "probable" narrow-ability classifications, the second classification is reported in parentheses. Only "probable" test classifications are included on this table (tests classified as "possible" measures are not included). This classification system was described in Chapter 4 of this text. The collection of tests in shaded boxes represent a WAIS-III/WJ/WMS-III cross-battery assessment, consisting of two qualitatively different indicators of each Gf-Gc broad ability.

[1] Because multiple indicators are available to represent this construct, it is important to select the most appropriate measures in light of specific referral concerns.

[2] The Listening Comprehension test on the WJ-R has been renamed to Oral Comprehension on the WJ-III.

[3] Cross-battery assessment strives to use only relatively pure measures of ability. This mixed measure is included because it is necessary to administer prior to the Logical Memory II test, which is considered to be a relatively pure measure of meaningful memory.

251

and therefore may unnecessarily penalize individuals with verbal impairments. Overall, the crossing of the WAIS-III with the WJ-R/III and/or WMS-III yields a comprehensive and useful set of measures for assessing a broad range of cognitive abilities with emphasis on selected memory functions.

The Cross-Battery Approach in Perspective

Although not without its limitations, since its formal introduction to the field, the *Gf-Gc* cross-battery approach has been well received (e.g., Borgas, 1999; Carroll, 1998; Daniel, 1997; Esters, Ittenbach, & Han, 1997; Genshaft & Gerner, 1998; see also foreword of this text). However, like any new approach, especially one that differs markedly from traditional methods, there are often a variety of questions and potential concerns (viz., practical, psychometric, theoretical, logistical) that arise with respect to its implementation. Table 6.5 includes a few misconceptions about cross-battery assessment that we have heard from practitioners and trainers who have become familiar with the method. This table also provides clarifications which can help elucidate some misunderstandings surrounding this new approach. After reviewing these misconceptions and clarifications, it should be clear that the *Gf-Gc* cross-battery approach is not only a viable and time-efficient method of measuring cognitive abilities, but it is better grounded in current theory and research than many single intelligence batteries and assessment approaches.

It is also important to understand that the cross-battery approach described in this chapter does not always have to be used to approximate the full range of broad cognitive abilities specified in *Gf-Gc* theory. The following "best practices" principles hold true for *Gf-Gc* designed Wechsler-based cross-battery assessments: (1) conducting assessments only after other preassessment activities have been completed (e.g., prevention, pre-referral interventions, instructional modifications, etc.); (2) pursuing intellectual assessments only when the results have direct relevance to well-defined referral questions; (3) embedding assessments in a multifactored approach; and (4) tailoring the assessment to the unique needs of the individual case. As stated earlier, for cases in which a comprehensive *Gf-Gc* assessment is not considered necessary, a *selective* cross-battery approach may be implemented. This approach is described in the next chapter.

Conclusion

Through a series of *Gf-Gc* cross-battery principles and steps, this chapter demonstrated how practitioners can augment the Wechsler Intelligence Scales to measure a wide range of broad cognitive abilities according to contemporary *Gf-Gc* theory and research—a result that cannot be achieved through the administration of any single Wechsler Scale. The foundational sources of information on which the *Gf-Gc* cross-battery approach was built (viz., the classification of the major intelligence batteries according to *Gf-Gc* theory) provide a means to systematically construct a more theoretically driven, comprehensive, and valid measure of cognitive abilities. When the cross-battery approach is applied to the Wechsler Intelligence Scales, it is possible to measure important abilities that would otherwise go

TABLE 6.5 Some Misconceptions about the Cross-Battery Approach and Corresponding Clarifications

Misconceptions	Clarifications
In order to conduct cross-battery assessments, I will need access to all the major intelligence batteries or at least most of them.	Only two intelligence batteries are needed to conduct proper cross-battery assessments. Access to additional batteries and tests may be required if more in-depth assessment in a given domain is necessary. As presented in the *Gf-Gc* worksheets (Appendix C), there are a variety of batteries from which to choose. It is recommended that practitioners review the worksheets to determine what batteries would be necessary to meet their needs (i.e., they may already have sufficient instrumentation to conduct comprehensive cross-battery assessments).
Cross-battery assessment takes more time than single-battery assessment.	The time of administration is dependent, in part, on whether or not a Full Scale score is needed. When compared to a single intelligence battery, there is no appreciable increase in time involved in conducting a cross-battery assessment. In fact, when conducting *selective* cross-battery assessments, the time required is often less than administering any one of the major intelligence batteries.
The cross-battery approach to assessment is complicated.	This method of assessment is characterized by an easy-to-follow set of six steps that guides the practitioner through designing, scoring, and interpreting cross-battery assessments.
The *Gf-Gc* theory underlying the cross-battery approach is supported by only factor-analytic evidence and, therefore, has limited interpretability.	*Gf-Gc* theory is supported by a network of validity evidence (developmental, neurocognitive, etc.) which exceeds that in support of any other psychometric theory of multiple cognitive abilities. Therefore, within the psychometric tradition, it is the theory around which cognitive functioning should be interpreted. See Chapter 2 for a summary of validity evidence for the *Gf-Gc* constructs.
Some *Gf-Gc* abilities do not correlate highly with *g* (or general intelligence) so why measure them (e.g., *Gs*)?	The importance of assessing certain *Gf-Gc* abilities should be guided by referral concerns as well as their established relations to outcome criteria (e.g., academic achievement). It is incorrect to assume that an ability is unimportant solely on the basis of its relation to *g* (this issue is discussed in Chapter 2).

(continued)

TABLE 6.5   Continued

Misconceptions	Clarifications
Combining tests from different intelligence batteries is an inappropriate and invalid use of intelligence tests.	The cluster scores derived from a cross-battery assessment are more reliable and valid than individual tests (i.e., subtests) because they are based on the aggregate of two qualitatively different and empirically strong narrow-ability indicators of a particular construct. Until new test batteries are developed or old ones are revised to be more comprehensive, *Gf-Gc* cross-battery assessment is the best available procedure for conducting reliable and valid assessments of cognitive abilities and processes that are grounded in the most well-validated psychometric theory of the structure of intelligence. It serves as a practical "bridge" to narrow the assessment-theory gap.
The *Gf-Gc* cluster scores yielded from cross-battery assessment cannot be entered into formulas to determine eligibility, so it is not worthwhile.	Because *Gf-Gc* cross-battery clusters should not be interpreted in the absence of their corresponding confidence bands, they should not be entered into *ability-achievement* discrepancy formulas. However, the information derived from cross-battery assessments can be used to identify cognitive ability and processing strengths and weaknesses, the latter of which is critical in documenting a learning disability. In light of the psychometric and theoretical rigor behind the construction of *Gf-Gc* clusters, the cross-battery approach is among the best methods available for examining intracognitive strengths and weaknesses (the *primary* discrepancy analysis in the assessment of learning disabilities; Mather, 1993).
Because the cross-battery approach involves using two or more measures that were normed on different populations, a cross-battery norm group does not exist. This leads to potential errors in interpretation.	Ideally, a comprehensive *Gf-Gc* assessment should be based on a single battery of tests normed on a single sample. However, currently this option does not exist nor is this option practical (e.g., to fully operationalize Carroll's [1993a] Three Stratum Model, a 70-subtest battery would need to be developed). The potential error that results from conducting an incomplete assessment of cognitive abilities through conventional methods is deemed greater than the error associated with the "crossing" of norm samples, especially if the cross-battery principles are followed (e.g., use only test batteries with large representative norm samples and minimize the number of different batteries used).

Traditional assessment data are easily interpreted through the plotting of test scores and well-established intraindividual and interindividual discrepancy procedures. Cross-battery data are not as easily interpreted.

The language of the cross-battery approach is not user-friendly.

Cross-battery data are interpreted in much the same way as traditional assessment data. However, the cross-battery intracognitive discrepancy procedure, in particular, is far in advance of those associated with traditional batteries (e.g., ipsative) because it is both psychometrically and theoretically defensible and is conducted as part of a *systematic* approach to assessment. Cross-battery assessment results can be plotted on a profile (see Appendix E) that allows for a graphic depiction of intracognitive discrepancies. The characteristics of the normal probability curve are used to make inferences regarding interindividual differences.

The language used in reports of cross-battery assessments is no more confusing or difficult than that used in a standard Wechsler-based psychoeducational report. Although the former uses *Gf-Gc* terminology (as opposed to verbal/nonverbal and simultaneous/successive terminology), it is the responsibility of the practitioner to communicate the meaning of any psychological term. It is no more difficult to describe Visual Processing (a broad ability within the *Gf-Gc* framework) than it is to describe Simultaneous Processing or Nonverbal ability. See Appendix G for simple and concise definitions and related information pertaining to the *Gf-Gc* abilities.

unassessed (e.g., *Gf, Ga, Glr*)—abilities that are important in understanding school learning and a variety of vocational/occupational outcomes.

The cross-battery approach allows for the effective measurement of the major cognitive areas specified in the *Gf-Gc* theoretical framework with emphasis on those considered most critical on the basis of history, observation and available test data. The *Gf-Gc* classifications of a multitude of cognitive ability tests (presented here and in McGrew and Flanagan [1998]) bring stronger content and construct validity evidence to the evaluation and interpretation process when the Wechsler Intelligence Scales are used as the core battery in assessment. As test development continues to evolve and become increasingly more sophisticated (psychometrically and theoretically), batteries of the future will undoubtedly be more comprehensive than the current Wechsler Scales and provide stronger content and construct validity. Notwithstanding, it is unrealistic from an economic and practical standpoint to develop a battery that operationalizes fully contemporary *Gf-Gc* theory (e.g., at the extreme, a 70-test battery, one for every narrow ability included in Carroll's Three Stratum Theory). Therefore, it is probable that *Gf-Gc*-organized cross-battery assessments will become increasingly important as the empirical support for the *Gf-Gc* model continues to mount and batteries of the future include more diverse measures of *Gf-Gc* constructs.

With a strong research base and a multiplicity of *Gf-Gc* measures available, *Gf-Gc* cross-battery procedures can aid practitioners in the selective measurement of cognitive abilities that are important with regard to the examinee's presenting problem(s). In particular, because of the well-supported psychometric and theoretical foundation on which the *Gf-Gc* cross-battery approach was developed, practitioners who use this method may be in a better position to address the underlying *cognitive processing deficit* component of all definitions of learning disability more reliably and validly. With the exception of the intracognitive discrepancy procedures of the WJ-R/III, the same cannot be said of any existing intracognitive analysis approaches used regularly in the fields of school and clinical psychology (two disciplines routinely involved in diagnosing learning disabilities).

In the past, the lack of theoretical clarity of the Wechsler Intelligence Scales confounded interpretation and adversely affected the examiner's ability to draw clear and useful conclusions from the data. The Wechsler-based *Gf-Gc* cross-battery approach provides a means for practitioners to ride the fourth wave of test interpretation for evaluating and supporting cognitive ability test performance within the context of sound theory and research. Guidelines for interpreting Wechsler-based *Gf-Gc* cross-battery data are presented in Chapter 7.

E N D N O T E S

1. In factor analysis a minimum of *three* variables are necessary to form a factor (Zwick & Velicer, 1986). The tests that are recommended for use in cross-battery assessments had either strong or moderate (but not mixed) loadings on their respective factors in studies in which three or more indicators typically formed a factor (see Chapter 4 for a summary). However, in the cross-battery approach a minimum of *two* narrow-ability measures is recommended for constructing *Gf-Gc*

broad ability composites for practical reasons (viz., time efficient assessment).

2. Mixed measures may be used in cross-battery assessment if they are a requisite to the administration of another measure of interest. For example, Stories on the CMS (a mixed measure of meaningful memory *[Glr]* and Listening ability *[Gc]*) must be administered prior to administering Stories 2 (a relatively pure measure of meaningful memory *[Glr]*). Definitions of *strong, moderate,* and *mixed* are provided in Chapter 4.

3. The *Gf-Gc* cluster average standard scores *should not* be combined to yield a Full Scale score (i.e., the average of the cluster averages should not be calculated and used in formulas that require Full Scale scores) because actual *normed* cluster scores are not always equal to the average of the individual standard scores that they comprise (see McGrew, 1994; and McGrew & Flanagan, 1998 for a discussion). This issue is addressed briefly in chapter 7. The *Gf-Gc* cross-battery approach is a method that allows for examination of relative strengths and weaknesses within ability domains.

4. Given the large number of individu be used in *Gf-Gc* cross-battery ass not practical to calculate and report the composite reliability and SEM estimates for every possible combination of tests. Since the WJ-R *Gf-Gc* broad-ability clusters are based on *Gf-Gc* theory (the foundation of cross-battery assessment) and are derived from two-test combinations (like the clusters in cross-battery assessments), the *Gf-Gc* cluster SEMs reported in the *WJ-R Technical Manual* (McGrew et al., 1991) were used to estimate a SEM value for the broad *Gf-Gc* cross-battery clusters. Likewise, it is not practical to report all published SEMs for all individual tests that might be interpreted in cross-battery assessments. The SEMs reported across the 21 WJ-R cognitive tests across all age ranges were reviewed to identify a reasonable SEM estimate that could be used as a general "rule-of-thumb" for all individual tests used in cross-battery assessments. Furthermore, the respective subtest and composite SEMs reported for other intelligence batteries (e.g., WISC-III) were reviewed to ensure that these SEM rules-of-thumb values were reasonable approximate values across a variety of instruments.

CHAPTER

7 Wechsler-Based *Gf-Gc* Cross-Battery Interpretation and Selective Cross-Battery Assessment

Strenuous and novel efforts must take place in order to ensure a closer relationship of science to practice

—Kamphaus (1998, p. 40).

The cross-battery assessment approach ensures that science and practice are closely linked in the measurement of cognitive abilities. This chapter provides general guidelines for interpreting Wechsler-based *Gf-Gc* cross-battery data within the context of current research. In addition, guidelines for conducting *Gf-Gc* selective cross-battery assessments are offered as they pertain to reading and mathematics referral concerns.

In this chapter, the results of the Wechsler-based *Gf-Gc* cross-battery assessment presented in Chapter 6 are interpreted. The interpretive approach described in this chapter, which includes both inter- and intra-analysis procedures, follows a scientific, practical, and well-conceived framework (Flanagan, Mascolo, & Genshaft, in press) based primarily on the work of Kaufman (1994a) and Kamphaus (1993; 1998).

A Conceptual Framework for Assessment and Interpretation

Bias is inherent in all aspects of the assessment process. Completely unbiased assessment may be inpossible to achieve; therefore, the goal in assessment should not be to eliminate all bias (this is likely to be a futile effort) but to reduce it as much as possible. Although equity and the reduction of bias in assessment may be accomplished in a variety of different ways (Cook, 1987), certain fundamental assumptions should be adhered to strictly throughout the process in order to ensure such fairness.

Comprehensive and fair assessment of individuals should not begin with a narrow focus or the presumption of pre-existing deficits. Rather, assessment should be guided by

258

the presumption that functioning is not impaired, that performance is within normal limits, and that the root or primary cause of any suspected difficulties lies outside the individual within the broader systems or ecology, until proven otherwise. Assessment should seek to ensure that all reasonable, external causes of suspected learning problems (e.g., lack of appropriate instruction, insufficient opportunity for learning, lack of school experience, unstable or dysfunctional home, language or cultural differences, etc.) have been carefully examined and ruled out as primary reasons for the observed learning difficulties prior to engaging in the process of standardized testing. Information derived from existing educational records, success or failure of prereferral interventions, health or developmental histories, and data from relevant sources (e.g., parents, siblings, teachers, friends, employers) should be used in an attempt to distinguish extrinsic causes from suspected intrinsic ones. Assessment should also include the development and systematic evaluation of appropriate prereferral and intervention approaches specifically designed to ameliorate the observed difficulties—an approach described as ecosystemic (Cook-Morales, 1994; Fine, 1985).

The adoption of such an approach can assist in preventing confirmation or confirmatory bias (Sandoval, 1998) wherein assessment begins with the assumption that the child has a deficit or disability and then results are obtained and evaluated only from the perspective of whether they do or do not support that notion. The fact that it may have been demonstrated satisfactorily that no external factors exist that account for, or can be considered the primary reasons for the observed learning difficulties does not automatically support the notion that a disability is present or warrant its adoption. Even when an assessor has reached the point where standardized, norm-referenced testing is warranted and deemed necessary in order to continue exploration of the nature of suspected learning difficulties, the basic hypothesis should remain in favor of the individual to the effect that there is no credible reason to believe that performance will be other than average.

A distinction should also be drawn between hypotheses that are to be tested and evaluated and opinion, conjecture, or supposition on the part of the assessor. Although there may be reason to entertain notions regarding the presence of a disability or data which supports an opinion regarding potentially superior or poor task performance, the hypotheses to be evaluated should remain in favor of the individual, no matter how much the assessor believes it to be unacceptable. Again, unless and until the data strongly suggest otherwise, the null hypothesis is not rejected. Therefore, in order to minimize any confirmation or confirmatory bias effects when using a hypothesis-driven approach, it is recommended that all *a priori* and *a posteriori* hypotheses adopt the null stance (i.e., performance will be average—whether across the board or on a particular subtest) even when there are strong suspicions and perhaps even other data which suggest differently. Thus, the data are allowed to speak for themselves and they are not interpreted to the advantage of the examiner who may be "bent" on supporting only one point of view or opinion.

The guidelines presented in this chapter are meant to help practitioners through the various stages of the assessment and interpretation process, in particular after the need for standardized testing has arisen. These stages, depicted in Figure 7.1, reflect, in part, Kamphaus's (1993) integrative method of test interpretation. It is important to note that the assessment and interpretation process described in this figure begins only when a focused evaluation of cognitive abilities through standardized testing is deemed necessary within the context of the broader, more comprehensive approach to assessment described above.

The interpretation process described herein continues to require careful evaluation of case history information (e.g., educational records and authentic measures of achievement, medical records), the inclusion of data from relevant sources (e.g., parents, siblings, teachers, friends, employers), and the framing of an individual's difficulties within the context of *Gf-Gc* theory and research. The various stages of *Gf-Gc* cross-battery interpretation are presented schematically in Figure 7.1 and are described briefly below.

Stage A: A Knowledge Base for *Gf-Gc* Theory and Research

An understanding of the presenting problems of a referral and the subsequent organization and interpretation of a battery of tests designed to assess referral concerns presupposes a

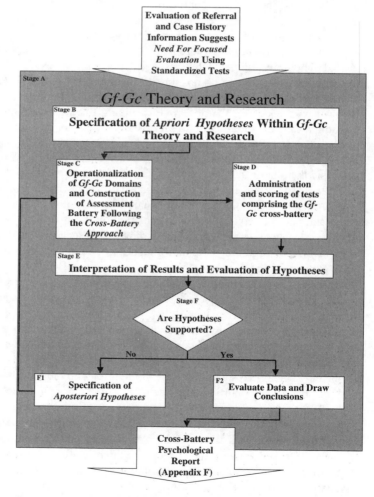

FIGURE 7.1   Stage of *Gf-Gc* Cross-Battery Assessment and Interpretation

sound *Gf-Gc* theory and research knowledge base. This stage of *Gf-Gc* cross-battery inter-pretation is represented by the shaded area in Figure 7.1 and is labeled *Stage A*. The *Gf-Gc* knowledge base requisite for sound interpretation includes an understanding of (1) the lit-erature on the relations between *Gf-Gc* cognitive abilities and specific academic and occu-pational outcomes; (2) the *Gf-Gc* cross-battery approach to assessing cognitive functioning; and (3) the network of validity evidence that exists in support of the *Gf-Gc* structure and nature of abilities.

This theory and research knowledge base is critical in the early stages of assessment because it guides the reasoning behind the possible connections between deficits in aca-demic (or other outcome) performance and suspected underlying cognitive deficits. It is from these logical deductions and presuppositions that the formation of *a priori* hypotheses which can be statistically evaluated ultimately occurs. It is important to note that reason and research are used to select relationships between ability and other manifest variables (achievement). However, it is the hypotheses that are formally tested, not the suspicions of the assessor, and the hypotheses are always specified with the null hypotheses representing average, normal functioning or the absence of any deficiencies as stated previously.

Stage B: Specification of *A Priori* Hypotheses within *Gf-Gc* Theory and Research

As may be seen in Figure 7.1, a connection should be made between an individual's pre-senting difficulties and research findings before *a priori* hypotheses can be generated. The *American Heritage Dictionary (1994)* defines *a priori* as follows: "From a known or assumed cause to a necessarily related effect; deductive . . . based on theory rather than on experiment." According to Kamphaus (1993), the *a priori* approach "forces consideration of research and theory because the clinician is operating on the basis of research and theory when the hypothesis is drawn" (p. 167). Thus, in the interpretive process outlined here, knowledge of *Gf-Gc* theory and research coupled with case history information and perhaps information from other fields (e.g., literature on learning disabilities, mental retardation, attention deficit disorder, etc.) is necessary in order to establish reasonable connections between outcome criteria (e.g., academic achievement, adaptive functioning, etc.) and cog-nitive functioning. Knowledge of these relationships informs assessment and is used as the foundation for specifying *a priori* hypotheses.

Stages C, D, and E: Construction of Assessment Battery, Administration and Scoring, Interpretation, and Evaluation of Hypotheses

Once a connection is established between an individual's difficulties and research findings and *a priori* hypotheses have been specified, knowledge of *Gf-Gc* theory and research is used to construct an appropriate assessment battery (see the process outlined in Figure 7.1) (Stage C). The cross-battery approach described in Chapter 6, for example, allows practi-tioners to draw empirically guided inferences regarding the nature and type of broad and narrow *Gf-Gc* cognitive abilities that are most likely to be related to the observed or reported difficulties of the examinee. The next stages reported in Figure 7.1 involve administering and scoring the tests comprising the selected *Gf-Gc* cross-battery (Stage D) and interpreting the *Gf-Gc Profile* of broad- and/or narrow-ability clusters (Stage E) to determine whether *a priori* hypotheses were supported or refuted or if the specification of *a posteriori* hypotheses is necessary.

Stage F: Are *A Priori* Hypotheses Supported?

Following the interpretation of initial *Gf-Gc* cross-battery results, Stage F in Figure 7.1 shows that one of two outcomes is likely: (F1) If one or more *a priori* hypotheses are not supported, then it is likely that additional assessment is warranted or (F2) if *a priori* hypotheses are supported by initial cross-battery data, then it is likely that further assessment is not warranted and conclusions may be drawn and presented in the form of a cross-battery psychological report (such as the one presented in Appendix F). In the former situation, *a priori* hypotheses do not explain one or more of the observed *Gf-Gc* scores and, therefore it is necessary to specify *a posteriori* hypotheses.

The *American Heritage Dictionary (1994)* defines *a posteriori* as follows: "Reasoning from particular facts to general principles; empirical." *A posteriori* hypotheses, which involve inferring causes from effects, have long been used in clinical assessment (Kamphaus, 1993). Following the specification of *a posteriori* hypotheses, it is necessary to again use knowledge of *Gf-Gc* theory and research to guide the selection of cognitive ability measures that will be used to test these hypotheses. As demonstrated by the arrow in Figure 7.1 leading from "specification of *a posteriori* hypotheses" (F1) to "operationalization of *Gf-Gc* domains and construction of an assessment battery . . . ," (Stage C) it is clear that both assessment and interpretation are iterative processes. That is, additional data collection (via the administration of more cognitive tests) or another "iteration" of assessment is necessary to corroborate findings or "narrow down the possibilities" for a particular finding after initial data collection (Kamphaus, 1993, p. 166). This iterative process of (1) assessment; (2) interpretation of results; and (3) evaluation of hypotheses within the context of *Gf-Gc* theory and research, case history, and literature from related fields in psychology continues until hypotheses either are supported or refuted and valid conclusions can be drawn.

The assessment and interpretation process depicted in Figure 7.1 will be followed in the next sections to demonstrate Examiner A's approach to understanding the nature of Christine's difficulties (following the case study information presented in Chapter 6). Specifically, brief descriptions of the commonly used interindividual and intraindividual analysis approaches to intelligence test interpretation will be presented along with procedures for conducting these analyses with Wechsler-based *Gf-Gc* cross-battery data using Christine's test performance as an example.

Interindividual Analysis with Wechsler-Based *Gf-Gc* Cross-Battery Data

Interindividual analysis provides population-relative information and reveals between-individual differences through the comparison of normative scores. *Normative scores* provide information about an individual's ability with respect to his or her same age peers (norm group; e.g., Anastasi & Urbina, 1997; Woodcock, 1994). Notably, an individual's normative score for one ability is not artificially altered by his or her scores on other abilities (as is the case with ipsative scores discussed later in this chapter)[1]. Interindividual analysis is used primarily to interpret global and scale (or cluster) performance (e.g., Wechsler Full Scale IQ, Verbal IQ, Performance IQ, etc.) and to aid in making diagnostic, classification, and educational placement decisions.

Unlike single battery assessment, cross-battery test scores come from different sources. In a typical evaluation of cognitive abilities, the majority (or all) of the data are gathered using one battery, such as a Wechsler Scale. As such, individual test scores on a given Wechsler battery are on the same scale and were standardized on the same population, allowing direct comparisons between scores. However, since more than one battery must be used to obtain a comprehensive assessment of *Gf-Gc* abilities, scores yielded by cross-battery assessments likely have different means and standard deviations (e.g., WISC-III subtests have a mean of 10 and SD of 3; WJ-R subtests have a mean of 100 and SD of 15). Moreover, cross-battery assessments may employ an unsystematic aggregate of standardized tests that were developed at different times, in different places, on different samples, with different scoring procedures, and for different purposes (Lezak, 1976; 1995).

In order to address these issues and make psychometrically defensible inter- (and intra-) cognitive ability comparisons (i.e., to make Wechsler-based cross-battery data comparisons necessary to understand cognitive functioning within the context of the *Gf-Gc* structure of abilities), it was necessary to (1) convert all scores to a common metric and (2) identify a normative standard to which test scores could be compared. As directed in Step 5 of the Wechsler-based cross-battery approach (see Chapter 6), all standard scores from cross-battery assessments were converted to a common metric with a mean of 100 and standard deviation of 15 (using the Percentile Rank and Standard Score Conversion Table in Appendix D). This step eliminates the concern regarding the accuracy and validity of conclusions drawn from test scores with different scales. Furthermore, this allows practitioners the ability to combine tests from two different batteries into reliable, construct-relevant clusters. The next step is to compare these scores to a *normative standard* (in lieu of a cross-battery norm group), thereby controlling for differences across normative samples in cross-battery assessments. The normal probability curve was selected because it is the most useful standard statistically and it can adequately address the reality of having to cross batteries (and in effect norm groups) to conduct more comprehensive and theoretically meaningful assessments (McGrew & Flanagan, 1998).

The normal probability curve "has very practical applications for comparing and evaluating psychological data in that the position of any test score on a standard deviation unit scale, in itself, defines the proportion of people taking the test who will obtain scores above or below a given score" (Lezak, 1976, p. 123). A description of *Gf-Gc* ability scores with respect to the normal probability curve is presented in Table 7.1 (e.g., percent of cases under portions of the normal curve). This table also provides commonly used "classification categories" (e.g., Low Average, Average, High Average, etc.) that correspond to different standard score and percentile rank ranges. Most of the information in this table can also be found on the *Gf-Gc* Profile (located in Appendix E). The guidelines presented below apply to Wechsler-based *Gf-Gc* cross-battery data that have been transferred from the *Gf-Gc* worksheets (Appendix C) to the profile and plotted (as described in Chapter 6).

It should also be noted that selecting tests that were normed within a few years of one another (e.g., WISC-III and WJ-R; WAIS-III and WJ-III) reduces the potential for error that may result from crossing batteries.

Interindividual Analysis of Christine's WISC-III-Based *Gf-Gc* Cross-Battery Evaluation

As discussed in Chapter 6, Christine was administered a select set of measures from the WISC-III, WJ-R, and CMS batteries following steps to address the specific referral concerns. Seven *Gf-Gc* clusters were calculated (see Figure 6.11) in an attempt to obtain a baseline level of functioning across a broad range of cognitive abilities.

Prior to the construction of a *Gf-Gc* cross-battery and the scoring of the *Gf-Gc* ability clusters, Examiner A suspected that Christine might have difficulties in the cognitive domains of *Gc, Ga, Gsm, Glr,* and *Gs*. This hypothesis was based on literature that suggests that narrow abilities within *Gc, Ga, Gsm, Glr,* and *Gs* have significant relations to reading achievement in the early elementary school years (McGrew & Flanagan, 1998). Examiner A next formed hypotheses to test the viability of the null hypothesis (that there is no difference in her functioning compared to the norm) versus the alternative hypothesis (that a difference does exist). The criteria for rejecting the null hypothesis was set at −1 SD below the mean (1 tailed test). Specifically, if the standard score range associated with each of these broad-ability clusters was above 85, the examiner would fail to reject the null hypothesis and conclude that Christine functions within normal limits in these cognitive domains.

TABLE 7.1   Description and Evaluation of Wechsler-Based *Gf-Gc* Ability Scores

Description of Performance			Evaluation of Performance
Standard Score Range	*Percentile Rank Range*	Gf-Gc *Ability Classification*	
≥131	98 to 99+	Very Superior	Normative Strength
121 to 130	92 to 97	Superior	(16% of the population)
111 to 120	76 to 91	High Average	(+1 standard deviation: SS = 115)
90 to 110	25 to 75	Average	Normal Range
80 to 89	9 to 24	Low Average	(68 % of the population)
			(−1 standard deviation: SS = 85)
70 to 79	3 to 8	Low	Normative Weakness
≥69	≥2	Very Low	(16% of the population)

Note: Gf-Gc ability classifications correspond to those used in McGrew and Flanagan (1998) and were adapted from Mather and Woodcock (1989; 1990).

Alternatively, if the standard score range associated with one or more of Christine's broad-ability clusters fell at or below −1 SD of the normative mean, the null hypothesis would be rejected in favor of the alternative hypotheses (i.e., a normative weakness would be inferred).[2]

Based on *Gf-Gc* domain specific knowledge, case history and referral information, and the current learning disabilities research, Examiner A was able to establish a basis for selective evaluation of cognitive functions as well as formulate *a priori* hypotheses to test these associations. The guidelines that follow are consistent with the aforementioned interpretive approach (see Figure 7.1), because they "force a link between research, theory, and test interpretation" (Kamphaus, 1998, p. 47).

Guideline 1: Evaluate Performance and Decide Whether Additional Measures Are Necessary to Administer

Careful evaluation of initial cross-battery assessment data allows practitioners to determine whether *a priori* hypotheses are supported or refuted. If *a priori* hypotheses are supported by the initial data, further assessment may not be necessary. Conversely, if *a priori* hypotheses are not supported, then *a posteriori* hypotheses are typically generated and another iteration of assessment may be conducted. In the latter scenario, the practitioner would most likely administer one or more tests to gather additional information to test hypotheses about *Gf-Gc* strengths and weaknesses.

Evaluator A reviewed Christine's Wechsler-based *Gf-Gc* cross-battery performance, which was recorded on the *Gf-Gc* profile presented in Chapter 6 (Figure 6.11). An initial review of Christine's broad-ability clusters revealed that her scores were in the average range in the areas of *Gf, Gc, Gv* and *Gs*. The remaining broad cognitive ability cluster scores (i.e., *Ga, Gsm,* and *Glr*) were low average and the bands associated with these clusters extended below −1 SD of the normative mean. These data meet the criterion set for the rejection of the null hypothesis and the acceptance of the alternative hypothesis. Therefore, the data is accepted as evidence that Christine's tested performance is below expectations compared to same-age peers in *Ga, Gsm,* and *Glr.* However, the data are inconclusive with regard to her *Gs* score because Christine scored in the average range on WISC-III Symbol Search and in the low average range on WISC-III Coding. Given the significant difference between the scores on these two tests, inferences about Christine's broad *Gs* ability must be made cautiously.

At this initial stage in the assessment process, the data support the conclusion that Christine's tested performance in *Ga, Gsm,* and *Glr* is below average. This is consistent with the research literature which has demonstrated that these *Gf-Gc* abilities explain a significant portion of the variance in reading achievement (McGrew & Flanagan, 1998). However, before drawing final conclusions from Christine's cross-battery data, it is necessary to evaluate her performance at the narrow-ability level to ascertain whether her tested performance is consistent within each broad-ability domain. If significantly disparate scores are found within broad-ability domains, the meaning of the discrepancy may not be readily apparent. Therefore, additional assessment may be necessary to determine whether this is a meaningful difference (Kamphaus, 1993). Interpretations and diagnostic conclusions should not be based on a single test score outlier (e.g., a subtest scaled score), regardless of the extent to which it deviates from all other scores. Outlier scores may be best accounted for by unreliability or chance (see Atkinson, 1991; Lezak, 1995). Therefore, assessment should be regarded as an iterative process.

Following the* Gf-Gc *Interpretation Flowchart.   In order to determine whether Christine should be given additional measures (i.e., whether another iteration of assessment was warranted), Examiner A used the interpretation flowchart presented in Figure 7.2 as a guide. According to this chart, Examiner A needs to determine whether or not Christine's performance on narrow-ability test indicators is uniform within broad *Gf-Gc* ability clusters. Following the procedures outlined for the WJ-R (McGrew et al., 1991), which take into account the reliability of the difference score, the following two guidelines are recommended for evaluating the differences between *Gf-Gc* confidence bands in cross-battery assessments: (1) if the confidence bands for any two test scores or clusters touch or overlap, the practitioner should assume that no significant difference exists between the examinee's true scores for the abilities being compared; (2) if the confidence bands for any two tests or clusters do not touch or overlap, then the practitioner should assume that a possible significant difference exists between the examinee's true scores for the abilities that are being compared (McGrew et al., 1991). According to McGrew and colleagues (1991), when the second, "nonoverlap" guideline is used, a practitioner can be 84 percent confident that a true difference in scores exists. This level of confidence was deemed to be appropriate for the clinical nature of the comparisons that are made in *Gf-Gc* cross-battery assessments.

It is noteworthy that individuals who score at a particular level on a given test often score at roughly the same level on other purported indicators of the construct being measured. "Or, more precisely, persons high on the construct should score high on a variety of indicators of that construct" (Messick, 1989, p. 51). Thus, within each of the broad *Gf-Gc* ability domains, a *convergence of indicators* is expected. However, because situational and method variables, for example, may differentially influence indicators of the same construct (see discussion of individual/situational and background/environmental variables in Chapter 4), "it is usually desirable to take the notion of convergence of indicators quite literally and base inferences on some combination of several indicators, preferably derived from quite different measurement methods" (Messick, 1989, p. 51). However, convergence can also be achieved legitimately through the combination of construct scores based on the same measurement method (e.g., inductive reasoning construct scores from several matrix analogies tests), which is sometimes the case when *Gf-Gc narrow*-ability constructs are represented following cross-battery procedures. Conversely, *broad*-ability constructs are typically measured through different measurement methods (e.g., *Gf* may be measured through a task requiring inductive reasoning with words and a task requiring deductive reasoning with numbers).

Since the *Gf-Gc* cross-battery classification system provides for reasonably accurate selection of multiple and varied indicators of constructs, it is expected that an individual's performance within broad-ability domains will be consistent. As such, interpretations and inferences about performance are made most appropriately at the broad-ability level (e.g., *Gf, Gc,* etc.). When performance within broad-ability domains is not consistent, however, it may be necessary to examine multiple indicators of the narrow abilities subsumed by the broad ability. In this latter situation, interpretation and inferences about performance are made most appropriately at the narrow-ability level (e.g., inductive reasoning, general sequential reasoning, etc.). Regardless of the level at which performance is examined (i.e., broad or narrow), interpretation necessitates well-represented constructs through two or more test indicators.

Examiner A reviewed the within *Gf-Gc* domain confidence bands of Christine's narrow-ability test indicator scores and found that the narrow-ability test indicator bands overlapped (i.e., converged) within all *Gf-Gc* domains except *Gv, Glr,* and *Gs* (see Figure 6.11). Since the confidence bands overlapped for the respective tests within the *Gf, Gc, Gsm,* and *Ga* clusters, Examiner A concluded that Christine's performance was uniform within these *Gf-Gc* domains (see Figure 7.2). However, since the within *Gv, Glr,* and *Gs* narrow-ability

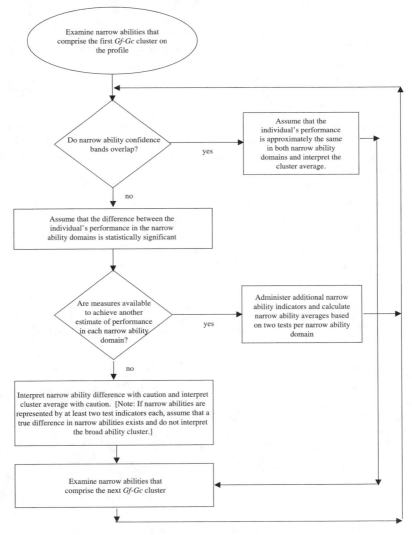

FIGURE 7.2   A Flowchart to Guide Interpretation at the Narrow *Gf-Gc* Ability Level

test indicator bands did not overlap, Examiner A assumed Christine's tested performance in the respective two narrow-ability domains comprising these clusters was significantly different.

In the area of *Gv* (see Figure 7.3), Christine's ability to quickly combine disconnected visual stimuli (e.g., scrambled puzzle pieces) into a meaningful whole (CS; WISC-III Object Assembly) appears to be better developed than her ability to rapidly perceive and manipulate visual patterns (SR; WISC-III Block Design). In the *Glr* domain (also depicted in Figure 7.3), her Associative Memory ability (MA; WJ-R Visual-Auditory Learning) was judged to be better developed than her Free Recall Memory ability (M6; CMS Word Lists). It is noteworthy that within the *Gv* and *Glr* domains, Christine's performance on decontextualized tasks (Block Design and Word Lists) was significantly below her performance on tasks that included meaningful contextual cues (Object Assembly and Visual-Auditory Learning; see interpretive report in Appendix F for a discussion). This suggests that method variables (i.e., contextually based versus noncontextually based stimuli) may have been responsible for the lack of convergence within these domains.

Finally, in the area of *Gs* (see Figure 7.4), Christine's rate of test taking (R9; WISC-III Coding) was significantly below her performance on a task of perceptual speed (P; WISC-III Symbol Search). However, it is not uncommon for young children who experience considerable difficulty in the early stages of reading to score below the mean on the Wechsler Coding test (see Mather, 1991 for a discussion). Also, as observed by Examiner A, Christine's performance on this task was adversely affected by her difficulty in tracking visual stimuli.

Since statements of statistical probability imply only that Christine performed differently on measures of two narrow abilities within the *Gv, Glr,* and *Gs* domains, Examiner A had to determine whether these differences had practical, educational, or diagnostic significance. That is, were these differences useful in understanding Christine's behavior or in planning for her educational instruction and service delivery (Kaufman, 1994; Mather & Woodcock, 1989, 1990; McGrew & Flanagan, 1998)? According to the flowchart in Figure

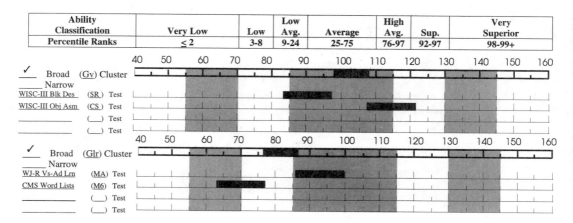

FIGURE 7.3   Christine's Initial Cross-Battery Performance in the Broad-Ability Domains of *Gv* and *Glr*

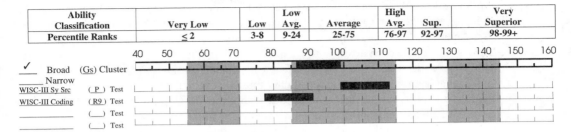

FIGURE 7.4   Christine's Cross-Battery Performance in the Broad-Ability Domain of *Gs*

7.2, ideally, Examiner A should administer additional measures—one for each of the narrow abilities measured in the *Gv* (SR and CS), *Glr* (MA and M6), and *Gs* (R9 and P) domains. In this way, narrow-ability averages (or clusters) could be calculated based on two tests (i.e., convergent indicators) of each narrow-ability domain. This is good practice givin that a two-test ability cluster is more *reliable* than a single subtest (Bracken, McCallum, & Crain, 1993; Jensen, 1998, p. 31; McGrew et al., 1991). Therefore, an examiner can more confidently assert that a true difference between two narrow-ability clusters exists when two two-test narrow-ability clusters (as opposed to individual subtests) are compared. For example, if the bands for the *narrow-ability averages* for SR and CS did not overlap, then Examiner A would be confident that a true difference existed between Christine's ability to rapidly perceive and manipulate visual patterns (SR) and her ability to quickly combine disconnected visual stimuli into a meaningful whole (CS), especially if supported by corroborating data relevant to the referral. In the absence of the latter condition, the meaningfulness of such a finding would be unclear and, therefore, of limited utility. Similarly, if significant differences were found within the *Glr* and *Gs* domains, respectively, Examiner A would be confident stating that a true difference exists between Christine's Associative Memory (MA) and her Free Recall Memory (M6) as well as between her rate of test taking (R9) and perceptual speed (P) abilities.

In addition to the increased reliability, the grounding of cross-battery assessments in contemporary *Gf-Gc* theory and research contributes to more valid test score inferences. It should be noted that the cross-battery approach differs markedly from the *shared abilities* approach inherent in traditional psychometric test interpretation. For example, in traditional test interpretation, when two or more individual test scores vary consistently from the individual's average performance (or from the normative mean), the aggregate of these scores (i.e., the cluster) is typically interpreted. However, unlike the clusters yielded by cross-battery assessments, many of the shared abilities clusters derived from traditional assessments lack validity evidence (Flanagan, Andrews, & Genshaft, 1997; Kamphaus, 1993; 1998; McDermott et al., 1992).

When statistically significant differences exist between narrow-ability averages, the respective broad-ability cross-battery cluster should not be interpreted, as it is likely a misleading estimate of the broad ability. For instance, if the MA and M6 narrow-ability confidence bands did not overlap, the broad *Glr* ability cluster should not be interpreted or should be interpreted with caution. Long-term Storage and Retrieval *(Glr)* in this case would be described most accurately in terms of performance in the different narrow-ability domains subsumed by *Glr* (i.e., MA and M6). It is important to realize that additional assessment within broad-ability domains is usually warranted when (1) a significant difference is found between narrow abilities in a broad domain; *and* (2) the lower of the two narrow abilities is suggestive of a significant normative weakness (i.e., ≤ 1 SD below the normative mean) that cannot be considered spurious due to the inhibiting influences of noncognitive factors, *or* both narrow abilities within the broad domain are ≤1 SD below the normative mean and significantly below that of most other *Gf-Gc* domains); *and* (3) the narrow ability (or abilities within the domain (or domains) is useful in understanding the individual's presenting difficulties (e.g., academic skill deficiencies). This decision-making process will be elaborated on in the text following.

Additional Considerations in the Decision-Making Process.   Following the interpretive flowchart in Figure 7.2, the next iteration of Christine's assessment would ideally consist of administering additional measures of narrow abilities within three broad *Gf-Gc* domains. However, it is wise to first review the practicality of this decision in light of relevant research and referral concerns. For example, with regard to *Gv*, Examiner A noted that Christine performed within the average range on the measure of Spatial Relations (SR; WISC-III Block Design = 90 ±7) and in the high-average range on the measure of Closure Speed (CS; WISC-III Object Assembly = 115 ± 7). Although the confidence bands for these scores do not overlap (suggesting a significant difference), Examiner A chose not to administer additional measures of SR and CS. This decision was based on two considerations.

First, Christine's Object Assembly test score suggested a normative strength, and her Block Design test score was within the normal range (see Table 7.1). These results suggest that tasks requiring visual processing do not present significant difficulties for Christine. Second, Christine's performance on tests of math calculation and applied problems (as measured by the WJ-R Tests of Achievement) indicated that she is functioning in the Average range in mathematics compared to same-age peers (see Appendix F). This finding is consistent with the cognitive abilities and achievement literature (see Chapter 3) that indicates that *Gv* abilities are most strongly related to high-level *mathematics* achievement (e.g., geometry, calculus) but do not relate significantly to reading achievement. Given that Christine's teachers were not concerned about her math achievement, Examiner A concluded that the observed difference between Christine's Spatial Relations and Closure Speed *Gv* abilities had no diagnostic or instructional implications. Examiner A concluded that it was not necessary to administer additional measures of *Gv*.

With regard to *Gs* (see Figure 7.4), Examiner A noted that Christine performed within the average range on the measure of Perceptual Speed (WISC-III Symbol Search = 105 ± 7) and within the low average range on the Rate-of-Test-Taking task (WISC-III Coding = 85 ± 7). The latter score is one standard deviation below the mean and therefore represents a normative weakness. Because Symbol Search and Coding measure highly related aspects of the broad ability of *Gs*, it is unusual to observe a significant disparity in performance on these subtests. However, observations of Christine's performance while taking the Coding test, coupled with the nature of her referral issues and supporting research, help explain this disparity.

In the area of *Gs*, Christine had difficulty with the basic rapid processing of *symbols,* suggesting that her difficulty may be attributed to difficulties processing symbols, rather than general processing speed. Examiner A noted that Christine's difficulty in searching, scanning, and tracking information inhibited her performance on the WISC-III Coding task (e.g., she was unable to maintain her place consistently, and often skipped lines). Christine's below-average Coding score is consistent with her academic history, Examiner A's behavioral observations of Christine, and studies which have found that children with reading disabilities often score significantly lower than controls on tests of coding speed (e.g., Wechsler Coding tests; Decker & DeFries, 1980; LaBuda & DeFries, 1988; cited in Mather, 1991). Within the context of this information and the conclusion that Christine has the ability to process certain types of information quickly and efficiently (e.g., Average performance on Symbol Search), Examiner A concluded that it was not necessary to administer additional *Gs* tests.

Examiner A's decisions to this point were that further assessment was not warranted in the areas of *Gf, Gc, Ga, Gv,* and *Gs*. Notwithstanding, on review of Christine's entire profile of *Gf-Gc* cognitive ability strengths and weaknesses (Figure 6.11) within the context of history, observations, and research, Examiner A was able to draw several conclusions. First, Examiner A reasoned that Christine might have a weakness in working memory (MW). This suspicion was derived from the fact that Christine performed one standard deviation below the mean on the CMS Sequences test and she was unable to repeat a string of three digits backwards on the WISC-III Digit Span test. According to the WISC-III manual, more than 75 percent of the children Christine's age in the standardization sample were able to repeat a sequence of three numbers backwards (The Psychological Corporation, 1997, Table B.6). Christine's performance on this task is below average. Because deficits in working memory have been associated with reading difficulties (see McGrew & Flanagan, 1998 for a summary), Examiner A concluded that it would be important to gather additional data in regard to Christine's working memory abilities.

Second, because memory in general was highlighted as an area of concern, and verbal short-term memory in particular has been found to be deficient in individuals who have significant reading problems (see Morris et al., 1998 for a review), Examiner A reasoned that Christine would likely experience difficulty on Memory Span tasks involving words as opposed to numbers. These types of tasks are similar to the verbal short-term memory tasks found in the literature (Aaron, 1997; Morris et al., 1998).

Third, based on initial performance in the area of *Glr,* Examiner A reasoned that Christine's long-term retrieval abilities would be weak when measured through tasks that require retrieval of noncontextual stimuli requiring either recall or recognition.

Fourth, Christine's initial test performance suggested weaknesses in *Ga* and working memory, two cognitive abilities that have been empirically linked to reading skill acquisition and performance. Examiner A therefore reasoned that Christine would likely demonstrate weaknesses on a task of rapid automatic naming (or naming facility [NA]), because poor readers who are deficient in *Ga* and/or working memory also have been found to have difficulty on tasks that require the rapid serial naming of objects, colors, and letters (e.g., Morris et al., 1998; Wolf, Bally, & Morris, 1986).

Examiner A's decision-making process to this point highlights the fact that the presumptions regarding the association between measured performance and strengths and weaknesses are grounded in the *Gf-Gc*/outcome criterion evidence knowledge base (see Chapter 2). In order to make these suspicions testable, however, Examiner A would need to specify *a posteriori* hypotheses. Although evidence exists to suggest deficits in Christine's performance, the null hypothesis specifies average or normal functioning in order to avoid confirmatory bias. If deficits are to be accepted as plausible, sufficient evidence should be gathered. In this instance, if differences are consistent with the criteria previously set forth (i.e., differences that equal or exceed –1 SD), then the examiner would reject the null hypotheses (or alternatively, fail to reject the alternative hypothesis). In other words, the interpretation would reflect true differences or deficits in ability. Once *a posteriori* hypotheses have been specified, Examiner A should determine what additional measures need to be administered in the broad domains of *Gsm* and *Glr* to allow for the proper evaluation of the hypotheses.

The Next Iteration.   Based on a review of the *Gsm* worksheet (in Appendix C), Examiner A decided to administer the Numbers Reversed and Memory for Words tests from the WJ-R. Numbers Reversed was selected because the task of repeating a string of digits in reverse sequence involves working memory. Therefore, Christine's performance on this test can be used to evaluate the *a posteriori* hypothesis that Christine's working memory is within normal limits. The Memory for Words test was selected to evaluate Examiner A's *a posteriori* hypothesis that Christine's memory span for words (as opposed to numbers) is within normal limits. This is an important determination given that performance on verbal short-term memory tasks is often low in children with poor reading skills. It is important to note that Examiner A selected tests from the WJ-R (a battery used to gather initial cross-battery data) in order to avoid the introduction of additional error, that may result from the crossing of multiple, independent norm samples, into the cross-battery assessment. Examiner A's decision reflects her adherence to the first guiding principle of cross-battery assessment (i.e., use the smallest number of batteries possible).

Examiner A next reviewed the *Glr* worksheet (in Appendix C) and decided to administer the WJ-R Memory for Names test. This Associative Memory test was selected to test Examiner A's *a posteriori* hypothesis that Christine's associative memory was within the average range. Although Examiner A has already reasoned that Christine is likely to demonstrate a weakness on tasks involving retrieval and recognition of noncontextual stimuli, by definition, the null hypothesis specifies normal functioning. To this point, Christine has scored low on a task involving the recall of noncontextual stimuli (i.e., CMS Word Lists) and average on a task involving storage and retrieval of contextually based information (i.e., WJ-R Visual-Auditory Learning). Nevertheless, Examiner A followed the hypothesis-driven approach in order to minimize bias. As such, Examiner A is operating under the assumption that cognitive functioning is average until the data suggest otherwise.

To this point in the assessment process, Examiner A has evaluated three *a posteriori* hypotheses using tests from a battery used in her initial evaluation of Christine (i.e., the WJ-R). However, in order to test the last *a posteriori* hypothesis, Examiner A needed to introduce a fourth battery to the evaluation.

Based on her knowledge of the *Gf-Gc* cognitive achievement literature (viz., *Ga* [phonological awareness]; *Gsm* [working memory]) that is related to reading achievement, Examiner A decided that it was necessary to assess another memory ability (i.e., rapid serial naming or naming facility) that has been associated with children with reading problems (e.g., Katz & Shankweiler, 1985; Morris et al., 1998; Stanovich, 1988; Wolf, Bally, & Morris, 1986). A review of the *Glr* worksheet reveals that the CAS, NEPSY, and WJ-III have Naming Facility tests. Due to the higher reliability of the NEPSY Naming Facility task as compared to the CAS task (and the fact that the WJ-III was not published at the time of this assessment), it was selected for inclusion in Christine's assessment. Examiner A's decision to administer a test from a fourth battery demonstrates one of the limitations of most intelligence batteries: Most (with the possible exception of the WJ-III) do not include a sufficiently broad range of ability measures to conduct an in-depth assessment of the core cognitive abilities that have been associated with reading disabilities.

Guideline 2: Use the Characteristics of the Normal Probability Curve to Evaluate Additional Data and Draw Conclusions

After repeating stages C, D, and E outlined in Figure 7.1 (with the assistance of the interpretive flowchart in Figure 7.2) and administering four additional measures, Examiner A used the characteristics of the normal probability curve to evaluate the *a posteriori* hypotheses in order to draw conclusions about Christine's *Gf-Gc* cross-battery performance (Stage F). Christine's complete profile of scores is presented in Figure 7.5, which is identical to Figure 6.11, with two notable exceptions. First, Figure 7.5 includes the WJ-R Memory for Words, Numbers Reversed and Memory for Names tests as well as the NEPSY test. Also, due to the administration of two additional tests each in the *Gsm* and *Glr* domains, Figure 7.5 includes *Gsm* and *Glr* clusters which have been recalculated based on four subtests per domain rather than two (as reported in Figure 6.11). The four additional tests and two recalculated clusters are represented in Figure 7.5 by the lighter shaded bars. Based on Christine's performance on these additional measures, Examiner A was able to test and evaluate her *a posteriori* hypotheses and draw the following conclusions.

In the area of *Gsm*, Christine obtained a score of 80 ± 7 (low) on the WJ-R Numbers Reversed test. Because the confidence bands associated with the numbers reversed and CMS Sequences test scores (85 ± 7; low average) overlapped, Examiner A concluded that Christine's performance on both tasks was about the same. Together these scores yielded a Working Memory cluster of 83 ± 5 (low average), a score that represents a *normative weakness* (i.e., her performance was more than 1 SD below the normative mean). This performance falls at the thirteenth percentile (see Appendix D for percentile ranks). Therefore, the *a posteriori* hypothesis that Christine will perform within normal limits in the area of working memory was not supported and the alternative hypothesis that she displays a deficit in working memory is accepted.

Christine obtained a score of 78 ± 7 (low) on the WJ-R Memory for Words test. Although her performance on this test is similar to her performance on the WISC-III Digit Span test (i.e., the respective confidence bands overlapped), suggesting uniform memory span ability across stimuli (i.e., *words* and *numbers*), when evaluated against the characteristics of the normal probability curve it is clear that Christine had more difficulty with the Memory for Words task (i.e., low performance with words versus average performance with numbers). In light of this finding Examiner A's *a posteriori* hypothesis (based on her

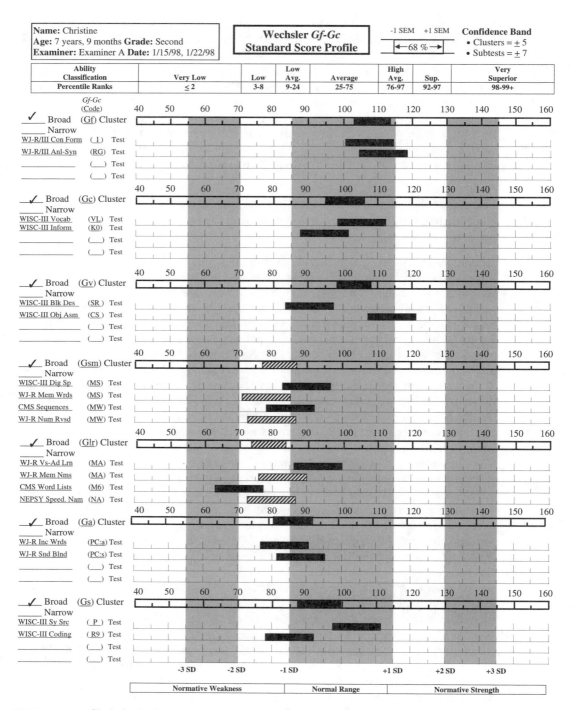

FIGURE 7.5.   Christine's Complete Profile of *Gf-Gc* Cross-Battery Performance

reading of the learning disabilities literature) that Christine would perform within normal limits on memory span tasks that involved words as opposed to numbers was not supported. The data suggest that the acceptance of the notion that Christine does, in fact, have a deficit in memory span. Moreover, the scores on the memory span tasks combined to yield a Memory Span cluster of 83 ± 5 (low average). Despite possible influences regarding the nature of the test stimuli, Christine's memory span ability is more than 1 SD below the normative mean and, therefore, is considered a normative weakness. Because all the individual test confidence bands overlapped within the *Gsm* domain, these tests can be combined to yield a broad *Gsm* cluster. Christine obtained a *Gsm* cluster of 83 ± 5 which falls in the low average range and is ranked at the thirteenth percentile. Therefore, *Gsm* appears to represent a normative weakness for Christine. As such, she experiences difficulty holding information in immediate awareness long enough to either use, transform, or encode it. This difficulty, in turn, likely interferes with the reading process.

In the area of *Glr,* Christine obtained a score of 83 ± 7 on the WJ-R Memory for Names test—a measure of associative memory. Although the confidence bands for both associative memory tests overlapped (as expected), Christine's performance on the contextually based associative memory task (i.e., Visual-Auditory Learning) is in the average range, while her performance on the noncontextually based associative memory task (i.e., Memory for Names) is greater than 1 SD below the mean. Thus, Examiner A's *a posteriori* hypothesis that Christine would perform similarly on contextually based and noncontextually based *Glr* tasks was not supported. The presence of this pattern within both the *Gsm* and *Gv* domains provides further support for rejecting the *Glr a posteriori* hypothesis of no differences in favor of the alternative. That is, Christine's functioning is dependent on the presence or absence of meaningful context.

Within the area of *Glr,* Examiner A had also suspected that Christine may have difficulty with rapid automatic naming tasks (i.e., Naming Facility). This suspicion was based on the research that has suggested that weaknesses in memory abilities and phonological processing (Christine's demonstrated areas of weakness) often covary with a rapid automatic naming weakness in children with reading problems (e.g., Morris et al., 1998; Snow, Burns, & Griffin, 1998; Stanovich, 1988; Torgeson, Wagner, Rashotte, Burgess, & Hecht, 1997; Torgeson, Wagner, & Rashotte, 1994). Specific cognitive weaknesses or deficits in these three specific cognitive abilities, therefore, are strong indicators of the presence of a specific reading disability, if corroborated with evidence from other data sources (Morris et al., 1998). Because Christine obtained a score of 80 ± 7 (low/low average) on the rapid automatic naming test (i.e., NEPSY; Speed Naming), she is regarded as having a normative weakness in this area. Thus, Examiner A's *a posteriori* hypothesis that functioning would be within normal limits is not supported. The data on Christine's performance in these three areas (phonological processing, verbal short-term memory, rapid automatic naming) is similar, which supports the alternative hypothesis that she demonstrated deficits in these areas.

Due to significant discrepancies among some of the narrow-ability indicators of *Glr,* performance in this area is likely explained better by the separate Associative Memory cluster and the Free Recall Memory and Naming Facility test indicator scores than by the broad *Glr* cluster. However, due to their relatively low reliability for an individual of Christine's chronological age, any interpretations based on the former two tests need to be corroborated with other sources of data or used only to provide support for a well-articulated and substantiated finding(s).

At this point in the assessment and interpretation process, Examiner A has sufficient data (historical, cognitive, academic, and behavioral; see interpretive report in Appendix F) to draw reasonable conclusions about the nature of Christine's referral concerns. Overall, Examiner A found that Christine showed specific and circumscribed weaknesses in *Gf-Gc* abilities that support a phonological processing-verbal short-term memory (VSTM) rate (i.e., rapid automatic naming or naming facility) subtype of reading disability (see Morris et al., 1998). Specifically, her *Ga* performance suggests a core problem with the development of phonological awareness skills and her performance within the areas of *Gsm* and *Glr* suggests specific weaknesses in other cognitive abilities that define this reading disability subtype (i.e., short-term memory, naming facility). Thus, Examiner A is reasonably confident that Christine's demonstrated below-average reading and spelling skills (as measured by the WJ-R ACH) are consistent with her demonstrated cognitive ability and processing weaknesses and case history information and classroom performance, and it also cannot be adequately explained by factors external to Christine at this time. Based on a comprehensive, systematic, and theory-driven approach to understanding Christine's academic achievement, Examiner A is reasonably confident that Christine's cognitive processing weaknesses help explain her current academic difficulties and inform appropriate interventions or remedial strategies.

In summary, corroborative information from Christine's *Gf-Gc* cross-battery assessment, combined with teacher and parent reports, as well as other assessment data (e.g., pre-referral and informal), led the team to conclude that significant information and evidence existed to support the presence of a learning disability. These data are also valuable for the development of appropriate interventions for Christine in the areas of reading and spelling (see Mather, 1991). Ongoing evaluation of the effectiveness of these interventions is necessary to determine the appropriateness of Christine's special education placement. An interpretive report containing a description of Christine's cross-battery performance and academic achievement as well as general impressions and recommendations is presented in Appendix F.

Cautions in* Gf-Gc *Cross-Battery Interpretation of Cluster Scores.   Cross-battery assessment in terms of the utility of the scores yielded by this approach are intended to identify normative (and intraindividual) strengths and weaknesses among multiple broad *Gf-Gc* abilities that, by and large, define the *Gf-Gc* structure of intelligence within the psychometric tradition. Through the use of "modern" principles of cognitive psychology, the cross-battery approach measures a broader range of skills and abilities that relate to learning and problem-solving processes than those measured by most all single intelligence batteries (see Embretson, 1996). As a result, the cross-battery approach yields seven reliable and valid *Gf-Gc* cluster scores that can help identify cognitive processing strengths or weaknesses when interpreted within the context of the systematic, scientific framework described herein. Because some of these scores represent the averages of tests from two or more different batteries, however, some words of caution are warranted.

Although standard scores, which reflect an individual's relative level of performance in a reference (norm) group, may be interpreted for individual tests, the *Gf-Gc* cluster average standard scores, which are calculated and plotted for cross-battery assessments, cannot be interpreted as if they represent actual cluster scores that were normed on a single norm group (McGrew & Flanagan, 1998). *Gf-Gc* cross-battery cluster-average standard scores should also not be interpreted as precise values that can be substituted or used as measures of aptitude or ability needed to make critical decisions about ability-achievement discrepancies according to *formal criteria* (e.g., *Gf-Gc* cluster scores should not be used in formulas that are designed to determine significant ability-achievement discrepancies). *The Gf-Gc cross-battery approach is a psychometrically and theoretically defensible procedure for identifying intracognitive ability and processing strengths and weaknesses.* Practitioners who must evaluate whether an individual has an ability-achievement or aptitude-achievement discrepancy in addition to determining intracognitive strengths and weaknesses are referred to Appendix H for guidelines to assist in this process, especially when the CB approach is utilized.

In addition to the issue of different norm groups (for tests that are combined from different batteries), the major reason *Gf-Gc* cross-battery cluster average standard scores should not be interpreted as actual normed standard scores is that *actual normed cluster scores do not always equal the average of the individual standard scores they comprise* (McGrew, 1994). This finding is related directly to the magnitude of the intercorrelations and number of tests in the cluster (Paik & Nebenzahl, 1987); the lower the intercorrelations between tests that contribute to a cluster score, the more extreme the difference will be between a cluster score that is *normed* and a cluster score that is based on the arithmetic average of tests. The only time when a cluster standard score will equal the average of the individual tests that comprise it is when all the tests of the cluster are correlated perfectly (see Paik & Nebenzahl, 1987, for details).

Gf-Gc cross-battery cluster scores provide useful information about where an individual is functioning relative to a normative standard (i.e., the normal probability curve) and relative to his or her own average performance. The information yielded by the *Gf-Gc* cross-battery clusters can aid in making diagnostic and classification decisions and, like the data derived from any assessment, should be corroborated by other sources of data (Kamphaus, 1993). The *clinical meaningfulness* of *Gf-Gc* cross-battery data will increase as a function of the extent to which these data are integrated with other quantitative and qualitative information (e.g., case history, informal assessment, behavioral observation) and interpreted within the context of relevant *Gf-Gc* theory and research and other significant variables (e.g., culture, environment, SES, etc.).

Intraindividual Analysis with Wechsler-Based *Gf-Gc* Cross-Battery Data

In contrast to interindividual analysis, information from an *intraindividual* analysis (or ipsative analysis) is *person relative* and reveals *within*-individual differences. In general, ipsative interpretation (the process of generating strength and weakness hypotheses about cognitive abilities) is based on an analysis of subtest scores that deviate significantly (either in a positive or negative direction) from the average (mean) of all of an individual's own subtest scores on the intelligence battery. Thus, the scaling of an ipsative score of a particular ability attribute for any given individual is dependent on the scores of every other ability attribute measured for that individual.

Ipsative analysis, or the "Kaufman Psychometric Approach" (Kamphaus et al., 1997), has been applied most frequently to the Wechsler Scales (Kaufman, 1979; 1990a; 1994a). Advanced as an alternative to global assessment of cognitive functioning, this popular approach to test interpretation rests on the assumption that uncovering an individual's pattern of relative strengths and weaknesses across a variety of specific cognitive functions or ability traits provides a more valid and viable basis from which to develop remedial strategies and plan interventions than do global measures of ability (e.g., global IQ). This emphasis on *within-* rather than *between-individual* comparisons holds intuitive appeal because it is commonly believed that only through the discovery of person-relative patterns of differential abilities can interventions be tailored to meet the unique needs of an individual. However, despite its popularity and intuitive appeal, ipsative analysis has significant limitations, which have led to considerable criticism (see Flanagan, Andrews, & Genshaft, 1997; Glutting, McDermott, Watkins, Kush, & Konold, 1997; McDermott & Glutting, 1997; McDermott et al., 1992).

Limitations of Ipsative Analysis

As reported in McDermott, Fantuzzo, and Glutting (1990), ipsative analysis has a number of major weaknesses. Specifically, these researchers asserted that ipsative scores (1) have no construct validity; (2) have near zero (and typically negative) intercorrelations; (3) are not stable over time; (4) have properties (e.g., their sum equals zero) which make any attempt at remediation a "no win" situation; (5) have poor predictive validity; and (6) do not carry any additional information that is not already provided by normative scores (Flanagan, Andrews, & Genshaft, 1997, p. 468). The major problem with ipsative score interpretation is that it is assumed that the ability constructs that underlie subtests are the same before and after ipsatization. However, "ipsatization automatically removes from a person's scores all common variance associated with Spearman's *g*" (McDermott et al., 1990, p. 293).

When common variance, typically the largest, most robust score variability for tests of intelligence batteries, is removed, only residual variance remains. Residual variance consists of reliable (unique variance) and unreliable components (error variance). However, the reliable variance that remains (viz., uniqueness or specificity) following subtest ipsatization is not valid because it does not reflect the construct originally purported to underlie the respective subtests (see McDermott et al., 1992). The result is confounded interpretation.

We concur with McDermott and Glutting's well-reasoned and empirically supported arguments against the practice of subtest level interpretation for the reasons cited above (see also McGrew, Flanagan, et al., 1997); there is no question that the procedure is inherently flawed. However, although we (and many others) have advised our students and colleagues to de-emphasize or eliminate subtest-level interpretation, the practice continues and will probably be commonplace for years to come. This is understandable given that the majority of assessment professionals are trained as scientist-practitioners. In light of this philosophy, assessment professionals have an obligation to explain behavior that deviates from the norm and to offer recommendations for remediation or treatment. However, the field of intelligence test interpretation, has been largely unsuccessful in grounding these efforts in a solid theoretical and research foundation. The result, at times, has been misinformed and misguided interpretations of individuals' intracognitive test performance.

While McDermott and Glutting believe that there is no merit in interpreting intracognitive test data, we contend that intracognitive test interpretation can be improved when it is linked to psychometrically defensible procedures, theory, and research. Therefore, we believe that the "gloom and doom" statements of McDermott and Glutting (see Foreword of this book) are premature. Rather we support the viewpoints of Prifitera, Weiss, and Saklofske (1998) who stated,

> If one accepts the tenet that tests do not diagnose but clinicians do and that most psychological tests are not in and of themselves conclusive diagnostic indicators (true of tests in medicine as well), then the large number of papers in the literature that criticize tests such as the WISC for failing to properly diagnose a disorder with a high level of accuracy are misguided in their emphasis. Perhaps these studies were needed to point out to practitioners that just looking at profiles of test scores (e.g., McDermott, Fantuzzo, & Glutting, 1990) leads to erroneous diagnostic decisions because subtest patterns in and of themselves are not conclusively diagnostic of a disorder. But the thrust of these papers seems to admonish clinicians for even looking at and comparing scores. Would one want a physician, for example, not to look at patterns of test results just because they in and of themselves do not diagnose a disorder? Would you tell a physician not to take your blood pressure and heart rate and compare them because these two scores in and of themselves do not differentially diagnose kidney disease from heart disease? (Prifitera et al., 1998, p. 6)

Although McDermott's and Glutting's research "has been helpful to put the breaks on cookbook, simplistic interpretations of test results devoid of the contextualism of the individual's unique life characteristics" (Prifitera et al., 1998, p. 6), it cannot be said that new approaches to identifying intracognitive strengths and weaknesses suffer from the same limitations as ipsative analysis. When placed within the context of an individual's unique characteristics and supported with converging sources of data, results of a *Gf-Gc* cross battery intracognitive analysis may assist in making meaningful diagnoses.

The purpose of this section is to address how the traditional practice of intraindividual analysis can be improved on, despite its inherent flaws. Based on the theory and measurement concepts presented in this book, we believe that *some* of the limitations of the intraindividual approach to interpretation can be circumvented. Specifically, we believe that ipsative interpretations based on the analysis of *Gf-Gc* cross-battery *clusters* are better supported theoretically and psychometrically than those made on individual test scores. The rationale for this belief is fourfold.

First, the "just say no to subtest analysis" admonition of McDermott and Glutting was based largely on research conducted with Wechsler Intelligence Scales, which reflect outdated conceptualizations of intelligence. Therefore, most ipsative test interpretation practice and research has not been grounded in an empirically validated structure of human cognitive abilities (McGrew & Flanagan, 1998; McGrew, Flanagan, et al., 1997; Vanderwood, McGrew, Flanagan, & Keith, 1999).

"The failure to find that specific abilities add anything to the prediction of achievement beyond that already provided by a *g* score from the Wechslers may be a correct interpretation for the set of constructs measured by the Wechsler batteries, but may be a *premature generalization* to apply to all intelligence batteries" or at least assessment batteries that reflect a current validated model of intelligence (McGrew et al., 1997, p.13). "Before the interpretation of specific abilities on intelligence tests is declared legally dead, the *g*/specific ability research needs to be reexamined in light of current theory and with instruments or combinations of instruments that provide a more accurate and complete measurement of most *Gf-Gc* abilities." A series of studies that examined the relationship of *g* and multiple *Gf-Gc* specific abilities (i.e., *Gf, Gc, Gv, Ga, Gs, Glr, Gsm*) to general and specific reading and math skills (Flanagan, Keith, Mascolo, Vanderwood, & McGrew, 1999; McGrew, Flanagan, et al., 1997, Vanderwood et al., 1999) has indicated that both general and specific cognitive abilities are important in understanding reading and math achievement (see Chapter 3 for a summary).[3]

Although these encouraging results require replication, they demonstrate that the *g*/specific abilities issue, although complex, is not dead and deserves a reexamination with contemporary research methodology within the context of the *Gf-Gc* theory (Flanagan, 1999; McGrew, Flanagan et al., 1997). The Wechsler-based *Gf-Gc* cross-battery approach presented in this book is grounded in contemporary theory and research and is based on sound measurement principles—conditions that greatly improve the practitioner's ability to draw clear and useful conclusions from the data (Daniel, 1997; Kamphaus, 1993; 1998; Kamphaus et al., 1997; Keith, 1988).

Second, the *Gf-Gc* cross-battery intraindividual interpretive process uses more valid and reliable cognitive ability indicators than the traditional subtest approach. Traditional ipsative approaches, which use individual subtest scores as the "raw material" for interpretation, yield data based on measures with relatively weak reliability. For example, the WISC-III Picture Completion, Coding, Picture Arrangement, Object Assembly, Comprehension, Arithmetic, Symbol Search, and Mazes subtests have *low* reliability (i.e., alpha coefficients < 0.80) for 9- to 11-year-olds (see Summary Pages in Chapter 4). Reliability theory informs us that combinations of tests (i.e., composites or clusters) are more reliable than the individual tests that comprise the cluster or composite. For example, for 12-year-olds, the individual WJ-R *Gs* tests of Visual Matching has *medium* reliability and Cross Out has *low* reliability (McGrew et al., 1991). However, the reliability coefficient of the WJ-R Processing Speed cluster (which is based on the combination of these two measures of *Gs,* a cluster analogous to *Gf-Gc* cross-battery clusters) is 0.90 (high) for the same group. Because *Gf-Gc* cross-battery interpretations are based on cluster (not subtest) test scores, the reliabilities of the cognitive ability composite estimates are typically higher than the reliabilities corresponding to the subtests used in the traditional approach. Cluster-level analysis includes more valid *and* reliable estimates of ability than subtest-level analysis.

Third, when a set of tests (e.g., all Wechsler Verbal tests) is ipsatized, the common variance or *g* is removed and the reliable residual variance that is left in each individual test is interpreted. As such, ipsative interpretation is based typically on the *smallest* portion of the test's reliable variance. Similarly, when the *Gf-Gc* cross-battery clusters are ipsatized, the variance that is common to all clusters (i.e., *Gf, Gc, Gv, Ga,* etc.) is removed. However, the variance that is shared by the two tests that combine to yield the respective *Gf-Gc* clusters remains. Therefore, when clusters that represent broad stratum II abilities are ipsatized in the cross-battery approach (as opposed to individual tests that represent stratum I abilities in the traditional approach), *proportionately more reliable variance remains.* We believe that intraindividual interpretations of cognitive abilities that are operationally defined by the reliable common variance shared by at least two strong indicators of each broad *Gf-Gc* ability represent a more promising practice than individual subtest analysis (see Messick, 1989).

Fourth, the validity of the *Gf-Gc* cross-battery clusters are supported further by the fact that they are comprised of two strong, qualitatively different narrow indicators of the respective broad *Gf-Gc* abilities. This composition of the cognitive ability clusters in *Gf-Gc* cross-battery assessment substantially reduces and, in many cases eliminates, *construct irrelevant variance* and *construct underrepresentation,* thereby reducing or largely eliminating invalidity in measurement and assessment. The increasing number of research investigations on the relations between the *Gf-Gc* constructs (which are represented by the *Gf-Gc* cross-battery clusters) and outcome criteria provides validation evidence that enriches and informs the interpretive process. Far less corresponding validity evidence is available to support subtest level interpretation (see McGrew & Flanagan, 1998).

In sum, the *traditional* subtest-based approach to ipsative interpretation of intelligence batteries has been found to be seriously flawed. This approach has been limited by the lack of a comprehensive and empirically supported theoretical framework to guide interpretation and by a reliance on individual subtests, many of which have low reliability and all of which, when interpreted in isolation, underrepresent the construct purported to be measured by the test. The *Gf-Gc* cross-battery intraindividual interpretive approach (described briefly in the following text) mitigates a number of the fundamental flaws of the traditional method of intracognitive interpretation through the use of more reliable and valid indicators of cognitive ability constructs.

Notwithstanding, because a significant degree of variation across tasks and item types is typical in the normal population, intraindividual differences alone are not sufficient grounds for making diagnostic, classification, and treatment decisions (Reschly & Grimes, 1995). Thus, even when significant intraindividual differences are found using *Gf-Gc* cross-battery data, corroboration with other sources of data is necessary. In the absence of supporting evidence, intraindividual differences alone, although statistically significant, should not be considered unusual, unique, or clinically meaningful.

Guidelines for Intraindividual Analysis with Wechsler-Based *Gf-Gc* Cross-Battery Data

The brief set of steps that follow is presented using Christine's *Gf-Gc* cross-battery cluster scores. The information derived from these steps is presented in Table 7.2. The first step is to sum an individual's *Gf-Gc* cross-battery cluster averages and divide by the total number of averages to obtain the individual's *overall Gf-Gc* cross-battery cluster average or the average of the averages (i.e., the average level of performance across all seven *Gf-Gc* cross-battery clusters). Examiner A obtained an overall *Gf-Gc* cross-battery cluster average of 95 by summing Christine's *Gf-Gc* cross-battery cluster standard score averages (sum = 663), reported in column two of Table 7.2, and dividing by the total number of cluster averages (i.e., 7). Christine's overall *Gf-Gc* cross-battery cluster average of 95 (663/7 = 94.7 ~ 95) is reported in column three of Table 7.2.

TABLE 7.2   Intraindividual Analysis Results of Christine's *Gf-Gc* Cross-Battery Evaluation

Gf-Gc Cluster	Cluster Standard Score Average	Overall *Gf-Gc* Cluster Average	Difference Score	Strength or Weakness
Gf	109	95	+14	ns
Gc	100	95	+5	ns
Gv	103	95	+8	ns
Gsm	88	95	−7	ns
Glr	82	95	−13	ns
Ga	86	95	−9	ns
Gs	95	95	0	ns

Note: The overall *Gf-Gc* cluster average is calculated by adding the seven individual cluster averages from column two together (sum = 663) and dividing by the total number of cluster averages (i.e., 7). Thus, 663/7 = 94.7 ~ 95. Strength = difference score of $\geq$ +15. Weakness = difference score of $\geq$ −15. ns = not significant.

The second step requires that the examiner obtain *difference scores* by subtracting the overall *Gf-Gc* cross-battery cluster average (column three in Table 7.2) from the individual *Gf-Gc* cross-battery cluster averages (located in column two). Christine's difference scores are reported in column four of Table 7.2. Note that the values reported in column four are preceded by either a "+" or "−" sign to indicate positive or negative differences between the *Gf-Gc* cross-battery individual cluster scores and the overall cluster score. The third step is to determine whether the absolute value of any of the difference scores is large enough for the corresponding *Gf-Gc* ability to be considered a significant intraindividual strength or weakness for the examinee.

Since it is contrary to our understanding of human behavior to expect an individual's abilities to be uniformly developed, a criterion must be specified so that *Gf-Gc* clusters which vary *significantly* from the individual's overall *Gf-Gc* cluster average can be identified. A criterion of ±15 is used to define significant intraindividual *Gf-Gc* cross-battery strengths and weaknesses because it is similar to the intraindividual analysis procedures used in other intelligence batteries. For example, Wechsler subtest scores that differ by 1 or more standard deviations (i.e., $\leq$ ±3, based on a subtest scaled score scale having a mean of 10 and a standard deviation of 3) from the average (mean) subtest scaled score are considered to represent possible strengths and weaknesses (Kaufman, 1979; 1990a). The ±15 standard score criterion is of similar magnitude to this Wechsler-based rule of thumb. As a result, all *Gf-Gc* cross-battery standard scores are converted to a scale with a mean of 100 and a standard deviation of 15. Thus, any individual *Gf-Gc* cluster standard score averages that differ from the overall standard score average by ±15 or more (i.e., $\geq$ 1 standard deviation above or below the mean) may be considered to indicate a *possible* intraindividual strength or weakness, respectively.

It is important to understand that a given standard score in an ipsative analysis that is identified as a *relative* strength or weakness because it deviates significantly from the average of a set of scores within a given profile, should not be interpreted as a significant *normative* strength or weakness. For example, if most standard scores in an individual's profile are greater than 115, then a standard score of 95 would differ significantly from the mean of this individual's set of scores. However, scores that fall within ±1 SD of the normative mean (i.e., between 85 and 115) are within normal limits. Thus, although a 95 is a significant relative weakness for this individual, it does not represent a normative weakness. Conversely, an ipsative analysis may not reveal any *relative* strengths or weaknesses among an individual's unique set of scores; however, from a normative perspective, one or more of the scores obtained by the individual may suggest significant normative strengths and/or weaknesses (i.e., the individual may have obtained a cluster score above 115 or below 85, respectively—a score that falls outside the standard score range associated with ±1 SD). This condition is particularly relevant to the use of intraindividual analysis in the identification and diagnosis of learning disability, as it applies specifically to the criterion of a deficit in one or more of the basic underlying cognitive processes.

Because an individual's performance relative to his or her same age peers (a normative group) is the standard against which a "deficit" is most appropriately determined, ipsative analysis is not sufficient for determining cognitive processing weaknesses. The flowchart presented in Figure 7.6 describes a process that may be used in *Gf-Gc* cross-battery ipsative analyses. The results of Christine's ipsative analysis using her obtained *Gf-Gc* cluster scores is interpreted in the text following.

In her review of the absolute value of Christine's difference scores located in column four of Table 7.2, Examiner A found that no difference scores exceeded the criterion value of 15. Thus, no significant intraindividual (i.e., *relative*) strengths or weaknesses were identified for Christine (see column five of Table 7.2). Based on these results, a practitioner may conclude that Christine does not demonstrate any significant cognitive processing strengths or weaknesses. This conclusion, however, may be premature and misinformed. Although the knowledge that Christine's performance in multiple cognitive ability domains did not differ significantly from the average of her performance across these multiple abilities is informative, this finding in isolation does not address whether or not Christine displayed any cognitive processing deficits.

After examining the results of Christine's *Gf-Gc* cross-battery ipsative analysis and finding no significant relative strengths or weaknesses, Figure 7.6 suggests that a practitioner should identify whether any *Gf-Gc* clusters fall greater than 1 SD below the mean. An examination of column two in Table 7.2 reveals that the *Glr* cluster standard score of 82 meets this criterion. As such, this cognitive processing area is considered a normative weakness or deficit (see Figure 7.6). It is also important to recall that Christine's *Gsm* performance after the administration of additional tests was estimated to be 83 (a value that meets the criterion for normative weakness).

Following the identificaton of significant intraindividual cognitive strengths and weaknesses, these findings should be translated into clinically meaningful descriptions of cognitive functioning (see Kaufman, 1994a; Kamphaus, 1993; McGrew, 1994; Sattler, 1988 for a discussion). In addition to identifying areas of cognitive processing deficit in learning disabilities evaluations, the goal of intraindividual analysis is to identify tasks that an individual is most adept at handling, and use this information to aid in planning instructional programs. It is important to remember that patterns of intraindividual subtest strengths and weaknesses are of limited utility diagnostically. However, although there is little research evidence to support making diagnostic decisions from a profile of Wechsler ipsatized subtest scores (Glutting, McDermott, & Konold, 1997; Kamphaus, 1993; Kam-

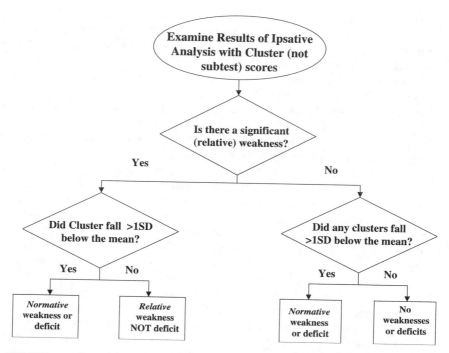

FIGURE 7.6   Determining Underlying Cognitive Processing Weaknesses

phaus et al., 1997; McDermott, et al., 1992; Watkins & Kush, 1994), research demonstrating specific reading disability subtypes based on individual tests is promising (e.g., Morris et al., 1998).

Together intraindividual and interindividual analyses may uncover clues about an individual's cognitive abilities, which may clarify the functional nature of learning problems and lead to more appropriate recommendations for clinical treatment, educational remediation, or vocational placement.

In the absence of empirical evidence that supports the practice of intraindividual or ipsative analysis, it is recommended that ipsative intracognitive analysis be de-emphasized or that it be used in conjunction with interindividual analysis to aid in understanding the unique learning and problem-solving processes of the individual (see also Kamphaus, 1993). Because there is no agreed upon litmus test for diagnosing learning problems, practitioners should be guided by a combination of resourcefulness, clinical experience, current theoretical and empirical research, and knowledge of the quantitative and qualitative characteristics of cognitive ability tests (McGrew & Flanagan, 1998) when interpreting an individual's performance on *Gf-Gc* cross-battery assessments.

Selective *Gf-Gc* Cross-Battery Assessment

According to Sattler (1998), "A prerequisite for effective assessment is the ability to plan assessment strategies and to choose tests to meet specific needs" (p. 7). *Gf-Gc* cross-battery assessments, like traditional assessments, should be designed to address specific referral concerns. Responding to every referral with a "knee-jerk" canned intelligence battery or a "complete" *Gf-Gc* cross-battery assessment is inconsistent with best practices in intellectual assessment. Best practices "require careful judgments about *when* intellectual assessment instruments are used, *how* they are used, the selection, administration, and interpretation of tests, and efforts to protect children and youth from misuses and misconceptions" (Reschly & Grimes, 1990). A description of *selective Gf-Gc* cross-battery approach, which we believe to be consistent with best practices follows.

Selective Gf-Gc cross-battery assessment is the process of tailoring a unique *Gf-Gc*-organized cross-battery assessment battery to address the specific concerns or questions of a referral. Although Examiner A found it necessary to gather information across the broad range of *Gf-Gc* abilities when evaluating Christine, depending on the nature of the referral, this may not always be necessary. With knowledge of referral concerns as well as the relations between *Gf-Gc* abilities and achievement or outcome criteria, practitioners can *tailor* cross-battery assessments that are time efficient and, more importantly, likely to provide information that results in more focused and referral-relevant recommendations. The selective cross-battery assessment approach described here focuses primarily on organizing a battery of measures to assess individuals referred for reading and/or mathematics difficulties. However, selective cross-battery assessments can be tailored to address any referral wherein cognitive abilities may be implicated.

The outcome-criterion evidence presented in Chapter 3 should serve as a useful starting point for the design of achievement-related (viz., reading and mathematics) *Gf-Gc* cross-battery assessments. If Examiner A had reviewed the outcome-criterion evidence summarized in Chapter 3, she would have discovered that all *Gf-Gc* abilities "are not created equal" in all contexts. For example, *Gv* abilities display no significant relation with reading achievement while *Ga* abilities are particularly important for the development of reading skills during the early elementary school years. These findings suggest that (1) *Ga* abilities should be featured prominently in all reading referrals during the early school years, and (2) the value of spending significant time (often as much as half of an intelligence battery in the case of the Wechslers) to measure *Gv* is highly questionable.

To facilitate the design of selective achievement-related cross-battery assessments, the main findings presented for reading and mathematics achievement in Chapter 3 are summarized in Table 7.3. Table 7.3, together with the discussion in Chapter 3, can facilitate the identification of *Gf-Gc* abilities that should receive priority consideration in the design of selective cross-battery assessments. Because a selective cross-battery case study is presented in the next chapter, general guidelines only will be presented here.

Guidelines for Selective Cross-Battery Assessment

All referrals for assessment are concerned with the unique circumstances of people who have individual needs and concerns. The decision-making process that ensues during the design and implementation of *Gf-Gc* selective cross-battery assessments is consistent with the "iterative process" of test interpretation described earlier in this chapter. According to Kamphaus, "[t]est interpretation is something like detective work, where the clinician follows clues and develops leads until eventually a clear picture of a crime emerges" (p. 166). This process can be seen in *Gf-Gc* selective cross-battery assessments where (1) initial

TABLE 7.3   Summary of Significant Relations Between *Gf-Gc* Abilities and Reading and Mathematics Achievement

Gf-Gc Ability	Reading Achievement	Mathematics Achievement
Gf	• Inductive (I) and general sequential (RG) reasoning abilities play a moderate role in reading comprehension	• **Inductive (I) and general sequential (RG) reasoning abilities are consistently very important at all ages**
Gc	• **Language development (LD), lexical knowledge (VL), and listening ability (LS) are important at all ages** • **These abilities become increasing more important with age**	• **Language development (LD), lexical knowledge (VL), and listening ability (LS) are important at all ages** • These abilities become increasing more important with age
Gsm	• Memory span (MS) is important especially when evaluated **within the context of working memory**	• Memory span (MS) is important especially when evaluated **within the context of working memory**
Gv		• May be important primarily for higher level or advanced mathematics (e.g., geometry, calculus)
Ga	• **Phonetic coding (PC) or *phonological awareness/processing* are very important during the elementary school years**	
Glr	• **Naming facility (NA) or *rapid automatic naming* is very important during the elementary school years.** • Associative memory (MA) abilities may be somewhat important at select ages (e.g., age 6)	
Gs	• **Perceptual speed (P) abilities are very important during all school years** • **These abilities are particularly important during the elementary school years**	• **Perceptual speed (P) abilities are very important during all school years** • **These abilities are particularly important during the elementary school years**

Note: This table represents a summary of research presented in Chapter 3. The absence of comments for a particular *Gf-Gc* ability and achievement area (e.g., *Ga* and mathematics) indicates that the research reviewed either did not report any significant relations between the respective *Gf-Gc* ability and the achievement area or, if significant findings were reported, they were weak and were for only a limited number of studies. Comments in bold represent the *Gf-Gc* abilities that showed the strongest and most consistent relations with the respective achievement domain.

design decisions are made; (2) testing of *a priori* (and *a posteriori*) hypotheses within the context of case history information is conducted; and (3) following evaluation of test results in conjunction with careful analysis of observations of the examinee during the assessment, additional data are gathered as necessary via further assessment. This iterative process continues until hypotheses are supported (or refuted) and a complete understanding of the individual's cognitive strengths and weaknesses emerges.

　　To aid practitioners in developing and implementing selective cross-battery assessments, the following guidelines are offered. First, selective cross-battery assessments should adhere to the same principles that guided the more complete *Gf-Gc* cross-battery assessment approach that was described in Chapter 6.

　　Second, the research literature on the relations between *Gf-Gc* abilities and achievement as well as other outcome-criterion variables should play a salient role in the selection of the *Gf-Gc* domains that will be assessed initially. Selective cross-battery assessments are only as good as the practitioner who designs and conducts them. A working knowledge of *Gf-Gc* achievement and outcome-criterion research and important areas of psychology (e.g., cognition, learning, etc.), together with an intimate familiarity with the characteristics of assessment tools (see Chapters 4 and 5 and McGrew & Flanagan, 1998), is necessary to design appropriate *Gf-Gc* cross-battery assessments.

　　Third, selective cross-battery assessment should be conceived of as "a work in progress." An iterative decision-making and assessment process is the norm. Initial assessments produce information that, in turn, may result in the generation of additional hypotheses and decisions to conduct additional assessment. Practitioners should always maximize their use of other sources of information (e.g., cumulative educational records, case histories, prior assessment results, parent and teacher comments) to aid in determining which *Gf-Gc* abilities should or should not be assessed.

　　Fourth, selective cross-battery assessments should not be pursued simply to save time. Rather, the time saved by either not assessing or by reducing the assessment coverage in a given *Gf-Gc* domain can be reallocated to more focused intellectual assessment activities (e.g., more in-depth assessment of narrow *Gf-Gc* abilities in a given domain) or to different types of assessment (e.g., classroom observation, criterion referenced) in other important domains that are relevant to the referral (e.g., self-concept). In short, *selective cross-battery assessments should have a purpose and specific focus.* The nature and type of referral concerns should drive the design of the assessment. Tests to be included should be selected in direct proportion to their potential relevance to the presenting referral concerns.

　　In conclusion, the iterative process in intellectual assessment and interpretation inherent in the *Gf-Gc* cross-battery approach is useful when unexpected findings emerge or when there is a need to test *a posteriori* hypotheses. Chapter 5 of this book as well as other sources (viz., McGrew & Flanagan, 1998) provide an array of cognitive ability tests from which to choose measures for subsequent iterations in the assessment process. Since all cognitive ability tests included in Chapter 5 and in McGrew and Flanagan were classified (empirically or logically) according to *Gf-Gc* theory, practitioners have the added benefit of grounding their selective assessments and interpretations within the context of current theory and research.

Conclusion

　　This chapter presented guidelines for the interpretation of *Gf-Gc* cross-battery data within the context of a systematic and integrative method of test interpretation. The procedures demonstrated how intercognitive and intracognitive analyses of individual cognitive ability *clusters* may provide diagnostic and prescriptive information that is more useful in the development of treatment and intervention plans than a traditional full scale or composite IQ. Guidelines were also offered for designing *selective Gf-Gc* cross-battery assessments that may prove to be more informative, useful, and efficient than the administration of any single intelligence battery.

Because selective *Gf-Gc* cross-battery assessments are supported by a body of research on the relations between *Gf-Gc* abilities and academic achievement, they (1) ensure that the abilities most closely associated with academic referrals are represented in the assessment; and (2) reduce or eliminate the evaluation of abilities that are unrelated to the achievement skill(s) in question. For these reasons, selective cross-battery assessments are more likely to provide adequate measurement of cognitive abilities and processes that underlie specific academic learning disabilities, than measurement provided by a single intelligence battery, and may be particularly useful in all types of special education evaluations.

While investigations of the predictive utility of cross-battery assessment over traditional assessment are available (see Chapter 3), the diagnostic and treatment validity of the *Gf-Gc* cross-battery approach, like traditional assessment approaches, is not yet available. For decades, the largely atheoretical Wechsler Intelligence test research has shown that "it is impossible to predict specific disabilities and areas of cognitive competency or dysfunction from the averaged ability test scores" (i.e., IQs; Lezak, 1995). Because Wechsler-based *Gf-Gc* cross-battery data are grounded in contemporary theory and research, they may prove to yield more clinically meaningful and diagnostically relevant information than IQ scores. Therefore, the study of the validity of *Gf-Gc* cross-battery assessments, currently underway, is a much needed and viable avenue for future research.

E N D N O T E S

1. Because cognitive ability tests show non-zero positive intercorrelations, the scores yielded by a given battery of tests will reflect these intercorrelations. That is, the higher the correlation between two cognitive ability measures, the greater the likelihood that the traits underlying these measures will vary consistently. This is because "average intercorrelations of normative attributes are determined mainly by the relationships among the contents of attribute scales and the psychological characteristics of the respondent population" (McDermott et al., 1992, p. 509). Conversely, ipsative scores have near zero (and often negative) intercorrelation. "The discovery of . . . near zero average relationships among ability attributes runs contrary to the theoretical expectation for constructs that might reflect some meaningful aspect of Spearman's *g*" (McDermott et al., 1992, p. 510). Thus, as opposed to normative scores, ipsative scores have "personological" ability dimensions (Broverman, 1961). That is, through factor analysis of ipsative measures, Broverman observed that the "consequent dimensions retained a certain reciprocally exclusive character whereby, as an individual exhibited greater ability in one area, commensurate inability was apparent in another area" (cited in McDermott et al., 1992, p. 518).

2. Typically, a score that is ≥ 1 SD above or below the mean is considered a normative strength or weakness, respectively (Lezak, 1976; 1995).

3. *Specific* abilities here are the *broad* (stratum II) *Gf-Gc* constructs of *Gf, Gc, Gv,* etc., which were represented in these studies by two or more strong test indicators. The term *specific* rather than *broad* is used in these studies to maintain consistency with the terminology of traditional *g*/specific ability research.

CHAPTER

8

Measuring Cognitive Abilities in Culturally and Linguistically Diverse Populations

Selective *Gf-Gc* Cross-Battery Assessment with the Wechsler Scales

Probably no test can be created that will entirely eliminate the influence of learning and cultural experiences. The test content and materials, the language in which the questions are phrased, the test directions, the categories for classifying the responses, the scoring criteria, and the validity criteria are all culture bound.

—Jerome M. Sattler (1992, p. 579)

Assessment of Culturally and Linguistically Diverse Populations

Few things create as much confusion or cause as much consternation for applied psychologists as the attempt to validly measure the cognitive abilities of individuals from diverse cultural and linguistic backgrounds. There are important implications when this task is not accomplished or is accomplished poorly. For example, failure to accurately distinguish normal, culturally based variations in behavior, first (L1) and second (L2) language acquisition, acculturation, and cognitive development from inherent disabilities has led to an overrepresentation of individuals from diverse populations in special education and other remedial programs (Cervantes, 1988). Because such misplacement can have adverse effects on children's learning, social, and psychological development (Collier, 1992; Dunn, 1968; Hobbs, 1975; Jones, 1972), it is important that psychologists using the Wechsler

Scales, or any other intelligence battery, understand both the nature and manner in which assessment can be biased as well as how to utilize systematic methods and procedures that may assist in reducing potential discrimination against culturally and linguistically diverse populations.

Defining Culture and Language

The assessment of culturally diverse individuals is a concern, particularly within the field of school psychology, because many psychologists are often ill-prepared to meet the unique needs of the growing number of these individuals in the U.S. population. Future projections concerning the diversity of the population in the United States reinforce the need for psychologists to be competent in serving diverse individuals. "It is estimated that by the year 2000, 38% of the U.S. population under the age of 18 will be non-Anglo whites and non-whites (Research and Policy Committee of the Committee for Economic Development, 1987) and by the year 2030, the number of Latino children, African American children, and children of other races, will increase by 5.5, 2.6, and 1.5 million, respectively, while the number of white, non-Latino children will decrease by 6.2 million from the 1985 figure (Children's Defense Fund, 1989)" (cf. Flanagan & Miranda, 1995).

Compounding the intricacies involved in evaluating diverse individuals fairly, is the nebulous nature and imprecise definition of culture. Matsumoto (1994) has described culture "as the set of attitudes, values, beliefs and behaviors, shared by a group of people, communicated from one generation to the next via language or some other means of communication" (p. 4; see also Barnouw, 1985). As defined, culture represents some consensus among a group of individuals as to what is important and valued by the members of that group in particular. Culture is, therefore, both a unique and shared experience, which has idiosyncratic but predictable effects on people's actions (including performance on standardized tests). For the purposes of this chapter, the phrase *culturally diverse* is used to describe individuals whose primary, personal and familial cultural experiences and knowledge differ from mainstream United States culture (Flanagan & Miranda, 1995).

Language also represents an important dimension in the understanding of an individual, since attitudes, values, beliefs, and behaviors are often revealed via interpersonal communication. Were all people speakers of the same language, there might be little concern for this topic. However, the increase in the linguistic diversity of the United States makes it likely that psychologists will, at some point, be required to assess individuals who do not come from English-only backgrounds. During the 1980s, the number of LEP (Limited English Proficient) students in the United States increased 2½ times faster than regular school enrollment (McLeod, 1994; cf. Ochoa et al., 1996). Moreover, according to Lopez (1997), "the nation's linguistic diversity is reflected in our school systems where educators often work with significant numbers of children from LEP and bilingual backgrounds. In New York City, for example, there are individual schools in which more than 50 languages and dialects are spoken by the student population (New York City Public Schools, 1993)" (p. 503).

A variety of labels have been used to identify individuals in the United States whose language histories are other than English-only. The most common of these is LEP (limited English proficient), however, others have been introduced in response to the pejorative connotations of the word *limited.* These include beginning English speaker (BES), dual-language learner (DLL), and English learner (EL; Hamayan & Damico, 1991). Regardless of the specific term used, the criteria for defining this group has been relatively consistent. According to the U.S. Department of Education, LEP refers to individuals (1) who were born in a country other than the United States and whose native language is not English, or (2) who originated from environments in which English is not the dominant language spoken (1994; p. 21). Generally speaking, individuals who are identified as LEP tend to be dominant (more fluent or comfortable, but not necessarily highly proficient) in their native language as compared to their English language abilities. Even when individuals are proficient in their native or primary language (L1) there is no guarantee that they will be proficient in a second language (L2, i.e., English) and are often considerably less proficient in English (Cummins, 1984). Whenever an individual is able to develop levels of proficiency in two languages, they may be described as *bilingual,* or as dual-language learners, although again, their proficiency in either language may be high, low or any combination thereof. It is important to appreciate that, by itself, the term *bilingual* does not necessarily imply any particular level of proficiency, comfort, or skill with the languages spoken. For a more detailed description of LEP and bilingual populations, see Lopez (1997), and Valdés and Figueroa (1994).

Given the preceding discussion, the phrase *linguistically diverse* will be used to represent the continuum of individuals who are non-native English speakers, specifically: (1) monolingual speakers with varying levels of proficiency in a language other than English, (2) dual-language learners with varying levels of L1 and L2 proficiency (i.e., LEP, BES, EL, etc.), and (3) those who are proficient in both L1 and L2 (balanced bilinguals).

Working with Diverse Populations

In recognition of the growing diversity of the United States population, the American Psychological Association (APA) published *Guidelines for Providers of Psychological Services to Ethnic, Linguistic, and Culturally Diverse Populations* (1990) in an effort to encourage psychologists to (1) consider the influence of language and culture on behavior when working with diverse groups, (2) consider the validity of the methods and procedures used to assess minority groups and (3) make interpretations of resultant psychological data within the context of an individual's linguistic and cultural characteristics (cf. Lopez, 1997). However, it appears that the degree of knowledge and level of skill necessary to meet these ideals is not automatically or routinely acquired through formal education in preservice psychology training programs (Ortiz, Ortiz, & Cook-Morales, 1994). This situation is compounded by the fact that there exists few national or state standards which define the basic professional competencies required in order to be considered a bilingual psychologist. Mere possession of the capacity to communicate in an individual's native language does not ensure appropriate, nondiscriminatory assessment of that individual. Traditional assessment practices and their inherent biases can be easily replicated in any number of languages. As a result, the lack of trained psychologists and shortage of qualified bilingual psychologists leads to a variety of difficulties in the assessment of individuals from diverse backgrounds. This chapter focuses primarily on the potential bias that may result from inappropriate subtest selection for use with culturally and linguistically diverse individuals and the corresponding meaning that is derived from test results on such populations. In short, it is diagnostic and interpretive bias which is of central concern in both general assessment of diverse individuals and the approach to be outlined in this chapter. Although assessment bias can never be eliminated entirely, comprehension of the manner in which bias operates in the process of using standardized tests can significantly reduce discrimination in the application of the Wechsler Scales or other intelligence batteries.

General Issues in Controlling Bias and Discrimination in Assessment

Most every aspect of the assessment process has the potential to create some form of bias and thus increase the likelihood that the results of such assessment will be questionable or uninterpretable. Although the bulk of the empirical attention aimed at identifying and controlling for potential bias has revolved primarily around presumptions of psychometric bias, there exists a number of means by which psychological assessment can be made less discriminatory. Cook (1987) has outlined some of the common approaches used to reduce bias and generate less discriminatory results in the various aspects of the assessment process. These approaches are summarized briefly in Table 8.1.

When assessment is conducted without regard for or knowledge of an individual's primary culture or native language, bias may be encountered in the cross-cultural transactions between examiner and examinee (Jones, 1988; Vazquez, Nutall, Deleon, & Valle, 1990). For example, inadvertent and unconscious interpersonal behaviors emitted by school personnel may unintentionally offend a student's parents causing them to feel uncomfortable and perhaps even withdraw or withhold cooperation. Moreover, an examinee's motivation or comfort during the testing process may be compromised by a failure to appreciate important cultural norms, values, behaviors, or expectations (Samuda, Kong, Cummins, Pascual-Leone, & Lewis, 1991). Therefore, attention should be paid to the transactions involved in the cross-cultural interactions inherent in assessing diverse individuals (Jones, 1988).

In similar fashion, the use of an ecological approach is one broad method which can assist in controlling bias that may arise as a result of not placing individual test performance or behavior within the appropriate cultural context. Sattler (1992) comments that "in fact, all human experience is affected by the culture, from prenatal development on" (p. 579). The culture of the individual and its role in defining the entire individual should not be ignored in evaluating performance of any kind, especially that on tests of intelligence.

Another commonly used bias-reduction technique involves measuring relevant constructs through means other than norm-referenced tests (which, as will be argued, may have questionable validity when used with individuals from diverse cultural and linguistic backgrounds) (Figueroa, 1990; 1990a, Valdés & Figueroa, 1994). For example, using authentic or skill-focused assessment techniques in the evaluation of academic achievement and using process-oriented methods (i.e., cognition-focused) in the evaluation of cognitive performance can yield data that are less susceptible to the discriminatory effects of cultural or linguistic variation from the mainstream (Gonzalez, Brusca-Vega, & Yawkey, 1997; Gopaul-McNicol, & Thomas-Presswood, 1998).

TABLE 8.1   Approaches Used to Control Bias in Assessment

Approach	Bias Control	Techniques/Procedures
Transactional	Attention to the assessors and the assessment process	■ Cultural knowledge bases ■ Culture-appropriate processes ■ Parent and child involvement ■ Cultural advocates
Ecological	Attention to ecological systems and child-in-ecologies	■ Ecosystems assessment ■ Culture-based hypotheses ■ Ecological assessment ■ Adaptive behavior evaluation
Alternative	Attention to different (i.e., not norm-referenced assessment questions)	*Authentic (skill focused)* ■ CBA/M, portfolio (work samples) ■ Criterion-referenced tests/procedures ■ Contextual-participant observation *Process (cognition focused)* ■ Dynamic assessment ■ Clinical observations ■ Piagetian assessment (Ordinal Scales)
Psychometric	Attention to the tests themselves	■ Underlying theory ■ Cultural and linguistic bias ■ Test adaptations ■ Test selection ■ Test interpretation
Interdisciplinary	Attention to the decision making process	■ Professional team ■ Parent inclusion

Source: Adapted from Cook, 1987.

Decisions based on discriminatory or insufficient data are unlikely to have positive or efficacious outcomes. Information about an individual's performance that is limited or confined to a narrow domain may not provide an accurate base on which to formulate appropriate intervention strategies (Salvia & Ysseldyke, 1998). Thus, in order for assessment results to be used in a nondiscriminatory manner, regardless of cultural heritage or linguistic background, an interdisciplinary approach is recommended. The importance of this approach has been consistently highlighted in the text of special education legislation since the passage of P.L. 94-142, the Education of Handicapped Children Act, now known as the Individuals with Disabilities Education Act (P.L. 105-17).

Of all the methods for controlling bias and discrimination in assessment, the one that continues to stir the most controversy and which remains at the heart of the present topic is the psychometric approach. The psychometric approach involves the use of instruments and procedures (i.e., standardized, norm-referenced tests) to measure various aspects of psychological functioning in a wide range of individuals. For some period of time, both theoretical and applied psychologists appear to have been quite successful in this approach creating what are today, instruments with superior technical and sophisticated statistical properties. With respect to culturally and linguistically diverse individuals, the major concern with such instruments has been the persistent finding of significant performance differences between different racial or ethnic groups (Figueroa, 1990; Jensen, 1974; 1976; 1980; Sattler, 1992; Valdés & Figueroa, 1994). These findings have been used to argue and advance hypotheses that suggest either a difference in the genetically based intellectual capabilities of members of different races (e.g., Jensen, 1969; 1973; Herrnstein & Murray, 1994; Terman, 1906; 1919; etc.) or that the tests themselves, particularly intelligence or IQ tests, are biased against members from nonmajority cultural groups (Figueroa, 1990; Gould, 1981; Mercer, 1979; Samuda et al., 1991; Williams, 1970). The emotional overlay and sociopolitical ramifications of this particular scientific debate are enormous and continue to generate considerable and current controversy, but this is not the central focus of this chapter. We will instead, attempt only to critically examine the issue of bias in intelligence tests in order to provide the reader with a clear understanding of the issues surrounding the use of intelligence and cognitive ability tests (in particular, the Wechsler Intelligence tests) with culturally and linguistically diverse individuals.

Due to their enormous popularity, the venerable Wechsler Intelligence Scales have been the primary targets and agents of investigation with respect to the issue of bias in tests of intelligence (Figueroa, 1990). Within this particular research tradition, there has emerged a broad spectrum of views ranging from the notion that intelligence batteries are heavily biased and should be abandoned altogether, to the view that the failure to use intelligence tests is a more discriminatory practice and does a greater disservice to individuals from nonmajority cultures (Sattler, 1992).

On the whole, it seems unlikely that many psychologists will quickly abandon their trusted Wechsler kits even when faced with the prospect of assessing individuals whose backgrounds might possibly cast doubt over the validity and interpretation of obtained results. In fact, a safe prediction would be that the intelligence test will remain a valued tool in the repertoire of applied psychologists for many generations to come regardless of the populations they are asked to assess. As intelligence tests continue to be used in the assessment of diverse individuals, professional standards and ethics governing such practice mandate that they be used in the most equitable manner possible (e.g., Professional Conduct Manual, National Association of School Psychologists, 1984; Standards for Educational and Psychological Testing, American Educational Research Association, American Psychological Association, American Council on Measurement, 1985).

The Wechsler scales have been applied to diverse populations in a variety of ways. Some of the more notable attempts with Spanish speaking populations have included direct translation of the WISC-R (Escala de Inteligencia Wechsler para Niños-Revisada; EIWN-R), the WISC-RM (a renormed version of the WISC-R using children from Mexico), and the WISC-R-PR (a renormed version of the WISC-R using children in the U.S. of Puerto Rican heritage living mainly in New York). Similar adaptations of the Wechsler Scales have been accomplished in many other languages as well (e.g., Japanese). Although these adaptations have been proven popular, they apparently have not been proven to be very successful. Figueroa (1990a) points out that the major problem with the use of these linguistically adapted Wechslers is that there is an underlying assumption "that the test takers are bilingual in the manner that the tests are 'bilingual'" (p. 102). In other words, assessing children in English with the WISC and in their native language with a translated version of the WISC does not provide an accurate or valid method of "bilingual" assessment, but rather monolingual assessment, albeit in two different languages.

The bilingual individual is not two monolinguals in one (Bialystok, 1991; Cummins, 1984; Hakuta, 1986) and valid assessment of bilingual individuals "requires that the tests be developed and normed on U.S. bilingual children (with full consideration of the many possible variant proficiencies in the home language and in English, as well as the various dialects and nationalities)" (Figueroa, 1990a, p. 102). Given that there are no Wechsler tests (or any other tests for that matter) available today which meet the criteria specified by Figueroa, the applied psychologist is left to other means in order to generate valid data on the intellectual capabilities of culturally and linguistically diverse individuals. In this regard, Figueroa (1990a) offered some avenues for investigation which included use of theoretical models for assessing bilingual populations and recognized the promise of using theoretical frameworks, should psychometric testing survive.

The selective Wechsler-based *Gf-Gc* cross-battery approach described in the previous chapters represents an advancement in the assessment of cognitive abilities primarily because it rests on current theory and empirically defensible methods. In keeping with Figueroa's (1990a) call for the application of theoretical frameworks in the assessment of culturally and linguistically diverse individuals, it is our contention that the psychometrically and theoretically based cross-battery approach outlined in the previous chapters is an ideal framework which can be extended via cultural and linguistic dimensions in order to increase the validity of obtained results. When the Wechsler Scales are used within a selective cross-battery assessment framework that also accommodates cultural and linguistic elements, they can be used to provide a defensible method that may lead to increases in specificity and validity with concomitant reductions in diagnostic and interpretive bias for diverse populations. The following sections outline the foundations and assumptions underlying selective cross-battery assessment and the manner in which diagnostic and interpretive bias is better controlled.

Bias in the Assessment of Intelligence

The Nature of Bias in Intelligence Batteries

The issues surrounding the nature of bias in the Wechsler Scales (and other intelligence batteries) developed and revised over the last 60 years have been discussed at length in the literature (e.g., Cronbach, 1984; Figueroa, 1983; 1990; Jensen, 1980; 1984; Kamphaus & Reynolds, 1987; Kaufman, 1994a; Reynolds & Gutkin, 1982; Salvia & Ysseldyke, 1998; Sattler; 1992; Valdés & Figueroa, 1994). With respect to the nature of the bias, the extant research literature has been rather unanimous: the Wechsler Scales (and some of the other major intelligence batteries) are not biased—at least not in the manner in which bias is normally conceptualized (Sattler, 1992).

Intelligence batteries have been accused of being biased on the grounds that there are differences in the mean IQs of different "cultural" groups (i.e., groups stratified on the basis of race or ethnicity) (Figueroa, 1990; Gould, 1981; Mercer, 1979; Samuda et al., 1991; Williams, 1970). Of course, any instrument specifically designed to assess differences between groups would be rather useless if, in fact, it did not show differences across groups. Bias is simply not definable on this basis (Sattler, 1992). Moreover, the attempt to discern *meaningful* differences between cultural group means is equally indefensible. Culture is not a monolithic entity and is poorly operationalized on the basis of race or ethnicity (Matsumoto, 1994; Valdés & Figueroa, 1994). To suppose that culture can be equated to race or ethnicity and that, as such, cultural differences alone should somehow interact with test performance, is an untenable position (Figueroa, 1990; 1990a; Valdés & Figueroa, 1994).

Research studies have consistently found that the WISC (all versions), as well as other intelligence batteries, predict academic achievement equally well for African Americans and Hispanic/Latinos as for White children (Bossard, Reynolds & Gutkin, 1980; Reschly & Sabers, 1979; Sattler, 1992). To date, the intelligence batteries' valid and reliable operationalization of *g*, expressed through the ubiquitous IQ, is still the single best predictor of academic success in the United States public school system (Neisser et al., 1996).

Another attempt to demonstrate the unbiased nature of intelligence batteries has been accomplished through studies that examine their factor structures across various ethnic groups. Such studies are based on the assumption that a replication of the battery's factor structure across different cultural groups implies that the battery measures the same abilities across those groups. With respect to the Wechsler Scales (primarily the WISC, WISC-R, and WPPSI) the basic verbal-performance factor structure has been reliably replicated in many diverse cultural groups including African Americans and Hispanics/Latinos (Greenberg, Stewart & Hansche, 1986; Gutkin & Reynolds, 1980; 1981; Sandoval, 1979; Sandoval, Zimmerman, and Woo, 1980). Similarly, the *Gf-Gc* structure of intelligence was found to be invariant across different cultural and racial groups (e.g., Keith, in press; see Carroll, 1993a and Chapter 2 for a review).

Because different factor-analytic methods have resulted in invariant Wechsler and *Gf-Gc* structures across cultures, cross-cultural validity has been inferred (Dana, 1993). Such validity, however, rests on the premise that cognitive abilities (i.e., those posited by Wechsler's conceptualization of intelligence or *Gf-Gc* theory) possess universal dimensions. Do cultural inventions (e.g., science, statistics, intelligence, etc.) exist, are they defined, and are they valued in precisely the same way from one culture to the next? Common sense, experientially based observation, and cross-cultural interactions suggest that the answer is most likely no. In all likelihood, culturally specific social behavior, patterns of communication, perceptual and cognitive styles all influence how a particular culture construes such things we call intelligence, and consequently, how it should or can be measured, if at all (Gould, 1981). The construct of intelligence can be measured uniquely in any selected culture. Yet being able to do so does not necessarily carry any significance or meaning for the culture being measured. The development of any construct, as well as any attempts to measure it in any population, remains a unique, idiosyncratic invention with little or limited utility for any other culture than that which developed it (Gould, 1981). There-fore, while it appears that *Gf-Gc* constructs can be validly measured in individuals from a particular culture (Loevinger, 1957; cf. Dana, 1993), interpretation of results from cognitive ability tests that measure the *Gf-Gc* constructs (specifically because they were developed in the United States) needs to be approached cautiously. It should be noted that establishing *construct equivalence* (through cross-cultural factor-analytic studies) for a test designed for the dominant culture (e.g., the U.S. population) is only one means of trans-forming the instrument into a measure that may be more appropriate for other specific cultural populations (Dana, 1993; Helms, 1997). Although construct equivalence is crucial (Dana, 1993), other types of equivalence not addressed here are also important to consider (e.g., functional equivalence, metric or scale equivalence, etc.; the reader is referred to Dana [1993], Helms [1997], and Valdés & Figueroa [1994] for a comprehensive discussion).

Another area in which intelligence batteries have been indicted for bias involves content. However, the literature does not support the argument that IQ tests include content, which is unfair or differentially difficult for individuals from diverse cultural and linguistic backgrounds, causing them to perform poorly. In fact, "inspection of standardized intelligence tests reveals few, if any, items that appear to be biased systematically in favor of one group over another" (Sattler, 1992; p. 567–568). Investigations of this type are relatively consistent in their conclusions that item content is not culturally biased and does not differentially affect the performance of individuals from one cultural group or another (Jensen, 1974; Sandoval, 1979; Sandoval, Zimmerman & Woo-Sam, 1983; Valdés & Figueroa, 1994).

In sum, despite the seemingly straightforward empirical findings that suggest little bias exists in contemporary intelligence batteries, there remains considerable concern in the field of applied psychology regarding the validity of using such batteries to assess the cognitive abilities of the growing number of individuals who come from diverse cultural and linguistic backgrounds. Although the majority of research appears on the surface to demonstrate that intelligence batteries are not biased per se, Figueroa (1990a) asserted that "the historical and contemporary literature is not unequivocal on the matter" (p. 95). At this time, Figueroa's observation regarding the question of test bias seems to ring as true as ever, to wit: "until the language proficiency factor, together with all the caveats in Chapter 13 of the *Standards* are taken into account, our knowledge about test bias and bilingualism will remain incomplete" (p. 95). Test bias, it would seem, is an elusive and complex matter.

Culture Bias versus Culture Loading

Perhaps, part of the answer to the question and nature of bias lies first in a reexamination of the basic assumptions made in the construction and development of intelligence batteries ever since their inception. Kamphaus (1993) has commented that "the traditions of Galton, Binet, Wechsler, Cattell, and others underlie all modern tests of intelligence. These tests emanated from French, British, German, North American, and other similarly European cultures" (p. 441). Gould's (1981) pointed rejoinder to the hereditarian argument for IQ illustrates the degree to which culture affects our views of nature and reality which we use almost unconsciously to make sense of data we collect. In this regard, it is necessary to understand that all tests of intelligence are reflections of the culture in which they were developed and are based on the cultural values and ideas held by the authors who developed them. As such, performance on these tests is contingent on the cultural experiences of the individual being assessed (Figueroa, 1990a; Samuda et al., 1991; Valdés & Figueroa, 1994). According to Neisser and colleagues (1996) "it is obvious that the cultural environment—how people live, what they value, what they do—has a significant effect on the intellectual skills developed by individuals" (p. 86). Clearly then, intelligence tests developed in the United States can be considered to be every bit as much cultural artifacts as jazz, the repeating rifle, and fins on cars. Adopting this perspective can be difficult because it requires a reevaluation of the ethnocentric viewpoints inculcated by cultural transmission. According to Matsumoto (1994), "sometimes we cannot separate ourselves from our own cultural backgrounds and biases to understand the behavior of others" (p. 6). Samuda and associates (1991) note that "we took for granted, also, the cultural orientation of the WASP mainstream. The school was, in fact, a reflection of the middle class societal norms and teachers were frequently the purveyors of information couched in terms of a collective mindset that almost totally disregarded any kind of minority sociocultural perspective" (p. vii). Nevertheless, in order to understand the influence of culture on test performance, psychologists need to recognize that "intelligence cannot be tested independently of the culture that gives rise to the test" (Cole & Cole, 1993, p. 502).

Users of standardized tests of intelligence should, therefore, recognize that performance on any intelligence battery reflects, at least in part, the extent to which the examinee is familiar with the social mores and conventions of the mainstream culture in which the battery was developed and normed (Cummins, 1981; Figueroa, 1990a; Samuda et al., 1991; Valdés & Figueroa, 1994). Given that the vast majority of tests used by psychologists in the United States were developed and normed in the United States, it is reasonable to conclude that the content of such tests will necessarily reflect native anthropological content as well as the culturally bound conceptualizations of intelligence of the test developers themselves. In order to serve children from diverse cultures in a more equitable manner, practitioners will need to acknowledge that "intelligence tests are not tests of intelligence in some abstract, culture-free way. They are measures of the ability to function intellectually by virtue of knowledge and skills in the culture of which they sample" (Scarr, 1978, p. 339). Although research indicates that most intelligence batteries appear to be technically sound, seem to be appropriately normed, and apparently are not culturally biased, they are, nevertheless, culturally loaded (Sattler, 1992; Valdés & Figueroa, 1994).

As discussed previously, tests of cognitive ability do not demonstrate cultural bias when culture is viewed as a unitary, monolithic construct expected to interact with performance or intended to differentiate one group of people from another (Figueroa, 1990; 1990a; Valdés & Figueroa, 1994). Indeed, tests of cognitive ability measure quite well the degree to which an individual has acquired and can readily access culturally specific information across most of the age-based developmental spectrum. However, exposure to mainstream United States culture (or lack thereof) has been identified as one of the most significant elements affecting the performance of individuals, in some cases quite dramatically, on tests of intelligence (Cummins, 1984; Figueroa, 1990a; Matsumoto, 1994; Valdés & Figueroa, 1994).

The process of acquiring culture (i.e., acculturation) remains invariant whether it is being learned natively by itself, simultaneously with another culture, or otherwise (Figueroa, 1983; 1990; 1990a; Valdés & Figueroa, 1994). The process of acculturation subsumes a fundamental notion of psychometric testing known as the "assumption of comparability" (Salvia & Ysseldyke, 1991, p. 18). According to Salvia and Ysseldyke (1991):

> When we test students using a standardized device and compare them to a set of norms to get an index of their relative standing, we assume that the students we test are similar to those on whom the test was standardized; that is, we assume their acculturation is comparable, but not necessarily identical, to that of the students who made up the normative sample for the test. (p. 18)

As such, bias exists in the inherent structure and design of tests that assume equivalent levels of acculturation across the variables of age or grade for individuals from other cultures. In order for such bias to be controlled, it should be noted that tests of intelligence and cognitive ability developed and normed in the United States will likely measure a lower range of ability in diverse individuals because they apparently fail to sample "cultural content that is part of the cognitive repertoire and processes available to the bicultural individual" (Valdés & Figueroa, 1994, p. 99). In this book this biasing influence is referred to as *cultural loading* in order to distinguish it from the common misconception that bias is a function of item content.

To summarize briefly, in order to increase the validity of results obtained in the assessment of individuals from diverse cultural backgrounds, users of standardized intelligence tests should seek to acquire two important and interrelated pieces of information: (1) the individual's level of acculturation and (2) the degree to which any given test contains or emphasizes culture specific knowledge. Mercer (1979), Valdés and Figueroa (1994), and others have addressed the few studies which attempted to measure the former issue. Our primary focus in this chapter concerns the latter and will be discussed in more detail in the text following.

Language Bias versus Language Loading

Although the linguistic barrier to reliable test performance seems obvious, it remains a poorly understood factor. Consistent with previous discussion, Valdés and Figueroa (1994) assert that "empirically established difficulty levels in psychometric tests are not altered by cultural differences. Neither are they because of proficiencies in the societal language" (p. 101). Language proficiency follows an experientially based developmental course every bit as invariant as that for acculturation. The effect of language proficiency as a variable that influences test performance is not seen in comparisons of performance within any single subtest. Rather, the effect is seen through the lack of concurrence between constructs measured through distinct channels (i.e., a set of verbal subtests versus a set of nonverbal subtests) (Cummins, 1984; Valdés & Figueroa, 1994). Herein lies the bias. Although there are few scientific studies in the literature that have utilized models of analysis comparing concurrence between verbal and nonverbal constructs, they are uniformly consistent in their findings—incidental learning is not measured equally by tasks that are linguistic versus perceptual in nature (Cummins, 1984; Jensen, 1974; 1976).

Much like an individual's standing on the acculturation spectrum, an individual's level of language proficiency and language background appears to directly influence test performance on tasks that require or presume a given level of language proficiency in order to either comprehend the instructions, formulate and verbalize the response, or otherwise use language ability in the performance of the given task (Cummins, 1984; Figueroa, Delgado, & Ruiz, 1984). Thus, as with culture, tests of intelligence may be linguistically biased because of expectations and assumptions regarding the comparability of language proficiency and development, which may not hold for linguistically diverse individuals any more than the assumption of comparability of acculturation. Figueroa (1990a) reinforces the notion that "language *background,* not just language proficiency, must be taken into account in every facet of assessment such as test development, selection, administration, and interpretation" (p. 94).

Language is acquired in a developmentally based sequence which begins at birth (perhaps sooner) and continues through adulthood (Cummins, 1984; Fromkin & Rodman, 1993; Krashen, 1985). Language acquisition is essentially universal; it occurs in nearly all human beings (i.e., those without physiological abnormalities that prevent or inhibit it) in approximately the same way (the basics are learned first, the complex follows thereafter) and at about the same time (Chomsky, 1986). However, when individuals attempt to learn a second language (e.g., English), their acquisition often begins at a point some years later than birth. The process of second language acquisition is much the same as it is for first language acquisition, differing only with respect to when the learning began (Baker, 1993; Cummins, 1984; Hamayan & Damico, 1991a; Krashen, 1985; Ortiz & Maldonado-Colon, 1986). Therefore, it would be unreasonable to expect a 12-year-old child who began learning English only two years ago to have the same level of English proficiency as another 12-year-old child who has been learning English from birth. The premise of linguistic equivalency with native English speakers rarely holds true for the English learner. Yet, the expectancy that the "average" 12-year-old, linguistically diverse child should already possess the given level of language proficiency we normally expect from 12-year-olds raised monolingually in the U.S. is embedded in virtually every assumption underlying tests of intelligence available today. Figueroa (1990a) asserted that intelligence "tests in English degenerate in unknown degrees into tests of English language proficiency" when used with bilingual children (p. 93).

In sum, there is powerful evidence suggesting that tests of intelligence and cognitive ability which carry high linguistic demands (e.g., vocabulary tests) may, in fact, be biased against individuals who are dual-language learners (Cummins, 1984; Figueroa, 1990; 1990a; Valdés & Figueroa, 1994). There is also evidence that dual-language learners are distinct linguistic entities quite distinct from their monolingual counterparts (Bialystok, 1991; Grosjean, 1989; Hakuta, 1986) who possess unique mental processing characteristics (Cummins, 1984; Valdés & Figueroa, 1994). Thus, in keeping with Figueroa's (1990a) call for the use of promising methods, until such conceptualizations of the bilingual mind are further researched and disseminated in the literature, nondiscriminatory assessment should continue to include, data on two closely related factors: the individual's level of proficiency in the specific language or languages (e.g., English, Spanish, Japanese, etc.) used to assess any given aspect of their functioning (e.g., intelligence or cognitive abilities) and the degree or level of linguistic demand contained in the test or tests used to assess that functioning.

Nonverbal Assessment of Intelligence

On the surface it would seem that difficult issues related to culture and language loading could be easily circumvented through the use of so-called "nonverbal" batteries. Publishers of such tests often promote them as being not only culture-free, but also language-free, since they can be administered in total pantomime (e.g., UNIT, Leiter-R). Assessors must be cautious, however, not to assume that even complete reduction of the verbal or oral language requirements of a particular test automatically eliminates linguistic bias. Although this approach to assessment can assist in generating less discriminatory results for individuals from diverse backgrounds (Figueroa, 1990a; McCallum & Bracken, 1997), they are not completely free of the influence of culture or language. In order to understand how such tests remain culture or language loaded, we must again examine the basic assumptions that underlie them.

The term *nonverbal intelligence* suggests that such tests measure a theoretical construct called nonverbal intelligence. However, the literature does not appear to support this premise. No theoretical model within the psychometric tradition (e.g., *Gf-Gc* theory) has identified a narrow or broad nonverbal ability or intelligence construct (see Carroll, 1993a; Kamphaus, 1993). A review of the published *Gf-Gc* ability classifications of tests that comprise the so-called nonverbal batteries (e.g., McGrew & Flanagan, 1998), and of tests that are often interpreted as measures of nonverbal abilities, seems to indicate that "the word *nonverbal* simply describes a methodology for assessing the same general intelligence that has been of interest to psychologists since the early part of the century" (Kamphaus, 1993, p. 323). The extant classifications demonstrate that most of these nonverbal tests appear to measure primarily *Gf* and *Gv* and, to a lesser extent, *Gs* and *Glr* (and not *nonverbal intelligence*). Moreover, tests and batteries of a nonverbal persuasion are characterized by either their measurement of a limited range of cognitive abilities or their redundancy in measurement of certain abilities (e.g., the Leiter-R includes four measures of *Gf*-I).

Another common assumption specific to nonverbal tests revolves around the idea that language does not influence or only minimally influences performance on these measures. Although they might not require oral expressive language ability per se, very often nonverbal tests demand a high level of receptive language skill in order to comprehend the examiner's instructions and expectations (e.g., Wechsler Block Design or WJ-R Analysis-Synthesis). When the individual does not possess the minimum required or expected level of receptive language (as is often the case for dual-language learners), performance is directly affected. Of course, there do exist tests that can be administered entirely through the use of gestures or pantomime (e.g., CTONI, Leiter-R, UNIT). These tests effectively eliminate most if not all oral (expressive or receptive) language requirements. Nevertheless, test performance continues to remain dependent on communication between the examiner and examinee and their ability to interact effectively in a nonverbal manner (i.e., the examiner's ability to clearly and correctly convey the nature of a given task and its expected response to the examinee—not to mention the examinee's ability to comprehend that communication and accurately re-convey an acceptable response to the examiner).

This nonverbal communication often carries more culturally based implications than verbal communication (Ehrman, 1996). Therefore, the influence of language on the test performance of linguistically diverse individuals on any test purported to be nonverbal cannot be presumed to operate solely within the verbal domain. Likewise, as described previously, nonverbal batteries do not necessarily eliminate the influence of culture either. In fact, there are indications that nonverbal tasks may carry as much if not more cultural content than that found in verbal tests (Greenfield, 1998) and, therefore, should not be presumed to be any more culture free. Additionally, the interpretation of the abilities that are measured by nonverbal tests or clusters can be quite confusing, are often much less defensible, and do not necessarily provide more valid assessment data (McCallum & Bracken, 1997).

Culture Loading, Language Loading, and Norms

One of the fundamental premises involved in the use of a standardized, norm-referenced instrument is that creation of a consistent, experimentally controlled setting allows examiners to measure performance on a variety of tasks and therefore make valid comparisons against a group of individuals tested under ostensibly equivalent conditions. The major intelligence batteries available today have more than adequate national norms and meet the strictest criteria with respect to the technical aspects of norm sample development. According to Sattler (1992), "national norms reflect the performance of the population as a whole. Because they describe the typical performance of our nation's children, they are important as a frame of reference and as a guide post for decision-making" (p. 570).

In order to enhance this guide post, test developers have, over the years, used particular strategies to create ever more representative norm samples. Today, it is common practice to stratify along several important variables including age, sex, race, ethnicity, education level, and geographic location when establishing suitable standardization samples. In broad terms, the idea is to generate a norm sample that minimizes and equalizes any systematic variation due to such variables, thereby allowing for comparisons of performance that are no more or less biased against any single individual for whom the sample is representative. There is no question that such stratification procedures produce state of the art norm samples that are sophisticated and technically valid.

A potential difficulty with norms in the case of culturally and linguistically diverse children rests with some of the assumptions underlying the stratification process—notably, what constitutes *representative* in the case of culturally different individuals. As stated previously, there is an assumption of comparability that when true, allows valid conclusions to be made regarding relative performance. When false, conclusions and interpretations of performance become questionable at best. As Salvia and Ysseldyke (1991) noted:

> When a child's general background experiences differ from those of the children on whom a test was standardized, then the use of the norms of the test as an index for evaluating that child's current performance or for predicting future performance may be inappropriate. Incorrect educational decisions may well be made. It must be pointed out that acculturation is a matter of experiential background rather than gender, skin color, race, or ethnic background. When we say that a child's acculturation differs from that of the group used as a norm, we are saying that the *experiential background* differs, not simply that the child is of different ethnic origin, for example, from the children on whom the test was standardized. (p. 18; emphasis in the original)

Too often, race and ethnicity are equated with culture. Although there is certainly some degree of correlation between them, culture is neither (Matsumoto, 1994). Thus, to suggest that any test controls well the potential influence of acculturation-based differences by simply assembling groups of racial or ethnic individuals in accordance with their frequency in the general population, is both misleading and difficult to defend (Valdés & Figueroa, 1994). It is not so much that racial differences should not be controlled or even that the stratification process is flawed, but rather the mistaken notion that controlling for race is equivalent to controlling for culture or acculturation. Even if cultural differences were easily operationalized, the expectation that they should necessarily interact with test performance in some disruptive fashion does not appear to be a reasonable assumption, as was discussed earlier (Figueroa, 1990; 1990a; Valdés & Figueroa, 1994).

Given the invariant nature of the acculturative process, from a statistical and structural point of view, it would probably matter little whether we included various cultural groups in accordance with their percentages in the general population or whether we included them in even greater numbers. If the intent is to create a norm group that is representative of individuals who are culturally different, numerical considerations are largely irrelevant because it is not the individual's culture per se, that affects performance; rather it is their level of acculturation (Cummins, 1984; Figueroa, 1990; 1990a; Valdés & Figueroa, 1994) which makes the difference. Again, from the standpoint of the developmental nature of the acculturation process, the patterns of differences in performance among individuals from the same cultural background would likely be no different than the patterns of differences found in performance among individuals raised within the cultural milieu in which the test was developed. However, in the former case, measured performance is more likely to reflect varying levels of individual acculturation more so than variation in actual or "true" cognitive ability (Cummins, 1984; Figueroa, 1990a; Valdés & Figueroa, 1994), whereas, in the latter case, measured performance can be taken as a valid reflection of the individual's standing compared to that of his or her peers.

In sum, until the Wechsler Scales (and other modern tests of intelligence and cognitive ability) specifically provide stratification within the norm sample on the basis of level of acculturation, we cannot presume that performance of children who are culturally different (i.e., raised outside the U.S. mainstream culture) can be validly compared to norm samples comprised of children who were reared in the U.S. mainstream (Cummins, 1984; Figueroa, 1990a; Samuda et al., 1991; Valdés & Figueroa, 1994). The norm samples for the current Wechsler Scales may be extremely well constructed, but the assumption of comparability may be violated any time such tests are used with culturally diverse individuals.

With respect to language proficiency, representation within the standardization sample is a similar issue. In the United States, every child entering school who does not speak English is immediately set on a path toward becoming a dual-language or English learner (circumstantial bilingual). However, dual-language learners or bilingual pupils tend not to be systematically included or accommodated in the design and norming of any of the currently available Wechsler Scales (or any other test of intelligence or cognitive ability). This remains true even when the sample is established in a language other than English, such as with the WISC-RM and WISC-R-PR. The WISC-RM, in particular, is comprised almost exclusively of monolingual Spanish speakers just as its English language counterpart is comprised of monolingual English speakers. Occasionally, some tests, such as the WISC-R-PR, include dual-language individuals, however, it is not done in any systematic manner or controlled method which distinguishes these individuals on the basis of their English language proficiency. Given the extant research on the nature of bilinguals (Cummins, 1984; Figueroa, 1990; Grosjean, 1989; Hamayan & Damico, 1991a; Valdés & Figueroa, 1994), it is difficult to accept that a group of monolingual individuals constitutes an acceptable comparison group for an individual who lies somewhere along the bilingual proficiency spectrum. As with acculturation, patterns of difference in performance among individuals from diverse linguistic backgrounds would be no different than the patterns of differences found in performance among individuals for whom the language of the test matches their native tongue (Cummins, 1984; Valdés & Figueroa, 1994). However, as outlined before, measured performance in the former case could reasonably be viewed more as a reflection of the individual's level of English language proficiency than any indication of actual cognitive ability (Cummins, 1984; Valdés & Figueroa, 1994). Figueroa (1990a) and others (e.g., Bialystok, 1991; Samuda et al., 1991) concluded that there are no Wechsler Scales (or other tests of intelligence or cognitive ability) for use with bilingual individuals that contain suitable norms for such dual-language learners. More to the point, "tests developed without accounting for language differences are limited in their validity and on how they can be interpreted" (Figueroa, 1990a; p. 94).

In sum, professionals engaged in the assessment of culturally and linguistically diverse individuals with the Wechsler Scales (or other standardized, norm-referenced instruments) should recognize three essential points: (1) the Wechsler Scales are culturally loaded and tend to reflect the values, beliefs, and knowledge that are deemed important for success in the culture in which the tests were developed—that is, U.S. mainstream culture; (2) the Wechsler Scales require language (or communication) on both the part of the examiner and the examinee and that linguistic factors can affect administration, comprehension, and performance on virtually all tests including the performance tests, such as Block Design; and (3) the individual Wechsler subtests vary on both dimensions; that is, the degree to which they are culturally loaded and require language.

A New Frame of Reference for Intelligence Tests

Culture and Language Classification

Well-standardized and psychometrically sound instruments represent one of the most important and valuable components in assessment. However, the preceding discussion has highlighted the extent to which cultural and linguistic factors should also be considered as equally important in light of the changing demographics of the United States (Dana, 1993) and the effect such factors have on test performance. The previous sections outlined both the general issues involved and the nature of bias that may be found in the assessment of intelligence of diverse individuals. To extend the practice of assessing culturally and linguistically diverse individuals, intelligence tests may benefit from an examination within a new frame of reference.

The frame of reference presented here is in line with Figueroa's (1990a) call for the application of defensible theoretical frameworks in the assessment of culturally and linguistically diverse individuals, as well as his admonition that relevancy to cultural and linguistic dimensions should be made. The methods proposed herein are also consistent with several of the propositions for testing bilinguals contained in Chapter 13 of the Standards of Educational and Psychological Testing (American Educational Research Association, American Psychological Association, American Council on Measurement, 1985). In particular, found here are the notions that idiosyncratic variations in cultural and linguistic background can lower test performance. These methods are also consistent with the APA *Guidelines for Providers of Psychological Services to Ethnic, Linguistic, and Culturally Diverse Populations* (1990).

The *Gf-Gc* classifications presented in earlier chapters provides the theoretical model for just such an approach. Table 8.2 represents an initial attempt to integrate cultural and linguistic elements into a broad, defensible framework for assessing culturally and linguistically diverse individuals with standardized, norm-referenced tests. Table 8.2 is a matrix of cognitive ability and special purpose tests (including all current Wechsler Scales, i.e., WPPSI-R, WISC-III, WAIS-III) that are organized according to three important test characteristics: (1) stratum I and stratum II abilities measured according to *Gf-Gc* theory; (2) degree of cultural loading; and (3) degree of linguistic demand. Together, these three test characteristics can be integrated in a manner that significantly advances methodology related to the assessment of culturally and linguistically diverse individuals. By providing such information, Table 8.2 becomes a potentially valuable tool that can aid in the compilation of a selective set of measures which may be less discriminatory and thus more valid for use with culturally and linguistically diverse populations. The following is a brief description of the characteristics of cognitive ability tests that are included.

The cognitive ability tests included in Table 8.2 are first classified according to the broad (stratum II) and narrow (stratum I) *Gf-Gc* abilities they measure. The tests listed in Table 8.2 are the same as those in Table 5.1, and are consistent with the *Gf-Gc* cross-battery worksheets found in Appendix C. The table also retains the same general formatting and structure found in the rest of the book. For example, tests printed in bold capital letters were defined empirically as strong measures of the respective broad (and narrow) *Gf-Gc* abilities reported in the column to the right of the test names in the table. Likewise, bold lowercase type represents tests with moderate loadings in these abilities, and lowercase regular type indicates tests that were classified logically (i.e., empirical support is not yet available or established). Table 8.2 also identifies the name of the battery in which the subtest is located, as well as the age range for which the subtest is appropriate. Classification along these dimensions does not strictly represent an accommodation to an issue particular to cultural or linguistic diversity. Rather, it is intended to reflect, as discussed in the first chapters, that the basis of valid assessment, including those conducted on diverse individuals, must first and foremost rest on the best available and most solid theoretical and empirical foundation.

The cognitive ability and special purpose tests included in Table 8.2 are also organized according to their Degree of Cultural Loading, which represents the degree to which their subtests require specific knowledge of and experience with mainstream U.S. culture. The *Gf-Gc* classifications of all tests included in the table were evaluated in terms of emphasis on process, content, and nature of response. It was reasoned that tests that are more process dominant (as opposed to product dominant), contain abstract or novel stimuli (as opposed to culture-specific stimuli), and which require simple, less culturally bound communicative responding (e.g., affirmative head nods, pointing) (see McCallum & Bracken, 1997) might yield scores that are less affected by an individual's level of exposure

TABLE 8.2   Test Classification by Degree of Cultural Loading and Linguistic Demand

Degree of Cultural Loading—Low

	Battery	Age	Subtest	Gf-Gc *Ability*
	CTONI	6–18	Geometric Sequences	*Gf* (I, RG)
	LEITER-R	5–18+	Design Analogies	*Gf* (I)
	LEITER-R	2–18+	Repeated Patterns	*Gf* (I)
	LEITER-R	2–18+	Sequential Order	*Gf* (I)
	LEITER-R	11–18+	Paper Folding	*Gv* (VZ)
	LEITER-R	11–18+	Figure Rotation	*Gv* (VZ, SR)
	UNIT	5–17	Cube Design	*Gv* (SR, VZ)
	UNIT	5–17	Mazes	*Gv* (SS)
	DAS	6–17	**MATRICES**	*Gf* (I)
	DAS	6–17	**SEQUENTIAL & QUANTITATIVE REASONING**	*Gf* (I, RG)
	DTLA-3	6–17	**Symbolic Relations**	*Gf* (I)
	MAT	5–17	Matrix Analogies Test	*Gf* (I, RG)
	Raven's	5–18+	Raven's Progressive Matrices	*Gf* (I)
	TONI-3	5–17	Test of Nonverbal Intelligence—Third Edition	*Gf* (I)
Degree of	DAS	3–17	Pattern Construction	*Gv* (SR)
Linguistic	DAS	2–3	Block Building	*Gv* (VZ)
Demand	DAS	4–5	Matching Letter-Like Forms	*Gv* (VZ)
	DAS	6–17	**RECALL OF DESIGNS**	*Gv* (MV)
Low	K-ABC	4–12	**TRIANGLES**	*Gv* (VZ, SR)
	KAIT	11–85+	**MEMORY FOR BLOCK DESIGNS**	*Gv* (MV)
	SB:IV	2–24	**PATTERN ANALYSIS**	*Gv* (VZ)
	WPPSI-R	3–7	Geometric Design	*Gv* (VZ, P2)
	CAS	5–17	Figure Memory	*Gv* (CF, MV)
	DTLA-3	6–17	Design Sequences	*Gv* (MV)
	DTLA-3	6–17	Design Reproduction	*Gv* (MV)
	TOMAL	5–19	Facial Memory	*Gv* (MV)
	TOMAL	5–19	Abstract Visual Memory	*Gv* (MV)
	TOMAL	5–19	Manual Imitation	*Gv* (MV)
	TOMAL	5–19	Delayed Recall of Visual Selective Reminding	*Gv* (MV)
	WMS-III	16–85+	Visual Reproduction I	*Gv* (MV)
	CAS	5–17	Matching Numbers	*Gs* (P, R9)
	CAS	5–17	Planned Codes	*Gs* (R9)
	CAS	5–17	Number Detection	*Gs* (R7, R9)
	DAS	3–17	Recall of Digits	*Gsm* (MS)
	K-ABC	2–12	**NUMBER RECALL**	*Gsm* (MS)
	SB:IV	7–24	**MEMORY FOR DIGITS**	*Gsm* (MS)
	WAIS-R	16–74	**DIGIT SPAN**	*Gsm* (MS)
	WISC-III	6–16	**DIGIT SPAN**	*Gsm* (MS)
Degree of	K-SNAP	11–85	Number Recall	*Gsm* (MS)
Linguistic	LAMB	20–60	Digit Span	*Gsm* (MS)
Demand	TOMAL	5–19	Digits Forward	*Gsm* (MS)
	TOMAL	5–19	Letters Forward	*Gsm* (MS)
Moderate	WMS-III	16–85+	Digit Span	*Gsm* (MS, MW)
	CMS	5–16	Dot Locations	*Gv* (MV)
	CMS	5–16	Numbers	*Gsm* (MS)
	WRAML	5–17	Number/Letter Memory	*Gsm* (MS)

306

TABLE 8.2   Continued

Degree of Cultural Loading—Low

	Battery	Age	Subtest	Gf-Gc Ability
	WJ-R	2–85+	**MEMORY FOR NAMES**	Glr (MA)
	WJ-R	4–85+	**DELAYED RECALL—MEMORY FOR NAMES**	Glr (MA)
	WRAML	5–17	Sound Symbol	Glr (MA)
	DAS	6–17	Speed of Information Processing	Gs (R7)
	DTLA-3	6–17	Word Sequences	Gsm (MS)
	TOMAL	5–19	Word Selective Reminding	Glr (M6)
	TOMAL	5–19	Delayed Recall of Word Selective Reminding	Glr (M6)
Degree of	SB:IV	7–24	**MATRICES**	Gf (I)
Linguistic	SB:IV	2–24	**Bead Memory**	Gv (MV)
Demand	WISC-III	6–16	Mazes	Gv (SS)
	WPPSI-R	3–7	**Mazes**	Gv (SS)
Moderate	WECHSLERS	3–74	**BLOCK DESIGN**	Gv (SR)
(continued)	LAMB	20–60	Simple Figure	Gv (MV)
	LAMB	20–60	Complex Figure	Gv (MV)
	WRAML	5–17	Design Memory	Gv (MV)
	WISC-III	6–16	Symbol Search	Gs (P, R9)
	WAIS-R	16–74	**DIGIT SYMBOL**	Gs (R9)
	WISC-III	6–16	**CODING**	Gs (R9)
	WJ-R/III	4–85+	**VISUAL MATCHING**	Gs (P, R9)
	WJ-R	4–85+	**CROSS OUT**	Gs (P, R9)
	WJ-III	4–85+	**PLANNING**	Gv (SS)
	SB:IV	7–24	Number Series	Gf (RQ)
Degree of	WJ-R/III	4–85+	**CONCEPT FORMATION**	Gf (I)
Linguistic	WJ-R/III	4–85+	**ANALYSIS SYNTHESIS**	Gf (RG)
Demand	WMS-III	16–85+	Letter-Number Sequencing	Gsm (MW)
	WJ-III	4–85+	**AUDITORY WORKING MEMORY**	Gsm (MW)
High	WJ-III	4–85+	**PAIR CANCELLATION**	Gs (R9)
	LAMB	20–60	Supraspan Digit	Gsm (MS)

Degree of Cultural Loading—Moderate

	Battery	Age	Subtest	Gf-Gc Ability
	LEITER-R	6–18+	Visual Coding	Gf (RG)
	LEITER-R	2–10	Matching	Gv (VZ)
	LEITER-R	2–18+	Attention Sustained	Gs (P, R9)
	DAS	2–5	Picture Similarities	Gf (I)
	CAS	5–17	Geometric Sequences	Gf (I)
Degree of	DAS	3–7	Recognition of Pictures	Gv (MV)
Linguistic	K-ABC	2–4	Face Recognition	Gv (MV)
Demand	SB:IV	7–24	**Memory for Objects**	Gv (MV)
	WECHSLERS	3–74	**OBJECT ASSEMBLY**	GV (CS)
Low	WJ-R/III	4–85+	**Picture Recognition**	Gv (MV)
	K-ABC	2–4	**WORD ORDER**	Gsm (MS)
	CAS	5–17	Receptive Attention	Gs (P, R4)
	K-ABC	2–4	Magic Window	Gv (PI)
	K-ABC	2–12	**Gestalt Closure**	Gv (CS)
	WJ-R	2–85+	**Visual Closure**	Gv (CS)

(continued)

TABLE 8.2   Continued

Degree of Cultural Loading—Moderate

	Battery	Age	Subtest	Gf-Gc *Ability*
	DAS	4–17	Recall of Objects	*Glr* (M6)
	TOMAL	5–19	Paired Recall	*Glr* (MA)
	CAS	5 - 17	Word Series	*Gsm* (MS)
	KAIT	11–85+	**REBUS LEARNING**	*Glr* (MA)
	KAIT	11–85+	**REBUS DELAYED RECALL**	*Glr* (MA)
	WJ-R/III	4–85+	**VISUAL-AUDITORY LEARNING**	*Glr* (MA)
	WJ-R/III	4–85+	**Delayed Recall—Visual Auditory Learning**	*Glr* (MA)
Degree of Linguistic Demand	KAIT	11–85+	**MYSTERY CODES**	*Gf* (I)
	K-SNAP	11–85	Four-Letter Words	*Gf* (I)
	CMS	5–16	Word Pairs	*Glr* (MA)
	CMS	5–16	Word Pairs	*Glr* (MA)
Moderate	WMS-III	16–85+	Verbal Paired Associates I	*Glr* (MA)
	WMS-III	16–85+	Verbal Paired Associates II	*Glr* (MA)
	WPPSI-R	3–7	Animal Pegs	*Gs* (R9)
	KAIT	11–85+	**LOGICAL STEPS**	*Gf* (I)
	LAMB	20–60	Word Pairs	*Glr* (MA, FI)
	DAS	3–5	Early Number Concepts	*Gq* (A3, KM)
	SB:IV	2–4	**QUANTITATIVE**	*Gq* (A3)
	WJ-III	4–85+	**RETRIEVAL FLUENCY**	*Glr* (FI)
	WJ-III	4–85+	**RAPID PICTURE NAMING**	*Glr* (NA)
	WECHSLERS	3–74	**ARITHMETIC**	*Gq* (A3)
	WJ-R/III	2–85+	**INCOMPLETE WORDS**	*Ga* (PC-A)
	WJ-R/III	4–85+	**SOUND BLENDING**	*Ga* (PC-S)
	TOPA	5–8	Test of Phonological Awareness	*Ga* (PC)
	SB:IV	12–24	**EQUATION BUILDING**	*Gf* (RQ)
Degree of Linguistic Demand	WPPSI-R	3–7	Sentences	*Gsm* (MS)
	WJ-R	4–85+	**MEMORY FOR WORDS**	*Gsm* (MS)
	CMS	5–16	Sequences	*Gsm* (MW)
	CMS	5–16	Word Lists	*Glr* (M6)
High	CMS	5–16	Word Lists 2	*Glr* (M6,MA)
	WMS-III	16–85+	Word Lists I	*Glr* (M6)
	WJ-III	4–85+	**AUDITORY ATTENTION**	*Ga* (UR)
	WJ-III	4–85+	**DECISION SPEED**	*Gs* (R7)
	WRAML	5–17	Verbal Learning	*Glr* (M6)

Degree of Cultural Loading—High

	Battery	Age	Subtest	Gf-Gc *Ability*
	LEITER-R	2–6	Classification	*Gf* (I)
	LEITER-R	2–10	Picture Context	*Gf* (RG)
	UNIT	5–17	Analogic Reasoning	*Gf* (I)
Degree of Linguistic Demand	LEITER-R	2–18+	Form Completion	*Gv* (VZ, SR)
	LEITER-R	4–10	Immediate Recognition	*Gv* (MV)
	LEITER-R	2–18+	Forward Memory	*Gv* (MV)
Low	LEITER-R	2–18+	Figure Ground	*Gv* (CF)
	LEITER-R	4–10	Delayed Recognition	*Glr* (MA)
	LEITER-R	2–18+	Associated Pairs	*Glr* (MA, MM)
	LEITER-R	6–18+	Delayed Pairs	*Glr* (MA, MM)
	K-BIT	4–90	Matrices	*Gf* (I)

TABLE 8.2 Continued

Degree of Cultural Loading—High

	Battery	Age	Subtest	Gf-Gc Ability
Degree of Linguistic Demand **Moderate**	DAS	2–5	Verbal Comprehension	Gc (LD, LS)
	WRAML	5–17	Picture Memory	Gv (MV)
	DAS	2–5	Naming Vocabulary	Gc (LD, VL)
	KAIT	11–85+	**FAMOUS FACES**	Gc (K2)
	WJ-R	4–85+	**ORAL VOCABULARY**	Gc (VL, LD)
	WJ-R	4–85+	**PICTURE VOCABULARY**	Gc (VL, K0)
	DTLA-3	6–17	Word Opposites	Gc (LD)
	K-BIT	4–90	Expressive Vocabulary	Gc (VL, K0, LD)
	DTLA-3	6–17	Picture Fragments	Gv (CS)
	K-SNAP	11–85	Gestalt Closure	Gv (CS)
	WMS-III	16–85+	Mental Control	Glr (MW)
Degree of Linguistic Demand **High**	CMS	5–16	Stories 2	Glr (MM)
	DAS	6–17	**SIMILARITIES**	Gc (LD)
	DAS	6–17	**WORD DEFINITIONS**	Gc (VL, LD)
	SB:IV	2–24	**VOCABULARY**	Gc (LD, VL)
	SB:IV	2–14	**Absurdities**	Gc (LD)
	WECHSLERS	3–74	**SIMILARITIES**	Gc (LD)
	WECHSLERS	3–74	**VOCABULARY**	Gc (LD, VL)
	WECHSLERS	3–74	**INFORMATION**	Gc (K0)
	DTLA-3	6–17	Story Construction	Gc (LD)
	DTLA-3	6–17	Basic Information	Gc (K0)
	PPVT-3	2–85	Peabody Picture Vocabulary Test—Third Edition	Gc (VL, K0, LD)
	WJ-R	4–85+	**LISTENING COMPREHENSION**	Gc (LS, LD)
	WJ-III	4–85+	**ORAL COMPREHENSION**	Gc (LS)
	WJ-III	2–85+	**VERBAL COMPREHENSION**	Gc (VL,LD)
	WJ-III	2–85+	**GENERAL INFORMATION**	Gc (K0)
	EVT	2–85+	Expressive Vocabulary Test	Gc (VL, LD)
	LAMB	20–60	Wordlist	Glr (M6, MA)
	SB:IV	12–24	**VERBAL RELATIONS**	Gc (LD)
	SB:IV	2–24	**Comprehension**	Gc (LD, K0)
	WECHSLERS	3–74	**COMPREHENSION**	Gc (LD, K0)
	WMS-III	16–85+	Logical Memory II	Glr (MM)

Note: CAS= Cognitive Assessment System; CMS= Children's Memory Scale; DAS= Differential Ability Scales; DTLA-3= Detroit Tests of Learning Aptitude —3; DTLA-4= Detroit Tests of Learning Aptitude—4; G-FTA= Goldman-Fristoe Test of Articulation; G-FTAD= Goldman-Fristoe-Woodcock Test of Auditory Discrimination; K-ABC= Kaufman Assessment Battery for Children; KAIT= Kaufman Adolescent and Adult Intelligence Test; Leiter-R= Leiter International Performance Scale—Revised; SB:IV= Stanford-Binet Intelligence Scale: Fourth Edition; TOPA= Test of Phonological Awareness; TPAT= The Phonological Awareness Test; UNIT= Universal Nonverbal Intelligence Test; W-ADT= Wepman's Auditory Discrimination Test—Second Edition; WMS-III= Wechsler Memory Scale—Third Edition; WJ-R= Woodcock-Johnson Psychoeducational Battery-Revised; WJ-III= Woodcock-Johnson Psychoeducational Battery—Third Edition.

Tests printed in bold/uppercase letters are strong measures as defined empirically; tests printed in bold/lowercase letters are moderate measures as defined empirically; tests printed in regular type/lowercase letters were classified logically (see McGrew and Flanagan, 1998). In the case where tests have two narrow-ability classifications, the second classification is reported in parentheses following the test description. Tests of the major batteries that were classified either empirically or logically as mixed measures are not included in this table.

Sources: Test definitions for the K-ABC and KAIT were adapted with permission from American Guidance Service. Test definitions for the Leiter-R were adapted with permission from Stoelting. Test definitions for the WMS-III, CMS, and DAS were adapted with permission from The Psychological Corporation. Test definitions for the Phonological Awareness Test were adapted with permission from LinguiSystems. Test definitions for the SB:IV, UNIT, WJ-R, and CAS were adapted with permission from Riverside. Test definitions for the DTLA-3/4 were adapted with permission from Pro-Ed.

to mainstream United States culture (Jensen, 1974; Valdés & Figueroa, 1994). Since these three characteristics (i.e., process-product dominance, nature of test stimuli, response requirements) represent continuous rather than dichotomous test features, the tests were classified as either low, moderate, or high with respect to their degree of cultural loading, and listed in this order. As noted previously, a given individual's relative standing on the acculturation continuum directly influences test performance (e.g., in general, low levels of acculturation lead to low test performance and high levels of acculturation lead to high test performance) (Cummins, 1984).

Classification of some of the Wechsler subtests in Table 8.2 is partially based on findings reported by Cummins (1984) wherein the WISC-R was administered to children living in Canada with varying levels of English proficiency and acculturation to Canadian mainstream. Results from this study indicated that the Information, Similarities, Vocabulary, and Comprehension subtests appeared to be the most culturally/linguistically biased (affected performance the most) against ESL (English as a Second Language) students. Arithmetic, Digit Span, Picture Arrangement, and Block Design fell more in the moderate range with respect to affecting performance; Picture Completion, Object Assembly, and Coding seemed to have the least effect. Thus, there is some support for the classification of these tests which is consistent with and supports the validity of the criteria used to classify the other tests in Table 8.2. Careful selection and use of tests listed in the table can reduce the distance between an individual's familiarity with mainstream culture and the cultural demands of the test, thereby offering the possibility of a fairer, less biased, and more valid interpretation of an individual's true functioning and potential.

With the exception of the *The Intelligence Test Desk Reference* (*ITDR*; McGrew & Flanagan, 1998), there are no guides currently available to help examiners determine the amount of linguistic skill required by various tests of intelligence and cognitive ability. Table 8.2 builds on and updates the information presented in the *ITDR* and provides the data needed in order to assist psychologists in selecting appropriate tests with which to assess linguistically diverse individuals. Accordingly, the tests included in Table 8.2 were classified based on their respective "Degree of Linguistic Demand."

In order to classify tests on this dimension, two particular factors were considered. First, tests were evaluated and classified according to the extent to which they require expressive and receptive language skills in order to be properly administered. Some tests have lengthy, verbose instructions (e.g., Wechsler Block Design subtest, WJ-R Analysis-Synthesis subtest, etc.), whereas, others can be given using only gestures or minimal language (e.g., CTONI, Leiter-R, UNIT, etc.). In addition, tests were evaluated according to the level of language proficiency required by the examinee in order to comprehend the administrator's instructions and provide appropriate responses. Responses on some tests require considerable expressive language skills (e.g., WISC/WAIS Vocabulary and Comprehension) while others may be accomplished without a word (e.g., WJ-R Visual Matching and Cross Out). Final classification was based on joint consideration of both factors using a three-dimensional categorization system that reflects the continuous nature of these variables (high, moderate, and low). In addition, the findings of Cummins (1984) served as a guide for the classification of some of the Wechsler subtests. These categories are presented vertically along the far left side of Table 8.2 and are arranged in order of increasing language demands for each of the three levels of cultural loading.

Given the present focus on the Wechsler Scales, an additional table has been included to assist in illustrating the nature of the classification scheme described above. The various Wechsler subtests have been placed in a comprehensive tabular matrix similar to the cultural loading-linguistic demand cubes contained in the Wechsler summary pages presented in Chapter 4. This matrix appears in Table 8.3 and provides a graphical representation of how the Wechsler Scales are arranged when classified according to the dimensions presented herein (i.e., degree of cultural loading and degree of linguistic demand). Once again, although some of the newer Wechsler subtests (e.g., Matrix Reasoning) have been classified on the basis of the criteria specified above, other legacy Wechsler subtests have been classified in accordance with both the criteria already mentioned and the results of the study by Cummins (1984).

A quick review of Table 8.3 highlights the relationship between the Wechsler Scales' emphasis on acquired or crystallized knowledge *(Gc)* and high levels of cultural loading and linguistic demand. The Wechsler Scales also contain many measures of processing speed *(Gs)* which, on the whole, have lower cultural loading, but moderate levels of linguistic demand (often due to the need for complex or long administration instructions). Measures of *Gsm,* which are seen as a function of facility and familiarity with verbal stimuli, require a higher level of language proficiency, but a somewhat lower degree of cultural loading.

When utilized within the context of a selective *Gf-Gc* cross-battery framework, the test classifications presented in Tables 8.2 and 8.3 can assist in constructing *Gf-Gc* cross-battery based tests for diverse individuals that are both scientifically more advanced and methodologically superior to the batteries presently available. Careful, deliberate selection and use of tests of cognitive ability that have lower linguistic demands can serve to reduce the distance between an individual's familiarity and proficiency with the English language and the inherent language demands of the test. For example, an individual's performance on the Leiter-R Design Analogies, Repeated Patterns, and Sequential Order tests (all measures of *Gf*-I) would be interpreted as reflecting an aspect of Fluid Intelligence (i.e., Induction) that is assessed via a nonverbal method (i.e., pantomime). Such a result would also not be misconstrued as reflecting the individual's nonverbal intelligence. When combined with other relevant information, interpretation of the test performance of individuals who are not native speakers of English can be made less biased and less discriminatory, perhaps yielding a more valid representation of actual ability or functioning.

The classifications of cognitive ability tests according to Degree of Cultural Loading and Degree of Linguistic Demand (reported in Tables 8.2 and 8.3) are by no means definitive and are not necessarily based on the most appropriate criteria. Except for some of the legacy Wechsler subtests which have some empirical basis, the majority of classifications are clearly subjective and were derived primarily through the integration of substantive issues presented in the literature as well as expert judgment. Apart from Cummins's (1984) study, empirically based findings for making such classifications is almost nonexistent and will require further investigation. Although the classifications are insufficient, by themselves, to establish a comprehensive basis for assessment of diverse individuals, they are, nevertheless, capable of greatly supplementing the assessment process in both the diagnostic and interpretive arenas. First, by guiding test selection, examiners may be able to construct batteries which are theoretically based and more fair to individuals from diverse

TABLE 8.3 Matrix of Cultural Loading and Linguistic Demand Classifications of the Wechsler Subtests

	Degree of Linguistic Demand		
Degree of Cultural Loading	Low	Moderate	High
Low	**MATRIX REASONING** (*Gf-I*) *Geometric Designs (*Gv-Vz*)	**BLOCK DESIGN** (*Gv-SR, Vz*) **SYMBOL SEARCH** (*Gs-R9*) **DIGIT SPAN** (*Gsm-MS*) **DIGIT SYMBOL-CODING** (*Gs-R9*) **CODING** (*Gs-R9*)	**LETTER-NUMBER SEQUENCING** (*Gsm-MW*)
Moderate	*OBJECT ASSEMBLY (*Gv-CS, SR*) *Mazes (*Gv-SS*)	*ARITHMETIC (*Gq-A3, Gf-RQ*) *Animal Pegs (*Gs-R9*) Picture Arrangement† (*Gv, Gc*)	*Sentences† (*Gsm-MS, Gc-LD*)
High	*Picture Completion† (*Gv-CF, Gc-K0*)		*INFORMATION (*Gc-K0*) *SIMILARITIES (*Gc-LD,VL*) *VOCABULARY (*Gc-LD,VL*) *COMPREHENSION (*Gc-LD, K0*)

Note: Tests printed in bold/uppercase letters are strong measures as defined empirically; tests printed in bold/lowercase letters are moderate measures as defined empirically; tests printed in regular type/lowercase letters were classified logically (see McGrew and Flanagan, 1998).

*Indicates subtests which appear on the WPPSI-R

†These tests demonstrate mixed loadings on the two separate factors indicated.

backgrounds. And second, by understanding that patterns of test performance for culturally and linguistically diverse individuals are reflected in the structure of the classifications, examiners may be able to guide their interpretation of obtained results in a less discriminatory manner. As such, examiners may be able to more appropriately and equitably meet the needs of culturally and linguistically diverse populations within the context of a broader, defensible system of multilingual, nondiscriminatory, cross-cultural assessment (cf. Dana, 1993; Gonzalez, Brusca-Vega, & Yawkey, 1997; Figueroa, 1990a; Hamayan & Damico, 1991a; Valdés & Figueroa, 1994).

These classifications may also serve as a starting point for researchers and practitioners to establish empirically supportable standards of practice with respect to test selection. Although it is clear that more research is necessary to provide an objective basis for understanding the cultural and linguistic demands on cognitive ability test performance, the classifications presented in Table 8.2 provide a viable framework to guide such research. Their limitations notwithstanding, these classifications offer a systematic and defensible method by which decisions regarding culturally fair assessment can be made. Used in conjunction with other information relevant to appropriate cross-cultural assessment (e.g., level of acculturation, language proficiency, socioeconomic status, academic history, and developmental data), these classifications should prove to be of practical value in decreasing the bias found in both test selection and interpretation.

Application of the Wechsler Scales with Diverse Populations

Instruments that are truly nondiscriminatory do not, and may never exist, especially when applied to individuals of diverse cultural and linguistic backgrounds. Coupled with the absence of practical frameworks to guide such assessments, it should come as no surprise that psychologists have had relatively little choice but to rely on the use of assessment techniques and Wechsler batteries that may be inappropriate or of limited utility in understanding the intellectual functioning of culturally and linguistically diverse individuals (Flanagan & Miranda, 1995; Lopez, 1997; Ochoa, Powell, & Robles-Pina, 1996). For example, the most commonly used instruments with culturally and linguistically diverse students include the WISC/WAIS (administered in English), the Bender, the Draw A Person, and the Leiter (see Ochoa et al., 1996). As discussed previously, this battery of tests is problematic for use with these populations for a variety of reasons (e.g., unidimensional assessments, linguistic and cultural confounds, etc.; see Lopez, 1997; McCallum & Bracken, 1997 for a discussion). Although a combination of tests is typically used to assess culturally and linguistically diverse populations because "no single instrument is a panacea for the complex problem of conducting cognitive assessment... fairly and equitably" in these groups (Holtzman & Wilkinson, 1991, p. 251; cf. Ochoa et al., 1996), the selection of instruments is typically unsystematic—reflecting a lack of understanding of the crucial issues in bilingual, cross-cultural assessment. It is recognized that substantive integration of the principles of *Gf-Gc* cross-battery assessment into a comprehensive bilingual, cross-cultural, nondiscriminatory assessment framework is well beyond the scope and purpose of this chapter. However, the general guidelines offered in this chapter may well complement the practice of assessment with diverse individuals and can assist in identifying more culturally and linguistically fair tests of intelligence and cognitive ability.

Hypothesis-Driven Assessment

The purpose of this section is to demonstrate how an appropriate cognitive assessment battery for individuals with varying levels of acculturation and English language proficiency can be designed using the Wechsler Scales and the descriptions of cognitive ability tests provided in Tables 8.2 and 8.3 as a guide. It is our contention that an empirically based selection of a set of tests known to assess a particular construct, combined with consideration of the relevant cultural and linguistic factors, may provide more valid assessment data than that which is ordinarily obtained through the use of a single intelligence battery. Even when one or more of the Wechsler Scales are used to form the foundation of any given assessment battery, the *Gf-Gc*-based cross-battery assessments developed from the matrices presented in Tables 8.2 and 8.3 will be unique to each individual being assessed, differing only as a function of the specific language competencies and cultural experiences of the examinee and the nature of the referral concerns. As will become evident in the example to follow, the ultimate goal in constructing a *Gf-Gc* cross-battery-based set of tests for use with diverse individuals is to ensure a balance between empirical issues and considerations related to cultural and linguistic factors.

The following example is consistent with Kamphaus' (1993) guidelines regarding the nature of the assessment and interpretation process. The reader is referred to Figure 7.1 in Chapter 7 for a review of the stages and decision points involved in the process as it applies within the context of a cross-battery approach. In the assessment of individuals from culturally and linguistically diverse backgrounds, it is recommended that hypotheses related to culture or language differences be developed and evaluated as potential contributors to the suspected learning problems before engaging in standardized testing. Moreover, as in the previous examples presented in this book, it is assumed that the assessment and interpretation process described in this chapter occurs as a result of a decision that standardized testing is warranted and that it forms but a single component of a broader ecosystemically based assessment framework.

Recall that both the broad approach to assessment and the hypothesis-driven format are necessary in order to prevent confirmation or confirmatory bias (Sandoval, Frisby, Geisenger, Scheuneman, & Grenier, 1998). Prereferral assessment and postreferral assessment should continue to operate under the notion that the child's learning difficulties are the result of some externally based systemic or environmental factor and that the child is not deficient or disabled. In every case where *a priori* and *a posteriori* hypotheses are evaluated, this stance forms the null hypothesis in the assessment process and should not be rejected in favor of an alternative hypothesis (that the child, may in fact have a deficit or disability) until the preponderance of data suggest otherwise (according to criteria set by the assessor or assessors). Use of a hypothesis-driven process couched within an ecosystemic framework helps to keep the assessment firmly rooted in more equitable and less discriminatory practices. By ensuring that all available data are evaluated fairly and carefully and that the data are allowed to support or refute any viable hypothesis, not simply the notion that the child is disabled, the practitioner is much less likely to identify a child as having a deficit, when in fact he does not. Conversely, the practitioner may also be more likely to fail in identifying a disability, when in fact one does exist. However, the negative implications of this latter type of error can be argued to be significantly less than that of the former type.

Use of the selective *Gf-Gc* cross-battery approach with diverse individuals is designed to reduce discrimination that arises from instrument selection and subsequent interpretation. Although the other potential sources of bias that may be found throughout the assessment process (e.g., inappropriate cross-cultural transactions, failure to use culture as the context for framing behavior; see Table 8.1) are not specifically attended to by this approach, the selective *Gf-Gc* framework focuses on issues that are quite common and well within the professional reach of practicing psychologists. The following case demonstrates only one of many test combinations that can be used to more effectively and accurately assess the cognitive abilities of children and adults from diverse cultural and linguistic backgrounds.

A Selective Wechsler-Based *Gf-Gc* Cross-Battery Example

Preassessment Considerations.   Let us suppose that Examiner B has been invited to an educational planning meeting to discuss the case of Belisa, a 5-year-old child who has been attending a Headstart program in her area for almost two years. Over the course of her preschool education, Belisa has experienced more difficulty than her classmates in mastering many of the readiness and preparatory skills being taught in the program. Even when compared to other children of the same age with comparable cultural and linguistic histories, Belisa is not developing at the rate which would ordinarily be expected. Because Belisa comes from both a culturally and linguistically diverse background, Examiner B's (and other professionals') presence at this meeting is extremely important in order to assist in evaluating whether or not these factors might be the primary cause of her learning difficulties.

After carefully reviewing Belisa's existing educational records, examining work samples provided by her present and previous teachers, evaluating information offered by the parent, comparing various aspects of performance with other children of similar cultural and linguistic backgrounds, and analyzing the interventions and modifications already attempted to ameliorate her learning difficulties, the members in attendance (including the parent) decided that Belisa's cultural and linguistic experiences were probably contributing to the observed learning difficulties, but were not necessarily the *primary* causes of them.

Because cultural and linguistic influences did not appear sufficient to fully account for the degree of academic impairment evident in Belisa's work, the members believed that a focused evaluation of her cognitive functioning through the use of standardized norm-referenced tests might be helpful. Examiner B, a psychologist, was asked to perform the evaluation in the hope that the results might lead to the development of appropriate curricular and teaching modifications and interventions. With permission from Belisa's parents, Examiner B began the process of cognitive assessment for the purpose of intervention, and not merely diagnosis.[1]

One of the most important preassessment considerations involves the relationship between assessment and intervention. Reschly (1990) comments that "cognitive assessment should be pursued only after interventions have been attempted systematically and evaluated rigorously, and then only when learning problems appear to be pervasive and persistent" (p. 262). Assessments that focus on diagnosis do not retain their link to intervention even when prior interventions have been unsuccessful. The process of measuring an individual's functioning is not, in and of itself, an intervention but a focused attempt to generate data that enhances the understanding of the individual's learning needs. Whether or not a particular case involves cultural or linguistic factors, practitioners should remain aware that implications for intervention exist irrespective of the success or failure of attempts to identify suspected cognitive functioning deficits.

A final preassessment consideration involves issues related to the language or languages to be used in assessment. In the case of individuals with dual-language backgrounds, it is preferable (if not legally required) that assessment be conducted by a professional who is competent in both the oral and written languages of the examinee and who is trained and prepared to assess the cultural and ethnic factors relevant to the individual being assessed.[2] In the event that no examiner with those qualifications is available to conduct the necessary assessment, modifications and adaptations to the testing situation will be required. Although the issues and problems inherent in such assessment are very important in nondiscriminatory assessment, they are well beyond the scope of this chapter (see Hamayan & Damico, 1991a or Valdés & Figueroa, 1994 for a comprehensive discussion of this topic). Cross-battery assessment in English in no way precludes identical or different cross-battery assessment in the native language. The major limitations in doing so will revolve around the availability (or lack thereof) of appropriate assessment instruments. Therefore, the following discussion provides a reasonable illustration of the process of selective cross-battery assessment irrespective of the language or languages in which the assessment is conducted.

Developing* A Priori *Hypotheses.   Examiner B's initial step involves the application of *Gf-Gc* theory and research as the basis for linking Belisa's observed patterns of learning difficulties with the logically related area or areas of disability; in this case, specific learning disability. This step requires knowledge of the relationships between cognitive abilities and processes and the development of academic skills which were outlined earlier in Chapter 3. For the sake of illustration, we will say that the members present at the educational planning meeting identified several particular difficulties including (1) inconsistent immediate recall of new but simple words and basic facts, even after numerous and repeated presentations; (2) exceedingly slow completion of relatively simple coloring and prewriting tasks; and (3) persistent orientation difficulties with forms and poor pattern matching with blocks.

On the basis of this information, Examiner B *reasoned* that Belisa would likely demonstrate difficulty on tasks that measure *Gsm, Gs,* and *Gv*. The basis for the decision to evaluate these particular cognitive domains was made after reviewing the literature on the relationship between developmental academic difficulties and cognitive processes (see Chapter 3 for a discussion), and considering the logical implications of the observed difficulties (McGrew, 1994; McGrew & Knopik, 1993). For example, Belisa's problems in immediately recalling words and facts might suggest problems with short-term memory *(Gsm)*. The observation that Belisa labored tremendously to complete simple worksheets seemed to implicate difficulties with processing speed *(Gs)*. And finally, Belisa's difficulties in learning and maintaining proper form and directional orientation as well as in matching and constructing simple patterns with blocks were viewed as potential indicators of visual processing difficulties *(Gv)*. It is important to note that Examiner B's reasoning and deductions assist in focusing the evaluation on the areas that appear to be most relevant to the referral question, thereby eliminating the need to investigate areas that are unlikely to offer useful information.

In keeping with Kamphaus' (1993) approach, Examiner B hypothesized *a priori* that Belisa's functioning in all areas to be tested would be within the average range (the null hypothesis—i.e., no deficits exist). The alternative hypothesis in each case would be that Belisa's functioning in one or more of the areas would not be within the average range (i.e., deficits may exist). To make these *a priori* hypotheses testable, Examiner B specified that in order to reject the null hypothesis, the standard score range associated with each of these broad-ability clusters would have to extend to or beyond –1 standard deviation from the normative mean, suggesting a normative weakness.[3] Standard score ranges that do not extend beyond this criterion level would be insufficient to reject the null hypothesis in favor of the alternative. At this point, Examiner B has integrated her knowledge of *Gf-Gc* theory and research with the available literature on developmental learning disabilities in order to formulate logical, specific, and testable *a priori* hypotheses, thereby creating defensible links between theory, research, and subsequent interpretation (Kamphaus, 1993).

Selection of *Gf-Gc* Cross-Battery Tests

Once the potential areas of difficulty believed to be related to Belisa's learning problems had been identified and the appropriate *a priori* hypotheses specified, Examiner B's next step involved constructing a battery of tests with reduced cultural content and minimal language demands for use in assessing the relevant cognitive abilities. Examiner B began by reviewing the tests contained in the upper portion of Table 8.2, since these measures were classified as having the lowest comparative language demands and a relatively low degree of cultural loading. However, in addition to considering cultural and linguistic factors, Examiner B attempted to adhere to the *Gf-Gc* cross-battery guiding principles when constructing the battery to allow for a psychometrically and theoretically defensible assessment. That is, she attempted to use the smallest number of different batteries, include two or more qualitatively different indicators of each broad *Gf-Gc* ability, and select tests of *Gf-Gc* abilities that were empirically (rather than logically) classified. Thus, Examiner B's task of building a battery of tests to measure Belisa's cognitive performance reflected a delicate and practical balance between (1) representing the breadth of *Gf-Gc* abilities that have been found to be related to the academic achievement areas in which Belisa demonstrated difficulty; (2) selecting tests that were classified as having low degrees of cultural loading and language demands; and (3) identifying the most empirically strong measures of all important *Gf-Gc* abilities, while keeping the number of tasks and batteries to a minimum.

In order to help illuminate the nature of this decision process, some of the most common intelligence batteries used with preschool-age children have been placed in a matrix that represents the cultural loadings and linguistic demands of their respective subtests. This information is available in Table 8.4.

Table 8.4 provides an illustration of the matrix formed when the preschool age-appropriate subtests from the WPPSI-R, DAS, and K-ABC are classified together according to degree of cultural loading, degree of linguistic demand, and *Gf-Gc* broad- and narrow-ability loadings. A cursory review of the table highlights several general, but important points related to the specifics of the decision-making process.

First, it is clear that no single battery used with preschool-age children provides adequate representation of more than three broad *Gf-Gc* abilities (see Flanagan, Mascolo, & Genshaft, in press for a review). While the WPPSI-R and the DAS have full representation of *Gv* and *Gc* and the K-ABC has adequate representation of *Gsm* and *Gv*, these batteries either underrepresent or do not measure the other broad *Gf-Gc* abilities. Depending on which of the many *Gf-Gc* abilities need to be assessed in preschool age children, it appears likely that such assessment can only be accomplished by crossing two or more distinct batteries (Flanagan et al., in press). Moreover, nearly one-third of the tests listed in Table 8.4 are classified as being high in cultural loading, linguistic demand, or both. The bulk of these tests have been shown to be measures of *Gc,* reflecting the acquisition of facts and knowledge, and they tend to be quite verbal in nature, especially in terms of the language skills required by examinees. As such, unless necessary, these tests are best avoided in the assessment of culturally and linguistically diverse individuals as they are less likely to provide valid estimates of true ability. Furthermore, those tests which are less culturally loaded and which have fewer language demands tend to converge primarily on the factor of visual processing *(Gv).* Of the 18 subtests that are classified as low or moderate on both cultural loading and linguistic demand, 10 are measures of *Gv.* Clearly, when the *Gf-Gc* abilities of interest are other than visual processing in nature, the examiner will be hard pressed to remain faithful to every one of the *Gf-Gc* guiding principles; defensible concessions will need to be made.

Decision Rationale: *Gsm*

In conjunction with the information presented above (gathered essentially from Table 8.2) and other relevant factors (including Belisa's age, the nature of the suspected relationship between cognitive abilities and academic achievement, and the need to assess particular *Gf-Gc* constructs), Examiner B selected what she believed to be the most appropriate combination of subtests for Belisa's assessment. The various subtests selected by Examiner B span across the WPPSI-R, K-ABC, and Leiter-R batteries. The following considerations illustrate the rationale for Examiner B's selections.

With respect to the assessment of Belisa's short-term memory ability *(Gsm),* Table 8.4 revealed that there were four possible subtest choices: Sentences (WPPSI-R), Recall of Digits (DAS), Word Order (K-ABC), and Number Recall (K-ABC). Although Examiner B was interested in utilizing Wechsler-based tests, she rejected Sentences (WPPSI-R) because it was classified as being high in linguistic demand and moderate in cultural loading, and because it was logically rather than empirically related to the construct. Examiner

TABLE 8.4 Matrix of Cultural Loading and Linguistic Demand Classifications of the WPPSI-R, DAS,* and K-ABC

Degree of Linguistic Demand

	Low	Moderate	High
Low (Cultural Loading)	WPS-Geometric Designs (Gv-Vz) DAS-Pattern Construction (Gv-Sr) DAS-Block Building (GV-Vz) DAS-Matching Letter-Like Forms (Gv-Vz)	**WPS-BLOCK DESIGN** (Gv-SR, Vz) DAS-Recall of Digits (Gsm-MS) **KBC-NUMBER RECALL** (Gsm-MS)	
Moderate (Cultural Loading)	**WPS-OBJECT ASSEMBLY** (Gv-CS,SR) **WPS-Mazes** (Gv-SS) DAS-Picture Similarities (Gf-I) DAS-Recognition of Pictures (Gv-MV) KBC-Face Recognition (Gv-MV) **KBC-WORD ORDER** (Gsm-MS) KBC-Magic Window (Gv-PI) **KBC-Gestalt Closure** (Gv-CS)	**WPS-ARITHMETIC** (Gq-A3, Gf-RQ) WPS-Animal Pegs (Gs-R9) DAS-Early Number concepts (Gq-A3,KM)	WPS-Sentences† (Gsm-MS, Gc-LD)
High (Cultural Loading)	WPS-Picture Completion† (Gv-CF, Gc-K0)	DAS-Verbal Comprehension (Gc-LD,LS) DAS-Naming Vocabulary (Gc-LD,VL)	**WPS-INFORMATION** (Gc-K0) **WPS-SIMILARITIES** (Gc-LD,VL) **WPS-VOCABULARY** (Gc-LD,VL) **WPS-COMPREHENSION** (Gc-LD,K0)

Degree of Cultural Loading

WPS = Wechsler Preschool and Primary Scale of Intelligence-Revised; DAS = Differential Abilities Scales; KBC = Kaufman Assessment Battery for Children.

Note: Tests printed in bold/uppercase letters are strong measures as defined empirically; tests printed in bold/lowercase letters are moderate measures as defined empirically; tests printed in regular type/lowercase letters were classified logically (see McGrew and Flanagan, 1998).

*Only the tests appropriate for children of at least three years of age are listed.

†These tests demonstrate mixed loadings on the two separate factors indicated.

B noticed that both Number Recall (K-ABC) and Recall of Digits (DAS) were moderate in linguistic demand and low in cultural loading and that Word Order (K-ABC) was moderate in cultural loading and low in linguistic demand. This made all three subtests appropriate for Belisa's case. Examiner B chose to go with the K-ABC subtests which have strong, empirical relationships to the construct, instead of the DAS subtest, which is classified logically, and therefore, less defensible. Moreover, this choice eliminated the need to use two separate batteries in assessing this construct, thereby maintaining efficiency in the assessment. It should be noted, however, that although there are two subtests measuring *Gsm*, both of these tests measure the same narrow ability (Memory Span [MS]). Therefore, they will yield a cluster average for that narrow ability which is only an estimate (rather than a statistically valid measure) of the *Gsm* broad factor. Since concessions are necessary at times in cross-battery assessment, having two measures of the same narrow ability for *Gsm* for this case is seen as acceptable.

Decision Rationale: *Gs*

Examiner B's attempts to select the best combination of tests with which to assess Belisa's processing speed ability *(Gs)* revealed a different obstacle in construct representation (viz., a dearth of subtests to choose from). For example, the only subtest from the three batteries classified in Table 8.4 which measures the broad *Gs* factor is Animal Pegs from the WPPSI-R. Animal Pegs is classified as being moderate in both cultural loading and linguistic demand and is classified logically with respect to representing the broad *Gs* factor. Although the properties of this subtest make it less than ideal for the purposes of this case, they do not make it inappropriate either. In wanting to adhere to the principle of parsimony in crossing batteries, Examiner B had hoped to supplement Animal Pegs with a subtest from the K-ABC. However, because none were available, Examiner B was forced to use the Attention Sustained subtest from the Leiter-R. A review of the classification of Attention Sustained in Table 8.2 reveals it to be low in linguistic demand, moderate in cultural loading, appropriate for children of Belisa's age, albeit logically rather than empirically classified. While these two subtests have certain shortcomings, in combination, they do have the advantage of measuring distinct narrow abilities (Animal Pegs: Rate-of-test-taking [R9]; and Attention Sustained: Perceptual Speed [P]) which will provide a valid measure of the broad *Gs* construct. As in the previous paragraph, the concessions made in this regard are seen as an appropriate and acceptable balance between the many factors and variables involved.

Decision Rationale: *Gv*

In her efforts to assess Belisa's visual processing *(Gv)* ability, Examiner B had significantly more choices and alternatives than she had when selecting tests to measure *Gsm* and *Gs*. This allowed Examiner B the luxury of weighing the advantages and disadvantages of all available *Gv* tests before making her selection. For example, while the DAS Pattern Construction and Block Building subtests had the advantage of being classified as low on both the cultural loading and linguistic demand dimensions, they had the disadvantage of being logically, rather than empirically classified. Moreover, because none of the DAS subtests had been selected as of yet (for use in assessing other constructs), this would have entailed crossing yet one more battery, for a total of four. Therefore, Examiner B looked at other test choices, including the three available subtests from the K-ABC, which were classified as having moderate cultural loading and low linguistic demand. However, as with the DAS subtests, two of the K-ABC tests were classified logically; only Gestalt Closure has an empirical relationship to the broad *Gv* factor. Finally, Examiner B came across two subtests which she believed were most appropriate: Object Assembly and Block Design from the WPPSI-R. Each subtest was moderate in one dimension and low in the other with respect to cultural loading and linguistic demand. In addition, each subtest has a strong, empirical relationship to the broad *Gv* factor and each one measures a qualitatively different narrow ability (Object Assembly: Closure Speed [CS]; Block Design: Spatial Relations [SR]) which will result in a valid broad factor score. And finally, since Examiner B had already selected a WPPSI-R subtest, this combination also kept the number of batteries crossed to a minimum—three subtests from the WPPSI-R, two from the K-ABC, and one from the Leiter-R.

Taken together, the decisions outlined above represent a reasonable balance between the relevant cultural and linguistic influences unique to Belisa's case and the need to retain empirically based, theoretically defensible methods and procedures. The specific combination of tests selected by Examiner B are presented in Table 8.5.

Interpretation of Results and Evaluation of Hypotheses

Once Examiner B concluded her administration and scoring of the tests comprising the *Gf-Gc* cross-battery developed for Belisa, she was then ready to evaluate the previously specified *a priori* hypotheses. In general, if the established criterion of −1 SD difference between the obtained standard score ranges and the normative mean was found in one or

TABLE 8.5   Belisa's *Gf-Gc* Cross-Battery Assessment

			Degree of Linguistic Demand			
		Low		*Moderate*		
		Battery	*Subtest*	*Battery*	*Subtest*	Gf-Gc *Ability*
Degree of Cultural Loading	*Low*			WPPSI-R K-ABC	**BLOCK DESIGN** **NUMBER RECALL**	*Gv* (SR) *Gsm* (MS)
	Moderate	WPPSI-R K-ABC Leiter-R	**OBJECT ASSEMBLY** **WORD ORDER** Attention Sustained	WPPSI-R	Animal Pegs	*Gv* (CS) *Gsm* (MS) *Gs* (P) *Gs* (R9)

Note: Tests in bold/capital letters are strong measures as defined empirically; bold/lower case letters indicate moderate measures as defined empirically; regular case letters signify logical classifications. Narrow-ability classifications are reported in parentheses.

more of the broad *Gf-Gc* factors assessed, Examiner B would have strong evidence to conclude that indeed, Belisa has deficits. Thus, the null hypothesis would be rejected in favor of the alternative. If, however, the criterion of –1 SD difference was not found in any of the broad *Gf-Gc* factors assessed, Examiner B would have to continue with the assertion that Belisa, in fact, has no such deficits. The null hypothesis would not be rejected and Belisa's observed educational difficulties could not be attributed to any underlying cognitive difficulties.

Evaluation of whether or not the hypotheses were supported is relatively straightforward when the two subtests used to assess the broad *Gf-Gc* factors measure distinct, and qualitatively different narrow abilities related to the broad factor. When two subtests measuring the *same* narrow ability are used to represent the broad factor, the examiner cannot be as certain that the result is a valid representation of functioning within that broad ability. For example, if the broad factor is assessed using subtests which measure only a single narrow ability, there is always the possibility that true weaknesses were missed. That is, an individual may, in fact, exhibit strength in one narrow ability, yet display significant normative weaknesses in another related, but distinct narrow ability. The converse of this situation (i.e., the individual is perceived to have a weakness in a broad ability when they actually have a strength) is equally problematic. In this case, an individual may perform poorly on a single narrow ability (even when measured twice), yet possess normative strengths in other related, but distinct narrow abilities.

Because the two measures of *Gsm* used to assess Belisa were of the same narrow ability (Memory Span [MS]), if the results indicated a normative weakness in this area, Examiner B would likely need to verify the finding with additional testing. However, because there were no other tests available on either the WPPSI-R, K-ABC, or Leiter-R batteries with which to assess a different narrow ability related to this broad factor (e.g., Working Memory [MW]), Examiner B would need to utilize subtests from another battery. In this example, a review of the *Gsm* Cross-battery Worksheet (see Appendix C) reveals that the Numbers Reversed subtest from the WJ-R/III would be appropriate for Belisa because it provides a measure of Working Memory for children as young as 4 years of age.

Specification of *A Posteriori* Hypotheses

In accordance with Kamphaus' (1993) guidelines regarding the nature of the assessment and interpretation process, Examiner B's next step would involve the specification of an *a posteriori* hypothesis. This hypothesis would be similar to that posited *a priori* (including criterion for evaluation, i.e., –1 SD). For example, Examiner B *reasoned* that because Belisa exhibited difficulties on previously administered measures of Memory Span, she might also demonstrate similar difficulties on tasks measuring Working Memory which is closely related to Memory Span. Results from additional testing that supported the presence of such a weakness might provide evidence in support of the presence of a deficit in short-term memory ability and strengthen the connection between these difficulties in cognitive functioning and Belisa's difficulties in academic performance, most notably reading. Conversely, if additional testing accomplished with Belisa did not demonstrate any difficulties related to Working Memory, Examiner B would need to conclude that these data are insufficient by themselves to support the presence of a true deficit in short-term memory functioning, let alone their relationship to academic performance.

Evaluation of the premises outlined above occurs in exactly the same manner as before. In this case, Examiner B hypothesized *a posteriori* that Belisa's functioning in Working Memory is within the average range (the null hypothesis—i.e., no deficit exists). The alternative hypothesis would be that Belisa's functioning in Working Memory is not within the average range (i.e., a deficit may exist). To test and evaluate this *a posteriori* hypothesis, Examiner B used the same criterion as before, namely that the standard score range associated with Belisa's measured performance on this Working Memory task would have to extend to or beyond −1 SD from the normative mean in order to be considered a true normative weakness and suggestive of a true deficit in functioning. If the obtained standard score range for Belisa on this task does not meet or exceed this criterion level, then the notion that Belisa's functioning in Working Memory is average can not be dismissed. As can be seen, the process of evaluating hypotheses is iterative and driven by the patterns seen in the data gathered in each cycle of assessment. At each step, however, the nature of the hypotheses and how they are specified, tested, and evaluated remains essentially the same.

Whether hypotheses are specified *a priori* or *a posteriori,* their systematic evaluation is both crucial and fundamental to the establishment of a record of rigorous, defensible, and most importantly, less biased assessment. The question as to how many iterations might be necessary rests on a complex and interrelated web of issues including such things as the nature of the referral issues, the specific *Gf-Gc* abilities to be measured, the availability of tests with the proper age range, the specific *Gf-Gc* abilities covered by various batteries, the specific narrow ability (or abilities) measured by each subtest, the empirical relationship of the subtests to the broad *Gf-Gc* factor, and, as was illustrated in this case, the presence and influence of unique cultural or linguistic variables.

In summary, the decision-making process involving a selective cross-battery framework for individuals from diverse cultural and linguistic backgrounds is complex and difficult. Not only must psychologists account for a wide variety of variables not ordinarily addressed in mainstream assessments, they must also gather information that spans the traditional boundaries of various disciplines. This can make the process intimidating and may discourage even those with the best of intentions when there is little time for learning and even less for assessment. We are of the belief, however, that well-reasoned use of the selective *Gf-Gc* cross-battery approach, combined with the hypothesis-driven assessment (Kamphaus, 1993) and interpretive guidelines espoused by Kamphaus and associates (1997) can lead to greater efficiency in the use of precious resources in assessment. Certainly, what has been presented here is not a complete solution to the dilemma posed by the need to assess diverse individuals. However, with proper planning and the use of the systematic approach outlined above, a psychologist should be able to select and assemble an appropriate set of tests that have a strong empirical basis and can reduce the potential discriminatory aspects involved in their use with diverse populations, without creating an inordinate burden on resources.

Conclusion

The nature of assessment with culturally and linguistically diverse individuals hinges on the examiner's ability to understand exactly the manner in which tests of intelligence may fail to accurately measure what they purport to measure in such individuals. The current Wechsler Scales (and other similar major intelligence batteries published in the United States today) continue to be the most utilized options for assessing cognitive functioning in culturally and linguistically diverse populations. However, when they are applied to individuals from diverse cultural and linguistic backgrounds, they should be used in a careful and systematic manner in order to reduce the potentially discriminatory aspects of their application. Astute examiners need to stay cognizant of the fact that although such tests are not biased per se, they are in every sense culturally loaded and linguistically demanding. Whenever such tests are used with individuals from diverse backgrounds, there exists the possibility that what is actually being measured is not cognitive functioning, but rather may be more reflective of acculturation and English language proficiency. Use of the selective *Gf-Gc* cross-battery approach, described in this chapter, offers one method by which systematic *selection* and interpretation of test and batteries can be accomplished, and which may help improve both the validity of the measurement as well as the interpretations that follow.

The information presented in this chapter can assist examiners in selecting tests within a *Gf-Gc* cross-battery framework that may ultimately prove to be a less discriminatory and more valid model for the assessment of the cognitive abilities in individuals from culturally and linguistically diverse backgrounds. Because selective *Gf-Gc* cross-battery assessments are supported by a body of research on the relations between *Gf-Gc* abilities and academic achievement, they (1) increase the likelihood that the abilities most closely associated with academic referrals are well represented in the assessment; and (2) can reduce or eliminate the evaluation of abilities unrelated to the achievement skill(s) in question. For these reasons alone, selective cross-battery assessments are more likely to provide adequate measurement of cognitive abilities and processes that underlie specific academic learning disabilities than that provided by a single intelligence battery. However, when combined with the proper considerations necessary to more equitably and fairly assess diverse individuals, (i.e., extensions related to the cultural and linguistic dimensions of tests) selective *Gf-Gc* cross-battery assessments can also facilitate the reduction of cultural loading and linguistic demand that may adversely affect test performance.

The latter portion of this chapter offered a theoretical case study example of a WPPSI-R/K-ABC/Leiter-R-based cross-battery assessment for a young child with cultural and linguistic differences. The example given illustrated the steps and decisions involved in creating an initial, but defensible framework for selecting cognitive ability tests that may provide fairer, and perhaps more valid, assessment of the cognitive capabilities of culturally and linguistically diverse populations. Careful and deliberate use of the classification tables presented in this chapter can help psychologists to evaluate and balance the issues relevant to such assessment, including (1) the underlying *Gf-Gc* ability measured by a test; (2) the extent to which a test is dependent on the prior acquisition of culturally based knowledge; and (3) the level and type of language skills required by a test in order for the examinee to comprehend and respond appropriately.

The treatment of the issues involved in bilingual, cross-cultural assessment presented in this chapter is rather brief and certainly not comprehensive or detailed. The primary focus has been on test selection and there are numerous other substantive issues that fall beyond the limits of this chapter. However, because the approach to conducting cognitive ability assessments of multilingual and multicultural populations offered in this chapter is grounded in contemporary theory and research, and because it is sensitive to cultural and linguistic influences on test performance, it is believed to offer a more appropriate means of assessing the cognitive abilities of individuals from diverse groups than does the use of a single intelligence battery or the unsystematic selection of various tests. Of course, the efficacy of such practice and its underlying assumptions awaits additional empirical support.

ENDNOTES

1. The nature of the decision process described in this paragraph is central to nondiscriminatory assessment of diverse children. In fact, the prereferral process is the appropriate forum for beginning the assessment and intervention process irrespective of whether a child is or is not referred for special education evaluation. Unfortunately, substantive discussion of these issues is well beyond the scope and intent of this chapter. The reader is referred to Gonzalez, Brusca-Vega, and Yawkey (1997), and Hamayan and Damico (1991) for a more in-depth treatment of the subject.

2. Prior to assessing individuals with multilingual backgrounds, measures of native (L1) and English (L2) language proficiency should be administered. Language proficiency data are used in many different ways and for various purposes in dual-language assessment including gauging the appropriateness of a normative comparison group, evaluating the need for test adaptations or modifications, determining the language or languages that will be used during evaluation, and guiding appropriate interpretation of results. According to Lopez (1997), "[t]he level of proficiency should be established in each of the two languages using measures that tap both expressive and receptive skills across context-embedded, interpersonal situations (i.e., BICS) as well as context-reduced, academic conditions (i.e., CALP)" (p. 507). There are a number of informal measures of English and Spanish language proficiency, including questionnaires of language background, observations, and language samples (Ramirez, 1990; cf. Lopez, 1997) and formal measures such as the Woodcock Language Proficiency Battery-Revised (Woodcock, 1991), the Woodcock-Muñoz Language Survey (Woodcock & Muñoz-Sandoval, 1996), and the Oral Language cluster of the Batería-R (Woodcock & Muñoz-Sandoval, 1996). However, formal language proficiency measures in languages other than Spanish are not readily available (Hamayan & Damico, 1991a; Lopez, 1997); the one exception to this is the Bilingual Verbal Ability Test (BVAT; Muñoz-Sandoval, Cummins, Alvarado, & Ruef, 1998) which can assess proficiency in 15 different languages, including Spanish.

3. Typically, a score that is ≥ 1 SD above or below the mean is considered a normative strength or weakness, respectively (Lezak, 1976; 1995).

APPENDIX A

A Network of Validity Evidence for the Wechsler Intelligence Scales

Type of validity evidence

Source	Battery					Substantive		Structural				External					Type of Sample							
	WPPSI WPPSI-R	WISC WISC-R WISC-III	WAIS WAIS-R WAIS-III	WMS WMS-R WMS-III	CMS	Theory development	Content validity	Item analyses	Factor analyses – exploratory	Factor analyses – confirmatory	MDS or cluster analyses	Developmental	Criterion: Concurrent	Criterion: Predictive	Heritability	Neurocognitive	Normal	LD	ADHD	MR	Gifted/talented	Standardization Sample	Developmental Disabilities	Other
Ackerman, P. T., Weir, N. L. et al. (1995)		✓											+					✓						
Allen, S. R. & Thorndike, R. M. (1995a)		✓	✓						+	+												✓		
Anaastopoulos, A. D., Spisto, M. A. et al. (1994)		✓											+						✓					✓
Alfonso, V. C., Zgondy, A. R. et al. (1998)	✓	✓																						
Allen, S. R. & Thorndike, R. M. (1995b)		✓							+	+												✓		
Beal, A. L. (1995)		✓																			✓			
Beal, A. L., Dumont, R., Cruse, C. L. et al. (199a)		✓											+	-				✓						
Beal, A. L., Dumont, R. Cruse, C. L. et al. (199b)		✓											+	+				✓						
Beck, N. C., Ray, J. S. et al. (1983)		✓												+										✓
Blaha, J. & Wallbrown, F. H. (1996)		✓							+													✓		

327

Type of validity evidence

Type of Sample

Source	WPPSI WPPSI-R	WISC WISC-R WISC-III	WAIS WAIS-R WAIS-III	WMS WMS-R WMS-III	CMS	Theory development	Content validity	Item analyses	Factor analyses – exploratory	Factor analyses – confirmatory	MDS or cluster analyses	Developmental	Criterion: Concurrent	Criterion: Predictive	Heritability	Neurocognitive	Normal	LD	ADHD	MR	Gifted/talented	Standardization Sample	Developmental Disabilities	Other
						Substantive		**Structural**				**External**												
Bolen, L. M., Aichinger, K. S. et al. (1995)		✓												+										✓
Boone, D. (1995)			✓									+												✓
Bornstein, R. A., & Chelune, G. J. (1988)			✓	✓					+															✓
Burton, D. B., Naugle, R. I. et al. (1995)			✓							+				+										✓
Callahan, C. D., Schopp, L., & Johnstone, B. (1997)			✓														✓							✓
Campbell, J. M., & McCord, D. M. (1996)			✓							+			-											
Chan, D. W. & Lin, W. Y. (1996)		✓																				✓		
Connery, S., Katz, D., Kaufman, A. S. et al. (1996)		✓											+											✓
Crockett, D. J. T., Hurwitz, T. A. et al. (1996)			✓											+								✓		✓

Type of validity evidence

Source	WPPSI WPPSI-R	WAIS WAIS-R WAIS-III	WISC WISC-R WISC-III	WMS WMS-R WMS-III	CMS	Theory development	Content validity	Item analyses	Factor analyses – exploratory	Factor analyses – confirmatory	MDS or cluster analyses	Developmental	Criterion: Concurrent	Criterion: Predictive	Heritability	Neurocognitive	Normal	LD	ADHD	MR	Gifted/talented	Standardization Sample	Developmental Disabilities	Other
					Battery		Substantive			Structural				External						Type of Sample				
Daley, C. E. & Nagle, R. J. (1996)			✓						+		+		-					✓						
Demsky, Y., Gass, C., & Golden, C. (1997)		✓											✓									✓		
Dixon, W. E. & Anderson, T. (1995)			✓							+												✓		
Donders, J. (1997)			✓							+	+											✓		
Donders, J. (1996)			✓																			✓		
Dumont, R. & Faro, C. (1993)			✓										+	+				✓						
Dumont, R., Cruse, C. L., Price, L. et al. (1996)			✓											+				✓						
Einstein, N. & Engelhart, C. I. (1997)		✓											+											✓
Elwood, R. W. (1991)				✓					-															✓
Faust, D. & Hollingsworth, J. (1991)	✓												+				✓							

329

Type of validity evidence — Type of Sample

Source	WPPSI WPPSI-R	WISC WISC-III	WAIS WAIS-R WAIS-III	WMS WMS-R WMS-III	CMS	Theory development	Content validity	Item analyses	Factor analyses – exploratory	Factor analyses – confirmatory	MDS or cluster analyses	Developmental	Criterion: Concurrent	Criterion: Predictive	Heritability	Neurocognitive	Normal	LD	ADHD	MR	Gifted/talented	Standardization Sample	Developmental Disabilities	Other
Fraboni, M. & Saltstone, R. (1992)			✓								+											✓		
Gaskill, F. W. I. & Brantley, J. C. (1996)		✓												−				✓						
Gerken, K. C. & Hodapp, A. F. (1992)	✓	✓											+	+						✓				
German, D. J. (1996)		✓												+			✓	✓						
Gfeller, Meldrum, & Jacobi (1995)				✓																				✓
Gluting, J. J., McDermott, P. A. et al. (1994)		✓									−		−	−		−						✓		
Gluting, J. J., Youngstrom, E. A. et al. (1997)		✓																				✓		✓
Gluting, J. J., Oakland, T., & Konold, T. R. (1994)		✓											+									✓		
Good, R. H. & Lane, S. (1990)		✓				+				+				−										✓
Graf, M. & Hinton, R. N. (1994)		✓															✓	✓						
Graf, M. & Hinton, R. N. (1997)		✓											+											✓

330

Type of validity evidence

Source	WPPSI-R	WISC WISC-R WISC-III	WAIS WAIS-R WAIS-III	WMS WMS-R WMS-III	CMS	Theory development	Content validity	Item analyses	Factor analyses – exploratory	Factor analyses – confirmatory	MDS or cluster analyses	Developmental	Criterion: Concurrent	Criterion: Predictive	Heritability	Neurocognitive	Normal	LD	ADHD	MR	Gifted/talented	Standardization Sample	Developmental Disabilities	Other
						Substantive		**Structural**				**External**					**Type of Sample**							
Grossman, I., Dennis, B., et al. (1993)			✓										+											✓
Gunter, C. M., Sapp, G. L., & Green, A. C. (1995)		✓												+				✓						
Gutkin, T. B., Reynolds, C. R. et al. (1984)			✓						+													✓		
Hale, R. L. (1981)		✓																						✓
Hale, R. L. (1983)		✓							+				+											✓
Herrera-Graf, M., Dipert, Z. J. et al. (1996)		✓												-										✓
Hoy, C., Gregg, N., Jagota, M. et al. (1993)			✓															✓						
Iverson, G. L., Myers, B. et al. (1996)			✓										+											✓
Johnstone, B., Holland D., & Hewett, J. E. (1997)			✓	✓					+				+											✓
Johnstone, Erdal, & Stadler (1995)				✓									-											✓

Type of validity evidence

Source	WPPSI / WPPSI-R	WISC / WISC-R / WISC-III	WAIS / WAIS-R / WAIS-III	WMS / WMS-R / WMS-III	CMS	Theory development	Content validity	Item analyses	Factor analyses – exploratory	Factor analyses – confirmatory	MDS or cluster analyses	Developmental	Criterion: Concurrent	Criterion: Predictive	Heritability	Neurocognitive	Normal	LD	ADHD	MR	Gifted/talented	Standardization Sample	Developmental Disabilities	Other
Kamphaus, R. W. & Platt, L. O.		✓						+														✓		
Kaplan, C. (1996)	✓													+			✓							
Kaplan (1993)	✓													-			✓							
Kaplan, C. H., Fox, L. M. & Paxton, L. (1991)	✓	✓												+										
Kavale & Forness (1984)																	✓	✓						✓
Karr, S., Crajaval, H., Elser, D. et al. (1993)	✓	✓											+				✓							
Kaufman, A. S., Kaufman, J. C. et al. (1996)		✓							+				-									✓		
Kaufman, A.S. & MacLean, J. E. (1987)		✓															✓							
Keith, T. Z. & Novak, C. G. (1987)		✓							+															✓
Keith, T. Z. & Witta, E. L. (1997)		✓								+												✓		
Kline, R. B., Snyder, J., Guilmette, S. et al. (1992)		✓									+			+										✓

332

Type of validity evidence — Type of Sample

Source	WPPSI-R	WISC WISC-R WISC-III	WAIS WAIS-R WAIS-III	WMS WMS-R WMS-III	CMS	Theory development	Content validity	Item analyses	Factor analyses – exploratory	Factor analyses – confirmatory	MDS or cluster analyses	Developmental	Criterion: Concurrent	Criterion: Predictive	Heritability	Neurocognitive	Normal	LD	ADHD	MR	Gifted/talented	Standardization Sample	Developmental Disabilities	Other
Konold, T. R., Kush, J. C., & Canivez, G. L. (1997)		✓								+								✓		✓				✓
Kush, J. C. (1996)		✓							+									✓						
Laicardi, C., Frustaci, A., & Lauriola, M. (1996)			✓						+								✓							
Lavin, C. (1996a)		✓											+											✓
Lavin, C. (1996b)		✓											+				✓							
Lavin, C. (1996c)		✓											+											✓
Law, J. G. & Faison, L. (1996)		✓											+											✓
Levinson, E. M. & Folino, L. (1994a)		✓											+								✓			
Levinson, E. M. & Folino, L. (1994b)		✓											-								✓			
Lowman, M. G., Schwanz, K. A. et al. (1996)		✓					-						-											
Lukens, J. & Hurrel, R. M. (1996)		✓											-							✓				
Lynn, R. & Cooper, C. (1994)		✓				+		+														✓		

333

Type of validity evidence

Source	Battery					Substantive		Structural				External					Type of Sample							
	WPPSI WPPSI-R	WISC WISC-R WISC-III	WAIS WAIS-R WAIS-III	WMS WMS-R WMS-III	CMS	Theory development	Content validity	Item analyses	Factor analyses – exploratory	Factor analyses – confirmatory	MDS or cluster analyses	Developmental	Criterion: Concurrent	Criterion: Predictive	Heritability	Neurocognitive	Normal	LD	ADHD	MR	Gifted/talented	Standardization Sample	Developmental Disabilities	Other
Lyon, M. A. (1995)		✓											+					✓						✓
Maller, S. J. (1996)		✓						-														✓		✓
McDermott, P. A., Glutting, J. J. et al. (1989)			✓								+											✓		
McDermott, P. A., Glutting, J. J. et al. (1989)		✓									+											✓		
McDermott, P. A., Glutting, J. J. et al. (1992)		✓											✓									✓		✓

Type of Sample · Type of validity evidence

Source	Battery: WPPSI/WPPSI-R	WISC/WISC-R/WISC-III	WAIS/WAIS-R/WAIS-III	WMS/WMS-R/WMS-III	CMS	Substantive: Theory development	Content validity	Structural: Item analyses	Factor analyses – exploratory	Factor analyses – confirmatory	MDS or cluster analyses	External: Developmental	Criterion: Concurrent	Criterion: Predictive	Heritability	Neurocognitive	Sample: Normal	LD	ADHD	MR	Gifted/talented	Standardization Sample	Developmental Disabilities	Other
McGeorge, P., Crawford, J. R. et al. (1996)			✓							+			+				✓							
McGhee, R. & Liberman, L. (1994)		✓				+			+								✓							
McGrew, K. S. & Pehl, J. (1988)		✓											+	+			✓							✓
Meinhardt, M., Hibbett, C., Koller, J. et al. (1993)	✓												+											
Milrod, R. & Rescorla, L. (1991)			✓						+				+				✓							
Morgan, A. W., Sullivan, S. A. et al. (1997)		✓											-				✓	✓						
McGrew, K. S. (1994)		✓											+				✓							
Moffitt & Silva (1987)												-				-								
Moses, Jr., J. A., Pritchard, D. A. et al. (1997)			✓										-			-								✓

335

Type of validity evidence

Type of Sample

Source	WPPSI / WPPSI-R	WISC / WISC-R / WISC-III	WAIS / WAIS-R / WAIS-III	WMS / WMS-R / WMS-III	CMS	Theory development	Content validity	Item analyses	Factor analyses – exploratory	Factor analyses – confirmatory	MDS or cluster analyses	Developmental	Criterion: Concurrent	Criterion: Predictive	Heritability	Neurocognitive	Normal	LD	ADHD	MR	Gifted/talented	Standardization Sample	Developmental Disabilities	Other
O'Gradey, K. E. (1983)			✓							+												✓		
O'Gradey, K. E. (1989)		✓								+												✓		
Nicks, S. D., Leonberger, T. P. et al. (1992)			✓	✓					+															✓
O'Mahoney & Doherty (1993)			✓	✓																				✓
Paolo, A. M. & Ryan, J. J. (1994)			✓										+				✓							
Paolo, A. M., Ryan, J. J. & Troster, A. I. (1997)			✓								+ ·	+ ·		+		+						✓		✓
Paolo, A. M., Ryan, J. J., Troster, A. I. et al. (1996)			✓											+		+								✓
Parker, K. (1983)			✓						+															
Parker, K. C. H. & Atkinson, L. (1995)			✓						+					+								✓		
Parker, K. C. H. & Atkinson, L. (1994)		✓								+												✓		
Pedersen, N. L., Plomin, R. et al. (1994)			✓												+									✓
Phelps, L. (1989)		✓											+ ·								✓			

Battery · Substantive · Structural · External

Type of validity evidence

Source	WPPSI WPPSI-R	WISC WISC-R WISC-III	WAIS WAIS-R WAIS-III	WMS WMS-R WMS-III	CMS	Theory development	Content validity	Item analyses	Factor analyses – exploratory	Factor analyses – confirmatory	MDS or cluster analyses	Developmental	Criterion: Concurrent	Criterion: Predictive	Heritability	Neurocognitive	Normal	LD	ADHD	MR	Gifted/talented	Standardization Sample	Developmental Disabilities	Other
						Battery			Structural			Substantive	External							Type of Sample				
Phelps, L. (1996)			✓										+					✓	✓					✓
Plante, T. & Skyora, C. (1994)		✓											+											✓
Prewett, P. N. (1995)		✓											+											✓
Prewett, P. N. & Matavich, M. A. (1994)		✓												-										✓
Prifitera, A. & Dersh, J. (1992)		✓											+					✓	✓			✓		
Qureshi, M. Y. & Seitz, R. (1994)	✓												-				✓							
Rawling, P. & Brooks, N. (1990)			✓											+										✓
Reitan, R. M. & Wolfson, D. (1996)			✓											+										✓
Reynolds, C. R., Chastain, R. L. et al. (1987)			✓																			✓		
Reynolds, C. R. & Ford, L. (1994)		✓							+				+ -									✓		
Riccio, C. A., Cohen, M. J., Hall, J. et al. (1997)		✓							+									✓	✓					✓
Roid, G. H. & Gyurke, J. (1991)	✓								+	+												✓		

337

Type of validity evidence / Type of Sample

Source	WPPSI WPPSI-R	WISC WISC-R WISC-III	WAIS WAIS-R WAIS-III	WMS WMS-R WMS-III	CMS	Theory development	Content validity	Item analyses	Factor analyses – exploratory	Factor analyses – confirmatory	MDS or cluster analyses	Developmental	Criterion: Concurrent	Criterion: Predictive	Heritability	Neurocognitive	Normal	LD	ADHD	MR	Gifted/talented	Standardization Sample	Developmental Disabilities	Other
					Battery				Structural				External							Type of Sample				
Roid, G. H. & Worrall, W. (1997)		✓								+			✓									✓		
Roszkowski, M. J. (1983)			✓						-				+							✓				
Rothlisberg, B. (1987)		✓											+				✓							
Rust, J. O. & Lindstrom, A. (1996)		✓											+				✓							
Rust, J. O. & Yates, A. G. (1997)		✓							-				+				✓							
Ryan, J. J., Bohac, D. L., & Trent, D. (1994)			✓						+															✓
Ryan, J. J., Paolo, A. M., Miller, D. A. et al. (1997)			✓						+															✓
Ryan, J. J., Dai, X. & Paolo, A. M. (1995)			✓										+											
Ryan, J. J., Weilage, M. E., Lopez, S. J. et al. (1997)			✓											+								✓		✓
Saklofske, D. H., Schwean, V. L. et al. (1994)		✓												+					✓					
Satterfield, W. A., Martin, C. W. et al. (1994)			✓											+										✓
Sattler, J. M. & Atkinson, L. (1993)	✓							+														✓		

338

Type of validity evidence

Source	Battery					Substantive		Structural				External					Type of Sample							
	WPPSI-R	WISC WISC-R WISC-III	WAIS WAIS-R WAIS-III	WMS WMS-R WMS-III	CMS	Theory development	Content validity	Item analyses	Factor analyses – exploratory	Factor analyses – confirmatory	MDS or cluster analyses	Developmental	Criterion: Concurrent	Criterion: Predictive	Heritability	Neurocognitive	Normal	LD	ADHD	MR	Gifted/talented	Standardization Sample	Developmental Disabilities	Other
Schneider, B. H. & Gervaais, M. D. (1991)	✓									+			+								✓			
Sherer, M., Nixon, S. J. et al. (1992)				✓									+			+	✓							✓
Sherman, E. M. S., Strauss, E.. et al. (1995)			✓						+				+			+								✓
Silverstein, A. B. (1982)			✓						+													✓		
Silverstein, A. B. (1976)		✓							+													✓		
Slate, R. (1994)		✓											+					✓						
Slate, R. (1995)		✓											+					✓		✓				
Slate, J. R. & Jones, C. H. (1995)		✓							+					+			✓	✓						
Slate, J. R. & Saarnio, D. A. (1995)		✓												+			✓	✓		✓				
Slate, J. R., Graham, L. S., & Bower, J. (1996)		✓												+			✓	✓		✓				
Smith, T. D., Smith, B. L., & Smithson, M. M.		✓											+											✓

339

Source	WPPSI WPPSI-R	WISC WISC-R WISC-III	WAIS WAIS-R WAIS-III	WMS WMS-R WMS-III	CMS	Theory development	Content validity	Item analyses	Factor analyses – exploratory	Factor analyses – confirmatory	MDS or cluster analyses	Developmental	Criterion: Concurrent	Criterion: Predictive	Heritability	Neurocognitive	Normal	LD	ADHD	MR	Gifted/talented	Standardization Sample	Developmental Disabilities	Other
Spruill, J. (1991)		✓											+							✓				
Stone, B. J. (1991)		✓								+							✓							
Stone, B. J., Gridley, B. E., & Gyurke, J. S. (1991)	✓									+							✓					✓		
Sullivan, P. M. & Montoya, L. A. (1997)		✓							+															✓
Tiholov, T. T., Zawallich, A. et al. (1996)		✓											+	+										✓
Tsushima, W. T. (1994)	✓												+				✓							
Urbina, S. P. & Clayton, J. P. (1991)	✓	✓											+				✓							
Vance, B. & Fuller, G. B. (1995)		✓											+											✓
Vance, H. Maddux, C. D., Fuller, G. B. et al. (1996)		✓												+										✓
Ward, L. C. & Ryan, J. J. (1996)		✓											+									✓		
Watkins, M. W. (1996)		✓											+											✓
Watkins, M. W. & Kush, J. C. (1994)		✓											-											✓

Type of validity evidence — Substantive / Structural / External

Battery

Type of Sample

Type of validity evidence

Source	Battery					Substantive		Structural				External					Type of Sample							
	WPPSI WPPSI-R	WISC WISC-R WISC-III	WAIS WAIS-R WAIS-III	WMS WMS-R WMS-III	CMS	Theory development	Content validity	Item analyses	Factor analyses – exploratory	Factor analyses – confirmatory	MDS or cluster analyses	Developmental	Criterion: Concurrent	Criterion: Predictive	Heritability	Neurocognitive	Normal	LD	ADHD	MR	Gifted/talented	Standardization Sample	Developmental Disabilities	Other
Watkins, M. W., Kush, J. C. et al. (1997)		✓											-					✓				✓		✓
Weiss, L. G. & Prifitera, A. (1995)		✓							+					+								✓		
Zillmer, E. A., Waechtler, C., Harris, B. et al. (1992)			✓																					✓
De Zubicary, G, Smith, G., & Anderson, D. (1996)			✓										-											✓

Note: WPPSI = Wechsler Preschool and Primary Scale of Intelligence (Wechsler, 1967); WPPSI-R = Wechsler Preschool and Primary Scale of Intelligence-Revised (Wechsler, 1989); WISC = Wechsler Intelligence Scale for Children (Wechsler, 1949); WISC-R = Wechsler Intelligence Scale for Children-Revised (Wechsler, 1974); WISC-III = Wechsler Intelligence Scale for Children-Third Edition (Wechsler, 1991); WAIS = Wechsler Adult Intelligence Scale (Wechsler, 1955); WAIS-R = Wechsler Adult Intelligence Scale-Revised (Wechsler, 1981); WAIS-III = Wechsler Adult Intelligence Scale- Third Edition (Wechsler, 1997); WMS = Wechsler Memory Scale (Wechsler, 1974); WMS-R = Wechsler Memory Scale-Revised (Wechsler, 1987); WMS-III = Wechsler Memory Scale-Third Edition (Wechsler, 1997); CMS = Children's Memory Scale (Cohen, 1997). "+" = study provides validity evidence. "-" = study does not provide validity evidence. Complete references may be found in the "References" section of this text.

APPENDIX B

Bibliography of Critical Reviews of the Wechsler Scales

Test Reviews

WAIS-III

None available.

WISC-III

Blumburg, T. A. (1995). A practitioner's view of the WISC-III. *Journal of School Psychology, 33*(1), 95–97.

Braden, J. P. (1995). Review of the Wechsler Intelligence Scale for Children, Third Edition. In J. C. Conoley & J. C. Impara (Eds.), *The twelfth mental measurements yearbook* (pp. 1098–1103). Lincoln, NE: Buros Institute.

Carroll, J. B. (1993). What abilities are measured by the WISC-III? *Journal of Psychoeducational Assessment: WISC-III Monograph,* 134–143.

Edelman, S. (1996). A review of the Wechsler Intelligence Scale for Children—Third Edition (WISC-III). *Measurement, and Evaluation in Counseling and Development, 28,* 219–224.

Edwards, R., & Edwards, J. L. (1993). The WISC-III: A practitioner perspective. *Journal of Psychoeducational Assessment: WISC-III Monograph,* 144–150.

Kaufman, A. S. (1992). Evaluation of the WISC-III and WPPSI-R for gifted children. *Roeper Review, 14*(3), 154–158.

Kaufman, A. S. (1994). King WISC the third assumes the throne. *Journal of School Psychology, 31,* 345–354.

Little, S. (1992). The WISC-III: Everything old is new again. *School Psychology Quarterly, 7*(2), 136–142

Post, K. R., & Mitchell, H. R. (1993). The WISC-III: A reality check. *Journal of School Psychology, 31,* 541–545.

Sandoval, J. (1995). Review of the Wechsler Intelligence Scale for Children, Third Edition. In J. C. Conoley & J. C. Impara (Eds.), *The twelfth mental measurements yearbook* (pp. 1103–1104). Lincoln, NE: Buros Institute.

Shaw, S. R., Swerdlik, M. E., & Laurent, J. (1993). Review of the WISC-III. *Journal of Psychoeducational Assessment, Monograph Series: WISC-III,* 151–160.

Sternberg, R. J. (1993). Rocky's back again: A review of the WISC-III. *Journal of Psychoeducational Assessment: WISC-III Monograph,* 161–164.

WPPSI-R

Bracken, B. A. (1992). Review of the Wechsler Preschool and Primary Scale of Intelligence—Revised. In J. J. Kramer & J. C. Conoley (Eds.), *The eleventh mental measurements yearbook* (pp. 1027–1029). Lincoln, NE: Buros Institute.

Braden, J. P. (1992). Review of the Wechsler Preschool and Primary Scale of Intelligence—Revised. In J. J. Kramer & J. C. Conoley (Eds.), *The eleventh mental measurements yearbook* (pp. 1029–1031). Lincoln, NE: Buros Institute.

Flanagan, D., & Alfonso, V. (1995). A critical review of the technical characteristics of new and recently revised intelligence tests for preschool children. *Journal of Psychoeducational Assessment, 13*(1), 66–90.

Kaufman, A. S. (1990). The WPPSI-R: You can't judge a test by its colors. *Journal of School Psychology, 29*(4), 387–394.

Kaufman, A. S. (1992). Evaluation of the WISC-III and WPPSI-R for gifted children. *Roeper Review, 14*(3), 154–158.

APPENDIX C

Wechsler-Based *Gf-Gc* Cross-Battery Worksheets

Note: The following information pertains to all *Gf-Gc Cross-Battery Worksheets* included in this Appendix. These worksheets were adapted from McGrew and Flanagan (1998).

The Wechsler tests and Wechsler-linked memory tests are enclosed in a bold-faced border. Tests printed in bold/uppercase letters are strong measures as defined empirically; tests printed in bold/lowercase letters are moderate measures as defined empirically; tests printed in regular face/lowercase letters were classified logically. In the case of tests with two probable narrow-ability classifications, the second classification is reported in parentheses. Only probable test classifications are included on the worksheet (tests classified as possible measures are not included). Tests that were classified either empirically or logically as mixed measures are not included on the worksheet. This classification system was described in Chapter 4 of this text. A description of how to use these worksheets appears in Chapter 6.

* If a test score is on a standard score scale other than 100 ± 15, record the score in the column marked by an asterisk. Then refer to the Standard Score Conversion Table (Appendix D) to convert the score to the scale of 100 ± 15. Record the new score in the next column.

** If the cluster includes two or more qualitatively different broad *Gf-Gc* indicators, then place a (✔) next to the word *Broad* and record the appropriate *Gf-Gc* code in the parentheses. If the cluster includes indicators from only one narrow ability subsumed by the broad *Gf-Gc* ability, then place a (✔) next to the word *Narrow* and record the respective narrow-ability code in the parentheses.

For a more complete description of the tests included on these worksheets see Table 5.1 in Chapter 5 of this text.

FLUID INTELLIGENCE (*Gf*) CROSS-BATTERY WORKSHEET
(Flanagan, McGrew, & Ortiz, 2000)

Battery or Test	Age	*Gf* Narrow Abilities Tests	SS*	SS (100±15)
		Induction (I)		
WAIS-III	16-89	**MATRIX REASONING**		
DAS	6-17	**MATRICES**		
DAS	2-5	Picture Similarities		
KAIT	11-85+	**MYSTERY CODES**		
SB:IV	7-24	**MATRICES**		
WJ-R/III	2-85+	**CONCEPT FORMATION**		
CAS	5-17	Nonverbal Matrices		
DTLA-3/4	6-17	**SYMBOLIC RELATIONS**		
Leiter-R	2-6	Classification		
Leiter-R	5-18+	Design Analogies		
Leiter-R	2-18+	Repeated Patterns		
Leiter-R	2-18+	Sequential Order		
UNIT	5-17	**ANALOGIC REASONING**		
Other				
		1. Sum of column		
		2. Divide by number of tests		
		3. **Induction** average		

General Sequential Reasoning (RG)

Battery or Test	Age	Tests	SS*	SS
KAIT	11-85+	**LOGICAL STEPS**		
WJ-R/III	4-85+	**ANALYSIS-SYNTHESIS**		
Leiter-R	2-10	Picture Context		
Leiter-R	6-18+	Visual Coding		
UNIT	5-17	**CUBE DESIGN**		
Other				
		1. Sum of column		
		2. Divide by number of tests		
		3. **General Sequential Reasoning** average		

Quantitative Reasoning (RQ)

Battery or Test	Age	Tests	SS*	SS
DAS	6-17	**SEQ & QUANT REASONING (I)**		
SB:IV	12-24	Equation Building		
SB:IV	7-24	Number Series		
Other				
		1. Sum of column		
		2. Divide by number of tests		
		3. **Quantitative Reasoning** average		

Name:_____
Age: _____
Grade:_____
Examiner:_____
Date of Evaluation: _____

Fluid Intelligence: Mental operations that an individual may use when faced with a relatively novel task that can not be performed automatically.

Induction: Ability to discover the underlying characteristic that governs a problem or set of materials.

General Sequential Reasoning: Ability to start with stated rules, premises or conditions and to engage in one or more steps to reach a solution to a problem.

Quantitative Reasoning: Ability to inductively and deductively reason with concepts involving mathematical relations and properties.

Cluster Average *

__ Broad (___)
__ Narrow (___)

CRYSTALLIZED INTELLIGENCE (*Gc*) CROSS-BATTERY WORKSHEET
(Flanagan, McGrew, & Ortiz, 2000)

Battery or Test	Age	*Gc* Narrow Abilities Tests	SS*	SS (100±15)
Language Development (LD)				
WECH	3-74	**COMPREHENSION (K0)**		
WECH	3-74	**SIMILARITIES (VL)**		
DAS	6-17	**SIMILARITIES**		
DAS	2-5	Verbal Comprehension (LS)		
SB:IV	12-24	**VERBAL RELATIONS**		
SB:IV	2-24	**Comprehension (K0)**		
SB:IV	2-14	**Absurdities**		
DTLA-3/4	6-17	Word Opposites		
DTLA-3/4	6-17	Story Construction		
Other				
		1. Sum of column		
		2. Divide by number of tests		
		3. **Language Development** average		
Lexical Knowledge (VL)				
WECH	3-74	**VOCABULARY (LD)**		
DAS	6-17	**WORD DEFINITIONS (LD)**		
DAS	2-5	Naming Vocabulary (LD)		
SB:IV	2-24	**VOCABULARY (LD)**		
WJ-R	2-85+	**ORAL VOCABULARY (LD)**		
WJ-R	2-85+	**PICTURE VOCABULARY (K0)**		
WJ-III	2-85+	**VERBAL COMP (LD)**		
NEPSY	3-4	Body Part Naming (K0)		
Other				
		1. Sum of column		
		2. Divide by number of tests		
		3. **Lexical Knowledge** average		
Listening Ability (LS)				
WJ-R	4-85+	**LISTENING COMP (LD)**		
WJ-III	4-85+	**ORAL COMP (LD)** (in ach. battery)		
NEPSY	3-12	Comp of Instructions (LD)		
Other				
		1. Sum of column		
		2. Divide by number of tests		
		3. **Listening Ability** average		
General Information (K0)				
WECH	3-74	**INFORMATION**		
DTLA-3/4	6-17	Basic Information		
WJ-III	2-85+	**GENERAL INFORMATION**		
Other				
		1. Sum of column		
		2. Divide by number of tests		
		3. **General Information** average		

Information About Culture (K2)				
KAIT	11-85+	**FAMOUS FACES**		
Other				
		1. Sum of column		
		2. Divide by number of tests		
		3. **Information About Culture** average		

Name:_____
Age: _____
Grade:_____
Examiner:_____
Date of Evaluation: _____

Crystallized Intelligence: The breadth and depth of a person's acquired knowledge of a culture and the effective application of this knowledge.

Language Development: General development, or the understanding of words, sentences, and paragraphs (not requiring reading) in spoken native language skills.

Lexical Knowledge: Extent of vocabulary that can be understood in terms of correct word meanings.

Listening Ability: Ability to listen and comprehend oral communications.

General Information: Range of general knowledge.
Information About Culture: Range of cultural knowledge (e.g., music, art).

Sum/No. of Narrow Ability Averages

**Cluster Average ** **
__ Broad (__)
__ Narrow (__)

VISUAL PROCESSING (*Gv*) CROSS-BATTERY WORKSHEET
(Flanagan, McGrew, & Ortiz, 2000)

Battery or Test	Age	*Gv* Narrow Abilities Tests	SS*	SS (100±15)
Spatial Relations (SR)				
WECH	3-74	**BLOCK DESIGN (Vz)**		
DAS	3-17	Pattern Construction		
K-ABC	4-12	**TRIANGLES**		
SB:IV	2-24	**PATTERN ANALYSIS**		
Leiter-R	11-18+	Figure Rotation (Vz)		
UNIT	5-17	Cube Design (Vz)		
Other				
		1. Sum of column		
		2. Divide by number of tests		
		3. **Spatial Relations** average		
Visualization (Vz)				
WPPSI-R	3-7	Geometric Designs (P2)		
DAS	2-3	Block Building		
DAS	4-5	Matching Letter-like Forms		
WJ-R/III	4-85+	**SPATIAL RELATIONS (SR)**		
Leiter-R	2-10	Matching		
Leiter-R	2-18+	Form Completion (SR)		
Leiter-R	11-18+	Paper Folding		
NEPSY	3-12	Block Construction		
Other				
		1. Sum of column		
		2. Divide by number of tests		
		3. **Visualization** average		
Visual Memory (MV)				
WMS-III	16-89	Visual Reproduction I		
CMS	5-16	Dot Locations		
CMS	5-16	Dot Locations 2		
CMS	5-16	Picture Locations		
DAS	6-17	**RECALL OF DESIGNS**		
DAS	3-7	Recognition of Pictures		
K-ABC	2-4	Face Recognition		
KAIT	11-85+	**MEM. FOR BLOCK DESIGNS**		
SB:IV	2-24	**Bead Memory**		
SB:IV	7-24	**Memory for Objects**		
WJ-R/WJIII	4-85+	**Picture Recognition**		
DTLA-3/4	6-17	Design Sequences		
DTLA-3/4	6-17	Design Reproduction		
Leiter-R	4-10	Immediate Recognition		
Leiter-R	2-18+	Forward Memory		
UNIT	5-17	**OBJECT MEMORY**		
UNIT	5-17	**SPATIAL MEMORY**		
UNIT	5-17	**SYMBOLIC MEMORY**		
NEPSY	3-12	Imitating Hand Positions		
Other				
		1. Sum of column		
		2. Divide by number of tests		
		3. **Visual Memory** average		

Name:_____
Age: _____
Grade:_____
Examiner:_____
Date of Evaluation: _____

Visual Processing: The ability to generate, perceive, analyze, synthesize, manipulate, transform, and think with visual patterns and stimuli.

Spatial Relations: Ability to rapidly perceive and manipulate visual patterns or to maintain orientation with respect to objects in space.

Visualization: Ability to mentally manipulate objects or visual patterns and to "see" how they would appear under altered conditions.

Visual Memory: Ability to form and store a mental representation or image of a visual stimulus and then recognize or recall it later.

VISUAL PROCESSING (*Gv*) CROSS-BATTERY WORKSHEET
(Flanagan, McGrew, & Ortiz, 2000)

Battery or Test	Age	*Gv* Narrow Abilities Tests	SS*	SS (100±15)
Closure Speed (CS)				
WECH	3-74	**OBJECT ASSEMBLY (SR)**		
K-ABC	2-12	**Gestalt Closure**		
WJ-R	2-85+	**Visual Closure**		
DTLA-3	6-17	Picture Fragments		
Other				
		1. Sum of column		
		2. Divide by number of tests		
		3. **Closure Speed** average		
Spatial Scanning (SS)				
WISC-III	6-16	**Mazes**		
WPPSI-R	3-7	**Mazes**		
UNIT	5-17	**Mazes**		
NEPSY	5-12	Route Finding		
Other				
		1. Sum of column		
		2. Divide by number of tests		
		3. **Spatial Scanning** average		
Flexibility of Closure (CF)				
CAS	5-17	Figure Memory (MV)		
Leiter-R	2-18+	Figure Ground		
Other				
		1. Sum of column		
		2. Divide by number of tests		
		3. **Flexibility of Closure** average		
Serial Perceptual Integration (PI)				
K-ABC	2-4	Magic Window		
Other				
		1. Sum of column		
		2. Divide by number of tests		
		3. **Serial Perceptual Integration** average		

Closure Speed: Ability to quickly combine disconnected, vague, or partially obscured visual stimuli or patterns into a meaningful whole, without knowing in advance what the pattern is.

Spatial Scanning: Ability to accurately and quickly survey a spatial field or pattern and identify a path through the visual field or pattern.

Flexibility of Closure: Ability to identify a visual figure or pattern embedded in a complex visual array, when knowing in advance what the pattern is.

Serial Perceptual Integration: Ability to identify a pictorial or visual pattern when parts of the pattern are presented rapidly in order.

Sum/No. of Narrow Ability Averages

Cluster Average **

__ Broad (___)
__ Narrow (___)

SHORT-TERM MEMORY (*Gsm*) CROSS-BATTERY WORKSHEET
(Flanagan, McGrew, & Ortiz, 2000)

Battery or Test	Age	*Gsm* Narrow Abilities Tests	SS*	SS (100±15)
Memory Span (MS)				
WAIS-III	6-89	**DIGIT SPAN (MW)**		
WISC-III	6-16	**DIGIT SPAN (MW)**		
CMS	5-16	Numbers (MW)		
CMS	5-16	Stories*** (*Gc*-LS)		
WMS-III	16-89	Logical Memory I*** (*Gc*-LS)		
WMS-III	16-89	Digit Span (MW)		
DAS	3-17	Recall of Digits		
K-ABC	2-12	**NUMBER RECALL**		
K-ABC	4-12	**WORD ORDER**		
SB:IV	7-24	**MEMORY FOR DIGITS (MW)**		
WJ-R/III	4-85+	**MEMORY FOR WORDS**		
CAS	5-17	Word Series		
DTLA-3	6-17	Word Sequences		
NEPSY	5-12	Repetition of Nonsense Words		
NEPSY	3-12	Sentence Repetition		
Other				
		1. Sum of column		
		2. Divide by number of tests		
		3. **Memory Span** average		
Working Memory (MW)				
WAIS-III	16-89	**LETTER-NUMBER SEQ.**		
WMS-III	16-89	Letter-Number Sequencing		
WMS-III	16-89	Mental Control		
CMS	5-16	Sequences		
WJ-R/III	4-85+	**NUMBERS REVERSED**		
WJ-III	4-85+	**AUDITORY WORKING MEM**		
NEPSY	5-12	Knock and Tap		
Other				
		1. Sum of column		
		2. Divide by number of tests		
		3. **Working Memory** average		

Name:_____
Age: _____
Grade:_____
Examiner:_____
Date of Evaluation: _____

Short-term Memory: The ability to apprehend and hold information in immediate awareness and then use it within a few seconds.

Memory Span: Ability to attend to and immediately recall temporally ordered elements in the correct order after a single presentation.

Working Memory: Ability to temporarily store and perform a set of cognitive operations on information that requires divided attention and the management of the limited capacity of short-term memory.

Sum/No. of Narrow Ability Averages

Cluster Average *

__ Broad (___)
__ Narrow (___)

*** Although these tests are mixed measures of two *Gf-Gc* abilities (i.e., they also involve Listening ability in addition to Memory Span), they are included on this worksheet because they are necessary to administer prior to administering Stories 2 and Logical Memory II, respectively (measures of *Glr*- MM).

LONG-TERM RETRIEVAL (*Glr*) CROSS-BATTERY WORKSHEET
(Flanagan, McGrew, & Ortiz, 2000)

Battery or Test	Age	*Glr* Narrow Abilities Tests	SS*	SS (100±15)
Associative Memory (MA)				
WMS-III	16-89	Verbal Paired Associates I		
WMS-III	16-89	Verbal Paired Associates II		
CMS	5-16	Word Pairs		
CMS	5-16	Word Pairs 2		
KAIT	11-85+	**REBUS LEARNING**		
KAIT	11-85+	**REBUS DELAYED RECALL**		
WJ-R	2-85+	**MEMORY FOR NAMES**		
WJ-R/III	2-85+	**VISUAL-AUD LEARNING (MM)**		
WJ-R	4-85+	**DEL REC: MEM FOR NAMES**		
WJ-R/III	4-85+	**Del Rec: Vis-Aud Learning (MM)**		
Leiter-R	4-10	Delayed Recognition		
Leiter-R	2-18+	Associated Pairs (MM)		
Leiter-R	6-18+	Delayed Pairs (MM)		
NEPSY	5-12	Memory for Names		
Other				
		1. Sum of column		
		2. Divide by number of tests		
		3. **Associative Memory** average		

Battery or Test	Age	Tests	SS*	SS
Ideational Fluency (FI)				
WJ-III	4-85+	**RETRIEVAL FLUENCY**		
Other				
		1. Sum of column		
		2. Divide by number of tests		
		3. **Ideational Fluency** average		

Battery or Test	Age	Tests	SS*	SS
Figural Fluency (FF)				
NEPSY	5-12	Design Fluency		
Other				
		1. Sum of column		
		2. Divide by number of tests		
		3. **Figural Fluency** average		

Battery or Test	Age	Tests	SS*	SS
Naming Facility (NA)				
WJ-III	4-85+	**RAPID PICTURE NAMING**		
CAS	5-17	Expressive Attention		
NEPSY	5-12	Speeded Naming		
Other				
		1. Sum of column		
		2. Divide by number of tests		
		3. **Naming Facility** average		

Name:_____
Age: _____
Grade:_____
Examiner:_____
Date of Evaluation: _____

Long-term Retrieval: Ability to store information (e.g., concepts, ideas, items, names) in long-term memory and to fluently retrieve it later through association.

Associative Memory: Ability to recall one part of a previously learned but unrelated pair of items when the other part is presented (i.e., paired-associative learning).

Ideational Fluency: Ability to rapidly produce a series of ideas, words, or phrases related to a specific condition or object.

Naming Facility: Ability to rapidly produce names for concepts.

Free Recall Memory: Ability to recall as many unrelated items as possible, in any order, after a large collection of items is presented.

LONG-TERM RETRIEVAL (*Glr*) CROSS-BATTERY WORKSHEET
(Flanagan, McGrew, & Ortiz, 2000)

Battery or Test	Age	*Glr* Narrow Abilities Tests	SS*	SS (100±15)
Free Recall Memory (M6)				
WMS-III	16-89	Word Lists I		
WMS-III	16-89	Word Lists II (MA)		
CMS	5-16	Word Lists		
CMS	5-16	Word Lists 2 (MA)		
DAS	4-17	Recall of Objects		
NEPSY	7-12	List Learning		
Other				
		1. Sum of column		
		2. Divide by number of tests		
		3. **Free Recall Memory** average		

Battery or Test	Age	*Glr* Narrow Abilities Tests	SS*	SS (100±15)
Meaningful Memory (MM)				
WMS-III	16-74	Logical Memory II		
CMS	5-16	Stories 2		
Other				
		1. Sum of column		
		2. Divide by number of tests		
		3. **Meaningful Memory** average		

Meaningful Memory: Ability to recall a set of items where there is a meaningful relation between items or the items create a meaningful story or connected discourse.

Sum/No. of Narrow Ability Averages

Cluster Average **

__ Broad (___)
__ Narrow (___)

AUDITORY PROCESSING (*Ga*) CROSS-BATTERY WORKSHEET
(Flanagan, McGrew, & Ortiz, 2000)

Battery or Test	Age	*Ga* Narrow Abilities Tests	SS*	SS (100±15)
Phonetic Coding: Analysis (PC:A)				
W-ADT	4-8	Wepman Aud. Discrim. Test		
GFW-TAD	3-70+	GFW Test of Aud. Discrim.		
G-FTA	2-16+	G-F Test of Articulation		
WJ-R/III	2-85+	**INCOMPLETE WORDS**		
TOPA	5-8	Test of Phonological Awareness		
TPAT	5-9	Segmentation		
TPAT	5-9	Isolation		
TPAT	5-9	Deletion		
TPAT	5-9	Rhyming		
NEPSY	3-12	Phonological Processing (PC:S)		
Other				
		1. Sum of column		
		2. Divide by number of tests		
		3. **Phonetic Coding: Analysis** average		

Battery or Test	Age	*Ga* Narrow Abilities Tests	SS*	SS (100±15)
Phonetic Coding: Synthesis (PC:S)				
WJ-R/III	4-85+	**SOUND BLENDING**		
TPAT	5-9	Substitution		
TPAT	5-9	Blending		
Other				
		1. Sum of column		
		2. Divide by number of tests		
		3. **Phonetic Coding: Synthesis** average		

Battery or Test	Age	*Ga* Narrow Abilities Tests	SS*	SS (100±15)
Speech/General Sound Discrimination (US/U3)				
WJ-III	4-85+	**AUDITORY ATTENTION**		
WJ-R	4-85+	**SOUND PATTERNS**		
Other				
		1. Sum of column		
		2. Divide by number of tests		
		3. **Speech/General Sound Disc.** average		

Name:_____
Age: _____
Grade:_____
Examiner:_____
Date of Evaluation: _____

Auditory Processing: Ability to perceive, analyze, and synthesize patterns among auditory stimuli.

Phonetic Coding (Analysis): Ability to process speech sounds, as in identifying, isolating, and analyzing sounds.

Phonetic Coding (Synthesis): Ability to process speech sounds, as in identifying, isolating, and blending or synthesizing sounds.

Speech/General Sound Discrimination: Ability to detect differences in speech sounds under conditions of little distraction or distortion.

Sum/No. of Narrow Ability Averages

Cluster Average *

__ Broad (___)
__ Narrow (___)

PROCESSING SPEED (*Gs*) CROSS-BATTERY WORKSHEET
(Flanagan, McGrew, & Ortiz, 2000)

Battery or Test	Age	*Gs* Narrow Abilities Tests	SS*	SS (100±15)
Perceptual Speed (P)				
WAIS-III	16-74	**SYMBOL SEARCH (R9)**		
WISC-III	6-16	**SYMBOL SEARCH (R9)**		
WJ-R/III	2-85+	**VISUAL MATCHING (R9)**		
WJ-R	4-85+	**CROSS OUT**		
CAS	5-17	Matching Numbers (R9)		
CAS	5-17	Receptive Attention (R4)		
Leiter-R	2-18+	Attention Sustained (R9)		
Other				
		1. Sum of column		
		2. Divide by number of tests		
		3. **Perceptual Speed** Average		
Rate -of-test-taking (R9)				
WAIS-III	16-74	**DIGIT SYMBOL-CODING**		
WISC-III	6-16	**CODING**		
WPPSI-R	3-7	Animal Pegs		
CAS	5-17	Planned Codes		
Other				
		1. Sum of column		
		2. Divide by number of tests		
		3. **Rate-of-test-taking** average		
Mental Comparison Speed (R7)				
DAS	6-17	Speed of Information Processing (R9)		
CAS	5-17	Number Detection (R9)		
WJ-III	4-84+	**DECISION SPEED**		
Other				
		1. Sum of column		
		2. Divide by number of tests		
		3. **Mental Comparison Speed** average		

Name:_____
Age: _____
Grade:_____
Examiner:_____
Date of Evaluation: _____

Processing Speed: Ability to fluently perform cognitive tasks automatically, especially when under pressure to maintain focused attention and concentration.

Perceptual Speed: Ability to rapidly search for and compare visual symbols presented side by side or separated in a visual field.

Rate-of-test-taking: Ability to rapidly perform tests that are relatively easy or that require very simple decisions.

Mental Comparison Speed: Reaction time when the stimuli must be compared for a particula attribute.

Sum/No. of Narrow Ability Averages

**Cluster Average **
__ Broad (__)
__ Narrow (__)

APPENDIX D

Percentile Rank and Standard Score Conversion Table

Percentile Rank and Standard Score Conversion Table

Percentile Rank	Standard Score			
				Wechslers (IQ & Memory Scales) K-ABC/KAIT DTLA 3/4 CAS, Leiter-R NEPSY CMS UNIT
	WJ-R/III (M=100;SD=15)	*DAS (M=50;SD=10)*	*SB-IV (M=50; SD=8)*	*(M=10; SD=3)*
99.99	160	90	82	
99.99	159	89		
99.99	158	89	81	
99.99	157	88		
99.99	156	87	80	
99.99	155	87		
99.99	154	86	79	
99.98	153	85		
99.98	153	85	78	
99.97	152	85		
99.96	151	84	77	
99.95	150	83		
99.94	149	83	76	
99.93	148	82		
99.93	147	81	75	
99.89	146	81		
99.87	145	80	74	19
99.84	144	79		
99.80	143	79	73	
99.75	142	78		
99.70	141	77	72	
99.64	140	77		18
99.57	139	76	71	
99	138	75		
99	138	75	70	
99	137	75		
99	136	74	69	
99	135	73		17
99	134	73	68	
99	133	72		
98	132	71	67	
98	131	71		
98	130	70	66	16
97	129	69		
97	128	69	65	

Percentile Rank	Standard Score			
				Wechslers (IQ & Memory Scales) K-ABC/KAIT DTLA 3/4 CAS, Leiter-R NEPSY CMS UNIT
	WJ-R/III (M=100;SD=15)	DAS (M=50;SD=10)	SB-IV (M=50; SD=8)	(M=10; SD=3)
97	127	68		
96	126	67	64	
95	125	67		15
95	124	66	63	
94	123	65		
93	123	65	62	
92	122	65		
92	121	64	61	
91	120	63		14
89	119	63	60	
88	118	62		
87	117	61	59	
86	116	61		
84	115	60	58	13
83	114	59		
81	113	59	57	
79	112	58		
77	111	57	56	
75	110	57		12
73	109	56	55	
71	108	55		
69	108	55	54	
67	107	55		
65	106	54	53	
65	105	53		11
62	104	53	52	
57	103	52		
55	102	51	51	
52	101	51		
50	100	50	50	10
48	99	49		
45	98	49	49	
43	97	48		
40	96	47	48	
38	95	47		9
35	94	46	47	

(continued)

Percentile Rank	Standard Score			
				Wechslers (IQ & Memory Scales) K-ABC/KAIT DTLA 3/4 CAS, Leiter-R NEPSY CMS UNIT
	WJ-R/III (M=100;SD=15)	DAS (M=50;SD=10)	SB-IV (M=50; SD=8)	(M=10; SD=3)
33	93	45		
31	93	45	46	
29	92	45		
27	91	44	45	
25	90	43		8
23	89	43	44	
21	88	42		
19	87	41	43	
17	86	41		
16	85	40	42	7
14	84	39		
13	83	39	41	
12	82	38		
11	81	37	40	
9	80	37		6
8	79	36	39	
8	78	35		
7	78	35	38	
6	77	35		
5	76	34	37	
5	75	33		5
4	74	33	36	
3	76	32		
3	72	31	35	
3	71	31		
2	70	30	34	4
2	69	29		
2	68	29	33	
1	67	28		
1	66	27	32	
1	65	27		3
1	64	26	31	
1	63	25		
1	63	25	30	
1	62	25		

Percentile Rank	Standard Score			
	WJ-R/III *(M=100;SD=15)*	*DAS* *(M=50;SD=10)*	*SB-IV* *(M=50; SD=8)*	*Wechslers (IQ & Memory Scales) K-ABC/KAIT DTLA 3/4 CAS, Leiter-R NEPSY CMS UNIT (M=10; SD=3)*
0.49	61	24	29	
0.36	60	23		2
0.30	59	23	28	
0.25	58	22		
0.20	57	21	27	
0.16	56	21		
0.16	55	20	26	1
0.11	54	19		
0.09	53	19	25	
0.07	52	18		
0.06	51	17	24	
0.05	50	17		
0.04	49	16	23	
0.03	48	15		
0.02	48	15	22	
0.02	47	15		
0.01	46	14	21	
0.01	44	13	20	
0.01	43	12		
0.01	42	11	19	
0.01	41	11		
0.01	40	10	18	

Wechsler *Gf-Gc* Standard Score Profile

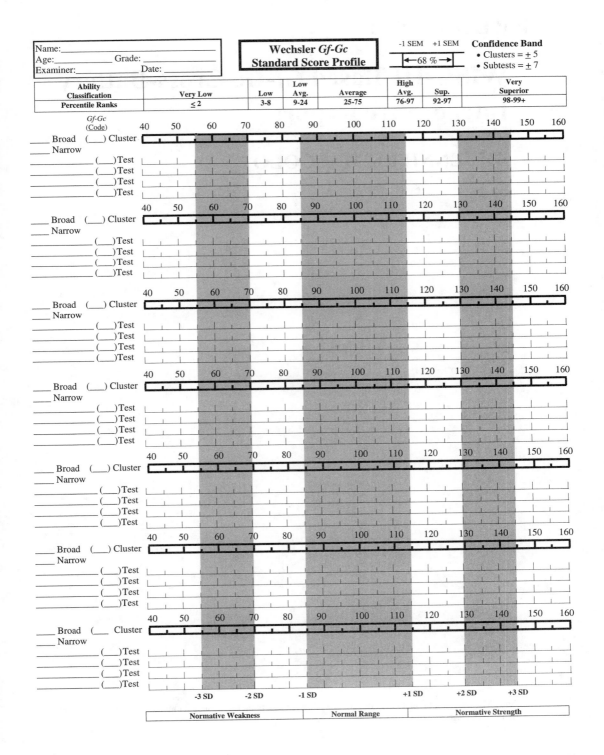

WISC-III-Based *Gf-Gc* Cross-Battery Interpretive Report

BY JENNIFER MASCOLO

Note: The rationale for test selection and procedures for deriving the clusters included in this report are described in detail in Chapters 6 and 7.

Name: Christine
D.O.B.: 4/9/90
Age: 7 years, 9 months
Home Language: English

Grade: 2nd
Evaluator: Examiner A
Date of Evaluation: 1/15/98, 1/22/98
Language of Instruction: English

Primary Referral Concerns

Christine was referred for a psychoeducational evaluation by the school's prereferral intervention team following unsuccessful intervention attempts designed to improve her academic performance in reading. The team, in particular Christine's second-grade teacher, had observed various difficulties in reading, especially with word recognition, decoding and sight-word vocabulary skills. The team also indicated in their referral that Christine had difficulty performing academic tasks that required spelling and written expression. This description of Christine's academic difficulties was corroborated by her reading teacher, who noted that Christine had made little progress, relative to her same-age peers. Likewise, Christine's parents were also in agreement that Christine's progress in reading continued to be slow, despite systematic and sustained modifications and interventions, including one-to-one tutoring, modified instruction and assignments, and the use of computer-assisted learning techniques.

Health and Developmental History

Christine resides with her biological mother and father, each of whom have a high school education. English is the only language spoken in Christine's home. Her family is of mixed Irish and German descent and have resided in the United States for several generations. Christine's mother reported an uneventful pregnancy. Developmental milestones were achieved within normal limits. Christine was reported to be in good health and her medical history is otherwise unremarkable.

Educational History

A review of Christine's academic records revealed that she has demonstrated consistent difficulty in learning the letters and sounds of the alphabet and learning to read and spell. In reading, Christine appeared to make progress through the use of visual context clues. Her mother reported that Christine has always had difficulty remembering information (e.g., nursery rhymes), despite numerous repetitions. This observation is consistent with teacher reports of Christine's difficulty with retaining and transferring information (e.g., writing words she hears). Although Christine achieves at a level commensurate with her peers in mathematics, whenever mathematical problems are complicated by verbal directions, her performance is hampered. Overall, Christine was described by her teachers as a very conscientious child who has good relations with her classmates. Based on a review of Christine's educational records, the nature and success (or failure) of previous instructional interventions, observations by classroom teachers, and other information gathered through the prereferral process, further examination of cognitive abilities through standardized testing appeared to be warranted.

Tests Administered

Wechsler Intelligence Scale for Children—Third Edition (WISC-III) (selected tests)

Woodcock-Johnson Psycho-Educational Battery—Revised, Tests of Cognitive Ability and Tests of Achievement (selected tests)

NEPSY (selected test)

Children's Memory Scale (CMS) (selected tests)

Clinical and Behavioral Observations

Christine approached the evaluation session in a cooperative manner and rapport was established easily. She worked diligently throughout the evaluation and persisted on items she found to be difficult. She also appeared attentive throughout the evaluation and maintained concentration on all tasks. Despite her cooperative and focused manner, Christine demonstrated difficulties on tasks that required visual tracking and she often skipped a line when required to read. Furthermore, when required to reproduce increasingly complex designs using three-dimensional blocks, Christine displayed considerable difficulty. Specifically, on the block design stimulus cards, when the lines that demarcate the blocks that comprise the design were removed, she failed to produce a correct response.

Assessment of Cognitive Functioning

A carefully selected set of tests from the WISC-III, WJ-R, CMS and NEPSY were combined via *Gf-Gc* cross-battery principles and procedures to yield seven broad cognitive ability clusters, including fluid reasoning *(Gf)*, crystallized intelligence *(Gc)*, visual processing *(Gv)*, short-term memory *(Gsm)*, long-term retrieval *(Glr)*, auditory processing *(Ga)*, and processing speed *(Gs)*. Because Christine demonstrated little progress across a wide range of academic tasks despite instructional interventions, an extensive evaluation of cognitive function was conducted. In addition to gathering baseline data across all the major cognitive areas, particular emphasis was placed on closely examining those areas which seemed logically related to the academic difficulties previously described and identified. In general, her performance across the cognitive ability clusters measured ranged from low to high average with some notable fluctuations evident within certain ability domains (see Table F.1). A detailed summary of Christine's performance within and across these cognitive ability domains follows.

***Cross-Battery Assessment of* Gf.**   Fluid Reasoning *(Gf)* is the ability to reason, form concepts, and solve problems using unfamiliar information or novel procedures. Christine's *Gf* ability was assessed through tasks that required her to analyze the parts of an incomplete logic puzzle and identify the missing parts (Analysis-Synthesis, SS = 111 ± 7; high average), as well as identify and state the rule for a concept about a set of colored geometric figures when shown instances and noninstances of the concept (Concept Formation, SS = 107 ± 7; average). More specifically, these tasks primarily measure Christine's ability to follow stated conditions to reach a solution to a problem (General Sequential Reasoning or

TABLE F.1 A Description of Christine's *Gf-Gc* Cross-Battery Performance

	Cluster Battery	Test	Standard Score	Confidence Interval	Percentile Rank	Classification
Cognitive	*Gf*		109	104–114	73	Average
	WJ-R	Concept Formation	107	100–114	67	Average
	WJ-R	Analysis-Synthesis	111	104–118	77	High Average
	Gc		100	95–105	50	Average
	WISC-III	Vocabulary	105	98–112	65	Average
	WISC-III	Information	95	88–102	38	Average
	Gv		103	98–108	57	Average
	WISC-III	Block Design	90	83–97	25	Average
	WISC-III	Object Assembly	115	108–122	84	High Average
	Gsm		83	78–88	13	Low Average
	WISC-III	Digit Span	90	83–97	25	Average
	WJ-R	Memory for Words	78	71–85	8	Low Average
	CMS	Sequences	85	78–92	16	Low Average
	WJ-R	Numbers Reversed	80	73–87	9	Low Average
	Glr		79	74–84	8	Low
	WJ-R	Memory for Names	83	76–90	13	Low Average
	WJ-R	Vis-Aud Learning	93	86–100	33	Average
	NEPSY	Speeded Naming	80	73–87	9	Low Average
	CMS	Word Lists	70	63–77	2	Low
	Ga		86	81–91	17	Low Average
	WJ-R	Incomplete Words	83	76–90	13	Low Average
	WJ-R	Sound Blending	88	81–95	21	Low Average
	Gs		95	90–100	38	Average
	WISC-III	Symbol Search	105	98–112	65	Average
	WISC-III	Coding	85	78–92	16	Low Average
Achievment	WJ-R ACH	Letter-Word Ident.	82	75–89	12	Low Average
	WJ-R ACH	Word Attack	74	67–81	4	Low
	WJ-R ACH	Reading Vocab.	83	76–90	13	Low Average
	WJ-R ACH	Passage Comp.	80	73–87	9	Low Average
	WJ-R ACH	Dictation	77	70–84	6	Low
	WJ-R ACH	Writing Samples	90	83–97	25	Average
	WJ-R ACH	Calculation	98	91–105	45	Average
	WJ-R ACH	Applied Problems	90	83–97	25	Average

Note: All standard scores are based on age norms

Deductive Reasoning) and discover the underlying rule that governs a set of materials (Inductive Reasoning), respectively. Christine's obtained scores on these reasoning tests combined to yield a cluster score of 109 ± 5 which is ranked at the seventy-third percentile and is classified as average. The variation in Christine's *Gf* test scores was not significant, indicating that her ability to reason inductively is approximately the same as her ability to reason deductively.

***Cross-Battery Assessment of* Gc.**   Crystallized Intelligence *(Gc)* is a broad ability that involves an individual's breadth and depth of general and cultural knowledge, verbal communication, and reasoning with previously learned procedures. Christine's *Gc* ability was assessed through tasks that required her to define orally presented words (Vocabulary, SS = 105 ± 7; average) and answer general factual knowledge questions (Information, SS = 95 ± 7; average). More specifically, these tasks measured Christine's knowledge of word meanings (Vocabulary Knowledge), understanding of words, sentences, and paragraphs in spoken native language skills (Language Development), and range of general knowledge (General [verbal] Information). Christine's cluster score of 100 ± 5 is ranked at the fiftieth percentile and is classified as average. The variation in scores Christine earned in this area was not statistically significant, suggesting uniform ability within this domain. Overall, Christine's ability to use her acquired knowledge and accumulated experiences to solve everyday problems is average. In other words, her ability to absorb and integrate the concepts, ideas, values, and knowledge of mainstream United States culture (as reflected in the WISC-III) and to reason with this culturally based information is within normal limits. Although Christine's performance on *Gf* and *Gc* tasks suggests that she ought to adapt, learn, and perform at an average level in a variety of environments, particularly academic, this is not the case in light of other cognitive skill weaknesses described in the text that follows.

***Cross-Battery Assessment of* Gv.**   Visual Processing *(Gv)* is the ability to analyze and synthesize visual stimuli and involves perceptions and manipulations of visual shapes and forms, typically when figural or geometric in nature. Christine's *Gv* ability was assessed through tasks that required her to assemble puzzles (Object Assembly, SS = 115 ± 7; high average) and copy designs using blocks (Block Design, SS = 90 ± 7; average). These tasks primarily assessed Christine's ability to combine disconnected visual stimuli or patterns into a meaningful whole (Closure Speed) and quickly perceive and manipulate visual patterns (Spatial Relations), respectively. Christine's obtained scores on these *Gv* tests combined to yield a cluster score of 103 ± 5, which is ranked at the fifty-seventh percentile and is classified as average. Christine demonstrated a significant strength on the Closure Speed test (Object Assembly), suggesting that this ability is better developed than her spatial relations ability. However, Christine's performance on the spatial relations task was hampered when the guided line structure was removed from the task stimulus cards. Because the lines serve as an added context, her relative weakness on this test, compared to the closure speed test, is consistent with teacher reports that Christine often needs to rely on contextual cues to facilitate her performance. Despite her relative weakness on the noncontextually based visual processing test, her performance on this test was estimated in the average range of ability. Moreover, Christine's high average ability to analyze and synthesize contextually based visual stimuli may actually aid her memory (in certain contexts) and assist with reasoning and problem solving.

***Cross-Battery Assessment of* Gsm.**   Short-term memory *(Gsm)* is the ability to hold information in immediate awareness and then use it within a few seconds. Christine's *Gsm* ability was assessed through tasks that required her to immediately recall digits in a given order (Digit Span, SS = 90 ± 7; average), repeat lists of unrelated words in correct sequence

(Memory for Words, SS = 78 ± 7; low), quickly perform simple tasks such as saying the days of the week forward and backward (Sequences, SS = 85 ± 7; low average), and repeat a series of random numbers backwards (Numbers Reversed, SS = 80 ± 7; low average). The first two tasks primarily measured Christine's ability to immediately recall temporally ordered elements in the correct order following a single presentation (Memory Span), whereas the latter two tasks primarily measured her ability to store and manipulate stimuli prior to producing a response (Working Memory). Christine obtained a *Gsm* cluster score of 83 ± 5 which is ranked at the thirteenth percentile and is classified as low average. On tasks of memory span, Christine demonstrated more difficulty on the task that used words as stimuli (low) than on the task that used numbers (average). Conversely, when Christine was required to store information (numerical or verbal) and manipulate or transform it prior to producing a response (working memory), she demonstrated low average ability. Furthermore, her performance on the working memory task with nonmeaningful or noncontextual stimuli (Numbers Reversed) was slightly lower than her performance on the more contextually based working memory task (Sequences). Christine's weaknesses in the *Gsm* area very likely impact her performance in reading, spelling, and retention of oral directions.

***Cross-Battery Assessment of* Glr.** Long-term storage and retrieval *(Glr)* is the ability to store information and fluently retrieve it later through association. Christine's *Glr* ability was assessed through tasks that required her to learn associations between unfamiliar auditory and visual stimuli (Memory for Names, SS = 83 ± 7; low average) and associate new visual symbols with familiar words and translate a series of these symbols into verbal sentences when presented as a reading passage (Visual-Auditory Learning, SS = 93 ± 7; average). In addition, Christine was required to rapidly name the color, size, and shape of a series of stimulus items (Speeded Naming, SS = 80 ± 7; low average), as well as recall orally presented paired words in any order (and, in a specified sequence later) (Word Lists, SS = 70 ± 7; low). Memory for Names and Visual-Auditory Learning measured Christine's ability to recall one part of a previously learned but unrelated pair of items when the other part is presented (Associative Memory); Speed Naming measured Christine's ability to rapidly produce names for concepts (Naming Facility); and Word Lists measured Christine's Free Recall Memory. Christine's obtained scores on these Memory tests yielded a *Glr* cluster score of 79 ± 5 which is ranked at the eigth percentile and is classified as low. As was the case with her short-term memory, Christine's level of performance on tasks of long-term storage and retrieval was dependent, in part, on the amount of contextual information provided. That is, her performance was weakest on tasks with the least amount of contextual information (e.g., Word Lists versus Visual-Auditory Learning). Of the three *Glr* abilities assessed, Christine's weakness in Naming Facility likely has a significant effect on her reading achievement. Overall, her specific weakness in this area, coupled with her additional memory weaknesses described above, help to explain her reported academic difficulties.

***Cross-Battery Assessment of* Ga.** Auditory Processing *(Ga)* is the ability to analyze and synthesize auditory stimuli. Christine's *Ga* ability was assessed through tasks that required her to listen to a recorded word with one or more phonemes missing and identify the word (Incomplete Words, SS = 83 ± 7; low average), as well as integrate auditorily presented syllables and/or phonemes into whole words (Sound Blending, SS = 88 ± 7; low average). These tasks primarily measured Christine's ability to analyze the individual sounds in words (Phonetic Coding: Analysis) and synthesize such sounds (Phonetic Coding: Synthesis), respectively. Christine obtained a *Ga* cluster score of 86 ± 5 which is ranked at the seventeenth percentile and is classified as low average. Since these tasks involve the analysis and synthesis of sounds, it seems likely that Christine's weakness in auditory processing (or poorly developed phonological awareness skills) has hindered the development of sound-symbol relationships, a critical component in the reading process.

Cross-Battery Assessment of* Gs.   Processing Speed *(Gs)* is defined as one's ability to quickly perform automatic cognitive tasks, particularly when pressured to maintain focused concentration. Christine's *Gs* ability was assessed through tasks that required her to quickly draw symbols that are paired with a series of simple shapes (Coding, SS = 85 ± 7; low average), and visually scan symbols to determine their presence or absence in a column (Symbol Search, SS = 105 ± 7; average). These tasks primarily measured Christine's ability to rapidly search for and compare visual symbols presented side-by-side (Perceptual Speed) as well as the ability to rapidly perform tests that are relatively easy or require very simple decisions (Rate-of-Test-Taking), respectively. Christine obtained a *Gs* cluster score of 95 ± 5 which is ranked at the thirty-eighth percentile and is classified as average. Christine demonstrated a normative weakness on the Coding task. Her performance on this task is consistent with her reported writing difficulties because this task involved writing symbols. Furthermore, the format of this task required Christine to visually track information from one line to the next in a continual up and down motion. Her observed visual tracking difficulty likely hindered her performance. In general, low scores on this task have been related to reading (and writing) difficulties, because this task involves the basic rapid processing of symbols. Thus, symbol-processing difficulties may also impact her reading performance.

Assessment of Academic Achievement

Christine's performance on measures of academic achievement was variable. On the Woodcock-Johnson—Revised Tests of Achievement (WJ-R ACH), Christine earned scores that ranged from low to average.

Reading.   Christine's performance in the area of reading reflects her skill in identifying isolated words and letters on a page (Letter-Word Identification SS = 82 ± 7), applying structural and phonic analysis to decode words (Word Attack SS = 74 ± 7), supplying opposite and similar word meanings (Reading Vocabulary SS = 83 ± 7), and using meaning (semantic) and grammatical (syntactic) cues to read and complete written passages with a contextually appropriate key word (Passage Comprehension SS = 80 ± 7). Christine's overall reading achievement is low average and consistent with referral concerns. Her basic reading skills as well as her ability to apply her knowledge to comprehend written discourse appear to be equally developed. Her primary area of difficulty appears to lie in her ability to decode words using phonetic analysis (e.g., Word Attack). This difficulty may hinder Christine's word identification ability which, in turn, may affect her ability to obtain meaning from written text. Although lack of vocabulary knowledge can also adversely affect one's performance in this area, Christine's performance in word knowledge, as evidenced by her scores on the cognitive battery *(Gc)* was average. Thus, her reading difficulties appear to be best explained by poor decoding ability (i.e., poorly developed phonological awareness skills). Because the ability to decode words is an important prerequisite for later reading skills (e.g., identifying words, reading comprehension) her difficulties with this skill help to explain her current level of reading performance.

Written Language.   Christine's performance in the area of writing was variable. On tasks designed to measure her skill in writing single word responses involving knowledge of punctuation, capitalization, spelling, and word usage, she performed poorly (Dictation SS = 77 ± 7). However, when faced with tasks that required her to produce written, single-word responses and sentences embedded in context she performed significantly better (Writing Samples SS = 90 ± 7). Christine's discrepant performance is likely due to the fact that she was not penalized on the Writing Samples test for misspellings when required to form sentences. As such, her basic decoding difficulties, as evidenced by her reading scores, did not play a major role in performance on this task. Additionally, this task involved contextual cues (i.e., pictures) which, as was the case with certain tasks in the cognitive domain *(Glr* and *Gsm*), may have aided Christine's performance in this area.

Mathematics.   In the area of mathematics, Christine's was required to perform basic mathematical operations (e.g., addition, subtraction) to solve problems (Calculation SS = 98 ± 7), as well as solve more involved word problems that were read to her (Applied Problems SS = 90 ± 7). Christine's overall performance in math was consistent with her teacher's report that Christine generally achieves at a level commensurate with her peers. Although Christine's teacher reported that Christine has difficulty following directions accompanying math problems, it is likely that this is a result of her reading difficulties rather than a reflection of her ability to perform mathematical computations.

Data Integration and Interpretation

Data derived from the administration of various cognitive, achievement, and special purpose batteries, suggest that Christine demonstrates low to average functioning across the various cognitive and academic domains that were evaluated. Overall, Christine's pattern of cognitive performance appears to aid in understanding the reason for referral. That is, specific and circumscribed cognitive weaknesses may contribute to her reported difficulties in academic performance, particularly reading. For example, although Christine appears to have a sufficient amount of information available to her *(Gc)* to read and understand age appropriate reading passages, her inability to hold information in immediate awareness long enough to use, transform, or encode it (*Gsm* [Memory Span, Working Memory]), coupled with her difficulty processing sound-symbol relationships (*Ga* [Phonetic Coding, phonological awareness]) and quickly retrieving previously learned information (*Glr* [Naming Facility]), very likely contribute to her difficulties in reading, spelling, and the comprehension of oral directions.

Of particular relevance to Christine's reading difficulty is her apparent weakness in phonetic coding (or phonological awareness). Christine has considerable difficulty discriminating individual sounds in words. Phonetic coding difficulties (e.g., analyzing and interpreting sounds in words) hinder the development of sound-symbol relationships which, in turn, limit opportunities for success in reading. Thus, Christine's difficulties in reading appear to stem primarily from a core phonological processing weakness. Christine's performance on *Ga* tests of phonetic coding as well as the Letter-Word Identification and Word Attack tests support this conclusion. This apparent phonological processing weakness may also help to explain her spelling difficulties, because spelling requires the ability to attend to the detailed sequence of sounds in words.

Although a core phonological processing weakness helps to explain Christine's difficulties in reading and spelling, her weaknesses in the areas of *Gsm* and *Glr* also appear likely to contribute to her poor reading and spelling abilities. Specifically, her demonstrated weaknesses on tasks of memory span and working memory indicate that her capacity to store relevant phonological information in memory is weak. This weakness can also negatively affect spelling skills because spelling requires the ability to maintain words in short-term memory long enough to encode the complete phonetic string. Finally, Christine's performance in the area of long-term storage and retrieval *(Glr)* also provides potentially important insights into her reading difficulties. Overall, Christine's *Glr* ability was found to be below average, however, the variation in performance within this domain suggests that her ability to arrange or organize material at the time of encoding is dependent, in part, on whether the information is presented in a contextual or noncontextual format. That is, she appears to encode and retrieve contextual information more efficiently than noncontextual material. Notwithstanding, of all the *Glr* abilities measured, her low ability on the rapid automatic naming (or Naming Facility) task may contribute most to her reading difficulties and is often present in combination with low phonological processing and short-term memory abilities in individuals with reading problems.

Christine's performance on various measures of achievement is consistent with referral concerns as well as consistent with and logically related to the outcomes found in the evaluation of her cognitive abilities. Specifically, she exhibited significantly weak word attack, word recognition, spelling, and comprehension skills. Despite these difficulties, Christine exhibited a relative strength in writing (i.e., Writing Samples). Her performance in this area, however, was aided by contextual cues. If similar contextual cues are not available in Christine's classroom assignments, then her difficulties in the area of writing will be pronounced. In fact, in all academic areas when numerous cognitive resources are being tapped simultaneously, and contextual cues are limited, the impact of Christine's individual cognitive weaknesses on overall classroom performance will likely be significant.

In summary, Christine's pattern of weaknesses is consistent with that often associated with a reading disability subtype that is characterized primarily by difficulties with phonological processing, verbal short-term memory (VSTM), and rate. Specifically, her performance suggests that her difficulty in analyzing and synthesizing speech sounds, as well as poorly developed sound-symbol relationships, interfere with her ability to read individual words in isolation, which, in turn, impacts on her ability to comprehend and spell. Because word recognition skills are not automatic for Christine, her reading comprehension is affected adversely. This is because the attention and cognitive resources that must be utilized to decode words detracts from the resources that are available for comprehension. Christine's weaknesses in short-term memory and long-term storage and retrieval exacerbate this core phonological processing problem and, as such, further limit opportunities for success in reading. In sum, the phonological processing-VSTM-rate reading disability subtype characterizing Christine's cognitive performance provides a basis for understanding her current level of reading achievement. Furthermore, Christine's phonological processing difficulties, in particular, and her memory problems, in general, help to explain her difficulties in spelling and understanding oral directions, respectively.

Recommendations for Intervention

The primary purpose of psychoeducational assessment is not so much diagnostic, as it is to generate data that may be used to develop effective interventions to resolve the issues that led to referral in the first place. Because of the close relationship created between theory and assessment in the *Gf-Gc* cross-battery approach, the resulting data provide a significant foundation from which learning difficulties can be clearly understood and appropriate instructional interventions developed. Regardless of the type of interventions that are developed, ongoing evaluation of their effectiveness must remain a part of whatever plan is developed to ameliorate the observed academic difficulties and concerns. The integration of corroborative information from standardized tests, teacher and parent reports, and prereferral data provided the basis for the following recommendations for Christine:

1. Christine's auditory processing weakness causes her difficulty in spelling and decoding words. Therefore, it is recommended that Christine receive training in phoneme segmentation and sound blending. Examples of these activities include identifying words beginning with the same sound (word matching), isolating individual sounds (e.g., recognizing the first sound in a word), identifying the numbers of phonemes in a word (phoneme counting), and identifying how the removal of a sound would change a given word (phoneme deletion). Additionally, teaching Christine how to organize sounds to construct a word (sound blending) is recommended. Finally, working with Christine on developing her sight word vocabulary may also serve to aid her reading performance.

2. Christine's auditory processing weakness in conjunction with her short-term memory weakness hinders her ability to understand and follow oral directions. Therefore, Christine should be encouraged to request repetition of instructions, and the use of elaborate or multistep instructions should be avoided. Given her above-average visual-processing ability, visual outlines and graphic organizers, as well as other visual learning strategies, may prove useful when instructing Christine. These strategies may also provide the added context which has been shown to optimize her performance on a variety of tasks. Additionally, Christine should be taught mnemonic aids and strategies for retaining information, such as the use of verbal mediation or rehearsal (e.g., saying the information to be remembered while looking at it).

3. Christine's long-term retrieval difficulties impact on her ability to relate previously acquired information to new information, especially when stimuli are not contextually

based. Furthermore, her ability to generalize what she has learned may be limited by this weakness. In an effort to facilitate her ability to generalize, Christine should be provided with intensive review and repetition at each step in the learning process, learning materials should be sequenced from simple to more complex, previously learned information should be reviewed prior to presenting new associations, and step-by-step instructions for completing a problem should be provided to Christine.

A User-Friendly Guide to Understanding Broad *Gf-Gc* Abilities and Their Relation to Achievement

Gf-Gc Broad (Stratum II) Ability	Definition	Relation to School Achievement
Gf	Fluid intelligence refers to a type of thinking that an individual may use when faced with a relatively new task that cannot be performed automatically. This type of thinking includes such things as forming and recognizing concepts (e.g., how are a dog, cat, and cow alike?), identifying and perceiving relationships (e.g., sun is to morning as moon is to *night*), drawing inferences (e.g., after reading a story, answering the question, "What will John do next?"), and reorganizing or transforming information. Overall, this ability can be thought of as a *problem-solving* type of intelligence.	Fluid intelligence or reasoning abilities have been shown to play a moderate role in reading. For example, the ability to reach general conclusions from specific information is important for reading comprehension. Fluid intelligence is also related to mathematical activities (e.g., figuring out how to set up math problems by using information provided in a word problem).
Gc	Crystallized intelligence refers to a person's knowledge base (or general fund of information) that has been accumulated over time. It involves knowledge of one's culture (e.g., who is the President of the United States?) as well as verbal- or language-based knowledge that has been developed during general life experiences, and formal schooling (e.g., knowledge of word definitions).	Crystallized abilities, especially one's language development, vocabulary knowledge, and the ability to listen are important for reading. This ability is related to reading comprehension in particular. Low crystallized intelligence may hamper an individual's ability to comprehend written text due to lack of vocabulary knowledge, basic concepts, and general life experiences that are needed to understand the text. This ability is also important for achievement in academic subjects such as geography, history, and science.
Gv	Visual processing is an individual's ability to think about visual patterns and visual stimuli (e.g., what is the shortest route from your house to school?). This type of intelligence also involves the ability to generate, perceive, analyze, synthesize, manipulate, and transform visual patterns and stimuli (e.g., draw a picture of what this shape would look like if I turned it upside down). Additional examples of this type of ability include putting puzzles together, completing a maze, and interpreting a graph or chart.	Visual processing is important for performing tasks that require higher-level or advanced mathematical skills and thinking (e.g., geometry and calculus).

Gsm	Short-term memory is the ability to hold information in one's mind and then use it within a few seconds. The most common example of short-term memory is holding a phone number in one's mind long enough to dial it.	A student with short-term memory difficulties may have problems following oral directions, comprehending long reading passages, spelling, acquiring word identification skills, and performing math computations (e.g., remembering a sequence of orally presented steps required to solve long math problems—first multiply, then add, then subtract).
Glr	Long-term retrieval refers to an individual's ability to take in and store a variety of information (e.g., ideas, names, concepts) in one's mind and then retrieve it quickly and easily at a later time by using association (e.g., remembering the names of one's teachers and classmates). This ability does not represent *what* is stored in long-term memory. Rather, it represents the *process* of storing and retrieving information.	Long-term retrieval abilities are particularly important for reading. For example, elementary school children who have difficulty naming objects or categories of objects rapidly may have difficulty in reading. Associative memory abilities also play a role in reading achievement. Overall, long-term retrieval is important in learning such things as the names of the letters of the alphabet or memorizing multiplication tables.
Ga	Auditory processing refers to the ability to perceive, analyze, and synthesize a variety of auditory stimuli (e.g., sounds). Examples of auditory processing would include listening to words with missing letters and saying the correct word (e.g., hearing "olipop" and saying "lollipop"), listening to piano music and identifying the key in which the piece is being played (e.g., C sharp).	Phonetic coding or *phonological awareness/processing* is very important during the elementary school years. Students who have difficulty with processing auditory stimuli may experience problems with learning grapheme-to-phoneme correspondence (e.g., listening to the sound *Ba* and identifying it as the letter *B* when given a list of letters to choose from), reading nonsense words (e.g., *bab*), and decoding words due to an inability to segment, analyze, and synthesize speech sounds. Students who are low in auditory processing abilities may also have difficulty in spelling, since this skill requires the ability to attend to the detailed sequence of sounds in words. Older students who are low in auditory processing abilities may have problems in decoding, spelling, foreign language learning, interpreting lectures, and understanding oral directions.

Gf-Gc Broad (Stratum II) Ability	Definition	Relation to School Achievement
Gs	Processing speed refers to an individual's ability to perform simple clerical-type tasks quickly, especially when under pressure to maintain attention and concentration. It can also be thought of as how quickly one can think or how quickly one can take simple tests that require simple decisions. For example, how quickly an individual can cross out all the letter "A"s when they are embedded in multiple rows of scrambled letters is a measure of processing speed.	Processing speed is important during all school years, particularly the elementary school years. Slow processing speed may impact upon reading skills since the basic rapid processing of symbols (e.g., letters) is often necessary for fluent reading. Additional difficulties may be evidenced in mathematics due to a lack of automaticity in basic math operations (e.g., addition, subtraction, multiplication).

APPENDIX H

Responsible Use of Ability-Achievement Discrepancies in Assessment

We shall not cease from exploration and the end of all our exploring will be to arrive where we started and know the place for the first time.

—Abrams (1962, p. 1970)

There are probably very few things more noxious to the applied psychologists involved in psychoeducational assessment than the need to integrate myriad legal mandates, school-based policies, statistical formulae, and conflicting theoretical perspectives into a defensible framework for identifying learning disabilities. Unquestionably, the lack of precision found in each of these arenas makes the task one of the more daunting processes facing psychologists today. However, the concept that appears to be most problematic revolves around the idea of establishing a discrepancy between ability and achievement through the many varied and far-ranging prescriptions offered throughout the fields of clinical, school, and neuropsychology.

Fully 98 percent of the states incorporate the notion of *discrepancy* in their translation of the federal definition (P.L. 105-17; IDEA) of learning disability as does the *Diagnostic and Statistical Manual—Fourth Edition (DSM-IV)* in its specification of learning disorder. Two-thirds of states provide criteria for determining how large a discrepancy must be between ability and achievement before it is considered severe (Mercer, Jordan, Allsopp, & Mercer, 1995). The *DSM-IV* also suggests criteria for determining a significant ability-achievement discrepancy. It is clear that the driving clinical force in diagnosing learning disability (Gridley & Roid, 1998, p. 250) involves a discrepancy between ability (aptitude or potential) and achievement (Lyons, 1996; Mather & Roberts, 1994). Despite the abundance of well-reasoned and empirically supported arguments *against* using ability-achievement discrepancy criteria to diagnose learning disability, "the fact remains that many clinicians are obligated by laws and regulations to determine such discrepancies on a daily basis" (Gridley & Roid, 1998, p. 252).

Given the degree to which the concept of ability-achievement discrepancies has been codified into various federal and state statutes, it is unlikely to disappear from the practical reality of psychological assessment any time soon. As such, we recognize that this endeavor, however precarious it may be, remains a fact of life for applied psychologists and involves many aspects of intellectual assessment that have been discussed in the text of this book. Therefore, we would like to offer the following discussion, not so much as a definitive treatise on the issue, but more as information that may assist practitioners in making the difficult decisions that face them with perhaps a greater degree of confidence and appreciation of the complexity inherent in the process. The ultimate purpose of this appendix is neither an attempt to refine the definition of learning disability nor endorse a set of existing procedures for identifying this disorder. Rather, the information presented herein is intended to highlight some of the most salient limitations and issues that have fueled controversies about the relevance and meaningfulness of ability-achievement discrepancy analysis and offer guidelines for interpreting ability-achievement discrepancies responsibly. The following material is presented and organized in a simple question-and-answer format designed to address the most common questions, concerns, and misconceptions involved in the assessment of learning disability and learning disorder.

1. What Is the Prevailing Scientific Definition of *Learning Disability?*

Although there are many definitions of *learning disability* within the fields of education and psychology, no universally accepted definition exists (Gridley & Roid, 1998). The definition that appears to represent a consensus within and between disciplines, as well as across most of the lifespan was developed by the National Joint Committee on Learning Disabilities (NJCLD) (Brinckerhoff, Shaw, & McGuire, 1993; Hammill, 1990)—a committee comprised of various professional and advocacy organizations. According to the NJCLD:

> Learning disabilities is a general term that refers to a heterogeneous group of disorders manifested by significant difficulties in the acquisition and use of listening, speaking, reading, writing, reasoning, or mathematical skills.
>
> These disorders are intrinsic to the individual and presumed to be due to a central nervous system dysfunction, and may occur across the life span. Problems in self-regulatory behaviors, social perception, and social interaction may exist with the learning disabilities but do not, by themselves, constitute a learning disability.
>
> Although learning disabilities may occur concomitantly with other disabilities (e.g., sensory impairment, mental retardation, serious emotional disturbance), or with extrinsic influences (such as cultural differences, insufficient or inappropriate instruction), they are not the result of those conditions or influences. (1990, p. 29)

2. What Is the Legal Definition of *Learning Disability* as Defined by Federal Law (P.L. 105-17)?

Specific Learning Disability (SLD), as a handicapping condition, is specified by federal statute in the recent reauthorization of the Individuals with Disabilities Education Act (IDEA). According to Section 300.7b(10), specific learning disability is defined as follows:

> (i) General. The term means a disorder in one or more of the basic psychological processes involved in understanding or in using language, spoken or written, that may manifest itself

in an imperfect ability to listen, think, speak, read, write, spell, or to do mathematical calculations, including such conditions as perceptual disabilities, brain injury, minimal brain dysfunction, dyslexia, and developmental aphasia.

(ii) Disorders not included. The term does not include learning problems that are primarily the result of visual, hearing, or motor disabilities, of mental retardation, of emotional disturbance, or of environmental, cultural, or economic disadvantage.

In addition to this definition, IDEA further specifies criteria for determining the existence of a specific learning disability. Section 300.541 states:

(a) A team may determine that a child has a specific learning disability if—
  (1) The child does not achieve commensurate with his or her age and ability levels in one or more of the areas listed in paragraph (a)(2) of this section, if provided with learning experiences appropriate for the child's age and ability levels; and
  (2) The team finds that a child has a severe discrepancy between achievement and intellectual ability in one or more of the following areas:
    (i) Oral expression.
    (ii) Listening comprehension.
    (iii) Written expression.
    (iv) Basic reading skills.
    (v) Reading comprehension.
    (vi) Mathematics calculation.
    (vii) Mathematics reasoning.
(b) The team may not identify a child as having a specific learning disability if the severe discrepancy between ability and achievement is primarily the result of—
  (1) A visual, hearing, or motor impairment;
  (2) Mental retardation;
  (3) Emotional disturbance; or
  (4) Environmental, cultural or economic disadvantage.

It is also important to note that many state educational agencies interpret this specification in IDEA somewhat differently. As long as the state educational agency does not compromise or subvert the intent or specification of the federal statute, they may operationalize the law in a manner deemed appropriate. The result has been that each state has developed slightly different procedures and regulations that guide compliance.

3. Since the Definition of *Learning Disability* Seems Relatively Straightforward, What Creates the Problem in Identification?

Continued efforts to refine and operationalize a meaningful theory-based definition of learning disability, notwithstanding, it is clear that the degree of consensus that exists with regard to the definition of *learning disability* is greater than that which exists with regard to the procedures, methods, and criteria that ought to be used to identify individuals with learning disability. According to Shaw, Cullen, McGuire, and Brinckerhoff (1995), "research indicates that the problem of identification is less a function of how a learning disability is conceived than of how it is operationally defined by practitioners" (p. 587). We believe, however, that practitioners who are knowledgeable about the critical issues surrounding the use and interpretation of discrepancy analysis will function at a higher level than the novice and thereby make more appropriate and informed decisions in the learning disability identification process. "It seems clear from the literature that despite the shortcomings of different methods used to operationalize ability-achievement discrepancies, that clinicians with adequate information make decisions that are more accurate and have greater interrater reliability than those for whom such information is not available (Ross, 1992)" (Gridley & Roid, 1998, p. 256).

4. How Valid Is the Use of Discrepancy Formulas in the Identification of Learning Disabilities?

Numerous formulas and methods for determining significant ability-achievement discrepancies exist, only a few of which are technically valid. Among the most common are deviation from grade level, expectancy formulas, scatter analysis, standard score difference (simple-difference method), and predicted-achievement methods using regression formulas (Heath & Kush, 1991). The first three methods are not recommended because they are technically limited and, therefore, interpretations that are drawn from the results of such methods are likely to be misleading (Flanagan & Alfonso, 1993a). The simple-difference method, although more psychometrically sound than the first three approaches, does not take into account the correlation between the ability and achievement measures or regression toward the mean. As such, this method yields false positives among individuals with above-average IQs and false negatives among individuals with below-average IQs (see Cone & Wilson, 1981; Gridley & Roid, 1998; Heath & Kush, 1991; McGrew, 1994; Reynolds, 1990; for a comprehensive discussion of the uses, advantages, and limitations of these discrepancy methods). Procedures that are based on the predicted-achievement method (and thus that account for regression toward the mean) are among the most statistically defensible approaches to determining whether an ability-achievement discrepancy is significant (Hintze, 1996a; 1996b; Gridley & Roid, 1998; Flanagan & Alfonso, 1993a; 1993b).

5. Why Is the Predicted-Achievement Method Superior and Can You Give Any Examples?

The predicted-achievement method (1) accounts for the imperfect correlation between the ability measure and the achievement measure; (2) takes into consideration the standard error of measurement in decision making; and (3) evaluates discrepancies relative to the frequency of occurrence of observed differences between the academic performance of the individual referred for evaluation and all other individuals that have the same level of global ability (e.g., the same IQ) (cited in Hintze, 1996b, p. 17). This method is used when evaluating discrepancies between a number of ability and achievement measures, including (1) WISC-III/WAIS-III/WPPSI-R FSIQ and WIAT subtests and composites; (2) WISC-III Verbal and Performance IQs and WIAT subtests and composites; (3) CAS Full Scale score and WJ-R achievement tests and clusters; (4) DAS General Cognitive Ability score and achievement clusters; and (5) WJ-R/III Broad Cognitive Ability, Scholastic Aptitude, and Achievement tests and clusters.

6. Are All Predicted-Achievement Methods Created Equal?

Although the predicted achievement method described above is technically valid, McGrew (1994) pointed out that among such methods for determining whether ability-achievement discrepancies are significant, some are superior to others. McGrew demonstrated this in a hierarchical presentation of discrepancy procedures. Table H.1 depicts McGrew's hierarchy and provides examples of ability-achievement analysis methods that correspond to qualitatively different levels of technical validity (and invalidity). An examination of Table H.1 demonstrates that the features of *conorming* and use of *aptitude* measures demarcate the most superior method among technically valid ability-achievement discrepancy procedures.

Tests that are conormed are those that were administered to the same individuals during the standardization process. A common standardization sample allows normative information for both measures to be generated from the same representative group of subjects. The use of conormed tests removes the possibility that aptitude and achievement discrepancy scores may contain error due to differences in the test norming samples. In the absence of conormed measures, clinicians need to evaluate whether the standardization sample from each measure is similar. According to McGrew (1994) "[t]his is largely a judgment call that requires clinicians to devote significant time to studying the norming procedures used for each test. The most efficient and optimal solution is to use aptitude and achievement tests from within the same conormed battery" (p. 213). (The difference between aptitude and ability measures within the context of the Discrepancy Model is discussed in the next section.) Another means of reducing error is to use ability and achievement measures that are statistically *linked* or *equated,* meaning that although the tests do not have the same large and representative standardization sample, they share a common sample nonetheless. The common sample is then used to generate the data (e.g., "pseudo" discrepancy norms; McGrew, 1994) necessary to determine significant ability-achievement discrepancies based on characteristics of the linking sample (see WIAT manual and CAS manual for details).

In order to understand the ability-achievement discrepancy literature, interpret the results of that literature appropriately, and address the discrepancy component of learning disability diagnostic and identification criteria more knowledgeably, it is necessary to clarify the distinction between ability and aptitude and contrast these constructs with *achievement*.

7. Is There Any Difference between Ability and Aptitude in Discrepancy Analysis?

Ability-achievement discrepancy analysis and *aptitude*-achievement discrepancy analysis are often used interchangeably. However, *ability* and *aptitude* are not synonymous. In general, "[a]bility measures represent aptitudes for learning in education and training settings when they predict important criteria of achievement . . . the measures can be used to classify students into different instructional treatments designed to be adaptive to particular ability types or levels" (Snow, 1994, p. 4).

TABLE H.1   Hierarchy of Discrepancy Procedures by Technical Validity and Select Examples

Levels	Description	Example
Actual Discrepancy Norms	(all measures must be conormed)	
Level 1	A differential scholastic aptitude measure and a measure of achievement	WJ-R/III
Level 2	A broad (general) ability measure and a measure of achievement	WJ-R/III DAS
Pseudo Discrepancy Norms	(based on a correction for regression)	
Level 3	A differentiated scholastic aptitude measure and a measure of achievement that are conormed	WJ-R/III
Level 4	A broad (general) ability measure and a measure of achievement that are conormed	DAS WJ-R/III
Level 5	A differentiated scholastic aptitude measure and a measure of achievement that are *not* conormed	WJ-R Scholastic Aptitude cluster and WIAT achievement score
Level 6	A broad (general) ability measure and a measure of achievement that are *not* conormed	WPPSI-R, WISC-III, WAIS-III/ WIAT; CAS/WJ-R ACH; WISC-III and WJ-R ACH; WJ-R and WIAT
Absolute Score Difference	(technically invalid)	
Level 7	An absolute score difference between a differentiated scholastic aptitude measure and a measure of achievement that are conormed	Same as Level 3 but using absolute score difference
Level 8	An absolute score difference between a broad (general) ability measure and a measure of achievement that are conormed	Same as Level 4 but using absolute score difference
Level 9	An absolute score difference between a differentiated scholastic aptitude measure and a measure of achievement that are *not* conormed	Same as Level 5 but using absolute score difference
Level 10	An absolute score difference between a broad (general) ability measure and a measure of achievement that are *not* conormed	Same as Level 6 but using absolute score difference

Note: Information in this table was adapted from McGrew (1994).

"An ability is a power to perform some specified act or task, either physical or mental" (Snow, 1994, p. 3). Factor-analytic techniques have been used extensively in the psychometric and intelligence literature to identify the mental abilities thought to comprise g or general intellectual ability (e.g., Carroll's 1993a Gf-Gc taxonomy described in this text). As presented in Chapter 3, a wealth of evidence is available to support the theoretical coherency, empirical replicability, and practical utility of the Gf-Gc hierarchical model of the structure of cognitive abilities. The general, broad and narrow abilities specified in Gf-Gc theory represent constructs that have been identified as important aspects of human cognitive *ability*. The Gf-Gc organization of abilities was derived largely from internal/structural validity studies (see Chapter 2).

Approximately 8 to 10 broad cognitive abilities and 70 narrow abilities have been found to exist (Carroll, 1993a). According to Snow (1994), "specific intellectual ability constructs and measures may come from different levels of hierarchical taxonomy for use in further research as well as in practical settings where ability differences among persons are a concern" (p. 3).

When we use a global or full scale score from an intelligence battery as the ability measure in an ability-achievement discrepancy formula, we essentially plug into the formula an aggregate (score) that is comprised of a wide mix of mental abilities believed (by the test author/developer) to be constituents of general intelligence *(g)*. As such, the array of abilities that make up the general intelligence aggregate may differ from battery to battery (this point will be demonstrated below). However, the assumption among many practitioners is that the ability component of a discrepancy formula means the same thing regardless of the battery, and hence total test score, used. This erroneous assumption could have potentially harmful consequences when we consider that the discrepancy model is a model of *prediction*—that is, one measure (ability) predicts the other (achievement). Because the degree of prediction will vary as a function of the relationship between the predictor and the criterion measure, a significant difference may be found in instances where the ability and achievement measures are not highly correlated, and a nonsignificant difference may be found when such measures are highly correlated. Specifically, the ability measure in the latter situation aids in explaining level of functioning in the criterion measure, whereas the ability measure in the former situation adds little to explanation of academic performance.

Depending on the aggregate in question, global ability scores from the major intelligence batteries account for approximately 25 to 35 percent of achievement variance (meaning that the ability measure cannot account for or explain 65 to 75 percent of the variance in achievement). Based on our knowledge of the relations between ability and achievement, it is clear that many Full Scale scores are comprised of cognitive abilities (e.g., Gv) that are irrelevant to (or explain little variance in) the academic criterion of interest (e.g., reading); however, some ability composites are very relevant to (explain much variance in) the criterion. This finding leads to the obvious question: Is there a better predictor (other than a global ability test score) that can be used in an ability-achievement discrepancy formula? The answer is yes, a measure of scholastic *aptitude*.

According to Snow (1994), "the concept of aptitude includes any enduring personal characteristics that are propaedeutic to successful performance in some particular situation. This definition includes affective, conative, and personality characteristics, as well as cognitive and psychomotor abilities (Snow, 1992). However, cognitive abilities are a particularly important source of aptitude for learning and performance in many school and work situations" (p. 4). Thus, aptitude measures are validated for a particular purpose through demonstrating that they predict important external criteria (e.g., specific academic skills). One of the best examples of the distinction between ability and aptitude as defined by Snow (1994) may be seen through an examination of the clusters yielded by the WJ-R.

The WJ-R Scholastic Aptitude clusters (e.g., the Reading, Math, and Written Language Aptitude clusters) are based on an equally weighted combination of four tests each from the cognitive battery. The aptitude clusters were developed through a series of stepwise multiple regression analyses conducted over the entire age range of the WJ-R (McGrew, Werder, & Woodcock, 1991). Consistent with the definition of *aptitude,* this statistical procedure identified "the optimal linear combination of variables that best predict[ed] a selected criterion variable" (p. 194). In the case of the WJ-R, these regression procedures identified the specific combinations of four WJ-R Tests of Cognitive Ability that best predicted performance on the Reading, Mathematics, and Written Language WJ-R Achievement clusters. Research on the differential prediction of the WJ-R Scholastic Aptitude clusters demonstrated that these clusters consistently predicted their respective outcome criterion better than both the 7-test and 14-test Broad Cognitive Ability clusters of the WJ-R, explaining up to 50 to 60 percent of the variance in the outcome criterion. Based on this research, McGrew (1994) concluded, "[t]he differential predictive validity evidence, when combined with the superior prediction of achievement when compared to other intelligence batteries (i.e., Wechslers, K-ABC, SB:IV) (McGrew et al., 1991), indicates that the WJTCA-R Scholastic Aptitude clusters are the best available measure to use when calculating aptitude/achievement discrepancies" (p. 211). Based on this WJ-R example, it is evident that aptitude measures derived through regression procedures are better predictors of certain outcome criteria than ability measures. Aptitude measures are designed for the purpose of prediction.

8. What Is the Relationship between Ability and Achievement?

As unusual as it may seem, an ability-achievement *dichotomy* is not recognized or supported in the cognitive psychology literature. The difference between ability and achievement is essentially a popular *verbal* distinction that does not correspond to an empirical distinction. For example, the *Gf-Gc* theoretical framework presented in this text—a framework based on the monumental contributions of Carroll (e.g., 1993a) and Horn (e.g., 1991)—includes *Grw* and *Gq* ability constructs (located at broad—stratum II in the integrated *Gf-Gc* model presented in this text). The narrow abilities subsumed by *Grw* and *Gq* are measured typically by achievement tests (e.g., WIAT, WJ-R ACH). However, many commonly used intelligence tests also include measures of *Grw* and *Gq* (achievement-like) abilities. For example, the Wechsler Scales include a measure of math achievement (*Gq* [Arithmetic]).

There are theorists (Horn, 1988) who argue that the ability-achievement distinction is primarily semantic, and that measures of cognitive abilities are every bit as much measures of achievement as measures of achievement are measures of cognitive abilities. Rather than being mutually exclusive, cognitive and academic abilities can be thought of as lying on a continuum with those abilities that develop largely through formal education and direct learning and instruction at one end (e.g., *Grw, Gq*) and abilities that develop as a result of informal and indirect learning and instruction at the other end (e.g., *Gf*). Thus, "abilities are achievements from past learning just as they are at the same time aptitudes for future learning.... Most abilities develop from extensive experience across learning history.... And ability differences are influenced by genetic factors as well as by experience" (Snow, 1994, p. 4).

9. If Ability and Achievement Are So Much Alike, Why Not Just Use One of Them to Assess Learning Disabilities?

Because it is difficult to make a clear-cut distinction between ability and achievement, it stands to reason that it is difficult to make a determination as to whether IQ *or* achievement tests should be used to understand the source of specific academic problems. Both intelligence and achievement tests yield useful information. The controversy surrounding what kind of test ought to be used in learning disability evaluations appears to have been sparked by a lack of understanding of what IQ and achievement tests measure. For example, the processes that Siegel (1998) identified as being low or problematic in children with learning disability (viz., auditory processing, short-term memory) are included in the *Gf-Gc cognitive abilities* framework. Achievement tests measure to some degree, the expression of those processes, whereas cognitive tests attempt to measure the underlying process itself. As a result of the continuous rather than dichotomous nature of cognitive abilities and achievements, coupled with the clarification of the distinction between ability and aptitude, it seems apparent that advocating for either an ability *or* an achievement measure in the identification and diagnosis of learning disability is unfounded.

10. Why Don't Aptitude Scores Seem to Result in a Significant Discrepancy as Often as Global Ability Scores?

Although logical as well as methodologically and technically sound, the use of aptitude clusters in discrepancy formulas creates a paradox of the sort described above. Specifically, the greater the predictive utility of the aptitude measure (i.e., the more variance in the criterion measure that can be explained by the aptitude measure) the *less likely* a finding of significant ability-achievement discrepancy will be for an individual whose academic skill deficiencies cannot be explained by conative, environmental, instructional, or other (exclusionary) factors. This is counter to the inherent meaning of an ability-achievement discrepancy found in most federal and state definitions of (and criteria for identifying) learning disabilities—that is, a significant discrepancy indicates the presence of a learning disability and a nonsignificant discrepancy indicates the absence of a learning disability.

When aptitude measures are developed that explain far more variance in academic achievement than can be explained currently through existing aptitude and ability measures, the term *discrepancy* could be replaced by the term *consistency*. That is, with greatly improved predictive power associated with aptitude measures, the probability of finding an aptitude-achievement *consistency* would be greater than the probability of finding an aptitude-achievement *discrepancy* in individuals with academic skill deficiencies, assuming all other exclusionary criteria were applied and evaluated appropriately. Notwithstanding, based on our current instrumentation as well as our current use of ability-achievement discrepancy procedures, "clinicians need to recognize that at least half of the equation in predicting achievement is accounted for by variables not included in the calculation of aptitude-achievement discrepancy scores. In short, the complexity of human behavior cannot be captured by any single number" (McGrew, 1994, p. 224).

11. If I Am Forced (by Law or Circumstance) to Use a Global Ability Score, Does It Matter Which One I Use?

The total test scores of the major intelligence batteries consist of a combination of abilities that reflect either the underlying theoretical model of the instrument or the author(s) conception of intelligence (i.e., his/her perception of those abilities that ought to be measured by an intelligence test). Table H.2 shows the differences in the underlying *Gf-Gc* abilities that contribute to the full scale or total test composites of many prominent and emerging intelligence batteries (based largely on a series of theory-driven joint factor-analytic studies presented in Chapters 3 and 4).

As may be seen in Table H.2, a significant amount of variation exists across intelligence batteries in terms of what *Gf-Gc* abilities are included in their respective total test composites. Based on the content differences across total test composites of different batteries, it seems that the results of ability-achievement discrepancy analyses will depend, in part, on the ability measure used. If all Full Scale scores do not consist of the same cognitive ability mix, then (assuming achievement is constant) the magnitude of an ability-achievement discrepancy will differ across ability measures. That is, differences in content across predictor variables will undoubtedly result in differing amounts of variance explained in the criterion variable. It appears that this condition alone undermines the utility and validity of the ability-achievement discrepancy procedure in learning disability diagnosis.

Confounding the issue related to differences in content across the total test scores of ability measures is the fact that different cognitive abilities have differential relations to academic skill areas (e.g., McGrew, 1993). For example, phonological awareness, verbal short-term memory and rate (rapid automatic naming or naming facility) are important in understanding reading acquisition and reading achievement (Morris et al., 1998). Many of the abilities listed in Table H.2 have been found to be strongly related to academic achievement. A review of the research on the differential effect of cognitive abilities on specific academic skills across the lifespan can be found in McGrew and Flanagan (1998) and Chapter 3 of this text.

12. Can You Give Me an Example of How the Use of Different Ability Scores Might Influence Discrepancy Analysis?

Suppose a fifth-grader has low *Ga, Gc,* and *Gs* abilities and concomitant reading acquisition deficits. Such an individual most likely will *not* demonstrate a severe ability-achievement discrepancy when her ability score is based on a global score that consists largely of *Ga, Gc,* and *Gs* abilities, because these abilities have been shown to be significantly pre-

TABLE H.2 *Gf-Gc* **Narrow (Stratum I) Abilities Measured by Cognitive and Special Purpose Batteries and Tests**

Gf-Gc Ability	WASI	WJ-R/III	WECH	K-ABC	SB:IV	DAS	KAIT	CAS	DTLA-3	Lieter-R
Gf										
RG	✓	✓✓					✓	✓	✓	✓
I	✓	✓✓	✓ WAIS-III	✓	✓	✓	✓	✓	✓	✓
RQ		✓✓	✓		✓	✓				
Gq										
A3			✓	✓	✓	✓				
KM					✓	✓				
Gc										
LD	✓	✓✓	✓		✓	✓	✓	✓	✓	
VL	✓	✓✓	✓			✓	✓		✓	
LS	✓	✓					✓	✓		
K0	✓	✓✓	✓		✓		✓		✓	
K2							✓			
Gsm										
MS	✓	✓✓		✓	✓	✓	✓	✓	✓	✓
MV (*Gv*)	✓	✓✓		✓	✓	✓	✓	✓	✓	✓
MW		✓✓	✓ WAIS-III							
Gv										
VZ		✓✓	✓	✓	✓	✓		✓		✓
SR			✓	✓	✓	✓			✓	
CS			✓	✓				✓		✓
CF	✓		✓					✓		✓
SS		✓								
PI				✓						
Ga										
PC-A		✓✓								
PC-S		✓✓								
UR		✓✓								
Glr										
MA		✓✓					✓			✓
MM		✓✓					✓			✓
M6						✓		✓		
NA		✓								
Gs										
P		✓✓						✓		✓
R9		✓✓	✓			✓		✓		✓
Gt										
R4								✓		
R7	✓					✓		✓		
Grw										
RD							✓			
V							✓			
SG							✓			

Note: Table includes primary and secondary abilities as well as "probable" and "possible" classifications (in a manner consistent with the ITDR) (McGrew & Flanagan, 1998). The Leiter-R and CAS may contain measures of Attention (AC). Some tests may measure psychomotor abilities (e.g., CAS Speech Rate) which are not reported in the table.

dictive of reading achievement in the elementary school years. Conversely, this same individual would likely show a significant ability-achievement discrepancy if her ability score was based on a global score that consisted largely of *Gf* and *Gv* abilities—abilities that do not demonstrate a significant relation to reading achievement in the elementary school years. In the former situation, many practitioners would conclude that the individual was not learning disabled (no ability-achievement discrepancy). In the latter situation, many practitioners would conclude that the individual is learning disabled (significant ability-achievement discrepancy). Neither conclusion is justified because neither conclusion is scientific, theory based, and consistent with the learning disability literature. Although this illustration is simplistic and lacks appropriate context (e.g., case history information), it demonstrates a common decision process (nonsignificant discrepancy = *No-learning disability*/significant discrepancy = *Yes-learning disability*) to which the practitioner is forced to adhere because of existing federal and state criteria. It is not a decision-making process that is grounded in theory and research.

13. Does the Identification of a Significant Discrepancy Automatically Imply the Presence of a Learning Disability?

Irrespective of the degree of technical validity inherent in the method used to establish the existence of a severe discrepancy, it is important to realize that by itself, a severe discrepancy between ability and achievement is *not* synonymous with (or mean that an individual has) a learning disability. An abundance of research (and legislative code) exists that argues unequivocally against the use of a significant ability-achievement discrepancy as the *sole* criterion on which to base a learning disability. Moreover, it is important to understand that discrepancy analysis will never be free from error entirely and we must practice in ways that serve to reduce it as much as possible. Within the content of the assessment approach presented in this text, a reduction in error of this type may be achieved by ensuring a convergence of indicators that support a particular diagnostic or eligibility decision following a systematic study of initial referral concerns. That is, data from multiple sources (e.g., behavioral observations, work samples, educational history and nature of instruction, background and environmental variables, cultural and linguistic differences, etc.), must point to (or converge on) the presence of a learning disability before identification and instructional decisions are made despite the presence of a significant (or nonsignificant) ability-achievement discrepancy.

14. Since the *Gf-Gc* Cross-Battery Approach Does Not Generate an Ability or Aptitude Score, How Can I Use It in the Identification of Specific Learning Disabilities?

If the state educational agency has specific mandates requiring the use of a particular type of standard score for discrepancy analysis in identifying learning disabilities, then the cross-battery approach will need to be augmented with additional subtests that allow for the calculation of such a score within one of the batteries used in the assessment. In such cases, it would be preferable to use the most reliable and technically valid score that can be obtained. Depending on the batteries used in cross-battery assessment, a global ability score (e.g., Wechsler FSIQ, WJ-R BCA) may be obtained with the administration of a relatively small number of additional tests. In other cases, it may not require the administration of any additional tests. Practitioners should use caution in attempting to substitute global scores drawn from a complete and comprehensive battery with those calculated from the use of an abbreviated or brief battery (e.g., Kaufman Brief Intelligence Test [K-BIT], Wechsler Abbreviated Scales of Intelligence [WASI], etc.). In some instances, a comprehensive battery will yield a score that is better-suited and more technically valid for the purposes of discrepancy analysis and formula calculations.

Although there may be occasion to use an abbreviated score, it is important to keep in mind that the validity of such practice will be as weak (or weaker than) that associated with the use of a comprehensive total test score. This is because the finding of a significant ability-achievement discrepancy, in and of itself, is not diagnostic of a learning disability, and the finding of a nonsignificant discrepancy does not rule out this disorder. Although an abbreviated battery that yields a highly reliable and valid general ability score may provide roughly the same ability-achievement discrepancy results as a full scale score from a comprehensive battery comprised of similar measures (e.g., WASI FSIQ-4 and WISC-III FSIQ), to support this claim. Until the use of abbreviated full scale scores in discrepancy analyses is supported empirically, full scale scores derived from abbreviated batteries should only be used to *screen* for ability-achievement discrepancies. Regardless of the total test score used in an ability-achievement discrepancy analysis (viz., a comprehensive or abbreviated full scale score), multiple data sources are necessary to support the practitioner's hypothesized meaning of a significant (or nonsignificant) ability-achievement discrepancy.

In some states (e.g., California), there are alternative methods (to standardized tests) that can be used to establish both the underlying cognitive processing deficit and a severe discrepancy requisite to the identification of a learning disability. In the example presented in the last paragraphs, a solid case for identifying the child as learning disabled (provided other relevant and sufficient sources of data were available to corroborate this diagnosis and alternative hypotheses were ruled out) can be made using the cross-battery approach (see Chapters 6 and 7). That is, rather than attempting to *find* an ability-achievement discrepancy through the use of standardized tests, a practitioner can use his/her knowledge of *Gf-Gc* theory and research (and related research on learning disability) to support the hypothesis that the child's reading deficiency is related to specific underlying cognitive processing deficits. This information could then be used as a basis for explaining why certain global scores may be attenuated (e.g., aptitude scores that consist largely of *Gc, Gs,* or *Ga* abilities) and, therefore, consistent with the outcome criterion (e.g., reading achievement). In cases such as this, the cross-battery approach can effectively assist in identifying the underlying cognitive processing deficit while other data are used to establish the presence of a severe discrepancy (e.g., work samples, curriculum-based assessment, school records, information provided by the parent, etc.). Not only may these procedures be effective in identifying learning disabilities, in some states they are also consistent with existing statutes.

15. Don't Children with Severe Ability-Achievement Discrepancies Perform Qualitatively Differently Than Those without Severe Discrepancies?

No. Aaron's (1997) review of the literature on the validity and utility of the (ability-achievement) discrepancy model of classifying *poor readers* into learning disabled (identified based on a severe discrepancy between ability and reading achievement) and non-learning disabled (those who did not have a severe ability-reading achievement discrepancy) groups rejected each of two fundamental premises of the discrepancy model classification procedure: (1) poor readers with discrepancies are qualitatively different (in terms of their cognitive makeup) than poor readers without discrepancies; and (2) as a consequence of the first premise, poor readers with discrepancies will respond differently to remedial treatment than poor readers without discrepancies. Aaron's review of the literature found little to no support for either premise.

According to Aaron, "studies which looked for differences between LD poor readers and non-LD poor readers from geographically diverse regions have provided no support for the premise that qualitative differences exist between LD poor readers and non-LD poor readers" (p. 466). This conclusion is consistent with the findings of other researchers and scholars in the field of learning disabilities (e.g., Lyon, 1995b; Siegel, 1992; 1998; Stanovich & Siegel, 1994). Indeed, the available evidence supports the conclusion that the method of separating poor readers on the *sole* basis of a severe ability-reading achievement discrepancy is of questionable significance.

Based on this conclusion, it is not surprising that Aaron's (1997) review found that poor readers with ability-reading achievement discrepancies did not respond differently to instruction than poor readers without this discrepancy. According to Aaron, "even though a few isolated studies report some difference in progress between poor readers classified as having LD and children with below average IQ, no overall, compelling evidence of educational gains has been obtained to warrant the continuation of the policy of classifying poor readers into LD and non-LD categories" (p. 475), based on the discrepancy model. In the same vein, Siegel (1998) concluded, "the IQ-achievement discrepancy scores serve no useful purpose in defining or understanding reading disabilities" (p. 131). Similarly, Gregg, Hoy, and Gay (1996) found that, "[w]hen compared to an extensive clinical model . . . [ability-achievement] discrepancy based models failed to differentiate adequately students with learning disabilities from non-learning disabled underachievers" (p. 80). The clinical model advocated by Gregg and colleagues is consistent with the approach presented in Part III of this text.

16. Can the *Gf-Gc* Cross-Battery Approach Help Identify Cognitive Processing Deficits More Accurately Than Other Methods?

Yes. The *Gf-Gc* taxonomy and the extant literature on the relations between *Gf-Gc* abilities and academic achievements at different ages can be used effectively to guide the selection of cognitive ability and achievement tests to assist in addressing referral concerns. As such, a comprehensive cognitive battery constructed following the procedures outlined in Chapter 6 would provide important information that may aid in explaining patterns of high and low achievement. Consistent with this notion is Swanson's (1991) suggestion that when investigating strategy development, processing competencies must be considered. Likewise, according to Brackett and McPherson (1996) "[a] major value of detecting severe discrepancies within and between areas of cognition is the focus on cognitive processing components of learning disabilities. However, the limited capacity of standardized instruments to assess isolated cognitive processes creates a major weakness in intracognitive discrepancy models" (p. 79). We believe that the *Gf-Gc* cross-battery approach more effectively addresses this longstanding weakness in intracognitive discrepancy models. Nevertheless, it is important to realize that some cognitive and achievement tasks involve very similar or identical skills, abilities, and processes. As such, the goal of assessment should be to uncover or identify the source of a learning problem through the convergence of cognitive *and* academic indicators that are related to the academic skill in question. Intracognitive analysis (via cross-battery assessment) and intra-achievement analysis appear quite appropriate for this purpose.

17. Do You Have any Guidelines for Interpreting Ability-Achievement Discrepancies in a Responsible Manner?

Yes. Figure H.1 provides an illustration of the points to be described herein. First, determine whether there is a significant ability-achievement discrepancy. Many test manuals contain *critical value* tables that provide the values necessary for determining whether a given ability-achievement standard score difference is significant (at either the 0.05 or 0.01 level of confidence) and some computer software scoring and report writing programs also include a set of functions for determining significant ability-achievement discrepancies.

Second, in addition to statistical significance, practitioners should determine whether the magnitude of the ability-achievement difference is *unusual*. This is accomplished typically by examining base rate or normative data. For example, if it is found that the magnitude of an individual's ability-achievement discrepancy occurred in less than 5 percent of same-age peers in the standardization sample, then the difference is considered unusual and likely clinically meaningful (see Sattler, 1992). Recall, however, that a significant and meaningful ability-achievement discrepancy, in and of itself, neither supports nor fails to support a learning disability.

Third, it is necessary to consider whether or not the cognitive abilities that have been found in the extant literature to predict the academic skill identified as problematic in the referral were included in the derivation of a total test ability score. If these abilities were assessed and were included as part of the ability measure in the discrepancy analysis, then the total test score may be attenuated. Conversely, if these abilities were not assessed and thus not reflected in the total test score, then it is assumed that the total test score is a valid estimate of general intelligence as defined by its cognitive ability constituents, provided there were not any individual/situational or background/environmental factors that inhibited performance.

Fourth, conduct an intracognitive discrepancy analysis using cross-battery principles and procedures (see Part III of this text). Prior to conducting cross-battery intracognitive analysis, the examiner should ensure that the cognitive abilities that are most predictive of

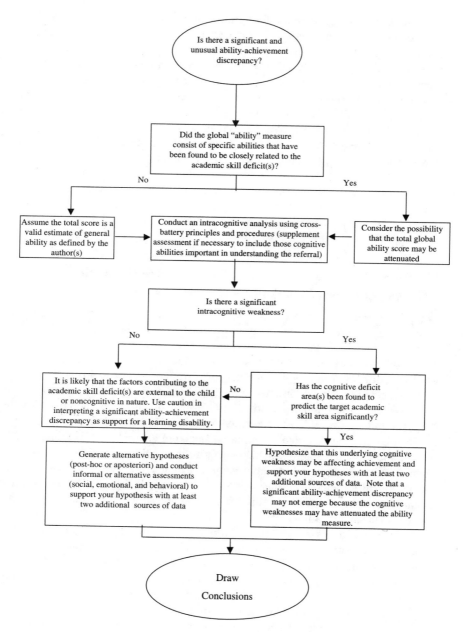

FIGURE H.1   A Flowchart for Interpreting Ability-Achievement Discrepancies

the presenting academic skill deficit(s) are represented in the assessment. If an intracognitive weakness was not found, based on this method, then it is assumed that factors contributing to the academic skill deficit(s) identified in the referral are external to the individual or noncognitive in nature. As such, an alternative to a learning disability hypothesis seems viable and caution should be exercised in interpreting a significant ability-achievement discrepancy as support for a learning disability diagnosis. If an intracognitive weakness is found, it is necessary to determine whether the identified cognitive ability weakness(es) are related to the academic skill deficit(s). As may be seen in Figure H.1, if the cognitive ability weakness(es) is closely associated with the academic skill deficit(s), then it may be hypothesized that underlying cognitive processes or weaknesses may be affecting academic achievement. In this situation, it is important to realize that an ability-achievement discrepancy may not emerge because the cognitive weakness(es) may have attenuated the ability measure (total test score) in the ability-achievement discrepancy analysis. As a result, the intracognitive analysis ought to supercede the ability-achievement discrepancy analysis in learning disability identification and diagnostic procedures. Figure H.1 shows that intracognitive weaknesses should be supported by other sources of data prior to drawing conclusions.

Conclusion

Although we explored the limitations of ability-achievement discrepancies in this appendix, we are nonetheless right back where we started from—that is, mandated by law to conduct an ability-achievement discrepancy analysis as part of a comprehensive learning disability evaluation. However, it is hoped that the information presented herein has allowed many practitioners to understand the nature of and meaning behind ability-achievement discrepancy analysis to the extent that it will represent an appropriate and defensible component of future learning disability evaluations.

To summarize, it is clear that the meaning of an ability-achievement discrepancy is largely dependent on (1) the content (i.e., cognitive mix) of the general ability measure and (2) the relations between the cognitive abilities that comprise the general ability score and the achievement domain in question. Ability-achievement *discrepancies,* in and of themselves, do not provide much insight into the nature of a learning disability. Unfortunately, the current criteria for documenting a learning disability has not caught up to (i.e., does not reflect) the current research that argues strongly against the reliance on an ability-achievement discrepancy model. Until the appropriate agencies and constituencies, that develop criteria for diagnosing learning disability, understand the often dangerous and misguided decisions that have resulted from uninformed interpretations of significant ability-achievement discrepancies—indeed, interpretations that are made out of legal necessity rather than in the context of scientific evidence—we are forced to couch these largely meaningless ability-achievement discrepancy results in a defensible framework that will allow us to make responsible decisions about special education eligibility and disability (e.g., in accordance with IDEA, *DSM-IV* criteria, the Americans with Disabilities Act, etc.) in spite of current legal constraints.

REFERENCES

Aaron, P. G. (1997). The impending demise of the discrepancy formula. *Review of Educational Research, 67*(4), 461–502.

Abrams, M. H. (Ed.). (1962). *The Norton anthology of English literature.* New York: W. W. Norton.

Ackerman, P. L., & Heggestad, E. D. (1997). Intelligence, personality, and interests: Evidence for overlapping traits. *Psychological Bulletin, 121*(2), 219–245.

Ackerman, P. T., Weir, N. L., Holloway, C. A., & Dykman, R. A. (1995). Adolescents diagnosed as dyslexic show major IQ declines on the WISC-III. *Reading and Writing, 7,* 163–170.

Adkins, D. C., & Kuder, G. F. (1940). The relation of primary mental abilities to activity preferences. *Psychometrika, 5,* 251–262.

Alfonso, V. C., & Flanagan, D. P. (1999). Cognitive assessment of preschoolers. In E. V. Nuttall (Ed.), *Assessing and screening preschoolers: Psychological and educational dimensions.* Boston: Allyn and Bacon.

Alfonso, V. C., Oakland, T. D., LaRocca, R., & Spanakos, A. (1998). *The course on individual cognitive assessment.* Manuscript submitted for publication.

Alfonso, V. C., Zgodny, A. R., Berdugo, H., & Gorman, B. S. (1998, August). *Confirmatory factor analysis of the WISC-III with individuals referred for academic difficulties.* Poster session presented at the annual meeting of the American Psychological Association, San Francisco, CA.

Allen, S. R., & Thorndike, R. M. (1995). Stability of the WPPSI-R and WISC-III factor structure using the cross-validation of covariance structure models. *Journal of Psychoeducational Assessment, 13,* 3–20.

American Educational Research Association, American Psychological Association, American Council on Measurement. (1985). *Standards for educational and psychological tests.* Washington, DC: American Psychological Association.

American Psychological Association. (1985). *Standards for educational and psychological testing.* Washington, DC: Author.

American Psychological Association. (1990). *Guidelines for providers of psychological services to ethnic, linguistic, and culturally diverse populations.* Washington, DC: Author.

Anaastopoulos, A. D., Spisto, M. A., & Maher, M. C. (1994). The WISC-III freedom from distractibility factor: Its utility in identifying children with attention deficit hyperactivity disorder. *Psychological Assessment, 6,* 368–371.

Anastasi, A. (1988). *Psychological testing* (6th ed.). New York: Macmillan.

Anastasi, A., & Urbina, S. (1997). *Psychological testing* (7th ed.). Upper Saddle River, NJ: Prentice-Hall.

Anderson, J. R. (1985). *Cognitive psychology and its implications* (2nd ed.). New York: W. H. Freeman.

Anokhin, P. K. (1969). Cybernetics and the integrative activity of the brain. In M. Cole & I. Maltzman (Eds.), *A handbook of contemporary Soviet psychology* (pp. 830–856). New York: Basic Books.

Armour-Thomas, E. (1992). Intellectual assessment of children from culturally diverse backgrounds. *School Psychology Review, 21,* 552–565.

Atkinson, L. (1991). On WAIS-R difference scores in the standardization sample. *Psychological Assessment, 3,* 292–294.

Baddeley, A. (1986). *Working memory.* Oxford: Oxford University Press.

Baddeley, A. (1992). Is working memory working?: The fifteenth Bartlett Lecture. *Quarterly Journal of Experimental Psychology, 44A,* 1–31.

Badian, N. A. (1988). A prediction of good and poor reading before kindergarten entry: A nine-year follow-up. *Journal of Learning Disabilities, 21*(2), 98–103, 123.

Bailey, K. D. (1994). *Typologies and taxonomies: An introduction to classification techniques.* Thousand Oaks, CA: Sage.

Baker, C. (1993). *Foundations of bilingual education and bilingualism.* Bristol, PA: Multilingual Matters, LTD.

Baker, L. A., Decker, S. N., & DeFries, J. C. (1984). Cognitive abilities in reading-disabled children: A longitudinal study. *Journal of Child Psychology & Psychiatry & Allied Disciplines, 25*(1), 111–117.

Bannatyne, A. (1974). Diagnosis: A note on recategorization of the WISC scaled scores. *Journal of Learning Disabilities, 7,* 272–274.

Barnouw, V. (1985). *Culture and personality.* Chicago: Dorsey Press.

Barona, M. S., & Barona, A. (1991). The assessment of culturally and linguistically different preschoolers. *Early Childhood Research Quarterly, 6,* 363–376.

Beal, A. L. (1995). A comparison of WISC-III and OLSAT for the identification of gifted students. *Canadian Journal of School Psychology, 11*(2), 120–129.

Beal, A. L., Dumont, R., Cruse, C. L., & Branche, A. H. (1996a). Practical implications of differences between the American and Canadian norms for the

WISC-III and a short form for children with learning disabilities. *Canadian Journal of School Psychology, 12,* 7–14.

Beal, A. L., Dumont, R., Cruse, C. L., & Branche, A. H. (1996b). Validation of a WISC-III short form for Canadian students with learning disabilities. *Canadian Journal of School Psychology, 12,* 1–6.

Beck, N. C., Ray, J. S., Seidenberg, M., Young, T. R., & Gamache, M. P. (1983). Development and cross-validation of a short form for the WISC-R. *Journal of Consulting and Clinical Psychology, 51*(6), 864–869.

Benson, J. (1998). Developing a strong program of construct validation: A test anxiety example. *Educational Measurement: Issues and Practice,* 10–22.

Benson, J., & Hagvet, K. (1996). The interplay between design, data analysis and theory in the measurement of coping. In M. Zeidner & N. Endler (Eds.), *Handbook of coping: Theory, research, applications* (pp. 83–106). New York: Wiley.

Berninger, V. W. (1990). Multiple orthographic codes: Key to alternative instructional methodologies for developing the orthographic-phonological connections underlying word identification. *School Psychology Review, 19*(4), 518–533.

Bialystok, E. (1991). *Language processing in bilingual children.* New York: Cambridge University Press.

Bishop, A. J. (1980). Spatial abilities and mathematics education: A review. *Educational Studies in Mathematics, 11,* 257–269.

Blaha, J., & Wallbrown, F. H. (1991). Hierarchical factor structure of the Wechsler Preschool and Primary Scale of Intelligence—Revised. *Psychological Assessment: A Journal of Consulting and Clinical Psychology, 3,* 455–463.

Blaha, J., & Wallbrown, F. H. (1996). Hierarchical factor structure of the Wechsler Intelligence Scale for Children—III. *Psychological Assessment, 8,* 214–218.

Boehm, A. E. (1991). Assessment of basic relational concepts. In B. Bracken (Ed.), *The psychoeducational assessment of preschool children* (2nd ed.) (pp. 86–106). Boston: Allyn and Bacon.

Bogen, J. E. (1969). The other side of the brain: Parts I, II, and III. *Bulletin of the Los Angeles Neurological Society, 34,* 73–105, 135–162, 191–203.

Bolen, L. M., Aichinger, C. W., Hall, C. W., & Webster, R. E. (1995). A comparison of the performance of cognitively disabled children on the WISC-R and WISC-III. *Journal of Clinical Psychology, 51*(1), 89–94.

Boone, D. (1995). A cross-sectional analysis of WAIS-R aging patterns with psychiatric inpatients: Support for Horn's hypothesis that fluid cognitive abilities decline. *Perceptual and Motor Skills, 81,* 371–379.

Borgas, K. (1999). Intelligence theories and psychological assessment: Which theory of intelligence guides your interpretation of intelligence test profiles? *The School Psychologist, 53*(1), 24–25.

Bornstein, R. A., & Chelune, G. J. (1988). Factor structure of the Wechsler Memory Scale—Revised. *The Clinical Neuropsychologist, 2*(2), 107–115.

Bossard, M. D., Reynolds, C. R., & Gutkin, T. B. (1980). A regression analysis of test bias on the Stanford-Binet Intelligence Scale. *Journal of Clinical Child Psychology, 9,* 52–54.

Bouchard, T. J., Jr. (1984, July 20). Review of the book *Frames of mind: The theory of multiple intelligences. American Journal of Orthopsychiatry, 54,* 506–508.

Bowey, J. A., Cain, M. T., & Ryan, S. M. (1992). A reading-level design study of phonological skills underlying fourth-grade children's word reading difficulties. *Child Development, 63,* 999–1011.

Bowey, J. A., & Patel, R. K. (1988). Metalinguistic ability and early reading achievement. *Applied Psycholinguistics, 9,* 367–383.

Boyle, G. J. (1991). Does item homogeneity indicate internal consistency of item redundancy in psychometric scales? *Personality & Individual Differences, 12*(3), 291–294.

Bracken, B. A. (1984). *Bracken Basic Concept Scale.* Columbus, OH: Charles E. Merrill.

Bracken, B. A. (1986). Incidence of basic concepts in the directions of five commonly used American tests of intelligence. *School Psychology International, 7,* 1–10.

Bracken, B. A. (1987). Limitations of preschool instruments and standards for minimal levels of technical adequacy. *Journal of Psychoeducational Assessment, 4,* 313–326.

Bracken, B. A., & Fagan, T. K. (Eds.). (1990). Intelligence: Theories and practice [Special Issue]. *Journal of Psychoeducational Assessment, 8*(3).

Bracken, B. A., & Howell, K. K. (1989). K-ABC subtest specificity recalculated. *Journal of School Psychology, 27,* 335–345.

Bracken, B. A., McCallum, R. S., & Crain, R. M. (1993). WISC-III subtest composite reliabilities and specificities: Interpretive aids. *Journal of Psychoeducational Assessment* [Monograph Series: WISC-III Monograph], 20–34.

Brackett, J., & McPherson, A. (1996). Learning disabilities diagnosis in postsecondary students: A comparison of discrepancy-based diagnostic models. In N. Gregg, C. Hoy, & A. F. Gay (Eds.), *Adults with learning disabilities: Theoretical and practical perspectives* (pp. 68–84). New York: Guilford.

Braden, J. P. (1995). Review of Wechsler Intelligence Scale for Children—Third Edition. In J. V. Mitchell (Ed.), *The tenth mental measurement yearbook* (vol. 1) (pp. 1098–1103). Lincoln, NE: Buros Institute of Mental Measurements.

Brady, S., Shankweiler, D., & Mann, V. (1983). Speech perception and memory coding in relation to reading ability. *Journal of Experimental Child Psychology, 35,* 345–367.

Briggs, S. R., & Cheek, J. M. (1986). The role of factor analysis in the development and evaluation of personality scales. Special issue: Methodological developments in personality research. *Journal of Personality, 54*(1), 106–148.

Brinckerhoff, L. C., Shaw, S. R., & McGuire, J. M. (1993). *Promoting postsecondary education for students with learning disabilities: A handbook for practitioners.* Austin, TX: Pro-Ed.

Broadbent, D. E. (1958). *Perception and communication.* Oxford, England: Pergamon.

Broverman, D. M. (1961). Effects of score transformations in the Q and R factor analysis techniques. *Psychological Review, 68,* 68–80.

Brown, L., Sherbenou, R. J., & Johnsen, S. K. (1997). *Test of Nonverbal Intelligence—Third Edition.* Itasca, IL: Riverside.

Bryant, P. E., Bradley, L., Maclean, M., & Crossland, J. (1989). Nursery rhymes, phonological skills and reading. *Child Language, 16,* 407–428.

Budoff, M. (1968). Learning potential as a supplementary assessment procedure. In J. Hellmuth (Ed.), *Learning disorders* (vol. 8) (pp. 295–343). Seattle, WA: Special Child.

Budoff, M. (1974). Measuring learning potential: An alternative to the traditional intelligence test. In G. R. Gredler (Ed.), *Ethical and legal factors in the practice of social psychology* (pp. 74–89). Philadelphia, PA: Temple University.

Budoff, M. (1987). The validity of learning potential assessment. In C. S. Lidz (Ed.), *Dynamic assessment* (pp. 52–81). New York: Guilford.

Burns, R. B. (1994, April). Surveying the cognitive domain. *Educational Researcher,* 35–37.

Burt, C. (1949). Alternative methods of factor analysis and their relations to Pearson's method of 'principal axes.' *British Journal of Psychology, Statistical Section, 2,* 98–121.

Burton, D. B., Naugle, R. I., & Schuster, J. M. (1995). A structural equation analysis of the Kaufman Brief Intelligence Test and the Wechsler Adult Intelligence Scale—Revised. *Psychological Assessment, 7,* 538–540.

Byrne, B., & Fielding-Barnsley, R. (1995). Evaluation of a program to teach phonemic awareness to young children: A 2 and 3 year follow-up and a new preschool trial. *Journal of Educational Psychology, 87*(3), 488–503.

Cacace, A. T., & McFarland, D. J., (1998). Central auditory processing disorder in school-aged children: A critical review. *Journal of Speech, Language, and Hearing Research, 41,* 355–373.

Callahan, C. D., Schopp, L., & Johnstone, B. (1997). Clinical utility of a seven subtest WAIS-R short form in the neuropsychological assessment of traumatic brain injury. *Archives of Clinical Neuropsychology, 12*(2), 133–138.

Campbell, D. P. (1971). *Handbook for the Strong Vocational Interest Blank.* Stanford, CA: Stanford University Press.

Campbell, J. M., & McCord, D. M. (1996). The WAIS-R Comprehension and Picture Arrangement subtests as measures of social intelligence: Testing traditional interpretations. *Journal of Psychoeducational Assessment, 14,* 240–249.

Campione, J., & Brown, A. (1987). Linking dynamic assessment with school achievement. In C. S. Lidz (Ed.), *Dynamic assessment* (pp. 85–115). New York: Guilford.

Carnine, L., Carnine, D., & Gersten, R. M. (1984). Analysis of oral reading errors made by economically disadvantaged students taught with a synthetic-phonics approach. *Reading Research Quarterly, 19*(3), 343–356.

Carroll, J. B. (1983). Studying individual differences in cognitive abilities: Through and beyond factor analysis. In R. F. Dillon (Ed.), *Individual differences in cognition* (vol. 1) (pp. 1–33). New York: Academic Press.

Carroll, J. B. (1989). Factor analysis since Spearman: Where do we stand? What do we know? In R. Kanfer, P. L. Ackerman, & R. Cudeck (Eds.), *Abilities, motivation, and methodology* (pp. 43–67). Hillside, NJ: Erlbaum.

Carroll, J. B. (1993a). *Human cognitive abilities: A survey of factor-analytic studies.* Cambridge, England: Cambridge University Press.

Carroll, J. B. (1993b). What abilities are measured by the WISC-III? *Journal of Psychoeducational Assessment* [WISC-III Monograph], 134–143.

Carroll, J. B. (1995a). Review of the book *Assessment of cognitive processes: The PASS theory of intelligence. Journal of Psychoeducational Assessment, 13,* 397–409.

Carroll, J. B. (1995b). On methodology in the study of cognitive abilities. *Multivariate Behavioral Research, 30*(3), 429–452.

Carroll J. B. (1996). A three-stratum theory of intelligence: Spearman's contribution. In I. Dennis & P. Tapsfield (Eds.), *Human abilities: Their nature and measurement* (pp. 1–17). New York: Academic Press.

Carroll, J. B. (1996). Mathematical abilities: Some results from factor analysis. In R. J. Sternberg & T. Ben-Zeev (Eds.), *The nature of mathematical thinking* (pp. 3–25). Mahwah, NJ: Erlbaum.

Carroll, J. B. (1997a). Psychometrics, intelligence, and public perception. *Intelligence, 24*(1), 25–52.

Carroll, J. B. (1997b). The three-stratum theory of cognitive abilities. In D. P. Flanagan, J. L. Genshaft, & P. L. Harrison (Eds.), *Contemporary intellectual assessment: Theories, tests, and issues* (pp. 122–130). New York: Guilford.

Carroll, J. B. (1998). Human cognitive abilities: A critique. In J. J. McArdle & R. W. Woodcock (Eds.), *Human cognitive abilities in theory and practice* (pp. 5–24). Mahwah, New Jersey: Lawrence Erlbaum Associates.

Carroll, J. B., & Maxwell, S. E. (1979). Individual differences in cognitive abilities. *Annual Review of Psychology, 30,* 603–640.

Cattell, R. B. (1941). Some theoretical issues in adult intelligence testing. *Psychological Bulletin, 38,* 592.

Cattell, R. B. (1957). *Personality and motivation structure and measurement.* New York: World Book.

Cattell, R. B. (1971). *Abilities: Their structure, growth, and action.* Boston: Houghton Mifflin.

Cervantes, H. T. (1988). Nondiscriminatory assessment and informal data gathering: The case of Gonzaldo L. In R. L. Jones (Ed.), *Psychoeducational assessment of minority group children: A casebook.* Berkeley, CA: Cobb & Henry.

Chan, D. W., & Lin, W. Y. (1996). The two- and three-dimensional models of the HK-WISC: A confirmatory factor analysis. *Measurement, and Evaluation in Counseling and Development, 28,* 191–199.

Chen, J.-Q., & Gardner, H. (1997). Alternative assessment from a multiple intelligences theoretical perspective. In D. P. Flanagan, J. L. Genshaft, & P. L. Harrison (Eds.), *Contemporary intellectual assessment: Theories, tests, and issues* (pp. 105–121). New York: Guilford.

Children's Defense Fund. (1989). *A vision for America's children.* Washington, DC: Author.

Chomsky, N. (1986). *Knowledge of language: Its nature, origin, and use.* New York: Praeger.

Clarke, L. A., & Watson, D. (1995). Constructing validity: Basic issues in objective scale development. *Psychological Assessment, 7,* 309–319.

Cohen, J. (1952). A factor-analytically based rationale for the Wechsler-Bellevue. *Journal of Consulting Psychology, 16,* 272–277.

Cohen, J. (1957). A factor-analytically based rationale for the Wechsler Adult Intelligence Scale. *Journal of Consulting Psychology, 21,* 451–457.

Cohen, J. (1959). The factorial structure of the WISC at ages 7-7, 10-6, and 13-6. *Journal of Consulting Psychology, 23,* 285–299.

Cohen, M. (1997). *Children's Memory Scale.* San Antonio, TX: The Psychological Corporation.

Cole, M., & Cole, S. R. (1993). *The development of children.* New York: Scientific American Books.

Collier, V. P. (1992). A synthesis of studies examining long-term language minority student data on academic achievement. *Bilingual Research Journal, 16,* 187–212.

Comrey, A. L. (1988). Factor-analytic methods of scale development in personality and clinical psychology. *Journal of Consulting and Clinical Psychology, 56*(5), 754–761.

Cook, V. J. (1987). Psychoeducational evaluation of ethnic minority children. In R. J. Velasquez & C. L. Uyeda (Eds.), *A cross-cultural perspective for the helping professional: Conference proceedings* (pp. 123–144). Fullerton: California State University.

Cook-Morales, V. J. (1994, February). *Ecosystems service delivery: Assessment and interventions.* Selected reading for CSP 710A, Ecosystems. Department of Counseling and School Psychology, San Diego State University.

Cone, T. E., & Wilson, L. R. (1981). Quantifying a severe discrepancy: A critical analysis. *Learning Disability Quarterly, 4,* 359–371.

Connery, S., Katz, D., Kaufman, A. S., & Kaufman, N. L. (1996). Correlations between two short cognitive tests and a WISC-III short form using a sample of adolescent inpatients. *Psychological Reports, 78,* 1373–1378.

Cooney, J. B., & Swanson, L. H. (1990). Individual differences in memory for mathematical story problems: Memory span and problem perception. *Journal of Educational Psychology, 82*(3), 570–577.

Costa, P. T., Jr., & McCrae, R. R. (1992a). Four ways five factors are basic. *Personality and Individual Differences, 13,* 653–665.

Costa, P. T., Jr., & McCrae, R. R. (1992b). "Four ways five factors are *not* basic": Reply. *Personality and Individual Differences, 13,* 861–865.

Crocker, L., & Algina, J. (1986). *Introduction to classical and modern test theory.* New York: Holt, Rinehart, and Winston.

Crockett, D. J. T., Hurwitz, T. A., Hart, S. D., MacDonald, J., & Welch, S. (1996). Prevalence of WAIS-R prototypal groups in neuropsychiatric participants. *Archives of Clinical Neuropsychology, 11*(8), 637–650.

Cronbach, L. (1971). Construct validation after thirty years. In R. Linn (Ed.), *Intelligence: Measurement, theory, and public policy: Proceedings of a syposium in honor of Lloyd Humphreys* (pp. 147–167). Urbana, IL: University of Chicago Press.

Cronbach, L. (1986). Signs of optimism for intelligence testing. *Educational Measurement: Issues and Practice, 5,* 23–24.

Cronbach, L. (1989). Construct validation after thirty years. In R. Linn (Ed.), *Intelligence: Measurement, theory, and public policy: Proceedings of a syposium in honor of Lloyd Humphreys* (pp. 147–167). Urbana, IL: University of Chicago Press.

Cronbach, L. J. (1984). *Essentials of psychological testing* (4th ed.). New York: Harper and Row.

Cronbach, L. J., & Meehl, P. (1955). Construct validity of psychological tests. *Psychological Bulletin, 52,* 281–302.

Cronbach, L. J., & Snow, R. E. (1977). *Aptitudes and instructional methods.* New York: Irvington.

Cummins, J. (1981). *Bilingualism and minority language children.* Toronto: The Ontario Institute for Studies in Education.

Cummins, J. C. (1984). *Bilingual and special education: Issues in assessment and pedagogy.* Austin, TX: Pro-Ed.

Daley, C. E., & Nagle, R. J. (1996). Relevance of WISC-III indicators for assessment of learning disabilities. *Journal of Psychoeducational Assessment, 14,* 320–333.

Dana, R. H. (1993). *Multicultural assessment perspectives for professional psychology.* Boston: Allyn and Bacon.

Daneman, M., & Carpenter, P. A. (1980). Individual differences in working memory and reading. *Journal of Verbal Learning and Verbal Behavior, 19,* 450–466.

Daniel, M. H. (1997). Intelligence testing: Status and trends. *American Psychologist, 52,* 1038–1045.

Das, J. P., Kirby, J. R., & Jarman, R. F. (1979). *Simultaneous and successive cognitive processes.* New York: Academic Press.

Das, J. P., & Naglieri, J. A. (1997). *Cognitive Assessment System.* Itasca, IL: Riverside.

Das, J. P., Naglieri, J. A., & Kirby, J. R. (1994). *Assessment of cognitive processes: The PASS theory of intelligence.* Needham Heights, MA: Allyn and Bacon.

Das, J. P., Naglieri, J. A., & Kirby, J. R. (1994). Assessment of cognitive processes: The PASS theory of intelligence. *Journal of Psychoeducational Assessment, 13,* 397–409.

Das, J. P., & Siu, I. (1982). Good and poor readers' word naming time, memory span, and story recall. *Journal of Experimental Education, 57*(2), 101–114.

Davidson, L., & Torff, B. (1994). Musical intelligence. In R. J. Sternberg (Ed.), *Encyclopedia of human intelligence* (pp. 744–746). New York: Macmillan.

Dawis, R. V. (1994). Occupations. In R. J. Sternberg (Ed.), *Encyclopedia of human intelligence* (pp. 781–785). New York: Macmillan.

Decker, S. N., & DeFries, J. C. (1980). Cognitive abilities in families with reading disabled children. *Journal of Learning Disabilities, 13*(9), 517–522.

Demsky, Y., Gass, C., & Golden, C. (1997). Common short forms of the Spanish Wechsler Adult Intelligence Scale. *Perceptual and Motor Skills, 85,* 1121–1122.

Detterman, D. K. (1979). Detterman's laws of individual differences research. In R. J. Sternberg & D. K. Detterman (Eds.), *Human intelligence: Perspectives on its theory and measurement.* Norwood, NJ: Ablex.

Detterman, D. K. (1985). Review of Wechsler Intelligence Scale for Children—Revised. In J. V. Mitchell (Ed.), *The ninth mental measurement yearbook* (vol. 2) (pp. 1715–1716). Lincoln, NE: Buros Institute of Mental Measurements.

DeZubicary, G., Smith, G., & Anderson, D. (1996). Comparison of IQs and Verbal-Performance IQ discrepancies estimated from two seven-subtest short forms of the WAIS-R. *Journal of Psychoeducational Assessment, 14,* 121–130.

Dixon, R. A., Kramer, D. A., & Baltes, P. B. (1985). Intelligence: A life-span developmental perspective. In B. B. Wolman (Ed.), *Handbook of intelligence: Theories, measurements, and applications* (pp. 301–350). New York: Wiley.

Dixon, W. E., & Anderson, T. (1995). Establishing covariance continuity between the WISC-R and the WISC-III. *Psychological Assessment, 7*(1), 115–117.

Donders, J. (1996). Cluster subtypes in the WISC-III standardization sample: Analysis of factor index scores. *Psychological Assessment, 8*(3), 312–318.

Donders, J. (1997). Sensitivity of the WISC-III to injury severity in children with traumatic head injury. *Psychological Assessment, 4*(1), 107–109.

Donders, J. (1997). A short form of the WISC-III for clinical use. *Psychological Assessment, 9*(1), 15–20.

Dumont, R., Cruse, C. L., Price, L., & Whelley, P. (1996). The relationship between the Differential Ability

Scales (DAS) and the Wechsler Intelligence Scale for Children—Third Edition (WISC-III) for students with learning disabilities. *Psychology in the Schools, 33*(3), 203–209.

Dumont, R., & Faro, C. (1993). A WISC-III short form for learning-disabled students. *Psychology in the Schools, 30,* 212–219.

Dunn, G., & Everitt, B. S. (1982). *An introduction to mathematical taxonomy.* New York: Cambridge University Press.

Dunn, L. (1968). Special education for the mildly retarded—Is much of it justifiable? *Exceptional Children, 35,* 5–22.

Dunn, L. M., Dunn, L. M., & Williams, K. T. (1997). *Peabody Picture Vocabulary Test—Third Edition.* Circle Pines, MN: American Guidance Service.

Eden, G. F., Stein, J. F., Wood, H. M., & Wood, F. B. (1996). Differences in visuospatial judgment in reading-disability and normal children. *Perceptual and Motor Skills, 82,* 155–177.

Eggen, P., & Kauchak, D. (1997). *Educational psychology: Windows on classrooms.* Upper Saddle River, NJ: Merrill.

Ehrman, M. E. (1996). *Understanding second language learning difficulties.* Thousand Oaks, CA: Sage.

Eisenstein, N., & Engelhart, C. I. (1997). Comparison of the K-BIT with short forms of the WAIS-R in a neuropsychological population. *Psychological Assessment, 9*(1), 57–62.

Elliott, C. D. (1990a). *Differential Ability Scales.* San Antonio, TX: Psychological Corporation.

Elliott, C. D. (1990b). *The Differential Ability Scales: Introductory and technical handbook.* San Antonio, TX: Psychological Corporation.

Elliott, C. D. (1994, April). *The measurement of fluid intelligence: Comparison of the Wechsler scales with the DAS and the KAIT.* Paper presented at the annual National Association of School Psychologists (NASP) Convention, Seattle, WA.

Ellwood, R. W. (1991). Factor structure of the Wechsler Memory Scale—Revised (WMS-R) in a clinical sample: A methodological reappraisal. *The Clinical Neuropsychologist, 5*(4), 329–337.

Embretson, S. E. (1996). Cognitive design principles and the successful performer: A study on spatial ability. *Journal of Educational Measurement, 33*(1), 29–39.

Engle, R. W., Cantor, J., & Carullo, J. J. (1992). Individual differences in working memory and comprehension: Test of four hypotheses. *Journal of Experimental Psychology, 18*(5), 972–992.

Engle, R. W., Nations, J. K., & Cantor, J. (1990). Is "working memory capacity" just another name for word knowledge? *Journal of Educational Psychology, 82*(4), 799–804.

Epstein, S. (1983). Aggression and beyond: Some basic issues on the prediction of behavior. *Journal of Personality, 51,* 360–392.

Esters, E. G., Ittenbach, R. F., & Han, K. (1997). Today's IQ tests: Are they really better than their historical predecessors? *School Psychology Review, 26*(2), 211–223.

Eysenck, H. J. (1991). Dimensions of personality: 16, 5 or 3? Criteria for a taxonomic paradigm. *Personality and Individual Differences, 12,* 773–790.

Eysenck, H. J. (1992). Four ways five factors are not basic. *Personality and Individual Differences, 13,* 667–673.

Farmer, M. F., & Klein, R. M. (1995). The evidence for a temporal processing deficit linked to dyslexia: A review. *Psychonomic Bulletin and Review, 2*(4), 460–493.

Faust, D., & Hollingsworth, J. (1991). Concurrent validation of the Wechsler preschool and primary scale of intelligence revised with two criteria of cognitive abilities. *Journal of Psychoeducational Assessment, 9,* 224–229.

Felton, R. H., & Pepper, P. P. (1995). Early identification and intervention of phonological deficits in kindergarten and early elementary children at risk for reading disability. *School Psychology Review, 24,* 405–414.

Feuerstein, R. (1970). A dynamic approach to the causation, prevention, and alleviaton of retarded performance. In H. C. Haywood (Ed.), *Sociocultural aspects of mental retardation* (pp. 341–377). New York: Appleton-Century-Crofts.

Feuerstein, R. (1972). Cognitive assessment of the socioculturally deprived child and adolescent. In L. J. Cornbach & P. J. D. Drenth (Eds.), *Mental tests and cultural adaptation* (pp. 265–275). The Hague: Mouton.

Feuerstein, R. (1979). *The dynamic assessment of retarded performance.* Baltimore, MD: University Park Press.

Feuerstein, R., Feuerstein, R., & Gross, S. (1997). The Learning Potential Assessment Device. In D. P. Flanagan, J. L. Genshaft, & P. L. Harrison (Eds.), *Contemporary intellectual assessment: Theories, tests, and issues* (pp. 297–313). New York: Guilford.

Feuerstein, R., Feuerstein, R., & Schun, Y. (1995). *The theory of structural cognitive modifiability.* Unpublished manuscript.

Figueroa, R. A. (1983). Test bias and Hispanic children. *Journal of Special Education, 17,* 431–440.

Figueroa, R. A. (1990). Assessment of linguistic minority group children. In C. R. Reynolds & R. W. Kamphaus (Eds.), *Handbook of psychological and educational assessment of children: Vol. 1. Intelligence and achievement.* New York: Guilford.

Figueroa, R. A. (1990a). Best practices in the assessment of bilingual children. In A. Thomas & J. Grimes (Eds.), *Best Practices in School Psychology—II.* Washington, DC: National Association of School Psychologists.

Figueroa, R. A., Delgado, G. L., & Ruiz, N. T. (1984). Assessment of Hispanic children: Implications for Hispanic hearing-impaired children. In G. L. Delgado (Ed.), *The Hispanic deaf: Issues and challenges for bilingual special education* (pp. 124–153). Washington, DC: Gallaudet College Press.

Fine, M. J. (1985). Interventions from a systems-ecological perspective. *Professional Psychology: Research and Practice, 16,* 262–270.

Flanagan, D. P. (1999). *Weschler-based* Gf-Gc *cross-battery assessment: Strengthening the validity of interpretations drawn from Wechsler test scores.* Manuscript submitted for publication.

Flanagan, D. P., & Alfonso, V. C. (1993a). Differences required for significance between Wechsler verbal and performance IQs and the WIAT subtests and composites: The predicted-achievement method. *Psychology in the Schools, 30,* 125–132.

Flanagan, D. P., & Alfonso, V. C. (1993b). WIAT subtest and composite predicted-achievement values based on WISC-III verbal and performance IQs. *Psychology in the Schools, 30,* 310–320.

Flanagan, D. P., & Alfonso, V. C. (1994, May). *A critical review of intelligence tests for culturally diverse preschoolers.* Paper presented at the meeting of the New York State Psychological Association, Bolton Landing, NY.

Flanagan, D. P., & Alfonso, V. C. (1995). A critical review of the technical characteristics of new and recently revised intelligence tests for preschool children. *Journal of Psychoeducational Assessment, 13,* 66–90.

Flanagan, D. P., Alfonso, V. C., & Flanagan, R. (1994). A review of the Kaufman Adolescent and Adult Intelligence Test: An advancement in cognitive assessment? *School Psychology Review, 23,* 512–525.

Flanagan, D. P., Alfonso, V. C., Kaminer, T., & Rader, D. E. (1995). Incidence of basic concepts in the directions of new and revised American intelligence tests for preschool children. *School Psychology International, 16,* 345–364.

Flanagan, D. P., Andrews, T. J., & Genshaft, J. L. (1997). The functional utility of intelligence tests with special education populations. In D. P. Flanagan, J. L. Genshaft, & P. L. Harrison (Eds.), *Contemporary*

intellectual assessment: Theories, tests, and issues (pp. 457–483). New York: Guilford.

Flanagan, D. P., & Genshaft, J. L. (1997). Guest editors' comments: Mini-series on issues related to the use and interpretation of intelligence testing in the schools. *School Psychology Review, 26,* 146–149.

Flanagan, D. P., Genshaft, J. L., & Harrison, P. L. (Eds.). (1997). *Contemporary intellectual assessment: Theories, tests, and issues.* New York: Guilford.

Flanagan, D. P., Keith, T. Z., Mascolo, J., Vanderwood, M. L., & McGrew, K. S. (1999). *Is g all there is? An investigation of the relationship between* Gf-Gc *specific cognitive abilities and math achievement in individuals in grades 1 through 12.* Manuscript in preparation.

Flanagan, D. P., Mascolo, J., & Genshaft, J. L. (in press). A conceptual framework for interpreting preschool intelligence tests. In B. A. Bracken (Ed.), *The psychoeducational assessment of preschool children.* Boston: Allyn and Bacon.

Flanagan, D. P., & McGrew, K. S. (1995, March). *Will you evolve or become extinct? Interpreting intelligence tests from modern* Gf-Gc *theory.* Paper presented at the meeting of the National Association of School Psychologists, Chicago.

Flanagan, D. P., & McGrew, K. S. (1997). A cross-battery approach to assessing and interpreting cognitive abilities: Narrowing the gap between practice and cognitive science. In D. P. Flanagan, J. L. Genshaft, & P. L. Harrison (Eds.), *Contemporary intellectual assessment: Theories, tests, and issues* (pp. 314–325). New York: Guilford.

Flanagan, D. P., & McGrew, K. S. (1998). Interpreting intelligence tests from contemporary *Gf-Gc* theory: Joint confirmatory factor analysis of the WJ-R and KAIT in a non-White sample. *Journal of School Psychology, 36,* 151–182.

Flanagan, D. P., & Miranda, A. H. (1995). Working with culturally different families. In A. Thomas & J. Grimes (Eds.), *Best practices in school psychology—III* (pp. 1039–1060). Washington, DC: The National Association of School Psychologists.

Flynn, J. R. (1984). The mean IQ of Americans: Massive gains 1932 to 1978. *Psychological Bulletin, 95,* 29–51.

Fraboni, M., & Saltstone, R. (1992). The WAIS-R number-of-factors quandary: A cluster analytic approach to construct validation. *Educational and Psychological Measurement, 52,* 603–613.

French, J. L., & Hale, R. L. (1990). A history of the development of psychological and educational testing. In C. R. Reynolds & R. W. Kamphaus (Eds.), *Handbook of psychological and educational assessment of children: Intelligence and achievement* (pp. 3–28). New York: Guilford.

French, J. W., Eckstrom, R. B., & Price, L. A. (1963). *Manual and kit of reference tests for cognitive factors*. Princeton, NJ: Educational Testing Service.

Friedman, L. (1995). The space factor in mathematics: Gender differences. *Review of Educational Research, 65*(1), 22–50.

Fromkin, V., & Rodman, R. (1993). *An introduction to language* (5th ed.). New York: Harcourt Brace Jovanovich.

Gagne, E. D. (1985). *The cognitive psychology of school learning*. Boston: Little, Brown.

Gardner, H. (1983). *Frames of mind: The theory of multiple intelligences*. New York: Basic Books.

Gardner, H. (1993). *Frames of mind: The theory of multiple intelligences* (10th anniversary ed.). New York: Basic Books.

Gardner, H. (1994). Multiple intelligences theory. In R. J. Sternberg (Ed.), *Encyclopedia of human intelligence* (pp. 740–742). New York: Macmillan.

Gardner, H. (1998). Are there additional intelligences? The case for naturalist, spiritual, and existential intelligences. In J. Kane (Ed.), *Education, information and transformation*. Englewood Cliffs, NJ: Prentice-Hall.

Gaskill, F. W. I., & Brantley, J. C. (1996). Changes in ability and achievement scores over time: Implications for children classified as learning disabled. *Journal of Psychoeducational Assessment, 14,* 220–228.

Geary, D. C. (1993). Mathematical disabilities: Cognitive, neuropsychological, and genetic components. *Psychological Bulletin, 114*(2), 345–362.

Genshaft, J. L., & Gerner, M. E. (1998). Gf-Gc cross-battery assessment: Implications for school psychologists. *Communique, 26*(8), 24–27.

Gerkne, K., & Hodapp, A. (1992). Assessment of preschoolers at-risk with the WPPSI-R and the Stanford-Binet. *Psychological Reports, 71,* 659–664.

German, D. J. (1996). The effects of word-finding difficulties on intellectual assessment. *Journal of Psychoeducational Assessment, 14,* 373–384.

Gfeller, J. D., Meldrum, D. L., & Jacobi, K. A. (1995). The impact of constructional impairment on the WMS-R visual reproduction subtests. *Journal of Clinical Psychology, 51*(1), 58–63.

Ghiselli, E. E. (1966). *The validity of occupational aptitude tests*. New York: Wiley.

Gide, A. (1913). *Journals 1889–1949, detached pages,* journal entry. Edited by Justin O'Brien, 1951.

Glutting, J. J., & Kaplan, D. (1990). Stanford-Binet Intelligence Scale—Fourth edition: Making the case for reasonable interpretations. In C. R. Reynolds & R.

W. Kamphaus (Eds.), *Handbook of psychological and educational assessment of children: Intelligence and achievement* (pp. 277–296). New York: Guilford.

Glutting, J. J., McDermott, P. A., & Konold, T. R. (1997). Ontology, structure, and diagnostic benefits of a normative subtest taxonomy from the WISC-III standardization sample. In D. P. Flanagan, J. L. Genshaft, & P. L. Harrison (Eds.), *Contemporary intellectual assessment: Theories, tests, and issues* (pp. 349–372). New York: Guilford.

Glutting, J. J., McDermott, P. A., Prifitera, A., & McGrath, E. A. (1994). Core profile types for the WISC-III and WIAT: Their development and application in identifying multivariate IQ-achievement discrepancies. *School Psychology Review, 23,* 619–639.

Glutting, J. J., McDermott, P. A., Watkins, M. M., Kush, J. C., & Konold, T. R. (1997). The base rate problem and its consequences for interpreting children's ability profiles. *School Psychology Review, 26,* 176–188.

Glutting, J. J., Oakland, T., & Konold, T. R. (1994). Criterion-Related Bias with the guide to the assessment of test session behavior for the WISC-III and WIAT: Possible race/ethnicity, gender, and SES effects. *Journal of School Psychology, 32*(4), 355–369.

Glutting, J. J., Youngstrom, E. A., Hale, R. L., Ward. T., & Ward, S. (1997). Incremental efficacy of WISC-III factor scores in predicting achievement: What do they tell us? *Psychological Assessment, 9*(3), 295–301.

Gonzalez, V., Brusca-Vega, R., & Yawkey, T. (1997). *Assessment and instruction of culturally and linguistically diverse students with or at-risk of learning problems: From research to practice*. Needham Heights, MA: Allyn and Bacon.

Good, R. H., & Lane, S. (1990). Confirmatory factor analysis of the K-ABC and WISC-R for at-risk students: A comparison of hierarchical models. *School Psychology Review, 19*(4), 492–504.

Gopaul-McNicol, S., & Thomas-Presswood, T. (1998). *Working with linguistically and culturally different children: Innovative clinical and educational approaches*. Needham Heights, MA: Allyn and Bacon.

Gould, S. J. (1981). *The mismeasure of man*. New York: W. W. Norton.

Graf, M., & Hinton, R. N. (1994). A 3-year comparison study of WISC-R and WISC-III IQ scores for a sample of special education students. *Educational and Psychological Measurement, 54*(1), 128–133.

Graf, M., & Hinton, R. N. (1997). Correlations for the developmental visual-motor integration test and the

Wechsler Intelligence Scale for Children—III. *Perceptual and Motor Skills, 84,* 699–702.

Greenberg, R. D., Stewart, K. J., & Hansche, W. J. (1986). Factor analysis of the WISC-R for white and black children evaluated for gifted placement. *Journal of Psychoeducational Assessment, 4,* 123–130.

Greenfield, P. M. (1998). The cultural evolution of IQ. In U. Neisser (Ed.), *The rising curve: Long-term gains in IQ and related measures.* Washington, DC: American Psychological Association.

Greenspan, S., & Driscoll, J. (1997). The role of intelligence in a broad model of personal competence. In D. P. Flanagan, J. L. Genshaft, & P. L. Harrison (Eds.), *Contemporary intellectual assessment: Theories, tests, and issues* (pp. 131–150). New York: Guilford.

Greg, N., Hoy, C., & Gay, A. F. (1996). *Adults with learning disabilities: Theoretical and practical perspectives.* New York: Guilford.

Gridley, B. E., & Roid, G. H. (1998). The use of the WISC-III with achievement tests. In A. Prifitera & D. Saklofske (Eds.), *WISC-III clinical use and interpretation: Scientist-practitioner perspectives* (pp. 249–288). San Diego, CA: Academic Press.

Grigorenko, E. L., & Sternberg, J. R. (1998). Dynamic testing. *Psychological Bulletin, 124*(1), 75–111.

Griswold, P. C., Gelzheiser, L. M., & Shepherd, M. J. (1987). Does a production deficiency hypothesis account for vocabulary learning among adolescents with learning disabilities? *Journal of Learning Disabilities, 20*(10), 620–626.

Grosjean, F. (1989). Neurolinguists beware! The bilingual is not two monolinguals in one person. *Brain and Language, 36,* 3–15.

Grossman, I., Dennis, B., & Kaufman, A. S. (1993). Validation of an "amazingly" short form of the WAIS-R for a clinically depressed sample. *Journal of Psychoeducational Assessment, 11,* 173–181.

Guilford, J. P. (1954). *Psychometric methods* (2nd ed.). New York: McGraw-Hill.

Guilford, J. P. (1967). *The nature of human intelligence.* New York: McGraw-Hill.

Gunter, C. M., Sapp, G. L., & Green, A. C. (1995). Comparison of scores on WISC-III and WISC-R of urban learning disabled students. *Psychological Reports, 77,* 473–474.

Gustafsson, J. E. (1984). A unifying model for the structure of intellectual abilities. *Intelligence, 8,* 179–203.

Gustafsson, J. E. (1988a). The "Spearman hypothesis" is false. *Multivariate Behavioral Research, 27,* 265–267.

Gustafsson, J. E. (1988b). Hierarchical models of individual differences in cognitive abilities. In R. J. Sternberg (Ed.), *Advances in the psychology of human intelligence* (vol. 4) (pp. 35–71). Hillsdale, NJ: Erlbaum.

Gustafsson, J. E. (1989). Broad and narrow abilities in research on learning and instruction. In R. Kanfer, P. L. Ackerman, & R. Cudeck (Eds.), *Abilities, motivation, and methodology: The Minnesota Symposium on Learning and Individual Differences* (pp. 203–237). Hillside, NJ: Erlbaum.

Gustafsson, J. E. (1994). General intelligence. In R. J. Sternberg (Ed.), *Encyclopedia of human intelligence* (pp. 469–475). New York: Macmillan.

Gustafsson, J. E., & Undheim, J. O. (1996). Individual differences in cognitive functions. In D. C. Berliner & R. C. Cabfee (Eds.), *Handbook of Educational Psychology* (pp. 186–242). New York: Macmillan.

Gutkin, T. B., & Reynolds, C. R. (1980). Factorial similarity of the WISC-R for Anglos and Chicanos referred for psychological services. *Journal of School Psychology, 18,* 34–39.

Gutkin, T. B., & Reynolds, C. R. (1981). Factorial similarity of the WISC-R for white and black children from the standardization sample. *Journal of Educational Psychology, 73,* 227–231.

Gutkin, T. B., Reynolds, C. R., & Galvin, G. A. (1984). Factor analysis of the Wechsler Adult Intelligence Scale—Revised (WAIS-R): An examination of the standardization sample. *Journal of School Psychology, 22,* 83–93.

Hakistan, A. R., & Bennet, R. W. (1977). Validity studies using the Comprehensive Ability Scale (CAB): I. Academic achievement criteria. *Educational and Psychological Measurement, 37,* 425–437.

Hakistan, A. R., & Cattell, R. B. (1978). Higher stratum ability structure on a basis of twenty primary abilities. *Journal of Educational Psychology, 70,* 657–659.

Hakuta, K. (1986). *Mirror of language: The debate on bilingualism.* New York: Basic Books.

Hale, R. L. (1979). The utility of the WISC-R subtest scores in discriminating among adequate and underachieving children. *Multivariate Behavioral Research, 14,* 245–253.

Hale, R. L. (1981). Concurrent validity of the WISC-R factor scores. *Journal of School Psychology, 19*(3), 274–278.

Hale, R. L. (1983). An examination for construct bias in the WISC-R across socioeconomic status. *Journal of School Psychology, 21,* 153–156.

Hale, R. L., & Landino, S. A. (1981). Utility of the WISC-R subtest analysis in discriminating among groups of conduct problem, withdrawn, mixed, and non-problem boys. *Journal of Consulting and Clinical Psychology, 41,* 91–95.

Hale, R. L., & Saxe, J. E. (1983). Profile analysis of the Wechsler Intelligence Scale for Children—Revised. *Journal of Psychoeducational Assessment, 1,* 155–162.

Hamayan, E. V., & Damico, J. S. (1991). Developing and using a second language. In E. V. Hamayan & J. S. Damico (Eds.), *Limiting bias in the assessment of bilingual students* (pp. 39–75). Austin, TX: Pro-Ed.

Hamayan, E. V., & Damico, J. S. (1991a). *Limiting bias in the assessment of bilingual students.* Austin, TX: Pro-Ed.

Hammill, D. D. (1990). On defining learning disabilities: An emerging consensus. *Journal of Learning Disabilities, 23,* 74–84.

Hammill, D. D., Brown, L. & Bryant, B. R. (1992). *A consumer's guide to tests in print.* Austin, TX: Pro-Ed.

Hammill, D. D., & Bryant, B. R. (1991). *Detroit Tests of Learning Aptitude—3.* Austin, TX: Pro-Ed.

Hammill, D. D., Pearson, N. A., & Wiederholt, J. L. (1996). *Comprehensive Test of Nonverbal Intelligence.* Austin, TX: Pro-Ed.

Hansen, J.-I. C., & Betsworth, D. G. (1994). Vocational abilities. In R. J. Sternberg (Ed.), *Encyclopedia of human intelligence* (pp. 1117–1122). New York: Macmillan.

Harrison, P. L., Flanagan, D. P., & Genshaft, J. L. (1997). An integration and synthesis of contemporary theories, tests, and issues in the field of intellectual assessment. In D. P. Flanagan, J. L. Genshaft, & P. L. Harrison (Eds.), *Contemporary intellectual assessment: Theories, tests, and issues* (pp. 533–562). New York: Guilford.

Harrison, P. L., Kaufman, A. S., Hickman, J. A., & Kaufman, N. L. (1988). A survey of tests used for adult assessment. *Journal of Psychoeducational Assessment, 6,* 188–198.

Heath, C. P., & Kush, J. C. (1991). Use of discrepancy formulas in the assessment of learning disabilities. In J. E. Obrzut & G. W. Hynd (Eds.), *Neuropsychological foundations of learning disabilities: A handbook of issues, methods, and practice.* New York: Academic Press.

Helms, J. E. (1997). The triple quandary of race, culture, and social class in standardized cognitive ability testing. In D. P. Flanagan, J. L. Genshaft, & P. L. Harrison (Eds.), *Contemporary intellectual assessment: Theories, tests, and issues* (pp. 517–532). New York: Guilford.

Herrera-Graf, M., Dipert, Z. J., & Hutton, R. N. (1996). Exploring the effective use of the Vocabulary/Block Design short form with a special school population. *Educational and Psychological Measurement, 56*(3), 522–528.

Herrnstein, R. J., & Murray, C. (1994). *The Bell Curve: The reshaping of American life by difference in intelligence.* New York: Free Press.

Hessler, G. (1993). *Use and interpretation of the Woodcock-Johnson Psycho-Educational Battery—Revised.* Chicago: Riverside.

Hintze, J. M. (1996a). Discrepancy analysis. *The Connecticut School Psychologist, 3*(2), 20–25.

Hintze, J. M. (1996b). A statistically justifiable approach to comparing multiple IQ and achievement test scores: Issues regarding multiple comparisons. *The Connecticut School Psychologist, 3*(3), 17–23.

Hitch, G. J. (1978). The role of short-term working memory in mental arithmetic. *Cognitive Psychology, 10,* 302–323.

Hobbs, N. (1975). *The futures of children.* San Francisco: Jossey-Bass.

Holland, J. L. (1973). *Making vocational choices: A theory of careers.* Englewood Cliffs, NJ: Prentice-Hall.

Holtzman, W. H., & Wilkinson, C. Y. (1991). Assessment of cognitive ability. In E. V. Hamayan & J. S. Damico (Eds.), *Limiting bias in the assessment of bilingual students* (pp. 247–280). Austin, TX: Pro-Ed.

Horn, J. L. (1965). *Fluid and crystallized intelligence: A factor analytic and developmental study of the structure among primary mental abilities.* Unpublished doctoral dissertation, University of Illinois, Champaign.

Horn, J. L. (1968). Organization of abilities and the development of intelligence. *Psychological Review, 75,* 242–259.

Horn, J. L. (1976). Human abilities: A review of research and theory in the early 1970s. *Annual Review of Psychology, 27,* 437–485.

Horn, J. L. (1982). The theory of fluid and crystallized intelligence in relation to learning and adult development. In F. I. M. Craik & S. Trehub (Eds.), *Aging and cognitive processes* (pp. 237–278). New York: Plenum Press.

Horn, J. L. (1985). Remodeling old theories of intelligence: Gf-Gc theory. In B. B. Wolman (Ed.), *Handbook of intelligence* (pp. 267–300). New York: Wiley.

Horn, J. L. (1988). Thinking about human abilities. In J. R. Nesselroade & R. B. Cattell (Eds.), *Handbook of multivariate psychology* (Rev. ed.) (pp. 645–685). New York: Academic Press.

Horn, J. L. (1989). Cognitive diversity: A framework for learning. In P. L. Ackerman, R. J. Sternberg, & R. Glaser (Eds.), *Learning and individual differences: Advances in theory and research* (pp. 61–114). New York: Freeman.

Horn, J. L. (1991). Measurement of intellectual capabilities: A review of theory. In K. S. McGrew, J. K.

Werder, & R. W. Woodcock, *Woodcock-Johnson technical manual* (pp. 197–232). Chicago: Riverside.

Horn, J. L. (1994). Theory of fluid and crystallized intelligence. In R. J. Sternberg (Ed.), *Encyclopedia of human intelligence* (pp. 443–451). New York: Macmillan.

Horn, J. L., & Cattell, R. B. (1967). Age differences in fluid and crystallized intelligence. *Acta Psychologica, 26,* 107–129.

Horn, J. L., & Noll, J. (1997). Human cognitive capabilities: Gf-Gc theory. In D. P. Flanagan, J. L. Genshaft, & P. L. Harrison (Eds.), *Contemporary intellectual assessment: Theories, tests, and issues* (pp. 53–91). New York: Guilford.

Hoy, C., Gregg, N., Jagota, M., King, M., Moreland, C., & Manglitz, E. (1993). Relationship between the Wechsler Adult Intelligence Scale—Revised and the Woodcock-Johnson Test of Cognitive Ability—Revised among adults with learning disabilities in university and rehabilitation settings. *Journal of Psychoeducational Assessment, Monograph Series WJ-R Monograph,* 54–63.

Humphreys, L. G. (1992). Commentary: What both critics and users of ability tests need to know. *Psychological Science, 3,* 271–274.

Hunt, E. (1990). A modern arsenal for mental assessment. *Educational Psychologist, 25*(3 & 4), 223–241.

Hunt, E., & Lansman, M. (1986). Unified model of attention and problem solving. *Psychological Review, 93,* 446–461.

Hynd, G. W., & Obrzut, J. E. (1981). *Neuropsychological assessment and the school-age child: Issues and procedures.* New York: Grune & Stratton.

Institute for Scientific Information. (1992). *Current contents on diskette.* Philadelphia, PA: Author.

Ittenbach, R. F., Esters, I. G., & Wainer, H. (1997). The history of test development. In D. P. Flanagan, J. L. Genshaft, & P. L. Harrison (Eds.), *Contemporary intellectual assessment: Theories, tests, and issues* (pp. 17–31). New York: Guilford.

Iverson, G. L., Myers, B., Bengston, M. L., & Adams, R. L. (1996). Concurrent validity of a WAIS-R seven subtest short form in patients with brain impairment. *Psychological Assessment, 8*(3), 319–323.

Iverson, L. L. (1979). The chemistry of the brain. *Scientific American, 241,* 134–149.

Jackson, N. E., Donaldson, G. W., & Cleland, L. N. (1988). The structure of precocious reading ability. *Journal of Educational Psychology, 80*(2), 234–243.

Jacobson, J. W., & Mulick, J. A. (Eds.). (1996). *Manual of diagnosis and professional practice in mental retardation.* Washington, DC: American Psychological Association.

Jensen, A. R. (1969). How much can we boost IQ and scholastic achievement? *Harvard Educational Review, 39,* 1–123.

Jensen, A. R. (1973). *Educability and group differences.* New York: Harper & Row.

Jensen, A. R. (1974). How biased are culture-loaded tests? *Genetic Psychology Monographs, 90,* 185–244.

Jensen, A. R. (1976). Construct validity and test bias. *Phi Delta Kappan, 58,* 340–346.

Jensen, A. R. (1980). *Bias in mental testing.* New York: Free Press.

Jensen, A. R. (1984). Test validity: g versus the specificity doctrine. *Journal of Social and Biological Structures, 7,* 93–118.

Jensen, A. R. (1992). Understanding g in terms of information processing. *Educational Psychology Review, 4,* 271–308.

Jensen, A. R. (1997, July). *What we know and don't know about the g factor.* Keynote address delivered at the bi-annual convention of the International Society for the Study of Individual Differences, Aarhus, Denmark.

Jensen, A. R. (1998). *The g factor: The science of mental ability.* Westport, CT: Praeger Publishers.

Jensen, A. R., & Weng, L. J. (1994). What is a good g? *Intelligence, 18,* 231–258.

Johnstone, B., Erdal, K., & Stadler, M. A. (1995). The relationship between the Wechsler Memory Scale—Revised (WMS-R) attention index and putative measures of attention. *Journal of Clinical Psychology in Medical Settings, 2*(2), 195–204.

Johnstone, B., Holland, D., & Hewett, J. E. (1997). The construct validity of the category test: Is it a measure of reasoning of intelligence? *Psychological Assessment, 9*(1), 28–33.

Jones, R. (1972). Labels and stigma in special education. *Exceptional Children, 38,* 553–546.

Jones, R. L. (Ed.). (1988). *Psychoeducational assessment of minority group children: A casebook.* Berkeley, CA: Cobb & Henry.

Just, M. A., & Carpenter, P. A. (1992). A capacity theory of comprehension: Individual differences in working memory. *Psychological Review, 99*(1), 122–149.

Kail, R. (1991). Developmental changes in speed of processing during childhood and adolescence. *Psychological Bulletin, 109,* 490–501.

Kamphaus, R., & Reynolds, C. (1987). *Clinical and research applications of the K-ABC.* Circle Pines, MN: American Guidance Services.

Kamphaus, R. W. (1990). K-ABC theory in historical and current contexts. *Journal of Psychoeducational Assessment, 8,* 356–368.

Kamphaus, R. W. (1993). *Clinical assessment of children's intelligence.* Boston: Allyn and Bacon.

Kamphaus, R. W., Kaufman, A. S., & Harrison, P. L. (1990). Clinical assessment practice with the Kaufman Assessment Battery for Children (K-ABC). In C. R. Reynolds & R. W. Kamphaus (Eds.), *Handbook of psychological and educational assessment of children* (pp. 259–276). New York: Guilford Press.

Kamphaus, R. W., Petoskey, M. D., & Morgan, A. W. (1997). A history of test intelligence interpretation. In D. P. Flanagan, J. L. Genshaft, & P. L. Harrison (Eds.), *Contemporary intellectual assessment: Theories, tests, and issues* (pp. 32–51). New York: Guilford.

Kamphaus, R. W., & Platt, L. O. (1992). Subtest specificities for the WISC-III. *Psychological Reports, 70,* 899–902.

Kamphaus, R. W., & Reynolds, C. R. (1984). Development and structure of the Kaufman Assessment Battery for Children (K-ABC). *The Journal of Special Education, 18*(3), 213–228.

Kaplan, C. (1993). Predicting first-grade achievement from pre-kindergarten WPPSI-R scores. *Journal of Psychoeducational Assessment, 11*(2), 133–138.

Kaplan, C. (1996). Predictive validity of the WPPSI-R: A four year follow up study. *Psychology in the Schools,* 211–220.

Karr, S., Crajaval, H., Elser, D., Bays, K., Logan, R., & Page, G. (1993). Concurrent validity of the WPPSI-R and the McCarthy Scales of children's abilities. *Psychological Reports, 72,* 940–942.

Katz, R. B., & Shankweiler, D. P. (1985). Receptive naming and the detection of word retrieval deficits in the beginning reader. *Cortex, 21,* 617–625.

Kaufman, A. S. (1975). Factor analysis of the WISC-R at eleven age levels between 6-1/2 and 16-1/2 years. *Journal of Consulting and Clinical Psychology, 43,* 135–147.

Kaufman, A. S. (1978). The importance of basic concepts in individual assessment of preschool children. *Journal of School Psychology, 16,* 207–211.

Kaufman, A. S. (1979). *Intelligent testing with the WISC-R.* New York: Wiley.

Kaufman, A. S. (1984). K-ABC and controversy. *Journal of Special Education, 18*(3), 409–444.

Kaufman, A. S. (1990a). *Assessing adolescent and adult intelligence.* Boston: Allyn and Bacon.

Kaufman, A. S. (1990b). The WPPSI-R: You can't judge a test by its colors. *Journal of School Psychology, 28,* 387–394.

Kaufman, A. S. (1994a). *Intelligent testing with the WISC-III.* New York: Wiley.

Kaufman, A. S. (1994b). King WISC the third assumes the throne. *Journal of School Psychology, 31,* 345–354.

Kaufman, A. S. (1996). Wechsler and Horn: A reply to McGrew and Flanagan. *Communique, 24*(6), 15–18.

Kaufman, A. S., Kaufman, J. C., Balgopal, R., & McLean, J. E. (1996). Comparison of three WISC-III short forms: Weighing psychometric, clinical, and practical factors. *Journal of Clinical Child Psychology, 25*(1), 97–105.

Kaufman, A. S., & Kaufman, N. L. (1983). *Kaufman Assessment Battery for Children.* Circle Pines, MN: American Guidance Service.

Kaufman, A. S., & Kaufman, N. L. (1990). *Kaufman Brief Intelligence Test.* Circle Pines, MN: American Guidance Service.

Kaufman, A. S., & Kaufman, N. L. (1993). *The Kaufman Adolescent and Adult Intelligence Test.* Circle Pines, MN: American Guidance Service.

Kaufman, A. S., & Kaufman, N. L. (1994). *Kaufman Short Neuropsychological Assessment Procedure.* Circle Pines, MN: American Guidance Service.

Kaufman, A. S., & Maclean, J. E. (1987). Joint factor analysis of the K-ABC and WISC-R normal children. *Journal of School Psychology, 25,* 105–118.

Kavale, K. A. (1982). Meta-analysis of the relationship between visual perceptual skills and reading achievement. *Journal of Learning Disabilities, 15*(1), 42–51.

Kavale, K. A., & Forness, S. R. (1984). A meta-analysis of the validity of Wechsler scale profiles and recategorizations: Patterns and parodies. *Learning Disabilities Quarterly, 7,* 136–156.

Keith, T. (1988). Research methods in school psychology: An overview. *School Psychology Review, 17,* 502–520.

Keith, T. Z. (1990). Confirmatory and hierarchical confirmatory analysis of the Differential Ability Scales. *Journal of Psychoeducational Assessment, 8,* 391–405.

Keith, T. Z. (1994). Intelligence is important, intelligence is complex. *School Psychology Quarterly, 9,* 209–221.

Keith, T. Z. (1997). Using confirmatory factor analysis to aid in understanding the constructs measured by intelligence tests. In D. P. Flanagan, J. L. Genshaft, & P. L. Harrison (Eds.), *Contemporary intellectual assessment: Theories, tests, and issues* (pp. 373–402). New York: Guilford.

Keith, T. Z. (in press). Effects of general and specific abilities on student achievement: Similarities and differences across ethnic groups. *School Psychology Quaterly.*

Keith, T. Z., & Novak, C. G. (1987). Joint factor structure of the WISC-R and K-ABC for referred school children. *Journal of Psychoeducational Assessment, 15,* 352–355.

Keith, T. Z., & Witta, E. L. (1997). Hierarchical and cross-age confirmatory factor analysis of the WISC-III: What does it measure? *School Psychology Quarterly, 12,* 89–107.

Kintsch, W. (1988). The role of knowledge in discourse comprehension: A construction-integration model. *Psychological Review, 95*(2), 163–182.

Kirby, J. R., & Becker, L. D. (1986). Cognitive components of reading problems in arithmetic. *RASE: Remedial & Special Education, 9*(5), 7–15, 27.

Kline, R. B., Snyder, J., Guilmette, S., & Castellanos, M. (1992). Relative usefulness of elevation, variability, and shape information from WISC-R, K-ABC, and Fourth Edition Stanford-Binet profiles on predicting achievement. *Psychological Assessment, 4*(4), 426–432.

Kochnower, J., Richardson, E., & DiBenedetto, B. (1983). A comparison of the phonic decoding ability of normal and learning disabled children. *Journal of Learning Disabilities, 16,* 348–351.

Konold, T. R., Kush, J. C., & Canivez, G. L. (1997). Factor replication of the WISC-III in three independent samples of children receiving special education. *Journal of Psychoeducational Assessment, 15,* 123–137.

Korkman, M., Kirk, U., & Kemp, S. (1998). *NEPSY: A developmental neuropsychological assessment.* San Antonio, TX: The Psychological Corporation.

Kosslyn, S. M. (1985). Mental imagery ability. In R. J. Sternberg (Ed.), *Human abilities: An information processing approach* (pp. 151–172). New York: W. H. Freeman.

Kranzler, J., Keith, T. Z., & Flanagan, D. P. (1999). *Joint confirmatory factor analysis of the Cognitive Assessment System.* Presentation submitted to the thirty-first annual meeting of the National Association of School Psychologists, New Orleans, LA.

Kranzler, J. H., & Keith, T. Z. (in press). Independent confirmatory factor analysis of the Cognitive Assessment System (CAS): What does the CAS measure? *School Psychology Review.*

Kranzler, J. H., & Weng, L. (1995). Factor structure of the PASS cognitive tasks: A reexamination of Naglieri et al. (1991). *Journal of School Psychology, 33,* 143–157.

Krashen, S. D. (1985). *Inquiries and insights: Second language teaching, immersion and bilingual education, literacy.* Englewood Cliffs, NJ: Alemany.

Kush, J. C. (1996). Factor structure of the WISC-III for students with learning disabilities. *Journal of Psychoeducational Assessment, 14,* 32–40.

Kyllonen, P. C., & Christal, R. E. (1990). Reasoning ability (little more than) working-memory capacity?! *Intelligence, 14,* 389–433.

LaBuda, M. C., & DeFries, J. C. (1988). Cognitive abilities in children with reading disabilities and controls: A follow-up study. *Journal of Learning Disabilities, 21*(9), 562–566.

Laicardi, C., Frustaci, A., & Lauriola, M. (1996). Factor structure of the WAIS-R Italian version compared with American and British solutions. *Psychological Reports, 79,* 1171–1177.

Laughon, P. (1990). The dynamic assessment of intelligence: A review of three approaches. *School Psychology Review, 14*(4), 459–470.

Lavin, C. (1996a). Scores on the Wechsler Intelligence Scale for Children—Third Edition and Woodcock-Johnson Tests of Achievement—Revised for a sample of children with emotional handicaps. *Psychological Reports, 79,* 1291–1295.

Lavin, C. (1996b). The relationship between the Wechsler Intelligence Scale for Children—Third Edition and the Kaufman Test of Educational Achievement. *Psychology in the Schools, 33,* 119–123.

Lavin, C. (1996c). The Wechsler Intelligence Scale for Children—Third Edition and the Stanford-Binet Intelligence Scale—Fourth Edition: A preliminary study of validity. *Psychological Reports, 78,* 491–496.

Law, J. G., & Faison, L. (1996). WISC-III and KAIT results in adolescent delinquent males. *Journal of Clinical Psychology, 52*(6), 699–703.

Leather, C. V., & Henry, L. A. (1994). Working memory span and phonological awareness tasks as predictors of early reading ability. *Journal of Experimental Child Psychology, 58,* 88–111.

Leckliter, I. N., Matarazzo, J. D., & Silverstein, A. B. (1986). A literature review of factor analytic studies of the WAIS-R. *Journal of Clinical Psychology, 42,* 332–242.

Lemaire, P., Abdi, H., & Fayol, M. (1996). The role of working memory resources in simple cognitive arithmetic. *European Journal of Cognitive Psychology, 8*(1), 73–103.

Levinson, E. M., & Folino, L. (1994a). Correlations of scores on the gifted evaluation scale with those on WISC-III and Kaufman Brief Intelligence Test for students referred for gifted evaluation. *Psychological Reports, 74,* 419–424.

Levinson, E. M., & Folino, L. (1994b). The relationship between the WISC-III and the Kaufman Brief Intelligence test with students referred for gifted evaluation. *Special Services in the Schools, 8*(2), 155–159.

Lezak, M. D. (1976). *Neuropsychological assessment.* New York: Oxford University Press.

Lezak, M. D. (1995). *Neuropsychological assessment* (3rd ed.). New York: Oxford University Press.

Lidz, C. S. (Ed.). (1987). *Dynamic assessment: An interactional approach to evaluation of learning potential.* New York: Guilford.

Lidz, C. S. (1991). *Practitioner's guide to dynamic assessment.* New York: Guilford.

Lidz, C. S. (1997). Dynamic assessment approaches. In D. P. Flanagan, J. L. Genshaft, & P. L. Harrison (Eds.), *Contemporary intellectual assessment: Theories, tests, and issues* (pp. 281–296). New York: Guilford.

Little, S. G. (1991). Is the WISC-III factor structure valid? *NASP Communiqué, 20*(2), 24.

Little, S. G. (1992). The WISC-III: Everything old is new again. *School Psychology Quarterly, 7*(2), 148–154.

LoBello, S. G., & Gulgoz, S. (1991). Factor analysis of the Wechsler Preschool and Primary Scale of Intelligence—Revised. *Psychological Assessment: A Journal of Consulting and Clinical Psychology, 3,* 130–132.

Loevinger, J. (1954). The attenuation paradox in test theory. *Psychological Bulletin, 51,* 493–504.

Loevinger, J. (1957). Objective tests as instruments of psychological theory. *Psychological Reports, 3,* 635–694.

Logie, R. (1996). The seven ages of working memory. In J. Richardson, R. Engle, L. Hasher, R. Logie, E. Stoltzfus, & R. Zacks (Eds.), *Working memory and human cognition* (pp. 31–65). New York: Oxford.

Lohman, D. F. (1989). Human intelligence: An introduction to advances in theory and research. *Review of Educational Research, 59*(4), 333–373.

Lohman, D. F. (1994). Spatial ability. In R. J. Sternberg (Ed.), *Encyclopedia of human intelligence* (pp. 1000–1007). New York: Macmillan.

Lopez, E. C. (1997). The cognitive assessment of limited English proficient and bilingual children. In D. P. Flanagan, J. L. Genshaft, & P. L. Harrison (Eds.), *Contemporary intellectual assessment: Theories, tests, and issues* (pp. 506–516). New York: Guilford.

Lord, F., & Novick, M. (1968). *Statistical theories of mental test scores.* Reading, MA: Addison Wesley.

Lorr, M. (1983). *Cluster analysis for social scientists.* San Francisco: Jossey-Bass.

Lowman, M., Schwanz, K., & Kamphaus, R. (1996). WISC-III third factor: Critical measurement issues. *Canadian Journal of School Psychology, 12*(1), 15–22.

Lubinski, D., & Benbow, C. P. (1995). An opportunity for empiricism. *Contemporary Psychology, 40*(10), 935–940.

Lukens, J., & Hurrel, R. M. (1996). A comparison of the Standford-Binet IV and the WISC-III with mildly retarded children. *Psychology in the Schools, 33,* 24–27.

Luria, A. R. (1966). *Human brain and psychological processes.* New York: Harper and Row.

Luria, A. R. (1970). The functional organization of the brain. *Scientific American, 222,* 66–78.

Luria, A. R. (1973). *The working brain: An introduction to neuropsychology.* New York: Basic Books.

Luria, A. R. (1976). *Cognitive development: Its cultural and social foundations.* Cambridge, MA: Harvard University Press.

Luria, A. R. (1980). *Higher cortical functions in man* (2nd ed., rev., and expanded). New York: Basic Books.

Luria, A. R. (1982). *Language and cognition.* New York: Wiley.

Lynn, R., & Cooper, C. (1994). A secular decline in the strength of Spearman's *g* in Japan. *Current Psychology, 13,* 3–9.

Lyon, G. R. (1995a). Toward a definition of dyslexia. *Annals of Dyslexia, 45,* 3–27.

Lyon, G. R. (1995b). Research initiatives in learning disabilities: Contributions from scientists supported by the National Institute of Child Health and Human Development. *Journal of Child Neurology, 10,* (Suppl. 1), 120–126.

Lyon, M. A. (1995). A comparison between WISC-III and WISC-R scores for learning disabilities. *Journal of Learning Disabilities, 28*(4).

MacDonald, G. W., & Cornwall, A. (1995). The relationship between phonological awareness and reading and spelling achievement eleven years later. *Journal of Learning Disabilities, 28*(8), 523–527.

Mackintosh, N. J. (1986). The biology of intelligence? *British Journal of Psychology, 77,* 1–18.

Maller, S. J. (1996). WISC-III verbal item invariance across samples of deaf and hearing children of similar measured ability. *Journal of Psychoeducational Assessment, 14,* 152–165.

Manger, T., & Eikeland, O.-J. (1996). Relationship between boys' and girls' nonverbal ability and mathematical achievement. *School Psychology International, 17,* 71–80.

Mann, V. A., & Liberman, I. Y. (1984). Phonological awareness and verbal short-term memory. *Journal of Learning Disabilities, 10,* 592–599.

Marjoribanks, K. (1976). Academic achievement, intelligence and creativity: A regression surface analysis. *Multivariate Behavioral Research, 11*(1), 105–118.

Matarrazzo, J. D. (1990). Psychological assessment versus psychological testing: Validation from Binet to the school, clinic, and courtroom. *American Psychologist, 45,* 999–1017.

Mather, N. (1991). *An instructional guide to the Woodcock-Johnson Psycho-Educational Battery—Revised.* Brandon, VT: Clinical Psychology Publishing.

Mather, N. (1993). Critical issues in the diagnosis of learning disabilities addressed by the Woodcock-Johnson Psycho-Educational Battery—Revised. *Journal of Psychoeducational Assessment, Monograph Series: Advances in Psychoeducational Assessment Woodcock-Johnson Psycho-Educational Battery—Revised.*

Mather, N., & Roberts, R. (1994). Learning disabilities: A field in danger of extinction? *Learning Disabilities Research & Practice, 9,* 49–58.

Mather, N., & Woodcock, D. (1989, 1990). *Examiner's manual for the Woodcock-Johnson Psycho-Educational Battery—Revised, Tests of Cognitive Ability.* Chicago, IL: Riverside.

Matheson, D. W., Mueller, H. M., & Short, R. H. (1984). The validity of Bannatyne's acquired knowledge category as a separate construct. *Journal of Psychoeducational Assessment, 2,* 279–291.

Matsumoto, D. (1994). *Cultural influences on research methods and statistics.* Pacific Grove: Brooks/Cole.

Mayer, R. E. (1994). Reasoning, inductive. In R. J. Sternberg (Ed.), *Encyclopedia of human intelligence* (pp. 935–938). New York: Macmillan.

McArdle, J. J., & Prescott, C. A. (1997). Contemporary models for the biometric genetic analysis of intellectual abilities. In D. P. Flanagan, J. L. Genshaft, & P. L. Harrison (Eds.), *Contemporary intellectual assessment: Theories, tests, and issues* (pp. 403–436). New York: Guilford.

McBride-Chang, C. (1995). Phonological processing, speech perception, and reading disability: An integrative review. *Educational Psychologist, 30*(3), 109–121.

McCallum, R. S., & Bracken, B. A. (1998). The Universal Nonverbal Intelligence Test. In D. P. Flanagan, J. L. Genshaft, & P. L. Harrison (Eds.), *Contemporary intellectual assessment: Theories, tests, and issues* (pp. 268–280). New York: Guilford.

McDermott, P. A., Fantuzzo, J. W., & Glutting, J. J. (1990). Just say no to subtest analysis: A critique on Wechsler theory and practice. *Journal of Psychoeducational Assessment, 8,* 290–302.

McDermott, P. A., Fantuzzo, J. W., Glutting, J. J., Watkins, M. W., & Baggaley, R. A. (1992). Illusions of meaning in the ipsative assessment of children's ability. *Journal of Special Education, 25,* 504–526.

McDermott, P. A., & Glutting, J. J. (1997). Informing stylistic learning behavior, disposition, and achievement through ability subtests—Or, more illusions of meaning? *School Psychology Review, 26,* 163–175.

McDermott, P. A., Glutting, J. J., Fantuzzo, J. W., Watkins, M. W., & Baggaley, A. R. (1992). Illusions of meaning in the ipsative assessment of children's ability. *The Journal of Special Education, 25*(4), 504–526.

McDermott, P. A., Glutting, J. J., Jones, J. N., & Noonan, J. V. (1989). Typology and prevailing composition of core profiles in the WAIS-R standardization sample. *Psychological Assessment: A Journal of Consulting and Clinical Psychology, 1*(2), 118–125.

McDermott, P. A., Glutting, J. J., Jones, J. N., Watkins, M. W., & Kush, J. (1989). Core profile types in the WISC-R national sample: Structure, membership, and applications. *Psychological Assessment: A Journal of Consulting and Clinical Psychology, 1*(4), 292–299.

McGeorge, P., Crawford, J. R., & Kelly, S. W. (1996). The relationship between WAIS-R abilities and speed of processing in a word identification task. *Intelligence, 23,* 175–190.

McGhee, R. L. (1993). Fluid and crystallized intelligence: Confirmatory factor analysis of the Differential Abilities Scale, Detroit Tests of Learning Aptitude—3, and Woodcock-Johnson Psycho-Educational Assessment Battery—Revised. *Journal of Psychoeducational Assessment, Monograph Series: Woodcock-Johnson Psycho-Educational Battery—Revised,* 20–38.

McGhee, R., & Liberman, L. (1994). *Gf-Gc* Theory of human cognition: Differentiation of short-term auditory and visual memory factors. *Psychology in the Schools, 31,* 297–304.

McGrew, K. S. (1984). Normative-based guides for subtest profile interpretation of the Woodcock-Johnson Tests of Cognitive Ability. *Journal of Psychoeducational Assessment, 2,* 325–332.

McGrew, K. S. (1985). Investigation of the verbal/nonverbal structure of the Woodcock-Johnson: Implications for subtest interpretations and comparisons with the Wechsler scales. *Journal of Psychoeducational Assessment, 3,* 65–71.

McGrew, K. S. (1993). The relationship between the WJ-R *Gf-Gc* cognitive clusters and reading achievement across the lifespan. *Journal of Psychoeducational Assessment, Monograph Series: WJ-R Monograph,* 39–53.

McGrew, K. S. (1994). *Clinical interpretation of the Woodcock-Johnson Tests of Cognitive Ability—Revised.* Boston: Allyn and Bacon.

McGrew, K. S. (1995, March). *Intelligence is a "many splendored" thing: Implications of theories of multiple intelligences.* Meeting of the National Association of School Psychologists, Chicago.

McGrew, K. S. (1996). *Clinical interpretation of the Woodcock-Johnson Tests of Cognitive Ability.* Orlando, FL: Grune and Stratton.

McGrew, K. S. (1997). Analysis of the major intelligence batteries according to a proposed comprehensive *Gf-Gc* framework. In D. P. Flanagan, J. L. Genshaft, & P. L. Harrison (Eds.), *Contemporary intellectual assessment: Theories, tests, and issues* (pp. 151–180). New York: Guilford.

McGrew, K. S. (1999). The Wechsler freedom-from-distractibility index: A tale of three subtests. *Communiqué, 27*(8), 24.

McGrew, K. S., & Flanagan, D. P. (1996). The Wechsler Performance Scale debate: Fluid intelligence *(Gf)* or visual processing *(Gv)? Communiqué, 24*(6), 14–16.

McGrew, K. S., & Flanagan, D. P. (1998). *The Intelligence Test Desk Reference (ITDR): Gf-Gc cross-battery assessment.* Boston: Allyn and Bacon.

McGrew, K. S., Flanagan, D. P., Keith, T. Z., & Vanderwood, M. (1997). Beyond *g:* The impact of *Gf-Gc* specific cognitive abilities research on the future use and interpretation of intelligence tests in the schools. *School Psychology Review,* 189–210.

McGrew, K. S., & Hessler, G. L. (1995). The relationship between the WJ-R *Gf-Gc* cognitive clusters and mathematics achievement across the life-span. *Journal of Psychoeducational Assessment, 13,* 21–38.

McGrew, K. S., & Knopik, S. N. (1993). The relationship between the WJ-R *Gf-Gc* cognitive clusters and writing achievement across the life-span. *School Psychology Review, 22,* 687–695.

McGrew, K. S., & Knopik, S. N. (1996). The relationship between intra-cognitive scatter on the Woodcock-Johnson Psycho-Educational Battery—Revised and school achievement. *Journal of School Psychology, 34,* 351–364.

McGrew, K. S., & Murphy, S. R. (1995). Uniqueness and general factor characteristics of the Woodcock-Johnson Tests of Cognitive Ability. *Journal of Psychoeducational Assessment, 2,* 141–148.

McGrew, K. S., & Pehl, J. (1988). Prediction of future achievement by the Woodcock-Johnson Psychoeducational Battery and the WISC-R. *Journal of School Psychology, 26,* 275–281.

McGrew, K. S., Untiedt, S. A., & Flanagan, D. P. (1996). General factor and uniqueness characteristics of the Kaufman Adolescent and Adult Intelligence Scale (KAIT). *Journal of Psychoeducational Assessment, 14,* 208–219.

McGrew, K. S., Werder, J. K., & Woodcock, R. W. (1991). *Woodcock-Johnson Psycho-Educational Battery—Revised technical manual.* Chicago: Riverside.

McGrew, K. S., & Wrightson, W. (1997). The calculation of new and improved WISC-III reliability, uniqueness, and general factor characteristics information through the use of data smoothing procedures. *Psychology in the Schools, 34,* 181–195.

McGue, M., & Bouchard, T. J., Jr. (1989). Genetic and environmental determinants of information processing and special mental abilities: A twin analysis. In R. J. Sternberg (Ed.), *Advances in the psychology of human intelligence* (vol. 5) (pp. 7–45). Hillsdale, NJ: Erlbaum.

McGuiness, D., McGuiness, C., & Donohue, J. (1995). Phonological training and the alphabet principle: Evidence for reciprocal causality. *Reading Research Quarterly, 30*(4), 830–852.

McLeod, B. (1994). Introduction. In B. McLeod (Ed.), *Language and learning: Educating linguistically diverse students* (pp. xiii–xxii). Albany, NY: State University of New York Press.

McNemar, Q. (1964). Lost: Our intelligence? Why? *American Psychologist, 19,* 871–882.

Meinhardt, M., Hibbett, C., Koller, J., & Busch, R. (1993). Comparison of the Woodcock-Johnson Psycho-Educational Battery—Revised and the Wechsler Intelligence Scale for Children—Revised with incarcerated adolescents. *Journal of Psychoeducational Assessment Monograph Series: WJ-R Monograph,* 64–70.

Mercer, C. D., Jordan, L., Allsopp, D. H., & Mercer, A. R. (1999). *Learning disabilities definitions and criteria used by state education departments.* Manuscript submitted for publication.

Meeker, M. N. (1969). *The structure of intellect.* Columbus, OH: Charles E. Merrill.

Mercer, J. R. (1979). *System of Multicultural Pluralistic Assessment: Technical Manual.* New York: The Psychological Corporation.

Meeker, M. N. (1975). *Glossary for SOI factor definitions: WISC-R Analysis.* Available from SOI Institute, 214 Main St., El Segundo, CA.

Messick, S. (1989). Validity. In R. Linn (Ed.), *Educational measurement* (3rd ed.) (pp. 131–104). Washington, DC: American Council on Education.

Messick, S. (1992). Multiple intelligences or multilevel intelligence? Selective emphasis on distinctive properties of hierarchy: On Gardner's *Frames of Mind* and Sternberg's *Beyond IQ* in the context of theory and research on the structure of human abilities. *Psychological Inquiry, 3*(4), 365–384.

Messick, S. (1995). Validity of psychological assessment: Validation of inferences from persons' responses and performances as scientific inquiry into score meaning. *American Psychologist, 50,* 741–749.

Messick, S. (1998). Validity of psychological assessment: Validation of inferences from persons' responses and performances as scientific inquiry into score meaning (pp. 241–261). In A. E. Kazdin (Ed.), *Methodological issues and strategies in clinical research* (2nd ed.). Washington, DC: American Psychological Association.

Meyer, M. (1997, September). The greening of learning: Using the eighth intelligence. *Educational Leadership, 32,* 34.

Milrod, R., & Rescorla, L. (1991). A comparison of the WPPSI-R and WPPSI with high IQ children. *Journal of Psychoeducational Assessment, 9,* 255–262.

Minton H. L., & Schneider, F. W. (1980). *Differential psychology.* Prospect Heights, IL: Waveland Press.

Mirsky, A. F. (1989). The neuropsychology of attention: Elements of a complex behavior. In E. Perecman (Ed.), *Integrating theory and practice in clinical neuropsychology.* Hillsdale, NJ: Erlbaum.

Moffitt, T. E., & Silva, P. A. (1987). WISC-R verbal and performance IQ discrepancy in an unselected cohort: Clinical significance and longitudinal stability. *Journal of Consulting and Clinical Psychology, 55*(5), 768–774.

Morgan, A. W., Sullivan, S. A., Darden, C., & Gregg, N. (1997). Measuring intelligence of college students with learning disabilities: A comparison of results obtained on the WAIS-R and the KAIT. *Journal of Learning Disabilities, 30*(5), 560–565.

Morris, R. D., Stuebing, K. K., Fletcher, J. M., Shaywitz, S. E., Lyon, G. R., Shankweiler, D. P., Katz, L., Francis, D. J., & Shaywitz, B. A. (1998). Subtypes of reading disability: Variability around a phonological core. *Journal of Educational Psychology, 90*(3), 347–373.

Moses, J. A., Jr., Pritchard, D. A., & Adams, R. L. (1997). Neuropsychological information in the Wechsler Adult Intelligence Scale—Revised. *Archives of Clinical Neuropsychology, 12*(2), 97–109.

Mueller, H. H., Dennis, S. S., & Short, R. H. (1986). A meta-exploration of WISC-R factor score profiles as a function of diagnosis and intellectual level. *Canadian Journal of School Psychology, 2,* 21–43.

Muñoz-Sandoval, A. F., Cummins, J., Alvarado, C. G., & Ruef, M. L. (1998). *The Bilingual Verbal Ability Tests.* Chicago, IL: Riverside.

Naglieri, J. A. (1985). *Matrix Analogies Test.* San Antonio, TX: Psychological Corporation.

Naglieri, J. A. (1997). Planning, attention, simultaneous, and successive theory and the cognitive assessment system: A new theory-based measure of intelligence. In D. P. Flanagan, J. L. Genshaft, & P. L. Harrison (Eds.), *Contemporary intellectual assessment: Theories, tests, and issues* (pp. 247–267). New York: Guilford.

Naglieri, J. A., & Das, J. P. (1990). Planning, attention, simultaneous, and successive (PASS) cognitive processes as a model for intelligence. *Journal of Psychoeducational Assessment, 8,* 303–337.

Naglieri, J. A., & Das, J. P. (1997). *Cognitive Assessment System: Interpretive Handbook.* Chicago: Riverside.

Näslund, J. C., & Schneider, W. (1996). Kindergarten letter knowledge, phonological skills, and memory processes: Relative effects on early literacy. *Journal of Experimental Child Psychology, 62,* 30–59.

National Association of School Psychologists. (1984). *Professional conduct manual.* Stratford, CT: NASP Publications Office.

National Joint Committee on Learning Disabilities (NJCLD). (1990). Operationalizing the NJCLD definition of learning disabilities for ongoing assessment in schools: A report from the National Joint Committee on Learning Disabilities. *Perspectives: The International Dyslexia Association, 23*(4), 29.

Neisser, U., Boodoo, G., Bouchard, T. J., Boykin, A. W., Brody, N., Ceci, S. J., Halpern, D. F., Loehlin, J. C., Perloff, R., Sternberg, R. J., & Urbina, S. (1996). Intelligence: Knowns and unknowns. *American Psychologist, 51,* 77–101.

Nettelbeck, T. (1994). Speediness. In R. J. Sternberg (Ed.), *Encyclopedia of human intelligence* (pp. 1014–1019). New York: Macmillan.

Newland, T. E. (1971). Psychological assessment of exceptional children and youth. In W. Cruickshank (Ed.), *Psychology of exceptional children and youth* (pp. 115–172). Englewood Cliffs, NJ: Prentice-Hall.

New York City Public Schools. (1993). *Answers to frequently asked questions about limited English proficient (LEP) students and bilingual ESL programs: Facts and figures, 1992–1993.* New York: Author.

Nunnally, J. S. (1978). *Psychometric theories.* New York: McGraw-Hill.

Ochoa, S. H., Powell, M. P., & Robles-Pina, R. (1996). School psychologists' assessment practices with bilingual and limited-English-proficient students. *Journal of Psychoeducational Assessment, 14,* 250–275.

O'Gradey, K. E. (1983). A confirmatory maximum likelihood factor analysis of the WAIS-R. *Journal of Consulting and Clinical Psychology, 51*(6), 826–831.

O'Gradey, K. E. (1989). Factor structure of the WISC-R. *Multivariate Behavioral Research, 24*(2), 177–193.

Olmedo, E. S. (1981). Testing linguistic minorities. *American Psychologist, 36,* 1078–1085.

O'Mahoney, J. F., & Doherty, B. (1993). Patterns of intellectual performance among recently abstinent alcohol abusers on WAIS-R and WMS-R sub-tests. *Archives of Clinical Neuropsychology, 8*(1), 373–380.

Ortiz, A. A., & Maldonado-Colon, E. (1986). Recognizing learning disabilities in bilingual children: How to lessen inappropriate referral of language minority students to special education. *Journal of Reading, Writing, and Learning Disabilities International, 43*(1), 47–56.

Ortiz, S. O., Ortiz, O. G., & Cook-Morales, V. J. (1994). *Preliminary Analysis: Survey of California school psychologists listed in the CASP Multilingual Directory.* Paper presented at the CASP Multicultural Affairs Committee Meeting and Workshop at the annual conference of the California Association of School Psychologists, Long Beach, CA.

Paik, M., & Nebenzahl, E. (1987). The overall percentile rank versus the individual percentile ranks. *The American Statistician, 41,* 136–138.

Paolo, A. M., & Ryan, J. J. (1994). WAIS-R Digital Symbol patterns for persons 75 years and older. *Journal of Psychoeducational Assessment, 12,* 67–75.

Paolo, A. M., Ryan, J. J., & Troster, A. I. (1997). Estimating Premorbid WAIS-R intelligence in the elderly: An extension and cross validation of new regression equations. *Journal of Clinical Psychology, 53*(7), 647–656.

Paolo, A. M., Ryan, J. J., Troster, A. I., & Hilmer, C. D. (1996). Demographically based regression equations to estimate WAIS-R subtest scaled scores. *The Clinical Neuropsychologist, 10*(2), 130–140.

Parker, K. (1983). Factor analysis of the WAIS-R at nine age levels between 16 and 74 years. *Journal of Consulting and Clinical Psychology, 51*(2), 302–308.

Perfetti, C. A. (1994). Reading. In R. J. Sternberg (Ed.), *Encyclopedia of human intelligence* (pp. 923–930). New York: Macmillan.

Phelps, L. (1996). Discriminative validity of the WRAML with ADHD and LD children. *Psychology in the Schools, 33,* 5–12.

Phelps, L., Bowen, J., Chaco, J., Howard, K., Leahy, S., & Lucenti, J. (1999, April). *Joint confirmatory factor analysis of the Woodcock-Johnson Psycho-Educational Battery—Third Edition (WJ-III) and the WISC-III.* Presentation at the thirtieth annual convention of the National Association of School Psychologists, Las Vegas, NV.

Plante, T., & Skyora, C. (1994). Are stress and coping associated with WISC-III performance among children? *Journal of Clinical Psychology, 50*(5), 759–762.

Plomin, R., DeFries, J. C., & McClearn, G. E. (1980). *Behavioral genetics.* San Francisco: Freeman.

Plomin, R., DeFries, J. C., & McClearn, G. E. (1990). *Behavioral genetics: A primer* (2nd ed.). New York: Freeman.

Plomin, R., & Lochlin, J. C. (1989). Direct and indirect IQ heritability estimates: A puzzle. *Behavior Genetics, 19*(3), 331–342.

Porteus, S. D. (1959). *The Maze Test and clinical psychology.* Palo Alto, CA: Pacific Books.

Porteus, S. D. (1965). *Porteus Maze Test: Fifty years' application.* New York: Psychological Corporation.

Prentky, R. A. (1994). Teaching machines. In R. J. Corsini & E. J. Lieberman (Reviewers), *Concise Encyclopedia of Psychology* (2nd ed.) (vol. 3) (p. 509). New York: Wiley.

Prewett, P. N. (1995). A comparison of two screening tests (the matrix analogies test—short form and the Kaufman Brief Intelligence Test) with the WISC-III. *Psychological Assessment, 7*(1), 69–72.

Prewett, P. N., & Matavich, M. A. (1994). A comparison of referred student's performance on the WISC-III and the Stanford-Binet Intelligence Scale: Fourth Edition. *Journal of Psychoeducational Assessment, 12,* 42–48.

Prifitera, A., & Dersh, J. (1992). Base rates of WISC-III diagnostic subtest patterns among normal, learning-disabled, and ADHD samples. *Journal of Psychoeducational Assessment, 43*–55.

Prifitera, A., Weiss, L. G., & Saklofske, D. H. (1998). The WISC-III in context. In A. Prifitera & D. Saklofske (Eds.), *WISC-III clinical use and interpretation* (pp. 1–39). San Diego, CA: Academic Press.

Prohovnik, I. (1980). *Mapping brainwork.* Malmo, Sweden: CWK Gleerup.

Psychological Corporation. (1997). *Wechsler Adult Intelligence Scale—Third Edition, Technical Manual.* San Antonio, TX: Psychological Corporation.

Quereshi, M. Y., & Seitz, R. (1994). Gender differences on the WPPSI, the WISC-R and the WPPSI-R. *Current Psychology, 13,* 117–123.

Ramirez, A. G. (1990). Prospectives on language proficiency assessment. In A. Barona & E. E. Garcia (Eds.), *Children at risk: Poverty, minority status, and other issues in educational equity* (pp. 305–323). Washington, DC: National Association of School Psychologists.

Rapaport, D., Gill, M. M., & Schafer, R. (1945–46). *Diagnostic psychological testing.* Chicago, IL: Year Book Publishers.

Rasanen, P., & Ahonen, T. (1995). Arithmetic disabilities with and without reading difficulties: A comparison of arithmetic errors. *Developmental Neuropsychology, 11*(3), 275–295.

Raven, J. C. (1938). *Progressive matrices: A perceptual test of intelligence.* San Antonio, TX: Psychological Corporation.

Rawling, P., & Brooks, N. (1990). Simulation index: A method for detecting factitious errors on the WAIS-R and WMS. *Neuropsychology, 4,* 223–238.

Reitan, R. M., & Wolfson, B. (1985). *The Halstead-Reitan Neuropsychological Test Battery: Theory and clinical interpretation.* Tuscon, AZ: Neuropsychology Press.

Reitan, R. M., & Wolfson, D. (1996). Relationships of age and education to Wechsler Adult Intelligence Scale IQ values in brain-damaged and non-brain-damaged groups. *The Clinical Neuropsychologist, 10*(3), 293–304.

Reschly, D. J. (1990). Found: Our intelligences: What do they mean? *Journal of Psychoeducational Assessment, 8,* 259–267.

Reschly, D. J., & Grimes, J. P. (1990). Best practices in intellectual assessment. In A. Thomas & J. Grimes (Eds.), *Best practices in school psychology—II* (pp. 425–439). Washington, DC: The National Association of School Psychologists.

Reschly, D. J., & Grimes, J. P. (1995). Intellectual assessment. In A. Thomas & J. Grimes (Eds.), *Best practices in school psychology—III* (pp. 763–774). Washington, DC: The National Association of School Psychologists.

Reschly, D. J., & Sabers, D. L. (1979). Analysis of test bias in four groups, with the regression definition. *Journal of Educational Measurement, 16,* 1–9.

Research and Policy Committee of the Committee for Economic Development. (1987). *Children in need—Investment strategies for the educationally disadvantaged.* New York: Author.

Reynolds, C. R. (1990). Conceptual and technical problems in learning disability diagnosis. In C. R. Reynolds & R. W. Kamphaus (Eds.), *Handbook of psychological and educational assessment of children: Intelligence and achievement* (pp. 571–592). New York: Guilford Press.

Reynolds, C. R., & Bigler, E. D. (1994). *Test of memory and learning.* Austin, TX: Pro-Ed.

Reynolds, C. R., Chaistain, R. L., Kaufman, A. S., & McLean, J. E. (1987). Demographic characteristics and IQ among adults: Analysis of the WAIS-R standardization sample as a function of the stratification variables. *Journal of School Psychology, 25,* 323–342.

Reynolds, C. R., & Ford, L. (1994). Comparative three-factor solutions of the WISC-III and WISC-R at 11 age levels between 6-1/2 and 16-1/2 years. *Archives of Clinical Neuropsychology, 9*(6), 553–570.

Reynolds, C. R., & Gutkin, T. B. (Eds.). (1982). *The handbook of school psychology.* New York: Wiley.

Reynolds, C. R., & Kamphaus, R. W. (Eds.). (1990). *Handbook of psychological and educational assessment of children: Intelligence and achievement.* New York: Guilford.

Reynolds, C. R., Kamphaus, R. W., & Rosenthal, B. (1988). Factor analysis of the Stanford-Binet Fourth Edition for ages 2 through 23. *Measurement and*

Evaluation in Counseling and Development, 21, 52–63.

Reynolds, C. R., & Kaufman, A. S. (1990). Assessment of children's intelligence with the Wechsler Intelligence Scale for Children—Revised (WISC-R). In C. R. Reynolds & R. W. Kamphaus (Eds.), *Handbook of psychological and educational assessment of children: Intelligence and achievement* (pp. 127–165). New York: Guilford.

Reynolds, M. C., & Lakin, K. C. (1987). Noncategorical special education: Models for research and practice. In M. C. Wang, M. C. Reynolds, & H. J. Walberg (Eds.), *Handbook of special education: Research and practice (Vol. 1). Learner characteristics and adaptive education* (pp. 331–356). New York: Pergamon.

Riccio, C. A., Cohen, M. J., Hall, J., & Ross, C. M. (1997). The third and fourth factors of the WISC-III: What they don't measure. *Journal of Psychoeducational Assessment, 15,* 27–39.

Richards, D. R., Stankov, L., Pallier, G., & Dolph, B. (1997). Charting the cognitive sphere: Tactile kinesthetic performance within the structure of intelligence. *Intelligence, 25*(2), 111–148.

Richards, R. D., Pallier, G., & Goff, G. N. (in press). Sensory processing within the structure of human cognitive abilities. In P. L. Ackerman, P. C. Kyllonen, & R. D. Roberts (Eds.), *The future of learning and individual differences research: Processing, traits, and content.* Washington, DC: American Psychological Association.

Richardson, J. (1996). Evolving concepts of working memory. In J. Richardson, R. Engle, L. Hasher, R. Logie, E. Stoltzfus, & R. Zacks (Eds.), *Working memory and human cognition* (pp. 3–30). New York: Oxford.

Richardson, J. T., Engle, R. W., Hasher, L., Logie, R. H., Stoltzfus, E. R., & Zacks, R. T. (1996). Working memory and human cognition. In M. Marschark (Series Ed.), *Counterpoints: Cognition, memory, and language.* Oxford, NY: Oxford University Press.

Roberts, R. D., & Stankov, L. (1998). *Individual differences in speed of mental processing and human cognitive abilities: Towards a taxonomic model.* Unpublished manuscript, USAF Armstrong Laboratory.

Roberts, R. D., Stankov, L., Pallier, G., & Dolph, B. (1997). Charting the cognitive sphere: Tactile-kinesthetic performance within the structure of intelligence. *Intelligence, 25,* 111–148.

Rogoff, B., & Chavajay, P. (1995). What's become of research on the cultural basis of cognitive development? *American Psychologist, 50,* 859–877.

Roid, G. H., & Gyurke, J. (1991). General-factor and specific variance in the WPPSI-R. *Journal of Psychoeducational Assessment, 9,* 209–223.

Roid, G. H., & Miller, L. J. (1997). *The Leiter International Performance Scale—Revised Edition.* Wood Dale, IL: Stoelting.

Roid, G. H., & Worrall, W. (1997). Replication of the Wechsler Intelligence Scale for Children—Third edition four-factor model in the Canadian normative sample. *Psychological Assessment, 9* (4), 512–515.

Ross, R. P. (1992). Aptitude-achievement discrepancy scores: Accuracy in analysis ignored. *School Psychology Review, 21,* 509–514.

Roszkowski, M. J. (1983). The Freedom-from-Distractibility factor: An examination of its adaptive behavior correlates. *Journal of Psychoeducational Assessment, 1* (3), 285–297.

Rothlisberg, B. A. (1987). Comparing the Stanford-Binet, fourth edition to the WISC-R: A concurrent validity study. *Journal of School Psychology, 25* (2), 193–196.

Rust, J. O., & Lindstrom, A. (1996). Concurrent validity of the WISC-III and Stanford-Binet IV. *Psychological Reports, 79* (2), 618–620.

Rust, J. O., & Yates, A. G. (1997). Concurrent validity of the Wechsler Intelligence Scale for Children—Third edition and the Kaufman Assessment Battery for Children. *Psychological Reports, 80* (1), 89–90.

Ryan, J. J., Bohac, D. L., & Trent, D. (1994). Speed of performance on the WAIS-R among persons 75 years of age and older. *Journal of Psychoeducational Assessment, 12* (4), 351–356.

Ryan, J. J., Dai, X., & Paolo, A. M. (1995). Verbal-performance IQ discrepancies on the mainland Chinese version of the Wechsler Adult Intelligence Scale (WAIS-RC). *Journal of Psychoeducational Assessment, 13* (4) 365–371.

Ryan, J. J., Paolo, A. M., Miller, D. A. & Morris, J. (1997). Exploratory factor analysis of the Wechsler Adult Intelligence Scale-Revised in a sample of brain-damaged women. *Archives of Clinical Neuropsychology, 12* (7), 683–689.

Ryan, J. J., Weilage, M. E., Lopez, S. J., Paolo, A. M., Miller, D. M., & Morris, J. (1997). Application of the seven-subtest short form of the WAIS-R in African Americans with brain damage. *Journal of Psychoeducational Assessment, 15* (4), 314–321.

Saklofske, D. H., Schwean, V. L., Yackulic, R. A., & Quinn, R. D. (1994). WISC-III and SB:FE performance of children with attention deficit hyperactivity disorder. *Canadian Journal of School Psychology, 10* (2), 167–171.

Salvia, J., & Ysseldyke, J. (1991). *Assessment in special and remedial education* (5th ed.). Boston: Houghton Mifflin.

Salvia, J., & Ysseldyke, J. E. (1995). *Assessment* (6th ed.). Boston: Houghton Mifflin.

Salvia, J., & Ysseldyke, J. E. (1998). *Assessment* (7th ed.). New York: Houghton Mifflin.

Samuda, R. J., Kong, S. L., Cummins, J., Pascual-Leone, J., & Lewis, J. (1991). *Assessment and placement of minority students.* New York: C.J. Hogrefe/Intercultural Social Sciences Publications.

Sandoval, J. (1979). The WISC-R and internal evidence of test bias with minority groups. *Journal of Consulting and Clinical Psychology, 47,* 919–927.

Sandoval, J. (1995). Review of Wechsler Intelligence Scale for Children—Third Edition. In J. V. Mitchell (Ed.), *The tenth mental measurement yearbook* (vol. 1) (pp. 1103–1104). Lincoln, NE: Buros Institute of Mental Measurements.

Sandoval, J. (1998). Critical thinking in test interpretation. In J. Sandoval, C. L. Frisby, K. F. Geisinger, J. D. Scheuneman, & J. R. Grenier (Eds.), *Test interpretation and diversity: Achieving equity in assessment* (pp. 31–50). Washington, DC: American Psychological Association.

Sandoval, J., Frisby, C. L., Geisinger, K. F., Scheuneman, J. D., & Grenier, J. R. (Eds.). (1998). *Test interpretation and diversity: Achieving equity in assessment.* Washington, DC: American Psychological Association.

Sandoval, J., Zimmerman, I. L., & Woo, J. M. (1980, September). *Cultural differences on WISC-R verbal items.* Paper presented at the annual convention of the American Psychological Association, Montreal, Canada.

Satterfield, W. A., Martin, C. W. & Leiker, M. (1994). A comparison of four WAIS-R short forms in patients referred for psychological/neuropsychological assessments. *Journal of Psychoeducational Assessment, 12* (4), 364–371.

Sattler, J. (1992). *Assessment of children* (Rev. and updated 3rd ed.). San Diego, CA: Sattler.

Sattler, J. M. (1988). *Assessment of children's intelligence and special abilities* (2nd ed.). San Diego, CA: Sattler.

Sattler, J. M. & Atkinson, L. (1993). Item equivalence across scales: The WPPSI-R and WISC-III. *Psychological Assessment, 5* (2), 203–206.

Sattler, J. M., & Ryan, J. J. (1999). *Assessment of children: Revised and updated third edition WAIS-III supplement.* San Diego, CA: Sattler.

Scarr, S. (1978). From evolution to Larry P., or what shall we do about IQ tests? *Intelligence, 2,* 325–342.

Scarr, S. (1985). An author's frame of mind: Review of *Frames of mind: The theory of multiple intelligences. New Ideas in Psychology, 3,* 95–100.

Scarr, S., & Carter-Saltzman, L. (1982). Genetics and intelligence. In R. J. Sternberg (Ed.), *Handbook of human intelligence* (pp. 792–896). Cambridge, England: Cambridge University Press.

Schaie, K. W. (1979). The primary mental abilities in adulthood: An exploration in the development of psychometric intelligence. In P. B. Baltes & O. G. Brim, Jr. (Eds.), *Life-span development and behavior* (vol. 2) (pp. 67–115). New York: Academic.

Schaie, K. W. (Ed.). (1983). *Longitudinal studies of adult psychological development.* New York: Guilford.

Schaie, K. W. (1994). The course of adult intellectual development. *American Psychologist, 49,* 304–314.

Schmidt, J. P., & Tombaugh, T. (1995). *Learning and Memory Battery.* North Tonawanda, NY: Multi-Health Systems.

Schneider, B., & Gervais, M. (1991). Identifying gifted kindergarten students with the brief screening measures and the WPPSI-R. *Journal of Psychoeducational Assessment, 9,* 201–208.

Seashore, H. G., Wesman, A. G., & Doppelt, J. E. (1950). The standardization of the Wechsler Intelligence Scale for Children. *Journal of Consulting Psychology, 14,* 99–110.

Shankweiler, D., Liberman, I. Y., Mark, L. S., Fowler, C. A., & Fischer, F. W. (1979). Human learning and memory. *Journal of Experimental Psychology, 5*(6), 531–545.

Shaw, S. E., Swerdlik, M. E., & Laurent, J. (1993). Review of the WISC-III [WISC-III Monograph]. *Journal of Psychoeducational Assessment,* 151–160.

Shaw, S. F., Cullen, J. P., McGuire, J. M., & Brinckerhoff, L. C. (1995). Operationalizing a definition of learning disabilities. *Journal of Learning Disabilities, 28,* 586–597.

Sherer, M., Nixon, S. J., Anderson, B. L., & Adams, R. L. (1992). Differential sensitivity of the WMS to the effects of IQ and brain damage. *Archives of Clinical Neuropsychology, 7,* 505–514.

Sherman, E. M. S., Strauss, E., Spellacy, F., & Hunter, M. (1995). Construct validity of WAIS-R factors: Neuropsychological test correlates in adults referred for evaluation of possible head injury. *Psychological Assessment, 7*(4), 440–444.

Sheslow, D., & Adams, W. (1990). *Wide Range Assessment of Memory and Learning.* Wilmington, NC: Wide Range Inc.

Siegel, L. S. (1992). An evaluation of the discrepancy definition of dyslexia. *Journal of Learning Disabilities, 25,* 618–629.

Siegel, L. S. (1998). The discrepancy formula: Its use and abuse. In B. K. Shapiro, P. J. Accardo, & A. J. Capute (Eds.), *Specific reading disability: A view of the spectrum* (pp. 123–136). Timonium, MD: York Press.

Silverstein, A. (1976). Variance components in the subtests of the WISC-R. *Psychological Reports, 39,* 1109–1110.

Silverstein, A. B. (1982). Factor structure of the Wechsler Adult Intelligence Scale—Revised. *Journal of Consulting and Clinical Psychology, 50,* 601–664.

Silverstein, A. B. (1982). Pattern analysis as simultaneous statistical inference. *Journal of Consulting and Clinical Psychology, 50,* 234–240.

Slate, J. R. (1994). WISC-III correlations with the WIAT. *Psychology in the Schools, 31,* 278–285.

Slate, J. R. (1995). Two investigations of the validity of the WISC-III. *Psychological Reports, 76,* 299–306.

Slate, J. R., & Jones, C. H. (1995). Preliminary evidence of the validity of the WISC-III for African American students undergoing special education evaluation. *Educational and Psychological Measurement, 55*(6), 1039–1046.

Slate, J. R., & Saarnio, D. A. (1995). Differences between WISC-III and WISC-R IQs: A preliminary investigation. *Journal of Psychoeducational Assessment, 13,* 340–346.

Slate, J. R., Spear Graham, L., & Bower, J. (1996). Relationships of the WISC-R and K-BIT for an adolescent clinical sample. *Adolescence, 31*(124), 776–782.

Smith, T. D., Smith, B. L., & Smithson, M. M. (1995). The relationship between the WISC-III and the WRAT3 in a sample of rural referred children. *Psychology in the Schools, 32,* 291–294.

Snider, V. E. (1989). Reading comprehension performance of adolescents with learning disabilities. *Learning Disability Quarterly, 12*(2), 87–96.

Snider, V. E., & Tarver, S. G. (1987). The effect of early reading failure on acquisition of knowledge among students with learning disabilities. *Journal of Learning Disabilities, 20*(6), 351–356, 373.

Snow, R. E. (1985). [Review of *Frames of mind: The theory of multiple intelligences*]. *American Journal of Education, 85,* 109–112.

Snow, R. E. (1986). Individual differences and the design of educational programs. *American Psychologist, 41,* 1029–1039.

Snow, R. E. (1989). Aptitude-treatment interaction as a framework for research on individual differences in learning. In P. L. Ackerman, R. J. Sternberg, & R. Glaser (Eds.), *Learning and individual differences: Advances in theory and research* (pp. 13–59). New York: Freeman.

Snow, R. E. (1989). Toward assessment of cognitive and conative structures in learning. *Educational Researcher, 18*(9), 8–14.

Snow, R. E. (1991). The concept of aptitude. In R. E. Snow & D. E. Wiley (Eds.), *Improving inquiring in social science* (pp. 249–284). Hillsdale, NJ: Erlbaum.

Snow R. E. (1992) Aptitude theory: Yesterday, today and tomorrow. *Educational Psychologist, 27*(1), 5–32.

Snow, R. E. (1994). Abilities and aptitudes. In R. J. Sternberg (Eds.), *Encyclopedia of human intelligence* (pp. 3–5). New York: Macmillan.

Snow, R. E., Burns, M. S., & Griffin, P. (1998). *Preventing reading difficulties in young children.* Washington, DC: National Academy Press.

Snow, R. E., Corno, L., & Jackson, D. (1996). Individual differences in affective and cognative functions. In D. C. Berliner & R. C. Colfee (Eds.), *Handbook of educational psychology.* New York: Macmillan.

Snow, R. E., & Swanson, J. (1992). Instructional psychology: Aptitude, adaptation, and assessment. *Annual Review of Psychology, 43,* 583–626.

Spearman, C. E. (1904). "General Intelligence," objectively determined and measured. *American Journal of Psychiatry, 15,* 201–293.

Spearman, C. E. (1927). *The abilities of man.* London: Macmillan.

Sperry, R. W. (1968). Hemisphere deconnection and unity in conscious awareness. *American Psychologist, 23,* 723–733.

Sperry, R. W. (1974). Lateral specialization in the surgically separated hemispheres. In F. O. Schmitt & F. G. Worden (Eds.), *The neurosciences: Third study program.* Cambridge, MA: MIT Press.

Spruill, J. (1991). A comparison of the Wechsler Adult Intelligence Scale—Revised with the Stanford-Binet Intelligence Scale (4th edition) for mentally retarded adults. *Psychological Assessment, 3,* 133–135.

Squire, L. R. (1987). *Memory and the brain.* New York: Oxford University Press.

Squire, L. R. (1992). Memory and the hippocampus: A synthesis from findings with rats, monkeys, and humans. *Psychological Review, 99,* 195–231.

Stahl, S. A., & Murray, B. A. (1994). Defining phonological awareness and its relationship to early reading. *Journal of Educational Psychology, 86*(2), 221–234.

Stankov, L. (1994). Auditory abilities. In R. J. Sternberg (Ed.), *Encyclopedia of human intelligence* (pp. 157–162). New York: Macmillan.

Stankov, L., & Horn, J. L. (1980). Human abilities revealed through auditory tests. *Journal of Educational Psychology, 72*(1), 21–44.

Stanovich, K. E. (1988). Explaining the differences between the dyslexic and the garden-variety poor reader: The phonological core variable difference model. *Journal of Learning Disabilities, 21,* 590–604.

Stanovich, K. E., Cunningham, A. E., & Cramer, B. B. (1984). Assessing phonological awareness in kindergarten children: Issues of task comparability. *Journal of Experimental Child Psychology, 38,* 175–190.

Stanovich, K. E., Cunningham, A. E., & Feeman, D. J. (1984). Intelligence, cognitive skills, and early reading progress. *Reading Research Quarterly, 19,* 278–303.

Stanovich, K. E., & Siegel, L. S. (1994). Phenotypic performance profile of children with reading disabilities: A regression-based test of the phonological-core variable-difference model. *Journal of Educational Psychology, 86,* 24–53.

Sternberg, R. J. (1985). *Beyond IQ: A triarchic theory of human intelligence.* New York: Cambridge University Press.

Sternberg, R. J. (1986). Intelligence, wisdom, and creativity: Three is better than one. *Educational Psychologist, 21*(3), 175–190.

Sternberg, R. J. (1992). Ability tests, measurements, and markets. *Journal of Educational Psychology, 84,* 134–140.

Sternberg, R. J. (1993). Rocky's back again: A review of the WISC-III. *Journal of Psychoeducational Assessment,* [WISC-III Monograph], 161–164.

Sternberg, R. J. (1994). A triarchic model for teaching and assessing students in general psychology. *General Psychologist, 30*(2), 42–48.

Sternberg, R. J. (1996). *Successful intelligence.* New York: Simon & Schuster.

Sternberg, R. J. (1997). The triarchic theory of intelligence. In D. P. Flanagan, J. L. Genshaft, & P. L. Harrison (Eds.), *Contemporary intellectual assessment: Theories, tests, and issues* (pp. 92–104). New York: Guilford.

Sternberg, R. J. (1997). Intelligence and lifelong learning: What's new and how do we use it? *American Psychologist, 52*(10), 1134–1139.

Sternberg, R. J., & Kaufman, J. C. (1998). Human abilities. *Annual Review of Psychology, 49,* 479–502.

Stevenson, H. W., Parker, T., Wilkinson, A., Hegion, A., & Fish, E. (1976). Longitudinal study of individual differences in cognitive development and scholastic achievement. *Journal of Educational Psychology, 68*(4), 377–400.

Stinnett, T. A., Havey, J. M., & Oehler-Stinnett, J. (1994). Current test usage by practicing school psychologists: A national survey. *Journal of Psychoeducational Assessment, 12,* 331–350.

Stone, B., & Brady, S. (1995). Evidence for phonological processing deficits in less-skilled readers. *Annals of Dyslexia, 45,* 51–78.

Stone, B. J. (1991). Joint confirmatory factor analyses of the DAS and WISC-R. *Journal of School Psychology,* 185–195.

Stone, B. J. (1992). Joint confirmatory factor analyses of the DAS and WISC-R. *Journal of School Psychology, 30,* 185–195.

Stone, B. J., Gridley, B. E., & Gyurke, J. S. (1991). Confirmatory factor analysis of the WPPSI-R at the extreme end of the age range. *Journal of Psychoeducational Assessment, 8,* 263–270.

Sullivan, P. M., & Montoya, L. A. (1997). Factor analysis of the WISC-III with deaf and hard-of-hearing children. *Psychological Assessment, 9*(3), 317–321.

Swanson, H. L. (1986). Learning disabled readers' verbal coding difficulties: A problem of storage or retrieval? *Learning Disabilities Research, 1,* 73–82.

Swanson, H. L. (1991). Operational definitions and learning disabilities: An overview. *Learning Disabilities Quarterly, 14*(4), 242–254.

Swanson, H. L. (1996). Individual and age-related differences in children's working memory. *Memory and Cognition, 24*(1), 70–82.

Swanson, H. L., & Berninger, V. W. (1995). The role of working memory in skilled and less skilled readers' comprehension. *Intelligence, 21,* 83–108.

Taylor, L. C., Brown, F. G., & Michael, W. B. (1976). The validity of cognitive, affecting, and demographic variables in the prediction of achievement in high school algebra and geometry: Implications for the definition of mathematical aptitude. *Educational and Psychological Measurement, 36,* 971–982.

Taylor, T. R. (1994). A review of three approaches to cognitive assessment, and a proposed integrated approach based on a unifying theoretical framework. *South African Journal of Psychology, 24*(4), 183–193.

Tellegen, A. (1982). *Brief manual for the Multidimensional Personality Questionnaire (MPQ).* Minneapolis, MN: Author.

Tellegen, A. T., & Waller, N. G. (in press). Exploring personality through test construction: Development of the Multidimensional Personality Questionnaire. In S. R. Briggs & J. M. Cheek (Eds.), *Personality measures: Development and evaluation* (vol. 1). Greenwich, CT: JAI Press.

Terman, L. M. (1906). Genius and stupidity. A study of some of the intellectual processes of seven "bright" and seven "stupid" boys. *Pedagogical Seminary, 13,* 307–373.

Terman, L. M. (1916). *The measurement of intelligence: An explanation of and a complete guide for the use of the Stanford revision and extension of the Binet-Simon intelligence scale.* Boston: Houghton Mifflin.

Terman, L. M. (1919). *The intelligence of school children.* Boston: Houghton Mifflin.

Terman, L. M., & Merrill, M. A. (1937). *Measuring intelligence:* Boston: Houghton Mifflin.

Terman, L. M., & Merrill, M. A. (1960). *Stanford-Binet Intelligence Scale: Manual for the Third Revision Form L-M.* Boston: Houghton Mifflin.

Terman, L. M., & Merrill, M. A. (1972). *Stanford-Binet Intelligence Scale: 1972 Norms Edition.* Boston: Houghton Mifflin.

Thorndike, R. L., Hagen, E. P., & Sattler, J. M. (1986). *Stanford-Binet Intelligence Scale: Guide for administering and scoring the Fourth Edition.* Chicago: Riverside.

Thorndike, R. M. (1997). The early history of intelligence testing. In D. P. Flanagan, J. L. Genshaft, & P. L. Harrison (Eds.), *Contemporary intellectual assessment: Theories, tests, and issues* (pp. 3–16). New York: Guilford.

Thorndike, R. M., & Lohman, D. F. (1990). *A century of ability testing.* Chicago: Riverside.

Thurstone, L. L. (1935). *The vectors of mind.* Chicago: University of Chicago Press.

Thurstone, L. L. (1938). Primary mental abilities. *Psychometric Monographs,* (1).

Thurstone, L. L. (1947). *Multiple factor analysis: A development and expansion of the vectors of mind.* Chicago: University of Chicago Press.

Thurstone, L. L., & Thurstone, T. G. (1941). Factorial studies of intelligence. *Psychometric Monographs,* No. 2.

Tiholov, T., Zawallich, A., & Jannzen, H. (1996). Diagnosis based on the WISC-III processing speed factor. *Canadian Journal of School Psychology, 12,* 23–34.

Torgesen, J. K. (1988). Studies of children with learning disabilities who perform poorly on memory-span tasks. *Journal of Learning Disabilities, 21*(10), 605–612.

Torgesen, J. K., & Bryant, B. R. (1994). *Test of Phonological Awareness.* Austin, TX: Pro-Ed.

Torgesen, J. K., Wagner, R. K., & Rashotte, C. A. (1994). Longitudinal studies of phonological processing and reading. *Journal of Learning Disabilities, 27*(5), 276–286.

Torgesen, J. K., Wagner, R. K., Rashotte, C. A., Burgess, S., & Hecht, S. (1997). Contributions of phonological awareness and rapid automatic naming ability to the growth of word-reading skills in second- to fifth-grade children. *Scientific Studies of Reading, 1*(2), 161–185.

Travers, J. F., Elliott, S. N., & Kratochwill, T. R. (1993). *Educational psychology: Effective teaching, effec-*

tive learning. Madison, WI: WCB Brown & Benchmark.

Tsushima, W. (1994). Short form of the WPPSI and WPPSI-R. *Journal of Child Clinical Psychology, 50,* 877–879.

Turner, M. L., & Engle, R. W. (1989). Is working memory capacity task dependent? *Journal of Memory and Language, 28,* 127–154.

Undheim, J. O., & Gustafsson, J. E. (1987). The hierarchical organization of cognitive abilities: Restoring general intelligence through the use of linear structural relations (LISREL). *Multivariate Behavioral Research, 22,* 149–171.

Urbina, S., & Clayton, J. (1991). WPPSI-R/WISC-R: A comparative study. *Journal of Psychoeducational Asessment, 9,* 247–254.

U.S. Department of Education. (1994). *Summary of the bilingual education state educational agency program survey of states' limited English proficient persons and available educational services (1992–1993): Final report.* Arlington, VA: Development Associates.

Valdés, G., & Figueroa, R. A. (1994). *Bilingualism and testing: A special case of bias.* Norwood, NJ: Ablex.

Vance, B., & Fuller, G. (1995). Relation of scores on WISC-III and WRAT-3 for a sample of referred children and youth. *Psychological Reports, 76,* 371–374.

Vance, H., Maddux, C. D., Fuller, G. B., & Awa, A. M. (1996). A longitudinal comparison of WISC-III and WISC-R scores of special education students. *Psychology in the Schools, 33,* 113–118.

Vandenberg, S. G., & Vogler, G. P. (1985). Genetic determinants of intelligence. In B. B. Wolman (Ed.), *Handbook of intelligence: Theories, measurements, and applications* (pp. 3–57). New York: Wiley.

Vanderwood, M. L., McGrew, K. S., Flanagan, D. P., & Keith, T. Z. (1999). *Examination of the contribution of general and specific cognitive abilities to reading achievement.* Manuscript submitted for publication.

Vazquez Nuttal, E., De Leon, B., & Valle, M. (1990). Best practices in considering cultural factors. In A. Thomas & J. Grimes (Eds.), *Best practices in school psychology—II.* Washington, DC: National Association of School Psychologists.

Vellutino, F. R., & Scanlon, D. M. (1982). Verbal processing in poor and normal readers. In C. Brainerd & M. Pressley (Eds.), *Verbal processing in children: Progress in cognitive development research* (pp. 189–264). Chicago: University of Chicago Press.

Vernon, P. A. (1990). An overview of chronometric measures of intelligence. *School Psychology Review, 19*(4), 399–410.

Vernon, P. A., & Mori, M. (1990). Physiological approaches to the assessment of intelligence. In C. R. Reynolds & R. W. Kamphaus (Eds.), *Handbook of psychological and educational assessment: Intelligence and achievement* (pp. 389–402). New York: Guilford Press.

Vernon, P. E. (1961). *The structure of human abilities* (2nd ed.). London: Methuen.

Vernon, P. E., Jackson, D. N., & Messick, S. (1988). Cultural influences on patterns of abilities in North America. In S. H. Irvine & J. W. Berry (Eds.), *Human abilities in cultural context* (pp. 208–231). New York: Cambridge University Press.

Vygotsky, L. S. (1978). In M. Cole, V. John-Steiner, S. Scribner, & E. Souberman (Eds.), *Mind in society: The development of higher psychological processes.* Cambridge, MA: Harvard University Press.

Wagner, R. K. (1986). Phonological processing abilities and reading: Implications for disabled readers. *Journal of Learning Disabilities, 19,* 623–630.

Wagner, R. K., & Torgesen, J. K. (1987). The nature of phonological processing and its causal role in the acquisition of reading skills. *Psychological Bulletins, 101*(2), 192–212.

Wagner, R. K., Torgesen, J. K., Laughton, P., Simmons, K., & Rashotte, C. A. (1993). Development of young readers' phonological processing abilities. *Journal of Educational Psychology, 85*(1), 83–103.

Wagner, R. K., Torgesen, J. K., & Rashotte, C. A. (1994). Development of reading related phonological processing abilities: New evidence of bidirectional causality from a latent variable longitudinal study. *Developmental Psychology, 30*(1), 73–87.

Ward, L. C., & Ryan, J. J. (1996). Validity and time saving in the selection of short forms of the Wechsler Adult Intelligence Scale—Revised. *Psychological Assessment, 8*(1), 69–72.

Watkins, M. W. (1996). Diagnostic utility of the WISC-III developmental index as a predictor of learning disabilities. *Journal of Learning Disabilities, 29*(3), 305–312.

Watkins, M. W., & Kush, J. C. (1994). Wechsler subtest analysis: The right way, the wrong way, or no way? *School Psychology Review, 23,* 640–651.

Watkins, M. W., Kush, J. C., & Glutting, J. J. (1997). Prevalence and diagnostic utility of the WISC-III SCAD profile among children with disabilities. *School Psychology Quarterly, 12*(3), 235–248.

Webster, R. E. (1979). Visual and aural short-term memory capacity deficits in mathematics disabled students. *Journal of Educational Research, 72*(5), 277–283.

Wechsler, D. (1939). *The measurement of adult intelligence.* Baltimore, MD: Williams & Wilkins.

Wechsler, D. (1944). *The measurement of adult intelligence* (3rd ed.). Baltimore: Williams & Wilkins.

Wechsler, D. (1949). *Manual for the Wechsler Intelligence Scale for Children.* San Antonio, TX: Psychological Corporation.

Wechsler, D. (1955). *Manual for the Wechsler Adult Intelligence Scale.* New York: Psychological Corporation.

Wechsler, D. (1958). *The measurement and appraisal of adult intelligence* (4th ed.). Baltimore, MD: Williams & Wilkins.

Wechsler, D. (1967). *Manual for the Wechsler Preschool and Primary Scale of Intelligence.* San Antonio, TX: Psychological Corporation.

Wechsler, D. (1974). *Manual for the Wechsler Intelligence Scale for Children—Revised.* New York: Psychological Corporation.

Wechsler, D. (1981). *Wechsler Adult Intelligence Scale—Revised.* San Antonio, TX: Psychological Corporation.

Wechsler, D. (1987). *Wechsler Memory Scale—Revised.* New York: Psychological Corporation.

Wechsler, D. (1989). *Wechsler Preschool and Primary Scale of Intelligence—Revised.* San Antonio, TX: Psychological Corporation.

Wechsler, D. (1991). *Wechsler Intelligence Scale for Children—Third Edition.* San Antonio, TX: Psychological Corporation.

Wechsler, D. (1997a). *Wechsler Adult Intelligence Scale—Third Edition.* San Antonio, TX: Psychological Corporation.

Wechsler, D. (1997b). *Wechsler Memory Scale—Third Edition.* San Antonio, TX: Psychological Corporation.

Weiss, L., & Prifitera, A. (1995). An evaluation of differential prediction of WIAT achievement scores for WISC-III FSIQ across ethnic and gender groups. *Journal of School Psychology, 33,* 297–304.

Williams, K. T. (1997). *Expressive Vocabulary Test.* Circle Pines, MN: American Guidance Service.

Williams, R. L. (1970). From dehumanization to black intellectual genocide: A rejoinder. *Clinical Child Psychology Newsletter, 9,* 6–7.

Wilson, B. C. (1992). The neuropsychological assessment of the preschool child: A branching model. In I. Rapm & S. I. Segalowitz (Eds.), *Handbook of Neuropsychology: Child Neuropsychology* (vol. 6) (pp. 377–394).

Wilson, M. S., & Reschly, D. J. (1996). Assessment in school psychology training and practice. *School Psychology Review, 25,* 9–23.

Witt, J. C., & Gresham, F. M. (1985). Review of Wechsler Intelligence Scale for Children—Revised. In J. V. Mitchell (Ed.), *The ninth mental measurement year-*

book (vol. 2) (pp. 1716–1719). Lincoln, NE: Buros Institute of Mental Measurements.

Wolf, M. (1991). Naming-speed and reading: The contribution of the cognitive neurosciences. *Reading Research Quarterly, 26*(2), 123–141.

Woodcock, R. (1989). *Emulation of the WISC-R type standard scores for users of the WJ-R.* Unpublished manuscript.

Woodcock, R. W. (1990). Theoretical foundations of the WJ-R measures of cognitive ability. *Journal of Psychoeducational Assessment, 8,* 231–258.

Woodcock, R. W. (1991). *Woodcock Language Proficiency Battery—Revised* (English Form). Chicago: Riverside.

Woodcock, R. W. (1993). An information processing view of *Gf-Gc* theory. *Journal of Psychoeducational Assessment* [Monograph Series: WJ-R Monograph], 80–102.

Woodcock, R. W. (1994). Measures of fluid and crystallized intelligence. In R. J. Sternberg (Ed.), *The encyclopedia of intelligence* (pp. 452–456). New York: Macmillan.

Woodcock, R. W. (1997). The Woodcock-Johnson Tests of Cognitive Ability—Revised. In D. P. Flanagan, J. L. Genshaft, & P. L. Harrison (Eds.), *Contemporary intellectual assessment: Theories, tests, and issues* (pp. 230–246). New York: Guilford.

Woodcock, R. W. (1998). Extending *Gf-Gc* theory into practice. In J. J. McArdle & R. W. Woodcock, (Eds.), *Human cognitive abilities in theory and practice* (pp. 137–156). Mahwah, NJ: Erlbaum.

Woodcock, R. W., & Johnson, M. B. (1977). *Woodcock-Johnson Psychoeducational Battery.* Allen, TX: DLM Teaching Resources.

Woodcock, R. W., & Johnson, M. B. (1989). *Woodcock-Johnson Psycho-Educational Battery—Revised.* Chicago: Riverside.

Woodcock, R. W., & Mather, N. (1989, 1990). WJ-R Tests of Cognitive Ability—Standard and Supplemental Batteries: Examiner's Manual. In R. W. Woodcock & M. B. Johnson, *Woodcock-Johnson Psycho-Educational Battery—Revised.* Chicago: Riverside.

Woodcock, R. W., McGrew, K. S., & Mather, N. (in press). *Woodcock-Johnson Psychoeducational Battery Third Edition (WJ-3).* Chicago: Riverside.

Woodcock, R. W., & Munoz-Sandoval, A. F. (1996). *Bateria Woodcock-Munoz Pruebas de habilidad cognoscitiva—Revisada.* Chicago: Riverside.

Woodcock, R. W., & Munoz-Sandoval, A. F. (1993). An IRT approach to cross-language test equating and interpretation. *European Journal of Psychological Assessment, 9,* 233–241.

Yopp, H. K. (1988). The validity and reliability of phonemic awareness tests. *Reading Research Quarterly, 23*(2), 159–177.

Ysseldyke, J. (1990). Goodness of fit of the Woodcock-Johnson Psycho-Educational Battery—Revised to the Horn-Cattell *Gf-Gc* theory. *Journal of Psychoeducational Assessment, 8,* 268–275.

Ysseldyke, J. E. (1979). Issues in psychoeducational assessment. In G. D. Phye & D. Reschly (Eds.), *School psychology: Methods and role.* New York: Academic Press.

Yuill, N., Oakhill, J., & Parking, A. (1989). Working memory, comprehension ability and the resolution of text anomaly. *British Journal of Psychology, 80,* 351–361.

Zachary, R. A. (1990). Wechsler's intelligence scales: Theoretical and practical considerations. *Journal of Psychoeducational Assessment, 8,* 276–289.

Zillmer, E., Waechtler, C., Harris, B., & Khan, F. (1992). The effects of unilateral and multifocal lesions on the WAIS-R: A factor analytic study of stroke patients. *Archives of Clinical Neuropsychology, 7,* 29–40.

Zimmerman, I. L., & Woo-Sam, J. M. (1985). Clinical applications. In B. B. Wolman (Ed.), *Handbook of intelligence: Theories, measurements, and applications* (pp. 873–898). New York: Wiley.

Zwick, W. R., & Velicer, W. F. (1986). Comparison of five rules for determining the number of components to retain. *Psychological Bulletin, 99*(3), 432–442.

INDEX